Fodor's 2011

SOUTH
FLORIDA

Be a Fodor's Correspondent

Share your trip with Fodor's.

Our latest guidebook to Florida—now in full color—owes its success to travelers like you. Throughout, you'll find photographs submitted by members of Fodors.com to our "Show Us Your . . . Florida" photo contest. We gratefully acknowledge the contest's sponsor, Visit Florida, whose support made the inclusion of these photos possible. Facing this page is a photograph of an alligator taken by Tim Souter from the boardwalk of the Anhinga Trail in Everglades National Park. We've also included "Word of Mouth" quotes from travelers who shared their experiences with others on our forums.

We are especially proud of this color edition. No other guide to Florida is as up to date or has as much practical planning information, along with hundreds of color photographs and illustrated maps. If you're inspired and can plan a better trip because of this guide, we've done our job.

We invite you to join the travel conversation: Your opinion matters to us and to your fellow travelers. Come to Fodors.com to plan your trip, share an experience, ask a question, submit a photograph, post a review, or write a trip report. Tell our editors about your trip. They want to know what went well and how we can make this guide even better. Share your opinions at our feedback center at fodors.com/feedback, or email us at editors@fodors.com with the subject line "South Florida Editor." You might find your comments published in a future Fodor's guide. We look forward to hearing from you.

Happy Traveling!

Tim Jarrell, Publisher

FODOR'S SOUTH FLORIDA 2011

Editors: Salwa Jabado *lead project editor*; Debbie Harmsen, Jess Moss

Editorial Contributor: Jacinta O'Halloran
Writers: Michael de Zayas, Teri Evans, Lynne Helm, Susan MacCallum-Whitcomb, Mary Thurwachter, Chelle Koster Walton

Production Editor: Carolyn Roth
Maps & Illustrations: David Lindroth and Mark Stroud, *cartographers;* Bob Blake, Rebecca Baer, *map editors;* William Wu, *information graphics*
Design: Fabrizio La Rocca, *creative director;* Guido Caroti, Siobhan O'Hare, *art directors;* Tina Malaney, Nora Rosansky, Chie Ushio, Jessica Walsh, Ann McBride, *designers;* Melanie Marin, *senior picture editor*
Cover Photo: (Florida Keys National Marine Sanctuary) Tom Stack
Production Manager: Amanda Bullock

ISBN 978-1-4000-0477-5

ISSN 1526-2219

SPECIAL SALES

This book is available at special discounts for bulk purchases for sales promotions or premiums. Special editions, including personalized covers, excerpts of existing books, and corporate imprints, can be created in large quantities for special needs. For more information, write to Special Markets/Premium Sales, 1745 Broadway, MD 6-2, New York, New York 10019, or e-mail specialmarkets@randomhouse.com.

AN IMPORTANT TIP & AN INVITATION

Although all prices, opening times, and other details in this book are based on information supplied to us at press time, changes occur all the time in the travel world, and Fodor's cannot accept responsibility for facts that become outdated or for inadvertent errors or omissions. So **always confirm information when it matters**, especially if you're making a detour to visit a specific place. Your experiences—positive and negative—matter to us. If we have missed or misstated something, **please write to us**. We follow up on all suggestions. Contact the South Florida editor at editors@fodors.com or c/o Fodor's at 1745 Broadway, New York, NY 10019.

PRINTED IN CHINA

10 9 8 7 6 5 4 3 2 1

CONTENTS

Fodor's Features

MAPS

ABOUT
THIS BOOK

Our Ratings

Sometimes you find terrific travel experiences and sometimes they just find you. But usually the burden is on you to select the right combination of experiences. That's where our ratings come in.

As travelers we've all discovered a place so wonderful that its worthiness is obvious. And sometimes that place is so experiential that superlatives don't do it justice: you just have to be there to know. These sights, properties, and experiences get our highest rating, **Fodor's Choice**, indicated by orange stars throughout this book.

Black stars highlight sights and properties we deem **Highly Recommended,** places that our writers, editors, and readers praise again and again for consistency and excellence.

By default, there's another category: Any place we include in this book is by definition worth your time, unless we say otherwise. And we will.

Disagree with any of our choices? Care to nominate a place or suggest that we rate one more highly? Visit our feedback center at www.fodors.com/feedback.

Budget Well

Hotel and restaurant price categories from ¢ to $$$$ are defined in the opening pages of each chapter. For attractions, we always give standard adult admission fees; reductions are usually available for children, students, and senior citizens. Want to pay with plastic? **AE, D, DC, MC, V** following restaurant and hotel listings indicate whether American Express, Discover, Diners Club, MasterCard, and Visa are accepted.

Restaurants

Unless we state otherwise, restaurants are open for lunch and dinner daily. We mention dress only when there's a specific requirement and reservations only when they're essential or not accepted—it's always best to book ahead.

Hotels

Hotels have private bath, phone, TV, and air-conditioning and operate on the European Plan (aka EP, meaning without meals), unless we specify that they use the Breakfast Plan (BP, with a full breakfast), Continental Plan (CP, with a continental breakfast), Full American Plan (FAP, all meals), or Modified American Plan (MAP, with breakfast and dinner), or

are all-inclusive (including all meals and most activities). We always list facilities but not whether you'll be charged an extra fee to use them, so always ask.

Listings	
★	Fodor's Choice
★	Highly recommended
⊠	Physical address
✛	Directions or Map coordinates
⌂	Mailing address
☎	Telephone
🖷	Fax
⊕	On the Web
✉	E-mail
✍	Admission fee
☉	Open/closed times
Ⓜ	Metro stations
☰	Credit cards
Hotels & Restaurants	
☷	Hotel
⌐♪	Number of rooms
⚭	Facilities
⑆⊙⑆	Meal plans
✕	Restaurant
⚏	Reservations
血	Dress code
⤓	Smoking
⑧⑨	BYOB
Outdoors	
🏌	Golf
⚠	Camping
Other	
☾	Family-friendly
⇨	See also
⊠	Branch address
☞	Take note

Experience
South Florida

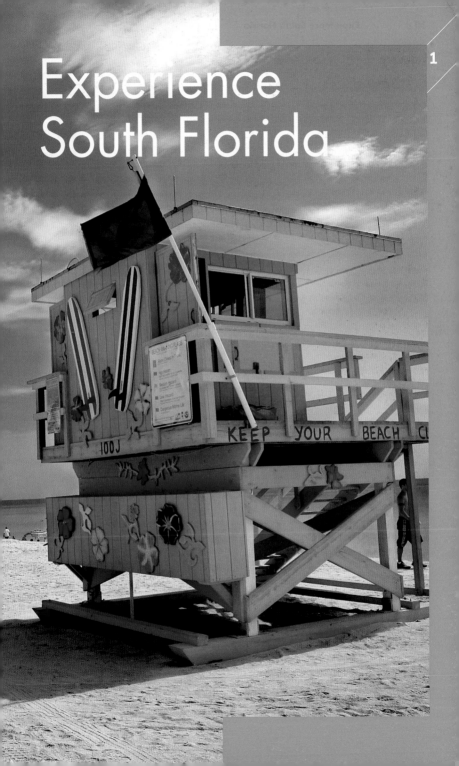

WHAT'S WHERE

The following numbers refer to chapters.

2 Palm Beach and the Treasure Coast. This area scores points for diversity. Palm Beach and environs are famous for their golden sand—and the golden bank accounts of their wealthy residents. Travelers who prefer nature's bounty can veer north to the Treasure Coast, where you'll discover outdoor opportunities and an "Old Florida" ambience.

3 Fort Lauderdale and Broward County. Like the college crowd that once turned this into the "Suds and Sun Capital of the Universe," Fort Lauderdale has grown up. The beaches that first drew them to Broward County still exist. But now the beaches are complemented by a refurbished waterfront with upscale lodging and entertainment options.

4 Miami and Miami Beach. Greater Miami is hot—and we're not just talking about the weather. Glass-skinned skyscrapers, art deco buildings, towering palms, and white sand beaches set the scene. Yet vacations here are as much about lifestyle as locale, so prepare for power shopping, club-hopping, and decadent dining.

5 The Everglades. Covering more than 1.5 million acres, the fabled River of Grass is Florida's greatest natural treasure. Neighboring Biscayne National Park (the country's largest marine park, 95% of which is underwater) runs a close second. Rounding out the eco-enthusiast's "top three" is the Big Cypress National Preserve.

6 Florida Keys. This slender necklace of landfalls, strung together by a 110-mi highway, marks the southern edge of the continental United States. Divided into Upper, Middle, and Lower, the Keys are nirvana for anglers, divers, and even literature lovers. They're also the place to go for a laid-back, living-in-a-Jimmy Buffet-song escape.

GEORGIA

Chattahoochee 19

Quincy

ALLAHASSEE 65 319

98 Perry

Eastpoint
Apalachicola 98 19

Osceola
National
Forest

St. Mary's R.

Amelia Island

95 Jacksonville

St. Johns R.

Lake City

St. Augustine

Santa Fe R.

75 Gainesville
301

Ocala
National
Forest

1

Suwannee R.

41

Ocala

27

Cedar Keys

40 Daytona Beach

4

Titusville

Orlando 50

Walt Disney World

Kissimmee

Tarpon Springs

75

Tampa

Clearwater

Tampa Bay

St. Petersburg

Bradenton

Sarasota

Venice 75

Winter Haven

Peace R.

27

Kennedy Space Center
Cape Canaveral
Cocoa Beach
Merritt Island

528

Melbourne

Florida's Turnpike

Sebastian Inlet
Recreation Area

95

Vero Beach

Fort Pierce

Kissimmee R.

Hutchinson
Island

70

Lake
Okeechobee

Singer Island
West Palm
2 Beach
Palm Beach

Caloosahatchee R.

Fort Myers

80

Cape Coral
Captiva Island
Sanibel Island

Naples

Big Cypress
National
Preserve

27

75

3 Boca Raton
Fort
Lauderdale

Miami Beach

41

4 Miami

Biscayne
Bay

Everglades City

Everglades
National
Park

Florida City

9336

5

Homestead

Key Largo

Cape Sable

Florida Bay

1 KEYS

0   50 miles

0   75 kilometers

Key West 6 FLORIDA

ATLANTIC OCEAN

Gulf of Mexico

SOUTH FLORIDA PLANNER

Oil Spill

The April 20, 2010 explosion of the Deepwater Horizon oil rig caused hundreds of thousands of gallons of oil to spill into the Gulf of Mexico. For up to date information on the impact of the oil spill on Florida's coast, see Florida's Department of Environmental Protection Web site: ⊕ www.dep.state.fl.us/ deepwaterhorizon as well as their Twitter feed: ⊕ twitter. com/FLDEPalert.

No Passport Required

On the streets of Miami's Little Havana, salsa tunes blare and the smell of roast pork fills the air. You can get a good whiff of tobacco, too, due to the cigar makers who still hand-roll their products here. For nearly 50 years, the neighborhood's undisputed heart has been Calle Ocho: the commercial thoroughfare that hosts Carnaval Miami each March. The festival's 10 frenetic days culminate in the world's longest conga line. Ambience- and amenity-wise, it is as close as you'll get to Cuba without running afoul of the federal government.

Getting to South Florida

Most visitors begin and end their trip to South Florida at Miami International (MIA). The state's second-busiest airport after Orlando, it provides nonstop service to more than 120 cities and handles some 34 million passengers annually. But if you're destined for the north side of Miami-Dade, try flying instead into Fort Lauderdale–Hollywood International (FLL), a 40-minute drive away. Its smaller size usually means easier access and shorter security lines. Moreover, lower landing costs attract budget carriers—among them jetBlue, Southwest, Spirit, and WestJet—that don't serve MIA. Checking out alternate airports elsewhere can also yield benefits in terms of time and money saved. The state's Department of Transportation Web site (⊕ www.dot.state. fl.us/aviation/commercialairports.shtm) has a handy airport map that makes researching your options easy.

Getting Around South Florida

If you're driving in Florida, you'll likely become acquainted with the three main highways that run into, then through Florida: I–95, I–75, and I–10. The first two (originating in Maine and Michigan, respectively) extend south; the last (starting in California) extends west.

Motorists going from Miami to the Keys must traverse the 110-mile Overseas Highway, also known as US 1. Notable for scenic views, 42 bridges, and peak-time traffic jams, it was recently designated as an "All-American Road" by the National Scenic Byways program—and is one of only 30 routes countrywide to be so honored. For a memorable drive, rent a convertible and enjoy the ocean breezes from Key Largo to Key West with the top down. Before you get your motor running, click on the state's Transportation Guide at ⊕ www.stateofflorida.com. It contains everything from mileage charts to details on turnpike tolls.

WHEN TO GO

South Florida is a year-round vacation venue, but it divides the calendar into regional tourism seasons. Holidays and school breaks are major factors. However, the clincher is weather, with the best months being designated as peak periods.

High season starts with the run-up to Christmas and continues through Easter. Snowbirds migrate down then to escape frosty weather back home, and festival-goers flock in because major events (such as Art Basel Miami Beach or the Orange Bowl) are held this time of year to avoid summer's searing heat and high humidity. Winter is also *the* time to visit the Everglades. Temperatures and mosquito activity are lower—as are water levels, making wildlife easier to see.

Climate

Florida is rightly called the Sunshine State, but it could also be dubbed the Humid State. June through September, 90% humidity levels aren't uncommon. Nor are accompanying thunderstorms; in fact, more than half of the state's rain falls during these months. Florida's two-sided coastline also makes it a target for tropical storms. Hurricane season officially begins June 1 and ends November 30. Severe storms can dampen your plans, disrupt public services, or worse. If you're advised of a Hurricane Watch before departing, consider postponing your trip.

THAT'S COOL

"Cool" is an adjective often applied to the Florida Keys, and understandably so. After all, geographic isolation long enabled locals to nurture a quirky, one-of-a-kind culture. Come in summer and you'll discover that this reef-rimmed paradise literally feels cooler, too, because ocean breezes help beat the heat. As an added bonus, the Keys get substantially less rain than the rest of South Florida (approximately 39 inches annually, compared with 60 in Miami or Palm Beach). It's one of the driest regions in the state.

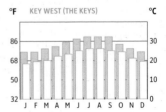

QUINTESSENTIAL SOUTH FLORIDA

Fabulous Food

Geography and gastronomy go hand in hand in Florida. Seafood, for instance, is a staple almost everywhere. Yet locals will point out that the way it is prepared changes considerably as you maneuver around the state. Northern restaurants show their regional roots with Cajun classics and Dixieland dishes. (It seems that virtually any fish can be crusted with pecans and served with greens!) Along the southeast coast, conversely, menus typically highlight Floribbean cuisine, which marries Floridian, Caribbean, and Latin flavors. (Think mahimahi with mango salsa.) Out in the Keys it's all about conch, whether served in fritters, chowder, or combined with key limes in ceviche. Inland, expect catfish, gator tails, and frogs' legs, all of which are best enjoyed at a Cracker-style fish camp with a side order of hush puppies.

The Arts

It's no secret that South Florida appeals to beach bums, boaters, fashionistas, and foodies. Now arts lovers are being drawn by a growing array of cultural offerings. Greater Miami, which is undergoing a renaissance of sorts, leads the way. For example, 2002 saw both the expansion of the Bass Museum and the launch of Art Basel, a December art fair that immediately became the hippest event of its kind in the country. Then in 2006, the ribbon was cut on the Adrienne Arsht Center for the Performing Arts (a world-class venue for the Florida Grand Opera, Miami City Ballet, and New World Symphony); followed by the debut of the new Frost Art Museum building in 2008. As if that wasn't enough, other projects—most notably a new home for the Miami Art Museum and enlarged digs for the Museum of Contemporary Art—are also in the works.

South Florida is synonymous with sunshine, and every year millions of heat-seeking visitors come to revel in it. However, the people who are lucky enough to actually live here know that the region's appeal rests on much more than those reliable rays.

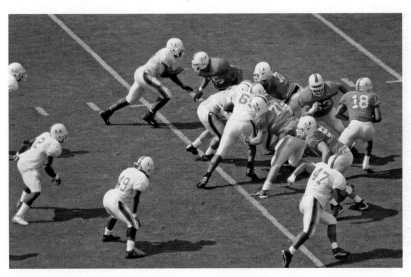

Water, Water Everywhere

Spanish explorer Ponce de León didn't find the Fountain of Youth when he swung through Florida in 1513. But if he'd lingered longer, he could have located 7,800 lakes, 1,700 rivers and creeks, and an estimated 350 springs. Over the centuries these have attracted American Indians, immigrants, opportunists, and, of course, countless outdoor adventurers. Boaters come for inland waterways and a 1,200-mi coast, and anglers are lured by 700 species of fish. (Florida claims 700 world-record catches, too, so concocting elaborate "fish tales" may not be necessary.) Snorkelers and divers curious to see what lies beneath can get face time with the marine life that thrives on the world's third-largest coral reef or bone up on maritime history in underwater archaeological preserves. Back on dry land, all those beaches are pretty impressive, too.

Superlative Sports

Panthers and Dolphins and Marlins, oh my! South Florida is teeming with teams—and residents take the games they play *very* seriously. Baseball fans can work themselves into a fever pitch both in season (when the MLB's Marlins take to the field in Miami) and off season (when Grapefruit League teams suit up for spring training in Juniper and Port St. Lucie). Football aficionados might cheer on the legendary Miami Dolphins or kick off the New Year by watching top-rated college teams battle it out in the FedEx Orange Bowl. Basketball lovers meanwhile feel the "Heat," and hockey addicts can applaud the Florida Panthers. When spectators feel a real need for speed, though, only one sport will suffice—jai-alai. Played professionally in Miami, Fort Pierce, and Dania Beach; it's the world's fastest game, with *pelotas* clocked at 188 mph.

SOUTH FLORIDA TOP ATTRACTIONS

The Florida Keys

(A) Little wonder these 800-plus islands are a prime destination for divers and snorkelers: they boast the world's third-largest reef and aquarium-clear waters that are brimming with sea life. Beneath the turquoise waves lies a colorful world populated by 40 species of coral and more than 600 of fish, which means you can observe purple sea fans, blue tangs, yellow-tailed snappers, green-finned parrot fish, and more. Locals debate the premiere area for viewing them, but John Pennekamp Coral Reef State Park is high on everyone's list. Underwater excursions organized by park concessionaires let you put your best flipper forward. (⇨ *See Chapter 6.*)

South Beach

(B) You can't miss the distinctive forms, vibrant colors, and extravagant flourishes of SoBe's architectural gems. The world's largest concentration of art deco edifices

is right here; and the Art Deco District, with more than 800 buildings, has earned a spot on the National Register of Historic Places (⇨ *see "A Stroll Down Deco Lane" In-Focus feature in Chapter 4*). The 'hood also has enough beautiful people to qualify for the Register of Hippest Places. The glitterati, along with vacationing hedonists, are drawn by über-trendy shops and a surfeit of celeb-studded clubs. Stellar eateries are the icing—umm, make that the ganache—on South Beach's proverbial cake. (⇨ *See Chapter 4.*)

The Everglades

(C) No trip to southern Florida is complete without seeing the Everglades. At its heart is a river—50 mi wide but merely 6 inches deep—flowing from Lake Okeechobee into Florida Bay. For an up-close look, speed demons can board an airboat that careens through the marshy waters. Purists, alternately, may placidly

canoe or kayak within the boundaries of Everglades National Park where amped-up modes of transport are forbidden. But remember to keep your hands in the boat. The critters that live in this unique ecosystem (alligators, Florida panthers, and cottonmouth snakes for starters) can add real bite to your visit! (⇨ *See Chapter 5.*)

Palm Beach

(D) If money could talk, you would hardly be able to hear above the din in Palm Beach. The upper crust started calling it home, during the winter months at least, back in the early 1900s. And today it remains a ritzy, glitzy enclave for both old money and the nouveau riche (a coterie led by "The Donald" himself, who owns the landmark Mar-a-Lago Club). Simply put, Palm Beach is the sort of community where shopping is a full-time pursuit and residents don't just wear Polo—they play it. Oooh and ahhh to your heart's content; then, for more conspicuous consumption, continue south along the aptly named Gold Coast to Boca Raton. (⇨ *See Chapter 2.*)

Fort Lauderdale

(E) Mariners frequently set their compass for Fort Lauderdale: a canal-laced coastal playground that's justifiably known as both "The Venice of America" and "The Yachting Capital of the World." Wannabe sailors who don't have their own vessel can cruise Broward County's 300 mi of inland waterways by water taxi and tour boat, or bob around the Atlantic Ocean in a chartered pleasure craft. If you happen to be in a buying mood, plan to arrive in late October for the Fort Lauderdale International Boat Show. Billed as the world's largest, it has $3 billion dollars' worth of boats in every conceivable size, shape, and price range. (⇨ *See Chapter 3.*)

IF YOU LIKE

Animal Encounters

South Florida makes an ideal habitat for party animals; however, there are other kinds of wildlife here, too. In terms of biodiversity, the state ranks third in the nation with approximately 1,200 different kinds of critters.

■ **Alligators.** Florida has more than 1.5 million resident alligators. You can see and even pet them at the Everglades Gator Park on Tamiami Trail, but "gator spotting" in swamps or roadside waterways is itself a favorite pastime. Eating the official state reptile in deep-fried nugget form is popular, too. Mmm . . . tastes like chicken.

■ **Birds.** Florida boasts 470 species of birds, and the 2,000-mi Great Florida Birding Trail (⊕ *www.floridabirdingtrail. com*) can help you find them. Through detailed guides and highway signs, it identifies sites where you might spy anything from bald eagles and burrowing owls to bubblegum-pink flamingos.

■ **Dolphins.** Not all Miami dolphins play football. Numerous boat cruises focus on the frolicking finned kind. If you dream of swimming with one, sign on for the Miami Seaquarium's Dolphin Odyssey program. Visiting the Keys? Try the Dolphin Research Center, a not-for-profit facility in Marathon.

■ **Manatees.** They're nicknamed sea cows and resemble walruses. Yet Florida's official marine mammals are most closely related to elephants, which may account for their slow pace and hefty frames. In winter, scan the water for a telltale glassy patch (called a "footprint"), indicating that a manatee swims below.

Blissful Beaches

South Florida is blessed with sun and sand. It has a surplus of grade-A beaches and an enviable range of beach activities. Whether you want to snorkel, surf, lounge, or people-watch, there's one to suit your preference.

■ **South Beach.** No American strand generates as much buzz as the one that hugs Ocean Drive in Miami Beach. Fringed with palms, backed by art deco architecture, and pulsating with urban energy, South Beach is arguably the top spot in the country for people-watchers eager to ogle the see-and-be-seen set.

■ **Dry Tortugas National Park.** Renowned for coral reefs, this cluster of seven islands in the Florida Keys offers outstanding snorkeling and scuba-diving opportunities. Considering that it is located 70 miles off Key West and can only be reached by boat or seaplane, simply getting there is an adventure.

■ **Sebastian Inlet State Park.** Contrary to popular belief, surfers don't have to head for California or Hawaii to catch a big wave. The Treasure Coast beach promises warm, easy access to water, plus the best breaks on the Eastern Seaboard. Just ask local hero—and international surfing legend—Kelly Slater.

■ **John D. MacArthur Beach State Park.** It isn't humans alone who love this sandy, barrier island park in North Palm Beach. Massive leatherback and loggerhead sea turtles lumber onto it to lay eggs each year between May and October. You can learn about them on ranger-led turtle watches in June and July.

Great Golf

Florida is home to more golf greens than any other state in the Union. Indeed, it's been said the southeast part of Florida has so many greens that you could tee off at a different course every week for two full years. Ready to go fore it?

■ **The Breakers.** Floridian's fascination with golf began in 1896 when the state's first course opened at this Palm Beach resort. (Rockefellers, Vanderbilts, and Astors signed the original guest book.) Today, the 70-par Ocean Course provides spectacular views of the Atlantic and challenging shots on 140 acres.

■ **PGA Village.** Owned by the PGA, this Port St. Lucie venue boasts three courses designed by Tom Fazio and Pete Dye, along with a Golf Learning and Performance Center that can transform duffers into scratch players. The PGA Historical Center, a free museum of golf memorabilia, is also on-site.

■ **Doral Golf Resort & Spa.** The Blue Monster grabs the spotlight here: after all, the famous par-72 course has been a stop on the PGA tour for more than 40 years. But the Miami resort has four other championship courses (including the new Jim McLean Signature one) and McLean's highly regarded golf school.

■ **Haulover Golf Course.** This par-27 public course at the north end of Miami Beach proves you can improve your handicap even if you are short on time or money. It has nine holes and you'll pay less than $9 to play them. The longest one, located directly on the intracoastal waterway, is 125 yards.

Unique Events

Give residents of this region the slimmest excuse to party and there's no holding them back. But nowhere are the festivities more exuberant than in Key West where the calendar is packed with outlandish events.

■ **Conch Republic Independence Celebration.** Each April, citizens assert the sovereignty of their pint-sized "island nation." The events, which span 10 days, include an impromptu parade and rollicking Royal Family Investiture, as well as a Great Battle involving water cannons and flying food.

■ **Hemingway Days.** Who's Your Papa? Ask that question in Key West and the answer will invariably be Ernest Hemingway. To understand the Importance of Being Ernest, come in late July for Hemingway Days. Highlights are a fishing tournament and look-alike contest featuring Papa impersonators.

■ **Pirates in Paradise Festival.** Ahoy Mateys! Key West embraces its piratical past for nine days starting in late November. Plank-walking contests, tall-ship trips, swashbuckling balls, and mock trials are on the agenda. There's also a pirate encampment at Fort Taylor. Parrots and eye patches optional.

■ **Sunset at Mallory Square.** Key West is the kind of town where simple sunsets warrant a celebration—which explains why thousands of onlookers join jugglers, clowns, and assorted eccentrics to applaud nature's nightly light show. The action centers around Mallory Square and the eponymous dock.

GREAT ITINERARIES

2 to 3 Days: Gold Coast and Treasure Coast

The opulent mansions of Palm Beach's Ocean Boulevard give you a glimpse of how the other half lives. For exclusive shopping and glittery sightseeing, sybarites should wander down "The Avenue" (that's Worth Avenue to non–Palm Beachers). The sporty set will find dozens of places to tee up (logically enough since the PGA is based here), along with tennis courts, polo clubs, even a croquet center. Those who'd like to see more of the Gold Coast can continue traveling south through Boca Raton to Fort Lauderdale. But to balance the highbrow with the low-key, turn north for a tour of the Treasure Coast. This stretch of the Atlantic shoreline was named for the booty spilled by a fleet of Spanish galleons that was shipwrecked here in 1715, and for centuries treasure kept washing up south of Sebastian Inlet. These days you're more likely to find manatees, sea turtles, and golden surfing opportunities.

2 to 3 Days: Miami Area

Greater Miami lays claim to America's most celebrated strand—South Beach—and lingering on it tops most itineraries. Anyone who longs to preen poolside by day, then strut supermodel-style through A-list eateries and clubs by night can do it all without leaving the Ocean Drive section of South Beach. Once you've been dazzled by the art deco architecture, merengue over to Calle Ocho: the epicenter of Miami's Cuban community. Elsewhere in the vicinity, Coconut Grove, Coral Gables, and the Miami Design District (an 18-block area crammed with showrooms and galleries) are well worth a visit. Since this is the sole U.S. city with two national parks and a national preserve in its backyard, it's also a convenient base

TIPS

■ If you're visiting multiple destinations, you can fly one-way into and out of different airports. Rent a car in between, picking it up at your point of arrival and leaving it at your point of departure.

■ Many national and state parks run no- or low-cost events—like walks, talks, and campfires—so ask about scheduled activities when visiting.

for eco-excursions. Take a day trip into the Everglades (if you've never seen alligator wrestling, here's your chance), hop a glass-bottom boat in Biscayne National Park, or suss out rare wood storks in Big Cypress National Preserve.

2 to 3 Days: Florida Keys

Some fantasize about "sailing away to Key Largo," others of "wasting away again in Margaritaville." In any case, almost everybody equates the Keys with relaxation. And they live up to their reputation, thanks to off-beat attractions and a come-as-you-are, do-as-you-please vibe. Key West is a good place to get initiated. The Old Town has a funky, laid-back feel; so take a leisurely walk, pay your respects to Hemingway, then rent a bike or moped to tour the rest of the island. Clear waters and abundant marine life make underwater exploration another must. After scoping out the parrot fish, you can return to town and join local "Parrotheads" in a Jimmy Buffett sing-along. When retracing your route to the mainland, plan a pit stop at Bahia Honda State Park for a visit to the Keys' best beach, or don your snorkel mask for one last look at the life aquatic in John Pennekamp Coral Reef State Park.

GONE FISHIN'

by Gary McKechnie

My favorite uncle has a passion for fishing.

It was one I didn't really understand—I'm more of a motorcycle guy, not a fishing pole–toting one. But one day he piqued my curiosity by telling me that fishing has many of the same enticements as motorcycling. Come again? He beautifully described the peaceful process of it all—how the serenity and solitude of the sport wash away concerns about work and tune him into the wonder of nature, just like being on a bike (minus the helmet and curvy highways).

I took the bait, and early one morning a few weeks later, my Uncle Bud and I headed out in a boat to a secluded cove on the St. Johns River near DeLand. We'd brought our rods, line, bait, and tackle—plus hot chocolate and a few things to eat. We didn't need much else. We dropped in our lines and sat silently, watching the fog hover over the water.

There was a peaceful stillness as we waited (and waited) for the fish to bite. There were turtles sunning themselves on logs and herons perched in the trees. We waited for hours for just a little nibble. I can't even recall now if we caught anything, but it didn't matter. My uncle was right: it was a relaxing way to spend a Florida morning.

REEL TIME

Florida is recognized as the "Fishing Capital of the World" as well as the "Bass Capital of the World." It's also home to some of the nation's most popular crappie tournaments.

Florida and fishing have a bond that goes back to thousands of years before Christ, when Paleo-Indians living along Florida's rivers and coasts were harvesting the waters just as readily as they were harvesting the land. Jump ahead to the 20th century and along came amateur anglers like Babe Ruth, Clark Gable, and Gary Cooper vacationing at central Florida fishing camps in pursuit of bream, bluegill, and largemouth bass, while Ernest Hemingway was scouring the waters off Key West in hopes of snagging marlin, tarpon, and snapper. Florida was, and is, a sportsman's paradise.

When he wasn't writing, Ernest Hemingway loved to fish in the Florida Keys. He's shown here in Key West in 1928.

A variety of fish and plentiful waterways—7,800 lakes and 1,700 rivers and creeks, not to mention the gulf and the ocean—are just two reasons why Florida is the nation's favorite fishing spot. And let's not forget the frost-free attributes: unlike their northern counterparts, Florida anglers have yet to drill through several feet of ice just to go fishing in the wintertime. Plus, a well-established infrastructure for fishing—numerous bait and tackle shops, boat rentals, sporting goods stores, public piers, and charters—makes it easy for experts and first-time fishermen to get started. For Floridians and the visitors hooked on the sport here, fishing in the Sunshine State is a sport of sheer ease and simplicity.

An afternoon on the waters of Charlotte County in southwest Florida.

CASTING WIDE

The same way Florida is home to rocket scientists and beach bums, it's home to a diverse variety of fishing methods. What kind will work for you depends on where you want to go and what you want to catch.

From the Panhandle south to the Everglades, fishing is as easy as finding a quiet spot on the bank or heading out on freshwater lakes, tranquil ponds, spring-fed rivers, and placid inlets and lagoons.

Perhaps the biggest catches are found offshore—in the Atlantic Ocean, Florida Straits, or the Gulf of Mexico. For saltwater fishing, you can join a charter, be it a private one for small groups or a large party one; head out along the long jetties or public piers that jut into the ocean; or toss your line from the shore into the surf (known as surf casting). Some attempt a tricky, yet effective form of fishing called net casting: tossing a circular net weighted around its perimeter; the flattened net hits the surface and drives fish into the center of the circle.

Surf casting on Juno Beach, about 20 mi north of Palm Beach.

FRESHWATER FISHING VS. SALTWATER FISHING

FRESH WATER

With about 8,000 lakes to choose from, it's hard to pick the leading contenders, but a handful rise to the top: Lake George, Lake Tarpon, Lake Weohyakapka, Lake Istokpoga, Lake Okeechobee, Crescent Lake, Lake Kissimmee, Lake George, and Lake Talquin. Florida's most popular freshwater game fish is the largemouth bass. Freshwater fishermen are also checking rivers and streams for other popular catches, such as spotted bass, white bass, Suwannee bass, striped bass, black crappie, bluegill, redear sunfish, and channel catfish.

SALT WATER

The seas are filled with some of the most challenging (and tasty) gamefish in America. From piers, jetties, private boats, and charter excursions, fishermen search for bonefish, tarpon, snook, redfish, grouper, permit, spotted sea trout, sailfish, cobia, bluefish, snapper, sea bass, dolphin (the short, squat fish, not Flipper), and sheepshead.

Tarpon

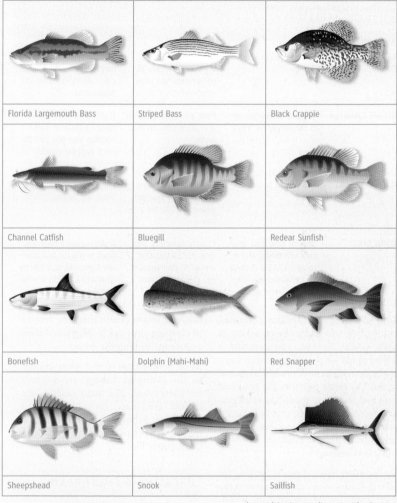

Florida Largemouth Bass

Striped Bass

Black Crappie

Channel Catfish

Bluegill

Redear Sunfish

Bonefish

Dolphin (Mahi-Mahi)

Red Snapper

Sheepshead

Snook

Sailfish

(top six) freshwater, (bottom six) saltwater

HERE'S THE CATCH

The type of fish you're after will depend on whether you fish in Florida's lake, streams, and rivers, or head out to sea. The Panhandle has an abundance of red snapper, while Lake Okeechobee is the place for bass fishing—although the largemouth bass is found throughout the state (they're easiest to catch in early spring, when they're in shallower wa-ters). If you're looking for a good charter, Destin has the largest charter-boat fishing fleet in the nation. In the Florida Keys, you can fish by walking out in the very shallow water for hundreds of yards with the water only up to your knees; the fish you might reel in this way include bonefish, tarpon, and permit.

CHARTING THE WATERS

TYPE OF TRIP	COST	PROS	CONS
LARGE PARTY BOAT	$40/person for 4 hrs.	The captain's fishing license covers all passengers; you keep whatever you catch.	Not much privacy, assistance, or solitude: boats can hold as many as 35 passengers.
PRIVATE CHARTER	Roughly $1,200 for up to six people for 9 hrs.	More personal attention and more time on the water.	Higher cost ($200 per person instead of $40); tradition says you split the catch with the captain.
GUIDED TRIP FOR INLAND WATERS	Around $300–$400 for one or two people for 6 hrs.	Helpful if your time is limited and you want to make sure you go where the fish are biting.	Can be expensive and may not be as exciting as deep-sea fishing.
GOING SOLO	Cost for gear (rod, line, bait, and tackle) and license ($30-$100 depending on where you fish and if you need gear).	Privacy, flexibility, your time and destination are up to you; you can get fishing tips from your fellow anglers.	If you require a boat, you need to pay for and operate it yourself, plus pay for gear and a fishing license and find a fishing spot!

With a little hunting (by calling marinas, visiting bait and tackle stores, asking at town visitor centers), you can find a fishing guide who will lead you to some of the best spots on Florida's lakes and rivers. The guide provides the boat and gear, and his license should cover all passengers. A guide is not generally necessary for freshwater fishing, but if you're new to the sport, it might be a worthwhile investment.

On the other hand, if you're looking for fishing guides who can get you into the deep water for tarpon, redfish, snook, snapper, and dolphin, your best bet is to hang out at the marinas along the Florida coast and decide whether price or privacy is more important. If it's price, choose one of the larger party boats. If you'd prefer some privacy and the privilege of creating an exclusive passenger list, then sign up for a private charter. The average charter runs about nine hours, but some companies offer overnight and extended trips, too. Gear is provided in both charter-boat methods, and charters also offer the service of cleaning your catch. All guided trips encourage tipping the crew.

Most people new to the sport choose to do saltwater fishing via a charter party boat. The main reasons are expert guidance, convenience, and cost. Plus, fishing with others can be fun. Charter trips depart from marinas throughout Florida.

CREATING A FLOAT PLAN

If you're fishing in a boat on your own, let someone know where you're headed by providing a float plan, which should include where you're leaving from, a description of the boat you're on, how many are in the boat with you, what survival gear and radio equipment you have onboard, your cell phone number, and when you expect to return. If you don't return as expected, your friend can call the Coast Guard to search for you. Also be sure to have enough life jackets for everyone on board.

RULES AND REGULATIONS

To fish anywhere in (or off the coast of) Florida, you need a license, and there are separate licenses for freshwater fishing and saltwater fishing.

For non-residents, either type of fishing license cost $47 for the annual license, $30 for the 7-day one, or $17 for a 3-day license. Permits/tags are needed for catching snook ($2), crawfish/lobster ($2), and tarpon ($51.50). License and permit costs help generate funds for the Florida Fish and Wildlife Conservation Commission, which reinvests the fees into ensuring healthy habitats to sustain fish and wildlife populations, to improve access to fishing spots, and to help ensure public safety.

You can purchase your license and permits at county tax collectors' offices as well as wherever you buy your bait and tackle, such as Florida marinas, specialty stores, and sporting goods shops. You can also buy it online at ⊕ www.myfwc.com/license and have it mailed to you; a surcharge is added to online orders.

If you're on a charter, you don't need to get a license. The captain's fishing license covers all passengers. Also, some piers have their own saltwater fishing licenses that cover you when you're fishing off them for recreational purposes—if you're pier fishing, ask the personnel at the tackle shop if the pier is covered.

RESOURCES

For the latest regulations on gear, daily limits, minimum sizes and seasons for certain fish, and other fishing requirements, consult the extraordinary **Florida Fish and Wildlife Conservation Commission** (☎ 888/347–4356 ⊕ www.myfwc.com).

WEB RESOURCES
Download the excellent, and free, Florida Fishing PDF at www.visitflorida.com/planning/guide. Other good sites: www.floridafishinglakes.net www.fishingcapital.com www.floridasportsman.com

Palm Beach and the Treasure Coast

WORD OF MOUTH

"If you really want to be close to restaurants and shops in the Palm Beach area, check out the Marriott in Delray Beach or even the adjacent Residence Inn by Marriott . . . about 30 minutes south of Palm beach."

—rattravlers

WELCOME TO PALM BEACH AND THE TREASURE COAST

TOP REASONS TO GO

★ **Beautiful Beaches:**
From Jupiter's sandy shoreline, where leashed dogs are welcome, to the broad stretches of sand in Delray Beach and Boca Raton, swimmers, sunbathers, and surfers—and sea turtles looking for a place to hatch their eggs—all find happiness.

★ **Exquisite Resorts:**
The Ritz-Carlton and the Four Seasons continue to sparkle with service fit for royalty. Two historic gems—the Breakers in Palm Beach and the Boca Raton Resort—perpetually draw the rich, the famous, and anyone else who can afford the luxury.

★ **Horse Around:**
Wellington, with its jumping events and its popular polo season, is often called the winter equestrian capital of the world.

★ **Have a Reel Good Time:** From Lake Okeechobee, a great place to catch bass and perch, to the Atlantic Ocean, teeming with kingfish, sailfish, dolphinfish, and wahoos, anglers will find the waters here a treasure chest.

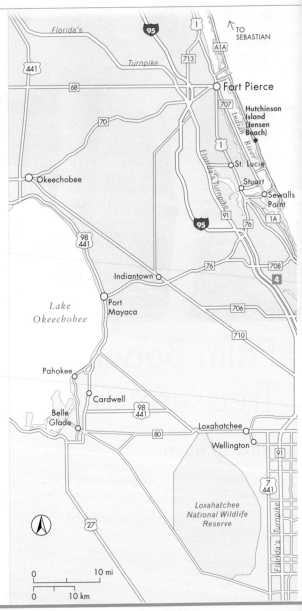

Wellington.

1 Palm Beach. With Gatsby-era architecture, stone-and-stucco estates, extravagant landscaping, and highbrow shops, Palm Beach is a must-see for travelers to the area. Plan to spend some time on Worth Avenue, also called the Mink Mile, a collection of more than 200 chic shops, and Whitehall, once the winter retreat for Henry Flagler, Palm Beach's founder.

2 West Palm Beach. Bustling with its own affluent identity, West Palm Beach has much to offer. Palm Beach–style homes line lovely Flagler Drive, and golf courses are abundant. Culture fans have plenty to cheer about, from the Kravis Center for the Performing Arts, to the Norton Museum of Art and the Armory Arts Center. Kids will love the Palm Beach Zoo.

3 South to Boca Raton. The territory from Palm Beach south to Boca Raton defines old-world glamour and new age sophistication. Delray Beach boasts a lively downtown, with galleries, shops, and restaurants. To the west are the Morikami Japanese Gardens and the headquarters of the American Orchid Society. Boca Raton's Mizner Park has tony boutiques, restaurants, and the Boca Raton Museum of Art.

4 Treasure Coast. Much of the shoreline north of Palm Beach remains blissfully undeveloped. Along the coast, the broad tidal lagoon separates barrier islands from the mainland.

GETTING ORIENTED

This South Florida region extends 120 mi from Sebastian to Boca Raton. The golden stretch of the Atlantic from Palm Beach southward defines old-world glamour and new age sophistication. North of Palm Beach, you'll uncover the comparatively undeveloped Treasure Coast, where towns and wide-open spaces along the road await your discovery. Altogether, there's a delightful disparity, from Palm Beach, pulsing fast with old-money wealth, to low-key Hutchinson Island and Manalapan. The burgeoning equestrian community of Wellington lies 10 mi west of Palm Beach. It is the site of much of the county's new development.

ATLANTIC OCEAN

◆ Jupiter Island
◆ Hobe Sound

1

○ Tequesta
Jupiter
1A

○ Juno Beach
Singer Island
◆ Palm Beach Gardens

● Palm Beach Shores

● Riviera Beach

West Palm **1** Beach
2 ○ Palm Beach
1A

○ Lake Worth
809
○○ South Palm Beach
Lantana ○ Manalapan

● Boynton Beach
95 **3**
◆ Gulf Stream

○ Delray Beach
○ Highland Beach
1A
○ Boca Raton
1

Worth Avenue.

PALM BEACH AND THE TREASURE COAST PLANNER

When to Go

The weather is optimal from November through May, but the trade-off is that roadways and facilities are more crowded and prices higher. In summer it helps to have a tolerance for heat, humidity, and afternoon downpours. Hurricane season runs from June through November, not necessarily a bad time for a trip here as there's always plenty of warning before the big storms. For the best lodging rates consider summer months or the early weeks of December. Make sure to bring insect repellent for outdoor activities.

Specialty Tours

DivaDuck Tours (✉ *Rosemary Ave. and Hibiscus St.* ☎ *561/844–4186* ⊕ *www.divaduck.com*) runs 75-minute amphibious tours of West Palm Beach/Palm Beach in and out of the water. Cruises run two or three times a day for $25.

Getting Here

The best place to fly into is **Palm Beach International Airport** (*PBI* ☎ *561/471–7420*). For a cab, call **Palm Beach Transportation** (☎ *561/689–4222*), the hotline for the Yellow cab company. **Tri-Rail Commuter Bus Service** (☎ *800/874–7245*), the commuter rail system, provides taxi and limousine service. For either, the lowest fares are $2.50 per mile, with the meter starting at $2.50. Tri-Rail has 18 stops altogether between West Palm Beach and Miami, where tickets can be purchased. The one-way fare is $5.50. The city's bus service, **Palm Tran** (☎ *561/841–4200*), runs routes 44 and 40 from the airport to Tri-Rail's nearby Palm Beach airport station daily. **Amtrak** (☎ *800/872–7245* ⊕ *www.amtrak.com*) connects West Palm Beach with cities along Florida's east coast and the northeast daily.

Getting Around

Interstate 95 runs north–south, linking West Palm Beach with Fort Lauderdale and Miami to the south and with Daytona, Jacksonville, and the rest of the Atlantic Coast to the north. Florida's turnpike runs from Miami north through West Palm Beach before angling northwest to reach Orlando. U.S. 1 threads north–south along the coast, connecting most coastal communities, whereas the more scenic Route A1A ventures out onto the barrier islands. Interstate 95 runs parallel to U.S. 1 but a few miles inland.

Alligator.

About the Restaurants

Numerous elegant establishments offer upscale Continental and contemporary fare, but the area also teems with casual waterfront spots serving affordable burgers and fresh seafood feasts. Grouper, fried or blackened, is especially popular here, along with the ubiquitous shrimp. An hour's drive west of the coast, around Lake Okeechobee, dine on catfish panfried to perfection and so fresh it seems barely out of the water. Early-bird menus, a Florida hallmark, typically entice the budget-minded with several dinner entrées at reduced prices offered during certain hours, usually before 5 or 6.

About the Hotels

Palm Beach has a number of smaller hotels in addition to the famous Breakers. Lower-priced hotels and motels can be found in West Palm Beach and Lake Worth. To the south, the coastal town of Manalapan has the Ritz-Carlton, Palm Beach; and the posh Boca Raton Resort & Club is near the beach in Boca Raton. To the north in suburban Palm Beach Gardens is the PGA National Resort & Spa. To the west, small towns near Lake Okeechobee offer country-inn accommodations.

Assume that hotels operate on the European Plan (EP, no meals), unless we specify that they use the Breakfast Plan (BP, with full breakfast), Continental Plan (CP, Continental breakfast), Full American Plan (FAP, all meals), or Modified American Plan (MAP, breakfast and dinner), or are all-inclusive (AI, all meals and most activities).

WHAT IT COSTS

	¢	$	$$	$$$	$$$$
Restaurants	under $10	$10–$15	$15–$20	$20–$30	over $30
Hotels	under $80	$80–$100	$100–$140	$140–$220	over $220

Restaurant prices are per person for a main course at dinner. Hotel prices are for a standard double room, excluding 6½% sales tax (more in some counties) and 1%–4% tourist tax.

Inland Sights

Want to get away from the water? Head 40 mi west of West Palm Beach on to Lake Okeechobee for some wildlife viewing, bird-watching, and fishing.

You are likely to see alligators in the tall grass along the shore, as well as birds, including herons, ibises, and bald eagles, which have made a comeback in the area. A 110-mi trail encircles Lake Okeechobee atop the 34-foot Herbert Hoover Dike. On the lake you'll spot happy anglers hooked on some of the best bass fishing in North America. There are 40 species of fish in "Lake O," including largemouth bass, bluegill, Okeechobee catfish, and speckled perch.

Since the **Okee-Tantie Recreation Area** (✉ 10430 Rte. 78 W., Okeechobee ☎ 863/763–2622) has direct lake access, it's a popular fishing outpost, with two public boat ramps, fish-cleaning stations, and a bait shop that stocks groceries. There are also picnic areas and a restaurant.

Getting Here: The best way to drive here from West Palm is to go west on Southern Boulevard from Interstate 95 past the cut-off road to Lion Country Safari. From there, the boulevard is designated U.S. 98/441.

2

PALM BEACH AND TREASURE COAST BEACHES

While not as white and fine as the shores on Florida's west coast, the beaches here provide good stomping grounds for hikers, well-guarded waters for swimmers, decent waves for surfers, and plenty of opportunities for sand-castle building and shell collecting.

Miles of sandy shoreline can be found here beside gorgeous blue-green waters you won't find farther north. The average year-round water temperature is 74°F, much warmer than Southern California beaches that average a comparatively chilly 62°F.

Humans aren't alone in finding the shores inviting. Migratory birds flock to the beaches, too, as do sea turtles, who come between May and August to lay their eggs in the sand. Locally organized watches take small groups out at night to observe mother turtles as they waddle onto shore, dig holes with their flippers and deposit their golf-ball-sized eggs into the sand. Hatchlings emerge about 45 days later.

WHEN TO GO

Palm Beach and Treasure Coast beaches are warm, clear, and sparkling all year long, but the best time to get in the water is between December and March. The shorelines are often more crowded then, but you don't have to worry about jellyfish or sea lice when you take a dip. Sea lice can cause welts, blisters, and rashes. The crowds thin out during summer and fall months, which is inviting, but jellyfish and sea lice can be a problem then.

PALM BEACH AND TREASURE COAST'S BEST BEACHES

DELRAY

If you're looking for a place to see and be seen, head for Delray's wide expanse of sand, which stretches 2 mi, half of it supervised by lifeguards. Reefs off the coast are popular with divers, as is a sunken Spanish galleon less than ½ mi offshore from the Seagate Club on the south end of the beach. **Pros:** good for swimmers and sunbathers; bars and restaurants across the street; cabanas and catamarans available for rent. **Cons:** often a long walk to the public restrooms.

JOHN D. MACARTHUR STATE PARK

If getting far from the madding crowd is your goal, John D. MacArthur State Park on the north end of Singer Island is a good choice. You will find a great place for snorkeling, kayaking, bird-watching, and fishing. Part of the beach was once dedicated to topless bathers, but that is no longer the case. **Pros:** guides to local flora and fauna are available; a good place to spot sea turtles. **Cons:** beach is a long walk from the parking lot.

JUNO BEACH

Juno Beach sports a 990-foot pier and a bait shop for those who like to spend their morning fishing. But the shoreline itself is a favorite for families with kids who drag along sand toys, build castles,

and hunt for shells. **Pros:** concession stand and a bait shop. **Cons:** beach isn't as wide as others.

RED REEF PARK

Looking for a great place to snorkel? This Boca Raton beach is just the ticket, and it doesn't matter if you're a beginner or a pro. The reef is only about 50 feet off shore. Expect to see tropical fish and maybe even a manatee or two. **Pros:** the park's showers and bathrooms are kept clean and there's a playground for kids. **Cons:** if you go at low tide, you're not going to see as many tropical fish.

STUART BEACH

When the waves robustly roll in at Stuart Beach, the surfers are rolling in, too. Beginning surfers are especially keen on Stuart Beach because of its ever-vigilant lifeguards, while pros to the sport like the challenges the choppy waters here bring. Beachgoers with kids like the snack bar known for its chicken fingers, and for those who like a side of museum musing with their day in the sun, there's an impressive collection of antique cars at a museum just steps from the beach. **Pros:** parking is easy to find, and there are three boardwalks for easy access to the beach. **Cons:** sand and surf can be rocky.

Updated
by Mary
Thurwachter

This golden stretch of Atlantic coast resists categorization, and for good reason. The territory from Palm Beach south to Boca Raton defines old-world glamour and new age sophistication.

North of Palm Beach you'll uncover the comparatively undeveloped Treasure Coast—liberally sprinkled with coastal gems—where towns and wide-open spaces along the road await your discovery. Altogether, there's a delightful disparity, from Palm Beach, pulsing fast with plenty of old-money wealth, to low-key Hutchinson Island and Manalapan. Seductive as the beach scene interspersed with eclectic dining options can be, you should also take advantage of flourishing commitments to historic preservation and the arts, as town after town yields intriguing museums, galleries, theaters, and gardens.

Palm Beach, with Gatsby-era architecture, stone-and-stucco estates, extravagant landscaping, and highbrow shops, can reign as the focal point for your sojourn any time of year. From Palm Beach, head off in any of three directions: south via the Gold Coast toward Boca Raton along an especially scenic route known as A1A, back to the mainland and north to the barrier-island treasures of the Treasure Coast, or west for more rustic inland activities such as bass fishing and biking on the dikes around Lake Okeechobee.

PALM BEACH

Long reigning as the place where the crème de la crème go to shake off winter's chill, Palm Beach continues to be a seasonal hotbed of platinum-grade consumption. Other towns like Jupiter Island may rank higher on the per-capita-wealth meter, but there's no competing with the historic social supremacy of Palm Beach. It has been the winter address for heirs of the iconic Rockefeller, Vanderbilt, Colgate, Post, Kellogg, and Kennedy families. Even newer power brokers, with names like Kravis, Peltz, and Trump, are made to understand that strict laws govern everything from building to landscaping, and not so much as a pool awning gets added without a town council nod. If Palm Beach were to fly a flag, it's been observed, there might be three interlocking Cs, standing not only for Cartier, Chanel, and Christian Dior but also for clean, civil, and capricious. Only three bridges allow access to the island, and huge tour buses are a no-no.

To learn who's who in Palm Beach, it helps to pick up a copy of the *Palm Beach Daily News*—locals call it the Shiny Sheet because its high-quality paper avoids smudging society hands or Pratesi linens—for, as it is said, to be mentioned in the Shiny Sheet is to be Palm Beach. All this fabled ambience started with Henry Morrison Flagler, Florida's premier developer, and cofounder, along with John D. Rockefeller, of Standard Oil. No sooner did Flagler bring the railroad to Florida in the 1890s than he erected the famed Royal Poinciana and Breakers hotels. Rail access sent real-estate prices soaring, and ever since, princely sums have been forked over for personal stationery engraved with 33480, the ZIP code of Palm Beach. To provide Palm Beach with servants and other workers, Flagler also developed an off-island community a mile or so west. West Palm Beach now bustles with its own affluent identity.

Setting the tone in this town of unparalleled Florida opulence is the ornate architectural work of Addison Mizner, who began designing homes and public buildings here in the 1920s and whose Moorish-Gothic style has influenced virtually all community landmarks. Thanks to Mizner and his lasting influence, Palm Beach remains a playground of the rich, famous, and discerning.

GETTING HERE AND AROUND

Palm Beach is 78 mi north of Miami. To access Palm Beach off Interstate 95, exit east at Southern Boulevard, Belvedere Road, or Okeechobee Boulevard. The city's Palm Tran buses run between Worth Avenue and Royal Palm Way in Palm Beach and major areas of West Palm Beach and require exact change. Regular fares are $1.50.

For a taste of what it's like to jockey for position in this status-conscious town, stake out a parking place on Worth Avenue or parallel residential streets, and squeeze in among the Mercedeses, Rolls-Royces, and Bentleys. Between admiring your excellent parking skills and feeling car-struck at the surrounding fine specimens of automobile, be sure to note the PARKING BY PERMIT ONLY and TWO-HOUR parking signs, as a $25 parking ticket might take the shine off your spot. ■ TIP→ The best course for a half-day visit is to valet-park at the parking deck next to Saks Fifth Avenue. Away from downtown, along County Road and Ocean Boulevard (the shore road, also designated as Route A1A), are Palm Beach's other defining landmarks: Mediterranean-style residences, some built of coral rock, that are nothing short of palatial, topped by barrel-tile roofs and often fronted by 10-foot ficus and sea grape hedges. The low wall that separates the dune-top shore road from the sea hides shoreline that varies in many places from expansive to eroded. Here and there, where the strand deepens, homes are built directly on the beach.

ESSENTIALS

Transportation Contact **Palm Tran** (☎ 561/841–4287).

Visitor Information **Town of Palm Beach Chamber of Commerce** (✉ 400 Royal Palm Way, Suite 106, Palm Beach ☎ 561/655–3282).

Draped in European elegance, The Breakers in Palm Beach sits on 140 acres along the oceanfront.

EXPLORING

Numbers in the margin correspond to the Palm Beach and West Palm Beach map.

TOP ATTRACTIONS

❸ Bethesda-by-the-Sea. Donald Trump and his wife Melania were married here in 2005, but this Spanish Gothic Episcopal church had a claim to fame upon its creation in 1925: it was built by the first Protestant congregation in southeast Florida. Guided tours follow 11 AM services on the second and fourth Sunday of the month. Adjacent are the formal, ornamental **Cluett Memorial Gardens.** ⌷ *141 S. County Rd.* ☎ *561/655–4554* ⊕ *www.bbts.org* ⌷ *Free* ☉ *Church and gardens daily 8–5.*

❷ The Breakers. Built by Henry Flagler in 1896 and rebuilt by his descendants after a 1925 fire, this magnificent Italian Renaissance–style resort helped launch Florida tourism with its Gilded Age opulence, attracting influential, wealthy Northerners to the state. The hotel, still owned by Flagler's heirs, is a must-see even if you aren't staying here. Walk through the 200-foot-long lobby, which has soaring arched ceilings painted by 72 Italian artisans and hung with crystal chandeliers, and the ornate Florentine Dining Room is decorated with 15th-century Flemish tapestries. ⌷ *1 S. County Rd.* ☎ *561/655–6611* ⊕ *www.thebreakers.com.*

Fodor'sChoice ★

❶ Henry Morrison Flagler Museum. The opulence of Florida's Gilded Age lives on at Whitehall, the palatial 55-room "marble palace" Henry Flagler commissioned in 1901 for his third wife, Mary Lily Kenan. Architects John Carrère and Thomas Hastings were instructed to create the finest home imaginable—and they outdid themselves. Whitehall

Fodor'sChoice ★

rivals the grandeur of European palaces and has an entrance hall with a baroque ceiling similar to Louis XIV's Versailles. Here you'll see original furnishings; a hidden staircase Flagler used to sneak from his bedroom to the billiards room; an art collection; a 1,200-pipe organ; and Florida East Coast Railway exhibits, along with Flagler's personal railcar, the *Rambler,* showcased in an 8,000-square-foot beaux arts–style pavilion behind the mansion. Tours take about an hour and are offered at frequent intervals. The café, open after Thanksgiving through mid-April, offers snacks and afternoon tea. ⊠ *1 Whitehall Way* ☏ *561/655–2833* ⊕ *www.flagler.org* ⊟ *$18* ⊘ *Tues.–Sat. 10–5, Sun. noon–5.*

❺ **Worth Avenue.** Called the Avenue by Palm Beachers, this ¼-mi-long
★ street is synonymous with exclusive shopping. Nostalgia lovers recall an era when faces or names served as charge cards, purchases were delivered home before customers returned from lunch, and bills were sent directly to private accountants. Times have changed, but a stroll amid the Moorish architecture of its shops offers a tantalizing taste of the island's ongoing commitment to elegant consumerism. Explore the labyrinth of eight pedestrian vias, on both sides of Worth Avenue, that wind past boutiques, tiny plazas, bubbling fountains, and the bougainvillea-festooned wrought-iron balconies of 2nd-floor apartments. ⊠ *Between Cocoanut Row and S. Ocean Blvd.*

WORTH NOTING

❻ **El Solano.** No Palm Beach mansion better represents the town's luminous legacy than the Spanish-style home built by Addison Mizner as his own residence in 1925. Mizner later sold El Solano to Harold Vanderbilt, and the property was long a favorite among socialites for parties and photo shoots. Vanderbilt held many a gala fund-raiser here. Beatle John Lennon and his wife, Yoko Ono, bought it less than a year before Lennon's death. It's still privately owned and not open to the public. ⊠ *721 S. County Rd.*

❼ **Mar-a-Lago.** Breakfast-food heiress Marjorie Merriweather Post commissioned a Hollywood set designer to create Ocean Boulevard's famed Mar-a-Lago, a 118-room, 110,000-square-foot Mediterranean-revival palace. Its 75-foot Italianate tower is visible from most areas of Palm Beach and from across the Intracoastal Waterway in West Palm Beach. Owner Donald Trump has turned it into a private membership club. ⊠ *1100 S. Ocean Blvd.* ☏ *561/832–2600* ⊕ *www.maralagoclub.com.*

❽ **Phipps Ocean Park.** In addition to the shoreline, tennis courts, picnic tables, and grills, this park has a Palm Beach County landmark in the **Little Red Schoolhouse.** Dating from 1886, it served as the first schoolhouse in what was then Dade County. No alcoholic beverages are permitted in the park. ⊠ *2185 S. Ocean Blvd.* ☏ *561/838–5400* ⊟ *Free* ⊘ *Daily dawn–dusk.*

❹ **Society of the Four Arts.** Despite widespread misconceptions of members-only exclusivity, this privately endowed institution—founded in 1936 to encourage appreciation of art, music, drama, and literature—is funded for public enjoyment. A gallery building—designed by Addison Mizner, of course—artfully melds an exhibition hall, library, and the Philip Hulitar Sculpture Garden, which underwent a major renovation

Palm Beach and
West Palm Beach

in 2006. Open from about Thanksgiving to Easter, the museum's programs are extensive, and there's ample free parking. In addition to showcasing traveling art exhibitions, the museum offers films, lectures, workshops, and concerts. ✉ *2 Four Arts Plaza* ☎ *561/655–7226* ⊕ *www.fourarts.org* ✉ *Program admission varies* ⊙ *Galleries Dec.–mid-Apr., Mon.–Sat. 10–5, Sun. 2–5; library, weekdays 10–5, Sat. 10–1; gardens 10–5 daily.*

SPORTS AND THE OUTDOORS

BIKING

Bicycling is a great way to get a closer look at Palm Beach. Only 14 mi long, ½ mi wide, flat as the top of a billiard table, and just as green, it's a perfect biking place. The palm-fringed **Lake Trail** (✉ *Parallel to Lake Way*) skirts the backyards of many palatial mansions and the edge of Lake Worth. The trail starts at the Society of the Four Arts, heading north 8 mi to the end and back—just follow the signs. A block from the bike trail, the **Palm Beach Bicycle Trail Shop** (✉ *223 Sunrise Ave.* ☎ *561/659–4583* ⊕ *www.palmbeachbicycle.com*) rents by the hour or day. It's open daily.

GOLF

Breakers Hotel Golf Club (✉ *1 S. County Rd.* ☎ *561/659–8407*) has the historic Ocean Course and the Todd Anderson Golf Academy and is open to members and hotel guests only. A $210 greens fee includes range balls, cart, and bag storage at Breakers West or at the redesigned Ocean Course. The **Town of Palm Beach Golf Club** (✉ *2345 S. Ocean Blvd.* ☎ *561/547–0598*) has 18 holes, including six on the Atlantic and three on the inland waterway; greens fee $45 riding, $32 to walk. The course was recently redesigned by Raymond Floyd and is a gem of a short-game course.

SHOPPING

★   One of the world's premier showcases for high-quality shopping, **Worth Avenue** runs ¼ mi east–west across Palm Beach, from the beach to Lake Worth. The street has more than 250 shops (more than 40 of them sell jewelry), and many upscale chain stores (Gucci, Hermès, Pucci, Saks Fifth Avenue, Neiman Marcus, Louis Vuitton, Emanuel Ungaro, Chanel, Dior, Cartier, Tiffany, and Tourneau) are represented—their merchandise appealing to the discerning tastes of the Palm Beach clientele. The six blocks of **South County Road** north of Worth Avenue have interesting (and somewhat less expensive) stores. For specialty items (out-of-town newspapers, health foods, and books), try the shops along the north side of **Royal Poinciana Way.** Most stores are closed on Sunday, and many go on hiatus in summer.

The thrift store **Church Mouse** (✉ *374 S. County Rd.* ☎ *561/659–2154*) is where many high-end resale boutique owners grab their merchandise. **Déjà Vu** (✉ *Via Testa, 219 Royal Poinciana Way* ☎ *561/833–6624*) could be the resale house of Chanel, as it has so many gently used, top-quality pieces. There's no digging through piles here; clothes are in impeccable condition and are well organized.

Giorgio's (⊠ *230 Worth Ave.* ☎ *561/655–2446*) is over-the-top indulgence, with 50 colors of silk and cashmere sweaters and 22 colors of ostrich and alligator adorning everything from bags to bicycles.

Jewelry is very important in Palm Beach, and for more than 100 years **Greenleaf & Crosby** (⊠ *236 Worth Ave.* ☎ *561/655–5850*) has had a diverse selection that includes investment pieces. **Spring Flowers** (⊠ *337 Worth Ave.* ☎ *561/832–0131*) has beautiful children's clothing. Little ones start with a newborn gown set by Kissy Kissy or Petit Bateau and grow into fashions by Cacharel and Lili Gaufrette.

Holding court for more than 60 years, **Van Cleef & Arpels** (⊠ *202 Worth Ave.* ☎ *561/655–6767*) is where legendary members of Palm Beach society shop for tiaras and formal jewels.

NIGHTLIFE AND THE ARTS

NIGHTLIFE
Palm Beach is teeming with restaurants that turn into late-night hot spots, plus hotel lobby bars perfect for tête-à-têtes. Popular for lunch and dinner, **Cucina Dell'Arte** (⊠ *257 Royal Poinciana Way* ☎ *561/655–0770*) later becomes the in place for the younger and trendy set. The old guard gathers at the **Leopard Lounge** (⊠ *Chesterfield Hotel, 363 Cocoanut Row* ☎ *561/659–5800*) for live music during cocktail hour and later to dance until the wee hours every night of the year. Thursday night happy hours spiked by creatively named cocktails and live jazz draw a local crowd to the lobby lounge and outdoor patio of the **Brazilian Court** (⊠ *301 Australian Ave.* ☎ *561/655–7740*).

THE ARTS
Society of the Four Arts (⊠ *2 Four Arts Plaza* ☎ *561/655–7226*) has concerts, lectures, and films November through March.

WHERE TO EAT

$$$
ITALIAN
✕ **Amici.** The town's premier celebrity-magnet bistro is still a crowd pleaser. When it moved across the street and down the block from its original location, the Palm Beach crowd followed. The northern Italian menu highlights house specialties such as rigatoni with spicy tomato sauce and roasted eggplant, potato gnocchi, grilled veal chops, risottos, and pizzas from a wood-burning oven. There are nightly pasta and fresh fish specials as well. To avoid the crowds, stop by for a late lunch or early dinner. ⊠ *375 S. County Rd.* ☎ *561/832–0201* ⊕ *www.amicipalmbeach.com* ⊘ *Reservations essential* ▭ *AE, DC, MC, V.*

$$$$
ITALIAN
✕ **Bice Ristorante.** The bougainvillea-laden trellises set the scene at the main entrance on Peruvian Way. Weather permitting, many patrons prefer to dine on the outdoor terrace on the narrow pedestrian walkway. A favorite of Palm Beach society and Hollywood celebs, both the restaurant and the bar become packed and noisy during high season. The aroma of basil, chives, and oregano fills the air as waiters carry out home-baked focaccia to accompany delectable dishes such as seafood

Worth Avenue is the place in Palm Beach for high-end shopping, from international boutiques to art galleries.

risotto, veal chops, and duck breast sautéed in mushroom sauce with venison-truffle ravioli. ⊠ *313½ Worth Ave.* ☎ *561/835–1600* ⌕ *Reservations essential* ▭ *AE, D, DC, MC, V.*

$$$$
FRENCH
Fodor's Choice
★

✕ **Café Boulud.** Celebrated chef Daniel Boulud opened his outpost of New York's Café Boulud in the Brazilian Court hotel. The warm and welcoming French-American venue is casual yet elegant, with a palette of honey, gold, and citron. Plenty of natural light spills through arched glass doors opening to a lush courtyard. Lunch and dinner entrées on Boulud's signature four-muse menu include classic French, seasonal, vegetarian, and a rotating selection of international dishes. The lounge, with its illuminated amber glass bar, is the perfect perch to take in the jet-set crowd that comes for a hint of the south of France in South Florida. A DJ plays on Saturday nights. ⊠ *Brazilian Court, 301 Australian Ave.* ☎ *561/655–6060* ⊕ *www.cafeboulud.com* ⌕ *Reservations essential* ▭ *AE, DC, MC, V.*

$$$$
ECLECTIC

✕ **Café L'Europe.** Even after 25 years, the favorite lunch spot of society's movers and shakers remains a regular stop on foodie itineraries. The management pays close attention to service and consistency, a big reason for its longevity. Best sellers include rack of lamb, Dover sole, and Wiener schnitzel, along with such inspired creations as crispy sweetbreads with poached pears and mustard sauce. Depending on your mood, the champagne-caviar bar can serve up appetizers or desserts. The place has an extensive wine list. A pianist plays nightly from 7 to 11 and a quartet plays dance music Friday and Saturday nights until 1 AM. ⊠ *331 S. County Rd.* ☎ *561/655–4020* ⊕ *www.cafeleurope.com* ▭ *AE, DC, MC, V* ☉ *No lunch May–Oct. Closed Mon.*

$$$$
FRENCH
Fodor's Choice
★
✕ **Chez Jean-Pierre.** With walls adorned with Dalí- and Picasso-like art, this is where the Palm Beach old guard likes to let down its guard, all the while partaking of sumptuous French cuisine and an impressive wine list. Forget calorie or cholesterol concerns and indulge in scrambled eggs with caviar or homemade duck foie gras, along with desserts like hazelnut soufflé or profiteroles au chocolat. Waiters are friendly and very attentive. Jackets are not required, although many men wear them. ⊠ *132 N. County Rd.* ☎ *561/833–1171* ⚞ *Reservations essential* ▭ *AE, DC, MC, V* ⊗ *Closed Sun. No lunch.*

$
AMERICAN
✕ **Hamburger Heaven.** A favorite with locals since 1945, the quintessential diner with horseshoe-shaped counter as well as booths and tables is loud and casual and has some of the best burgers on the island. Fresh salads, homemade pastries, and daily soup and hot-plate specials featuring comfort foods like meat loaf and chicken potpie are also available. During the week, it's a popular lunch stop for working stiffs. The staff is friendly and efficient. ⊠ *314 S. County Rd.* ☎ *561/655–5277* ▭ *MC, V* ⊗ *Closed Sun.*

$$
PIZZA
✕ **Pizza Al Fresco.** The secret-garden setting is the secret to the success of this popular European-style pizzeria, where you can dine under a canopy of century-old banyans in a charming courtyard. Specialties are 12-inch hand-tossed brick-oven pizzas with such interesting toppings as prosciutto, arugula, and caviar. There's even a dessert pizza topped with Nutella. Piping-hot calzones, salads, and sandwiches round out the selection. Look for the grave markers of Addison Mizner's beloved pet monkey, Johnnie Brown, and Rose Sachs's dog Laddie (she and husband Morton bought Mizner's villa and lived there 47 years) next to the patio. Delivery is available—by limo, of course. This bistro is dog-friendly. ⊠ *14 Via Mizner, at Worth Ave.* ☎ *561/832–0032* ⊕ *www.pizzaalfresco.com* ▭ *AE, MC, V.*

$$$
AMERICAN
★
✕ **Ta-boó.** This 60-year-old landmark with peach stucco walls and green shutters attracts Worth Avenue shoppers looking for a two-hour lunch and a dinner crowd ranging from tuxed and sequined theatergoers to polo-shirted vacationers. Entrées include Black Angus dry-aged beef or roast duck. Don't miss Coconut Lust, a signature dessert. Drop in late night during the winter season when the nightly music is playing and you'll probably spot a celebrity or two. ⊠ *221 Worth Ave.* ☎ *561/835–3500* ⊕ *www.taboorestaurant.com* ▭ *AE, DC, MC, V.*

$$$
CAFÉ
✕ **Testa's Palm Beach.** Attracting a loyal clientele since 1921, this restaurant is still owned by the Testa family. Lunches range from burgers to crab salad, and dinner specialties include snapper Florentine and jumbo lump-crab cakes. You can dine inside in an intimate pine-paneled room with cozy bar, out back in a gazebo-style room for large groups, or outside at tables with pink tablecloths next to planters of pink hibiscus, with a view of the Breakers in the distance. Don't miss the signature strawberry pie made with fresh Florida berries. ⊠ *221 Royal Poinciana Way* ☎ *561/832–0992* ⊕ *www.testasrestaurants.com* ▭ *AE, D, MC, V.*

WHERE TO STAY

$$$$ ★ **Brazilian Court.** A short stroll from Worth Avenue, the yellow-stucco Spanish-style facade and red tile roof, and lobby with cypress ceilings and stone floors, underscore this boutique hotel's Roaring '20s origins. All of the studio and one- and two-bedroom suites have rich limestone baths and showers, wine refrigerators, and personal butler service. Bay windows look out into the impeccably maintained gardens and enchanting flower-filled courtyards. Amenities include a state-of-the-art business center, a hair salon and spa, and Café Boulud, a local outpost from famed restaurateur Daniel Boulud; hotel guests reportedly have a better shot than outsiders at procuring a table. Don't feel like dressing up for a table? There's 24-hour in-room dining by Café Boulud. **Pros:** one of the best restaurants in town; attracts a hip crowd; gorgeous courtyard; close to shopping and not far from the beach; free shuttle to the hotel's sister property on the beach, The Omphoy. **Cons:** fitness center is tiny; small pool. ✉ *301 Australian Ave.* ☎ *561/655–7740* 🌐 *www.thebraziliancourt.com* *80 rooms* *In-room:a/c, refrigerator, Internet, Wi-Fi. In-hotel: restaurant, room service, bar, pool, gym, spa, bicycles, laundry facilities, some pets allowed* 💳 *AE, D, DC, MC, V.*

$$$$ Fodor's Choice ★ **The Breakers.** Dating from 1896 and on the National Register of Historic Places, this Italian Renaissance–style resort, owned by Henry Flagler's heirs, sprawls over 140 oceanfront acres. Cupids frolic at the main Florentine fountain, and majestic frescoes grace hallways leading to restaurants. For added luxury, cabanas come with personal concierge. More than an opulent hotel, the Breakers is a modern resort packed with amenities, from a 20,000-square-foot luxury spa and beach club to clubhouses for the 10 tennis courts and two 18-hole golf courses. One of the most extensive wine collections in the world is housed here, keeping the hotel's three sommeliers busy. **Pros:** fine attention to detail throughout; beautiful room views; top-rate golf and tennis facilities. **Cons:** big price tag. ✉ *1 S. County Rd.* ☎ *561/655–6611 or 888/273–2537* 🌐 *www.thebreakers.com* *540 rooms, 68 suites* *In-room: a/c, Internet, safe, refrigerator (some), Wi-Fi. In-hotel: 9 restaurants, room service, bars, golf courses, tennis courts, pools, gym, spa, beachfront, water sports, children's programs (ages 3–12), Internet terminal, parking (paid)* 💳 *AE, D, DC, MC, V.*

$$$$ **The Chesterfield.** Two blocks north of Worth Avenue, the distinctive white-stucco hotel with coral-colored stucco walls and red-and-white-striped awnings offers 54 inviting rooms ranging from small to spacious. All have plush upholstered chairs, paintings, and marble baths. Settle on a leather couch near the cozy library's fireplace and peruse an international newspaper or classic book, or have a cigar in Churchill's, the only public smoking room on the island. Room keys here are brass and maid service is twice a day. A quiet area surrounds a large pool where you can relax, and the Leopard Lounge draws a convivial crowd. **Pros:** turndown service; complimentary beverages in king rooms and suites; elegant rooms; you can open guest-room windows, which is a treat for those who hate air-conditioning **Cons:** small elevator; narrow steps leading to presidential suite. ✉ *363 Cocoanut Row* ☎ *561/659–5800 or 800/243–7871* 🌐 *www.chesterfieldpb.com* *44 rooms, 11*

suites ⚒ *In-room: a/c, refrigerator (some), safe Internet. In-hotel: restaurant, room service, bar, pool, Internet terminal, parking (free), some pets allowed* ☰ *AE, D, DC, MC, V.*

$$$$ 🖫 **The Colony.** What distinguishes this legendary British colonial–style hotel is that it's only one block from Worth Avenue and one block from a beautiful beach on the Atlantic Ocean. The hotel's lobby and pool area has ornamental plants, fountains, wicker furniture, and billowing white panels reminiscent of South Beach's luxurious hotels. An attentive staff, youthful yet experienced, is buzzing with competence and a desire to please. Guest rooms are decorated in Caribbean-colonial, with sunny yellow walls and dark mahogany desks, and pineapple-carved poster beds grace some rooms. Roomy suites and luxurious two-bedroom villas have laundry facilities and full kitchens. The pool is shaped like the state of Florida, although the panhandle is severely reduced in size. Reserve early for the dinner cabaret shows, which have featured entertainers such as Faith Prince and Andrea Marcovicci. **Pros:** close to shopping; rich history; lots of luxury. **Cons:** elevators are small; price tag is high. ⊠ *155 Hammon Ave.* ☎ *561/655–5430 or 800/521–5525* ⊕ *www. thecolonypalmbeach.com* ⤶ *64 rooms, 16 suites, 3 penthouse suites, 7 2-bedroom villas with Jacuzzis* ⚒ *In-room: a/c, safe, refrigerator upon request, Wi-Fi. In-hotel: restaurant, bar, pools, spa, bicycles, Internet terminal, parking (paid) some pets allowed* ☰ *AE, DC, MC, V.*

$$$$ 🖫 **Four Seasons Resort Palm Beach.** Relaxed elegance is the watchword
★ at this four-story resort, which sits on 6 acres with a delightful beach at the south end of town. Fanlight windows, marble columns, chintz curtains, and swaying palms are serene and inviting. A fabulous new spa opened in 2008, and guest-room bathrooms were remodeled in 2009. Rooms are spacious, with separate seating areas and private balconies; many have ocean views. On weekends, live music accompanies cocktails in the Living Room lounge. Jazz groups perform on some weekends in season. The restaurants are worth sampling, and all three have children's menus. Children eat free (except for room service). **Pros:** outstanding restaurants; all rooms have balconies and ocean views; kids eat free; well-established spa. **Cons:** far from nightlife; pricey. ⊠ *2800 S. Ocean Blvd.* ☎ *561/582–2800 or 800/432–2335* ⊕ *www.fourseasons. com* ⤶ *210 rooms, 13 suites* ⚒ *In-room: a/c, safe, Internet. In-hotel: 3 restaurants, room service, bars, tennis courts, pool, gym, spa, beachfront, bicycles, children's programs (ages 3–12), laundry service, some pets allowed, parking (paid)* ☰ *AE, D, DC, MC, V.*

$$$$ 🖫 **The Omphoy Ocean Resort.** This Zenlike boutique hotel on 3 acres opened in 2009 and is a hit with young and hip travelers. From exotic ebony pillars in the lobby to bronze-infused porcelain tile floors and a lounge area with a row of gongs guests are welcome to bang on, the hotel has a sexy, sophisticated look. Asian-style guest rooms come with private balconies, flat-screen TVs and sleek four-poster beds that are nothing like your grandmother's. **Pros:** Michelle Bernstein restaurant; rooms have ocean views and most have balconies. **Cons:** the infinity pool is surrounded by a parking lot and you have to walk through or around the hotel to get to the beach from it. ⊠ *2842 S. Ocean Blvd.* ☎ *561/540–6440 or 888/344–4321* ⊕ *www.omphoy.com* ⤶ *134 rooms,*

10 suites ♿ In-room: a/c, safe, Wi-Fi. In-hotel: 2 restaurants, room service, bars, pool, gym, spa, beachfront, laundry service, Internet terminal, parking (paid), some pets allowed ═ AE, D, DC, MC, V.

WEST PALM BEACH

Across the Intracoastal Waterway from Palm Beach.

Long considered Palm Beach's less-privileged stepsister, sprawling West Palm has evolved into an economically vibrant destination of its own, ranking as the cultural, entertainment, and business center of the entire county and territory to the north. High-rise buildings like the mammoth Palm Beach County Judicial Center and Courthouse and the State Administrative Building underscore the breadth of the city's governmental and corporate activity. The glittering Kravis Center for the Performing Arts is Palm Beach County's principal entertainment venue.

GETTING HERE AND AROUND

West Palm Beach is across the Intracoastal Waterway from Palm Beach. The city's Palm Tran buses run between Worth Avenue and Royal Palm Way in Palm Beach and major areas of West Palm Beach and require exact change. Regular fares are $1.50. Alternatively, share space with local lawyers and shoppers on the free and frequent Molly's Trolleys, which makes continuous loops down Clematis Street, the city's main street, and through CityPlace, a shopping-restaurant-theater district. Hop on and off at any of the seven stops. The trolleys run Sunday to Wednesday 11–9 and Thursday to Saturday 11–11.

ESSENTIALS

Transportation Contacts Molly's Trolleys (☎ 561/838–9511). **Palm Tran** (☎ 561/841–4200).

Visitor Information Chamber of Commerce of the Palm Beaches (✉ 401 N. Flagler Dr. ☎ 561/833–3711). **Palm Beach County Convention & Visitors Bureau** (✉ 1555 Palm Beach Lakes Blvd., Suite 800 ☎ 561/233–3000).

EXPLORING

The heart of revived West Palm Beach is a small, attractive, easy-to-walk downtown area, spurred on by active historic preservation. Along five blocks of beautifully landscaped Clematis Street, which ends at the Intracoastal Waterway, are boutiques and outdoor cafés, plus the 400-seat Cuillo Centre for the Arts, which features shows and concerts; and Palm Beach Dramaworks, an intimate theater that often shows new plays. An exuberant nightlife has taken hold of the area. In fact, downtown rocks every Thursday from 6 PM on with Clematis by Night, a celebration of music, dance, art, and food at Centennial Square. Even on downtown's fringes there are sights of cultural interest.

West Palm Beach's outskirts, flat stretches lined with fast-food outlets and car dealerships, may not inspire, but are worth driving through to reach attractions scattered around the city's southern and western reaches. Several sites are especially rewarding for children and other animal and nature lovers.

The Armory Art Center in West Palm Beach helps students of all ages create works or art in various media.

DOWNTOWN

⑩ Ann Norton Sculpture Gardens. This monument to the late American sculptor Ann Weaver Norton, second wife of Norton Museum founder Ralph H. Norton, includes a complex of art galleries in the main house and studio, plus 2½ acres of gardens, where you'll find 300 varieties of palm trees, seven granite figures, and six brick megaliths. The plantings were designed to attract native birds. Call ahead—hours sometimes vary. ✉ *253 Barcelona Rd.* ☎ *561/832–5328* ⊕ *www.ansg.org* ✉ *$5* ⊙ *Wed.–Sun. 10–4.*

⑫ Armory Art Center. Built by the WPA in 1939, the facility is now a visual-arts center hosting rotating exhibitions and art classes throughout the year. ✉ *1703 Lake Ave.* ☎ *561/832–1776* ⊕ *www.armoryart.org* ✉ *Free* ⊙ *Weekdays 10–4, weekends 10–2.*

⑪ Currie Park. Frequent weekend festivals, including an annual celebration of seafood, take place at the scenic city park next to the Intracoastal Waterway. Sit on one of the piers and watch the yachts and fishing boats pass by. Put on your jogging shoes—the park is at the north end of a 6.3-mi biking-jogging-skating path. ✉ *N. Flagler Dr. at 23rd St.*

⑨ Norton Museum of Art. Constructed in 1941 by steel magnate Ralph H. and Elizabeth Norton, the museum has an extensive collection of 19th- and 20th-century American and European paintings—including works by Picasso, Monet, Matisse, Pollock, and O'Keeffe—and Chinese, contemporary, and photographic art. There are a sublime outdoor covered loggia, Chinese bronze and jade sculptures, and a library. Galleries, including the Great Hall, also showcase traveling exhibits. There's a good museum store, and lectures, programs and concerts for children

Fodor's Choice
★

and adults. ■TIP→ One of the city's best-kept secrets is this museum's Café 1451, with its artfully presented dishes that taste as good as they look. ⊠ *1451 S. Olive Ave.* ☏ *561/832–5196* ⊕ *www.norton.org* 🖃 *$12* ⊘ *Tues.–Sat. 10–5, Sun. 1–5.*

AWAY FROM DOWNTOWN
TOP ATTRACTIONS

⑱ **Lion Country Safari.** Drive your own vehicle along 8 mi of paved roads through a 500-acre cageless zoo with a thousand free-roaming animals. Lions, elephants, white rhinos, giraffes, zebras, antelopes, chimpanzees, and ostriches are among the wild things in residence. Lions are fenced away from roads, but there's a good chance you'll have a giraffe or two nudging at your window. Exhibits include the Kalahari, designed after a South African bush plateau and containing water buffalo and nilgai (the largest type of Asian antelope), and the Gir Forest, modeled after a game forest in India and showcasing a pride of lions. (For obvious reasons, no convertibles or pets are allowed.) A walk-through area has bird feeding and a petting zoo. You can also take a pontoon-boat tour, go paddleboating, play miniature golf, or send the kids off to the play area with rides and sports fields. There's also a restaurant and a snack shop. ⊠ *2003 Lion Country Safari Rd., at Southern Blvd. W, Loxahatchee* ☏ *561/793–1084* ⊕ *www.lioncountrysafari.com* 🖃 *$26; $5 parking fee* ⊘ *Daily 9:30–5:30; last entrance 4:30.*

⑲ **Mounts Botanical Gardens.** Take advantage of balmy weather by walking among the tropical and subtropical plants here. Join a free tour or explore the 14 acres of exotic trees, rain-forest area, and butterfly and water gardens on your own. Many plants were significantly damaged during the 2004 and 2005 hurricanes, and new plantings will take years to reach maturity. There are lots of free brochures about tropical trees, flowers, and fruits in the main building. If you're feeling inspired, be sure to check out the gift shop's wide range of gardening books. ⊠ *531 N. Military Trail* ☏ *561/233–1757* ⊕ *www.mounts.org* 🖃 *Gardens: $5 suggested donation; tours $5* ⊘ *Mon.–Sat. 8–4, Sun. noon–4.*

⑮ **National Croquet Center.** The world's largest croquet complex, the 10-acre center is also the headquarters for the U.S. Croquet Association. Vast expanses of manicured lawn are the stage for fierce competitions—in no way resembling the casual backyard games where kids play with wide wire wickets. There's also a clubhouse with a pro shop and Café Croquet, with verandas for dining and viewing, and a museum hall. You have to be a member, or a guest of a member, to reserve a lawn every day but Saturday, when lessons are free and lawns are open to all. ⊠ *700 Florida Mango Rd., at Summit Blvd.* ☏ *561/478–2300* ⊕ *www.croquetnational.com* 🖃 *Free admission. Full day of play $25.* ⊘ *June–Sept., Tues.–Sat. 9–5; Oct.–May, daily 9–5.*

⑬ **Palm Beach Zoo.** At this 23-acre wild kingdom there are more than 125 species of animals, from Florida panthers to the giant Aldabra tortoise. Here you'll find the country's first outdoor exhibit of Goeldi's monkeys. The Tropics of America exhibit has 6 acres of rain forest plus an aviary, Maya ruins, and an Amazon River village. Also notable are a nature trail, the otter exhibit, a children's petting zoo, merry-go-round, interactive fountain and a restaurant overlooking the river. ✉ *1301 Summit Blvd.* ☎ *561/533–0887* ⊕ *www.palmbeachzoo.org* 🎫 *$14.95* ☉ *Daily 9–5.*

WORTH NOTING

⑰ Okeeheelee Nature Center. Explore 5 mi of trails through 90 acres of western Palm Beach County's native pine flatwoods and wetlands. A visitor center gift shop has hands-on exhibits and offers guided walks by the center's volunteers. ✉ *7715 Forest Hill Blvd. 33413* ☎ *561/233–1400* 🎫 *Free* ☉ *Visitor center Tues.–Fri. 1–4:35, Sat. 8:15–4:30; trails daily dawn–dusk.*

⑯ Pine Jog Environmental Education Center. The draw here is 135 acres of mostly undisturbed Florida pine flatwoods with 2½-mi of self-guided trails. Formal landscaping around five one-story buildings includes native plants; dioramas and displays illustrate ecosystems. School groups use the trails during the week; special events include camping and campfires. The gift shop is closed on Saturday. Call for an event schedule. ✉ *6301 Summit Blvd.* ☎ *561/686–6600* ⊕ *www.pinejog.org* 🎫 *Free* ☉ *Weekdays 9–4, Sat. 9–2.*

⑭ South Florida Science Museum. Here at the museum, which includes the Aldrin Planetarium and McGinty Aquarium, there are hands-on exhibits with touch tanks and laser shows with music by the likes of Dave Matthews. Galaxy Golf is a 9-hole science challenge. Weather permitting you can observe the heavens Friday night through the most powerful telescope in South Florida. ✉ *4801 Dreher Trail N* ☎ *561/832–1988* ⊕ *www.sfsm.org* 🎫 *$9, planetarium $4, laser show $5, galaxy golf $2* ☉ *Weekdays 10–5, Sat. 10–6, Sun. noon–6.*

OFF THE BEATEN PATH

Forty miles west of West Palm Beach, rimming the western edges of Palm Beach and Martin counties, **Lake Okeechobee,** the second-largest freshwater lake completely within the United States, is girdled by 120 mi of road yet remains shielded from sight for almost its entire circumference. Lake Okeechobee—the Seminole's Big Water and the gateway of the great Everglades watershed—measures 730 square mi, roughly 33 mi north–south, and 30 mi east–west, with an average natural depth of only 10 feet (flood control brings the figure up to 12 feet and deeper). Six major lock systems and 32 separate water-control structures manage the water. Encircling the lake is a 34-foot-high grassy levee—locals call it "the wall"—and the Lake Okeechobee Scenic Trail, a segment of the Florida National Scenic Trail, an easy, flat ride for bikers. ■TIP→ There's no shade, so wear a hat, sunscreen, and bug repellent. Be sure to bring lots of bottled water, too, because restaurants and stores are few and far between.

SPORTS AND THE OUTDOORS

GOLF

The **Palm Beach National Golf & Country Club** (✉ *7500 St. Andrews Rd., Lake Worth* ☎ *561/965–3381* ⊕ *www.palmbeachnational.com*) has an 18-hole classic course with a Joe Lee championship layout; greens fees $49/$75. The Joanne Carner Golf Academy is based here.

SHOPPING

★   West Palm's **Antique Row**, aka South Dixie Highway, is the destination for those who are interested in interesting home decor. From thrift shops to the most exclusive stores, it is all here—furniture, lighting, art, junk, fabric, frames, tile, and rugs. So if you're looking for an art deco, French-provincial, or Mizner pièce de résistance, big or small, schedule a few hours for an Antique Row stroll. You'll find bargains during the off-season (May to November). Antique Row runs north–south from Okeechobee Road to Forest Hill Boulevard, although most stores are bunched between Belvedere Road and Southern Boulevard.

If you're looking for a mix of food, art, performance, landscaping, and retailing, then head to renewed downtown West Palm around **Clematis Street**, which runs east–west from Dixie Highway to Flagler Drive. Water-view parks with attractive gardens—and fountains where kids can cool off—add to the pleasure of browsing, window-shopping, and resting at an outdoor café. Hip national retailers such as Design Within Reach, Ann Taylor Loft, and Z Gallerie blend in with restaurants, pubs, and nightclubs.

The 55-acre **CityPlace** (⌂ *700 S. Rosemary Ave.* ☎ *561/366–1000* ⊕ *www.cityplace.com*), a four-block-by-four-block commercial and residential complex centered on Rosemary Avenue, attracts people of all ages to enjoy restaurants, cafés, outdoor bars, a 20-screen Muvico, the Harriet Himmel Theater, and a 36,000-gallon dance, water, and light show. This family-friendly dining, shopping, and entertainment complex has plenty to see and do. Among CityPlace's stores are popular national retailers Macy's, Armani Exchange, Pottery Barn, Lucky Brand Jeans, Nine West, Sephora, and Restoration Hardware; designer boutiques include Betsey Johnson, Kenneth Cole, and Nicole Miller, and several shops unique to Florida. Behind the punchy, brightly colored clothing in the front window of **C. Orrico** (☎ *561/832–9203*) are family fashions and accessories by Lily Pulitzer and girlie casual gear by Three Dots and Trina Turk. **Rhythm Clothiers** (☎ *561/833–7677*) attracts fashion-forward types with a stock of men's and women's clothing by Dolce & Gabbana, Catherine Malandrino, Diesel, Miss Sixty, and J. Lindeberg.

The free downtown trolley runs a continuous loop linking Clematis Street and CityPlace, so you won't miss a shop.

NIGHTLIFE AND THE ARTS

NIGHTLIFE

CityPlace comes alive at **Blue Martini** (⌂ *550 S. Rosemary Ave.* ☎ *561/835–8601*), a bar with eclectic music that attracts a diverse crowd. There are guitars hanging above the bar and a DJ booth made from a 1957 Chevy at **Dr. Feelgood's Rock Bar & Grill** (⌂ *219 Clematis St.* ☎ *561/833–6500*). Vince Neil, Mötley Crüe's lead singer, is the owner. **ER Bradley's Saloon** (⌂ *104 Clematis St.* ☎ *561/833–3520*) is an open-air restaurant and bar where people of all ages congregate to hang out and socialize while overlooking the Intracoastal Waterway.

THE ARTS

★ Starring amid the treasury of local arts attractions is the **Raymond F. Kravis Center for the Performing Arts** (⊠ *701 Okeechobee Blvd.* ☎ *561/832–7469* ⊕ *www.kravis.org*), which includes the 2,200-seat Dreyfoos Hall, a glass, copper, and marble showcase just steps from the restaurants and shops of CityPlace. The center also boasts the 300-seat Rinker Playhouse and the Gosman Amphitheatre, which holds 1,400 in seats and on the lawn. A packed year-round schedule unfolds here with drama, dance, and music, including Kravis on Broadway, which features a blockbuster lineup of Broadway's biggest touring productions; and Florida Stage, a theater company that presents new and emerging plays.

Palm Beach Opera (⊠ *415 S. Olive Ave.* ☎ *561/833–7888* ⊕ *www.pbopera.org*) stages five productions, including the Vocal Competition Grand Finals, from December to April at the Kravis Center with English translations projected above the stage. The family opera series includes matinee performances such as *Hansel & Gretel*; tickets are $20 to $165.

WHERE TO EAT

$$$ ✕ **Forte.** Its style says "South Beach," but this Italian eatery makes
ITALIAN   its home in West Palm Beach. And Clematis Street is happy to host the energy. Stephen Asprino, the city's answer to Emeril Lagasse, put together a great wine list and serves up Italian dishes with French, American, and Japanese influences. Be sure to try the spring garlic soup. Also good is buccatini alla carbonara—a tasty pasta with cheese, eggs, and bacon. Honey-ricotta gelato is a good choice for dessert. ⊠ *225 Clematis St.* ☎ *561/833–3330* ⊕ *www.fortepalmbeach.com* ▭ *AE, D, DC, MC, V.*

$ ✕ **Havana.** Decorated with vintage travel posters of its namesake city,
CUBAN   this two-level restaurant serves such authentic Cuban specialties as roast-pork sandwiches and chicken slowly cooked in Spanish sauce. Lunch and dinner dishes are enhanced by the requisite black beans and rice. Open until 1 AM Friday and Saturday, this friendly place attracts a late-night crowd. The popular walk-up window serves strong Cuban coffee, sugary fried churros, and fruit juices in exotic flavors like mamey, mango, papaya, guava, and guanabana. ⊠ *6801 S. Dixie Hwy.* ☎ *561/547–9799* ⊕ *www.havanacubanfood.com* ▭ *AE, MC, V.*

$ ✕ **Howley's.** Since 1950 this diner's eat-in counter and "cooked in sight,
SEAFOOD   it must be right" motto has made a congenial setting for meeting old friends and making new ones. Forgo the counter for the 1950s-style tables or sit out on the patio. The café attracts a loyal clientele for breakfast, lunch, and dinner with such specialties as turkey and dressing, burgers, and chicken salad. ⊠ *4700 S. Dixie Hwy.* ☎ *561/833–5691* ▭ *AE, D, MC, V.*

$$ ✕ **Il Bellagio.** In the center of CityPlace, this European-style bistro offers
ITALIAN   Italian specialties and a wide variety of fine wines. The menu includes classics like chicken parmigiana, risotto, and fettuccine Alfredo. Pizzas from the wood-burning oven are especially tasty. Service is friendly and efficient, but the overall noise level tends to be high. Sit at the outdoor

tables next to the main plaza's dancing fountains. ⊠ *CityPlace, 600 S. Rosemary Ave.* ☎ *561/659–6160* ⊕ *www.ilbellagiocityplace.com* ⊟ *AE, D, MC, V.*

¢ ✕ **Middle East Bakery**. This hole-in-the-wall Middle Eastern bakery, deli,
MEDITERRANEAN and market is packed at lunchtime with regulars who are on a first-name basis with the gang behind the counter. From the nondescript parking lot the place doesn't look like much, but inside, delicious hot and cold Mediterranean treats await. Choose from traditional gyro sandwiches and lamb salads with sides of grape leaves, tabbouleh, and couscous. ⊠ *327 5th St., at Olive Ave.* ☎ *561/659–7322* ⊟ *AE, MC, V* ⊘ *Closed Sun.*

WHERE TO STAY

$$$ ⛺ **Grandview Gardens Bed & Breakfast**. This 1923 Spanish-style inn is
★ the new kid on the B&B block in West Palm Beach. The cheery yellow building is conveniently located next to Howard Park, across from the Armory Art Center, and a short walk from the Convention Center, CityPlace, and the Kravis Center. It is warmly decorated with terra-cotta floors, a coral-stone fireplace, and terraces overlooking a swimming pool and gardens. Each spacious room has Mediterranean flair, as well as French doors opening to private terraces overlooking the pool. **Pros:** private entrances; pool; multilingual owners. **Cons:** not close to the beach; steps to climb. ⊠ *1608 Lake Ave.* ☎ *561/833–9023* ⊕ *www.grandview-gardens.net* ⟿ *5 rooms, 1 cottage* ⟁ *In-room: a/c, Internet. In-hotel: pool, parking (free)* ⊟ *AE, DC, MC, V* ⦿ *BP.*

$$$$ ⛺ **Hampton Inn & Suites in Wellington**. Taking its cues from the polo fields and the equestrian center nearby, the Hampton sports a handsome look and an equestrian theme. The four-story hotel, about 10 mi west of downtown West Palm Beach, has the feeling of a ritzy clubhouse, with rich wood paneling, hunt prints, and elegant chandeliers. One-bedroom suites have sleeper sofas, refrigerators, and microwaves. All rooms have coffeemakers. Some rooms have a lake view. **Pros:** complimentary hot breakfast; free high-speed Internet access; near shopping. **Cons:** no restaurant. ⊠ *2155 Wellington Green Dr.* ☎ *561/472–9696* ⊕ *www.hamptoninn.com* ⟿ *122 rooms, 32 suites* ⟁ *In-room: a/c, refrigerator (some), Wi-Fi. In-hotel: pool, gym* ⊟ *AE, D, MC, V* ⦿ *BP.*

$$$ ⛺ **Hotel Biba**. In the El Cid historic district, this 1940s-era motel has gotten a fun, stylish revamp from designer Barbara Hulanicki. Each of the 43 rooms has a vibrant mélange of colors, along with handcrafted mirrors, mosaic bathroom floors, and custom mahogany furnishings. Luxury touches include Egyptian-cotton sheets, down pillows and duvets, and lavender-scented closets. The hotel is one block from the Intracoastal Waterway and about a mile from Clematis Street nightlife, and the lobby bar attracts a hip happy-hour crowd. **Pros:** cool design; popular wine bar. **Cons:** water pressure is weak; bathrooms are tiny; noisy when the bar is open late. ⊠ *320 Belvedere Rd.* ☎ *561/832–0094* ⊕ *www.hotelbiba.com* ⟿ *43 rooms* ⟁ *In-room: a/c, Wi-Fi. In-hotel: bar, pool* ⊟ *AE, DC, MC, V.*

SOUTH TO BOCA RATON

Strung together by Route A1A, the towns between Palm Beach and Boca Raton are notable for their variety, from high-rise condominiums to small-town public beaches. In one town you'll find a cluster of art galleries and fancy dining, and the very next town will yield mostly hamburger joints and mom-and-pop stores.

LAKE WORTH

2 mi south of West Palm Beach, off I–95 or Federal Hwy.

For years, tourists looked here mainly for inexpensive lodging and easy access to Palm Beach, since a bridge leads from the mainland to a barrier island with Lake Worth's beach. Now Lake Worth has several blocks of restaurants and art galleries, making this a worthy destination on its own.

ESSENTIALS

Visitor Information **Lake Worth Chamber of Commerce** (⊠ *501 Lake Ave.* ☎ *561/582–4401*).

EXPLORING

The **Museum of Polo & Hall of Fame** is a good place to start if you're looking for an introduction to polo. See polo memorabilia, art, and a film on the history of the sport. ⊠ *9011 Lake Worth Rd.* ☎ *561/969–3210* ⊕ *www.polomuseum.com* ⊡ *Free* ☉ *May–Dec., weekdays 10–4; Jan.–Apr., weekdays 10–4, Sat. 10–2.*

WHERE TO EAT

¢ ✕ **Benny's on the Beach.** Perched on the Lake Worth Pier, Benny's has
AMERICAN diner-style food that's cheap and filling, but the spectacular view of the sun glistening on the water and the waves crashing directly below is what dining here is all about. Get here early—it doesn't serve dinner. ⊠ *10 Ocean Ave.* ☎ *561/582–9001* ⊟ *MC, V* ☉ *No dinner.*

$ ✕ **Bizaare Avenue Café.** Decorated with a mix of artwork and antiques,
ECLECTIC this cozy bistro fits right into downtown Lake Worth's groovy, eclectic scene. Artwork and furnishings can be purchased. Daily specials are available on both the lunch and dinner menus, where crepes, pizzas, pastas, and salads are the staples. ⊠ *921 Lake Ave. 33460* ☎ *561/588–4488* ⊟ *www.bizaareavecafe.com* ☉ *AE, D, DC, MC, V.*

$$$ ✕ **Paradiso.** Arguably downtown Lake Worth's finest Italian restaurant,
ITALIAN this is the place to go for a romantic evening. Veal chops, seafood, cheese ravioli, and risotto are all good choices. Don't miss the chocolate Grand Marnier soufflé for dessert. As the name implies, the food is heavenly. ⊠ *625 Lucerne Ave.* ☎ *561/547–2500* ⊕ *www.paradisolakeworth.com* ⊟ *AE, MC, V.*

WHERE TO STAY

$$$–$$$$ ☷ **Mango Inn.** It's only a 15-minute walk to the beach from this B&B
★ dating from 1915. The two ground-floor rooms have French doors opening onto a patio. A poolside cottage has two bedrooms and two bathrooms. Have your complimentary breakfast of homemade raspberry buttermilk pancakes on the veranda overlooking the heated pool

The posh Palm Beach area has its share of luxury villas on the water; many are Mediterranean in style.

or in the courtyard next to the fountain. **Pros:** close to shops and restaurants; breakfasts served poolside; some suites have whirlpool tubs. **Cons:** some rooms are quite small. ✉ *128 N. Lakeside Dr.* ☎ *561/533–6900 or 888/626–4619* 🌐 *www.mangoinn.com* *7 rooms, 3 suites, 1 cottage* *In-room: a/c, kitchen, refrigerator (some), Internet. In-hotel: pool, no kids under 16* *AE, D, MC, V* *BP.*

$$$–$$$$ ★ **Sabal Palm House.** Built in 1936, this two-story B&B is a short walk from the Intracoastal Waterway. Three rooms and a suite are in the main house, and three others are across a brick courtyard in the carriage house. Each room is inspired by a different artist—including Renoir, Dalí, Norman Rockwell, and Chagall—and all have oak floors, antique furnishings, and private balconies. There's an inviting parlor where afternoon tea and weekend wine and appetizers are served. A full breakfast is offered indoors or in the courtyard, under the palms. **Pros:** fresh flowers in guest rooms; extra pillows; close to shops and restaurants. **Cons:** no pool. ✉ *109 N. Golfview Rd.* ☎ *561/582–1090 or 888/722–2572* 🌐 *www.sabalpalmhouse.com* *5 rooms, 2 suites* *In-hotel: some pets allowed, no kids under 14* *AE, MC, V* *BP.*

LANTANA

2 mi south of Lake Worth, off I–95 or Federal Hwy.

Lantana—just a bit farther south from Palm Beach than Lake Worth—has inexpensive lodging and a bridge connecting the town to its own beach on a barrier island. Tucked between Lantana and Boynton Beach is **Manalapan,** a tiny but posh residential community.

ESSENTIALS

Visitor Information Lantana Chamber of Commerce (✉ *212 Iris Ave.* ☎ *561/585–8664*).

SPORTS AND THE OUTDOORS

BEACH

Lantana Public Beach. Ideal for sprawling, beachcombing, or power-walking, Lantana is also worthy for its proximity to one of the most popular food concessions in town, the **Dune Deck Café.** Here the choices are standard, but the food is particularly fresh and the portions are hearty. Try an omelet with a side of fries and melon wedges, Greek salad, homemade yogurt with seasonal fruit topped with honey, or a side of banana-nut bread. There are daily breakfast and lunch specials; dining is outdoors under yellow canopies perched over the beach. ✉ *100 N. Ocean Ave.* ☎ *561/582–0472* *Parking 25¢ for 15 mins* ⏲ *Daily 9–4:45.*

FISHING

B-Love Fleet (✉ *314 E. Ocean Ave.* ☎ *561/588–7612*) offers three deep-sea fishing excursions daily: 8–noon, 1–5, and 6:30–10:30. No reservations are needed; just show up 30 minutes before the boat is scheduled to leave. The cost is $37 per person and includes fishing license, bait, and tackle.

WHERE TO EAT AND STAY

$$$ SEAFOOD ✕ **Old Key Lime House.** Overlooking the Intracoastal Waterway, the 1889 Lyman family house has grown in spurts over the years and its latest addition is the Manatee Observation Deck. This is an informal seafood house covered by a chiki hut built by the Seminole Indians after the restaurant was damaged by Hurricane Wilma. It's also the largest viewing home for Gator Football. The panoramic water views are the main appeal here for adults—kids love to feed the fish and rock in the glider seats on the dock. Don't miss key lime pie—the house specialty was featured in *Bon Appetite* magazine. ✉ *300 E. Ocean Ave.* ☎ *561/533–5220* 🌐 *www.oldkeylimehouse.com* 💳 *AE, MC, V.*

$$$ SEAFOOD ✕ **Station House.** The best Maine lobster in South Florida might well reside at this delicious dive, where all the seafood is cooked to perfection. Sticky seats and tablecloths are an accepted part of the scene, so don't wear your best duds. Although it's casual and family-friendly, reservations are recommended since it's a local favorite. Station Grill, across the street, is less seafood oriented but every "bite" as good. ✉ *233 Lantana Rd.* ☎ *561/547–9487* 🌐 *www.stationhouserestaurants.com* 💳 *AE, D, DC, MC, V* ⏲ *No lunch.*

$$$ JAPANESE ★ ✕ **Suite 225.** On a quaint street lined with shops and boutiques is this historic house that's been transformed into a sleek sushi bar. Glass doors open up to outdoor dining areas, and a bar is nestled under large banyan trees. Start with a sampler platter from the extensive list of eclectic "suite rolls," which includes nearly 40 choices, including the spicy tuna roll and the fantasy roll with salmon and cream cheese. Among the other choices are grilled sake-skirt steak with ginger-barbecue sauce and pork chops with Asian-pear chutney. ✉ *225 E. Ocean Ave.* ☎ *561/582–2255* 💳 *AE, D, MC, V* ⏲ *No lunch.*

$$$$　⊡ **Ritz-Carlton, Palm Beach.** Despite its name, this triple-tower landmark
★　is actually in Manalapan, halfway between Palm Beach and Delray
Beach. A huge double-sided marble fireplace dominates the elegant
lobby and foreshadows the luxury of the guest rooms, which have
richly upholstered furnishings and marble tubs. Most rooms have ocean
views, and all have balconies. A 2006 expansion added a 3,000-square-
foot oceanfront terrace, a second pool, two restaurants, and a grand
spa. Coconut palms shade the pools and courtyard—all of which are
served by attendants who can fulfill whims from iced drinks to cool face
towels. **Pros:** gorgeous rooms; magnificent ocean views; shops across the
street. **Cons:** not close to golf course; 15-minute drive to Palm Beach.
⊠ *100 S. Ocean Blvd., Manalapan* ☎ *561/533–6000 or 800/241–3333*
⊕ *www.ritz-carlton.com* ⌁ *310 rooms* ⌂ *In-room: a/c, safe, refrigerator, Internet, Wi-Fi. In-hotel: 3 restaurants, room service, bars, tennis
courts, pools, spa, beachfront, water sports, bicycles, children's programs (ages 5–17), laundry service, Internet terminal, parking (paid)*
⊟ *AE, D, DC, MC, V.*

BOYNTON BEACH

3 mi south of Lantana, off I–95 or Federal Highway.

In 1884, when fewer than 50 settlers lived in the area, Nathan Boynton, a Civil War veteran from Michigan, paid $25 for 500 acres with a
mile-long stretch of beachfront thrown in. How things have changed,
with today's population at about 118,000 and property values still on
an upswing. Far enough from Palm Beach to remain low-key, Boynton
Beach has two parts, the mainland and the barrier island—the town of
Ocean Ridge—connected by two bridges.

ESSENTIALS

Visitor Information **Boynton Beach Chamber of Commerce** (⊠ *1880 N.
Congress Ave., Suite 106* ☎ *561/732–9501*).

EXPLORING

Arthur R. Marshall–Loxahatchee National Wildlife Refuge. The most robust
part of the Everglades, this 221-square-mi refuge is one of three huge
water-retention areas accounting for much of the Everglades outside
the national park. These areas are managed less to protect natural
resources, however, than to prevent flooding to the south. Start from the
visitor center, where there is a marsh trail to a 20-foot-high observation
tower overlooking a pond. The boardwalk takes you through a dense
cypress swamp. There's also a 5½-mi canoe trail, best for experienced
canoeists since it's overgrown. Wildlife viewing is good year-round,
and you can fish for bass and panfish. ⊠ *10216 Lee Rd., off U.S. 441
between Rte. 804 and Rte. 806* ☎ *561/734–8303* ⌁ *$5 per vehicle,
pedestrians $1* ☉ *Daily sunrise to sunset; visitor center, weekdays 9–4,
weekends 9–4:30.*

☾　**Schoolhouse Children's Museum.** Boynton Beach's history is highlighted
★　through interactive exhibits that make the museum a kid and parent
pleaser. In this 1913 schoolhouse children can milk a mock cow or
pick and wash plastic vegetables at the Pepper Patch Farm. Kids can

buy tickets and dress up for a "time travel" train ride that immerses them in Boynton's history. A great outdoor playground castle is adjacent to the museum. ⊠ *129 E. Ocean Ave.* ☎ *561/742–6780* ⊕ *www. schoolhousemuseum.org* ⊠ *$5* ⊙ *Tues.–Sat. 10–5.*

SPORTS AND THE OUTDOORS

BEACH

An inviting beach, boardwalk, concessions, grills, and playground await at **Boynton Beach Oceanfront Park** (⊠ *6415 Ocean Blvd.* ☎ *No phone* ⊠ *Parking $10 per day* ⊙ *Daily 7:30* AM–11 PM).

FISHING

West of Boynton Beach, fish the canal at the **Arthur R. Marshall–Loxahatchee National Wildlife Refuge** (⊠ *10119 Lee Rd., off U.S. 441 between Rte. 804 and Rte. 806* ☎ *561/734–8303*). There's a boat ramp, and the waters are decently productive, but bring your own equipment. On the other side of town, catch fish swimming between the Atlantic and Intracoastal Waterway at the **Boynton Beach Inlet Pier** (⊠ *6990 N. Ocean Blvd.* ☎ *No phone*).

GOLF

Links at Boynton Beach (⊠ *8020 Jog Rd.* ☎ *561/742–6500*) has 18-hole and 9-hole executive courses; greens fees $27–$59 champion course, $39–$49 family course (rates vary with time of day; it's busier and costs more in the morning).

WHERE TO EAT

$
AMERICAN
✕ **Banana Boat.** A mainstay for local boaters who cruise up and down the Intracoastal Waterway, Banana Boat is easily recognizable by the lighthouse on its roof. On weekends, casual crowds clad in tank tops, flip-flops, and bikinis dance to live island music while downing frozen drinks. The kitchen serves fish-and-chips, burgers, and ribs. ⊠ *739 E. Ocean Ave.* ☎ *561/732–9400* ⊕ *www.bananaboatboynton.com* ☐ *AE, MC, V.*

DELRAY BEACH

2 mi south of Gulf Stream via I–95 or Federal Hwy.

A onetime artists' retreat with a small settlement of Japanese farmers, Delray has grown into a sophisticated beach town. Atlantic Avenue, the once dilapidated main drag, has evolved into a more-than-a-mile-long stretch of palm-dotted sidewalks, lined with stores, art galleries, and dining establishments. Running east–west and ending at the beach, it's a pleasant place for a stroll, day or night. Another active pedestrian way begins at the eastern edge of Atlantic Avenue and runs along the big, broad swimming beach that extends north to George Bush Boulevard and south to Casuarina Road.

ESSENTIALS

Visitor Information Delray Beach Chamber of Commerce (⊠ *64-A SE 5th Ave.* ☎ *561/278–0424*).

Morikami Museum and Japanese Gardens gives a taste of the Orient through its exhibits and tea ceremonies.

EXPLORING

Colony Hotel. The chief landmark along Atlantic Avenue since 1926 is this Mediterranean revival–style hotel, which is a member of the National Trust for Historic Preservation. Walk through the lobby to the parking lot of the hotel where original stable "garages" still stand— relics of the days when hotel guests would arrive via horse and carriage. ⊠ *525 E. Atlantic Ave.* ☎ *561/276–4123.*

Old School Square Cultural Arts Center. Just off Atlantic Avenue is this cluster of several museums set in restored school buildings dating from 1913 and 1926. The **Cornell Museum of Art & History** offers ever-changing art exhibits. During its season, the **Crest Theatre** showcases performances by local and touring troupes in the restored 1925 Delray High School building. ⊠ *51 N. Swinton Ave.* ☎ *561/243–7922* ⊕ *www.oldschool. org* ⊠ *$6* ⊙ *Tues.–Sat. 10:30–4:30, Sun. 1–4:30.*

Fodor'sChoice
★ **Morikami Museum and Japanese Gardens.** Out in the boonies west of Delray Beach seems an odd place to encounter the East, but this is exactly where you can find a cultural and recreational facility heralding the Yamato Colony of Japanese farmers. The on-site Cornell Café serves light Asian fare. If you don't get your fill of orchids, the American Orchid Society's 20,000-square-foot headquarters is across the street. ⊠ *4000 Morikami Park Rd.* ☎ *561/495–0233* ⊕ *www.morikami.org* ⊠ *$12* ⊙ *Tues.–Sun. 10–5.*

2

SPORTS AND THE OUTDOORS

BEACHES

★ Enjoy many types of water-sports rentals—sailing, kayaking, windsurfing, Boogie boarding, surfing, snorkeling—or scuba diving at a sunken Spanish galleon less than ½ mi offshore at **Seagate Beach** (⊠ *½ mi south of Atlantic Ave. at Rte. A1A*. A scenic walking path follows the main stretch of the public **Delray Beach Municipal Beach** (⊠ *Atlantic Ave. at Rte. A1A*) , which stretches 2 mi, half of it supervised by lifeguards. Reefs off the coast are popular with divers.

BIKING

There's a bicycle path in Barwick Park and a special oceanfront lane along Route A1A. **Richwagen's Bike & Sport** (⊠ *298 NE 6th Ave.* ☎ *561/276–4234*) rents bikes by the hour or day and provides lock, basket, helmet, and maps.

WATERSKIING

At **Lake Ida Park** (⊠ *2929 Lake Ida Rd.*) you can water-ski whether you're a beginner or a veteran. The park has a boat ramp, a slalom course, and a trick ski course.

SHOPPING

Atlantic Avenue is a showcase for art galleries, shops, and restaurants. This charming area, from Swinton Avenue east to the ocean, has maintained much of its small-town integrity.

In the historic Colony Hotel, **Escentials Apothecaries** (⊠ *533 Atlantic Ave.* ☎ *561/276–7070*) is packed with all things good smelling for your bath, body, and home. **Snappy Turtle** (⊠ *1100 Atlantic Ave.* ☎ *561/276–8088*) is where Mackenzie-Childs and Lilly Pulitzer mingle with other fun fashions for the home and family.

NIGHTLIFE

Boston's on the Beach (⊠ *40 S. Ocean Blvd.* ☎ *561/278–3364*) grooves to reggae on Monday night and live music from jazz to country to rock most other nights. At **Dada** (⊠ *52 N. Swinton Ave.* ☎ *561/330–3232*), bands play in the living room of a historic house. It's a place where those who don't drink will also feel comfortable. **Delux** (⊠ *16 E. Atlantic Ave.* ☎ *561/279–4792*) is where a young, hip crowd goes to dance all night long.

WHERE TO EAT

$$$
AMERICAN
★
✕ **32 East.** Although restaurants come and go on a trendy street like Atlantic Avenue, 32 East remains one of the best restaurants in Delray Beach. A daily menu of wood-oven pizzas, salads, soups, seafood, and meat is all based on what is fresh and plentiful. Dark-wood accents and dim lighting make this large restaurant seem cozy. There's a packed bar in front and an open kitchen in back. ⊠ *32 E. Atlantic Ave.* ☎ *561/276–7868* ⊕ *www.32east.com* ▭ *AE, D, MC, V* ⊗ *No lunch.*

$$
BRITISH
✕ **Blue Anchor.** Yes, this pub was actually shipped from England, where it stood for 150 years in London's historic Chancery Lane. There it was a watering hole for famed Englishmen, including Winston Churchill. The Delray Beach incarnation has stuck to authentic British pub fare. Chow down on a ploughman's lunch (a chunk of Stilton cheese, a hunk of bread, and pickled onions), shepherd's pie, fish-and-chips, and

bangers and mash (sausages with mashed potatoes). Don't be surprised to find a rugby game on TV. English beers and ales are on tap and by the bottle. It's a late-night place open until at least 2. ⊠ *804 E. Atlantic Ave.* ☎ *561/272–7272* ⊕ *www.theblueanchor.com* 🗎 *AE, D, MC, V.*

$$$ ✕ **Kyoto.** An energetic crew keeps this bustling Japanese eatery running
JAPANESE into the wee hours all week long. Sushi and sake are the main draws here, but there are also less traditional dishes on offer. The dining room is stylish and contemporary, with a sleek black sushi bar. You can dine among a bar crowd and watch your sushi being assembled, or take a table in the front courtyard and watch the crowds meander along happening Pineapple Grove. ⊠ *25 NE 2nd Ave.* ☎ *561/330–2404* 🖃 *AE, DC, MC, V.*

¢ ✕ **Old School Bakery.** This place concentrates on sandwich making at
AMERICAN its best. Particularly worthy is the cherry chicken salad sandwich with
★ Brie on multigrain. Apart from sandwiches and soups served for lunch every day, order from a diverse baked-goods menu with artisan breads, pastries, several kinds of cookies, and even biscotti. The bakery is primarily takeout, but there are a few small tables in an adjacent open-air courtyard. ⊠ *814 E. Atlantic Ave.* ☎ *561/243–8059* 🖃 *No credit cards* ☺ *AE, MC, V.*

WHERE TO STAY

$$$$ 🏨 **Colony Hotel & Cabana Club.** In the heart of downtown Delray, this charming building dates back to 1926. Today it's listed on Delray's local Register of Historic Places and maintains an air of the 1920s with its Mediterranean-revival architecture. The Cabana Club is a separate property on the ocean about a mile away, with a private beach, club, and heated saltwater pool. A convivial bar and live music on weekend nights make the lobby area a great place to wind down. In fact, yoga classes are held there daily (except Monday). Fine shops selling leather goods, body products, and stationery fill the lower-level storefronts. **Pros:** great location; close to restaurants; shuttle to the beach. **Cons:** air-conditioning units can be loud; breakfast buffet servings are repetitious. ⊠ *525 E. Atlantic Ave.* ☎ *561/276–4123 or 800/552–2363* ⊕ *www. thecolonyhotel.com* ⇥ *69 rooms* ♿ *In-room: a/c, Internet, Wi-Fi. In-hotel: bar, pool, beachfront, parking (free)* 🖃 *AE, DC, MC, V* ⵏⵉⵍ *CP.*

$$$$ 🏨 **Delray Beach Marriott.** By far the largest property in Delray Beach, this five-story hotel has a stellar location at the east end of Atlantic Avenue. It sits across the road from the beach and is within walking distance of restaurants, shops, and galleries. Rooms and suites are spacious, and many have stunning ocean views. If you want a bit of pampering, there's also a spa. The free-form pool is surrounded by a comfortable deck. **Pros:** great location; near nightlife; luxurious spa. **Cons:** sprawling resort; chain-hotel feel; service can be impersonal. ⊠ *10 N. Ocean Blvd.* ☎ *561/274–3200* ⊕ *www.delraybeachmarriott.com* ⇥ *268 rooms, 88 suites* ♿ *In-room: a/c, safe, Internet. In-hotel: 3 restaurants, room service, bars, pool, gym, spa, beachfront, laundry facilities, parking (free)* 🖃 *AE, DC, MC, V.*

$$$$ 🏨 **Sundy House.** Just about everything in this bungalow-style B&B is exe-
★ cuted to perfection. Guest rooms are luxuriously decorated, and apartments offer full kitchens and laundry facilities. Situated a few blocks

south of Atlantic Avenue, this lodging's only real downside is a long walk to the beach (although the complimentary beach shuttle lessens the inconvenience). Even if you do not stay here, come see the extraordinary tropical gardens. Dine at the exceptional restaurant De la Tierra under an expansive indoor canopy, or on the patios set among koi ponds. **Pros:** beautiful property; excellent restaurant; quiet area. **Cons:** not on the beach. ⌧ *106 Swinton Ave.* ☎ *561/272–5678 or 877/434–9601* ⊕ *www.sundyhouse.com* ↪ *10 rooms, 1 apartment* ⌂ *In-room: Wi-Fi. In-hotel: restaurant, bar, pool, Internet terminal* ▭ *AE, DC, MC, V.*

BOCA RATON

6 mi south of Delray Beach, off I–95.

Less than an hour south of Palm Beach and anchoring the county's south end, upscale Boca Raton has much in common with its fabled cousin. Both reflect the unmistakable architectural influence of Addison Mizner, their principal developer in the mid-1920s. The meaning of the name Boca Raton (pronounced boca rah-*tone*) often arouses curiosity, with many folks mistakenly assuming it means "rat's mouth." Historians say the probable origin is Boca Ratones, an ancient Spanish geographical term for an inlet filled with jagged rocks or coral. Miami's Biscayne Bay had such an inlet, and in 1823 a mapmaker copying Miami terrain confused the more northern inlet, thus mistakenly labeling this area Boca Ratones. No matter what, you'll know you've arrived in the heart of downtown when you spot the town hall's gold dome on the main street, Federal Highway.

TOURS The **Boca Raton Historical Society** (⌧ *71 N. Federal Hwy.* ☎ *561/395–6766* ⊕ *www.bocahistory.org*) offers trolley tours of city sites during season on Thursday. **Old Northwood Historic District Tours** (☎ *No phone* ⊕ *www.oldnorthwood.org*) leads two-hour walking tours that include visits to historic home interiors. During season they typically start Sunday at 2; a $5 donation is suggested. Tours for groups of six or more can be scheduled almost any day.

ESSENTIALS
Visitor Information Boca Raton Chamber of Commerce (⌧ *1800 N. Dixie Hwy.* ☎ *561/395–4433*).

EXPLORING
2 East El Camino Real. Built in 1925 as the headquarters of the Mizner Development Corporation, this is an example of Mizner's characteristic Spanish-revival architectural style, with its wrought-iron grilles and handmade tiles. As for Mizner's grandiose vision of El Camino Real, the architect-promoter once prepared brochures promising a sweeping wide boulevard with Venetian canals and arching bridges. Camino Real is attractive, heading east to the Boca Raton Resort & Club, but don't count on feeling like you're in Venice. ⌧ *2 E. Camino Real.*

Boca Raton Museum of Art. An interactive children's gallery and changing exhibition galleries showcase internationally known artists at this museum in a spectacular building in the Mizner Park shopping center. The permanent collection upstairs includes works by Picasso, Degas,

Matisse, Klee, and Modigliani, as well as notable pre-Columbian art. ⊠ *501 Plaza Real* ☎ *561/392–2500* ⊕ *www.bocamuseum.org* ✉ *$8* ☽ *Tues., Thurs., and Fri. 10–5, Wed. 10–9, weekends noon–5.*

☼ **Children's Science Explorium.** This hands-on science center offers interactive exhibits, programs and camps designed to enhance 5- to 12-year-old explorers' understanding of everyday physical sciences. The Explorium is in Sugar Sand Community Center. ⊠ *300 S. Military Trail* ☎ *561/347–3913* ⊕ *www.scienceexplorium.org* ✉ *Suggested donaton: $2* ☽ *Weekdays 9–6, weekends 10–5.*

☼ **Gumbo Limbo Nature Center.** A big draw for kids, this nifty nature center has four huge saltwater tanks brimming with sea life—from coral to stingrays—and a boardwalk through dense forest with a 40-foot tower you can climb to overlook the tree canopy. In spring and early summer, staffers lead nocturnal turtle walks: you can watch nesting females come ashore and lay eggs. (Purchase tickets in advance; see Web site for details.) A great hiking spot, the park has a sturdy boardwalk and a 40-foot observation tower. Spend a little time there and you're likely to see brown pelicans and osprey. Kids love the aquariums, insect tanks, and the butterfly garden. ⊠ *1801 N. Ocean Blvd.* ☎ *561/338–1473* ⊕ *www.gumbolimbo.org* ✉ *Free but $3 donation suggested; turtle walks $5* ☽ *Mon.–Sat. 9–4, Sun. noon–4; turtle walks May–July, Mon.–Thurs. 9* PM–*midnight.*

Old Floresta. This residential area was developed by Addison Mizner starting in 1925 and landscaped with palms and cycads. It includes houses that are mainly Mediterranean in style, many with balconies supported by exposed wood columns. Home tours are held twice a year. ⊠ *Behind the Boca Raton Art School on Palmetto Park Rd.*

SPORTS AND THE OUTDOORS
BEACHES
Red Reef Park (⊠ *1400 N. Rte. A1A*) has a beach and playground plus picnic tables and grills, and the beach is a good spot for snorkeling. The reef is only about 50 feet offshore. **South Beach Park** (⊠ *400 N. Rte. A1A*) is a pretty stretch of sand popular with sunbathers. In addition to its beach, **Spanish River Park** (⊠ *3001 N. Rte. A1A*) has picnic tables, grills, and a large playground.

BOATING
For the thrill of blasting across the water at up to 80 mph, **Palm Breeze Charters** (⊠ *107 E. Palmetto Park Rd., Suite 330* ☎ *561/368–3566*) offers a variety weekly cruises and boat charters.

GOLF
Two championship courses are at **Boca Raton Resort & Club** (⊠ *501 E. Camino Real* ☎ *561/447–3078*) ; greens fees $180/$210, includes cart with GPS. The Dave Pelz Golf School is at the country club course.

SHOPPING
★ **Mizner Park** (⊠ *Federal Hwy., 1 block north of Palmetto Park Rd.*) is a distinctive 30-acre shopping center with apartments and town houses among its gardenlike retail and restaurant spaces. Some three dozen

stores, including national and local retailers, mingle with fine restaurants, sidewalk cafés, galleries, a movie theater, museum, and amphitheater.

NIGHTLIFE

Drop by **Gatsby's Boca** (✉ *5970 SW 18th St., Shoppes at Village Point* ☎ *561/393–3900*) any night of the week to mingle with a lively crowd. Shoot pool at one of 18 tables or watch sporting events on several giant screens. **Pranzo** (✉ *402 Plaza Real* ☎ *561/750–7442*) has a happening weekend bar scene.

WHERE TO EAT

$$
VIETNAMESE
★
✕ **La Tre.** An adventuresome menu distinguishes this simple Vietnamese eatery. Try the crispy eggplant or the crepe stuffed with pork, shrimp, and vegetables. Tamarind-flavored squid is another winner. The restaurant's black-lacquer furniture seems to date from the 1980s. Don't anticipate a romantic dinner experience, as there's an odd purple hue cast from fluorescent lighting. The food makes it worth the trip, however. ✉ *249 E. Palmetto Park Rd.* ☎ *561/392–4568* ▭ *AE, DC, MC, V* ☉ *No lunch.*

$$$
ITALIAN
✕ **Tiramisu.** The food is an extravaganza of taste treats; veal chops, tuna, and anything with mushrooms draw raves, but count on hearty fare rather than a light touch. Start with the portobello mushroom with garlic or the Corsican baby sardines in olive oil. For a main course, try ricotta ravioli; scaloppine of veal stuffed with crabmeat, lobster, and Gorgonzola; or Tuscan fish stew. Enjoy it all in an intimate setting as Andrea Bocelli music plays in the background. ✉ *170 W. Camino Real.* ☎ *561/338–9692* ▭ *AE, DC, MC, V* ☉ *No lunch Sun.*

$$$$
SEAFOOD
✕ **Truluck's.** This popular chain is so serious about seafood that it boasts its own fleet of 16 boats. Stone crabs are the signature dish, and you can have all you can eat on Monday night from December to May. Other recommended dishes include jalapeño salmon topped with blue crabmeat, hot and crunchy trout, crab cakes, and bacon-wrapped shrimp. Portions are huge, so you might want to make a meal of appetizers. The place comes alive each night with its popular piano bar. ✉ *Mizner Park, 351 Plaza Real* ☎ *561/391–0755* ⊕ *www.trulucks.com* ▭ *AE, D, MC, V.*

$$$
CHINESE
✕ **Uncle Tai's.** The draw at this upscale eatery is some of the best Szechuan food on Florida's east coast. Specialties include sliced duck with snow peas and water chestnuts in a tangy plum sauce, and orange beef delight—flank steak stir-fried until crispy and then sautéed with pepper sauce, garlic, and orange peel. They'll go easy on the heat on request. The service is quietly efficient. ✉ *5250 Town Center Circle* ☎ *561/368–8806* ⊕ *www.uncle-tais.com* ▭ *AE, MC, V* ☉ *No lunch Sun.*

WHERE TO STAY

$$$$
★
⊞ **Boca Raton Resort & Club.** Addison Mizner built this Mediterranean-style hotel in 1926, and additions over time have created this sparkling, sprawling resort. There are many lodging options: traditional rooms are small but warmly decorated; beachfront rooms are light and airy; yacht-club rooms are the most luxurious, with custom-designed Venetian-style canopy beds and carved gold-leaf lamps. The beach is accessible by shuttle. In addition to a redesigned golf course with a two-story

clubhouse, there's an expansive tennis and fitness center and the largest spa in Florida. It has 44 treatment rooms reserved for guests and offers treatments that take advantage of local flora. Chef Angela Hartnett opened a restaurant here, immediately drawing locals. **Pros:** historical property; loaded with luxury; plenty of activities. **Cons:** all this luxury is costly; conventions crowd common areas. ⊠ *501 E. Camino Real* ☎ *561/447–3000 or 800/327–0101* ⊕ *www.bocaresort.com* ⤵ *1,047 rooms, 134 suites, 60 1-bedroom bungalows* ♿ *In-room: a/c, safe, kitchen (some), Wi-Fi. In-hotel: 12 restaurants, room service, bars, golf course, tennis courts, pools, gym, water sports, children's programs (ages 2–17), laundry service, parking (paid)* ▭ *AE, DC, MC, V.*

$$ 🏨 **Ocean Breeze Inn.** If golf is your game, this smaller resort is an excellent choice. Guests can play the outstanding course at the adjoining Ocean Breeze Golf & Country Club, otherwise available only to club members. Rooms are in a three-story building, and most have a patio or balcony. **Pros:** great spot for golfers; bargain rates. **Cons:** rooms are dated. ⊠ *5800 NW 2nd Ave.* ☎ *561/994–0400 or 800/344–6995* ⊕ *www.oceanbreezegolf.com* ⤵ *46 rooms* ♿ *In-room: a/c, refrigerator. In-hotel: restaurant, golf course, tennis courts, pool, laundry facilities, parking (free)* ▭ *AE, DC, MC, V.*

$$$$ 🏨 **Radisson Bridge Resort of Boca Raton.** This resort on the Intracoastal Waterway has views of the ocean that can't be beat, especially from the top-floor restaurant. The ground-floor restaurant, Water Color, offers great views of passing boats. The beach is a five-minute walk away, as are restaurants, galleries, and boutiques. Comfortable accommodations and an ideal location are the main draws. Rooms are decorated in typical Boca style, with pale woods and rattan and a watercolor palette—nothing spectacular, yet quite presentable. **Pros:** great location; affordable rates. **Cons:** can be noisy if you're near the bridge. ⊠ *999 E. Camino Real* ☎ *561/368–9500 or 800/333–3333* ⊕ *www. bocaratonbridgehotel.com* ⤵ *110 rooms, 11 suites* ♿ *In-room: a/c, refrigerator (some), Internet. In-hotel: 2 restaurants, room service, bars, pool, gym, beachfront, laundry facilities, parking (free)* ▭ *AE, DC, MC, V.*

THE TREASURE COAST

In contrast to the Gold Coast—as the Palm Beach/West Palm Beach area is known—is the more rural Treasure Coast, covering northernmost Palm Beach County, plus Martin, St. Lucie, and Indian River counties. Along the coast are barrier islands all the way to Sebastian and beyond. Inland there's cattle ranching in tracts of pine and palmetto scrub, along with sugar and citrus production. Shrimp farming uses techniques for acclimatizing shrimp from saltwater—land near seawater is costly—to freshwater, all the better to serve demand from restaurants popping up all over the region. Despite, a growing number of malls and beachfront condominium, much of the Treasure Coast remains largely blissfully undeveloped.

PALM BEACH SHORES

7 mi north of Palm Beach, on Singer Island.

Rimmed by mom-and-pop motels, this residential town is at the southern tip of Singer Island, across Lake Worth Inlet from Palm Beach. To travel between the two, however, you must cross over to the mainland before returning to the beach.

GETTING HERE AND AROUND

The best way to drive to Palm Beach Shores from West Palm Beach is to head 7 mi north on Interstate 95. Head east on Blue Heron Boulevard/Route 708 across the Intracoastal Waterway to Atlantic Avenue. Head south and you'll be in Palm Beach Shores.

ESSENTIALS

Visitor Information **Northern Palm Beach County Chamber of Commerce** (✉ *800 N. U.S. 1, Jupiter* ☎ *561/694–2300*).

SPORTS AND THE OUTDOORS

In the Intracoastal Waterway between Palm Beach Shores and Riviera Beach, 79-acre **Peanut Island** was opened in 1999 as a recreational park. There's a 20-foot-wide walking path surrounding the island, a 19-slip boat dock, a 170-foot T-shape fishing pier, six picnic pavilions, a visitor center, and 20 overnight campsites. The small **Palm Beach Maritime Museum** (☎ *561/832–7428*) is open daily except Friday and showcases the "Kennedy Bunker," a bomb shelter prepared for President John F. Kennedy. Call for tour hours. To get to the island, you can take a water taxi. ☎ *561/339–2504* ⊕ *www.pbmm.org* ⌨ *$2 donation* ☉ *Daily dawn–dusk for noncampers.*

FISHING

The **Sailfish Marina and Resort** (✉ *98 Lake Dr.* ☎ *561/844–1724* ⊕ *www.sailfishmarina.com*) has seasoned captains and a large fleet of 28- to 60-foot boats. Book a full or half day of deep-sea fishing for up to six people.

WHERE TO EAT AND STAY

$$
SEAFOOD
✕ **Sailfish Marina Restaurant.** This waterfront restaurant overlooking Peanut Island is a great place to chill out after a long day of mansion-gawking, boating, or beach-bumming. Choose a table in the dining room or under an umbrella on the terrace and enjoy mainstays like conch chowder or grilled swordfish. More upscale entrées—this, after all, is still Palm Beach County—include lobster tail and baby sea scallops sautéed in garlic and lemon butter. Breakfast is a winner here, too. Sportfishing charters are available at Sailfish's store. ✉ *98 Lake Dr.* ☎ *561/842–8449* ⊟ *www.sailfishmarina.com* ☉ *AE, MC, V.*

$$
▥ **Sailfish Marina Resort.** This waterfront lodging has a marina with deepwater slips and accommodations that include motel-style rooms, efficiencies, and even a three-bedroom house. All rooms open to landscaped grounds, although five rooms are directly on the water. Rooms have peaked ceilings, carpeting, flat-screen TVs and stall showers; all have ceiling fans. From the seawall, you'll see fish through the clear inlet water. **Pros:** inexpensive rates; on the Intracoastal Waterway; water taxi stops here. **Cons:** can be noisy; area attracts a party crowd; dated

Florida's Sea Turtles: The Nesting Season

From May to October it's turtle-nesting season all along the Florida coast. Female loggerhead, Kemp's ridley, and other species living in the Atlantic Ocean or Gulf of Mexico swim up to 2,000 mi to the Florida shore. By night they drag their 100- to 400-pound bodies onto the beach to the dune line. Then each digs a hole with her flippers, drops in 100 or so eggs, covers them up, and returns to sea.

The babies hatch about 60 days later. Once they burst out of the sand, the hatchlings must get to sea rapidly or risk becoming dehydrated from the sun or being caught by crabs, birds, or other predators.

Instinctively, baby turtles head toward bright light, probably because for millions of years starlight or moonlight reflected on the waves was the brightest light around, serving to guide hatchlings to water. But now light from beach development can lead the babies in the wrong direction, towards the street rather than the water. To help, many coastal towns enforce light restrictions during nesting months. Florida home owners are requested to dim their lights on behalf of baby sea turtles.

At night, volunteers walk the beaches, searching for signs of turtle nests. Upon finding telltale scratches in the sand, they cordon off the sites, so beachgoers will leave the spots undisturbed. Volunteers also keep watch over nests when babies are about to hatch and assist if the hatchlings get disoriented.

It's a hazardous world for baby turtles. They can die after eating tar balls or plastic debris, or they can be gobbled by sharks or circling birds. Only about one in a thousand survives to adulthood. After reaching the water, the babies make their way to warm currents. East Coast hatchlings drift into the Gulf Stream, spending years floating around the Atlantic.

Males never return to land, but when females attain maturity, in 15–20 years, they return to shore to lay eggs. Remarkably, even after migrating hundreds and even thousands of miles out at sea, most return to the very beach where they were born to deposit their eggs. Each time they nest, they come back to the same stretch of beach. In fact, the more they nest, the more accurate they get, until eventually they return time and again to within a few feet of where they last laid their eggs. These incredible navigation skills remain for the most part a mystery despite intense scientific study. To learn more, check out the Sea Turtle Survival League's and Caribbean Conservation Corporation's Web site at ⊕ *www.cccturtle.org*.

—Pam Acheson

rooms. ⊠ *98 Lake Dr.* ☎ *561/844–1724 or 800/446–4577* ⊕ *www. sailfishmarina.com* ⇆ *30 units* ⚇ *In-room: a/c, kitchen (some), Internet. In-hotel: restaurant, bar, pool* ⊟ *AE, MC, V.*

PALM BEACH GARDENS

5 mi north of West Palm Beach, off I–95.

About 15 minutes northwest of Palm Beach is this relaxed, upscale residential community known for its high-profile golf complex, the PGA National Resort & Spa. Although not on the beach, the town is less than a 15-minute drive from the ocean.

ESSENTIALS

Visitor Information Northern Palm Beach County Chamber of Commerce (⊠ *800 N. U.S. 1, Jupiter* ☎ *561/694–2300*).

SPORTS AND THE OUTDOORS

GOLF

If you're the kind of traveler who takes along a set of clubs, the **PGA National Resort & Spa** (⊠ *1000 Ave. of the Champions* ☎ *561/627–1800*) is for you. The resort has five championship courses that are challenging enough for the pros. Among them are the Champion Course, designed by Tom Fazio and Jack Nicklaus (greens fee $350); the General Course, designed by Arnold Palmer ($250); the Haig Course, the first course opened at the resort ($210); the Estate Course, with a practice range and putting green ($210); and the Tom Fazio–designed Squire Course ($210). Lessons are available at the Golf Digest Academy.

EN
ROUTE

John D. MacArthur Beach State Park & Nature Center. Almost 2 mi of beach, good fishing and shelling, and one of the finest examples of subtropical coastal habitat remaining in southeast Florida are among the treasures here. To learn about what you see, take an interpretive walk to a mangrove estuary along the upper reaches of Lake Worth. The nature center, open daily 9–5, has exhibits on the coastal environment. ⊠ *10900 Rte. A1A, North Palm Beach* ☎ *561/624–6950* ⊕ *www.macarthurbeach.org* ⊠ *$5 per vehicle, up to 8 people* ⊙ *Daily 8–sundown.*

WHERE TO EAT

$$$
AMERICAN
★

✕ **Café Chardonnay.** At the end of a strip mall, Café Chardonnay is surprisingly elegant. Soft lighting, warm woods, and cozy banquettes set the scene for a quiet lunch or romantic dinner. The place consistently receives praise for its innovative menu and outstanding wine list. Starters include wild-mushroom strudel and truffle-stuffed diver sea scallops. Entrées might include Gorgonzola-crusted filet mignon or pan-seared veal scaloppine with rock shrimp. ⊠ *4533 PGA Blvd.* ☎ *561/627–2662* ⊕ *www.cafechardonnay.com* ⊟ *AE, D, MC, V* ⊙ *No lunch weekends.*

$$$
AMERICAN

✕ **Ironwood Grille.** Opened in 2008, this new kid on the block is part of the PGA National Resort & Spa. The contemporary eatery specializes in beef and seafood dishes made with locally grown organic produce. Other good choices include she-crab soup with sherry and grilled filet mignon. The chic lobby restaurant and the adjoining bar share an extensive wine cellar and a room for private wine tastings. On Thursday nights, a DJ plays music from 6 until 9. ⊠ *400 Ave. of* the Champions ☎ 561/627–2000 ⌨ www.ironwoodgrille.com ⊙ AE, D, MC, V.

$$ **✗ Spoto's.** If you like oysters, head
SEAFOOD to this place where black-and-white photographs of oyster fisherman adorn the walls. The polished tables give the eatery a country club look. A local chain, Spoto's serves up a delightful bowl of New England clam chowder and an impressive variety of oysters and clams. The prime rib Caesar salad with crispy croutons never disappoints. Sit outside on the patio to take advantage of the area's perfect weather. There's a popular brunch on Sunday. ⊠ 4560 PGA Blvd. ☎ 561/776–9448 ⊕ www. spotosoysterbar.com ⊟ AE, DC, MC, V.

WHERE TO STAY

$$$$ ⌂ **PGA National Resort & Spa.** With five championship courses, this
★ resort has hosted more championship tournaments than any other golf destination in the country. A top-to-bottom renovation has made the facilities even more attractive, as is clear once you step into the massive clubhouse. But while golf is a big draw, only 40% of guests are golfers. The rest come for the other amenities, such as the extensive sports facilities, the excellent dining, and the 240-acre nature preserve. At the pool, simply raise a flag and a server rushes over to take your drink order. The spa is in a building styled after a Mediterranean fishing village, and six outdoor therapy pools are joined by a collection of imported mineral saltwater pools. Guest rooms have luxurious maple furnishings, flat-screen TVs, and private balconies. **Pros:** a golfer's paradise; short drive to shopping; large rooms. **Cons:** not on the beach. ⊠ 400 Ave. of the Champions ☎ 561/627–2000 or 800/633–9150 ⊕ www.pgaresort.com ⇆ 280 rooms, 59 suites ⌂ In-room: a/c, safe, kitchen (some), refrigerator (some), Internet, In-hotel: 7 restaurants, room service, bars, golf courses, tennis courts, pools, gym, spa, Wi-Fi hotspot, parking (free) ⊟ AE, D, DC, MC, V.

JUPITER

12 mi north of Palm Beach Shores via I–95 and Rte. 706.

Jupiter is one of the few little towns in the region not fronted by an island. Beaches here are part of the mainland, and Route A1A runs for almost 4 mi along the beachfront dunes and beautiful estates.

ESSENTIALS

Visitor Information **Northern Palm Beach County Chamber of Commerce** (⊠ 800 N. U.S. 1, Jupiter ☎ 561/694–2300).

EXPLORING

Dubois Home. Take a look at how life once was at this modest pioneer outpost dating from 1898. Sitting atop an ancient Jeaga Indian mound 20 feet high and looking onto Jupiter Inlet, it has Cape Cod as well as Cracker (Old Florida) design. It's in Dubois Park, worth a visit for its

Away from developed shorelines, Blowing Rocks Preserve on Jupiter Island lets you wander the dunes.

lovely beaches and swimming lagoons. The park is open dawn to dusk. ⊠ *19075 Dubois Rd.* ☎ *561/747–8380* ⊕ *www.lrhs.org* ✉ *$2* ☼ *Tues. and Wed. 1–4.*

★ **Jupiter Inlet Lighthouse.** Designed by Civil War hero General George Meade, this brick lighthouse has been operated by the Coast Guard since 1860. Tours of the 105-foot-tall landmark unfold every half hour. (Children must be at least 4 feet tall to go to the top.) There's a small museum that tells about efforts to restore this graceful spire to the way it looked from 1860 to 1918. ⊠ *500 Capt. Armour's Way, U.S. 1 and Beach Rd.* ☎ *561/747–8380* ⊕ *www.jupiterlighthouse.org* ✉ *Tour $7* ☼ *Tues.–Sun. 10–5; last tour at 4.*

SPORTS AND THE OUTDOORS

BASEBALL

Both the **St. Louis Cardinals** and **Florida Marlins** (⊠ *4751 Main St.* ☎ *561/775–1818*) train at the 7,000-seat Roger Dean Stadium.

BEACHES

Carlin Park. A beach is just one of the draws here. The park also has picnic pavilions, hiking trails, a baseball diamond, a playground, six tennis courts, and fishing sites. The Lazy Loggerhead Café, serving snacks and burgers, is open daily 9–5. ⊠ *A1A at Juno Beach* ☎ *561/799–0185* ☼ *Daily dawn–dusk.* **Juno Beach.** A 990-foot pier and a bait shop are the big draws here, but a section is available for surfing, and there's a snack bar, too. ⊠ *14775 S. Rte. A1A* ☎ *561/624–0065* ☼ *Daily dawn–dusk.*

CANOEING

Canoe Outfitters of Florida (⊠ *9060 W. Indiantown Rd.* ☎ *561/746–7053*) leads trips along 8 mi of the Loxahatchee River, where you can see animals in the wild, from otters to eagles. Canoe or kayak rental for two to three hours is $25, including drop-off and pickup.

GOLF

The 18-hole **Abacoa Golf Club** (⊠ *105 Barbados Dr.* ☎ *561/622–0036*) is a good alternative to nearby private courses; greens fee $60/$119. The **Golf Club of Jupiter** (⊠ *1800 Central Blvd.* ☎ *561/747–6262*) has 18 holes of varying difficulty; greens fee $49/$69. **Jupiter Dunes Golf Club** (⊠ *401 Rte. A1A* ☎ *561/746–6654*) has an 18-hole golf course named Little Monster and a putting green near the Jupiter River estuary; greens fee $36/$65.

WHERE TO EAT AND STAY

$$
SEAFOOD
✕ **Food Shack.** This local favorite is a bit tricky to find, but worth the search. The fried-food standards you might expect at such a casual place are not found on the menu; instead there are fried-tuna rolls with basil and fried grouper cheeks with a fruity slaw. A variety of beers are fun to pair with the creatively prepared seafood dishes that include wahoo, mahimahi, and snapper. ⊠ *103 South U.S. 1* ☎ *561/741–3626* ⊕ *www.littlemoirsfoodshack.com* ▭ *DC, MC, V* ☉ *Closed Sun.*

$$$
SEAFOOD
✕ **Sinclair's Ocean Grill.** This popular spot in the Jupiter Beach Resort has sunlight streaming through the glass doors overlooking the pool. The menu has a daily selection of fresh fish, such as cashew-encrusted grouper, Cajun-spice tuna, and mahimahi with pistachio sauce. There are also thick, juicy steaks—filet mignon is the house specialty—and chicken and veal dishes. The Sunday buffet is a big draw. ⊠ *5 N. Rte. A1A* ☎ *561/745–7120* ⊕ *www.jupiterbeachresort.com* ▭ *AE, D, MC, V.*

$$$$
🏨 **Jupiter Beach Resort.** This time-share resort looks great after a complete renovation that added a 7,500-square-foot spa. Caribbean-style rooms with mahogany sleigh beds and armoires fill the nine-story tower. Most rooms have balconies, and those on higher floors have great ocean views. Some overlook Jupiter Lighthouse, and others face Juno Pier. Families love the casual approach and the plentiful activities, such as turtle-watches from May to October. Snorkeling equipment and bicycles are available for rent. **Pros:** fabulous views; good location. **Cons:** very high beds; pricey rates. ⊠ *5 N. Rte. A1A* ☎ *561/746–2511 or 800/228–8810* ⊕ *www.jupiterbeachresort.com* ⇱ *133 rooms, 44 suites* ⚭ *In-room: a/c, safe, Wi-Fi. In-hotel: 3 restaurants, bars, tennis court, pool, gym, spa, beachfront, water sports, bicycles, laundry facilities, parking (free)* ▭ *AE, D, MC, V.*

JUPITER ISLAND AND HOBE SOUND

5 mi north of Jupiter, off Rte. A1A.

Northeast across the Jupiter Inlet from Jupiter is the southern tip of Jupiter Island. Here expansive and expensive estates often retreat from the road behind screens of vegetation, and at the north end of the island turtles come to nest in a wildlife refuge. To the west, on the mainland, is the little community of Hobe Sound.

GETTING HERE AND AROUND

The best way to get to Jupiter Island and Hobe Sound from Jupiter is to drive north 5 mi on Interstate 95 to Indiantown Road. From there, head east to Federal Highway (U.S. 1), then north on U.S. 1.

EXPLORING

Blowing Rocks Preserve. Protected within this 73-acre preserve are plants native to beachfront dune, coastal strand (the landward side of the dunes), mangrove forests, and tropical hardwood forests. The best time to visit is when high tides and strong offshore winds coincide, causing the sea to blow spectacularly through holes in the eroded outcropping. Park in the lot; police ticket cars parked along the road. ⊠ *574 South Beach Rd., Rte. 707, Jupiter Island* ☎ *561/744–6668* ⊠ *$2* ☼ *Daily 9–4:30.*

Hobe Sound National Wildlife Refuge. Two tracts make up this refuge: 232 acres of sand-pine and scrub-oak forest in Hobe Sound, and 735 acres of coastal sand dune and mangrove swamp on Jupiter Island. Trails are open to the public in both places. Turtles nest and shells wash ashore on the 3½-mi-long beach, which has been severely eroded by high tides and strong winds. ⊠ *13640 SE Federal Hwy., Hobe Sound* ☎ *772/546–6141* ⊠ *$5 per vehicle* ☼ *Daily dawn–dusk.*

☾ **Hobe Sound Nature Center.** It's located in the Hobe Sound National Wildlife Refuge, but this nature center is an independent organization. Its museum, which has baby alligators and crocodiles and a scary-looking tarantula, is a child's delight. A ½-mi trail winds through a forest of sand pine and scrub oak—one of Florida's most unusual and endangered plant communities. It lost its original building in 2004 due to hurricanes and moved into a new building in 2007. A new visitor center opened in 2009. ⊠ *13640 SE Federal Hwy., Hobe Sound* ☎ *772/546–2067* ⊕ *www.hobesoundnaturecenter.com* ⊠ *Donation suggested* ☼ *Trail daily dawn–dusk; nature center weekdays 9–3.*

Jonathan Dickinson State Park. From Hobe Mountain, an ancient dune topped with a tower, you are treated to a panoramic view of this park's 10,285 acres of varied terrain and the Intracoastal Waterway. The Loxahatchee River, which cuts through the park, is home to manatees in winter and alligators all year. Two-hour boat tours of the river depart daily at 9, 11, 1, and 3 and cost $14.50 per person. Among amenities are a dozen cabins for rent, tent sites, bicycle and hiking trails, a campground, and a snack bar. ⊠ *16450 SE Federal Hwy., Hobe Sound* ☎ *772/546–2771* ⊠ *$6 per vehicle* ☼ *Daily 8–dusk.*

SPORTS AND THE OUTDOORS

OUTFITTER

Jonathan Dickinson's River Tours (⊠ *Jonathan Dickinson State Park, 16450 SE Federal Hwy., Hobe Sound* ☎ *561/746–1466*) offers boat tours of the Loxahatchee River and canoe, kayak, and boat rentals from 9 to 5 daily.

STUART

7 mi north of Hobe Sound.

This compact little town on a peninsula that juts out into the St. Lucie River has a remarkable amount of shoreline for its size and also has a charming historic district. The ocean is about 5 mi east.

GETTING HERE AND AROUND

To get to Stuart from Jupiter and Hobe Sound, drive north on Federal Highway (U.S. 1).

ESSENTIALS

Visitor Information **Stuart Main Street** (✉ 201 SW Flagler Ave. ☎ 772/286–2848). **Stuart/Martin County Chamber of Commerce** (✉ 1650 S. Kanner Hwy. ☎ 772/287–1088).

EXPLORING

Strict architectural and zoning standards guide civic-renewal projects. Stuart has antiques shops, restaurants, and more than 50 specialty shops within a two-block area. A self-guided walking-tour pamphlet is available at assorted locations downtown to clue you in on this once-small fishing village's early days.

★ **Maritime & Yachting Museum.** Linking the watery past with a permanent record of maritime and yachting events contributing to Treasure Coast lore, this museum near a marina has many old ships as well as historic exhibits to explore. Among those leading Saturday tours is a retired ship captain who has many interesting stories to share. ✉ *1707 NE Indian River Dr.* ☎ *772/692–1234* ⊕ *www.mymflorida.com* ✂ *$5* ☾ *Mon.– Sat. 10–5, Sun. 1–4.*

SPORTS AND THE OUTDOORS

BEACHES

Stuart Beach. With its ever-vigilant lifeguards, this is a good spot for beginning surfers. More experienced wave riders enjoy the challenges of the choppy waters. Fishing and shelling are also draws. ✉ *801 NE Ocean Blvd.* ☎ *772/221–1418.*

FISHING

Deep-sea charters are available at the **Sailfish Marina** (✉ *3565 SE St. Lucie Blvd.* ☎ *772/221–9456*).

SHOPPING

More than 60 restaurants and shops with antiques, art, and fashion have opened downtown along Osceola Street.

Operating for more than two decades, the **B&A Flea Market**, the oldest and largest such enterprise on the Treasure Coast, has a street-bazaar feel, with shoppers happily scouting for the practical and unusual. ✉ *2885 SE Federal Hwy.* ☎ *772/288–4915* ✂ *Free* ☾ *Weekends 8–3.*

THE ARTS

On the National Register of Historic Places, the **Lyric Theatre** (✉ *59 SW Flagler Ave.* ☎ *772/286–7827* ⊕ *www.lyrictheatre.com*) has been revived for live performances. A gazebo has free music performances.

WHERE TO EAT AND STAY

$$ ✕ **Courtine's.** A husband-and-wife team oversees this quiet and hos-
FRENCH pitable restaurant under the Roosevelt Bridge. French and American influences are clear in the Swiss chef's dishes, from rack of lamb with Dijon mustard to grilled filet mignon stuffed with Roquefort and fresh spinach. The formal dining room has subtly elegant touches, such as fresh flowers on each table. A more casual menu is available at the bar. ⊠ *514 N. Dixie Hwy.* ☎ *772/692–3662* ⊕ *www.courtines.com* ▭ *AE, MC, V* ☺ *Closed Sun. and Mon. No lunch.*

$$ ✕ **Finz Waterfront Grille.** Located on the southern end of the Manatee
SEAFOOD Pocket in Port Salerno, the popular island-style restaurant is surrounded by boatyards and a lively gallery scene. Sit on the covered dock and take in the breeze while eating the tastiest crab cakes south of Chesapeake Bay. The kitchen also serves up savory teriyaki-marinated steak tips, Maryland crab soup, peel-and-eat shrimp, and maple-glazed salmon. There's live island music on Sunday afternoons from 2–5 and entertainment every Saturday and Sunday night. ⊠ *4290 SE Salerno Rd.* ☎ *772/283–1929* ⊕ *www.finzwaterfrontgrille.com* ▭ *AE, D, MC, V.*

$$$ ⌷ **Pirate's Cove Resort & Marina.** On the banks of the St. Lucie River, this cozy enclave is the perfect place to recoup after a day at sea. The resort is relaxing and casual but packed with plenty of recreational activities. The tropically furnished rooms are spacious and have balconies to enjoy the waterfront views. The few suites include microwaves and refrigerators. A Continental breakfast is included. **Pros:** pretty location; great for boaters. **Cons:** lounge gets noisy at night. ⊠ *4307 SE Bayview St., Port Salerno* ☎ *772/287–2500 or 800/332–1414* ⊕ *www. piratescoveresort.net* ⇗ *48 rooms, 2 suites* ⌂ *In-room: a/c, refrigerator, Wi-Fi. In-hotel: restaurant, room service, pool, bar, parking (free)* ⍾⃝ *BP* ▭ *AE, D, DC, MC, V.*

HUTCHINSON ISLAND (JENSEN BEACH)

5 mi northeast of Stuart.

The down-to-earth town of Jensen Beach, occupying the core of the island, stretches across both sides of the Indian River. Between late April and August more than 600 turtles come here to nest along the town's Atlantic beach. Area residents have taken pains to curb the runaway development that has created the commercial crowding found to the north and south, although some high-rises have popped up along the shore.

GETTING HERE AND AROUND

The best way to reach Jensen Beach from Stuart is to drive north on Federal Highway (U.S. 1) to Northwest Jensen Boulevard, then east on Jensen Beach Boulevard.

ESSENTIALS

Visitor Information **Jensen Beach Chamber of Commerce** (⊠ *1900 NE Ricou Terr., Jensen Beach* ☎ *772/334–3444*).

EXPLORING

Elliott Museum. This pastel-pink museum was erected in 1961 in honor of Sterling Elliott, inventor of an early automated-addressing machine and a four-wheel cycle. The museum, with its antique cars, dolls, toys, and vintage baseball cards, is a nice stop for anyone fond of nostalgic goods. There are also antique fixtures from an early general store, blacksmith shop, and apothecary shop. ⊠ *825 NE Ocean Blvd., Jensen Beach* ☎ *772/225–1961* ⊕ *www.elliottmuseumfl.org* ⊡ *$8* ⊙ *Mon.–Sat. 10–4, Sun. 1–4.*

★ **Florida Oceanographic Coastal Center.** Explore a ½-mi interpretive boardwalk through coastal hardwood and mangrove forest. Guided nature walks through trails and stingray feedings are offered at various times during the day. Boat tours, which include a 20-minute stop at a bird sanctuary, cost $23 per person. Dolphins, manatees, and turtles are often seen on the boat tour, for which reservations are required. ⊠ *890 NE Ocean Blvd., Jensen Beach* ☎ *772/225–0505* ⊕ *www. floridaoceanographic.org* ⊡ *$8* ⊙ *Mon.–Sat. 10–5, Sun. noon–4; guided nature walks Mon.–Sat. 11 and 3, Sun. at 2; boat tours Tues., Fri., and Sat. at 11, Thurs. at 11 and 4.*

Gilbert's House of Refuge Museum. Built in 1875 on Hutchinson Island, the museum is the only remaining building of nine such structures built by the U.S. Life-Saving Service (a predecessor of the Coast Guard) to aid stranded sailors. Exhibits include antique lifesaving equipment, maps, artifacts from nearby wrecks, and boatbuilding tools. ⊠ *301 SE MacArthur Blvd., Jensen Beach* ☎ *772/225–1875* ⊡ *$6* ⊙ *Mon.–Sat. 10–4, Sun. 1–4.*

SPORTS AND THE OUTDOORS

BASEBALL

The **New York Mets** (⊠ *525 NW Peacock Blvd., Port St. Lucie* ☎ *772/871–2115*) train at Tradition Field. It's also the home of the St. Lucie Mets Minor League Team.

BEACHES

At the north end of the Indian River Plantation, **Bathtub Reef Park** (⊠ *MacArthur Blvd., off Rte. A1A, Jensen Beach*) is ideal for children because the waters are shallow and usually calm. At low tide you can walk to the reef. Facilities include restrooms and showers.

GOLF

Hutchinson Island Marriott Golf Club (⊠ *555 NE Ocean Blvd., Jensen Beach* ☎ *772/225–6819*) has 18 holes for members and hotel guests; greens fee $60 for 18 holes. With three separate courses, the PGA–operated **PGA Golf Club at the PGA Villages** (⊠ *1916 Perfect Dr., Port St. Lucie* ☎ *772/467–1300 or 800/800–4653*) is a public facility designed by Pete Dye and Tom Fazio; greens fee $55/$99.

WHERE TO EAT AND STAY

$$$

CONTINENTAL

★ ✕ **11 Maple Street.** This cozy spot is as good as it gets on the Treasure Coast. Soft music and a friendly staff set the mood in the antiques-filled dining room, which holds only 16 tables. Appetizers run from panfried conch to crispy calamari, and entrées include seared rainbow trout, wood-grilled venison with onion-potato hash, and beef tenderloin with white-truffle-and-chive butter. Desserts like white-chocolate custard with blackberry sauce are seductive, too. ⊠ *3224 Maple Ave., Jensen Beach* ☎ *772/334–7714* ⊕ *www.11maplestreet.net* ⌖ *Reservations essential* ≡ *MC, V* ⊘ *Closed Mon. and Tues. No lunch.*

$ ✕ **Conchy Joe's.** Like a hermit crab sliding into a new shell, Conchy
SEAFOOD Joe's moved up from West Palm Beach in 1983. Built in the 1920s, this rustic stilt house is full of antique fish mounts, gator hides, and snakeskins. It's a popular tourist spot, but the waterfront location, casual vibe, and delicious seafood attract locals, too. Staples include grouper marsala, broiled sea scallops, and fried cracked conch. There's live reggae Thursday through Sunday. ⊠ *3945 NE Indian River Dr., Jensen Beach* ☎ *772/334–1130* ⊕ *www.conchyjoes.com* ≡ *AE, D, MC, V.*

$$$–$$$$ ⊞ **Hutchinson Island Marriott Beach Resort & Marina.** With a 77-slip marina, a full water-sports program, a golf course and tennis courts, and a wide range of restaurants, this self-contained resort is excellent for families. Many of the rooms are in a trio of four-story buildings that form an open courtyard with a large pool. Additional rooms and apartments are scattered throughout the 200-acre property; some overlook the Intracoastal Waterway, others gaze at the ocean or tropical gardens. **Pros:** attentive staff; challenging golf course. **Cons:** no children's program. ⊠ *555 NE Ocean Blvd., Hutchinson Island* ☎ *772/225–3700 or 800/775–5936* ⊕ *www.marriott.com* ⌁ *213 rooms, 70 suites* ⌖ *Inroom: a/c, kitchen (some), Internet. In-hotel: 3 restaurants, room service, bars, golf course, tennis courts, pools, gym, spa, beachfront, laundry facilities, Wi-Fi hotspot, parking (free) , some pets allowed* ≡ *AE, D, DC, MC, V.*

FORT PIERCE

11 mi north of Stuart, off Federal Hwy. (U.S. 1).

About an hour north of Palm Beach, this community has a distinctive rural feel, focusing on ranching and citrus farming. There are several worthwhile stops, including those easily seen while following Route 707.

ESSENTIALS

Visitor Information **St. Lucie County Tourist Development Council** (⊠ *2300 Virginia Ave.* ☎ *800/344–8443*).

EXPLORING

Heathcote Botanical Gardens. Take a self-guided tour of this 3½-acre park, which includes a palm walk, a Japanese garden, and an orchid house. There is also a gift shop with whimsical and botanical knickknacks. Guided tours are available Tuesday through Saturday by appointment. ⊠ *210 Savannah Rd.* ☎ *772/464–4672* ⊕ *www. heathcotebotanicalgardens.org* ⊡ *$6* ⊘ *May–Oct., Tues.–Sat. 9–5; Nov.–Apr., Tues.–Sat. 9–5, Sun. 1–5.*

★ **Navy SEAL Museum.** Commemorating more than 3,000 troops who trained here during World War II, the museum has weapons and equipment on view and exhibits depicting the history of the Underwater Demolition Teams. Patrol boats and vehicles are displayed outdoors.

⊠ *3300 N. Rte. A1A* ☏ *772/595–5845* ⊕ *www.navysealmuseum.com* ⊠ *$6* ☉ *Tues.–Sat. 10–4, Sun. noon–4.*

Savannas Recreation Area. Once a reservoir, the 550 acres have been returned to a natural state. Today the wilderness area has campsites, boat ramps, and trails. ⊠ *1400 E. Midway Rd.* ☏ *772/464–7855* ☉ *Daily 8–6.*

Smithsonian Marine Ecosystems Exhibit. Run by the Smithsonian Institute and housed in the St. Lucie County Marine Center, this is where scientists come to study local ecosystems. A highlight is the 3,000-gallon coral-reef tank, originally shown in the Smithsonian's National Museum of Natural History in Washington, D.C. The parklike setting, where children love to play, makes it an ideal picnic destination. ⊠ *420 Seaway Dr.* ☏ *772/462–3474* ⊠ *$3, free the first Tues. of the month* ☉ *Tues.–Sat. 10–4.*

SPORTS AND THE OUTDOORS

Fort Pierce Inlet State Recreation Area. Sand dunes and coastal forests cover this 340-acre reserve. The park has swimming, surfing, picnic facilities, and a self-guided nature trail. ⊠ *905 Shorewinds Dr.* ☏ *772/468–3985* ⊠ *$6 per vehicle* ☉ *Daily 8–dusk.*

Fort Pierce State Park. Accessible only by footbridge, the reserve has 4 mi of trails around Jack Island. The 1½-mi Marsh Rabbit Trail across the island traverses a mangrove swamp to a 30-foot-tall observation tower overlooking the Indian River. ⊠ *Rte. A1A* ☏ *772/468–3985* ⊠ *$4 for one, $6 for a vehicle* ☉ *Daily 8–5:30.*

FISHING

For charter boats and fishing guides, contact the dockmaster at the **Dockside Harborlight Resort** (⊠ *1160 Seaway Dr.* ☏ *772/461–4824*).

SCUBA DIVING

On North Hutchinson Island, the **Urca de Lima Underwater Archaeological Preserve,** 200 yards from shore and under 10–15 feet of water, contains remains of a flat-bottom, round-bellied store ship. Once part of a treasure fleet bound for Spain, it was destroyed by a hurricane. ⊠ *3375 N. A1A.*

THE ARTS

Home of the Treasure Coast Art Association, the **A.E. "Bean" Backus Museum & Gallery** displays works of one of Florida's foremost landscape artists. It also mounts changing exhibits and offers exceptional buys on work by local artists. ⊠ *500 N. Indian River Dr.* ☏ *772/465–0630* ⊕ *www.backusgallery.com* ⊠ *Free but $2 donation suggested* ☉ *Wed.–Sun. 11–4.*

WHERE TO EAT AND STAY

$$$
SEAFOOD
✕ **Mangrove Mattie's.** This upscale spot on Fort Pierce Inlet provides dazzling waterfront views and delicious seafood. Dine on the terrace or in the dining room, and don't forget to try the coconut-fried shrimp or the chicken and scampi. Go during happy hour (weekdays 5–8) for a free buffet. Many locals come by for Sunday brunch. ⊠ *1640 Seaway Dr.* ☏ *772/466–1044* ⊕ *www.mangrovematties.com* ⊟ *AE, D, DC, MC, V.*

$–$$ ☐ **Dockside Harborlight Resort Inn.** Formerly two adjacent motels, this resort is the best of the lodgings lining the Fort Pierce Inlet along Seaway Drive. Spacious, nicely decorated units on two floors have kitchens or wet bars. Some have a waterfront porch or balcony. A cluster of apartments is across the street, away from the water. Overnight boat docking is available for an additional $25 per night. **Pros:** good value; reasonable rates at marina. **Cons:** basic decor; some steps to climb. ☒ *1160 Seaway Dr.* ☎ *772/468–3555 or 800/286–1745* ⊕ *www.docksideinn. com* ↪ *72 rooms, 4 apartments* ☖ *In-room: a/c, refrigerator (some). In-hotel: pools, laundry facilities, parking (free)* ▤ *AE, D, DC, MC, V.*

VERO BEACH

12 mi north of Fort Pierce.

Tranquil and charming, this Indian River County town has a strong commitment to the environment and the arts. There are plenty of outdoor activities here, even though many visitors gravitating to the training camp of the Los Angeles Dodgers opt to do little at all. In the town's exclusive Riomar Bay area, roads are shaded by massive live oaks, and a popular cluster of restaurants and shops is just off the beach.

GETTING HERE AND AROUND

To get here, you have two options—Route A1A, along the coast, or Route 605 (also called Old Dixie Highway), on the mainland. As you approach Vero on the latter, you pass through an ungussied landscape of small farms and residential areas. On the beach route, part of the drive is through an unusually undeveloped section of the Florida coast.

ESSENTIALS

Visitor Information **Indian River Chamber of Commerce** (☒ *1216 21st St.* ☎ *772/567–3491*).

EXPLORING

Environmental Learning Center. In addition to aquariums filled with Indian River creatures, the 51 acres here have a 600-foot boardwalk through the mangrove shoreline and a 1-mi canoe trail. The center is on the northern edge of Vero Beach, and the pretty drive is worth the trip. ☒ *255 Live Oak Dr.* ☎ *772/589–5050* ⊕ *www.elcweb.org* ☒ *Donation suggested* ☉ *Tues.–Fri. 10–4, Sat. 9–noon, Sun. 1–4.*

Heritage Center and Indian River Citrus Museum. You'll learn that more grapefruit is shipped from the Indian River area than anywhere else in the world at this museum. The memorabilia harks back to when families washed and wrapped the luscious fruit to sell at roadside stands, and oxen hauled citrus-filled crates with distinctive Indian River labels to the rail station. ☒ *2140 14th Ave.* ⊕ *www.veroheritage.org* ☎ *772/770–2263* ☒ *Free* ☉ *Tues.–Fri. 10–4.*

Fodor's Choice **McKee Botanical Garden.** On the National Register of Historic Places, the
★ 18 acres here are both a tropical garden and a horticulture museum. The historic Hall of Giants, a rustic structure built from cedar and hearts of pine, features a beautiful stained glass, bronze bells, and the world's largest single-plank mahogany table. There's a 529-square-foot bamboo pavilion, a gift shop, and the Garden Café, which serves tasty snacks

DID YOU KNOW?

Vero Beach is known for its arts. But like many of Florida's coastal towns, some of the top attractions here are the natural offerings, from Vero Beach's citrus trees to its beautiful sunrises.

and sandwiches and locally grown tea. This is the place to see spectacular water lilies. ✉ *350 U.S. 1* ☎ *772/794–0601* 🌐 *www.mckeegarden.org* 🎫 *$9* ⏲ *Tues.–Sat. 10–5, Sun. noon–5.*

Vero Beach Museum of Art. Part of a 26-acre campus dedicated to the arts, the museum is where a full schedule of exhibitions, art movies, lectures, workshops, and classes are hosted. The museum's five galleries and sculpture garden make it the largest art facility in the Treasure Coast. ✉ *3001 Riverside Park Dr.* ☎ *772/231–0707* 🌐 *www.vbmuseum.org* ⏲ *Mon.–Sat. 10–4:30, Sun. 1–4:30.*

SPORTS AND THE OUTDOORS

BEACHES

Humiston Park (✉ *Ocean Dr. below Beachland Blvd. Vero Beach* ☎ *772/231–5790* 🎫 *Free*) is one of the beach-access parks along the east edge of town that have lifeguards, boardwalks, and steps bridging the dunes, plus there are picnic tables and a children's play area. There are picnic tables, restrooms, and a nice playground for kids at **Treasure Shores Park** (✉ *11300 A1A, 3 mi north of County Rd. 510* ☎ *772/581–4997*). **Wabasso Beach Park** (✉ *County Rd. 510, east of A1A* ☎ *772/581–4998*) has lifeguards, restrooms, a boardwalk, and showers.

GOLF

Sandridge Golf Club (✉ *5300 73rd St.* ☎ *772/770–5000*) has two public 18-hole courses designed by Ron Garl; greens fee $49.

SHOPPING

Along Ocean Drive near Beachland Boulevard, a shopping area includes art galleries, antiques shops, and upscale clothing stores. The eight-block area of Oceanside has an interesting mix of boutiques, specialty shops, and eateries.

Just west of Interstate 95, **Outlets at Vero Beach** (✉ *1824 94th Dr.* ☎ *772/770–6171*) is a discount shopping destination with 70 brand-name stores, including Ann Taylor, Ralph Lauren Polo, and Jones New York.

THE ARTS

Riverside Children's Theatre (✉ *Agnes Wahlstrom Youth Playhouse, 3280 Riverside Park Dr.* ☎ *772/234–8052* 🌐 *www.riversidetheatre.com*) offers a series of professional touring and local productions. The **Riverside Theatre** (✉ *3250 Riverside Park Dr.* ☎ *772/231–6990* 🌐 *www.riversidetheatre.com*) stages five productions each season in its 650-seat Mainstage and three in its 200-seat Second Stage.

WHERE TO EAT AND STAY

$$$ SEAFOOD

✕ **Ocean Grill.** Opened as a hamburger shack in 1938, the Ocean Grill combines its ocean view with Tiffany-style lamps, wrought-iron chandeliers, and paintings of pirates. Count on at least three kinds of seafood any day on the menu, along with steaks, pork chops, soups, and salads. The house drink, "Pusser's Painkiller"—a curious blend first mixed by British sailors in the Virgin Islands and rationed in a tin cup. It commemorates the 1894 wreck of the *Breconshire,* which occurred offshore and from which 34 British sailors escaped. ✉ *Sexton Plaza, 1050 Ocean Dr.* ☎ *772/231–5409* 🌐 *www.ocean-grill.com* 💳 *AE, D, DC, MC, V* ⏲ *Closed 2 wks after Labor Day. No lunch weekends.*

2

$–$$ ⊡ **Aquarius Oceanfront Resort.** Right on beautiful South Beach, this small, unpretentious resort has loyal guests who book a year in advance. Ask for Rooms 125 and 126, which have balconies overlooking the beach. Others, most with kitchens, face the parking lot. Walk across the street to the excellent Italian restaurant Monte's and to South Beach Pizza. **Pros:** relaxed vibe; great location; faces the beach. **Cons:** steps to climb; nothing too fancy. ⊠ *1526 Ocean Dr.* ☎ *772/231–5218 or 877/767– 1526* ⊕ *www.aquariusverobeach.com* ⌇ *28 rooms* ⌂ *In-room: a/c, kitchen (some). In-hotel: pool, beachfront, laundry facilities, parking (free)* ⊟ *AE, DC, MC, V.*

$$$–$$$$ ⊡ **Costa d'Este.** Many people know this hotel because of its famous own- ers, singer Gloria Estefan and producer Emilio Estefan. They bought the property in 2004, just before hurricanes ripped the former Palm Court apart. They brought in a new design and a lively ambience. The architecture features geometrical designs, something you will notice as soon as you arrive at the porte-cochere entrance. Rooms are sleek and filled with custom-made furnishings. You get the feel of being in a modern yacht with broad ocean views. Oriente, the resort's restaurant, has become a favorite of locals who come for the Cuban cuisine. **Pros:** great location; huge showers; faces the beach. **Cons:** marble floors can be cold. ⊠ *3244 Ocean Dr.* ☎ *772/562–9919* ⊕ *www.costadeste.com* ⌇ *90 rooms, 4 suites* ⌂ *In-room: a/c, safe, refrigerator, Wi-Fi. In-hotel: restaurant, room service, pool, gym, spa, laundry service, parking (free)* ⊟ *AE, MC, V.*

$–$$ ⊡ **Driftwood Resort.** On the National Register of Historic Places, this 1935 inn was built entirely from ocean-washed timbers and decorated with such artifacts as ship bells, Spanish tiles, and a cannon from a 16th-century Spanish galleon. The time-share complex includes nine buildings on the beach with both modern and historic rooms. The inn attracts guests from around the world, who sit in wooden rock- ers facing the beach. **Pros:** great seaside location; near restaurants and shops. **Cons:** older property; rooms can be musty. ⊠ *3150 Ocean Dr.* ☎ *772/231–0550* ⊕ *www.thedriftwood.com* ⌇ *96 1- and 2-bedroom suites, 4 hotel rooms* ⌂ *In-room: a/c, kitchen refrigerator. In-hotel: restaurant, bar, pools, beachfront, parking (free)* ⊟ *AE, DC, MC, V.*

SEBASTIAN

14 mi north of Vero Beach, off Federal Hwy. (U.S. 1).

One of the few sparsely populated areas on Florida's east coast, this fishing village has as remote a feeling as you're likely to find between Jacksonville and Miami Beach. That adds to the appeal of the recreation area around Sebastian Inlet, where you can walk for miles along quiet beaches and catch some of Florida's best waves for surfing.

ESSENTIALS

Visitor Information Sebastian Chamber of Commerce (⊠ *700 Main St.* ☎ *772/589–5969*).

EXPLORING

McLarty Treasure Museum. A National Historical Landmark, this museum underscores this credo: "Wherever gold glitters or silver beckons, man will move mountains." It has displays of coins, weapons, and tools salvaged from a fleet of Spanish treasure ships that sank in the 1715 storm, leaving some 1,500 survivors struggling to shore between Sebastian and Fort Pierce. The museum's last video showing begins at 3. ⊠ *13180 N. Rte. A1A* ☎ *772/589–2147* ⊠ *$2* ☉ *Daily 10–4.*

Mel Fisher's Treasures. You'll really come upon hidden loot when you enter this museum operated by the late Mel Fisher's family. See some of what was recovered in 1985 from the Spanish treasure ship *Atocha* and its sister ships of the 1715 fleet. The museum certainly piques one's curiosity about what is still buried at sea: treasures continue to be discovered each year. ⊠ *1322 U.S. 1* ☎ *772/589–9875* ⊕ *www.melfisher. com* ⊠ *$6.50* ☉ *Mon.–Sat. 10–5, Sun. noon–5.*

Pelican Island National Wildlife Refuge. Within the Indian River Lagoon and on the barrier island across from Sebastian, Pelican Island was founded in 1903 by President Theodore Roosevelt as the nation's first national wildlife refuge. The island is a closed wilderness area. The historic Pelican Island rockery is viewable from a distance by commercial boat and kayak tours and from a public observation tower on the adjacent barrier island. The Refuge has more than 6 mi of foot trails through the barrier island habitats. A boardwalk and observation tower enable visitors to see birds, endangered species, and habitats. ⊠ *1339 20th St.* ☎ *772/562–3909 Ext. 275* ⊠ *Free* ☉ *Daily 7:30–sunset.*

Sebastian Inlet State Recreation Area. Because of the highly productive fishing waters of Sebastian Inlet, this 578-acre property at the north end of Orchid Island is one of the Florida park system's biggest draws. Both sides of the high bridge spanning the inlet—views are spectacular—attract anglers as well as those eager to enjoy the fine sandy shores, known for having some of the best waves in the state. A concession stand on the inlet's north side sells short-order food, rents various craft, and has a small apparel and surf shop. There's a boat ramp, and not far away is a dune area that's part of the **Archie Carr National Wildlife Refuge.** ⊠ *9700 S. Rte. A1A, Melbourne Beach* ☎ *321/984–4852* ⊕ *www. floridastateparks.org* ⊠ *$5 per vehicle* ☉ *Daily 7–sunset.*

SPORTS AND THE OUTDOORS

FISHING

For sportfishing, try **Big Easy Fishing Charters** (⊠ *Capt. Hiram's Restaurant, 1606 N. Indian River Dr.* ☎ *772/664–4068*). For bottom fishing, try **Incentive Charter Fishing** (⊠ *Capt. Hiram's Restaurant, 1606 N. Indian River Dr.* ☎ *321/676–1948*).

Fort Lauderdale and Broward County

WORD OF MOUTH

"The train curved in to the shoreline, leaving the wild interior behind and entering the highly developed sun playgrounds of South Florida, where palm trees seemingly sprouted out of the roofs of the high-rise hotels and speedboats spewed jets of water behind them in the rivers near Lake Worth."

—Daniel Williams

WELCOME TO FORT LAUDERDALE AND BROWARD COUNTY

TOP REASONS TO GO

★ **Blue Waves:** Sparkling Lauderdale beaches— from Deerfield Beach and Pompano Beach through Dania Beach and Hollywood—are Florida's first to capture Blue Wave Beach status from the Clean Beaches Council.

★ **Inland Waterways:** More than 300 mi of inland waterways including downtown Fort Lauderdale's historic New River create what's known as the Venice of America.

★ **Everglades Access:** Just minutes from luxury hotels and golf courses, the rugged Everglades tantalize with alligators, colorful birds, and other wildlife.

★ **Vegas-Style Gaming:** In 2008, Vegas-style slots came to Hollywood's glittering Seminole Hard Rock Hotel & Casino, adding to video slots already in play there and at other Broward "racinos."

★ **Cruise Gateway:** Port Everglades—homeport for Royal Caribbean's new *Oasis of the Seas*, the world's largest cruise vessel—hosts cruise ships from major lines.

1 **Fort Lauderdale.** Anchored by historic New River and its attractive Riverwalk, Fort Lauderdale embraces high-rise condos along with single-family homes, museums, parks, and attractions. Las Olas Boulevard, lined with boutiques, sidewalk cafés, and restaurants, links downtown and the beaches.

2 **North on Scenic A1A.** Stretching north on Route A1A, seaside attractions range from high-rise Galt Ocean Mile to low-rise resort communities—and a glimpse of a lighthouse, inspiration for the community of Lighthouse Point.

3 **South Broward.** From Hollywood's beachside Broadwalk and historic Young Circle (the latter transformed into an Arts Park) to Seminole gaming, South Broward provides grit, glitter, and diversity in attractions.

Fort Lauderdale Beach.

441
811
Deerfield Beach
A1A
Coconut Creek
91
Hillsboro Beach
811
Hillsboro Lighthouse
Sample Rd.
834
7 **Butterfly World**
Margate
Powerline Rd.
Federal Hwy.
2
Coconut Cr. Pkwy.
North Lauderdale
Atlantic Blvd.
Dixie Hwy.
Pompano Beach
95
1
Cypress Creek Rd.
Sawgrass Expwy.
Commercial Blvd.
Lauderdale-by-the-Sea
Oakland Park Blvd.
Lauderdale Lakes
N. Andrews Ave.
A1A
441
Sunrise Blvd.
Seminole Dr.
S.W. 31st Ave.
Fort Lauderdale
Broward Blvd.
Las Olas Blvd.
1
Davie Blvd.
Melrose Park
S.E. 17th St. Causeway
84
7
Port Everglades
595
Fort Lauderdale-Hollywood International Airport
Griffin Rd.
1
Stirling Rd.
Dania Beach Blvd.
Dania Beach
A1A
Sheridan St.
822
95
Hollywood Blvd.
Hollywood
Pembroke Rd.
3
Dixie Hwy.
Hallandale Blvd.
Hallandale

ATLANTIC OCEAN

0   3 mi
0   3 km

GETTING ORIENTED

3

Along the southeast's Gold Coast, Fort Lauderdale and Broward County anchor a delightfully chic middle ground between the historically elite Palm Beaches and the international hubbub of Miami. From downtown Fort Lauderdale, it's about a four-hour drive to either Orlando or Key West, but there's plenty to keep you in Broward. All told, Broward boasts 31 communities from Deerfield Beach to Hallandale Beach along the coast, and from Coral Springs to Southwest Ranches closer to the Everglades. Big—in fact, huge—shopping options await in Sunrise, home of Sawgrass Mills, the upscale Colonnade Outlets at Sawgrass, and IKEA Sunrise.

Las Olas Labor Day Art fair.

FORT LAUDERDALE AND BROWARD COUNTY PLANNER

When to Go

Peak season runs Thanksgiving through March, when concert, art, and entertainment seasons go full throttle. Expect rain, heat, and humidity in summer. Hurricane winds come most notably in August and September, sometimes as late as November. Golfing tee-time waits are longer on weekends year-round. Fort Lauderdale sunshine can burn even in cloudy weather.

Top Festivals

Fort Lauderdale International Film Festival. Beginning in late October, this event showcases over 200 feature, documentary, and short films from around the world. In addition to 23 days of screenings, you can expect seminars and Hollywood-style parties. Directors and actors in attendance add star power. ☎ 954/760-9898 ⊕ www.fliff.com.

Seminole Hard Rock Winterfest Boat Parade. In mid-December, 100-plus vessels decked out with festive decorations light up the Intracoastal Waterway in Fort Lauderdale. Over the years, celebrity grand marshals have included Regis Philbin, Joan Rivers, and Kim Kardashian. ☎ 954/767-0686 ⊕ www. winterfestparade.com.

Getting Here and Around

Serving more than 21 million travelers a year, **Fort Lauderdale–Hollywood International Airport** (FLL ☎ 954/359-6100) is 4 mi south of downtown Fort Lauderdale, just off U.S. 1 between Fort Lauderdale and Hollywood, and near Port Everglades and Fort Lauderdale Beach. Other options include **Miami International Airport (MIA),** about 35 mi to the south, and the far less chaotic **Palm Beach International Airport** (PBI ☎ 561/471-7420) , about 45 mi to the north. All three airports link to **Tri-Rail** (☎ 800/874-7245), a commuter train operating seven days through Palm Beach, Broward, and Miami-Dade counties.

Broward County Transit (☎ 954/357-8400) operates bus route No. 1 between the airport and its main terminal at Broward Boulevard and Northwest 1st Avenue, near downtown Fort Lauderdale. Service from the airport is every 20 minutes and begins daily at 5:40 AM; the last bus leaves the airport at 11:15 PM. The fare is $1.50. Broward County Transit (BCT) also covers the county on 275 fixed routes. The fare is $1.50. Service starts at 5 AM and continues to 11:30 PM, except on Sunday.

Amtrak provides daily service to Fort Lauderdale and stops at Deerfield Beach and Hollywood.

By car, access to Broward County from north or south is via Florida's Turnpike, Interstate 95, U.S. 1, or U.S. 441. Interstate 75 (Alligator Alley, requiring a toll despite being part of the nation's interstate-highway system) connects Broward with Florida's west coast and runs parallel to State Road 84 within the county. East–west Interstate 595 runs from westernmost Broward County and links Interstate 75 with Interstate 95 and U.S. 1, providing handy access to the airport and seaport. Route A1A, designated a Florida Scenic Highway by the state's Department of Transportation, generally parallels the beach.

About the Restaurants

References to "Fort Liquordale" from spring-break days of old have given way to au courant allusions for the decidedly cuisine-oriented "Fork Lauderdale." Greater Fort Lauderdale offers some of the finest, most varied dining of any U.S. city its size, spawned in part by the advent of new luxury hotels and upgrades all around. From among more than 4,000 wining-and-dining establishments in Broward, choose from basic Americana or cuisines of Asia, Europe, or Central and South America, and enjoy more than just food in an atmosphere with subtropical twists.

About the Hotels

Not as posh as Palm Beach or as deco-trendy as Miami Beach, Fort Lauderdale has a growing roster of more-than-respectable lodging choices, from beachfront luxury suites to intimate bed-and-breakfasts to chain hotels along the Intracoastal Waterway. Relatively new on the luxury beachfront are the Atlantic, the Hilton Fort Lauderdale Beach Resort, the Ritz-Carlton, Fort Lauderdale, and Florida's first W resort, and more upscale places to hang your hat are on the horizon while smaller family-run lodging spots disappear. If you want to be *on* the beach, be sure to ask specifically when booking your room, since many hotels advertise "waterfront" accommodations that are along inland waterways or overlooking the beach from across Route A1A. Opened just in time for Superbowl 2010, the iconic Yankee Clipper (shaped like a ship's prow) has regained luster with a major revamp as the Sheraton Fort Lauderdale Beach Hotel, and it's *definitely* smack on the beach.

Assume that hotels operate on the European Plan (EP, no meals), unless we specify that they use the Breakfast Plan (BP, with full breakfast), Continental Plan (CP, Continental breakfast), Full American Plan (FAP, all meals), or Modified American Plan (MAP, breakfast and dinner), or are all-inclusive (AI, all meals and most activities).

WHAT IT COSTS

	¢	$	$$	$$$	$$$$
Restaurants	under $10	$10–$15	$15–$20	$20–$30	Over $30
Hotels	under $80	$80–$100	$100–$140	$140–$220	over $220

Restaurant prices are per person for a main course at dinner. Hotel prices are for a standard double room, excluding 6% sales tax (more in some counties) and 1%–5% tourist tax.

Boat Tours

Carrie B (✉ *Riverwalk at SE 5th Ave., Fort Lauderdale* ☎ *954/768–9920* ⊕ *www.carriebcruises.com*), a 300-passenger day cruiser, gives 90-minute tours on the New River and Intracoastal Waterway. Cruises depart at 11, 1, and 3 each day and cost $19.95.

Fort Lauderdale Duck Tours (✉ *17 S. Fort Lauderdale Beach Blvd., Fort Lauderdale* ☎ *954/761–4002* ⊕ *www.fortlauderdaleducktours.com*), provides 90 minutes of land/water family fun aboard a 45-passenger amphibious hydra terra, cruising Venice of America neighborhoods, historic areas, and the Intracoastal Waterway. Tours depart daily (schedule varies) and cost $30.

Jungle Queen (✉ *Bahia Mar Beach Resort, 801 Seabreeze Blvd., Fort Lauderdale* ☎ *954/462–5596* ⊕ *www.junglequeen.com*) operates *Jungle Queen III* and *Jungle Queen IV*, tour boats seating more than 500 for cruises up New River through the heart of Fort Lauderdale. Sightseeing cruises at 9:30 and 1:30 cost $17.50, and the 6 PM BBQ dinner cruise costs $39.95.

Pro Dive International (✉ *515 Seabreeze Blvd., Fort Lauderdale* ☎ *954/761–3413* ⊕ *www.prodiveusa.com*) operates the 60-foot glass-bottom boat *Pro Diver II* for taking in offshore reefs. Daily two-hour trips cost $28 or $35 to snorkel, equipment provided.

FORT LAUDERDALE AND BROWARD COUNTY BEACHES

A wave-capped, 20-mi shoreline with wide ribbons of golden sand for beachcombing and sunbathing remains the anchor draw for Fort Lauderdale and Broward County.

Fort Lauderdale isn't just for spring breakers. In fact, ever since investors started pouring money into the waterfront scene, beginning in the '90s, the beach has lured a more upscale clientele. That said, it still has great people-watching and opportunities for partying.

Beyond the city, Broward County's beachfront extends for miles without interruption, although character of communities along the shoreline varies. To the south in Hallandale, the beach is backed by towering condominiums, while tee times and nightlife beckon in Hollywood. Deerfield Beach and Lauderdale-by-the-Sea to the north are magnets for active families, and nearby Pompano Beach attracts anglers. Many places along Broward shorelines—blessedly, for purists—are uncluttered with nothing but sand and turquoise waters.

SAFETY TIPS

⚠ Avoid unguarded waters, and be aware of color codes. In Fort Lauderdale, double red flags mean water is closed to the public, often because of lightning or sharks; a lone red flag signals strong currents; purple signals presence of marine pests like men-of-war, jellyfish, or sea lice; green means calm conditions. In Hollywood, orange signals rip currents with easterly onshore winds; blue warns of marine life like jellyfish; red means hazardous; green signals good conditions.

FORT LAUDERDALE'S BEST BEACHES

FORT LAUDERDALE BEACH

Alone among Florida's major beach-front communities, Fort Lauderdale's beach remains gloriously open and uncluttered. A wave theme unifies the Fort Lauderdale Beachfront setting—from the low, white, wave-shaped wall between the beach and beachfront promenade to the widened and bricked inner promenade in front of shops, restaurants, and hotels. Walkways line both sides of the beach roadway, and traffic has been trimmed to two gently curving northbound lanes, where in-line skaters skim past slow-moving cars. On the beach side, a low masonry wall doubles as an extended bench, separating sand from the promenade. At night the wall is accented with pretty ribbons of fiber-optic color, often on the blink despite an ongoing search for a permanent fix. The beach is most crowded between Las Olas and Sunrise boulevards.

HOLLYWOOD'S BROADWALK

The name might be Hollywood, but there's nothing hip or chic about Hollywood North Beach Park, which sits at the north end of Hollywood (Route A1A and Sheridan Street). And that's a good thing. It's just a laid-back, old-fashioned place to enjoy the sun, sand, and sea. No high-rises overpower the scene here. Parking is $5. The main part of the

Broadwalk is quite a bit more fashionable. Thanks to a $14 million makeover, this popular beach has spiffy new features like a pedestrian walkway, a concrete bike path, a crushed-shell jogging path, an 18-inch decorative wall separating the Broadwalk from the sand, and places to shower off after a dip. Fido fans take note: the 2008 film *Marley & Me*, starring Jennifer Aniston and Owen Wilson and filmed in Greater Fort Lauderdale, spurred a comeback for dog beaches in South Florida, including the year-round Dog Beach of Hollywood.

LAUDERDALE-BY-THE-SEA

For a small village with a pier, Lauderdale-by-the-Sea packs a big punch for beach pleasure. Especially popular with divers and snorkelers, this laid-back stretch of sand provides great access to lovely coral reefs. When you're not down in the waters, look up and you'll likely see a pelican flying by. Gentle trade winds make this an utterly relaxing retreat from the hubbub of the Fort Lauderdale party scene. Things do liven up with nightly entertainment at a couple of local watering holes, but L-B-T-S, as it's known, still provides a small-town, easygoing, family-friendly feel.

Updated by
Lynne Helm

Collegians of the 1960s returning to Fort Lauderdale would be hard-pressed to recognize the onetime "Sun and Suds Spring Break Capital of the Universe." Back then, Fort Lauderdale's beachfront was lined with T-shirt shops, and downtown consisted of a lone office tower and dilapidated buildings waiting to be razed.

The beach and downtown have since exploded with upscale shops, restaurants, and luxury resort hotels equipped with enough high-octane amenities to light up skies all the way to western Broward's Alligator Alley. At risk of losing small-town 45-rpm magic in iPod times—when hotel parking fees alone eclipse room rates of old—Greater Fort Lauderdale somehow seems to meld disparate eras into nouveau nirvana, seasoned with a little Gold Coast sand.

The city was named for Major William Lauderdale, who built a fort at the river's mouth in 1838 during the Seminole Indian wars. It wasn't until 1911 that the city was incorporated, with only 175 residents, but it grew quickly during the Florida boom of the 1920s. Today's population hovers around 150,000, and suburbs keep growing—1.6 million live in Broward County's 31 municipalities and unincorporated areas. As elsewhere, many speculators busily flipping property here got caught when the sun-drenched real-estate bubble burst, leaving Broward's foreclosure rate to skyrocket.

Despite economic downturns, gaming options have expanded. South Florida's Indian tribes have long offered bingo, poker, and machines resembling slots. In 2005, Broward became Florida's first county to offer gambling with true slot machines at four wagering facilities referred to as racinos: Gulfstream Park Racing & Casino, the Mardi Gras Racetrack & Gaming, Dania Jai Alai Casino, and the Isle Casino & Racing of Pompano Park. In 2008, Hollywood's Seminole Hard Rock Hotel & Casino, which ranks as the most glittering example of Vegas-style gaming with a tropical twist cut a deal with the state to replace bingo-style machines with genuine Vegas-style slots.

FORT LAUDERDALE

Like many southeast Florida neighbors, Fort Lauderdale has long been revitalizing. In a state where gaudy tourist zones often stand aloof from workaday downtowns, Fort Lauderdale exhibits consistency at both ends of the 2-mi Las Olas corridor. The sparkling look results from upgrades both downtown and on the beachfront. Matching the downtown's innovative arts district, cafés, and boutiques is an equally inventive beach area, with hotels, cafés, and shops facing an undeveloped shoreline, and new resort-style hotels replacing faded icons of yesteryear. Despite wariness of pretentious overdevelopment, city leaders have allowed a striking number of glittering high-rises. Some nostalgia buffs fret over the diminishing vision of sailboats bobbing in waters near downtown, now that a boxy high-rise has erased one of the area's oldest marinas. Sharp demographic changes are also altering the faces of Greater Fort Lauderdale communities, increasingly cosmopolitan with more minorities, including Hispanics and people of Caribbean descent, as well as gays and lesbians. In Fort Lauderdale, especially, a younger populace is growing, whereas longtime residents are dying off or heading north, to a point where one former city commissioner likens the change to that of historic New River—moving with the tide and sometimes appearing at a standstill. "The river of our population is at still point, old and new in equipoise, one pushing against the other."

GETTING HERE AND AROUND

The Fort Lauderdale metro area is laid out in a grid system, and only myriad canals and waterways interrupt the mostly straight-line path of streets and roads. Nomenclature is important here. Streets, roads, courts, and drives run east–west. Avenues, terraces, and ways run north–south. Boulevards can (and do) run any which way. For visitors, trendy Las Olas Boulevard is one of the most important east–west thoroughfares from the beach to downtown, whereas Route A1A—referred to as Atlantic Boulevard, Ocean Boulevard, and Fort Lauderdale Beach along some stretches—runs along the north–south oceanfront. These names can confuse visitors, since there are separate streets called Atlantic and Ocean in Hollywood and Pompano Beach. Boulevards, composed of either pavement or water, give Fort Lauderdale its distinct "Venice of America" character.

The city's transportation system, though less congested than elsewhere in South Florida, suffers from traffic overload. Interstate 595 connects the city and suburbs and provides a direct route to the Fort Lauderdale–Hollywood International Airport and Port Everglades, but lanes slow to a crawl during rush hours. The Intracoastal Waterway, paralleling Route A1A, is the nautical equivalent of an interstate highway. It runs north–south between downtown Fort Lauderdale and the beach and provides easy boating access to neighboring beach communities.

The major taxi company serving the area is Yellow Cab, with vehicles equipped for major credit cards.

TOURS Honeycombed with some 300 mi of navigable waterways, Fort Lauderdale is home port for about 44,000 privately owned vessels, but you don't need to be a boat owner to ply the waters. For a scenic way to

This couple tours Fort Lauderdale via a three-wheeled scooter; photo by rockindom, Fodors.com member.

really see this canal-laced city, simply hop on a Water Taxi, sometimes called a Water Bus, part of Fort Lauderdale's water-transportation system, made up of a fleet of vessels carrying up to 70 passengers each. Providing transport and quick, narrated tours, a water taxi is a good way to bar-hop or access many waterfront hotels and restaurants. Larger, multiple-deck touring vessels and motorboat rentals for self-guided adventure are other sightseeing options.

Boats won't get you everywhere; you may need to call for taxi service when getting to and from the airport, seaport, or major hotels. Meters run at rates of $4.50 for the first mile and $2.40 for each additional mile; waiting time is 40¢ per minute. There's a $10-fare minimum (at press time reportedly rising to $15) from seaport or airport, and an additional $2 service charge when you are collected from the airport.

Catch an orange-bottomed, yellow-topped Sun Trolley, running every 15 minutes, either free or for $1 or so, depending on routes. Sun Trolley's *Convention Connection*, 50¢ per person, runs round-trip from Cordova Road's Harbor Shops near Port Everglades (where you can park free) to past the Convention Center, over the 17th Street Causeway, and north along Route A1A to Beach Place. Wave at trolley drivers— yes, they will stop—for pickups anywhere along the route.

ESSENTIALS

Transportation Contacts Sun Trolley (☎ *954/761–3543* ⊕ *www.suntrolley. com*). **Water Taxi** (☎ *954/467–0008* ⊕ *www.watertaxi.com*). **Yellow Cab** (☎ *954/565–5400*).

Visitor Information Greater Fort Lauderdale Convention and Visitors Bureau (☎ *954/765–4466* ⊕ *www.sunny.org*).

EXPLORING

Numbers in the margin correspond to the Fort Lauderdale map.

DOWNTOWN

The jewel of downtown along New River is the Arts and Entertainment District, with Broadway shows, ballet, and theater at the riverfront Broward Center for the Performing Arts. Clustered within a five-minute walk are the Museum of Discovery & Science, the expanding Fort Lauderdale Historical Museum, and the Museum of Art, home to stellar touring exhibits. Restaurants, sidewalk cafés, bars, and blues, folk, jazz, reggae, and rock clubs flourish. Tying this district together is the Riverwalk, extending 2 mi along the New River's north and south banks. Tropical gardens with benches and interpretive displays fringe the walk on the north, boat landings on the south.

TOP ATTRACTIONS

❺ Fort Lauderdale History Center. Surveying city history from the Seminole era to more recent times, the Fort Lauderdale Historical Society's museum has expanded into several adjacent buildings, including the historic King-Cromartie House, New River Inn, and the Hoch Heritage Center, a public research facility archiving original manuscripts, maps, and more than 250,000 photos. ⊠ *231 SW 2nd Ave.* ☎ *954/463–4431* ⊕ *www.oldfortlauderdale.org* ✉ *$10* ☾ *Tues.–Sun. noon–4.*

❸ Museum of Art Fort Lauderdale. Currently in an Edward Larrabee Barnes–
★ designed building that's considered an architectural masterpiece, activists started this museum in a nearby storefront about 50 years ago. MOAFL now coordinates with Nova Southeastern University to host world-class touring exhibits and has an impressive permanent collection of 20th-century European and American art, including works by Picasso, Calder, Dalí, Mapplethorpe, Warhol, and Stella, as well as works by celebrated Ashcan School artist William Glackens. ⊠ *1 E. Las Olas Blvd.* ☎ *954/763–6464* ⊕ *www.moafl.org* ✉ *$10* ☾ *Tues.–Sat. 11–5, Sun. noon–5.*

❼ Museum of Discovery & Science/AutoNation IMAX Theater. Open 365 days
☾ barring weather-related events, the aim here is to entertain children—
★ *and* adults—with wonders of science. The courtyard's 52-foot-tall Great Gravity Clock lets arrivals know cool experiences await. Exhibits include Kidscience, encouraging youngsters to explore the world; and Gizmo City, a look at how gadgets work. Florida Ecoscapes has a living coral reef, plus sharks, rays, and eels. The AutoNation IMAX theater, part of the complex, shows films, some in 3-D. A Subway sandwich shop is on premises. ⊠ *401 SW 2nd St.* ☎ *954/467–6637 museum, 954/463–4629 IMAX* ⊕ *www.mods.org* ✉ *Museum $11, $16 with one IMAX show* ☾ *Mon.–Sat. 10–5, Sun. noon–6.*

❻ Riverwalk. Lovely views and entertainment prevail on this paved prom-
★ enade on the New River's north bank. On the first Sunday of every month a free jazz brunch attracts visitors. The walk has been extended 2 mi on both sides of the urban stream, connecting the facilities of the Arts and Science District.

A Black Heritage Gem

West of downtown Fort Lauderdale's Arts and Sciences District, in the heart of the African-American community along Sistrunk Boulevard, lies a gem once discounted as a grand idea unlikely to get off the ground.

Yet in 2002, Fort Lauderdale's **African-American Research Library and Cultural Center** soared into reality as a $14 million repository of history and heritage of African, African-American, and Caribbean cultures, with historic books, papers, and art, much of it pertaining to the African diaspora. There's a 300-seat auditorium, a story-time area, and 5,000 square feet of gallery space for exhibits. African symbols appear as part of the decor.

For Samuel F. Morrison, now-retired Broward County Library director, the center is the culmination of his dream, a vision to create a worthy showcase reflecting African-American heritage. Broward County anted up $5 million for the 60,000-square-foot center, and Morrison raised the rest.

Of the nation's major African-American public research facilities, Fort Lauderdale's also has a Caribbean focus. Offerings include the Alex Haley Collection, with eight unfinished manuscripts. Other components range from Fisk University research of slave narratives to books on Jamaica. You'll also find the Kitty Oliver Oral Histories Collection on Broward and Okeechobee and the Niara Sudarkasa Collection of papers, artwork, and other materials of the former president of Lincoln University.

And there's the collection of Dorothy Porter Wesley—in some eyes the greatest of the black bibliophiles. Her collection includes about 500 inscribed and autographed books—some date to 1836—with personal narratives, histories, fiction, and reference works, which Wesley's daughter, Constance Porter Uzelac, refers to as "Mama's stuff." Wesley was known for going to homes of the recently deceased to make sure nothing of value got tossed. "She'd get to the house before the body was cold," her daughter recalls, heading straight to attics and basements to retrieve bits and scraps of history.

Passionate about his dream, Morrison also remains adamant about the library's widespread appeal, noting that "these pieces provide glimpses [into] the hearts and minds of people who have made a difference in the lives of not only people of color and African culture, but people of many colors and cultures."

✉ *2650 Sistrunk Blvd.* ☎ *954/625–2800* ⊕ *www.broward.org/library/aarlcc.htm* 🎟 *Free* ⊗ *Mon.–Thurs. 10–9, Fri. and Sat. 10–6, Sun. 1–5.*

❶ **Stranahan House.** The city's oldest residence, on the National Register of Historic Places, and increasingly dwarfed by high-rise development, was once home for businessman Frank Stranahan, who arrived in 1892. With his wife, Ivy, the city's first schoolteacher, he befriended and traded with Seminole Indians, and taught them "new ways." In 1901 he built a store and later made it his home. After financial reverses, Stranahan tied himself to a concrete sewer grate and jumped into New River, leaving his widow to carry on. Ivy died in 1971, and now her home (at various

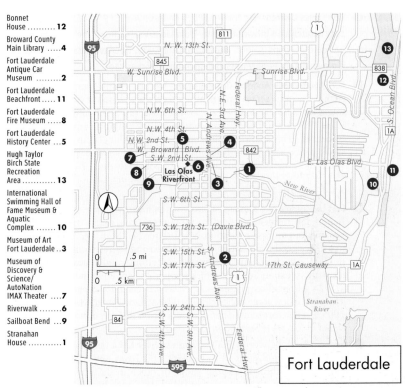

Fort Lauderdale

times a post office, general store, and restaurant) is a museum, with many period furnishings, and tours. ⊠ *335 SE 6th Ave., at Las Olas Blvd.* ☎ *954/524–4736* ⊕ *www.stranahanhouse.org* ⊠ *$12* ⊗ *Wed.– Sat. 10–3, Sun. 1–3.*

QUICK BITES

The sweet smell of waffle cones lures pedestrians to **Kilwin's of Las Olas** (⊠ **809 E. Las Olas Blvd.** ☎ **954/523–8338**), an old-fashioned confectionery that also sells hand-paddled fudge and scoops of homemade ice cream.

WORTH NOTING

4 **Broward County Main Library.** One of more than 30 libraries in the Broward County system, this eight-story building of Florida limestone (with a terraced glass facade standing up remarkably well to occasional hurricane-force winds) was designed by Marcel Breuer to showcase the green, leafy surrounding environment, outdoor plaza, and reflecting pool. Works are displayed here from Broward's Public Art and Design Program, including paintings, sculpture, and photographs by nationally renowned and Florida artists. A technology center has personal computers for public use and devices for patrons with disabilities. A 300-seat theater hosts productions from theater to poetry readings. ⊠ *100 S. Andrews Ave.* ☎ *954/357–7444* ⊕ *www.broward.org/library* ⊠ *Free* ⊗ *Mon.–Thurs. 9–9, Fri. and Sat. 9–5, Sun. noon–5:30.*

Don't miss **Charcuterie Too** (⊠ *100 S. Andrews Ave.* ☎ *954/463–9578*), a cozy cafeteria on Broward County Main Library's 2nd floor. The lunch menu has quiche, soups, salads, and homemade cakes. Open weekdays 10–2:30, it draws library bookworms and downtown worker bees.

② **Fort Lauderdale Antique Car Museum.** Retired floral company owner Arthur O. Stone set up a foundation to preserve these eye-poppers. Nostalgia includes around two dozen Packards (all in running condition) from 1900 to the 1940s, along with a gallery saluting Franklin Delano Roosevelt. This sparkling museum sports everything from grease caps, spark plugs, and gearshift knobs to Texaco Oil signage, plus a newer wing and an enlarged library. ⊠ *1527 SW 11th Ave. (Packard Ave.)* ☎ *954/779–7300* ⊕ *www.antiquecarmuseum.net* ⊠ *$8* ⊙ *Weekdays 10–4, Sat. 10–3.*

❽ **Fort Lauderdale Fire Museum.** Following its harrowing fire of 1912, Fort Lauderdale residents pushed for more protection, finally opening what became known as Fire Station No. 3 (later No. 8) in 1927. This landmark, designed by architect Francis Abreu and retired from active duty in 2004, now functions as a historical, cultural, and educational facility with an expanding array of Roaring '20s era equipment including a 1928 Ahrens-Fox piston pumper, as well as a 1942 parade engine. There's also a vintage police car. ⊠ *1022 W. Las Olas Blvd.* ☎ *954/763–1005* ⊕ *www.fortlauderdalefiremuseum.com* ⊠ *Free, donations appreciated* ⊙ *Sat. 9–1, Sun. noon–5.*

❾ **Sailboat Bend.** Between Las Olas and the river lies a neighborhood with a character reminiscent of Key West's Old Town and Miami's Coconut Grove. Although without shops or much in the way of services, it's still worth a visit to be reminded of days gone by. The circa 1927 Fire Station No. 3, designed by local architect Francis Abreu and now housing the Fort Lauderdale Fire Museum, is at the corner of West Las Olas Boulevard and Southwest 11th Avenue. Across the river lies the tree-lined Tarpon River neighborhood, alluding to the canal-like river looping off New River from the southeast quadrant and running to the southwest section, returning to New River near Sailboat Bend.

ALONG THE BEACH

⓬ ★ **Bonnet House.** A 35-acre oasis in the heart of the beach area, this subtropical estate on the National Register of Historic Places stands as a tribute to the history of Old South Florida. The charming home was the winter residence of the late Frederic and Evelyn Bartlett, artists whose personal touches and small surprises are evident throughout. For architecture, artwork, or the natural environment, this place is special. Be on the lookout for playful monkeys swinging from trees, a source of amusement at even some of the most solemn weddings on the grounds. Hours can vary, so call first. ⊠ *900 N. Birch Rd.* ☎ *954/563–5393* ⊕ *www.bonnethouse.org* ⊠ *$20 for house tours, $10 for grounds only* ⊙ *Tues.–Sat. 10–4, Sun. noon–4.*

⓫ **Fort Lauderdale Beachfront.** Fort Lauderdale's increasingly stylish beachfront offers easy access not only to a wide band of beige sand but also to restaurants and shops. Heading north for 2 mi, beginning at the Bahia

Mar yacht basin along Route A1A, you'll have clear ocean views (typically across rows of colorful beach umbrellas) to ships passing in and out of nearby Port Everglades. If you're on the beach, gaze back on an exceptionally graceful promenade.

⑬ Hugh Taylor Birch State Recreation Area. Amid the tropical greenery of this 180-acre park, stroll along a nature trail, visit the Birch House Museum, picnic, play volleyball, or paddle a rented canoe. Since parking is limited on Route A1A, park here and take a walkway underpass to the beach (which can be accessed 9–5, daily). ⊠ *3109 E. Sunrise Blvd.* ☎ *954/564–4521* ⊕ *www.floridastateparks.org* ⊠ *$6 per vehicle, $2 per pedestrian* ⊙ *Daily 8–sunset.*

⑩ International Swimming Hall of Fame Museum & Aquatic Complex. This monument to underwater accomplishments has two 50-meter pools plus a dive pool open daily to the public. The exhibition building has photos, medals, and other souvenirs from major swim events, and the Huizenga Theater provides an automated video experience where you can select vintage-Olympic coverage or old films such as Esther Williams' *Million Dollar Mermaid.* ⊠ *1 Hall of Fame Dr., 1 block south of Las Olas at Rte. A1A* ☎ *954/462–6536* ⊕ *www.ishof.org* ⊠ *Museum $8, pool $4* ⊙ *Museum mid-Jan.–late Dec., weekdays 9–7, weekends 9–5; pool mid-Jan.–late Dec., weekdays 8–4, weekends 9–5.*

NEED A BREAK?
For respite from the sun, duck into **Undergrounds Coffeehaus** (⊠ *2743 E. Oakland Park Blvd.* ☎ *954/630–1900*), a few blocks west of the beach. It's cozy and one-of-a-kind, with consignment art, new and used books, teas, desserts, and a swoon-worthy PB&J latte. Owner Aileen Liptak promises coffee "so good, we drink it ourselves" along with free Wi-Fi with a beverage purchase. Closed Mon. and Fri., no lunch weekends.

SPORTS AND THE OUTDOORS

BIKING

Among the most popular routes are Route A1A and Bayview Drive, especially in early morning before traffic builds, and a 7-mi bike path that parallels State Road 84 and New River and leads to Markham Park, which has mountain bike trails. ■TIP→ Alligator alert: do not dangle your legs from seawalls.

BIRD-WATCHING

North of Fort Lauderdale's 17th Street Causeway, within the Gothic intrigue of **Evergreen Historic Cemetery** (⊠ *1300 SE 10th St.* ☎ *954/745–2140* ⊕ *www.browardcemeteries.com*), lies a bird-watchers' haven. The circa 1879 graveyard, shaded by gumbo limbo and strangler figs, doubles as a place of fleeting repose for Bahama mockingbirds and other species winging through urban Broward. Warblers are big here, and there are occasional sightings of red-eyed vireos, northern waterthrushes, and scarlet tanagers.

Cruising for a Taxi

Shout "Taxi! Taxi!" in Fort Lauderdale, and look for your ship to come in.

Actually, you'll be catching what's also called a water bus, as the original fleet of tiny water taxis has been replaced by vessels accommodating up to 70 passengers. Either way, they're floating cabs, and a great way to get around.

For sightseeing, the water-taxi-cum-bus can pick you up at any of several docks along the Intracoastal Waterway or New River, and you can stop off at attractions like the Performing Arts Center, the Museum of Discovery & Science, Stranahan House, or the Gallery at Beach Place. For lunch, sail away to restaurants on Las Olas Boulevard or Las Olas Riverfront. As the sun disappears, water taxis are a superb way to head out for dinner or bar-hop, letting your pilot play the sober role of designated driver.

The water-transport venture was started by Bob Bekoff, a longtime Broward resident and outspoken tourism promoter, who decided to combine the need for transportation with one of the area's most captivating features:

waterways that make Fort Lauderdale the Venice of America.

Ride all you want with a day pass, purchased onboard or at a kiosk at the Gallery at Beach Place, 10:30 AM–12:30 AM, for $13. Family all-day passes for two adults and up to four youths are $48, and after 7 PM passes are $7. Annual passes are $180. A dozen or so scheduled stops include Bahia Mar, Gallery at Beach Place, Galleria Mall, Seville Street, Pier 66, Convention Center, and Downtowner Saloon. The winter season South Beach Express, a socko day-trip to the Art Deco District of Miami Beach ($35), leaves Fort Lauderdale around 9 AM, returning to Fort Lauderdale about four hours after arrival in the Miami area at around noon, with the length of the boat ride each way depending on weather conditions, tides, and other variables. For family reunions and such, group tours like the Sunset Cruise, or Mansions and Marinas are on tap. To get around town by boat, contact **Water Bus** (☏ *954/467–6677* ⊕ *www.watertaxi.com*).

FISHING

If you're interested in a saltwater charter, check out the **Bahia Mar Beach Resort** (✉ *801 Seabreeze Blvd.* ☎ *954/627–6357*). Sportfishing and drift-fishing bookings can be arranged.

SCUBA DIVING AND SNORKELING

Lauderdale Diver (✉ *1334 SE 17th St. Causeway* ☎ *954/467–2822*), which is PADI–affiliated, arranges dive charters up and down Broward's shoreline. Dive trips typically last four hours. Nonpackage reef trips are open to divers for around $50; scuba gear is extra. **Pro Dive** (✉ *429 Seabreeze Blvd.* ☎ *954/761–3413*), a five-star PADI facility, is the area's oldest diving operation. Snorkelers can go out for $35 on a two-hour snorkeling trip, including equipment. Scuba divers pay $55 using their own gear or $115 with full scuba- and snorkel-rental gear included.

SHOPPING

MALLS

Just north of Las Olas Boulevard on Route A1A is **The Gallery at Beach Place** (✉ *17 S. Fort Lauderdale Beach Blvd.*). Browse shops, enjoy lunch or dinner, or carouse at assorted nightspots. Lower-level eateries tend toward the more upscale, whereas upper-level prices are lower (go figure), with superior ocean views. ■ TIP→ Beach Place has covered parking, but you can pinch pennies by using a nearby municipal lot that's metered. Just west of the Intracoastal Waterway, the split-level **Galleria Mall** (✉ *2414 E. Sunrise Blvd.*) entices with Neiman Marcus, Dillard's, and Macy's, plus 150 specialty shops for anything from cookware to exquisite jewelry. Chow down at Capital Grille, Blue Martini, Mama Sbarro's, and Seasons 52, or head for the food court, a decided cut above at this upscale mall open 10–9 Monday through Saturday, noon–5:30 Sunday. The **Swap Shop** (✉ *3291 W. Sunrise Blvd.*) is the South's largest flea market, with 2,000 vendors open daily. While exploring this indoor–outdoor entertainment and shopping complex, hop on the carousel or stick around for movies at the 14-screen Swap Shop drive-in.

Sawgrass Mills (✉ *12801 W. Sunrise Blvd., at Flamingo Rd., Sunrise*), 10 mi west of downtown Fort Lauderdale, has 26 million visitors a year, ranking it Florida's second-biggest tourist attraction (after the one with the mouse). The ever-growing complex has a basic alligator shape, and walking it all amounts to about a 2-mi jaunt. Count on 11,000 self-parking spaces (note your location, or you'll be working those soles), valet parking, and two information centers. More than 400 shops—many manufacturer's outlets, retail outlets, and name-brand discounters—include Abercrombie & Fitch Outlet, Chico's Outlet, Super Target, and Ron Jon Surf Shop. Restaurants such as Cajun Grill, the Cheesecake Factory, Mangia La Pasta, and Rainforest Café are on-site. Wannado City, an "interactive-empowerment environment" is geared toward ages four and up. The adjacent Shops at Colonnade cater to well-heeled patrons with a David Yurman jewelry outlet and other shops including Valentino, Burberry, Kate Spade, and Barneys New York.

Sand can sometimes be forgiving if you fall, and bicyclists also appreciate the ocean views.

SHOPPING DISTRICTS

When you're downtown, check out **Las Olas Riverfront** (✉ *1 block west of Andrews Ave. along New River*), a shopping, dining, and entertainment complex with constantly evolving shops for everything from meals and threads to cigars and tattoos. If only for a stroll and some high-end window-shopping, don't miss **Las Olas Boulevard** (✉ *1 block off New River east of Andrews Ave.*). The city's best boutiques plus top restaurants and art galleries line a beautifully landscaped street.

NIGHTLIFE AND THE ARTS

For the most complete weekly listing of events, check "Showtime!" the *South Florida Sun-Sentinel*'s tabloid-sized entertainment section and events calendar published on Friday. "Weekend," in the Friday Broward edition of *The Herald,* also lists area happenings. The weekly *City Link* is principally an entertainment and dining paper with an "underground" look. *New Times* is a free alternative weekly circulating a Broward–Palm Beach County edition. *East Sider* is another free weekly entertainment guide.

THE ARTS

Broward Center for the Performing Arts (✉ *201 SW 5th Ave.* ☎ *954/462–0222*) is the waterfront centerpiece of Fort Lauderdale's arts district. More than 500 events unfold annually at the 2,700-seat architectural gem, including Broadway-style musicals, plays, dance, symphony, opera, rock, film, lectures, comedy, and children's theater. An enclosed elevated walkway links to a parking garage across the street. **Cinema Paradiso** (✉ *503 SE 6th St.* ☎ *954/525–3456* ⊕ *www.cinemaparadiso.*

org) operates as an art-house movie theater from a former church, south of New River near the county courthouse. The space doubles as headquarters for FLIFF, the Fort Lauderdale International Film Festival. Screenings stretch from extreme sports to anime.

★ At **Chef Jean-Pierre Cooking School** (✉ *1436 N. Federal Hwy.* ☎ *954/563– 2700* ⊕ *www.chefjp.com* ✉ *$65 per demonstration class, $120 hands- on class* ⊙ *Store Mon.–Sat. 10–7, class schedules vary*), catering to locals, seasonal snowbirds, and folks winging in for even shorter stays, Jean-Pierre Brehier (former owner of the much missed Left Bank Res- taurant on Las Olas) teaches the basics, from boiling water onward. The enthusiastic Gallic transplant has appeared on NBC's *Today* and CNN's *Larry King Live.* For souvenir hunters, this fun cooking facility also sells nifty pots, pastas, oils, and other irresistibles.

NIGHTLIFE

BARS AND LOUNGES

Coyote Ugly (✉ *214 SW 2nd St.* ☎ *954/764–8459*) continues a tradi- tion of being one of the hottest spots in Broward. **Hooters of Beach Place** (✉ *The Gallery at Beach Place, 17 S. Fort Lauderdale Beach Blvd.* ☎ *954/767–0014*) extends its reputation for tacky and unrefined fun to this seaside setting with a fabulous view.

Around since 1948, **Kim's Alley Bar** (✉ *1920 E. Sunrise Blvd.* ☎ *954/763– 2143*) has two bar areas, a jukebox, and pool tables that provide endless entertainment. **Maguire's Hill 16** (✉ *535 N. Andrews Ave.* ☎ *954/764–4453*) hosts live music in classic Irish-pub surroundings. **Parrot Lounge** (✉ *911 Sunrise La.* ☎ *954/563–1493*) favored by Phila- delphia Eagles fans, backs up libations and revelry with wings, fingers, poppers, and skins.

WHERE TO EAT

$$$ ╳ **15th Street Fisheries & Dockside Cafe.** A prime Intracoastal Waterway
SEAFOOD view is a big part of the allure at this two-story seafood landmark alternately drawing praise and pans from patrons, some complaining about lackluster service during financial seminars—also known as plate lickers—booked upstairs. Despite fluctuating tides in quality, the old 15th carries on solidly with spicy conch chowder, cold seafood sal- ads, and homemade breads. Grilled mahimahi and fried alligator are among the more than 50 entrées, and there's key lime pie. You can feed giant tarpon at the dock with shrimp from the dock store around 5 PM. Valet parking costs $2 at dinner, but it's free at lunch. ✉ *1900 SE 15th St.* ☎ *954/763–2777* ⊕ *www.15streetfisheries.com* ▭ *AE, D, DC, MC, V.*

$$ ╳ **Alligator Alley.** At this taproom and music hall big on nightly music
AMERICAN from rockabilly to funk rock, chefs ladle up memorable gumbo, and alli- gator ribs so good they once were featured on the Food Network. Wash down your beer with Gator Bites or Buffalo Fingers, or for delicacy, go for an appetizer of scallopini of gator with Szechuan sauce. Vegetarians can bulk up on cheese fries, or keep trim with a garden salad. ✉ *1321 E. Commercial Blvd.* ☎ *954/771–2220* ⊕ *www.alligatoralleyflorida. com* ▭ *AE, D, MC, V.*

3

$$$$ ✕ **Blue Moon (EAST) Fish Company.** Most tables have stellar views of the
SEAFOOD Intracoastal Waterway, but Blue Moon East's true magic comes from the
★ kitchen, where chefs Baron Skorish and Bryce Statham create moon-and-
stars-worthy seafood dishes. Start with the raw bar, a sushi sampler, or
pan-seared fresh-shucked oysters. Salads include hydroponic lettuce with
candied walnuts, and among the entrée favorites are lump crab and corn-
roasted grouper with asparagus risotto and peppercorn-crusted big-eye
tuna with sticky rice. Carnivores might opt for prosciutto-stuffed veal
tenderloin. Wrap up an evening with the tartelette of bananas Foster.
For Sunday champagne brunches book early, even in the off-season. For
the record, a Blue Moon West has risen in Coral Springs. ✉ *4405 W.
Tradewinds Ave.* ☎ *954/267–9888* ▭ *AE, D, DC, MC, V.*

$$$$ ✕ **By Word of Mouth.** Unassuming but outstanding, this restaurant never
AMERICAN advertises, hence its name. Mere word has sufficed for nearly a quar-
★ ter century because locals consistently put this dining spot along the
railroad tracks just off Oakland Park Boulevard at the top of "reader's
choice" polls. Although bare at lunch, a dozen interior tables are dressed
in champagne-colored cloths at dinner, but what's magnetic here is the
food, not the vaguely Tuscan decor. There's no menu per se, but you'll
be shown the day's specials on display to make your choice. Count on
a solid gourmet lineup of fish, fowl, beef, pasta, and vegetarian entrées
to be enjoyed inside or out on the patio, perhaps with a glass of wine.
✉ *3200 NE 12th Ave.* ☎ *954/564–3663* ⊕ *www.bywordofmouthfoods.
com* ▭ *AE, D, MC, V.*

$$$$ ✕ **Canyon Southwest Cafe.** Southwestern fusion fare helps you escape the
SOUTHWESTERN ordinary at this small, stylish enclave. It's been run for the past dozen
years by owner and executive chef Chris Wilber. Order, for example,
bison medallions with scotch bonnets, a tequila-jalapeño smoked salmon
tostada, coriander-crusted tuna, or blue-corn fried oysters. Chipotle,
wasabi, mango, and red chilies accent fresh seafood and wild game.
Start off with a prickly pear margarita or choose from a well-rounded
wine list or beer selection. ✉ *1818 E. Sunrise Blvd.* ☎ *954/765–1950*
⊕ *www.canyonfl.com* ▭ *AE, MC, V* ☾ *No lunch.*

$ ✕ **Carlos & Pepe's.** In a strip shopping center west of the 17th Causeway,
MEXICAN this local favorite has long been known for icy margaritas, crunchy
chips and salsa, and tasty fare from omelets to pizza. On the downside,
its iconic margaritas for the past few years have been served in beer-style
tumblers rather than stemmed margarita ware of old. (Management
mumbles about breakage.) On the upside, the tuna dip that goes so
well with libations retains its luster. ✉ *1302 SE 17th St., Harbor Beach*
☎ *954/467–7192* ▭ *AE, D, MC, V* ☾ *No lunch weekdays.*

$$$ ✕ **Casa D'Angelo.** Owner-chef Angelo Elia has created a gem of a Tuscan-
ITALIAN style white-tablecloth restaurant, tucked in the Sunrise Square shopping
center. Casa D'Angelo's oak oven turns out marvelous seafood and beef
dishes. The pappardelle with porcini mushrooms takes pasta to pleasant
heights. Another favorite is the calamari and scungilli salad with garlic
and lemon. Ask about the oven-roasted fish of the day or the snapper
oreganta at market price. ✉ *1201 N. Federal Hwy.* ☎ *954/564–1234*
⊕ *www.casa-d-angelo.com* ▭ *AE, D, DC, MC, V* ☾ *No lunch.*

$$$ ✕**Casablanca Cafe.** You'll get a fabulous ocean view and a good meal to
AMERICAN   boot at this historic two-story Moroccan-style villa, built in the 1920s
Fodor'sChoice   by local architect Francis Abreu. This piano bar's menu is a potpourri
★   with both tropical and Asian influence (try the Korean-style roasted
duck) along with North African specialties like lamb shank and cous-
cous. There's a deck for outside dining. It's a lively spot with friendly
service. ⊠ *Rte. A1A and Alhambra St.* ☎ *954/764–3500* ⊕ *www.
casablancacafeonline.com* ⊟ *AE, D, MC, V.*

$ ✕**Elbo Room.** You can't go wrong wallowing in the past, lifting a drink,
AMERICAN   and exercising your elbow at the Elbo, a noisy, suds-drenched hot spot
since 1938. This watering hole phased out food (except for light nibbles)
ages ago, but kept a hokey sense of humor: upstairs a sign proclaims
WE DON'T SERVE WOMEN HERE. YOU HAVE TO BRING YOUR OWN. ⊠ *241 S.
Fort Lauderdale Beach Blvd.* ☎ *954/463–4615* ⊕ *www.elboroom.com*
⊟ *AE, D, MC, V.*

$ ✕**Ernie's Barbecue.** Walls once plastered with philosophical quotes from
SOUTHERN   a former owner have been scrubbed clean at Ernie's, where the menu
proclaims CONCH IS KING, BARBECUE IS A WAY OF LIFE, AND THE BAR IS OPEN
LATE. Fortunately for patrons, barbecue platters of pork or beef and
conch chowder are as lip-smacking as ever. Bimini bread, thick-sliced
for sandwiches, is also sold by the loaf to go, along with racks of ribs
and conch chowder by the quart. Seafood, salads, and burgers pass
muster here, and there's a children's menu. Eat downstairs, or, if you
don't mind the Federal Highway traffic buzz, take the stairs to 2nd-
floor open-air patio tables near a pool table. ⊠ *1843 S. Federal Hwy.*
☎ *954/523–8636* ⊟ *AE, D, MC, V.*

$$ ✕**Floridian.** This Las Olas landmark is plastered with photos of Monroe,
AMERICAN   Nixon, and local notables past and present in a succession of brightly
painted rooms with funky chandeliers. The kitchen dishes up some of
the best breakfasts around (no matter the hour), with oversize omelets
that come with biscuits, toast, or English muffins, plus a choice of grits
or tomato. With sausage or bacon on the side, you'll forget about eating again soon. Count on savory sandwiches and hot platters for lunch,
tempting meat-loaf plates for dinner, and friendly, efficient service. It's
open 24 hours—even during hurricanes, as long as the power holds out.
Feeling flush? Try the Fat Cat Breakfast (New York strip steak, hash
browns or grits, toast, and worthy champagne) or the Not-So-Fat-Cat,
with the same grub and a lesser-quality vintage. ⊠ *1410 E. Las Olas
Blvd.* ☎ *954/463–4041* ⊟ *No credit cards.*

$$$ ✕**Le Café de Paris.** Serving the classics for lunch and dinner under own-
FRENCH   ership of Swiss-born (and jeans-clad) Louis Flematti since 1962, Le
Café seats upward of 150 in several rooms but keeps everything cozy
with comfort foods like crusty bread, onion soup, and savory crepes,
as well as duck, lamb, and beef dishes. A celebration dinner (under
$90 for two) includes a bottle of wine and baked Alaska. There's also a
mouthwatering pastry wagon. ⊠ *715 Las Olas Blvd.* ☎ *954/467–2900*
⊕ *www.cafedeparislasolas.com* ⊟ *AE, D, DC, MC, V* ☉ *Closed Sun.
No lunch Sat.*

$ ✕**Lester's Diner.** Home to steaming coffee and a tempting skip-your-
AMERICAN   dinner dessert display, Lester's has stood as a 24-hour haven for the

hungry along State Road 84 since 1967. Truckers stop here on their way to Port Everglades, as do workers from the area's thriving marine industry, suits from downtown toting briefcases, along with sunburned visitors. A stick-to-the-ribs menu includes breakfast anytime, home-made soups, sandwiches (try the Monte Cristo), salads, and dinners of generous portions. If your cholesterol count can take the hit, try the country-fried steak or the chicken-liver omelet. Two other Lester's—in western Broward's Margate and Sunrise—close at midnight on week-nights. ☒ *250 State Rd. 84* ☎ *954/525–5641* ☒ *4701 Coconut Creek Pkwy., Margate* ☎ *954/979–4722* ☒ *1399 NW 136th Ave., Sunrise* ☎ *954/838–7473* ▭ *D, MC, V.*

$ ✕ **Maguire's Hill 16.** With the requisite lineup of libations and sand-
IRISH wiches, this long-popular Irish pub also has a very tasty potato soup, shepherd's pie, bangers and mash, fish-and-chips, corned beef and cab-bage, and Irish stew, daily specials, and nightly live music. ☒ *535 N. Andrews Ave.* ☎ *954/764–4453* ⊕ *www.maguireshill16.com* ▭ *AE, D, DC, MC, V.*

$$$ ✕ **Oasis Cafe.** On a spit of land near Route A1A, this outdoor-only
AMERICAN spot has swing-glide tables covered by green-striped awnings afford-ing plenty of shade. Friendly staffers serve up libations and casual fare from burgers and wraps to salads and steak. Try the club sandwich for lunch. Be aware that a 15% gratuity is tacked on no matter what your party size. A free valet assists with cramped parking. ☒ *600 Seabreeze Blvd.* ☎ *954/463–3130* ▭ *AE, D, MC, V.*

$$$ ✕ **Primavera.** You could drive past this unremarkable-looking spot
ITALIAN tucked into an unremarkable shopping plaza, but you'd be missing out on a remarkable dining experience. Among chef-owner Giacomo Dresseno's favorites is a double-cut veal chop, but there's also fresh pasta with rich sauces and risotto entrées, and creative fish, poultry, and beef dinners. If you're in town for a while, check out the chef's two-hour cooking classes ($40), accompanied by a light meal. Ticket holders appreciate the reasonably priced pre-theater menu. ☒ *830 E. Oakland Park Blvd.* ☎ *954/564–6363* ⊕ *www.trueitalian.com* ▭ *AE, D, DC, MC, V* ☾ *Closed Mon. No lunch.*

$$$$ ✕ **Shula's on the Beach.** For anyone getting positively misty-eyed at mere
STEAK mention of Don Shula's Miami Dolphins 17–0 Perfect Season of '72,
Fodor's Choice the good news for steak—and sports—fans is that this beachfront spot
★ also turns out culinary winners. Certified Angus beef is grilled over a super-hot fire for quick charring. Steak Mary Anne, named for Shula's wife, consists of two sliced fillets in a savory sauce, and for hearty appetites there's the humongous Shula-cut porterhouse that just might qualify you for the famed 48-ounce Club, for folks who can tuck all that away in one sitting. Seafood is excellent, too, as is the apple cobbler à la mode. Patio tables provide views of sand and ocean, and inside seating gives you access to sports memorabilia and large-screen TVs. ☒ *Westin Beach Resort, 321 N. Fort Lauderdale Beach Blvd.* ☎ *954/355–4000* ⊕ *www.shulas.com* ▭ *AE, D, DC, MC, V.*

$ ✕ **Siam Cuisine.** Some locals claim that this eatery, tucked away in a
THAI small storefront in Wilton Manors, serves the best Thai in the Fort Lauderdale area, and they may be right. The family-run kitchen turns

out appealing, flavorful delights including sushi and crispy whole fish, usually red snapper. Curry dishes with chicken, beef, pork, or shrimp are favorites, along with steamed dumplings and roast duck. Wines are by the bottle or glass. ⊠ *2010 Wilton Dr.* ☏ *954/564–3411* ⊕ *www. siamcuisineflorida.com* ⊟ *AE, MC, V.*

$ ✕ **Southport Raw Bar.** You can't go wrong at this unpretentious spot
SEAFOOD where the motto, on bumper stickers for miles around, proclaims EAT FISH, LIVE LONGER, EAT OYSTERS, LOVE LONGER, EAT CLAMS, LAST LONGER. Raw or steamed clams, raw oysters, and peel-and-eat shrimp are market priced. Sides range from Bimini bread to key lime pie, with conch fritters, beer-battered onion rings, and corn on the cob in between. Order wine by the bottle or glass, and beer by the pitcher, bottle, or can. Eat outside overlooking a canal, or inside at booths, tables, or in the front or back bars. Limited parking is free, and a grocery-store parking lot is across the street. ⊠ *1536 Cordova Rd.* ☏ *954/525–2526* ⊕ *www. southportrawbar.com* ⊟ *MC, V.*

$ ✕ **Tom Jenkins.** Big portions of deliciously dripping barbecue are dis-
SOUTHERN pensed at this handy spot for eat-in or takeout, south of the New River Tunnel and north of the 17th Street Causeway. Think you don't have time to stop? Roll down your window and inhale on the way by, and you're likely to change your mind. Furnishings include an old Singer sewing machine and a wringer washer, and diners partake at picnic-style tables. Side dishes with dinners for around $10 include baked beans, collards, and mighty tasty macaroni and cheese. For lunch, Tom's pork, beef, and catfish sandwiches are a shortcut to satisfaction. Leave room for sweet-potato pie or peach cobbler. Heading to a park or the beach? Family samplers ($49.95) with pork spare ribs, chicken, beef, and sides feed four to six. ⊠ *1236 S. Federal Hwy.* ☏ *954/522–5046* ⊕ *www. tomjenkinsbbq.com* ⊟ *MC, V* ☻ *Closed Sun. and Mon.*

¢ ✕ **Tortillería Mexicana.** With a machine cranking out 1,000 pounds of
MEXICAN cornmeal tortillas daily (double that on weekends), this hole-in-the-wall Tortillería Mexicana, near Oakland Park City Hall, has authentic fare attracting Broward's growing Mexican population and plenty of gringos to boot. Staples include tacos, tamales, chicken with rice and beans, enchiladas, quesadillas, and flautas with chicken, salad, and hot pepper slices. Owner Eliseo Martinez opened a second tortilla haven, in Pompano Beach, this one with a bakery and butcher shop. ⊠ *4115 N. Dixie Hwy., Oakland Park* ☏ *954/563–2503* ⊠ *1614 E. Sample Rd., Pompano Beach* ☏ *954/943–0057* ⊟ *MC, V.*

$$$ ✕ **Tropical Acres.** The Studiale family's sprawling restaurant has served
STEAK up sizzling steaks from a fireplace grill since 1949—a millennium by South Florida standards. Juicy prime rib is big at this bastion of yester-year ambience. Choose from more than 35 entrées, including sautéed frogs' legs, rack of lamb, and boneless New York strip for two, or ask friendly servers for recommendations. You'll find some of the best early-bird specials around, including prime rib for well under $20. A wine list of some 60 labels ranges from $20 to $70, with a dozen or so poured by the glass. ⊠ *2500 Griffin Rd.* ☏ *954/989–2500* ⊕ *www. tropical-acres.com* ⊟ *AE, DC, MC, V.*

WHERE TO STAY

3

DOWNTOWN AND BEACH CAUSEWAYS

$$$–$$$$
Fodor's Choice
★

Hyatt Regency Pier Sixty-Six Resort & Spa. Unfortunately, the trademark of this high-rise resort—the rooftop Pier Top Lounge—has closed. Happily, that space with the most eye-popping views around is open to the public for a pricey Sunday brunch with unlimited champagne ($65 per head). The iconic 17-story tower dominates a lovely 22-acre spread that includes the full-service Spa 66. Each room has a balcony with views of the 142-slip marina, pool, ocean, or the Intracoastal Waterway. Some guests prefer the ground-level lanai rooms. Lush landscaping and convenience to beach and causeway, shopping, and restaurants add to overall allure, plus each room has complimentary Wi-Fi. Hail the Water Taxi at the resort's dock for access to downtown or the beach. **Pros:** great views; plenty of activities; ideal location. **Cons:** not on the beach; spa's location seems like an afterthought. ⊠ *2301 SE 17th St. Causeway* ☎ *954/525–6666 or 800/327–3796* ⊕ *www.pier66.com* ⊅ *380 rooms, 8 suites* ⚭ *In-room: safe, refrigerator, Wi-Fi. In-hotel: 6 restaurants, bars, tennis courts, pools, gym, spa, water sports, Wi-Fi hotspot* ⊟ *AE, D, DC, MC, V.*

$$$–$$$$

Riverside Hotel. On Las Olas Boulevard, just steps from boutiques, restaurants, and art galleries, Fort Lauderdale's oldest hotel debuted in 1936. Frequent renovations have kept it looking great. Penthouse suites in the newer 12-story executive tower have balconies with sweeping views of Las Olas, New River, and the downtown skyline. Historic photos grace hallways, and rooms are outfitted with antique oak furnishings and framed prints. Enjoy afternoon tea in the spruced-up lobby with free Wi-Fi, and dine at Indigo, where American favorites include steaks and seafood. For private dining, the hotel's Wine Room has a 4,000-bottle cellar; a reservations-only English afternoon-tea program (choose from Classic, Full, or Royal) unfolds in the lobby. **Pros:** historic appeal; in the thick of Las Olas action; nice views. **Cons:** no quick access to beach. ⊠ *620 E. Las Olas Blvd.* ☎ *954/467–0671 or 800/325–3280* ⊕ *www.riversidehotel.com* ⊅ *203 rooms, 10 suites* ⚭ *In-room: Internet, safe, refrigerator. In-hotel: 2 restaurants, bars, pool* ⊟ *AE, DC, MC, V.*

$$$–$$$$

Schubert Resort. This restored 1950s art-deco hotel is an all-male, clothing-optional boutique resort tucked into tropical landscaping within the Victoria Park neighborhood. Suites are oversize and have marble-and-granite baths; most have either a king-size bed or two double beds. Continental breakfast is served overlooking the pool. The pet-friendly property feels secluded yet is a short walk from shopping and restaurants. **Pros:** friendly staff; well-managed property; clean and tidy. **Cons:** somewhat dated decor. ⊠ *855 NE 20th Ave.* ☎ *954/763–7434 or 866/338–7666* ⊕ *www.schubertresort.com* ⊅ *31 rooms* ⚭ *In-room: kitchen (some). In-hotel: pool* ⊟ *AE, D, MC, V* ⦿ *CP.*

ALONG THE BEACH

$–$$$

The Alcazar Resort. Once a family-oriented Sea Chateau, this two-story enclave is now a clothing-optional resort for gay men. A heated pool and shaded courtyard are within the now-fenced property, and corner efficiencies with kitchenettes have been renamed junior suites. Most beds are kings, although some rooms have pairs of queen-size beds. All rooms

Lago Mar Resort & Club in Fort Lauderdale has its own private beach on the Atlantic Ocean.

have complimentary Wi-Fi. **Pros:** interesting architecture; nice pool area. **Cons:** not on the beach; no view. ⊠ *555 N. Birch Rd.* ☎ *954/567–2525* ⊕ *www.alcazarresort.com* ↗ *15 rooms, 5 suites* ⅃ *In-room: kitchen (some), refrigerator. In-hotel: pool* ⊟ *AE, D, DC, MC, V.*

$$$$ ⌂ **The Atlantic Hotel.** Functional but elegant, this luxury condo hotel
★ is steps from Las Olas Boulevard and the Atlantic. A British-colonial scheme is picked up throughout, from the marble and wood and beiges and browns of the lobby to the spacious, unfussy rooms, decorated with simple, dark-wood furniture, ample marble kitchen areas, creamy fabrics, and plush carpeting. The decor chooses to frame, rather than compete with, balcony views of city or ocean (choose the latter if available). Among on-premises amenities are a European-style spa offering treatments and massages within the spa or in-room, the tony lobby-level Trina lounge and restaurant, and the 5th-floor Ocean Terrace, for light fare with a pool view. **Pros:** sophisticated lodging option; rooms have high-tech touches. **Cons:** across highway from beach; some traffic noise. ⊠ *601 N. Fort Lauderdale Beach Blvd.* ☎ *954/567–8020* ⊕ *www.atlantichotelfl* ↗ *61 rooms, 58 suites, 4 penthouses* ⅃ *In-room: kitchen, refrigerator (some), Internet, Wi-Fi. In-hotel: 2 restaurants, bar, pool, gym, spa, laundry service, parking (paid), Wi-Fi hotspot* ⊟ *AE, D, DC, MC, V.*

$$–$$$ ⌂ **Lago Mar Resort and Club.** The sprawling Lago Mar, owned by the
⟳ Banks family since the early 1950s, has retained its sparkle thanks to
★ frequent renovations. Most accommodations are spacious suites with pullout sofas and kitchens, making then ideal for families. Brilliantly colored bougainvilleas edge the swimming lagoon, and you have direct access to a large private beach in an exclusive neighborhood. Acquario serves northern Italian cuisine nightly and a divine filet mignon; kids and

kids-at-heart gravitate toward the Soda Shop, a bakery and ice-cream parlor. **Pros:** secluded setting; plenty of activities; on the beach. **Cons:** not the easiest to find. ✉ *1700 S. Ocean La.* ☎ *954/523–6511 or 800/524–6627* ⊕ *www.lagomar.com* 🛏 *52 rooms, 160 suites* ⚭ *In-room: kitchen, Wi-Fi. In-hotel: 3 restaurants, tennis court, pools, Wi-Fi hotspot* ▭ *AE, DC, MC, V.*

WORD OF MOUTH

"Loved Lago Mar. The rooms are spacious and clean, nice pools and nice beach. Restaurant is very good. You would need a car to get to other places in Fort Lauderdale but I think it is worth it."
—lindafromNJ

3

$$$-$$$$ 🏨 **Pelican Grand Beach Resort.** Smack on the beach, this already lovely property has been transformed with a new tower, restaurant and lounge, an old-fashioned ice-cream parlor, and a circulating lazy-river pool that allows guests to float 'round and 'round. Most rooms and one-bedroom suites have ocean views. (Pelican fans of old may care to know that the original Sun Tower has gotten a makeover but now operates separately from the resort). Free Wi-Fi is available in public spaces and by the pool. **Pros:** you can't get any closer to the beach in Fort Lauderdale. **Cons:** you'll need wheels to access Las Olas beach-area action. ✉ *2000 N. Atlantic Blvd.* ☎ *954/568–9431 or 800/525–6232* ⊕ *www.pelicanbeach.com* 🛏 *121 rooms (remainder of 155 total are condominiums)* ⚭ *In-room: safe, refrigerator, Internet. In-hotel: restaurant, bar, pool, Wi-Fi hotspot* ▭ *AE, DC, MC, V.*

$$$-$$$$ 🏨 **The Pillars Hotel at New River Sound.** A "small secret" kept by locals in the know, this gem is one block from the beach and on the Intracoastal Waterway. Its design recalls the colorful architecture of 18th-century British colonial Caribbean plantations. Most rooms have views of the waterway or pool, with French doors opening to individual patios or balconies. Rooms have rattan-and-mahogany headboards and antique-reproduction desks and nightstands; suites include wet bars with refrigerators and microwaves. The Secret Garden is a tiny restaurant for hotel guests. **Pros:** attentive staff; lovely decor; idyllic pool area. **Cons:** small rooms; not for families with young kids given proximity to dock and water with no lifeguard on duty. ✉ *111 N. Birch Rd.* ☎ *954/467–9639* ⊕ *www.pillarshotel.com* 🛏 *17 rooms, 5 suites* ⚭ *In-room: refrigerator (some), Internet, Wi-Fi. In-hotel: restaurant, room service, pool, no kids under 12* ▭ *AE, D, DC, MC, V.*

$$$-$$$$ 🏨 **Ritz-Carlton, Fort Lauderdale.** After a short-lived debut as the St. Regis, this shimmering luxury tower became a Ritz-Carlton in 2008. It's an eye-popper, with 24 dramatically tiered, glass-walled stories rising behind a tropical sundeck and a pool looking out toward the ocean. A sun-filled lobby and public areas sparkle with white-and-charcoal marble floors, crystal chandeliers, leather banquettes, and murals inspired by work of French artist Jean Cocteau. Cero, serving breakfast, lunch, and dinner, and the Lobby Bar, with a King Neptune mural, provide ocean views. The Wine Room, separated by glass from the bar, beckons with fine vintages from a 5,000-bottle collection. Guest rooms, overlooking the Atlantic or the Intracoastal Waterway, are intended to evoke the golden era of luxury travel with vintage photographs of the

city. Luxury also awaits at the spa, with exotic therapies and a treatment suite for couples. **Pros:** golfers have privileges at the private Grande Oaks Golf Course, where *Caddyshack* was filmed. **Cons:** golf facilities off-site; no complimentary Wi-Fi in public spaces. ⊠ *1 N. Fort Lauderdale Beach Blvd.* ☎ *954/465–2300* ⊕ *www.ritzcarlton.com* ➘ *138 rooms, 54 suites* ⸦ *In-room: safe, Wi-Fi. In-hotel: 2 restaurants, bar, pool, gym, spa* ⊟ *AE, D, MC, V.*

NORTH ON SCENIC A1A

North of Fort Lauderdale's Birch Recreation Area, Route A1A edges away from the beach through a stretch known as Galt Ocean Mile, and a succession of oceanside communities line up against the sea. Traffic can line up, too, as it passes through a changing pattern of beach-blocking high-rises and modest family vacation towns and back again. Here and there a scenic lighthouse or park dots the landscape, and other attractions and recreational activities are found inland.

Towns are shown on the Broward County map.

LAUDERDALE-BY-THE-SEA

5 mi north of Fort Lauderdale.

Just north of Fort Lauderdale's northern boundary, this low-rise family resort town traditionally digs in its heels at mere mention of high-rises. The result is choice shoreline access that's rapidly disappearing in nearby communities, and Lauderdale-by-the-Sea takes delight in enhancing the beachgoing experience, adding such amenities as showers and bike racks.

GETTING HERE AND AROUND

Lauderdale-by-the-Sea is just north of Fort Lauderdale. If you're driving from Interstate 95, exit east onto Commercial Boulevard and head over the Intracoastal Waterway. From U.S. 1 (aka Federal Highway), turn east on Commercial Boulevard.

Catch free rides on the Pelican Hopper, a pelican-white, air-conditioned bus running south to the top of the Galt Ocean Mile and north to Terra Mar Drive. Lauderdale-by-the-Sea's 25-seat shuttle operates seven days with various stops, including the Publix Supermarket at the Village Shopping Center in Sea Ranch Lakes.

ESSENTIALS

Transportation Contact **Pelican Hopper** (☎ *954/776–0576*).

Visitor Information **Lauderdale-by-the-Sea Chamber of Commerce** (⊠ *4201 N. Ocean Dr., Lauderdale-by-the-Sea* ☎ *954/776–1000* ⊕ *www.lbts.com*).

SPORTS AND THE OUTDOORS

★ **Anglin's Fishing Pier** (☎ *954/491–9403*), a longtime favorite for 24-hour fishing, has a fresh, renovated appearance after shaking off repeated storm damage that closed the pier at intervals during the past decade. What's more, Anglin's Café (☎ *954/491–6007*) has reopened, 7 AM to 4 PM.

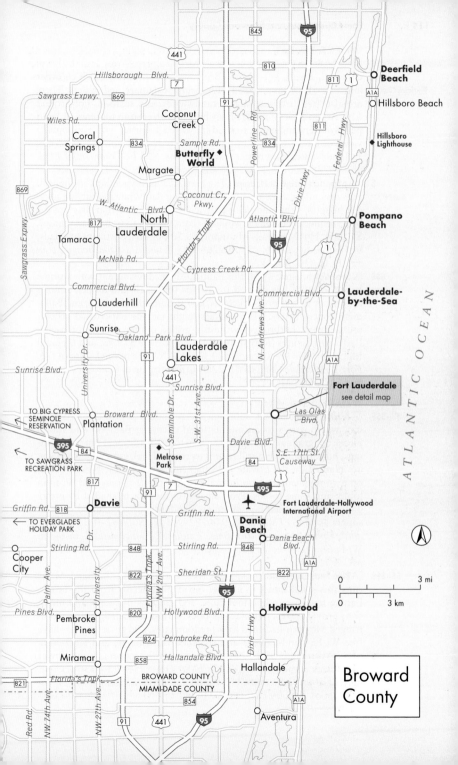

WHERE TO EAT

$$ ✕ **Aruba Beach Café.** A big beachside barn of a place—very casual, always
CAFÉ crowded, always fun—Aruba Beach serves Caribbean conch chowder
Fodor's Choice and a Key West soup loaded with shrimp, calamari, and oysters. There
★ are also fresh tropical salads, sandwiches, and seafood. For around
$10, Aruba serves a mighty juicy burger with custom toppings. A band
performs day and night, so head for the back corner with eye-popping
views of the beach if you want conversation while you eat and drink.
A Sunday breakfast buffet starts at 9 AM. ⊠ *1 E. Commercial Blvd.*
☎ *954/776–0001* ⊕ *www.arubabeachcafe.com* ▭ *AE, D, DC, MC, V.*

$ ✕ **LaSpada's Original Hoagies.** The crew at this seaside hole-in-the-wall
AMERICAN puts on quite a show of ingredient-tossing flair while assembling take-
out hoagies, subs, and deli sandwiches. Locals rave that they are the
best around. Fill up on the Monster (ham, cheese, roast beef, and turkey,
$10.95), Hot Meatballs Marinara ($8.50), or an assortment of salads.
⊠ *4346 Seagrape Dr.* ☎ *954/776–7893* ⊕ *www.laspadashoagies.com*
▭ *AE, D, DC, MC, V.*

$$$ ✕ **Sea Watch.** Since 1974, this nautical-themed restaurant with a prime
SEAFOOD beach location has catered to crowds for lunch and dinner. Among
appetizers are oysters Rockefeller, gulf shrimp, clams casino, and Baha-
mian conch fritters. Main courses might include oat-crusted yellow-
tail snapper, charbroiled swordfish, grilled orange roughy, or paella.
Early-bird dinners (May through December) are $19.95, and 6-pound
Maine lobsters are around $100. ⊠ *6002 N. Ocean Blvd. (Rte. A1A),*
Fort Lauderdale ☎ *954/781–2200* ⊕ *www.seawatchontheocean.com*
▭ *AE, D, DC, MC, V.*

WHERE TO STAY

$$–$$$ ▭ **A Little Inn by the Sea.** Subtropical charm flourishes at this two-story
inn, which caters to an international clientele. Bamboo and rattan
pieces are gradually being replaced by more traditional hotel furnishings, but this Little Inn still retains its tropical feel, especially when you
are planted on the private balconies, many facing the beach. Count
on a complimentary Continental-breakfast buffet, plus free Wi-Fi in
lobby and some rooms. **Pros:** smack on the beach; shaded by pretty
palms. **Cons:** casual housekeeping standards; towels can be in short
supply. ⊠ *4546 El Mar Dr.* ☎ *954/772–2450 or 800/492–0311* ⊕ *www.*
alittleinnhotel.com ⌁ *10 rooms, 7 suites, 12 efficiencies* ♿ *In-room:*
Wi-Fi (some). In-hotel: pool, beachfront, Wi-Fi hotspot ▭ *AE, D, DC,*
MC, V ⦿| *CP.*

$$–$$$ ▭ **Blue Seas Courtyard.** Innkeeper Cristie Furth, with her husband, Marc,
runs this small motel in a quiet resort area across from the beach.
Lattice fences, gurgling fountains, and gardens of cactus and impa-
tiens provide privacy around the brick patio and heated pool. A palm-
fringed Mexican-hacienda look predominates, and guest quarters have
free Wi-Fi, hand-painted and stenciled furnishings, and terra-cotta
tiles. **Pros:** south-of-the-border vibe; friendly owners. **Cons:** lower
rooms lack ocean views. ⊠ *4525 El Mar Dr.* ☎ *954/772–3336* ⊕ *www.*
blueseascourtyard.com ⌁ *12 rooms* ♿ *In-room: kitchen, Wi-Fi. In-*
hotel: pool, laundry facilities ▭ *MC, V.*

$–$$ 🛏 **Great Escape Hotel.** For comfortable accommodations amid palms and other tropical plants, this two-story property could be your great—and economical—escape. Guests tend to congregate around the pretty pool (despite free Wi-Fi in rooms!). **Pros:** walk to the beach; bargain rates. **Cons:** no ocean view. ✉ *4620 N. Ocean Dr.* ☎ *954/772–1002* ⊕ *www. greatescapehotel.com* ⤳ *11 units* ♿ *In-room: Wi-Fi. In-hotel: pool, laundry facilities* ☰ *AE, MC, V.*

$$–$$$ 🛏 **High Noon Beach Resort.** Flanked by the Nautilus Resort to the north
★ and the Sea Foam Resort to the south, High Noon—family-run since 1961—plays the central role for this resort trio on the beach, where you'll find a comfortable place to relax morning, noon, or night. Accommodations, poolside or oceanfront, range from standard rooms to efficiencies with kitchens to apartments with separate bedrooms and one or two baths. Nine rooms have private balconies. There's also a two-bedroom beach house. Wicker furnishings prevail at all three properties, and there's free Wi-Fi in common areas and most rooms. **Pros:** smack on the beach; friendly vibe. **Cons:** early booking required. ✉ *4424 El Mar Dr.* ☎ *954/776–1121 or 800/382–1265* ⊕ *www.highnoonresort. com* ⤳ *40 rooms* ♿ *In-room: kitchen (some), refrigerator (some), Wi-Fi. In-hotel: pool, beachfront, Wi-Fi hotspot* ☰ *AE, D, DC, MC, V.*

$$ 🛏 **Tides Inn Oceanfront Resort.** Set on the beach, you'll find this small lodging oasis convenient to pier and surrounding activity yet with a private courtyard and a well-located (if not overly landscaped) rectangular pool. Units, from rooms to oceanview and oceanfront efficiencies, plus a 2nd-floor "penthouse," are well-appointed, and the phone system allows for private voice-mail. **Pros:** on the beach. **Cons:** older property. ✉ *4628 El Mar Dr.,* ☎ *954/772–2933* ⊕ *www.tidesinnresort.com* ⤳ *5 rooms, 4 efficiencies, 1 one-bedroom unit.* ♿ *In-room: Wi-Fi in rooms. In-hotel: pool* ☰ *AE, D, MC, V* ⧖ *CP.*

$$–$$$ 🛏 **Tropic Seas Resort Motel.** This two-story property has an unbeatable location—directly on the beach and two blocks from municipal tennis courts. Built in the 1950s and renovated in 2007, tiled units are clean and comfortable, with tropical rattan furniture and ceiling fans. Coffee and Danish pastry are served daily. **Pros:** family-owned friendliness; great location. **Cons:** must reserve far ahead; basic decor. ✉ *4616 El Mar Dr.* ☎ *954/772–2555 or 800/952–9581* ⊕ *www.tropicseasresort. com* ⤳ *3 rooms, 6 efficiencies, 7 apartments* ♿ *In-hotel: pool, beachfront* ☰ *AE, D, DC, MC, V* ⧖ *CP.*

POMPANO BEACH AND DEERFIELD BEACH

Pompano Beach and Deerfield Beach are 3 mi and 6½ mi north of Lauderdale-by-the-Sea, respectively.

As Route A1A enters this town directly north of Lauderdale-by-the-Sea the high-rise scene resumes. Sportfishing is big in Pompano Beach, as its name implies, but there's more to beachside attractions than the popular Fisherman's Wharf. Behind a low coral-rock wall, Alsdorf Park (also called the 14th Street boat ramp) extends north and south of the wharf along the road and beach. Farther north is Deerfield Beach.

GETTING HERE AND AROUND

From Interstate 95, Pompano Beach exits include Sample Road, Copans Road, or Atlantic Boulevard. For Deerfield Beach, take the Hillsboro Boulevard exit east.

ESSENTIALS

Visitor Information Greater Pompano Beach Chamber of Commerce (☎ 954/941–2940 ⊕ www.pompanobeachchamber.com). **Greater Deerfield Beach Chamber of Commerce** (☎ 954/427–1050 ⊕ www.deerfieldchamber.com).

EXPLORING

☙ **Quiet Waters Park**. Its name belies what's in store for kids here. Splash Adventure is a high-tech water-play system with slides and tunnels, among other activities. A Rent-A-Tent program ($35 per night for up to four campers) provides already set-up tents or teepees. There's also cable water-skiing and boat rental on this county park's lake, and a skate park. ✉ *401 S. Powerline Rd., Deerfield Beach* ☎ *954/360–1315 wwww.broward.org/parks/qw.htm* ☗ *Park $1 weekends, free weekdays* ☉ *Apr.–Sept., daily 8–6; Oct.–Mar., daily 8–5:30.*

SPORTS AND THE OUTDOORS

FISHING

Pompano Pier. The 24-hour pier extends more than 1,000 feet into the Atlantic. Upscale seafood and steak restaurants, part of a planned renovation, have been delayed by the economic downtown. Meanwhile, the pier tackle shop sells beer and snacks. Admission is $4 to fish, $1 to sightsee; rod-and-reel rental is $16.50 (including admission, plus a $20 deposit) for the day. Anglers brag about catching barracuda, jack, and snapper here in the same sitting, along with bluefish, cobia, and, yes, even pompano. ☎ 954/226–6411.

OUTFITTERS The **Cove Marina** (✉ *Hillsboro Blvd. and the Intracoastal Waterway, Deerfield Beach* ☎ 954/427–9747) has a deep-sea charter fleet. In winter there are excellent runs of sailfish, kingfish, dolphin, and tuna. A half-day charter for six costs about $600, or $1,000 for a full day. For drift-fishing, try **Fish City Pride** (✉ *Fish City Marina, 2621 N. Riverside Dr., Pompano Beach* ☎ 954/781–1211). Morning, afternoon, and evening trips cost $37 and include fishing gear and bait. Arrange for a saltwater-charter boat through the **Hillsboro Inlet Marina** (✉ *2705 N. Riverside Dr., Pompano Beach* ☎ 954/943–8222). The eight-boat fleet offers half-day charters for $550, six hours for $750, or a full day for $950, including gear for up to six anglers.

SCUBA DIVING

As namesake of the **SS Copenhagen State Underwater Archaeological Preserve**, the wreck of the SS*Copenhagen* lies in 15- to 30-foot depths just outside the second reef on the Pompano Ledge, 3.6 miles south of Hillsboro Inlet. The 325-foot-long steamer's final voyage, from Philadelphia bound for Havana, began May 20, 1900, ending six days later when the captain—attempting to avoid gulf currents—crashed onto a reef off what's now Pompano Beach. In 2000, the missing bow section was identified a half mile to the south. The wreck, a haven for colorful fish and corals and a magnet for skin and scuba divers, became

Florida's fifth Underwater Archaeological Preserve in 1994, listed on the National Register of Historic Places in 2001.

Among the area's most popular dive operators, **Dixie Divers** (⊠ *Cove Marina, Hillsboro Blvd. and the Intracoastal Waterway, Deerfield Beach* ☎ *954/420–0009* ⊕ *www.dixiedivers.com*) has morning and afternoon dives aboard the 48-foot *Lady-Go-Diver,* plus evening dives on weekends. Snorkelers and certified divers can explore the marine life of nearby reefs and shipwrecks. The cost is $60; ride-alongs are welcome for $35.

SHOPPING

Bargain hunters head to the **Festival Flea Market Mall** (⊠ *2900 W. Sample Rd., Pompano Beach* ☎ *954/979–4555* ⊕ *www.festival.com*), where more than 800 vendors sell new, brand-name merchandise at discounts. The Hillsboro Antiques Mall relocated here (you'll find it at the south-east corner), adding classy antiquity to good, old-fashioned, shopping fun. For diversion, there's also a food court.

WHERE TO EAT
DEERFIELD BEACH

$$$
FRENCH
★
✕ **Brooks.** This is one of Broward's more elegant dining spots, thanks to French perfectionist Bernard Perron. Brooks is now run by Perron's son-in-law John Howe. Updated Continental fare is served in a series of rooms filled with old-master replicas, cut glass, antiques, and floral wallpaper. Fresh ingredients go into distinctly Floridian dishes, including sautéed Key Largo yellowtail snapper. Roast rack of lamb is also popular. Put your order in early for the chocolate or Grand Marnier soufflé. ⊠ *500 S. Federal Hwy.* ☎ *954/427–9302* ▭ *AE, D, MC, V.*

$
SEAFOOD
★
✕ **Olympia Flame Diner.** The family-owned Flame burned white-hot in 2009 when finance guru Suze Orman did a star turn as a waitress here for an Oprah TV segment. Orman has a condo nearby, and her fitness trainer—who dines here regularly—suggested the blue-awning diner as an illuminated best bet for a hot, home-style meal accompanied by megawatt chatter. Greek specialties from spinach pie to baklava dominate the menu, but you can order seafood, deli-style sandwiches, and burgers along with beer or wine. And no, Oprah and Ormon mega-exposure hasn't changed the homey mood here at all. ⊠ *80 S. Federal Hwy.* ☎ *954/480–8402* ⊕ *www.olympiaflamediner.com* ▭ *MC, V.*

$$
SEAFOOD
★
✕ **Whale's Rib.** For a casual, almost funky, nautical experience near the beach, look no farther. If you want to blend in, order a fish special with whale fries—thinly sliced potatoes that look like hot potato chips. Those with smaller appetites can choose from salads and fish sand-wiches, or raw-bar favorites like Ipswich clams. ⊠ *2031 NE 2nd St.* ☎ *954/421–8880* ▭ *AE, MC, V.*

POMPANO BEACH

$$$$
ECLECTIC
★
✕ **Cafe Maxx.** New-wave epicurean dining had its South Florida start here in the early 1980s, and Cafe Maxx remains fresh. The menu changes nightly but showcases tropical appeal with jerk-spiced sea scal-lops or jumbo stone crab claws with honey-lime mustard sauce and black-bean-and-banana-pepper chili with Florida avocado. Appetiz-ers include caviar pie and crispy sweetbreads. Desserts such as Trio of

Sorbet (or ice cream) with a flurry of fruit sauces including mango stay the tropical course. Select from 300 wines by the bottle, and many by the glass. ✉ *2601 E. Atlantic Blvd.* ☎ *954/782–0606* ⊕ *www.cafemaxx. com* ⊟ *AE, D, DC, MC, V* ☺ *No lunch.*

WHERE TO STAY

DEERFIELD BEACH

$$$–$$$$ 🏨 **Royal Flamingo Villas.** This cluster of villas sits near the Intracoastal Waterway on more than 7 acres of manicured grounds. Roomy one- and two-bedroom villas are decorated in sunny pastels, rattan, and wicker, all keeping with the tropical theme. If you don't need lavish public facilities, this is your upscale choice at a reasonable price with complimentary Wi-Fi. **Pros:** serene atmosphere; attractive landscaping. **Cons:** don't look for vibrant decor. ✉ *1225 Hillsboro Mile (Rte. A1A), Hillsboro Beach* ☎ *954/427–0660 or 800/241–2477* ⊕ *www. royalflamingovillas.com* ⇗ *40 villas* ⌂ *In-hotel: pool, beachfront, laundry facilities* ⊟ *D, MC, V.*

POMPANO BEACH

$$–$$$ 🏨 **Beachcomber Resort & Villas.** This property's beachfront location is close to most local attractions and a mile from the Pompano Pier. Ocean views are everywhere, from the oversize guest-room balconies to dining rooms. Although there are also villas and penthouse suites atop the eight-story structure, the standard rooms are spacious, and all units have free Wi-Fi. The multilingual staff is attentive to guest requests. **Pros:** Old Florida feel; lots of laid-back charm. **Cons:** worn around the edges. ✉ *1200 S. Ocean Blvd.* ☎ *954/941–7830 or 800/231–2423* ⊕ *www.beachcomberresort.com* ⇗ *143 rooms, 9 villas, 4 suites* ⌂ *In-room: Internet. In-hotel: restaurant, bar, pools, beachfront* ⊟ *AE, D, DC, MC, V.*

$$–$$$ 🏨 **Wyndham Palm-Aire.** In its heyday (and hey, that's many a day ago), stars like Elizabeth Taylor checked in here to slim down and chill out. Now a time-share, this resort has studios and one-, two-, and four-bedroom apartments that are individually owned but share similar decor. Some units have whirlpool tubs and washers and dryers; kitchens range from partial to full. Housekeeping is provided weekly, and more frequently for a charge. The spa and fitness complex has a sauna, steam room, and fitness equipment. Five championship golf courses at the Palm-Aire Country Club are just a chip shot away. The Palms Café serves lunch and dinner, and drinks are on tap at the Tiki Hut. **Pros:** roll out of bed onto the golf course; home-away-from-home feel. **Cons:** a bit past its prime. ✉ *2601 Palm-Aire Dr. N* ☎ *954/972–3300* ⊕ *www.wyndhampalmaire.com* ⇗ *298 units* ⌂ *In-room: safe, refrigerator, Wi-Fi. In-hotel: restaurant, bar, golf courses, tennis courts, pools, gym, spa* ⊟ *AE, D, DC, MC, V.*

SOUTH BROWARD

South Broward's roots are in early Florida settlements. Thus far it has avoided some of the glitz and glamour of neighbors to the north and south, and folks here like it that way. Still, there's plenty to see and do—

Early-bird anglers at Dania Beach get not only a jump-start on fishing, but can watch the sunrise.

excellent restaurants in every price range, world-class pari-mutuels, and a new focus on the arts.

DANIA BEACH

Dania Beach is 4 mi south of Fort Lauderdale.

This town at the south edge of Fort Lauderdale is probably best known for its antiques dealers, but there are other attractions as well.

GETTING HERE

From Interstate 95, exit east on Griffin Road or Stirling Road.

ESSENTIALS

Visitor Information **Greater Dania Beach Chamber of Commerce** (⊠ *102 W. Dania Beach Blvd., Dania Beach* ☎ *954/926–2323* ⊕ *www.greaterdania.org*).

EXPLORING

Dania Beach Hurricane. Accessed via Boomers! fun park, and visible from Interstate 95, this isn't the world's highest, fastest, or longest roller coaster, but it's near the top in all those categories, and ranks as the tallest wooden coaster south of Atlanta. This retro-feel ride creaks like an old staircase while you race along 3,200 feet of track and plummet from 100 feet at speeds up to 55 mph. Access to the park is free, but the Hurricane will cost you $6 per ride, or $13 for an all-day wristband. ⊠ *1760 NW 1st St.* ☎ *954/921–7433* ⊕ *www.boomersparks.com* ✉ *$6* ⊙ *Sun.–Thurs. 11–11, Fri. and Sat. 10 AM–1 AM.*

★ **IGFA Fishing Hall of Fame and Museum.** This creation of the International Game Fishing Association is a shrine to the sport. It has an extensive museum and research library where seven galleries feature fantasy fishing and other interactive displays. At the Catch Gallery, you can cast off virtually to reel in a marlin, sailfish, trout, tarpon, or bass. (If you suddenly get an urge to gear up for your own adventures, a Bass Pro Shops Outdoor World is next door.) ⊠ *300 Gulfstream Way* ☎ *954/922–4212* ⊕ *www.igfa.org* 🎟 *$8* ⊙ *Daily 10–6.*

SPORTS AND THE OUTDOORS

FISHING

The 920-foot, 24-hour **Dania Pier** (☎ *954/367–4423*) has gussied up with chickee huts, restrooms, and a concessionaire restaurant of sorts, offering peel-and-eat shrimp and other dishes, doled out with a take-it-or-leave it attitude. If you leave it, you can get hot dogs with much friendlier service at the bait shop. Fishing is $3 (with parking another $5 for the day), tackle rental $6, bait about $3, and spectators pay $2.

MINIATURE GOLF

🐣 **Boomers!** (⊠ *1801 NW 1st St.* ☎ *954/921–1411* ⊕ *www.boomersparks. com* 🎟 *Free* ⊙ *Mon.–Thurs. noon–11, Fri. noon–1 AM, Sat. 10 AM–1 AM, Sun. 10 AM–11 PM*) has action games for kids of all ages—go-karts, miniature golf, batting cages, bumper boats, and a skycoaster.

WHERE TO EAT

$ ✕ **Jaxson's Ice Cream Parlour & Restaurant.** This local landmark whips up
AMERICAN malts, shakes, and jumbo sundaes from ice creams prepared daily on premises, plus sandwiches and salads, amid an antique-license-plate decor. Owner Monroe Udell's trademarked Kitchen Sink—a small sink full of ice cream, topped by sparklers—for parties of four or more goes for $12.95 per person. Less ambitious appetites lean toward Jaxson's Sampler (Junior or Senior). ⊠ *128 S. Federal Hwy.* ☎ *954/923–4445* ⊕ *www.jaxsonsicecream.com* 🍴 *AE, D, MC, V.*

HOLLYWOOD

Hollywood is 3 mi south of Dania Beach.

Hollywood has had a face-lift, with more nips and tucks to come. Young Circle, once down-at-heel, has become Broward's first Arts Park. On Hollywood's western outskirts, the flamboyant Seminole Hard Rock Hotel & Casino has permanently etched the previously downtrodden section of State Road 7/U.S. 441 corridor on the map of trendy excitement, drawing local weekenders, architecture buffs, and gamblers. But Hollywood's redevelopment effort doesn't end there: new shops, restaurants, and art galleries open at a persistent clip, and the city has spiffed up its Broadwalk—a wide pedestrian walkway along the beach—where rollerbladers are as commonplace as snowbirds from the north.

GETTING HERE AND AROUND

From Interstate 95, exit east on Sheridan Street or Hollywood Boulevard.

ESSENTIALS

Visitor Information Hollywood Chamber of Commerce (⊠ *330 N. Federal Hwy., Hollywood* ☎ *954/923–4000* ⊕ *www.hollywoodchamber.org*).

EXPLORING

Art and Culture Center of Hollywood. This is a visual- and performing-arts facility with an art reference library, outdoor sculpture garden, and arts school. It's southeast of Young Circle, melding urban open space with a fountain, a 2,000-plus-seat amphitheater, and an indoor theater. Nearby, on trendy Harrison Street and Hollywood Boulevard, are chic lunch places, bluesy entertainment spots, and shops. ⊠ *1650 Harrison St.* ☎ *954/921–3274* ⊕ *artandculturecenter.org* ⊡ *$7* ⊙ *Mon.–Sat. 10–5, Sun. noon–4.*

SPORTS AND THE OUTDOORS

Ⓒ **West Lake Park.** Rent a canoe, kayak, or take the 40-minute boat tour at this park bordering the Intracoastal Waterway. At 1,500 acres, it is one of Florida's largest urban nature facilities. Extensive boardwalks traverse mangrove forests that shelter endangered and threatened species. A 65-foot observation tower showcases the entire park. At the free **Anne Kolb Nature Center,** named after Broward's late environmental advocate, there's a 3,500-gallon aquarium. The center's exhibit hall has 27 interactive displays. ⊠ *1200 Sheridan St.* ☎ *954/926–2410* ⊡ *Weekends $1.50, weekdays free* ⊙ *Daily 9–5.*

BEACH

Ⓒ **Broadwalk.** With the Intracoastal Waterway to the west and the beach

Fodor'sChoice and ocean immediately east, this spiffed-up 2-mi paved promenade

★ has lured pedestrians and cyclists since 1924. With a recent $14 million makeover, this stretch has taken on added luster for the buff, the laid-back, and the retired. Kids also thrive here: there are play areas, rental bikes, trikes, and other pedal-powered gizmos. Expect to hear French spoken here, since Hollywood Beach has long been a favorite getaway for Quebecois. Conversations in Spanish and Portuguese are also frequently overheard on this path. ⊠ *Rte. A1A and Sheridan St.* ⊡ *Parking $7* ⊙ *Wed.–Mon. 8–6.*

FISHING

Sea Leg's III (⊠ *5398 N. Ocean Dr.* ☎ *954/923–2109*) runs drift-fishing trips during the day and bottom-fishing trips at night. Trips cost $35–$38, including rod rental.

GOLF

The **Diplomat Country Club & Spa** (⊠ *501 Diplomat Pkwy., Hallandale* ☎ *954/883–4000*) has 18 holes and a spa; greens fee $69/$209. The course at **Emerald Hills** (⊠ *4100 N. Hills Dr.* ☎ *954/961–4000*) has 18 holes; greens fee $55/$190.

HORSE RACING

Gulfstream Park Racing & Casino is the winter home of top thoroughbreds, as well as the year-round home of slot-machine and bingo action. The season is capped by the $1 million Florida Derby, with Kentucky Derby hopefuls. Racing unfolds January through April. After 37 years on Miami Beach, **Christine Lee's,** known for Asian specialties and prime steaks, has opened shop here. ⊠ *901 S. Federal Hwy., Hallandale* ☎ *954/454–7000 or 800/771–8873* ⊕ *www.gulfstreampark. com* ⊡ *Grandstand free, clubhouse $5* ⊙ *Racing Wed.–Mon. at 1* PM.

NIGHTLIFE AND THE ARTS

THE ARTS

Harrison Street Art and Design District in downtown Hollywood has galleries featuring original artwork (eclectic paintings, sculpture, photography, and mixed media). Friday night the artists' studios, galleries, and shops stay open later while crowds meander along Hollywood Boulevard and Harrison Street. **The Shade Post** (⊠ *2028 Harrison St.* ☎ *954/920–0029* ⊕ *www.artofshade.com*) features Kayce Armstrong's Art of Shade creations, fashioned from recycled garments, old shower curtains, etc., showcased in a boutique outfitted with racks made of old masts and rigging. Hours are also offbeat, Tuesday through Saturday, 4–10. **Mosaica** (⊠ *2020 Hollywood Blvd.* ☎ *954/923–7006*) is a design studio with handcrafted, one-of-a-kind mosaic-tile tables, mirrors, and art.

WHERE TO EAT

$$$
SEAFOOD
✕ **Giorgio's Grill.** Good food and service are hallmarks of this expansive 400-seat restaurant overlooking the Intracoastal Waterway. Seafood is a specialty, but you'll also find pasta and meat dishes, and a solid Sunday brunch for around $20. A great watery view especially around sunset and friendly staff add to the experience, and there's a surprisingly extensive, reasonably priced wine list. ⊠ *606 N. Ocean Dr.* ☎ *954/929–7030* ⊕ *www.giorgiosgrill.com* ▤ *AE, D, DC, MC, V.*

$$$
ARGENTINE
✕ **Las Brisas.** Next to the beach, this cozy bistro offers seating inside or out, and the food is Argentine with Italian flair. A small pot, filled with *chimichurri*—a paste of oregano, parsley, olive oil, salt, garlic, and crushed pepper—for spreading on steaks, sits on each table. Grilled fish is a favorite, as are pork chops, chicken, and pasta entrées. Desserts include a flan like *mamacita* used to make. ⊠ *600 N. Surf Rd.* ☎ *954/923–1500* ▤ *AE, D, DC, MC, V* ⊗ *No lunch.*

$$
AMERICAN
✕ **LeTub.** Formerly a Sunoco gas station, this quirky waterside saloon has an enduring affection for claw-foot bathtubs. Hand-painted porcelain is everywhere—under ficus, sea grape, and palm trees. If a potty doesn't appeal, there's a secluded swing facing the water north of the main dining area. Despite molasses-slow service and an abundance of flies at sundown, this eatery is favored by locals, and management seemed genuinely appalled when hordes of trend-seeking city slickers started jamming bar stools and tables after Oprah declared its thick, juicy Angus burgers the best around. A plain burger and small fries will run you around $15. ⊠ *1100 N. Ocean Dr.* ☎ *954/921–9425* ⊕ *www.theletub.com* ▤ *No credit cards.*

$$
JAPANESE
✕ **Sushi Blues Café.** Run by husband-and-wife-team Kenny Millions and Junko Maslak, this place proves that sushi has gone global. Japanese chefs prepare conventional and macrobiotic-influenced dishes, including lobster teriyaki and steamed snapper with miso sauce. Poached pears steamed in cabernet sauce and cappuccino custard are popular desserts. Music is a big part of the appeal of this place, especially when the Sushi Blues Band performs on weekends. ⊠ *2009 Harrison St.* ☎ *954/929–9560* ⊕ *www.sushiblues.com* ▤ *AE, MC, V.*

WHERE TO STAY

$$–$$$ ⚇ **Driftwood on the Ocean.** Facing the beach at Surf Road's secluded south end, this sprawling motel has been around since the 1950s. The setting is what draws guests, but attention to maintenance and refurbishing in recent seasons makes it an improved value. Accommodations range from a studio to a deluxe two-bedroom, two-bath suite. Most units have a kitchen; all have balconies or terraces and free wireless Internet access. **Pros:** wide ribbon of beachfront; bargain rates. **Cons:** not all rooms face ocean; no restaurant or bar. ⊠ *2101 S. Surf Rd.* ☎ *954/923–9528 or 800/944–3148* ⊕ *www.driftwoodontheocean.com* ↳ *7 rooms, 9 2-bedroom apartments, 13 1-bedroom apartments, 20 efficiencies* ⚭ *In-room: kitchen (some), Wi-Fi. In-hotel: pool, beachfront, bicycles, laundry facilities* ⊟ *AE, D, MC, V.*

$$–$$$ ⚇ **Manta Ray Inn.** Canadians Donna and Dwayne Boucher run this
★ immaculate, affordable, two-story inn on the beach. Dating from the 1940s, the inn, with new pale-pink tile in downstairs rooms and moss-green carpet in upstairs rooms, offers casual, comfortable beachfront accommodations with wicker or rattan furnishings, and cable TV, free Wi-Fi, and off-street parking. Kitchens are equipped with microwaves, pots, pans, and serving utensils. One-bedroom apartments have marble shower stalls, and two-bedroom units also have tubs. Manta Ray guests also have access to the pool next door at the Enchanted Isle time-share. **Pros:** on the beach; low-key atmosphere. **Cons:** no restaurant. ⊠ *1715 S. Surf Rd.* ☎ *954/921–9666 or 800/255–0595* ⊕ *www.mantarayinn.com* ↳ *12 units* ⚭ *In-room: Wi-Fi. In-hotel: beachfront* ⊟ *AE, D, MC, V.*

$$$–$$$$ ⚇ **The Westin Diplomat Resort & Spa.** This 39-story property had its 15
★ minutes recently as host to Senator John Edwards's mistress, Reille Hunter, but the central atrium with ceilings soaring to 60 feet are worth talking about, too. A signature of the resort is its 120-foot, bridged infinity pool, extending from lobby to oceanfront. Rooms are light and spacious, and patio furnishings are recyclable. A Mediterranean-inspired spa offers more than a dozen pampering treatments, including a caviar facial. The hotel's country club, across the Intracoastal Waterway, has golf and tennis facilities. Shuttle service takes you across in no time. Enjoy sushi and other Asian specialties at Aizia, or head across to the Links Restaurant and Lounge for American fare. **Pros:** Heavenly beds for adults and kids now, too; in-room workouts and great spa; eye-popping architecture. **Cons:** beach is eroding. ⊠ *1995 E. Hallandale Beach Blvd.* ☎ *954/602–6000 or 800/327–1212* ⊕ *www. starwoodhotels.com* ↳ *900 rooms, 100 suites* ⚭ *In-room: refrigerator, Internet, Wi-Fi. In-hotel: 5 restaurants, bars, golf course, tennis courts, pools, gym, spa* ⊟ *AE, DC, MC, V.*

Miami and Miami Beach

WORD OF MOUTH

"South beach is perfect . . . plenty of shopping, beautiful beach . . .
great restaurants, lots of fun."

—flep

WELCOME TO MIAMI AND MIAMI BEACH

TOP REASONS TO GO

★ **The Beach:** Miami Beach has been rated as one of the 10 best in the world. White sand, warm water, and bronzed bodies everywhere provide just the right mix of relaxation and people-gazing.

★ **Dining Delights:** Miami's eclectic residents have transformed the city into a museum of epicurean wonders, ranging from Cuban and Argentine fare to fusion haute cuisine.

★ **Wee-Hour Parties:** A 24-hour liquor license means clubs stay open until 5 AM, and after-parties go until noon the following day.

★ **Picture-Perfect People:** Miami is a watering hole for the vain and beautiful of South America, Europe, and the Northeast. Watch them—or join them—as they strut their stuff on Lincoln Road, chow down in style at the Forge, and flaunt their tans on the white beds of the Shore Club hotel.

★ **Art Deco District:** Candy colors and neon as far as the eye can see will put a lift in your step.

1 Downtown Miami. Weave through the glass-and-steel labyrinth of new condo construction to catch a Miami Heat game at the American Airlines Arena or a ballet at the spaceship-like Adrienne Arsht Center for the Performing Arts. To the far north is Little Haiti. To the southwest is Little Havana.

2 South Beach. People-watch from sidewalk cafés along Ocean Drive, lounge poolside at posh Collins Avenue hotels, and party 'til dawn at the nation's hottest clubs.

3 Coral Gables. Dine and shop on family-friendly Miracle Mile, and take a driving tour of the Mediterra-nean-style mansions in the surrounding neighborhoods.

4 Coconut Grove. Catch dinner and a movie and listen to live music at CocoWalk, or cruise the bohemian shops and locals' bars in this hip neighborhood.

5 Key Biscayne. Pristine parks and tranquility make this upscale enclave a total antithesis to the South Beach party.

South beach.

South beach.

LITTLE
HAITI

N.W. 79th St.

9

N.W. 62nd St.

N.W. 54th St.   944

Robert Frost Expwy.

N.W. 36th St.

N.W. 20th St.

DOWNTOWN
MIAMI

W. Flagler St.

S.W. 8th St.

LITTLE
HAVANA

S.W. 22nd St.

JFK Causeway

MIAMI
BEACH

Julia Tuttle Causeway   195

2

SOUTH
BEACH

A1A

Art Center

Venetian Causeway

Watson
Island

American
Airlines
Arena

MacArthur Causeway

41

Art Deco
District

Fisher
Island

Marine
Stadium

Rickenbacker
Causeway

Virginia
Key

COCONUT
GROVE

Grove Isle

Coco Walk

Biscayne
Bay

5 KEY
BISCAYNE

ATLANTIC OCEAN

Cape Florida
Lighthouse

GETTING ORIENTED

Long considered the gateway to Latin America, Miami is as close to Cuba and the Caribbean as you can get within the United States. The 36-square-mi city is located at the southern tip of the Florida peninsula, bordered on the east by Biscayne Bay. Over the bay lies a series of barrier islands, the largest being a thin 18-square-mi strip called Miami Beach. To the east of Miami Beach is the Atlantic Ocean. To the south are the Florida Keys.

Miami beach.

MIAMI AND MIAMI BEACH PLANNER

When to Go

Miami and Miami Beach are year-round destinations. Most visitors come October through April, when the weather is close to perfect; hotels, restaurants, and attractions are busiest; and each weekend holds a festival or event. "Season" kicks off in December with Art Basel Miami Beach, and hotel rates don't come down until after the college kids have left from spring break.

It's hot and steamy from May through September, but nighttime temperatures are usually pleasant. Also, summer is a good time for the budget traveler. Many hotels lower their rates considerably, and many restaurants offer discounts—especially during **Miami Spice** in August, when slews of top restaurants offer special tasting menus at a steep discount (sometimes Spice runs for two months, check *www.iLoveMiamiSpice.com* for details).

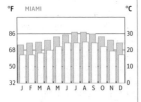

Getting Here

By Air: Miami is serviced by Miami International Airport (MIA) near downtown and Fort Lauderdale-Hollywood International Airport (FLL) 18 mi north. Many discount carriers, like Spirit Airlines, Southwest Airlines, and AirTran fly into FLL, making it a smart bargain if you are renting a car. Otherwise, look for flights to MIA on American Airlines, Delta, and Continental. MIA is undergoing extensive renovations that are expected to conclude in the summer of 2011; delays and long walks to gates are a common occurrence.

By Car: Interstate 95 is the major expressway connecting South Florida with points north; State Road 836 is the major east–west expressway and connects to Florida's Turnpike, State Road 826, and Interstate 95. Seven causeways link Miami and Miami Beach, Interstate 195 and Interstate 395 offering the most convenient routes; the Rickenbacker Causeway extends to Key Biscayne from Interstate 95 and U.S. 1. **Remember U.S. 1** (*aka* **Biscayne Boulevard**)—you'll hear it often in directions. It starts in Key West, hugs South Florida's coastline, and heads north straight through to Maine.

By Train: Amtrak provides service from 500 destinations to the Greater Miami area. The trains make several stops along the way; north–south service stops in the major Florida cities of Jacksonville, Orlando, Tampa, West Palm Beach, and Fort Lauderdale. For extended trips, or if you want to visit other areas in Florida, you can come via Auto Train (where you bring your car along) from Lorton, Virginia, just outside Washington, D.C., to Sanford, Florida, just outside Orlando. From there it's less than a four-hour drive to Miami. Fares vary, but expect to pay between $269 and $346 for a basic sleeper seat and car passage each way. ■TIP→ You must be traveling with an automobile to purchase a ticket on the Auto Train.

Getting Around

Greater Miami resembles Los Angeles in its urban sprawl and traffic. You'll need a car to visit many attractions and points of interest. If possible, avoid driving during the rush hours of 7–9 AM and 5–7 PM—the hour just after and right before the peak times also can be slow going. During rainy weather, be especially cautious of flooding in South Beach and Key Biscayne.

Some sights are accessible via the public transportation system, run by the **Metro-Dade Transit Agency** (☎ *305/770–3131* ⊕ *www.miamidade.gov/transit*), which maintains 650 Metrobuses on 70 routes; the 21-mi Metrorail elevated rapid-transit system; and the Metromover, an elevated light-rail system. The bus stops for the **Metrobus** are marked with blue-and-green signs with a bus logo and route information. The fare is $1.50 (exact change only). Transfers cost 50¢. Some express routes carry surcharges of $1.85. Elevated **Metrorail** trains run from downtown Miami north to Hialeah and south along U.S. 1 to Dadeland. The system operates daily 5 AM–midnight. The fare is $2; 50¢ transfers to Metrobus must be purchased at the station where you originally board the system. **Metromover** resembles an airport shuttle and runs on two loops around downtown Miami, linking major hotels, office buildings, and shopping areas. The system spans 4 mi, including the 1-mi Omni Loop and the 1-mi Brickell Loop. There is no fee to ride; transfers to Metrorail are $2.

Tri-Rail (☎ *800/874–7245* ⊕ *www.tri-rail.com*), South Florida's commuter-train system, offers shuttle service to and from MIA from 3797 NW 21st Street. Tri-Rail stops at 18 stations along a 71-mi route. Prices range from $3.50 to $9.25 for a round-trip ticket.

Cab It

Except in South Beach, it's difficult to hail a cab on the street; in most cases you'll need to call a cab company or have a hotel doorman hail one for you. Fares run $4.50 for the first mile and $2.40 every mile thereafter; flat-rate fares are also available from the airport to a variety of zones. Many cabs now accept credit cards; inquire before you get in the car.

Taxi Companies: **Central Cabs** (☎ *305/532–5555*). **Diamond Cab Company** (☎ *305/545–5555*). **Flamingo Taxi** (☎ *305/599–9999*). **Metro Taxi** (☎ *305/888–8888*). **Society Cab Company** (☎ *305/757–5523*). **Super Yellow Cab Company** (☎ *305/888–7777*). **Tropical Taxi** (☎ *305/945–1025*). **Yellow Cab Company** (☎ *305/633–0503*).

Visitor Information

For additional information about Miami and Miami Beach, contact the city's visitors bureaus:

Greater Miami Convention & Visitors Bureau (✉ *701 Brickell Ave., Suite 2700, Miami* ☎ *305/539–3000, 800/933–8448 in U.S.* ⊕ *www.miamiandbeaches.com*). **Miami Beach Chamber of Commerce & Visitors Center** (✉ *1920 Meridian Ave., Miami Beach* ☎ *305/674–1300 or 800/666–4519* ⊕ *www.miamibeachchamber.com*).

4

MIAMI BEACHES

Almost every side street in Miami Beach dead-ends at the ocean. Sandy shores also stretch along the southern side of the Rickenbacker Causeway to Key Biscayne, where you'll find more popular beaches.

Beaches tend to have golden, light brown, or gray-tinted sand with coarser grains than the fine white stuff on Florida's Gulf Coast beaches. Although pure white-sand beaches are many peoples' idea of picture-perfect, darker beach sand is much easier on the eyes on a sunny day and—bonus!—your holiday photos (and the people in them) will have a subtle warm glow rather than harsh highlights.

Expect gentle waves, which can occasionally turn rough, complete with riptides, depending on what weather systems are lurking out in the ocean—always check and abide by the warnings posted on the lifeguard's station. One thing that isn't perfect here is shelling, but for casual shell collectors Bal Harbour Beach is the best bet; enter at 96th Street and Collins Avenue.

SOUTH BEACH PARKING TIPS

Several things are plentiful in South Beach. Besides the plethora of cell phones and surgically enhanced bodies, there are a lot of cars for a small area, and plenty of seriously attentive meter maids. On-street parking is scarce, tickets are given freely, and towing charges are high. Check your meter to see when you must pay to park; times vary. It's $1 for meters north and $1.25 for meters south of 23rd Street. There are also public parking lots that accept cash and credit cards. Or, buy a Parking Meter Card at Miami Beach Visitors Center and Publix supermarkets for $25.

MIAMI'S BEST BEACHES

LUMMUS PARK BEACH

Want glitz and glamour? On South Beach's Ocean Drive from 6th to 14th streets, this beach is crowded with beautiful people working hard on their tans, muscle tone, and social lives. It's also the place for golden sands, blue water, and gentle waves. However, as this place is all about seeing and being seen, the less perfect among us may feel intimidated or bored.

MATHESON HAMMOCK PARK BEACH

Kids will thrill to the tender waves and warm water of the beach at 4000 Crandon Boulevard in Key Biscayne. The golden sands of this 3-mi beach are only part of the attraction: the park includes children's rides and a playground, picnic areas—even a golf course. The man-made lagoon is perfect for inexperienced swimmers, and it's the best place in Miami for a picnic. But the water can be a bit murky, and with the emphasis on families, it's not the best place for singles.

BILL BAGGS CAPE FLORIDA STATE PARK

All the way at the end of Key Biscayne, at 1200 S. Crandon Boulevard, is a wide peachy-brown beach with usually gentle waves. The picnic area is popular with local families on the weekends, but the beach itself never feels crowded. The

park also includes miles of nature trails; bike, boat, beach chair, and umbrella rentals; and casual dining at the Lighthouse Café. You can fish off the piers by the marina, too. Come here for an escape from city madness.

HOLLYWOOD BEACH

Halfway between Miami and Fort Lauderdale, Hollywood Beach is a perfect retreat. Sun yourself on the pristine golden-white sands, join a volleyball game, take a tai chi or yoga lesson, then walk along the 2-mi boardwalk and visit its small shops, cafés, and restaurants. Head north on the boardwalk and you'll find North Beach Park's sea turtle hatchery, part of the Endangered Sea Turtle Protection Program (kids love it); it's open Thursday through Monday. Meander south and you end up at the Ocean Walk Mall.

HAULOVER BEACH

Want to bare it all? Just north of Bal Harbour, at 10800 Collins Avenue in Sunny Isles, sits the only legal clothing-optional beach in the area. Haulover has more claims to fame than its casual attitude toward swimwear—it's also the best beach in the area for body-boarding and surfing as it gets what passes for impressive swells in these parts. Plus the sand here is fine-grain white, unusual for the Atlantic coast.

Updated by
Teri Evans

Think of Miami as a teenager: a young beauty with growing pains, cocky yet confused, quick to embrace the latest fads, exasperating yet lovable. This analogy may help you understand how best to tackle this imperfect paradise.

As cities go, Miami and Miami Beach really are young. Just a little more than 100 years ago, Miami was mosquito-infested swampland, with an Indian trading post on the Miami River. Then hotel builder Henry Flagler brought his railroad to the outpost known as Fort Dallas. Other visionaries—Carl Fisher, Julia Tuttle, William Brickell, and John Sewell, among others—set out to tame the unruly wilderness. Hotels were erected, bridges were built, the port was dredged, and electricity arrived. The narrow strip of mangrove coast was transformed into Miami Beach—and the tourists started to come.

Greater Miami is many destinations in one. At its best it offers an unparalleled multicultural experience: melodic Latin and Caribbean tongues, international cuisines and cultural events, and an unmistakable joie de vivre—all against a beautiful beach backdrop. In Little Havana the air is tantalizing with the perfume of strong Cuban coffee. In Coconut Grove, Caribbean steel drums ring out during the Miami/Bahamas Goombay Festival. Anytime in colorful Miami Beach restless crowds wait for entry to the hottest new clubs.

Many visitors don't know that Miami and Miami Beach are really separate cities. Miami, on the mainland, is South Florida's commercial hub. Miami Beach, on 17 islands in Biscayne Bay, is sometimes considered America's Riviera, luring refugees from winter with its warm sunshine; sandy beaches; graceful, shady palms; and tireless nightlife. The natives know well that there's more to Greater Miami than the bustle of South Beach and its Art Deco district. In addition to well-known places such as Coconut Grove and Bayside, the less reported spots—like the Museum of Contemporary Art in North Miami, the burgeoning Design District in Miami, and the mangrove swamps of Matheson Hammock Park in Coral Gables—are great insider destinations.

EXPLORING MIAMI AND MIAMI BEACH

If you had arrived here 40 years ago with a guidebook in hand, chances are you'd be thumbing through listings looking for alligator wrestlers and you-pick strawberry fields or citrus groves. Things have changed. While Disney sidetracked families in Orlando, Miami was developing a unique culture and attitude that's equal parts beach town/big business, Latino/Caribbean meets European/American—all of which fuels a great art and food scene, as well as an exuberant nightlife and myriad festivals.

To find your way around Greater Miami, learn how the numbering system works. Miami is laid out on a grid with four quadrants—northeast, northwest, southeast, and southwest—which meet at Miami Avenue and Flagler Street. Miami Avenue separates east from west and Flagler Street separates north from south. Avenues and courts run north–south; streets, terraces, and ways run east–west. Roads run diagonally, northwest–southeast. But other districts—Miami Beach, Coral Gables, and Hialeah—may or may not follow this system, and along the curve of Biscayne Bay the symmetrical grid may shift diagonally. It's best to buy a detailed map, stick to the major roads, and ask directions early and often. However, make sure you're in a safe neighborhood or public place when you seek guidance; cabdrivers and cops are good resources.

DOWNTOWN MIAMI, LITTLE HAVANA, AND LITTLE HAITI

Downtown Miami dazzles from a distance. The skyline is fluid, thanks to the sheer number of sparkling glass high-rises between Biscayne Boulevard and the Miami River. Business is the key to downtown Miami's daytime bustle. Traffic congestion from the high-rise offices and expensive parking tend to keep the locals away, unless they're bringing out-of-town guests to touristy Bayside Marketplace. But change is in the air—the influx of condos and offices is bringing in shops and restaurants, most notably Mary Brickell Village, which serves as a culinary oasis for the starved business district. Thanks to the free Metromover, which runs inner and outer loops through downtown and to nearby neighborhoods to the south and north, this is an excellent tour to take by rail. Attractions are conveniently located within about two blocks of the nearest station. If you're coming from north or east of downtown, leave your car near a Metromover stop and take the Omni Loop downtown. If you're coming from south or west, park your car at a Metrorail station and take a leg of the 21-mi elevated commuter system downtown.

Little Havana is southwest of downtown Miami. See our "Caribbean Infusion" spotlight for a map of this neighborhood as well as one of Little Haiti in north Miami.

EXPLORING

Numbers correspond to the Downtown Miami map.

DOWNTOWN MIAMI

1 **Adrienne Arsht Center for the Performing Arts.** Lovers of culture and other artsy types are drawn to this stunning home of the Florida Grand Opera, Miami City Ballet, New World Symphony, Concert Association of Florida, and other local and touring groups, which have included Broadway hits like *Wicked* and *Mamma Mia!* Think of it as a sliver of savoir faire to temper Miami's often-over-the-top vibe. Designed by architect César Pelli, the massive development contains a 2,400-seat opera house, 2,200-seat concert hall, a black-box theater, and an outdoor Plaza for the Arts. ⊠ *1300 Biscayne Blvd., at NE 13th St., Downtown* ☎ *305/949–6722* ⊕ *www.arshtcenter.org.*

2 **Freedom Tower.** In the 1960s this ornate Spanish-baroque structure was the Cuban Refugee Center, processing more than 500,000 Cubans who entered the United States after fleeing Fidel Castro's regime. Built in 1925 for the *Miami Daily News,* it was inspired by the Giralda, an 800-year-old bell tower in Seville, Spain. Preservationists were pleased to see the tower's exterior restored in 1988. Today, it is owned by Miami-Dade College, and continues to maintain the tower as a cultural and educational center, which includes a museum depicting Cuban history, the experiences of refugees, and the achievements of Cuban-Americans. ⊠ *600 Biscayne Blvd., at NE 6th St., Downtown* ☎ *No phone* ⊙ *Tues.–Sun. noon–7.*

3 **Miami-Dade Cultural Center.** Containing three cultural resources, this fortress-like 3-acre complex is a downtown focal point. **The Miami ★ Art Museum** (☎ *305/375–3000* ⊕ *www.miamiartmuseum.org* 🎟 *$8 [free for families every second Sat.]* ⊙ *Tues.–Fri. 10–5 [until 9 the third Thurs. of month], weekends noon–5*) is waiting to move into its new 120,000-square-foot home in Museum Park, which is to be completed in 2012. Meanwhile, the museum presents major touring exhibitions of work by international artists, with an emphasis on art since 1945. Every second Saturday entrance is free for families. Discover a treasure trove of colorful stories about the region's history at **HistoryMiami** (☎ *305/375–1492* ⊕ *www.hmsf.org* 🎟 *$8 museum, $10 combo ticket art and history museums* ⊙ *Tues.–Fri. 10–5, weekends noon–5*), formerly known as the Historical Museum of Southern Florida. Exhibits celebrate Miami's multicultural heritage, including an old Miami streetcar, and unique items chronicling the migration of Cubans to Miami. The **Main Public Library** (☎ *305/375–2665* ⊕ *www.mdpls.org* ⊙ *Aug.–May, Mon.–Wed., Fri., and Sat. 9–6, Thurs. 9–9, Sun. 1–5*) contains nearly 4 million holdings and a Florida Department that includes rare books, documents, and photographs recording Miami history. It also has art exhibits in the auditorium and in the 2nd-floor lobby. ⊠ *101 W. Flagler St., between NW 1st and 2nd Aves., Downtown.*

4 **Wynwood Art District.** Just north of downtown Miami, the up-and-com-★ ing Wynwood Art District is peppered with galleries, art studios, and private collections accessible to the public. Visit during Wynwood's monthly gallery walk on the second Saturday evening of each month

Continued on page 143

Downtown Miami

← TO AIRPORT

395

TO LITTLE HAITI ↑

SCHOOL BOARD

N.E. 15th St.

N.W. 14th St.

N.E. 14th St.

OMNI

1

4

N.W. 13th St.

N.E. 13th St.

Dolphin Expressway

41

MacArthur

Causeway

N.W. 12th St.

Biscayne Blvd.

TO SOUTH BEACH/ MIAMI BEACH →

CULMER

N.W. 11th St.

N.E. 11th St.

BICENTENNIAL PARK

N.W. 10th St.

N.E. 10th St.

ELEVENTH STREET

Bicentennial Park

95

N.W. 9th St.

N.E. 9th St.

OMNI EXTENSION

N.W. 8th St.

N.E. 8th St.

PARK WEST

AmericanAirlines Arena

N.W. 7th St.

OVERTOWN/ ARENA

N.E. 7th St.

South American Way

TO PORT OF MIAMI →

N.W. 6th St.

STATE PLAZA/ ARENA

N.E. 6th St.

FREEDOM TOWER

2

N.W. 5th St.

METROMOVER

COLLEGE NORTH

N.W. 4th St.

N.E. 4th St.

COLLEGE BAYSIDE

Bayside Marketplace

N.E. 3rd St.

N.E. 2nd St.

GOVERNMENT CENTER

N.E. 1st St.

FIRST STREET

Bayfront Park

N.W. 1st St.

W. Flagler St.

W. Flagler St.

MIAMI AVE.

Gusman Center for the Performing Arts

E. Flagler St.

3

S.W. 1st St.

THIRD STREET

KNIGHT CENTER

S.E. 1st St.

BAYFRONT PARK

S.W. 2nd St.

S.E. 2nd St.

S.W. 3rd St.

S.E. 4th St.

S.W. 4th St.

S.W. 4th St.

Biscayne Blvd. Way

S.W. 5th St.

Miami

BRICKELL EXTENSION

S.W. 6th St.

River

S.E. 5th St.

FIFTH STREET

Brickell Key

95

S.W. 7th St.

S.E. 6th St.

S.W. 7th St.

METRORAIL

Mary Brickell Village

S.E. 7th St.

Brickell Park

S.W. 8th St.

S.W. 2nd Ave.

S. Miami Ave.

S.E. 8th St.

EIGHTH STREET

← **5 6**

0   1/4 mile

0   1/4 km

KEY

Ⓜ *Metro stops*

– – – *Metromover*

CARIBBEAN INFUSION

by Michelle Delio

Miami has sun, sand, and sea, but unlike some of Florida's other prime beach destinations, it also has a wave of cultural traditions that spice up the city.

It's with good reason that people in Miami fondly say that the city is an easy way for Americans to visit another country without ever leaving the United States. According to the U.S. Census Bureau, more than half of Miami's population is foreign born and more than 70% speak a language other than English at home (in comparison, only 36.7% of New York City residents were born in another country). The city's Latin/Caribbean immigrants and exiles make up the largest segments of the population.

Locals merrily merge cultural traditions, speaking "Spanglish" (a mix of Spanish and English), sipping Cuban coffee with Sicilian pastries, eating Nuevo Latino fusion food, and dancing to the beat of other countries' music. That said, people here are just as interested in keeping to their own distinct ways—think of the city as a colorful mosaic composed of separate elements rather than a melting pot.

Miami's diverse population creates a city that feels alive in a way that few other American cities do. Nothing is set in stone here, for better or worse, and there's always a new flavor to explore, a new holiday to celebrate, a new accent to puzzle over.

No visit to Miami would be complete without a stop at one of the two neighborhoods famed for their celebrations of cultural traditions— Little Haiti and Little Havana—places that have a wonderful foreign feel even amid cosmopolitan Miami.

Playing dominoes is a favorite pastime at Maximo Gomez Park in Little Havana (left).

LA PETITE HAÏTI—LITTLE HAITI

Little Haiti is a study in contrasts. At first glance you see the small buildings painted in bright oranges, pinks, reds, yellows, and turquoises, with signs, some handwritten, touting immigration services, lunch specials with *tassot* (fried cubed goat), and voodoo supplies.

But as you adjust to this dazzle of color, you become aware of the curious juxtapositions of poverty and wealth in this evolving neighborhood. Streets dip with potholes in front of trendy art galleries, and dilapidated houses struggle to survive near newly renovated soccer fields and arts centers.

Miami's Little Haiti is the largest Haitian community outside of Haiti itself, and while people of different ethnic backgrounds have begun to move to the neighborhood, people here tend to expect to primarily see other Haitians on these streets. Obvious outsiders may be greeted with a few frozen stares on the streets, but owners of shops and restaurants tend to be welcoming. Creole is commonly spoken, although some people—especially younger folks—also speak English.

WHEN TO GO

The neighborhood is best visited during the daytime, combined with a visit to the nearby Miami Design District, an 18-block section of art galleries, interior design showrooms, and restaurants between N.E. 41st Street and N.E. 36th Street, Miami Avenue, and Biscayne Boulevard.

CREOLE EXPRESSIONS

Creole, one of Haiti's two languages (the other is French), is infused with French, African, Arabic, Spanish, and Portuguese words.

Komon ou ye? How are you? *(also spelled Kouman)
N'ap boule! Great!
Kisa ou ta vla? What would you like?
Mesi. Thanks.
Souple. Please.

LITTLE HAITI

Sweat Records
(Churchill's Pub)

Chez Le
Bebe

Morningside
Bayfront
Park

Biscayne Bay

0   1/2 mi

0   1/2 km

MANGÉ KRÉYOL (HAITIAN FOOD)

Traditional Caribbean cuisines tend to combine European and African culinary techniques. Haitian can be a bit spicier—though never mouth-scorching hot—than many other island cuisines. Rice and beans are the staple food, enlivened with a little of whatever people might have: fish, goat, chicken, pork, usually stewed or deep-fried, along with peppers, plantains, and tomatoes.

Chez Le Bebe (✉ *114 N.E. 54th St.* ☎ *305/751–7639* ⊕ *www.chezlebebe. com*) offers Haitian home cooking—if you want to try stewed goat, this is the place to do it. Chicken, fish, oxtail, and fried pork are also on the menu; each plate comes with rice, beans, plantains, and salad for less than $12.

Tap Tap restaurant (✉ *819 Fifth St.* ☎ *305/672–2898*) is outside of Little Haiti, but this Miami institution will immerse you in the island's culture with an extensive collection of Haitian folk art displayed everywhere in the restaurant. On the menu is pumpkin soup, *spageti kreyol* (pasta, shrimp, and a Creole tomato sauce), goat stewed in Creole sauce (a mildly spicy tomato-based sauce), conch, and "grilled goat dinner." You can eat well here for $15 or less.

GETTING ORIENTED

Little Haiti, once a small farming community outside of Miami proper, is slowly becoming one of the city's most vibrant neighborhoods. Its northern and southern boundaries are 85th Street and 36th Street, respectively, with Interstate–95 to the west and Biscayne Boulevard to the east. The best section to visit is along North Miami Avenue from 54th to 59th streets. Driving is the best way to get here; parking is easy to find on North Miami Avenue. Public transit (☎ *305/891–3131*) is limited.

SHOPPING

The cluster of botanicas at N.E. 54th Street and N.E. 2nd Avenue offer items intended to sway the fates, from candles to plastic and plaster statues of Catholic saints that, in the voodoo tradition, represent African deities. While exploring, don't miss **Sweat Records** (✉ *5505 N.E. 2nd Ave.* ☎ *305/342–0953* ⊕ *www. sweatrecordsmiami.com*). Sweat sells a wide range of music—rock, pop, punk, electronic, hip-hop, and Latino. Check out the vegan-friendly organic coffee bar at the store, which is open from noon to 10 PM every day but Sunday.

LITTLE HAVANA

First settled en masse by Cubans in the early 1960s, after that country's Communist revolution, Little Havana is a predominantly working-class area and the core of Miami's Hispanic community. Spanish is the main language, but don't be surprised if the cadence is less Cuban than Salvadoran or Nicaraguan: the neighborhood is now home to people from all Latin American countries.

If you come to Little Havana expecting the Latino version of New Orleans's French Quarter, you're apt to be disappointed—it's not yet that picturesque. But if great, inexpensive food (not just Cuban; there's Vietnamese, Mexican, and Argentinean here as well), distinctive, affordable art, cigars, and coffee interest you, you'll enjoy your time in Little Havana. It's not a prefab tourist destination, so don't expect Disneyland with a little Latino flair—this is real life in Miami.

WHEN TO GO

The absolute best time to visit Calle Ocho is the last Friday evening of every month, between 6:30 and 11 PM on 8th Street from 14th to 17th avenues. Known as **Viernes Culturales** (⊕ www.viernesculturales.com), it's a big block party that everyone is welcome to attend. Art galleries, restaurants, and stores stay open late, and music, mojitos, and avant-garde street performances bring a young, hip crowd to the neighborhood where they mingle with locals.

If you come in mid-March, your visit may coincide with the annual **Calle Ocho festival** (⊕ www.carnavalmiami.com), which draws more than a million visitors in search of Latin music, food, and shopping.

LITTLE HAVANA

S.W. 6th St.

S.W. 16th Ave.

S.W. 14th Ave.

S.W. 13th Ave.

S.W. 12th Ave.

S.W. 10th Ave.

S.W. 7th St.

El Pub Restaurant ✕

Walk of Stars ◆ Lily's Records ◆

Calle Ocho

El Credito Cigar Factory ◆

S.W. 8th St.

Tamiami Trail

Casa Panza ✕ Restaurant

Los Pinareños Frutería ◆

El Rey de los Habanos ◆

El Titan de Bronze ◆

Dominio ◆ Park

S.W. 9th St.

S.W. 17th Ave.

S.W. 16th Ave.

S.W. 15th Ave.

S.W. 14th Ave.

S.W. 13th Ave.

S.W. 11th Ave.

S.W. 10th St.

0   1/8 mile

S.W. 11th St.

0   1/8 km

4

GETTING ORIENTED

Little Havana's semi-official boundaries are 27th Avenue to 4th Avenue on the west, Miami River to the north, and S.W. 11th Street to the south. Much of the neighborhood is residential, but its heart and tourist hub is Calle Ocho (8th Street), between 14th and 18th avenues.

The best way to get here is by car. Park on the side streets off **Calle Ocho** (some spots have meters; most don't). Other options include the free **Metromover** (☎ 305/891–3131) and a cab ride. From Miami Beach the 15-minute ride should cost just under $30 each way.

THE SIGHTS

Stroll down Calle Oche from 12th to 17th avenues and look around you: cafés are selling guava pastries and rose petal flan, a botanica brims with candles and herbs to heal whatever ails you. Over there at a tropical fruit stand someone is hacking off the top of a coconut with a machete, while nearby, thimble-size cups of liquid energy (aka *café cubano*) are passed through the open windows of coffee shops. Small galleries showcasing modern art jostle up next to mom-and-pop food shops and high-end Cuban clothes and crafts. At Dominio Park (officially Maximo Gomez Park), guayabera-clad seniors bask in the sun and play dominoes, while at corner bodegas and coffee shops (particularly Versailles) regulars share neighborhood gossip and political opinions. A few steps away is the "Paseo de las Estrellas" (Walk of Stars). The Latin version of its Hollywood namesake, the strip of sidewalk embedded with stars honors many of the world's top Hispanic celebrities, among them the late salsa queen Celia Cruz, crooner Julio Iglesias, and superstar Gloria Estefan.

SPANISH EXPRESSIONS

Qué deseaba? Can I help you?

Algo más? Anything else?

Muchas gracias! Thank you very much!

No hay de qué. / De nada. You're welcome.

No entiendo. I don't understand.

Oye! All-purpose word used to get attention or express interest, admiration, and appreciation.

Calle Ocho Carnaval

Rolling cigars by hand in a Little Havana factory.

THE SOUNDS

Salsa and merengue pour out of storefronts and restaurants, while other businesses cater to the snap and shuffles of flamenco performances and Sevillaña *tablaos* (dances performed on a wood-plank stage, using castanets). If you want to join in the merriment along Calle Ocho, dance with locals on the patio of **El Pub Restaurant** (near 15th Avenue), or snack on tapas at **Casa Panza Restaurant** (near 16th), where the background music is the restaurant owner's enthusiastic singing. Any time of day, you can hear the constant backbeat of people speaking Spanish and the occasional crowing of a stray, time-confused rooster. To take these sounds home with you, wander over to **Lily's Records** (✉ *1419 S.W. 8th St, near 14th* ☎ *305/856–0536*), for its huge selection of Latin music.

THE SCENTS

Bottled, the essence of Little Havana would be tobacco, café cubano, and a whiff of tropical fruit. To indulge your senses in two of these things, head to **Los Pinareños Frutería** on Calle Ocho just west of 13th Avenue. Here you can sip a sweet, hot *cortadito* (coffee with milk), a *cafecito* (no milk), or a cool *coco frio* (coconut water). For more subsistence, dig into a Cuban-style tamale. There are stools out front of the shop, or take your drink to go and wander over to S.W. 13th Avenue, which has monuments to Cuban heroes, and sit under the ceiba trees. For cigars, head to Calle Ocho near 11th Avenue and visit any of these three stores: **El Credito Cigar Factory, El Rey de los Habanos**, and **El Titan de Bronze**. At these family-owned businesses employees deftly hand-roll millions of stogies a year.

TOURS

If a quick multicultural experience is your goal, set aside an hour or two to do your own self-guided walking tour of the neighborhood. For real ethnic immersion, allow more time; eating is a must, as well as a peek at the area's residential streets lined with distinctive homes.

Especially illuminating are **Little Havana tours by Dr. Paul George** (✉ *101 W. Flagler St.* ☎ *305/375–1621* ✎ *historictours@ hmsf.org*). A history professor at Miami Dade College and historian for the Historical Museum of Southern Florida, George covers architecture and community history on his tours. These take place only a few times a year. Private three-hour tours are available for groups of up to 20 people for $400 ($20 per person above 20 people).

For customized offerings, try **Miami Cultural Tours** (✉ *305/416-6868* ⊕ *www. miamiculturaltours.com*), interactive tours that introduce people to Little Havana and Little Haiti. Group and private tours are available, with prices ranging from $39 to $79 a person.

when studios and galleries are all open at the same time. Make sure a visit includes a stop at the **Margulies Collection at the Warehouse** (✉ *591 NW 27th St., between NW 5th and 6th Aves., Downtown* ☎ *305/576–1051* ⊕ *www.margulieswarehouse.com*). Martin Margulies's collection of vintage and contemporary photography, videos, and installation art in a 45,000-square-foot space makes for eye-popping viewing. Entrance fee is a $10 donation, which goes to a local homeless shelter for women and children. It's open October to April, Wednesday to Saturday 11–4. Fans of edgy art will appreciate the **Rubell Family Collection** (✉ *95 NW 29th St., between N. Miami Ave. and NW 1st Ave., Downtown* ☎ *305/573–6090* ⊕ *www.rfc.museum*). Mera and Don Rubell have accumulated work by artists from the 1970s to the present, including Jeff Koons, Cindy Sherman, Damien Hirst, and Keith Haring. Admission is $10, and the gallery is open Wednesday to Saturday 10–6.

4

LITTLE HAVANA

❺ Cuban Memorial Boulevard. Two blocks in the heart of Little Havana are filled with monuments to Cuba's freedom fighters. Among the memorials are the *Eternal Torch of the Brigade 2506*, commemorating those who were killed in the failed Bay of Pigs invasion of 1961; a bust of 19th-century hero Antonio Maceo; and a bas-relief map of Cuba depicting each of its *municipios*. There's also a bronze statue in honor of Tony Izquierdo, who participated in the Bay of Pigs invasion, served in Nicaragua's Somozan forces, and was also on the CIA payroll. ✉ *SW 13th Ave., south of SW 8th St., Little Havana.*

❻ El Credito Cigar Factory. A peek at the intently focused cigar rollers through the giant windows doesn't prepare you for the rich, pungent scent that jolts your senses as you step inside the store. Many of the workers at this once family-owned business date back three generations, as they learned their trade in prerevolutionary Cuba. Today the tobacco leaf they use comes from Cuban seeds grown in the Dominican Republic, Ecuador, and Nicaragua. A walk-in humidor has many brands of full-bodied cigars with varying blends of tobacco favored by customers such as Arnold Schwarzenegger, Bill Clinton, Robert De Niro, and Bill Cosby. Informational tours are available weekdays. ✉ *1106 SW 8th St., near SW 11th Ave., Little Havana* ☎ *305/858–4162* ⊕ *www. elcreditocigars.com* ⊗ *Weekdays 8–5, Sat. 9–4. Factory closed Sat. but store is open.*

MIAMI BEACH

The hub of Miami Beach is South Beach (SoBe, but you'll never hear locals calling it that), with its energetic Ocean Drive. Here, life unfolds 24 hours a day. Beautiful people pose in hotel lounges and sidewalk cafés, tanned cyclists zoom past palm trees, and visitors flock to see the action. On Lincoln Road, café crowds spill onto the sidewalks, weekend markets draw all kinds of visitors and their dogs, and thanks to a few late-night lounges the scene is just as alive at night.

Quieter areas to the north on Collins Avenue are Surfside (from 88th to 96th streets), fashionable Bal Harbour (beginning at 96th Street), and Sunny Isles (between 157th and 197th streets). If you're interested in these areas and you're flying in, the Fort Lauderdale airport might be a better choice.

EXPLORING

Numbers correspond to the Miami Beach and South Beach map.

SOUTH BEACH
TOP ATTRACTIONS

❺ Española Way. There's a bohemian feel to this street lined with Mediterranean-revival buildings constructed in 1925. Al Capone's gambling syndicate ran its operations upstairs at what is now the Clay Hotel, a youth hostel. At a nightclub here in the 1930s, future bandleader Desi Arnaz strapped on a conga drum and started beating out a rumba rhythm. Visit this quaint avenue on a weekend afternoon, when merchants and craftspeople set up shop to sell everything from handcrafted bongo drums to fresh flowers. Between Washington and Drexel avenues the road has been narrowed to a single lane and Miami Beach's trademark pink sidewalks have been widened to accommodate sidewalk cafés and shops selling imaginative clothing, jewelry, and art. ⊠ *Española Way, between 14th and 15th Sts. from Washington to Jefferson Aves.*

❼ Holocaust Memorial. A bronze sculpture depicts refugees clinging to a giant bronze arm that reaches out of the ground and 42 feet into the air. Enter the surrounding courtyard to see a memorial wall and hear the music that seems to give voice to the 6 million Jews who died at the hands of the Nazis. It's easy to understand why Kenneth Treister's dramatic memorial is in Miami Beach: the city's community of Holocaust survivors was once the second-largest in the country. ⊠ *1933–1945 Meridian Ave., at Dade Blvd.* ☎ *305/538–1663* ⊕ *www.holocaustmmb. org* ⊡ *Free (donations welcome)* ☉ *Daily 9–9.*

❻ Lincoln Road Mall. A playful 1990s redesign spruced up this open-air pedestrian mall, adding a grove of 20 towering date palms, five linear pools, and colorful broken-tile mosaics to the once-futuristic 1950s vision of Fontainebleau designer Morris Lapidus. Some of the shops are owner-operated boutiques with a delightful variety of clothing, furnishings, jewelry, and decorative design. Others are the typical chain stores of American malls. Remnants of tired old Lincoln Road—beauty supply and discount electronics stores on the Collins end of the strip—somehow fit nicely into the mix. The new Lincoln Road is fun, lively, and friendly for people old, young, gay, and straight—and their dogs. Folks skate, scoot, bike, or jog here. The best times to hit the road are during Sunday morning farmers' markets and on weekend evenings, when cafés bustle, art galleries open shows, street performers make the sidewalk their stage, and stores stay open late.

Two of the landmarks worth checking out at the eastern end of Lincoln Road are the massive 1940s keystone building at 420 Lincoln Road, which has a 1945 Leo Birchanky mural in the lobby, and the 1921 mission-style Miami Beach Community Church, at Drexel Avenue. The Lincoln Theatre (No. 541–545), at Pennsylvania Avenue, is a classical four-story art deco gem with friezes. The New World Symphony, a national advanced-training orchestra led by Michael Tilson Thomas,

Fodor's Choice ★

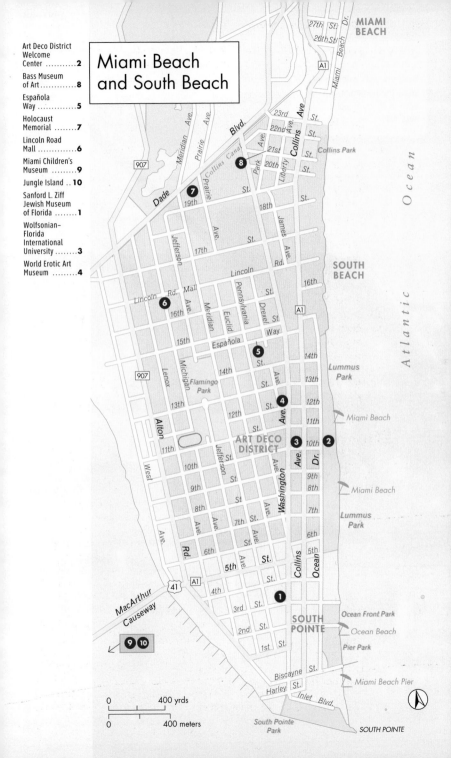

Miami Beach and South Beach

MIAMI BEACH

SOUTH BEACH

ART DECO DISTRICT

SOUTH POINTE

SOUTH POINTE

Ocean

Atlantic

Ocean

Collins Park

Lummus Park

Miami Beach

Miami Beach

Lummus Park

Ocean Front Park

Ocean Beach

Pier Park

Miami Beach Pier

South Pointe Park

MacArthur Causeway

0   400 yrds

0   400 meters

rehearses and performs here, and concerts are often broadcast via loud-speakers, to the delight of visitors. Just west, facing Pennsylvania, a fabulous Cadillac dealership sign was discovered underneath the facade of the Lincoln Road Millennium Building, on the south side of the mall. At Euclid Avenue there's a monument to Lapidus, who in his 90s watched the renaissance of his whimsical creation. At Lenox Avenue, a black-and-white art deco movie house with a Mediterranean barrel-tile roof is now the Colony Theater (No. 1040), where live theater and experimental films are presented. ⊠ *Lincoln Rd., between Collins Ave. and Alton Rd.*

WORTH NOTING

❷ Art Deco District Welcome Center. Run by the Miami Design Preservation League, the center provides information about the buildings in the district. A gift shop sells 1930s–50s art deco memorabilia, posters, and books on Miami's history. Several tours—covering Lincoln Road, Española Way, North Beach, and the entire Art Deco district, among others—start here. You can rent audiotapes for a self-guided tour, join one of the regular morning (Friday through Wednesday) or Thursday-evening walking tours. All of the options provide detailed histories of the art deco hotels. Don't miss the special boat tours during Art Deco Weekend, in early January. ⊠ *1001 Ocean Dr., at Barbara Capitman Way (10th St.)* ☎ *305/531–3484* ⊠ *Tours $20* ☉ *Sun.–Thurs. 10–7, Fri. and Sat. 10–6.*

▅TIP→ For a map of the Art Deco district and info on some of the sites there, see our "A Stroll Down Deco Lane" in-focus feature.

❽ Bass Museum of Art. The Bass, in historic Collins Park, is part of the Miami Beach Cultural Park, which includes the Miami City Ballet's Arquitectonica-designed facility and the Miami Beach Regional Library. The original building, constructed of keystone, has unique Maya-inspired carvings. The expansion designed by Japanese architect Arata Isozaki houses another wing and an outdoor sculpture garden. Special exhibitions join a diverse collection of European art. Works on permanent display include *The Holy Family,* a painting by Peter Paul Rubens; *The Tournament,* one of several 16th-century Flemish tapestries; and works by Albrecht Dürer and Henri de Toulouse-Lautrec. Special exhibits often cost a little extra. ⊠ *2121 Park Ave., at 21st St.* ☎ *305/673–7530* ⊕ *www.bassmuseum.org* ⊠ *$8* ☉ *Wed.–Sun. noon–5.*

❶ Sanford L. Ziff Jewish Museum of Florida. Listed on the National Register of Historic Places, this former synagogue, built in 1936, contains art deco chandeliers, 80 impressive stained-glass windows, and a permanent exhibit, MOSAIC: Jewish Life in Florida, which depicts more than 235 years of the Florida Jewish experience. The museum, which includes a store filled with books, jewelry, and other souvenirs, also hosts traveling exhibits and special events. ⊠ *301 Washington Ave., at 3rd St.* ☎ *305/672–5044* ⊕ *www.jewishmuseum.com* ⊠ *$6, free on Sat.* ☉ *Tues.–Sun. 10–5. Museum store closed Sat.*

❸ Wolfsonian–Florida International University. An elegantly renovated 1926
★ storage facility is now a research center and museum showcasing a 120,000-item collection of modern design and "propaganda arts"

amassed by Miami native Mitchell ("Micky") Wolfson Jr., a world traveler and connoisseur. Broad themes of the 19th and 20th centuries—nationalism, political persuasion, industrialization—are addressed in permanent and traveling shows. Included in the museum's eclectic holdings, which represent art deco, art moderne, art nouveau, Arts and Crafts, and other aesthetic movements, are 8,000 matchbooks collected by Egypt's King Farouk. ⊠ *1001 Washington Ave., at 10th St.* 🕿 *305/531–1001* ⊕ *www.wolfsonian.org* 🖃 *$7, free after 6 PM Fri.* 🕐 *Mon., Tues., and weekends noon–6, Thurs. and Fri. noon–9.*

❹ **World Erotic Art Museum (WEAM).** The sexy collection of more than 4,000 erotic items, all owned by millionaire Naomi Wilzig, unfolds with unique art of varying quality—fertility statues from around the globe and historic Chinese shunga books (erotic art offered as gifts to new brides on the wedding night) share the space with some kitschy knickknacks. If this is your thing, an original phallic prop from Stanley Kubrick's *A Clockwork Orange* and an over-the-top Kama Sutra bed is worth the price of admission, but the real standout is "Miss Naomi," who is usually on hand to answer questions and provide behind-the-scenes anecdotes. Kids 17 and under are not admitted. ⊠ *1205 Washington Ave., at 12th St.* 🕿 *305/532–9336* ⊕ *www.weam.com* 🖃 *$15* 🕐 *Daily 11 AM–midnight.*

WATSON ISLAND

❿ **Jungle Island.** South Florida's original tourist attraction, the park is
🧒 home to just about every unusual and endangered species you would want to see, including a rare albino alligator, a liger (lion and tiger mix), a 28-foot-long "crocosaur," and a myriad of exotic birds. The most intriguing offerings are the interactive animal tours, including the Lemur Experience ($45 for 45 minutes), in which the highly social primates make themselves at home on your lap or shoulders, and the Penguin Encounter ($30 for 30 minutes), where you can pet and feed warm-weather South African penguins. ⊠ *1111 Parrot Jungle Trail, off MacArthur Causeway (I–395)* 🕿 *305/400–7000* ⊕ *www.jungleisland. com* 🖃 *$29.95, $23.95 for kids, plus $7 parking* 🕐 *Daily 10–6.*

❾ **Miami Children's Museum.** This Arquitectonica-designed museum, both
🧒 imaginative and geometric in appearance, is directly across the MacArthur Causeway from Jungle Island. Twelve galleries house hundreds of interactive, bilingual exhibits. Children can scan plastic groceries in the supermarket, scramble through a giant sand castle, climb a rock wall, learn about the Everglades, and combine rhythms in the world-music studio. ⊠ *980 MacArthur Causeway* 🕿 *305/373–5437* ⊕ *www. miamichildrensmuseum.org* 🖃 *$12, parking $1 per hr* 🕐 *Daily 10–6.*

CORAL GABLES

You can easily spot Coral Gables from the window of a Miami-bound jetliner—just look for the massive orange tower of the Biltmore Hotel rising from a lush green carpet of trees concealing the city's gracious homes. The canopy is as much a part of this planned city as its distinctive architecture, all attributed to the vision of George E. Merrick nearly 100 years ago.

The story of this city began in 1911, when Merrick inherited 1,600 acres of citrus and avocado groves from his father. Through judicious investment he nearly doubled the tract to 3,000 acres by 1921. Merrick dreamed of building an American Venice here, complete with canals and homes. Working from this vision, he began designing a city based on centuries-old prototypes from Mediterranean countries. Unfortunately for Merrick, the devastating no-name hurricane of 1926, followed by the Great Depression, prevented him from fulfilling many of his plans. He died at 54, an employee of the post office. Today Coral Gables has a population of about 43,000. In its bustling downtown, more than 150 multinational companies maintain headquarters or regional offices, and the University of Miami campus in the southern part of the Gables brings a youthful vibrancy to the area. A southern branch of the city extends down the shore of Biscayne Bay through neighborhoods threaded with canals. The gorgeous Fairchild Tropical Botanic Garden and beachfront Matheson Hammock Park dominate this part of the Gables.

ESSENTIALS

Visitor Information Coral Gables Chamber of Commerce (✉ *224 Catalonia Ave., Coral Gables* ☎ *305/446–1657* ⊕ *www.gableschamber.org*).

EXPLORING

Numbers correspond to the Coral Gables, Coconut Grove, and Key Biscayne map.

TOP ATTRACTIONS

❶ **Biltmore Hotel.** Bouncing back stunningly from its dark days as an Army
★ hospital, this hotel has become the jewel of Coral Gables—a dazzling architectural gem with a colorful past. First opened in 1926, it was a hot spot for the rich and glamorous of the Jazz Age until it was converted to an Army–Air Force regional hospital in 1942. Until 1968, the Veterans Administration continued to operate the hospital after World War II. The Biltmore then lay vacant for nearly 20 years before it underwent extensive renovations and reopened as a luxury hotel in 1987. Its 16-story tower, like the Freedom Tower in downtown Miami, is a replica of Seville's Giralda Tower. The magnificent pool, reportedly the largest hotel pool in the continental United States, is steeped in history— Johnny Weissmuller of Tarzan fame was a lifeguard here, and in the 1930s grand aquatic galas featuring alligator wrestling, synchronized swimming, and bathing beauties drew thousands. More recently it was President Clinton's preferred place to stay and golf. To the west is the Biltmore Country Club, a richly ornamented beaux arts–style structure with a superb colonnade and courtyard; it was reincorporated into the hotel in 1989. Sunday champagne brunch is a local legend; try to get a

table in the courtyard. Afterward join one of the free tours offered at 1:30, 2:30, and 3:30. ⊠ *1200 Anastasia Ave., near De Soto Blvd., Coral Gables* ☎ *305/445–1926* ⊕ *www.biltmorehotel.com.*

❻ Fairchild Tropical Botanic Garden. With 83 acres of lakes, sunken gardens, a 560-foot vine pergola, orchids, bellflowers, coral trees, bougainvillea, rare palms, and flowering trees, Fairchild is the largest tropical botanical garden in the continental United States. The tram tour highlights the best of South Florida's flora; then you can set off exploring on your own. A 2-acre rain-forest exhibit showcases tropical plants from around the world complete with a waterfall and stream. The conservatory, Windows to the Tropics, is home to rare tropical plants, including the Titan Arum (*Amorphophallus titanum*), a fast-growing variety that attracted thousands of visitors when it bloomed in 1998. (It was only the sixth documented bloom in this country in the 20th century.) The Keys Coastal Habitat, created in a marsh and mangrove area in 1995 with assistance from the Tropical Audubon Society, provides food and shelter to resident and migratory birds. Check out the Montgomery Botanical Center, a research facility devoted to palms and cycads. Spicing up Fairchild's calendar are plant sales, afternoon teas, and genuinely special events year-round, such as the International Mango Festival the second weekend in July. The excellent bookstore–gift shop carries books on gardening and horticulture, and the Garden Café serves sandwiches and, seasonally, smoothies made from the garden's own crop of tropical fruits. ⊠ *10901 Old Cutler Rd., Coral Gables* ☎ *305/667–1651* ⊕ *www.fairchildgarden.org* ✑ *$20* ⊘ *Daily 9:30–5.*

Fodor's Choice ★

❸ Venetian Pool. Sculpted from a rock quarry in 1923 and fed by artesian wells, this 825,000-gallon municipal pool completed a major face-lift in 2010. It remains quite popular because of its themed architecture— a fantasy version of a waterfront Italian village—created by Denman Fink. The pool has earned a place on the National Register of Historic Places and showcases a nice collection of vintage photos depicting 1920s beauty pageants and swank soirees held long ago. Paul Whiteman played here, Johnny Weissmuller and Esther Williams swam here, and you should, too (but no kids under 3). A snack bar, lockers, and showers make this must-see user-friendly as well. ⊠ *2701 De Soto Blvd., at Toledo St., Coral Gables* ☎ *305/460–5356* ⊕ *www.gablesrecreation. com* ✑ *$11 adults, free parking across De Soto Blvd.* ⊘ *June–Aug., weekdays 11–7:30, weekends 10–4:30; Sept., Oct., Apr., and May, Tues.–Fri. 11–5:30, weekends 10–4:30; Nov.–Mar., Tues.–Fri. 10–4:30, weekends 10–4:30.*

Fodor's Choice ★

WORTH NOTING

❷ Coral Gables Congregational Church. With George Merrick as a charter member (he donated the land on which it stands) this parish was organized in 1923. Rumor has it that Merrick built this small church, the first in the Gables, in honor of his father, a congregational minister. The original interior is still in magnificent condition, and a popular concert series is held here every other Thursday evening in the summer. ⊠ *3010 De Soto Blvd., at Anastasia Ave., Coral Gables* ☎ *305/448–7421* ⊕ *www.coralgablescongregational.org* ⊘ *Weekdays 8:30–5, Sun. services at 9 and 11.*

4 Coral Gables Merrick House and Gardens. In 1976 the city of Coral Gables acquired Merrick's boyhood home. Restored to its 1920s appearance, it contains Merrick family furnishings and artwork. The breezy veranda and coral-rock construction are details you'll see repeated on many of the grand homes along Coral Way. ⊠ *907 Coral Way, at Toledo St., Coral Gables* ☎ *305/460–5361* 🖼 *House $5, grounds free* ☉ *House tours Wed. and Sun. at 1, 2, and 3; grounds daily 8–sunset.*

5 Miracle Mile. Even with competition from some impressive malls, this half-mile stretch of retail stores continues to thrive because of its intriguing mixture of unique boutiques, bridal shops, art galleries, charming restaurants, and upscale nightlife venues. ⊠ *Coral Way between SW 37th and SW 42nd Aves., Coral Gables.*

OFF THE BEATEN PATH

Metrozoo. Don't miss a visit to this top-notch zoo, 14 mi south of Miami. The only subtropical zoo in the continental United States, it has 340 acres that are home to more than 2,000 animals, including 40 endangered species, which roam on islands surrounded by moats. Take the monorail ($3 for an all-day pass) for a cool overview, then walk around for a closer look, including the latest attraction Amazon & Beyond, which encompasses 27 acres of simulated tropical rain forests showcasing 600 animals indigenous to the region, such as giant river otters, harpy eagles, anacondas, and jaguars. Other exhibits include Tiger Temple, where white tigers roam, and the African Plains exhibit, where giraffes, ostriches, and zebras graze in a simulated natural habitat. You can even feed veggies to the giraffes at Samburu Station. The Wings of Asia aviary has about 300 exotic birds representing 70 species flying free within the junglelike enclosure. There's also a petting zoo with a meerkat exhibit and interactive opportunities, such as those at Dr. Wilde's World and the Ecology Theater, where kids can touch Florida animals like alligators and opossums. An educational and entertaining wildlife show is given three times daily. ⊠ *12400 Coral Reef Dr. (SW 152nd St.), Richmond Heights, Miami* ☎ *305/251–0400* ⊕ *www.miamimetrozoo. com* 🖼 *$15.95, $11.95 children ages 3 to 12; 45-min tram tour $4.95* ☉ *Daily 9:30–5:30, last admission 4.*

OFF THE BEATEN PATH

Everglades Alligator Farm. Here's your chance to see gators, gators, gators—2,000 or so—and other wildlife such as blue herons, snowy egrets, and perhaps a rare roseate spoonbill. You can also take in alligator wrestling, reptile shows, and other animal exhibits as well as an airboat ride (they're not allowed inside Everglades National Park). This place is a little more than 30 mi south of Miami, just south of the former pioneer town of Homestead. ⊠ *40351 SW 192nd Ave., Florida City* ☎ *305/247–2628* ⊕ *www.everglades.com* 🖼 *$15.50, $23 with airboat tour* ☉ *Daily 9–6.*

COCONUT GROVE

Eclectic and intriguing, Miami's Coconut Grove can be considered the tropical equivalent of New York's Greenwich Village. A haven for writers and artists, the neighborhood has never quite outgrown its image as a small village. During the day it's business as usual in Coconut Grove, much as in any other Miami neighborhood. But in the evening,

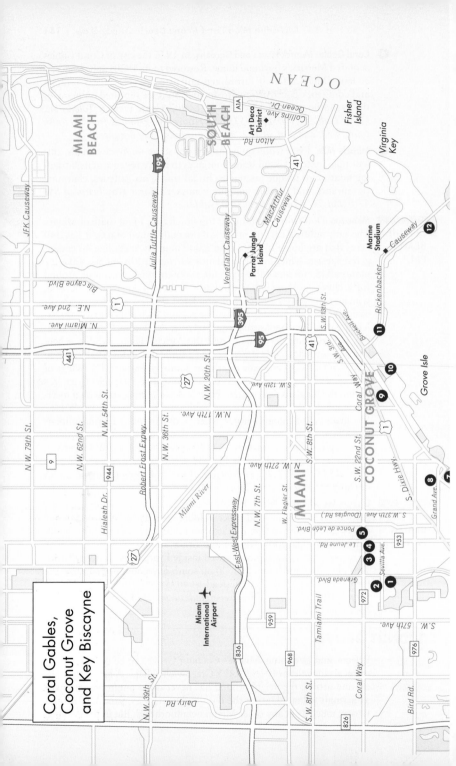

ATLANTIC

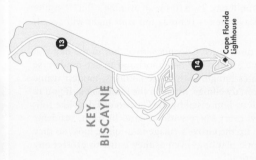

Biscayne Bay

KEY BISCAYNE

● Cape Florida Lighthouse
13
14

CORAL GABLES

Coral Gables

Maynada St.
Sunset Dr.
Ponce de León Rd.
Old Cutler Rd.
Red Rd.
Ponce de León Blvd.
S.W. 72nd St.

Watertus
Cartagena Plaza

SOUTH MIAMI

986

7
6

0   3 miles
0   3 km

especially on weekends, it seems as if someone flips a switch and the streets come alive. Locals and tourists jam into small boutiques, sidewalk cafés, and stores lodged in two massive retail-entertainment complexes. For blocks in every direction, students, honeymooning couples, families, and prosperous retirees flow in and out of a mix of galleries, restaurants, bars, bookstores, comedy clubs, and theaters. With this weekly influx of traffic, parking can pose a problem. There's a well-lighted city garage at 3315 Rice Street, or look for police to direct you to parking lots where you'll pay $5–$10 for an evening's slot. If you're staying in the Grove, leave the car behind, and your night will get off to an easier start.

Nighttime is the right time to see Coconut Grove, but in the day you can take a casual drive around the neighborhood to see its diverse architecture. Posh estates mingle with rustic cottages, modest frame homes, and stark modern dwellings, often on the same block. If you're into horticulture, you'll be impressed by the Garden of Eden–like foliage that seems to grow everywhere without care. In truth, residents are determined to keep up the Grove's village-in-a-jungle look, so they lavish attention on exotic plantings even as they battle to protect any remaining native vegetation.

ESSENTIALS

Visitor Information Coconut Grove Chamber of Commerce (✉ *2820 McFarlane Rd., Coconut Grove, Miami* ☎ *305/444–7270* ⊕ *www.coconutgrovechamber.com).*

EXPLORING

Numbers correspond to the Coral Gables, Coconut Grove, and Key Biscayne map.

❼ Barnacle Historic State Park. A pristine bay-front manse sandwiched between cramped luxury developments, Barnacle is Miami's oldest house still standing on its original foundation. To get here, you'll hike along an old buggy trail through a tropical hardwood hammock and landscaped lawn leading to Biscayne Bay. Built in 1891 by Florida's first snowbird—New Yorker Commodore Ralph Munroe—the large home, built of timber that Munroe salvaged from wrecked ships, has many original furnishings, a broad sloping roof, and deeply recessed verandas that channel sea breezes into the house. If your timing is right, you may catch one of the monthly Moonlight Concerts, and the old-fashioned picnic on the Fourth of July is popular. ✉ *3485 Main Hwy.* ☎ *305/442–6866* ⊕ *www.floridastateparks.org/thebarnacle* 🖱 *$1, concerts $5* ☾ *Fri.–Mon. 9–5; tours at 10, 11:30, 1, and 2:30; group tours for 10 or more Weds. and Thurs. by reservation; concerts Sept.–May on evenings near the full moon 6–9, call for dates.*

❽ CocoWalk. This indoor-outdoor mall has three floors of nearly 40 name-brand (Victoria's Secret, Gap, Banana Republic, etc.) and independent shops that stay open almost as late as its popular restaurants and clubs. Kiosks with beads, incense, herbs, and other small items are scattered around the ground level; street entertainers hold court on weekends; and the movie theaters and nightspots are upstairs. If you're ready for an evening of touristy people-watching, this is the place. ✉ *3015 Grand*

Ave. ☎ *305/444–0777* ⊕ *www.cocowalk.net* ☾ *Sun.–Thurs. 10–10, Fri. and Sat. 10* AM*–11* PM.

⑨ Miami Museum of Science and Planetarium. This small, fun museum is ☺ chock-full of hands-on sound, gravity, and electricity displays for children and adults alike. For animal lovers, its wildlife center houses native Florida snakes, turtles, tortoises, and birds of prey. Check the museum's schedule for traveling exhibits that appear throughout the year. If you're here the first Friday of the month, stick around for a laser-light rock-and-roll show, presented in the planetarium at 9, 10, and 11 PM, or gaze at the planets through two powerful Meade telescopes at the Weintraub Observatory for free. ⊠ *3280 S. Miami Ave.* ☎ *305/646–4200* ⊕ *www. miamisci.org* ⊡ *Museum exhibits, planetarium shows, and wildlife center $14.95, laser show $7* ☾ *Museum daily 10–6.*

⑩ Vizcaya Museum and Gardens. Of the 10,000 people living in Miami
Fodor'sChoice between 1912 and 1916, about 1,000 of them were gainfully employed
★ by Chicago industrialist James Deering to build this European-inspired residence. Once comprising 180 acres, this national historic landmark now occupies a 30-acre tract that includes a native hammock and more than 10 acres of formal gardens with fountains overlooking Biscayne Bay. The house, open to the public, contains 70 rooms, 34 of which are filled with paintings, sculpture, antique furniture, and other fine and decorative arts. The collection spans 2,000 years and represents the Renaissance, baroque, rococo, and neoclassical periods. So unusual and impressive is Vizcaya that visitors have included many major heads of state. Guided tours are available. Moonlight tours, offered on evenings that are nearest the full moon, provide a magical look at the gardens; call for reservations. ⊠ *3251 S. Miami Ave.* ☎ *305/250–9133* ⊕ *www. vizcayamuseum.org* ⊡ *$15* ☾ *Daily 9:30–4:30.*

KEY BISCAYNE AND VIRGINIA KEY

Once upon a time, these barrier islands were an outpost for fishermen and sailors, pirates and salvagers, soldiers and settlers. The 95-foot Cape Florida Lighthouse stood tall during Seminole Indian battles and hurricanes. Coconut plantations covered two-thirds of Key Biscayne, and there were plans as far back as the 1800s to develop the picturesque island as a resort for the wealthy. Fortunately, the state and county governments set much of the land aside for parks, and both keys are now home to top-ranked beaches and golf, tennis, softball, and picnicking facilities. The long and winding bike paths that run through the islands are favorites for in-line skaters and cyclists. Incorporated in 1991, the village of Key Biscayne is a hospitable community of about 10,500; Virginia Key remains undeveloped at the moment, making these two playground islands especially family-friendly.

ESSENTIALS

Visitor Information **Key Biscayne Chamber of Commerce and Visitors Center** (⊠ *88 W. McIntyre St., Suite 100, Key Biscayne* ☎ *305/361–5207* ⊕ *www. keybiscaynechamber.org*).

Not all the fun is for grown-ups. With sandy shores great for kite flying, Miami beaches appeal to kids, too.

EXPLORING

Numbers correspond to the Coral Gables, Coconut Grove, and Key Biscayne map.

14 **Bill Baggs Cape Florida State Park.** Thanks to inviting beaches, sunsets, and a tranquil lighthouse, this park at Key Biscayne's southern tip is worth the drive. It has 19 picnic shelters, and two cafés that serve light lunches. A stroll or ride along walking and bicycle paths provides wonderful views of Miami's dramatic skyline. From the southern end of the park you can see a handful of houses rising over the bay on wooden stilts, the remnants of Stiltsville, built in the 1940s and now protected by the Stiltsville Trust. The nonprofit group was established in 2003 to preserve the structures as they showcase the park's rich history. Bill Baggs has bicycle rentals, a playground, fishing piers, and guided tours of the **Cape Florida Lighthouse,** South Florida's oldest structure. The lighthouse was erected in 1845 to replace an earlier one damaged in an 1836 Seminole attack, in which the keeper's helper was killed. The restored cottage and lighthouse offer free tours at 10 AM and 1 PM Thursday to Monday. Be there a half hour beforehand. ✉ *1200 S. Crandon Blvd., Key Biscayne* ☎ *305/361–5811 or 305/361–8779* ⊕ *www. floridastateparks.org/capeflorida* 💲 *$4 per single-occupant vehicle, $8 per vehicle with 2–8 people; $2 per person on bicycle, bus, motorcycle, or foot* ☉ *Daily 8–dusk, tours Thurs.–Mon. at 10 and 1; sign up 1 hr beforehand (on weekdays you can almost always simply show up shortly before tour time).*

Fodor's Choice ★

⑬ Crandon Park North Beach. This
relaxing oasis in northern Key Biscayne is popular with families, and
many educated beach enthusiasts
rate the 3-mi beach here among
the top 10 beaches in North America. The sand is soft, there are no
riptides, there's a great view of the
Atlantic, and parking is both inex-

WORD OF MOUTH

"Stay in South Beach and take a
drive out to Key Biscayne—you'll
love it!! Nice place to ride bikes."

—JerseySue

pensive and plentiful. The park is dotted with picnic tables and grills,
so it's a weekend favorite of locals often showcasing Miami's a multicultural flavor with salsa and hip-hop, jerk chicken and barbecue ribs.
Crandon Gardens at Crandon Park was once the site of a zoo. There are
swans, waterfowl, and dozens of huge iguanas running loose. Nearby
are a restored carousel (open weekends and major holidays), outdoor
roller rink, and playground. At the north end of the beach is the free
Marjory Stoneman Douglas Biscayne Nature Center (☎ 305/361–6767
⊕ www.biscaynenaturecenter.org ☽ Daily 10–4), where you can explore
sea-grass beds on a tour with a naturalist; see red, black, and white
mangroves; and hike along the beach and hammock in the Bear Cut
Preserve. The park also sponsors hikes and tours. (⇨ Crandon Park in
Beaches section, under Sports and the Outdoors.) ⊠ 4000 Crandon
Blvd., Key Biscayne ☎ 305/361–5421 ⊕ www.biscaynenaturecenter.
org ☞ $5 per vehicle ☽ Daily 8–sunset.

⑫ Miami Seaquarium. This classic family attraction stages shows with sea
lions, dolphins, and Lolita the killer whale. The Crocodile Flats exhibit
has 26 Nile crocodiles. Discovery Bay, an endangered mangrove habitat,
is home to sea turtles, alligators, herons, egrets, and ibis. You can also
visit a shark pool, a tropical reef aquarium, and West Indian and Florida
manatees. But the newest interactive attraction is the Stingray Touch
Tank, where you can touch and feed cownose rays and southern stingrays. Another big draw is the Swim with Our Dolphins program. For
$199, a two-hour session allows you to touch, kiss, and swim with the
gentle marine mammals on the Dolphin Odyssey, $139 ($99 for kids) to
participate in the shallow water Dolphin Encounter. It may seem pricey
but it does include park admission, towel, and a wet suit. Reservations
required. Children 9 and younger pay $10 less. ⊠ 4400 Rickenbacker
Causeway, Virginia Key ☎ 305/361–5705 ⊕ www.miamiseaquarium.
com ☞ $37.95, dolphin swim program $199, parking $8 ☽ Daily 9–6,
last admission 4:30; dolphin swim daily at 9:30 10,11:30, 1, and 2:30;
dolphin encounter daily at 12:15 and 3:15.

⑪ Old Rickenbacker Causeway Bridge. Here you can watch boat traffic pass
through the channel, pelicans and other seabirds soar and dive, and dolphins cavort in the bay. Park at the bridge entrance, about a mile from
the tollgate, and walk past anglers tending their lines to the gap where
the center draw span across the Intracoastal Waterway was removed.
On the right, on cool, clear winter evenings, the water sparkles with
dots of light from hundreds of shrimp boats. ⊠ Rickenbacker Causeway
south of Powell Bridge, east of Coconut Grove.

SPORTS AND THE OUTDOORS

Sun, sand, and crystal-clear water mixed with an almost nonexistent winter and a cosmopolitan clientele make Miami and Miami Beach ideal for year-round sunbathing and outdoor activities. Whether the priority is showing off a toned body, jumping on a Jet Ski, or relaxing in a tranquil natural environment, there's a beach tailor-made to please. But tanning and water sports are only part of this sun-drenched picture. Greater Miami has championship golf courses and tennis courts, miles of bike trails along placid canals and through subtropical forests, and skater-friendly concrete paths amidst the urban jungle. For those who like their sports of the spectator variety, the city offers up a bonanza of pro teams for every season. The Miami Dolphins remain the only NFL team to have ever played a perfect season, the scrappy Florida Marlins took the World Series title in 2003, and the Miami Heat were the 2006 NBA champions. There's even a crazy ball-flinging game called jai alai that's billed as the fastest sport on earth.

In addition to contacting the venues *below* directly, get tickets to major events from **Ticketmaster** (☎ *800/745–3000* ⊕ *www.ticketmaster.com*).

AUTO RACING

★ **Homestead–Miami Speedway.** For NASCAR Nextel Cup events, head south to this famous speedway, which hosts the Ford 400 Nextel Cup Series season finale. The highlight of the speedway schedule, it's held the third Sunday in November in conjunction with the NASCAR Craftsman Truck Series season finale and other races. The speedway, built in 1995 and improved with steeper banking in 2003, is also home to the Toyota Indy 300 IRL season opener each February and other Indy-car racing. ⊠ *1 Speedway Blvd., Exit 6 of Florida's Tpke. (Rte. 821) at SW 137th Ave., Homestead* ☎ *866/409–7223* ⊕ *www.homesteadmiamispeedway. com* ☾ *Weekdays 9–5* 🎫 *Prices vary according to event.*

BASEBALL

☾ **Florida Marlins.** Miami's baseball team won't be playing at Dolphin Stadium much longer. In 2012 it will move into a brand-new stadium on the grounds of Miami's famous Orange Bowl. Go see the team that came out of nowhere to beat the New York Yankees and win the 2003 World Series before they move. Home games are April through early October. ⊠ *Land Shark Stadium, 2267 NW 199th St., 16 mi northwest of Downtown, between I–95 and Florida's Tpke.* ☎ *305/626–7400 or 877/627–5467* ⊕ *www.marlins.com* 🎫 *$9–$315, parking $10.*

BASKETBALL

Miami Heat. The 2006 NBA champs play at the 19,600-seat, waterfront AmericanAirlines Arena. The state-of-the-art venue features restaurants, a wide patio overlooking Biscayne Bay, and a silver sun-shape special-effects scoreboard with rays holding wide-screen TVs. During Heat games, when the 1,100 underground parking spaces are reserved for

MIAMI TOURS

BOAT TOURS

Duck Tours Miami (✉ *1665 Washington Ave., Miami Beach* ☎ *877/382–5849 or 786/276–8300* ⊕ *www.ducktoursmiami.com* ✉ *$32*) uses amphibious vehicles to offer daily 90-minute tours of Miami that combine land and sea views. Comedy and music are part of the mix. Tickets are $18 for children 4–12.

Island Queen, Island Lady, and *Miami Lady* (✉ *401 Biscayne Blvd., Miami* ☎ *305/379–5119* ⊕ *www. islandqueencruises.com* ✉ *$25*) are 140-passenger double-decker tour boats docked at Bayside Marketplace. Daily 90-minute narrated tours of the Port of Miami and Millionaires' Row cost of $17 for those 11 and under.

For something a little more private and luxe, **RA Charters** (☎ *305/666–7979 or 305/989–3959* ⊕ *www. racharters.com* ✉ *Call for prices*) sails out of the Dinner Key Marina in Coconut Grove. Full- and half-day charters include sailing lessons, with occasional extended trips to the Florida Keys. For a romantic night, have Captain Masoud pack some gourmet fare and sail sunset to moonlight while you enjoy Biscayne Bay's spectacular skyline view of Miami.

WALKING TOURS

Operated by the Miami Design Preservation League, the **Art Deco District Tour** (✉ *1001 Ocean Dr., South Beach, Miami Beach* ☎ *305/531–3484* ⊕ *www.mdpl.org* ✉ *$20 guided tour, $15 audio tour*) is a 90-minute guided walking tour that departs from the league's welcome center at Ocean Drive and 10th Street. It starts at 10:30 AM Friday through Wednesday, and at 6:30 PM Thursday. Alternatively, you can go at your own pace with the league's self-guided audio tour, which takes roughly an hour and a half.

season-ticket holders, you can park across the street at Miami's Bayside Marketplace ($20), at metered spaces along Biscayne Boulevard, or in lots on side streets, where prices range from $5 to $25, depending on the distance from the arena (a limited number of spaces for people with disabilities are available on-site for non-season-ticket holders). Better yet, take the Metromover to the Park West or Freedom Tower station. Home games are held November through April. ✉ *AmericanAirlines Arena, 601 Biscayne Blvd., Downtown* ☎ *786/777–4328, 800/462–2849 ticket hotline* ⊕ *www.nba.com/heat* ✉ *$10–$425.*

BEACHES

MIAMI BEACH

NORTH MIAMI BEACH

Haulover Beach Park. This popular clothing-optional beach is embraced by naturists of all ages, shapes, and sizes. Once you park in the North Lot, you'll walk through a short tunnel covered with trees and natural habitat until you emerge on the unpretentious beach, where nudity is rarely met by gawkers. There are volleyball nets, and plenty of beach chair and umbrella rentals to protect your birthday suit from too much exposure—to the sun, that is. The sections of beach requiring swimwear are popular, too, given the park's ample parking and relaxed atmosphere. Lifeguards stand watch. More active types might want to check out the kite rentals, charter-fishing excursions, and a par-3, nine-hole golf course. ⊠ *10800 Collins Ave., north of Bal Harbour in Sunny Isles* ☎ *305/947–3525* ⊿ *$6 per vehicle* ☉ *Daily sunrise–sunset.*

☃ ★ **Oleta River State Park.** Tucked away in North Miami Beach is a ready-made family getaway. Nature lovers will find it easy to embrace the 1,128 acres of subtropical beauty along Biscayne Bay. Swim in the calm bay waters and bicycle, canoe, kayak, and bask among egrets, manatees, bald eagles, and fiddler crabs. Dozens of picnic tables, along with 10 covered pavilions, dot the stunning natural habitat, which has recently been restored with red mangroves to revitalize the ecosystem and draw endangered birds, like the roseate spoonbill. There's a playground for tots, a mangrove island accessible only by boat, 15 mi of mountain-bike trails, a half-mile exercise track, concessions, and outdoor showers. If you want to continue the nature adventure into the evening, then reserve an overnight stay in minimalist (but still air-conditioned) cabins, which run $62.15 per night. ⊠ *3400 NE 163rd St., North Miami Beach* ☎ *305/919–1844* ⊕ *www.floridastateparks. org/oletariver* ⊿ *$1 per person on foot or bike; $3 for single-occupant vehicle; $5 per vehicle up to 8 people; $1 each additional. Free entrance if renting a cabin.* ☉ *Daily 8–sunset.*

Surfside Beach. *Parlez-vous français?* If the answer is "*Oui,*" you'll feel quite comfortable at this serene stretch of beach, which draws many French Canadian snowbird tourists who come to thaw out from the winter here. ⊠ *Collins Ave. between 88th and 96th Sts., Surfside.*

SOUTH BEACH
Fodor's Choice
★

The 10-block stretch of white sandy beach hugging the turquoise waters along **Ocean Drive**—from 5th to 15th streets—is one of the most popular in America, known for drawing unabashedly modelesque sunbathers and posers. The beaches crowd quickly on the weekends with a blend of European tourists, young hipsters, and sun-drenched locals offering Latin flavor. Separating the sand from the traffic of Ocean Drive is palm-fringed Lummus Park, with its volleyball nets and chickee huts (huts made of palmetto thatch over a cypress frame) for shade. The beach at 12th Street is popular with gays, a section often marked with rainbow flags. Locals hang out on 3rd Street beach, where they watch fit Brazilians play foot volley, a variation of volleyball that uses everything but the hands. Because much of South Beach leans toward skimpy sunning—women are often in G-strings and casually topless—many families prefer the tamer sections of Mid- and North Beach. Metered parking spots next to the ocean are a rare find. Instead, opt for a public garage a few blocks away and enjoy the people-watching as you walk to find your perfect spot on the sand. ⊠ *Ocean Dr., between 1st and 22nd Sts., Miami Beach* ☎ *305/673–7714.*

KEY BISCAYNE AND VIRGINIA KEY

Fodor's Choice
★

Bill Baggs Cape Florida State Park. The picturesque drive down to the southern tip of Key Biscayne is only a hint of the natural beauty you will find when exploring this 410-acre park. For swimmers, the beach here is frequently ranked among the top 10 in North America by the

University of Maryland's esteemed sandman, Dr. Beach. Families often picnic here, choosing the shade under any of the 19 shelters. For active wanderers, explore the nature trails, try your hand at the fishing piers, or take a breezy bike ride along paths that offer breathtaking views of the bay and Miami's skyline. History buffs can enjoy guided tours of the Cape Florida Lighthouse, South Florida's oldest structure. ⊠ *1200 S. Crandon Blvd., Key Biscayne* ☎ *305/361–5811 or 305/361–8779* ⊿ *$2 per person on foot, bike, motorbike, or bus; $8 per vehicle with 2 to 8 people* ☉ *Daily 8–sunset, lighthouse tours Thurs.–Mon. 10 and 1.*

☾ ★ **Crandon Park North Beach.** The 3-mi sliver of beach paradise is dotted with palm trees to provide a respite from the steamy sun, until it's time to take a dip in the clear-blue waters. On weekends, be prepared for a long hike from your car to the beach. There are bathrooms, outdoor showers, plenty of picnic tables, and concession stands. The family-friendly park offers abundant options for kids who find it challenging to simply sit and build sand castles. There are marine-theme play sculptures, a dolphin-shaped spray fountain, an old-fashioned outdoor roller rink, and a restored carousel (it's open weekends and major holidays 10–5, until 6 in summer, and you get three rides for $1). (⇨ *Crandon Park in Exploring section for more on the park.*) ⊠ *4000 Crandon Blvd., Key Biscayne* ☎ *305/361–5421* ⊿ *$5 per vehicle* ☉ *Daily 8–sunset.*

BICYCLING

Perfect weather and flat terrain make Miami-Dade County a popular place for cyclists; however, biking here can also be quite dangerous. Be very vigilant when biking on Miami Beach, or better yet, steer clear and bike the beautiful paths of Key Biscayne.

Key Cycling (⊠ *328 Crandon Blvd., Key Biscayne* ☎ *305/361–0061* ⊕ *www.keycycling.com*) rents bikes for $15 for two hours, $24 for the day, and $80 for the week.

BOATING AND SAILING

Boating, whether on sailboats, powerboats, luxury yachts, Wave Runners, or Windsurfers, is a passion in greater Miami. The Intracoastal Waterway, wide and sheltered Biscayne Bay, and the Atlantic Ocean provide ample opportunities for fun aboard all types of watercraft.

The best windsurfing spots are on the north side of the Rickenbacker Causeway at Virginia Key Beach or to the south at, go figure, Windsurfer Beach. Kitesurfing adds another level to the water-sports craze. The shallow waters off the parking lot in Matheson Hammock Park are like catnip for local kiteboarders. They also blast off from 87th Street in Miami Beach at North Shore Open Space Park.

MARINAS

Haulover Marine Center (⊠ *15000 Collins Ave., north of Bal Harbour, Miami Beach* ☎ *305/945–3934* ⊕ *www.haulovermarinecenter.net*), which has a bait-and-tackle shop and a 24-hour marine gas station, is low on glamour but high on service.

Near the Art Deco district, **Miami Beach Marina** (⊠ *MacArthur Causeway, 300 Alton Rd., Miami Beach* ☎ *305/673–6000* ⊕ *www. miamibeachmarina.com*) has plenty to entice sailors and landlubbers alike: restaurants, charters, boat rentals, a complete marine-hardware store, a dive shop, excursion vendors, a large grocery store, a fuel dock, concierge services, and 400 slips accommodating vessels of up to 250 feet. There's also a U.S. Customs clearing station and a charter service, Florida Yacht Charters. Picnic tables along the docks make this marina especially visitor-friendly.

Busy **Bayshore Landing Marina** (⊠ *2560 S. Bayshore Dr., Coconut Grove* ☎ *305/854–7997*) is home to a lively seafood restaurant that's good for viewing the nautical eye candy.

OUTFITTERS AND EXPEDITIONS

You can rent 18- to 68-foot powerboats through **Club Nautico** (⊠ *Miami Beach Marina, 300 Alton Road, #112, Miami Beach* ☎ *305/673–2502* ⊕ *www.clubnauticousa.com* ⊠ *Crandon Park Marina, 5400 Crandon Blvd., Key Biscayne* ☎ *305/361–9217*), a national powerboat-rental company. You can also get a 100-foot powerboat, but make sure to call a week in advance. Half- to full-day rentals range from $200 to $699. You may want to consider buying a club membership; it'll cost a bundle at first, but you'll save about 50% on all your future rentals.

Playtime Watersports (⊠ *Collins Ave., Miami Beach* ☎ *786/234–0184* ⊕ *www.playtimewatersport.com* ⊠ *Eden Roc, 4525 Collins Ave.* ⊠ *Miami Beach Resort and Spa, 4833 Collins Ave.* ⊠ *Ritz-Carlton, 455 Grand Bay Dr.* ⊠ *Alexander Hotel, 5225 Collins Ave.*) sells and rents high-end water-sports equipment, including Wave Runners and wind-driven devices. n addition to renting equipment, the friendly folks at **Sailboards Miami** (⊠ *Site E1 Rickenbacker Causeway, Key Biscayne* ☎ *305/361–7245* ⊕ *www.sailboardsmiami.com*) say they teach more windsurfers each year than anyone in the United States, and promise to teach you to windsurf within two hours—for $69. Rentals average $30 for the first hour and $25 for each additional hour.

FOOTBALL

Fodor's Choice
★   The **Miami Dolphins** have one of the largest average attendance figures in the league. September through January, on home-game days the Metro Miami-Dade Transit Agency runs buses to the stadium. ⊠ *Dolphin Stadium, 2267 NW 199th St., 16 mi northwest of Downtown, between I–95 and Florida's Tpke.* ☎ *305/620–2578* ⊕ *www.miamidolphins.com.*

GOLF

Greater Miami has more than 30 private and public courses. Costs at most courses are higher on weekends and in season, but you can save by playing on weekdays and after 1 or 3 PM, depending on the course—call ahead to find out when afternoon-twilight rates go into effect. For information on most courses in Miami and throughout Florida, you can visit ⊕ *www.floridagolferguide.com.* The 18-hole, par-71 championship **Biltmore Golf Course** (⊠ *1210 Anastasia Ave., Coral Gables*

Continued on page 168

A STROLL DOWN

DECO LANE

by Susan MacCallum Whitcomb

"It was an age of miracles, it was an age of art,

it was an age of excess, and it was an age of satire."

—F. Scott Fitzgerald, *Echoes of the Jazz Age*

The 1920s and '30s brought us flappers and gangsters, plunging stock prices and soaring skyscrapers, and plenty of headline-worthy news from the arts scene, from talking pictures and the jazz craze to fashions where pearls piled on and sequins dazzled. These decades between the two world wars also gave us an art style reflective of the changing times: art deco.

Distinguished by geometrical shapes and the use of industrial motifs that fused the decorative arts with modern technology, art deco became the architectural style of choice for train stations and big buildings across the country (think New york's Radio City Music Hall and Empire State Building).

Using a steel-and-concrete box as the foundation, architects dipped into art deco's grab bag of accessories, initially decorating facades with spheres, cylinders, and cubes. They later borrowed increasingly from industrial design, stripping elements used in ocean liners and automobiles to their streamlined essentials.

The style was also used in jewelry, furniture, textiles, and advertising. The fact that it employed inexpensive materials, such as stucco or terrazzo, helped art deco thrive during the Great Depression.

MIAMI BEACH'S ART DECO DISTRICT

With its warm beaches and tropical surroundings, Miami Beach in the early 20th century was establishing itself as America's winter playground. During the roaring '20s luxurious hostelries resembling Venetian palaces, Spanish villages, and French châteaux sprouted up. In the 1930s, middle-class tourists started coming, and more hotels had to be built. Designers like Henry Hohauser chose Art Deco for its affordable yet distinctive design.

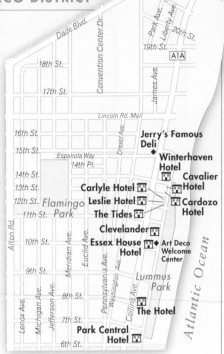

An antidote to the gloom of the Great Depression, the look was cheerful and tidy. And with the whimsical additions of portholes, colorful racing bands, and images of rolling ocean waves painted or etched on the walls, these South Beach properties created an oceanfront fantasy world for travelers.

Many of the candy-colored hotels have survived and been restored. They are among the more than 800 buildings of historical significance in South Beach's art deco district. Composing much of South Beach, the 1-square-mi district is bounded by Dade Boulevard on the north, the Atlantic Ocean on the east, 6th Street on the south, and Alton Road on the west.

Because the district as a whole was developed so rapidly and designed by like-minded architects—**Henry Hohauser, L. Murray Dixon, Albert Anis,** and their colleagues—it has amazing stylistic unity. Nevertheless, on this single street you can trace the evolution of period form from angular, vertically emphatic early deco to aerodynamically rounded Streamline Moderne. The relatively severe Cavalier and more curvaceous Cardozo are fine examples of the former and latter, respectively.

To explore the district, begin by loading up on literature in the **Art Deco Welcome Center** (✉ *1001 Ocean Dr.* ☎ *305/531–3484* ⊕ *www.mdpl.org*). If you want to view these historic properties on your own, just start walking. A four-block stroll north on Ocean Drive gets you up close to camera-ready classics: the **Clevelander** (1020), the **Tides** (1220), the **Leslie** (1244), the **Carlyle** (1250), the **Cardozo** (1300), the **Cavalier** (1320), and the **Winterhaven** (1400).

ART DECO TOURS

See the bold looks of classic Art Deco architecture along Ocean Drive.

SELF-GUIDED AUDIO TOURS

Expert insight on the architecture and the area's history is yours on the Miami Design Preservation League's (MDPL) 90-minute self-guided walks that use an iPod or cell phone and include a companion map. You can pick up the iPod version and companion map at the Art Deco Welcome Center from 9:30 AM to 5 PM daily; the cost is $15. The cell-phone option ($10) is available anytime by calling 786/312–1229 and charging the amount to your credit card; your payment allows you access to audio commentary for up to 24 hours after purchase.

WALKING TOURS

The MDPL's 90-minute "Ocean Drive and Beyond" group walking tour gives you a guided look at area icons, inside and out. (A number of interiors are on the itinerary, so it's a good chance to peek inside spots that might otherwise seem off-limits.) Morning tours depart at 10:30 AM from the Art Deco Welcome Center Gift Shop on Tuesday, Wednesday, Friday, Saturday, and Sunday. An evening tour departs at 6:30 PM on Thursdays. Reservations can't be made in advance, so arrive 15–20 minutes early to buy tickets ($20).

Celebrate the 1930s during Art Deco Weekend.

BIKE TOURS

Rather ride than walk? Three-hour cycling tours of the city's art deco history are organized daily for groups (5 or more) by **South Beach Bike Tours** (☎ *305/673–2002*⊕ *www.southbeach-biketours.com*). The $59 cost includes equipment, snacks, and water.

ART DECO WEEKEND

Tours, lectures, film screenings, and dozens of other '30s-themed events are on tap every January, during the annual **Art Deco Weekend** (☎ *305/672–2014*, ⊕ *www.ArtDecoWeekend. com*). Festivities—many of them free—kick off with a Saturday morning parade and culminate in a street fair. More than a quarter of a million people join in the action, which centers on Ocean Drive between 5th and 15th streets. The 2011 dates are Jan. 14–16.

ARCHITECTURAL HIGHLIGHTS

FRIEZE DETAIL, CAVALIER HOTEL

The decorative stucco friezes outside the Cavalier Hotel at 1320 Ocean Drive are significant for more than aesthetic reasons. Roy France used them to add symmetry (adhering to the "Rule of Three") and accentuate the hotel's verticality by drawing the eye upward. The pattern he chose also reflected a fascination with ancient civilizations engendered by the recent rediscovery of King Tut's tomb and the Chichén Itzá temples.

Cavalier Hotel

LOBBY FLOOR, PARK CENTRAL HOTEL

Terrazzo—a compound of cement and stone chips that could be poured, then polished—is a hallmark of deco design. Terrazzo floors typically had a geometric pattern, like this one in the Park Central Hotel, a 1937 building by Henry Hohauser at 640 Ocean Drive.

Park Central Hotel

CORNER FACADE, ESSEX HOUSE HOTEL

Essex House Hotel, a 1938 gem that appears permanently anchored at 1001 Collins Avenue, is a stunning example of Maritime deco (also known as Nautical Moderne). Designed by Henry Hohauser to evoke an ocean liner, the hotel is rife with marine elements, from the rows of porthole-style windows and natty racing stripes to the towering smokestack-like sign. With a prow angled proudly into the street corner, it seems ready to steam out to sea.

Essex House Hotel

NEON SPIRE, THE HOTEL

The name spelled vertically in eye-popping neon on the venue's iconic aluminum spire—Tiffany—bears evidence of the hotel's earlier incarnation. When the L. Murray Dixon–designed Tiffany Hotel was erected at 801 Collins Avenue in 1939, neon was still a novelty. Its use, coupled with the spire's rocket-like shape, combined to create a futuristic look influenced by the sci-fi themes then pervasive in popular culture.

The Hotel

ENTRANCE, JERRY'S FAMOUS DELI

Inspired by everything from car fenders to airplane noses, proponents of art deco's Streamline Moderne look began to soften buildings' hitherto boxy edges. But when Henry Hohauser designed Hoffman's Cafeteria in 1940 he took moderne to the max. The landmark at 1450 Collins Avenue (now Jerry's Famous Deli) has a sleek, splendidly curved facade. The restored interior echoes it through semicircular booths and rounded chair backs.

Jerry's Famous Deli

ARCHITECTURAL TERMS

The Rule of Three: Early deco designers often used architectural elements in multiples of three, creating tripartite facades with triple sets of windows, eyebrows, or banding.

Eyebrows: Small shelf-like ledges that protruded over exterior windows were used to simultaneously provide much-needed shade and serve as a counterpoint to a building's strong vertical lines.

Tropical Motifs: In keeping with the setting, premises were plastered, painted, or etched with seaside images. Palm trees, sunbursts, waves, flamingoes, and the like were particularly common.

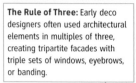

Banding: Enhancing the illusion that these immobile structures were rapidly speeding objects, colorful horizontal bands (also called "racing stripes") were painted on exteriors or applied with tile.

Stripped Classic: The most austere version of art deco (sometimes dubbed Depression Moderne) was used for buildings commissioned by the Public Works Administration.

(top) Hotel Marlin; (left) Sherbrooke Hotel; (right) U.S. Post Office in Miami Beach.

4

IN FOCUS A STROLL DOWN DECO LANE

☏ *305/460–5364*), known for its scenic layout, has been restored to its original Donald Ross design, circa 1925. Greens fees in season range from $145 to $165 for nonresidents. The optional cart is $27. Overlooking the bay, the **Crandon Golf Course** (⊠ *6700 Crandon Blvd., Key Biscayne* ☏ *305/361–9129* ⊕ *www.crandongolfclub.com*) is a top-rated 18-hole, par-72 public course in a beautiful tropical setting. Expect to pay $160 for a round in winter, $63.50 in summer, cart included. Twilight rates from $40 apply after 3 PM. **Don Shula's Hotel & Golf Club** (⊠ *7601 Miami Lakes Dr., 154th St. Exit off Rte. 826, Miami Lakes* ☏ *305/820–8106* ⊕ *www.donshulahotel.com*), in northern Miami, has one of the longest championship courses in the area (7,055 yards, par 72), a lighted par-3 course, and a golf school. Greens fees are $134–$175, depending on the season. Hotel guests get discounted rates. You'll pay in the lower range on weekdays, more on weekends, and $45 after 3 PM. Golf carts are included. The par-3 course is $12 weekdays, $15 weekends. The club hosts more than 75 tournaments a year.

Among its five courses and many annual tournaments, the **Doral Golf Resort and Spa** (⊠ *4400 NW 87th Ave., 36th St. Exit off Rte. 826, Doral, Miami* ☏ *305/592–2000 or 800/713–6725* ⊕ *www.doralresort.com*), just west of Miami proper, is best known for the par-72 Blue Monster course and the PGA's annual World Golf Championship. (The week of festivities planned around this tournament, which offers $8 million in prize money, brings hordes of pro-golf aficionados in late March.) Greens fees range from $95 to $325. Carts are not required. it the links in the heart of South Beach at the lovely 18-hole, par-72 **Miami Beach Golf Club** (⊠ *2301 Alton Rd., Miami Beach* ☏ *305/532–3350* ⊕ *www. miamibeachgolfclub.com*). Greens fees are $125 in summer, $200 in winter, including mandatory cart.

IN-LINE SKATING

Miami Beach's ocean vistas, wide sidewalks, and flat terrain make it a perfect locale for in-line skating—and don't the locals know it. Very popular is the **Lincoln Road Mall** from Washington Avenue to Alton Road; many of the restaurants along this pedestrian mall have outdoor seating where you can eat without shedding your skates. For a great view of the Art Deco district and action on South Beach, skate along the sidewalk on the east side of **Ocean Drive** from 5th to 14th streets. In South Miami an often-traversed concrete path winds **under the elevated Metrorail** from Vizcaya Station (across U.S. 1 from the Miami Museum of Science) to Red Road at U.S. 1 (across from the Shops at Sunset Place). You don't have to bring your own; a number of in-line skate shops offer rentals that include protective gear.

OUTFITTER

Fritz's Bike, Skate and Surf (⊠ *1620 Washington Ave., Miami Beach* ☏ *305/532–1954* ⊕ *www.fritzsmiamibeach.com* ☉ *Daily 10–10*) charges $10 an hour or $24 for 24 hours, which includes a helmet. A deposit of $100 is required.

For locals, the beach scene is often incorporated into daily life, from getting exercise to walking the dog.

SCUBA DIVING AND SNORKELING

Diving and snorkeling on the offshore coral wrecks and reefs on a calm day can be comparable to the Caribbean. Chances are excellent you'll come face-to-face with a flood of tropical fish. One option is to find Fowey, Triumph, Long, and Emerald reefs in 10- to 15-foot dives that are perfect for snorkelers and beginning divers. On the edge of the continental shelf a little more than 3 mi out, these reefs are just ¼ mi away from depths greater than 100 feet. Another option is to paddle around the tangled prop roots of the mangrove trees that line the coast, peering at the fish, crabs, and other creatures hiding there.

It's a bit of a drive, but the best diving and definitely the best snorkeling to be had in Miami-Dade is on the incredible living coral reefs in **Biscayne Underwater Park** (⊠ *9710 SW 328th St., Exit 6 of Florida's Tpke., Homestead* ☎ *305/230–1100* ⊕ *www.nps.gov/bisc*), in the rural southeast corner of the county. With 95% of its 173,000 acres underwater, this is the national-park system's largest marine park. The huge park includes the northernmost islands of the Florida Keys and the beginning of the world's third-longest coral reef. Guided snorkeling and scuba trips, offered from the concession near the visitor center, cost $35.95 for a three-hour snorkel trip (daily 1:30–4:30), including equipment, and $54 for a four-hour, two-tank dive trip (weekends 8:30–1). Scuba equipment is available for rent. ⇨ *See the Everglades chapter for more on Homestead.*

Perhaps the area's most unusual diving options are its **artificial reefs** (⊠ *1920 Meridian Ave., Miami Beach* ☎ *305/672–1270*). Since 1981,

Miami-Dade County's Department of Environmental Resources Management has sunk tons of limestone boulders and a water tower, army tanks, and almost 200 boats of all descriptions to create a "wreck-reational" habitat where divers can swim with yellow tang, barracudas, nurse sharks, snapper, eels, and grouper. Most dive shops sell a book listing the locations of these wrecks. Information on wreck diving can be obtained from the Miami Beach Chamber of Commerce.

Divers Paradise of Key Biscayne (⊠ *5400 Crandon Blvd., Key Biscayne* ☎ *305/361–3483* ⊕ *www.keydivers.com*) has a complete dive shop and diving-charter service next to the Crandon Park Marina, including equipment rental and scuba instruction with PADI and NAUI affiliation. Dive trips are offered Tuesday through Friday at 10 and 1, weekends 8:30 and 1:30. The trip is $60. **South Beach Dive and Surf Center** (⊠ *850 Washington Ave., Miami Beach* ☎ *305/531–6110* ⊕ *www.southbeach-divers.com*), an all-purpose dive shop with PADI affiliation, runs dives with instructors on Tuesday, Thursday, and Saturday at 10 AM, night dives on Wednesday at 5 PM, and wreck and reef dives on Sunday at 11:45 AM. The center also runs dives in Key Largo's Spiegel Grove, the second-largest wreck ever to be sunk for the intention of recreational diving, and in the Neptune Memorial Reef, inspired by the city of Atlantis and created in part using the ashes of cremated bodies. Boats depart from marinas in Miami Beach and Key Largo, in the Florida Keys.

SHOPPING

Miami teems with sophisticated shopping malls and the bustling avenues of commercial neighborhoods. But this is also a city of tiny boutiques tucked away on side streets—such as South Miami's Red, Bird, and Sunset roads intersection—and outdoor markets touting unusual and delicious wares. Stroll through Spanish-speaking neighborhoods where shops sell clothing, cigars, and other goods from all over Latin America. At an open-air flea-market stall, score an antique glass shaped like a palm tree and fill it with some fresh Jamaican ginger beer from the table next door. Or stop by your hotel gift shop and snap up an alligator magnet for your refrigerator, an ashtray made of seashells, or a bag of gumballs shaped like Florida oranges. Who can resist?

MALLS

People fly to Miami from all over the world just to shop, and the malls are high on their list of spending spots. Stop off at one or two of these climate-controlled temples to consumerism, many of which double as mega-entertainment centers, and you'll understand what makes Miami such a vibrant shopping destination.

Fodor's Choice ★ **Bal Harbour Shops.** Local and international shoppers flock to this swank collection of 100 high-end shops, boutiques, and department stores, which include such names as Christian Dior, Gucci, Hermès, Salvatore Ferragamo, Tiffany & Co., and Valentino. Many European designers open their first North American signature store at this outdoor, pedestrian-friendly mall, and many American designers open their first boutique outside of New York here. Restaurants and cafés, in tropical garden settings, overflow with style-conscious diners. People-watching at outdoor café Carpaccio is the best in town. ✉ *9700 Collins Ave., Bal Harbour* ☎ *305/866–0311* ⊕ *www.balharbourshops.com.*

CocoWalk. This popular three-story outdoor mall is busier than ever after a beautiful renovation. Chain stores like Victoria's Secret and Gap blend with specialty shops like Koko & Palenki and Edward Beiner, blending the bustle of a mall with the breathability of an open-air venue. Kiosks with cigars, beads, incense, herbs, and other small items are scattered around the ground level, and restaurants and nightlife (Cheesecake Factory, Fat Tuesday, and a 16-screen AMC theater, to name a few) line the upstairs perimeter. Hanging out and people-watching is something of a pastime here. The stores stay open almost as late as the popular restaurants and clubs. ✉ *3015 Grand Ave., Coconut Grove, Miami* ☎ *305/444–0777* ⊕ *www.cocowalk.net.*

Fodor's Choice
★ **Village of Merrick Park.** At this Mediterranean-style shopping and dining venue Neiman Marcus and Nordstrom anchor 115 specialty shops. Designers such as Etro, Tiffany & Co., Burberry, Carolina Herrera, and Gucci fulfill most high-fashion needs, and Brazilian contemporary-furniture designer Artefacto provides a taste of the haute-decor shopping options. International food venues like C'est Bon and a day spa, Elemis, offer further indulgences. ✉ *358 San Lorenzo Ave., Coral Gables* ☎ *305/529–0200* ⊕ *www.villageofmerrickpark.com.*

SHOPPING DISTRICTS

If you're over the climate-controlled slickness of shopping malls and can't face one more food-court "meal," you've got choices in Miami. Head out into the sunshine and shop the city streets, where you'll find big-name retailers and local boutiques alike. Take a break at a sidewalk café to power up on some Cuban coffee or fresh-squeezed OJ and enjoy the tropical breezes.

DOWNTOWN MIAMI

★ Miami is synonymous with good design, and this visitor-friendly shopping district is an unprecedented melding of public space and the exclusive world of design. Covering a few city blocks around NE 2nd Avenue and NE 40th Street, the **Miami Design District** (⊕ *www.miamidesigndistrict.net*) contains more than 200 showrooms and galleries, including Kartell, Ann Sacks, Poliform, and Luminaire. Recent openings of Michael's Genuine Food & Drink and Domo Japones sushi also make this trendy neighborhood a hip place to dine. Unlike most showrooms, which are typically the beat of decorators alone, the Miami Design District's showrooms are open to the public and occupy windowed, street-level spaces. Bring your quarters, as all of the parking is on the street and metered. The neighborhood even has its own high school (of art and design, of course) and hosts street parties and gallery walks. Although in many cases you'll need a decorator to secure your purchases, browsers are encouraged to consider for themselves the array of rather exclusive furnishings, decorative objects, antiques, and art.

MIAMI BEACH

★ Give your plastic a workout in South Beach shopping at the many high-profile tenants on this densely packed two-block stretch of **Collins Avenue between 5th and 10th streets.** Think Club Monaco, M.A.C, Kenneth Cole, Barney's Co-Op, and A/X Armani Exchange. Sprinkled among the upscale vendors are hair salons, spas, cafés, and such familiar stores as the Gap, Urban Outfitters, and Banana Republic. Be sure to head over one street east and west to catch the shopping on Ocean Drive and Washington Avenue.

Fodor'sChoice The eight-block-long pedestrian **Lincoln Road Mall** is the trendiest place
★ on Miami Beach. Home to more than 150 shops, 20-plus art galleries and nightclubs, about 50 restaurants and cafés, and the renovated Colony Theatre, Lincoln Road, between Alton Road and Washington Avenue, is like the larger, more sophisticated cousin of Ocean Drive. The see-and-be-seen theme is furthered by outdoor seating at every restaurant, where well-heeled patrons lounge and discuss the people (and pet) parade passing by. An 18-screen movie theater anchors the west end of the street, which is where most of the worthwhile shops are; the far east end is mostly discount and electronics shops. Sure, there's a Pottery Barn, a Gap, and a Williams-Sonoma, but the emphasis is on emporiums with unique personalities, like En Avance, Chroma, Base, and Jonathan Adler.

DOWNTOWN CORAL GABLES

Lined with trees and busy with strolling shoppers, **Miracle Mile** is the centerpiece of the downtown Coral Gables shopping district (⊕ *www. shopcoralgables.com*), which is home to men's and women's boutiques, jewelry and home-furnishings stores, and a host of exclusive couturiers and bridal shops. Running from Douglas Road to LeJeune Road and Aragon Avenue to Andalusia Avenue, more than 30 first-rate restaurants offer everything from French to Indian cuisine, and art galleries and the Actors' Playhouse give the area a cultural flair.

SPECIALTY STORES

Beyond the shopping malls and the big-name retailers, Greater Miami has all manner of merchandise to tempt even the casual browser. For consumers on a mission to find certain items—art deco antiques or cigars, for instance—the city streets burst with a rewarding collection of specialty shops.

ANTIQUES

★ **Architectural Antiques** (✉ *2520 SW 28th La., Coconut Grove* ☎ *305/285–1330* ⊕ *www.miamiantique.com*) carries an enormous selection of antique lighting, as well as large and eclectic items—railroad crossing signs, statues, English roadsters. There's also antique furniture, paintings, and silverware, all in a cluttered setting that makes shopping an adventure.

Artisan Antiques Art Deco (✉ *110 NE 40th St., Miami Design District* ☎ *305/573–5619*) purveys china, crystal, mirrors, and armoires from the French–art deco period, but an assortment of 1930s radiator covers, which can double as funky sideboards, is what's really neat here. The shop is open Monday through Friday.

★ **Senzatempo** (✉ *1680 Michigan Ave., Suite 1015, South Beach, Miami Beach* ☎ *305/534–5588* ⊕ *www.senzatempo.com*), once a popular showroom, is now a warehouse, but buyers can stop in its Lincoln Road area offices to place orders for great vintage home accessories by European and American designers of the 1930s through the 1970s, including electric fans, klieg lights, and chrome furniture.

Valerio Antiques (✉ *250 Valencia Ave., Coral Gables* ☎ *305/448–6779*) carries fine French art deco furniture, bronze sculptures, shagreen boxes, and original art glass by Gallé and Loetz, among others.

BEAUTY

Fodor'sChoice **Brownes & Co.** (✉ *841 Lincoln Rd., Miami Beach* ☎ *305/532–8703*
★ ⊕ *www.brownesbeauty.com*) provides luxurious products to those who appreciate them the most. Cosmetics include Molton Brown, Nars, Le Clerc, and others. It also sells herbal remedies and upscale hair and body products from Bumble and bumble. Just try to resist something from the collection of French, Portuguese, and Italian soaps in various scents and sizes. A popular in-house salon, **Some Like It Hot** (☎ *305/538–7544*), offers some of the best waxing in town.

BOOKS

Fodor'sChoice **Books & Books, Inc.** (✉ *265 Aragon Ave., Coral Gables* ☎ *305/442–4408*
★ ✉ *927 Lincoln Rd., Miami Beach* ☎ *305/532–3222* ✉ *9700 Collins Ave., Bal Harbour* ☎ *305/864–4241*), Greater Miami's only independent English-language bookshops, specialize in contemporary and classical literature as well as in books on the arts, architecture, Florida, and Cuba. At any of its three locations you can lounge at a café or, at the Coral Gables store, browse the photography gallery. All stores host regular poetry and other readings.

CIGARS

El Credito Cigars (✉ *1106 SW 8th St., Little Havana* ☎ *305/858–4162*), in the heart of Little Havana, employs rows of workers at wooden benches. They rip, cut, and wrap giant tobacco leaves, and press the cigars in vises. El Credito cigars are known for their good quality and relatively low price. Dedicated smokers find their way here to pick up a $90 bundle or to peruse the *gigantes*, *supremos*, *panatelas*, and Churchills available in natural or *maduro* wrappers. **Sabor Havana Cigars** (✉ *2309 Ponce de León Blvd, Coral Gables* ☎ *305/444–1764* ⊕ *www.saborhavanacigar.com*) offers rare cigars and Spanish wine to help you relax. **Sosa Family Cigars** (✉ *3475 SW 8th St., Little Havana* ☎ *305/446–2606*), once known as Macabi, carries a wide selection of premium and house cigars in a humidified shop. There's a selection of wines for purchase. Humidors and other accessories are also available.

CLOTHING FOR MEN AND WOMEN

★ **Base** (✉ *939 Lincoln Rd., Miami Beach* ☎ *305/531–4982* ⊕ *www. baseworld.com*) is a constantly evolving shop with an intriguing magazine section, an international CD station with DJ, and groovy home accessories. Stop here for men's and women's eclectic clothing, shoes, and accessories that mix Japanese design with Caribbean-inspired materials. The often-present house-label designer may help select your wardrobe's newest addition.

Intermix (✉ *634 Collins Ave., Miami Beach* ☎ *305/531–5950* ⊕ *www. intermixonline.com*) is a modern New York–based boutique with the variety of a department store. You'll find fancy dresses, stylish shoes, slinky accessories, and trendy looks by sassy and somewhat pricey designers like Chloé, Stella McCartney, Marc Jacobs, Moschino, and Diane von Furstenberg.

Kristine Michael (✉ *7271 SW 57th Ave., South Miami* ☎ *305/665–7717*) is a local fashion institution for suburban moms and University of Miami students. The store's hip and up-to-the-minute selection of pieces from Theory, Alice & Olivia, Kors, and C & C California stands out from the national retailers across the street at the Shops at Sunset Place.

★ **Silvia Tcherassi** (✉ *350 San Lorenzo Ave., Coral Gables* ☎ *305/461–0009* ⊕ *www.silviatcherassi.com*), the Colombian designer's signature boutique in the Village of Merrick Park, features feminine and frilly dresses and separates accented with chiffon, tulle, and sequins.

SWIMWEAR

South Beach Surf & Dive Shop (✉ *850 Washington Ave., Miami Beach* ☎ *305/531–6110* ⊕ *www.southbeachdivers.com*) is a one-stop shop for beach gear—from clothing and swimwear for guys and gals to wake-, surf-, and skateboards. The shop also offers multilingual surfing, scuba, snorkeling, and dive lessons and trips.

JEWELRY
Fodor'sChoice

★ **Beverlee Kagan** (✉ *5831 Sunset Dr., South Miami* ☎ *305/663–1937* ⊕ *kaganjewelry.com*) deals in a wide selection of vintage and antique jewelry, including art deco–era bangles, bracelets, and cuff links.

Jose Roca Fine Jewelry Designs (✉ *297 Miracle Mile, Coral Gables* ☎ *305/448–2808*) designs fine jewelry from precious metals and stones. If you have a particular piece that you would like to create, this is the place to have it meticulously executed.

Me & Ro (✉ *Shore Club hotel, 1901 Collins Ave., Miami Beach* ☎ *305/ 672–3566* ⊕ *www.meandrojewelry.com*) is a trendy New York–based jewelry shop run by Michele Quan and Robin Renzi, with a celebrity clientele that reads like a who's who. Designs are crafted from silver, gold, and semiprecious stones.

★ **MIA Jewels** (✉ *1439 Alton Rd., Miami Beach* ☎ *305/532–6064* ⊕ *www. miajewels.com*) is an Alton Road jewelry and accessories boutique known for its colorful, gem- and bead-laden, gold and silver earrings, necklaces, bracelets, and brooches by lines such as Cousin Claudine, Amrita, and Alexis Bittar. This is a shoo-in store for everyone: you'll find things for trend lovers (gold-studded chunky Lucite bangles), classicists (long, colorful, wraparound beaded necklaces), and ice lovers (long Swarovski crystal cabin necklaces) alike.

ONLY IN MIAMI

★ **Dog Bar** (✉ *1684 Jefferson Ave., Miami Beach* ☎ *305/532–5654*), just north of Lincoln Road's main drag, caters to enthusiastic animal owners with a variety of unique items for the pampered pet, including a luxurious, over-the-top pet sofa imported from Italy and offered in cowhide, leather, or vinyl fitted into a chrome frame.

La Casa de las Guayaberas (✉ *5840 SW 8th St., Little Havana* ☎ *305/266–9683*) sells custom-made guayaberas, the natty four-pocket dress shirts favored by Latin men. Hundreds are also available off the rack.

SHOES

★ Design your own couture stiletto or stylish sandal in just a half hour (cobblers are fast at work while you wait) at **Morgan Miller Shoes** (✉ *618 Lincoln Rd., Miami Beach* ☎ *305/672–8700* ⊕ *www.morganmillershoes. com*). The selection of materials is seemingly endless: wood, resin, or cork heels or sandals; leather, alligator, snake, or ostrich straps in a myriad of vibrant colors; and more than 100 crystals and jewels to choose from. Prices range from a basic sandal with a denim strap for about $70 to an over-the-top pair of strappy lime-green, snakeskin stilettos laced with Swarovski crystals, colored tacks, and hanging jewels, topping $500. This is a great store for footwear fashionistas, but you don't have to be a shoe addict to enjoy finding the right fit here.

OUTDOOR MARKETS

Pass the mangoes! Greater Miami's farmers' markets and flea markets take advantage of the region's balmy weather and tropical delights to lure shoppers to open-air stalls filled with produce and collectibles.

★ **Coconut Grove Farmers Market.** The most organic of Miami's outdoor markets specializes in a mouthwatering array of local produce as well as such ready-to-eat goodies as cashew butter, homemade salad dressings, and fruit pies (some of the offerings can taste stodgy to the nonorganic eater). If you are looking for a downright granola crowd and experience, pack your Birkenstocks because this is it. ✉ *Grand Ave. and Margaret St., Coconut Grove* ☎ *305/238–7747.*

Coral Gables Farmers Market. Some 25 local produce growers and plant vendors sell herbs, fruits, fresh-squeezed juices, chutneys, cakes, and muffins at this market between Coral Gables' City Hall and Merrick Park. Artists also join in. Regular events include gardening workshops, children's activities, and cooking demonstrations offered by Coral Gables' master chefs. Mid-January through late March only. ✉ *405 Biltmore Way, Coral Gables* ☎ *305/460–5311.*

★ **Lincoln Road Antique and Collectibles Market.** Interested in picking up samples of Miami's ever-present modern and moderne furniture and accessories? This outdoor show offers eclectic goods that should satisfy post impressionists, deco-holics, Edwardians, Bauhausers, Goths, and '50s junkies. ✉ *Lincoln and Alton Rds., Miami Beach* ☎ *305/673–4991.*

Lincoln Road Farmers Market. With all the familiar trappings of a farmers' market (except for farmers—most of the people selling veggies appear to be resellers), this is quickly becoming a must-see event before or after visiting the Antique and Collectibles Market. It brings local produce and bakery vendors to the Lincoln Road Mall and often features plant workshops, art sales, and children's activities. This is a good place to pick up live orchids, too. ⊠ *Lincoln Rd. between Meridian and Euclid Aves., Miami Beach* ☎ *305/673–4166.*

NIGHTLIFE

Miami's pulse pounds with nonstop nightlife that reflects the area's potent cultural mix. On sultry, humid nights with the huge full moon rising out of the ocean and fragrant night-blooming jasmine intoxicating the senses, who can resist Cuban salsa, Jamaican reggae, and Dominican merengue, with some disco and hip-hop thrown in for good measure? When this place throws a party, hips shake, fingers snap, bodies touch. It's no wonder many clubs are still rocking at 5 AM.

FIND OUT WHAT'S GOING ON

The *Miami Herald* (⊕ *www.miamiherald.com*) is a good source for information on what to do in town. The Weekend section of the newspaper, included in the Friday edition, has an annotated guide to everything from plays and galleries to concerts and nightclubs. The "Ticket" column of this section details the week's entertainment highlights. Or, you can pick up the free weekly tabloid *Miami New Times* (⊕ *www. miaminewtimes.com*), the city's largest free alternative newspaper, published each Thursday. It lists nightclubs, concerts, and special events; reviews plays and movies; and provides in-depth coverage of the local music scene. "Night & Day" is a rundown of the week's cultural highlights. *Ocean Drive* (⊕ *www.oceandrive.com*), Miami Beach's model-strewn, upscale fashion and lifestyle magazine, squeezes club, bar, restaurant, and events listings in with fashion spreads, reviews, and personality profiles. Paparazzi photos of local party people and celebrities give you a taste of Greater Miami nightlife before you even dress up to paint the town.

The Spanish-language *El Nuevo Herald* (⊕ *www.elnuevoherald.com*), published by the *Miami Herald,* has extensive information on Spanish-language arts and entertainment, including dining reviews, concert previews, and nightclub highlights. Spanish-language radio, primarily on the AM dial, is also a good source of information about arts events. Tune in to WXDJ (95.7 FM), Amor (107.5 FM), or Radio Mambi (710 AM).

BARS AND LOUNGES

One of Greater Miami's most popular pursuits is barhopping. Bars range from intimate enclaves to showy see-and-be-seen lounges to loud, raucous frat parties. There's a New York–style flair to some of the newer lounges, which are increasingly catering to the Manhattan party crowd who escape to South Beach for long weekends. If you're looking for

From salsa and merengue to disco and hip-hop, Miami's dance clubs cater to diverse styles of music.

a relatively non-frenetic evening, your best bet is one of the chic hotel bars on Collins Avenue.

COCONUT GROVE

Monty's in the Grove. The outdoor bar here has Caribbean flair, thanks especially to live calypso and island music. It's very kid-friendly on weekends, when Mom and Dad can kick back and enjoy a beer and the raw bar while the youngsters dance to live music. Evenings bring a DJ and reggae music. ⊠ *2550 S. Bayshore Dr., at Aviation Ave.* ☎ *305/856–3992* ⊕ *www.montysbayshore.com.*

CORAL GABLES

Bar at Ponce and Giralda. One of the oldest bars in South Florida, the old Hofbrau has been reincarnated and now serves vibrant, live reggae music on Saturday nights and a non-touristy vibe. ⊠ *172 Giralda Ave., at Ponce de León Blvd., Coral Gables* ☎ *305/442–2730.*

Globe. The centerpiece of Coral Gables's emphasis on nightlife draws crowds of twentysomethings who spill into the street for live jazz on Saturday evenings and a bistro-style menu nightly. Free appetizers and drink specials every weekday attract a strong happy-hour following. Outdoor tables and an art-heavy, upscale interior are comfortable, if you can find space to squeeze in. ⊠ *377 Alhambra Circle, at Le Jeune Rd.* ☎ *305/445–3555* ⊕ *www.theglobecafe.com.*

John Martin's Restaurant and Irish Pub. The cozy upscale Irish pub hosts an Irish cabaret on Saturday night with live contemporary and traditional music—sometimes by an Irish band—storytelling, and dancers. ⊠ *253 Miracle Mile, at Ponce de León Blvd.* ☎ *305/445–3777* ⊕ *www. johnmartins.com.*

THE VELVET ROPES

How to get past the velvet ropes at the hottest South Beach nightspots? First, if you're staying at a hotel, use the concierge. Decide which clubs you want to check out (consult *Ocean Drive* magazine celebrity pages if you want to be among the glitterati), and the concierge will e-mail, fax, or call in your names to the clubs so you'll be on the guest list when you arrive. This means much easier access and usually no cover charge (which can be upward of $20) if you arrive before midnight. Guest list or no guest list, follow these pointers: make sure there are more women than men in your group. Dress up—casual chic is the dress code. For men this means no sneakers, no shorts, no sleeveless vests, and no shirts unbuttoned past the top button. For women, provocative and seductive is fine; overly revealing is not. Black is always right. At the door: don't name-drop—no one takes it seriously. Don't be pushy while trying to get the doorman's attention. Wait until you make eye contact, then be cool and easygoing. If you decide to tip him (which most bouncers don't expect), be discreet and pleasant, not big-bucks obnoxious—a $10 or $20 bill quietly passed will be appreciated, however. With the right dress and the right attitude, you'll be on the dance floor rubbing shoulders with South Beach's finest clubbers in no time.

DOWNTOWN MIAMI

Fodor's Choice
★

Tobacco Road. Opened in 1912, this classic holds Miami's oldest liquor license: No. 0001! Upstairs, in a space that was occupied by a speak-easy during Prohibition, local and national blues bands perform nightly. There is excellent bar food, a dinner menu, and a selection of single-malt scotches, bourbons, and cigars. This is the hangout of grizzled journalists, bohemians en route to or from nowhere, and club kids seeking a way station before the real parties begin. ⊠ *626 S. Miami Ave., Downtown Miami* ☎ *305/374–1198* ⊕ *www.tobacco-road.com.*

SOUTH BEACH

★ **Buck 15.** This hidden lounge above popular Lincoln Road eatery Miss Yip Café is one of Miami's best-kept secrets. The tiny club manages to play amazing music—a rock-heavy mix of songs you loved but haven't heard in ages—and maintain a low-key, unpretentious attitude. The drinks are reasonable, and the well-worn couches are great to dance on. The club attracts local hipsters and some gay couples. ⊠ *707 Lincoln Rd., Miami Beach* ☎ *305/538–3815* ⊕ *www.buck15.com.*

Club Deuce. Although it's completely unglam, this pool hall attracts a colorful crowd of clubbers, locals, celebs—and just about anyone else. Locals consider it the best spot for a cheap drink. ⊠ *222 14th St., at Collins Ave., Miami Beach* ☎ *305/531–6200.*

Lost Weekend. Players at this pool hall are serious about their pastime, so it's hard to get a table on weekends. The full bar, which has 150 kinds of beers, draws an eclectic crowd, from yuppies to drag queens to slumming celebs like Lenny Kravitz and the guys in Hootie and the Blowfish. ⊠*218 Española Way, at Collins Ave., Miami Beach* ☎*305/672–1707.*

Mynt Ultra Lounge. The name of this upscale nightclub, which opens its doors at midnight, is meant to be taken literally—not only are the walls bathed in soft green shades, but an aromatherapy system pumps out different fresh scents, including mint. Celebs like Enrique Iglesias, Angie Everhart, and Queen Latifah have cooled down here. ⊠*1921 Collins Ave., Miami Beach* ☎*786/276–6132* ⊕*www.myntlounge.com.*

★ **The National.** Don't miss a drink at the hotel's nifty wooden bar, one of many elements original to the 1939 building, which give it such a sense of its era that you'd expect to see Ginger Rogers and Fred Astaire hoofing it along the polished lobby floor. The adjoining Martini Room has a great collection of cigar and old airline stickers and vintage Bacardi ads on the walls. Don't forget to take a peek at the long, sexy pool. ⊠*1677 Collins Ave., Miami Beach* ☎*305/532–2311* ⊕*www. nationalhotel.com.*

Fodor'sChoice ★ **Rose Bar at the Delano.** The airy lobby lounge at South Beach's trendiest hotel manages to look dramatic but not cold, with long, snow-white, gauzy curtains and huge white pillars separating conversation nooks (this is where Ricky Martin shot the video for "La Vida Loca"). A pool table brings the austerity down to earth. There's also an expansive poolside bar, dotted with intimate poolside beds (bottle service required) and private cabanas to reserve for the evening—for a not-so-nominal fee, of course. ⊠*1685 Collins Ave., South Beach, Miami* ☎*305/672–2000.*

Santo Restaurant. This Lincoln Road lounge is where Miami's Latin crowd (and anyone who loves Latin music) comes to party. During the day, Santo serves eclectic fare with a Latin twist. On Thursday through Saturday evenings, the back half of the venue turns into a stage for nightly live and DJ performances, ranging from salsa to reggaeton. ⊠*430 Lincoln Rd., Miami Beach* ☎*305/532–2882 or 305/531–0900.*

Fodor'sChoice ★ **SkyBar at the Shore Club.** Splendor-in-the-garden is the theme at this haute spot by the sea, where multiple lounging areas are joined together. Daybeds, glowing Moroccan lanterns, and maximum atmosphere make a visit to this chic outdoor lounge worthwhile. Groove to dance music in the Red Room, or enjoy an aperitif and Japanese bar bites at Nobu Lounge. The Red Room, Nobu Restaurant and Lounge, Italian restaurant Ago, and SkyBar all connect around the Shore Club's pool area. ⊠*1901 Collins Ave., Miami Beach* ☎*305/695–3100.*

CABARET, COMEDY, AND SUPPER CLUBS

You can still find the kind of song-and-dance extravaganzas that were produced by every major Miami Beach hotel in the 1950s (think scantily clad showgirls and feathered headdresses). But also on tap are modern-day affairs like flamenco shows, salsa dancing, and comedy clubs.

COCONUT GROVE

Improv Comedy Club. This long-standing comedy club hosts nationally touring comics nightly. Comedy-club regulars will recognize Margaret Cho and George Wallace, and everyone knows Damon Wayans and

Chris Rock, both of whom have taken the stage here. Urban Comedy Showcase is held Tuesday and Wednesday, with an open-mike part of the evening on Wednesday. A full menu is available. ✉ *Streets of Mayfair, 3390 Mary St., at Grand Ave.* ☎ *305/441–8200* ⊕ *www. miamiimprov.com.*

LITTLE HAVANA

Casa Panza. The visionary Madrileñan owners of this Little Havana restaurant have energized the neighborhood with a twice-weekly tribute to *La Virgen del Rocío* (the patron saint of a province in Andalusia), in which the room is darkened and diners are handed lighted candles and sheet music. Everyone readily joins in the singing, making for a truly enjoyable evening. There is flamenco dancing on Friday and Saturday. ✉ *1620 SW 8th St.* ☎ *305/643–5343.*

DANCE CLUBS

DOWNTOWN MIAMI

Lombardi's. You can shake it salsa- or merengue-style until midnight to live bands that perk up diners on Friday, Saturday, and Sunday nights at this downtown restaurant and bar. ✉ *Bayside Marketplace, 401 Biscayne Blvd.* ☎ *305/381–9580* ⊕ *www.lombardisbayside.com.*

Space. Want 24-hour partying? Here's the place. Created from four downtown warehouses, Space has two levels (one blasts house music; the other reverberates with hip-hop), an outdoor patio, a New York–style industrial look, and a 24-hour liquor license. It's open on weekends only, and you'll need to look good to be allowed past the velvet ropes. ✉ *34 NE 11th St.* ☎ *305/375–0001* ⊕ *www.clubspace.com.*

SOUTH BEACH

Greater Miami's gay action centers on the night clubs in South Beach. That tiny strip of sand rivals New York and San Francisco as a hub of gay nightlife—if not in the number of clubs then in the intensity of the partying. The neighborhood's large gay population and the laissez-faire attitudes of the hip straights that live and visit here encourage gay-friendliness at most South Beach venues that are not specifically gay.

Fodor's Choice ★ **Cameo.** One of Miami's ultimate dance clubs, Cameo, formerly known as Crobar, has gotten a welcome face-lift. Gone is the industrial feel, but all-star DJs and plentiful dance space remain, and plush VIP lounges have been added. If you can brave the velvet rope, Saturday-night parties are the best. ✉ *1445 Washington Ave.* ☎ *305/532–2667.*

Nikki Beach Club. With its swell on-the-beach location, the full-service Nikki Beach Club has become a favorite pretty-people and celeb hangout. Tepees and hammocks on the sand, dance floors both under the stars and inside, and beach parties make this a true South Beach experience. ✉ *1 Ocean Dr.* ☎ *305/538–1111.*

Score. This popular bar is the see-and-be-seen central of Miami's gay community. DJs spin every night of the week except Sunday, a popular karaoke night where everything goes. ✉ *727 Lincoln Rd.* ☎ *305/535–1111* ⊕ *www.scorebar.net.*

LIVE MUSIC

DOWNTOWN MIAMI

Fodor's Choice ★ **Tobacco Road.** Live blues, R&B, and jazz bands are on tap seven days a week along with food and drink at this Miami institution. ⊠ *626 S. Miami Ave.* ☎ *305/374–1198* ⊕ *www.tobacco-road.com.*

SOUTH BEACH

★ **Jazid.** If you're looking for an unpretentious alternative to the velvet-rope nightclubs, this unassuming, live-music hot spot is a standout on the strip. Eight-piece bands play danceable Latin rhythms, as well as reggae, hip-hop, and fusion sounds. Get ready for a late night though, as bands are just getting started at midnight. They play every night of the week. Call ahead to reserve a table. ⊠ *1342 Washington Ave.* ☎ *305/673–9372* ⊕ *www.jazid.net.*

WHERE TO EAT

Updated by Michael de Zayas

Miami's restaurant scene has exploded in the last few years, with dozens of great new restaurants springing up left and right. The melting pot of residents and visitors has brought an array of sophisticated, tasty cuisine. Little Havana is still king for Cuban fare, while Miami Beach is swept up in a trend of fusion cuisine, which combines Asian, French, American, and Latin cuisine with sumptuous—and pricy—results. Downtown Miami and the Design District especially are home to some of the city's best spots, and they're all new. Since Miami dining is a part of the trendy nightlife scene, most dinners don't start until 8 or 9 PM, and may go well into the night. Hot spots fill up quickly, so come before 7 or make reservations. Attire is usually casual-chic, but patrons like to dress to impress. Prices tend to stay high in hot spots like Lincoln Road; but if you venture off the beaten path, you can find delicious food for reasonable prices. When you get your bill, check whether a gratuity is already included; most restaurants add between 15% and 18% (ostensibly for the convenience of, and protection from, the many Latin American and European tourists who are used to this practice in their homelands), but supplement it depending on your opinion of the service.

WHAT IT COSTS				
¢	$	$$	$$$	$$$$
AT DINNER under $10	$10–$15	$15–$20	$20–$30	over $30

Price per person for a median main course or equivalent combination of smaller dishes.

COCONUT GROVE, CORAL GABLES, AND KEY BISCAYNE

COCONUT GROVE

$–$$ FRENCH ✕ **Le Bouchon du Grove.** This French bistro with a supercharged atmosphere is a great spot in the heart of the Grove. Waiters tend to lean on chairs while taking orders, and managers and owners freely mix with

BEST BETS FOR MIAMI DINING

Fodor's writers and editors have selected their favorite restaurants by price, cuisine, and experience in the Best Bets lists *below*. In the first column, Fodor's Choice designations represent the "best of the best" in every price category. Find specific details about a restaurant in the full reviews, listed alphabetically by neighborhood.

Fodor's Choice ★

Azul, Downtown Miami, p. 187

Big Pink, South Beach, p. 191

The Forge, Mid-Beach, p. 189

Havana Harry's, Coral Gables, p. 183

Joey's, Wynwood, p. 184

Michael's Genuine Food & Drink, Design District, p. 186

Michy's, Design District, p. 186

Palacio de los Jugos, Coral Gables, p. 183

Pascal's on Ponce, Coral Gables, p. 184

Sra. Martinez, Design District, p. 186

Timó, Sunny Isles, p. 190

By Price

¢

Palacio de los Jugos, Coral Gables, p. 183

$

Big Pink, South Beach, p. 191

Las Culebrinas, Coral Gables, p. 183

Tobacco Road, Downtown Miami, p. 187

Tutto Pasta, Little Havana, p. 188

Versailles, Little Havana, p. 188

$$

Hy-Vong Vietnamese Cuisine, Little Havana, p. 188

Joey's, Wynwood, p. 184

Novecento, Downtown Miami, p. 187

Sra. Martinez, Design District, p. 186

$$$

Michael's Genuine Food & Drink, Downtown Miami, p. 186

$$$$

Azul, Downtown Miami, p. 187

The Forge, Mid-Beach, p. 189

Pascal's on Ponce, Coral Gables, p. 184

By Cuisine

AMERICAN

Big Pink, South Beach, p. 191

Michael's Genuine Food & Drink, Downtown Miami, p. 186

News Café, South Beach, p. 195

ASIAN

Hy-Vong Vietnamese Cuisine, Little Havana, p. 188

SushiSamba Dromo, South Beach, p. 195

ITALIAN

Café Prima Pasta, North Beach, p. 189

Osteria del Teatro, South Beach, p. 195

Timo, Sunny Isles, p. 190

SEAFOOD

Joe's Stone Crab, South Beach, p. 191

La Marea, South Beach, p. 194

Nemo, South Beach, p. 194

Prime One Twelve, South Beach, p. 195

Tuscan Steak, South Beach, p. 198

By Experience

CHILD-FRIENDLY

Tutto Pasta, Little Havana, p. 188

Versailles, Little Havana, p. 188

HOT SPOTS

Blue Door at the Delano, South Beach, p. 191

Meat Market, South Beach, p. 194

Michael's Genuine Food & Drink, Downtown Miami, p. 186

the clientele, making Le Bouchon perhaps the last remaining vestige of the Grove's bohemian days. The result is one big happy family, all enjoying traditional French pâtés, gratins, quiches, chicken fricassee, mussels, duck-leg confit, and steak frites. The lively mood inside is matched by the throngs that parade outside the French doors. Breakfast is served daily. ⊠ *3430 Main Hwy.* ☎ *305/448–6060* ⊕ *www.lebouchondugrove. com* ⊟ *AE, MC, V* ⊹ *5C.*

CORAL GABLES

$ ✕ **Havana Harry's.** When Cuban families want a home-cooked meal but
CUBAN don't want to cook it themselves, they come to this big, unassuming
Fodor'sChoice restaurant. In fact, you're likely to see whole families here, from babes
★ in arms to grandmothers. The fare is traditional Cuban: the long thin steaks known as *bistec palomilla* (a panfried steak), roast chicken with citrus marinade, and fried pork chunks; contemporary flourishes— mango sauce and guava-painted pork roast—are kept to a minimum. Most dishes come with white rice, black beans, and a choice of ripe or green plantains. The sweet ripe ones offer a good contrast to the savory dishes. This is an excellent value. Start with the $5.95 *mariquitas* (plantain chips) with guacamole. ⊠ *4612 Le Jeune Rd.* ☎ *305/661–2622* ⊟ *AE, D, MC, V* ⊹ *5C.*

$ ✕ **Las Culebrinas.** Each of Las Culebrinas' five locations in Miami tends
SPANISH to draw throngs of adoring diners for Spanish tapas and Cuban steaks. Tapas here are not small; some are entrée size like the Frisbee-size Spanish *tortilla* (omelet). Our suggestion: indulge in a tender fillet of crocodile, fresh fish, or the grilled pork stuffed with mashed bananas, followed by a dessert of *crema Catalana,* caramelized at your table with a blowtorch—this is a good time to remind your kids not to touch. ⊠ *4700 W. Flagler St., at NW 47th Ave.* ☎ *305/445–2337* ⊕ *www. culebrinas.com* ⊟ *AE, MC, V* ⊹ *4C.*

$$$$ ✕ **Ortanique on the Mile.** Cascading ortaniques, a Jamaican hybrid
CARIBBEAN orange, are hand-painted on columns in this warm, welcoming yellow dining room. Food is vibrant in taste and color, as delicious as it is beautiful. Though there is no denying that the strong, full flavors are imbued with island breezes, chef-partner Cindy Hutson's personal cuisine goes beyond Caribbean refinements. The menu centers on fish, since Hutson has a special way with it, and the Caribbean bouillabaisse is not to be missed. On Sunday there is live jazz. ⊠ *278 Miracle Mile* ☎ *305/446–7710* ⊕ *www.cindyhutsoncuisine.com* ⊟ *AE, DC, MC, V* ⊘ *No lunch weekends* ⊹ *5C.*

¢ ✕ **Palacio de los Jugos.** This joint is one of the easiest and truest ways
CUBAN to see Miami's local Latin life in action. It's also one of the best fruit-
Fodor'sChoice shake shacks you'll ever come across (ask for a juice of—"*jugo de*"—
★ mamey, melón, or guanabana, a sweet-tart equatorial fruit, and you can't go wrong). Besides the rows and rows of fresh tropical fruits and vegetables, and the shakes you can make with any of them, this boisterous indoor-outdoor market has numerous food counters where you can get just about any Cuban food—tamales, rice and beans, a *pan con lechón* (roast pork on Cuban bread), fried pork rinds, or a coconut split before you and served with a straw. Order your food at a counter and eat it along with local families at rows of outdoor picnic-style tables

4

next to the parking lot. It's disorganized, chaotic, and not for those cutting calories, but it's delicious and undeniably the real thing. ✉ *5721 W. Flagler St.* ☎ *305/264–4557* ⊕ *www.elpalaciodelosjugosonline.com* ▭ *No credit cards* ✛ *4B.*

$$$$
FRENCH
Fodor's Choice
★

✕ **Pascal's on Ponce.** This French gem amid the Coral Gables restaurant district is always full, thanks to chef-proprietor Pascal Oudin's assured and consistent cuisine. Oudin forgoes the glitz and fussiness often associated with French cuisine, and instead opts for a simple, small, refined dining room that won't overwhelm patrons. The equally sensible menu includes a superb gnocchi appetizer (ask for mushrooms on top). The main course is a tough choice between oven-roasted duck with poached pears, milk-fed veal loin, and diver sea scallops with beef short rib. It opened in 2000. Ask your expert waiter to pair dishes with a selection from Pascal's impressive wine list, and, for dessert, order the bittersweet chocolate soufflé. ✉ *2611 Ponce de León Blvd.* ☎ *305/444–2024* ⊕ *www.pascalmiami.com* ▭ *AE, D, DC, MC, V* ☾ *Closed Sun. No lunch Sat.* ✛ *5C.*

KEY BISCAYNE

$$$$
ITALIAN

✕ **Cioppino.** Few visitors think to venture out to the far end of Key Biscayne for dinner, but making the journey to the soothing grounds of this quiet Ritz-Carlton property on the beach is worth it. Choose your view: the ornate dining room near the exhibition kitchen or the alfresco area with views of landscaped gardens or breeze-brushed beaches. Choosing your dishes may be more difficult, given the many rich, luscious Italian options, including imported cheeses, olive oils, risottos and fresh fish flown in daily. Items range from the creamy burrata mozzarella and authentic pasta dishes to tantalizing risotto with organic spinach and roasted quail, all expertly matched with fine, vintage, rare, and boutique wines. An after-dinner drink and live music at the old-Havana-style RUMBAR inside the hotel is another treat. ✉ *Ritz-Carlton, 455 Grand Bay Dr.* ☎ *305/365–4286* ▭ *AE, D, DC, MC, V* ✛ *6E.*

MIAMI

DESIGN DISTRICT

$$
ITALIAN
Fodor's Choice
★

✕ **Joey's.** This joyfully good and merrily buzzing new place is literally the only restaurant in Wynwood, an emerging neighborhood to the south of the Design District. But this new restaurant already has that rarest of blessings—the sizzling vibe of a thriving neighborhood restaurant that everyone seems to adore. Its contagious charm begins with the service: informal, but focused, very professional, and attentive. Then comes the food: Veneto native chef Ivo Mazzon does homage to fresh ingredients prepared simply and perfectly. A full line of original flatbread pizzas contend for tops in Miami. The *dolce e piccante* has figs, Gorgonzola, honey, and hot pepper; it's unexpectedly sweet at first bite, and at bite 10 you'll be swearing it's the best you've ever had. The wine list is small but the product of much discernment. Because it's little and in a weird spot, Joey's makes you feel that you're the first to discover it; and that you've made a new friend in Miami—one you'll need to visit

again very soon. ⊠ *2506 NW 2 Ave., Design District* ☎ *305/438–0488* ⊕ *www.joeyswynwood.com* ☰ *AE, D, MC, V* ✛ *4D.*

$$$
AMERICAN
Fodor's Choice
★

✕ **Michael's Genuine Food & Drink.** Though it's new, Michael's is already frequently cited as Miami's top restaurant. This indoor-outdoor bistro in Miami's Design District relies on fresh ingredients and a hip but unpretentious vibe to lure diners. Beautifully arranged combinations like crispy beef cheek with whipped celeriac, and sweet-and-spicy pork belly with kimchi explode with unlikely but satisfying flavor. Owner and chef Michael Schwartz, famous for South Beach's popular Nemo restaurant, aims for sophisticated American cuisine with an emphasis on local and organic ingredients. He gets it right. Portions are divided into small, medium, and large plates, and the smaller plates are more inventive, so you can order several and explore. Reserve two weeks in advance for weekend tables; also, consider brunch. ⊠ *130 NE 40th St., Design District* ☎ *305/573–5550* ⊕ *www.michaelsgenuine.com* ☰ *AE, MC, V* ⊙ *No lunch weekends* ✛ *3D.*

$$$
MEDITERRANEAN
Fodor's Choice
★

✕ **Michy's.** Miami's homegrown star chef Michelle Bernstein made a huge splash with the shabby-chic decor and self-named restaurant on the north end of Miami's Design District. Bernstein serves exquisite French- and Mediterranean-influenced seafood dishes at over-the-causeway (read: non-tourist-trap) prices. Plates come in half portions and full portions, which makes the restaurant even more of a deal. Can't-miss entrées include the blue cheese and *jamón serrano* (serrano ham) *croquetas*, the beef short rib, and the steak frites au poivre. ⊠ *6927 Biscayne Blvd., Design District* ☎ *305/759–2001* ⊕ *www.chefmichellebernstein. com* ☰ *AE, D, DC, MC, V* ⊙ *Closed Mon. No lunch* ✛ *3E.*

$$$
SEAFOOD

✕ **Pacific Time.** Veteran travelers to Miami Beach will remember Pacific Time from Lincoln Road, where it was a favorite for nearly 15 years. The restaurant has reopened in an airy setting in the Design District that is hip and airy and unpretentious. The food is as fresh as ever, and the drinks are superb. The dinner menu has 20 inexpensive small plates, including local black grouper with red curry. Entrées include a pan-seared salt-and-pepper skate wing served over a bed of celery root with lemon butter and green apple. Try sitting in the courtyard, a pleasing lunch spot for blue-cheese burgers or tasty shrimp po' boys served on focaccia. (Note: Pacific Time is a convenient backup if you can't get a reservation at Michael's Genuine, one of the city's most popular restaurants; it's a short block away.) Finally, something amazing at PT: a truly sophisticated kids tasting menu; if you're a foodie with young kids, bring 'em here. ⊠ *35 NE 40th St., Design District* ☎ *305/722–7369* ⊕ *www.pacifictimerestaurant.com* ☰ *AE, D, MC, V* ✛ *3D.*

$$
SPANISH
Fodor's Choice
★

✕ **Sra. Martinez.** For a good time with food, dial up Sra. Martinez. Michelle Bernstein's second restaurant (her, first, Michy's, is a must-visit for Miami foodies) opened in November 2008; the name is a sly take on her name—her husband is David Martinez—which is good, because something as artful as this new restaurant deserves a signature. Bernstein anchors her menu at Sra. Martinez in traditional Spanish cuisine, a brilliant jumping-off point for her wildly successful experiments in flavor, texture, and plate composition. Order several dishes from the Cold & Crisp ($5–$18) and Warm & Lush ($8–$23) sections, which feature small plates of takes on traditional tapas. The cuisine is modern, colorful and, above all, fun. Cocktail lovers will be delighted by the inventive, high-quality selections like the Jalisco Mule, a sly (and spicy) take on the traditional Moscow Mule, made with tequila and ginger beer, and laced with chili syrup. It's no wonder this restaurant has already become one of the best and most exciting in the city. ✉ *4000 NE 2 Ave., Design District* ☎ *305/573–5474* ⊕ *www.chefmichellebernstein.com* ▭ *AE, D, DC, MC, V* ☾ *Closed Sun. No Lunch Sat.* ✛ *3D.*

DOWNTOWN MIAMI

$$$$
ECLECTIC
Fodor's Choice
★

✕ **Azul.** From chef Clay Conley's exotically rendered Asian-Mediterranean cuisine to the thoughtful service staff who graciously anticipate your broader dining needs, Azul has sumptuously conquered the devil in the details. Does your sleeveless blouse leave you too cold to properly appreciate the Moroccan lamb and seared red snapper? Forgot your reading glasses and can't decipher the hanger steak with foie-gras sauce? Request a pair from the host. A risotto with Alba white truffles is typical of the way Azul will reach across the globe for the finest ingredients. The Moroccan-inspired Colorado lamb with eggplant and harissa is a perennial favorite. There is a lot of new competition for dining attention in town, but Azul is still at the pinnacle of its game. ✉ *Mandarin Oriental Hotel, 500 Brickell Key Dr., Downtown Miami* ☎ *305/913–8358* ⌕ *Reservations essential* ▭ *AE, MC, V* ☾ *Closed Sun. No lunch weekends* ✛ *5D.*

$$
MEDITERRANEAN

✕ **Eos.** This new restaurant at the snazzy Viceroy Hotel on Brickell is definitely worth a visit if you're downtown. Chef Michael Psilakis and restaurateur Donatella Arpaia are culinary superstars whose involvement gives this restaurant a lot of attention. The sophisticated, bold design is by Kelly Wearstler, who was also responsible for La Marea at the Tides in South Beach. The large menu of inexpensive light dishes is divided by ingredients—cheese and crostini; vegetable and potato; pasta; fish; and meats, poultry, and game. The influences are vast, with Greek, Italian, French, and Spanish flavors all evident. There's also a sushi and sashimi selection. ✉ *485 Brickell Ave., Downtown* ☎ *305/503–4400 or 866/781–9923* ⊕ *www.viceroymiami.com* ▭ *AE, D, DC, MC, V* ✛ *4D.*

$$
ARGENTINE

✕ **Novecento.** This Argentine eatery is the Financial District's answer to Ocean Drive: the people are still beautiful, but now they're wearing suits. Known for its empanadas (tender chicken or spinach and cheese), simple grilled meats (luscious grilled skirt steak with chimichurri sauce), and the innovative Ensalada Novecento (grilled skirt steak, french fries, and baby mixed greens), it's no wonder Novecento is Brickell Avenue's best power-lunch and happy-hour spot. Come for Sunday brunch and enjoy the signature *parillada*, a small grill with an assortment of steaks, sausages, and sweetbreads (not sweet bread, but rather the sweet pancreas of a lamb or calf). ✉ *1414 Brickell Ave., Downtown Miami* ☎ *305/403–0900* ⊕ *www.bistronovecento.com* ▭ *AE, D, DC, MC, V* ✛ *5D.*

$
AMERICAN

✕ **Tobacco Road.** If you like your food (or your drink) the way you like your blues—gritty, honest, and unassuming—then this almost-100-year-old joint will earn your respect. This is Miami's oldest bar and restaurant, and it manages to stay up the latest, too: 5 AM. A live band plays daily, making this hangout one of Miami's low-key gems. The road burger is a popular choice, as are appetizers like nachos and chicken wings; the chili may induce a call for a fire hose. Fine single-malt scotches are stocked behind the bar. ⊠ *626 S. Miami Ave., Downtown Miami* ☎ *305/374–1198* ⊕ *www.tobacco-road.com* ▭ *AE, D, DC, MC, V* ✢ *4D.*

LITTLE HAVANA

$$$$ ✕ **Casa Juancho.** This meeting place for the movers and shakers of the
SPANISH   Cuban *exilio* community is also a haven for lovers of fine Spanish regional cuisine. Strolling balladeers serenade amid brown brick, rough-hewn dark timbers, hanging smoked meats, ceramic plates, and oil still lifes: a bit of old España dropped on Calle Ocho. Try the hake prepared in a fish stock with garlic, onions, and Spanish white wine or the *carabineros a la plancha* (jumbo red shrimp with head and shell on, split and grilled). For dessert, *crema Catalana* is a rich pastry custard with a delectable crust of burnt caramel. The house features one of the largest lists of reserve Spanish wines in the United States. Jackets are recommended for men at dinner. ⊠ *2436 SW 8th St., Little Havana* ☎ *305/642–2452* ⊕ *www.casajuancho.com* ▭ *AE, D, DC, MC, V* ✢ *5C.*

$$ ✕ **Hy-Vong Vietnamese Cuisine.** Spring springs forth in spring rolls of
VIETNAMESE   ground pork, cellophane noodles, and black mushrooms wrapped in homemade rice paper. People are willing to wait on the sidewalk for hours—come before 7 PM to avoid a wait—to sample the fish panfried with mango or with *nuoc man* (a garlic-lime fish sauce), not to mention the thinly sliced pork barbecued with sesame seeds, almonds, and peanuts. Beer-savvy proprietor Kathy Manning serves a half-dozen top brews (Double Grimbergen, Peroni, and Spaten, among them) to further inoculate the experience from the ordinary—well, as ordinary as a Vietnamese restaurant on Calle Ocho can be. ⊠ *3458 SW 8th St., Little Havana* ☎ *305/446–3674* ⊕ *www.hyvong.com* ▭ *AE, D, MC, V* ☉ *Closed Mon. and Tues. No lunch* ✢ *5C.*

$ ✕ **Tutto Pasta.** Tourists might pay $30 for linguine elsewhere, but locals
ITALIAN   are more likely to frequent Tutto Pasta, where they feast on the delicious
☉   homemade pasta for less than $15. Start with fresh-baked goat-cheese foccacia with truffle oil. Then try the famous lobster ravioli garnished with plantain chips, or the tilapia sautéed with shrimp, calamari, scallops, and tomato sauce. Hop over to Tutto Pizza next door to enjoy innovative Brazilian-inspired thin pizzas like the Portuguesa, topped with ham, mozzarella, black olives, eggs, and onions. Finish with Tutto chocolate cake or creamy Brazilian Pave. ⊠ *1751 SW 3rd Ave. at SW 18th Rd., Little Havana* ☎ *305/857–0709* ⊕ *www.tuttopasta.com* ▭ *MC, V* ✢ *5D.*

$ ✕ **Versailles.** ¡*Bienvenido a Miami!* To the area's Cuban population,
CUBAN   Miami without Versailles is like rice without black beans. The storied eatery, where old émigrés opine daily about all things Cuban, is a stop on every political candidate's campaign trail, and it should be a stop for you as well. Order a heaping platter of *lechon asado* (roasted pork loin), *ropa vieja* (shredded beef), or *picadillo* (spicy ground beef), all served with rice, beans, and fried plantains. Battle the oncoming food coma with a cup of the city's strongest cafecito, which comes in the

tiniest of cups but packs a lot of punch. Versailles operates a bakery next door as well—take some pastelitos home. ⊠ *3555 SW 8th St., between SW 35th and SW 36th Aves., Little Havana* ☎ *305/444–0240* ⊕ *www. versaillescuban.com* ▭ *AE, D, DC, MC, V* ✛ *5C.*

MIAMI BEACH

MID-BEACH AND NORTH

$$$
ITALIAN
✕**Café Prima Pasta.** If Tony Soprano lived in Miami, this is where you'd find him. This famous, bustling Italian eatery is infused with the energy of the Argentine Cea family, whose clan cooks, serves, and operates this place, while somehow finding the time to pose for photos with the hundreds of celebrities who have eaten here over the years (see them in the photos on the walls). It's on a busy street, yet the low light, soothing music, and intimate seating on this restaurant's outdoor veranda can make Café Prima Pasta a romantic spot. Everything is made in-house— from the fragrant rosemary butter to the pasta, which tastes best as crab-stuffed ravioli or as linguine dyed in squid ink and served with sea- food in a lobster sauce. ⊠ *414 71st St., North Beach* ☎ *305/867–0106* ⊕ *www.primapasta.com* ▭ *MC, V* ⊗ *No lunch.* ✛ *3F.*

$$$
CONTINENTAL
✕**Chef Allen's.** Chef Allen Susser has long been a figure of Miami's culi- nary scene, a member of the original, self-designated "Mango Gang," who created contemporary American masterpieces from a global menu. Over the past couple of years, though, his namesake restaurant been renovated with a new look and jolt of fresh energy as a "modern sea- food bistro," focusing on sustainable fish. The restaurant is still the best in northern Miami. After trying the famous Devil's on a Horseback (manchego- and mango-stuffed dates wrapped in bacon), order a salad of baby greens and warm wild mushrooms or a rock-shrimp hash with roasted corn. Allen serves only locally caught seafood, so you may want to consider the swordfish with conch-citrus couscous, macadamia nuts, and lemon. It's hard to resist the dessert soufflé; order it when you order your appetizer to eliminate a mouthwatering wait at the end of your meal. ⊠ *19088 NE 29th Ave., Aventura* ☎ *305/935–2900* ⊕ *www. chefallens.com* ▭ *AE, D, MC, V* ✛ *1F.*

$$$–$$$$
STEAKHOUSE
Fodor'sChoice
★
✕**The Forge.** Legendary for its opulence, this restaurant has been wow- ing patrons in its present form since 1968. The Forge is a steak house, but a steak house the likes of which you haven't seen before. Antiques, gilt-framed paintings, a chandelier from the Paris Opera House, and Tiffany stained-glass windows from New York's Trinity Church are the fitting background for some of Miami's best steaks. The tried-and-true menu also includes prime rib, bone-in fillet, lobster thermidor, chocolate soufflé, and decadent side dishes like creamed spinach and roasted- garlic mashed potatoes. The focaccia bread is to die for. For its walk-in humidor alone, the over-the-top Forge is worth visiting. ⊠ *432 Arthur Godfrey Rd., Miami Beach* ☎ *305/538–8533* ⌂ *Reservations essential* ⊕ *www.theforge.com* ▭ *AE, MC, V* ⊗ *No lunch.* ✛ *4F.*

$$$
CANTONESE
★
✕**Hakkasan.** This stateside sibling of the Michelin-starred London res- taurant is one of the best-looking restaurants on Miami Beach. Intri- cately carved, lacquered-black-wood Chinois panels divide seating sections, creating a deceptively cozy dining experience. The music is

Pink as cotton candy and bubble gum, the Big Pink diner fits right in with its art deco surroundings.

clubby, the waitresses' matching outfits are slinky, and the shadowy lighting is thoughtfully designed to make everyone look about as good as they can. Chef Alan Yau, a pioneer of the haute-Chinese-food movement, has collected mostly simple and authentic Cantonese recipes, many featuring fresh seafood. Don't overlook the tofu dishes in lieu of other proteins: this isn't supermarket soy. The braised tofu and aubergine claypot in black bean pairs glorious little pillows of silken tofu with expertly cooked eggplant in a perfectly seasoned, thick, funky sauce. Unfortunately, not all dishes are as successful. ⊠ *4441 Collins Ave., Miami Beach* ☎ *305/538–2000* ⊟ *AE, D, DC, MC, V* ☼ *No lunch* ⊹ *2F.*

$$$
ITALIAN
Fodor's Choice
★

✕ **Timó.** Located in a glorified strip mall 5 mi north of South Beach, Timo (Italian for "thyme") is worth the trip from anywhere in South Florida. It's a kind of locals' secret that it's the best food in South Florida. The handsome bistro, co-owned by chef Tim Andriola and Rodrigo Martinez (former general manager and wine director at Norman's), has dark-wood walls, Chicago brick, and a stone-encased wood-burning stove. Andriola has an affinity for robust Mediterranean flavors: sweetbreads with bacon, honey, and aged balsamic vinegar; inexpensive, artisanal pizzas; and homemade pastas. Wood-roasted meats and Parmesan dumplings in a truffled broth are not to be missed. Every bite of every dish attests to the care given, and the service is terrific. ⊠ *17624 Collins Ave., Sunny Isles* ☎ *305/936–1008* ⊕ *www.timorestaurant.com* ⊟ *AE, DC, MC, V* ☼ *No lunch weekends* ⊹ *1F.*

SOUTH BEACH

$
AMERICAN
Fodor's Choice
★

✕ Big Pink. The decor in this innovative, super-popular diner may remind you of a roller-skating rink—everything is pink Lucite, stainless steel, and campy (think sports lockers as decorative touches)—and the menu is 3 feet tall, complete with a table of contents. Food is solidly all-American, with dozens of tasty sandwiches, pizzas, turkey or beef burgers, and side dishes, each and every one composed with gourmet flair. Big Pink also makes a great spot for brunch. ⊠ *157 Collins Ave., South Beach* ⊕ *www.mylesrestaurantgroup.com* ☎ *305/532–4700* ▤ *AE, MC, V* ⊹ *5H.*

$$$$
STEAK

✕ BLT Steak. Miami suddenly has a plethora of good steak houses. This 2009 newbie is in the light-filled, open lobby of the snazzy Betsy Hotel at the very northern end of Ocean Drive and has the distinction of being open for breakfast daily—get the sensational steak and eggs. The clever name stands for Bistro Laurent Tourondel, Mr. T being the highly regarded chef who created the chain of BLTs. You can count on the highest quality cuts of USDA prime, certified Black Angus, and American Wagyu beef, in addition to blackboard specials and raw-bar selections. The grilled Kobe beef–skirt salad is juicy and delicious. ⊠ *1440 Ocean Dr., South Beach* ☎ *305/673–0044* ⊕ *www.bltrestaurants.com* ▤ *AE, D, DC, MC, V* ⊹ *2H.*

$$$$
FRENCH

✕ Blue Door at the Delano. In a hotel where style reigns supreme, this high-profile restaurant provides both glamour and solid cuisine. The four white-curtained, high-ceilinged walls make it the most theatrically focused dining room in the city. Acclaimed consulting chef Claude Troisgros combines the flavors of classic French cuisine with South American influences to create a seasonal menu that might include foie gras with berries or lobster with caramelized banana. Equally pleasing is dining with the crème de la crème of Miami (and New York and Paris) society. Don't recognize the apparent bigwig next to you? If you hear bits of his cell-phone conversation, you'll be filled in pronto. ⊠ *1685 Collins Ave., South Beach* ☎ *305/674–6400* ⌂ *Reservations essential* ▤ *AE, D, DC, MC, V* ⊹ *2H.*

$$$
SEAFOOD

✕ Joe's Stone Crab Restaurant. In South Beach's decidedly new-money scene, the stately Joe's Stone Crab is an old-school testament to good food and good service. South Beach's most storied restaurant started as a turn-of-the-century eating house when Joseph Weiss discovered succulent stone crabs off the Florida coast. Almost a century later, the restaurant stretches a city block and serves 2,000 dinners a day to local politicians and moneyed patriarchs. Stone crabs, served with legendary mustard sauce, crispy hash browns, and creamed spinach, remain the staple. But don't think you need a trust fund to eat here: Joe's serves sensational fried chicken for $5.95. Finish your meal with tart key lime pie, baked fresh daily. ■TIP➔ Joe's famously refuses reservations, and weekend waits can be three hours long—yes, you read that correctly—so come early or order from Joe's Take Away next door. ⊠ *11 Washington Ave., South Beach* ☎ *305/673–0365, 305/673–4611 for takeout, 800/780–2722 for overnight shipping* ⌂ *Reservations not accepted* ⊕ *www.joesstonecrab.com* ▤ *AE, D, DC, MC, V* ☉ *Closed May–mid-Oct. No lunch Sun. and Mon.* ⊹ *5G.*

CUBAN FOOD

If the tropical vibe has you hankering for Cuban food, you've come to the right place. Miami is the top spot in the country to enjoy authentic Cuban cooking.

The flavors and preparations of Cuban cuisine are influenced by the island nation's natural bounty (yucca, sugarcane, guava), as well as its rich immigrant history, from near (Caribbean countries) and far (Spanish and African traditions). Chefs in Miami tend to stick with the classic versions of beloved dishes, though you'll find some variation from restaurant to restaurant as recipes have often been passed down through generations of home cooks. Try the popular **Versailles** (⌧ *3555 SW 8th St.* ☎ *305/444–0240*) in Little Havana or Coral Gables' **Havana Harry's** (⌧ *4612 Le Jeune Rd.* ☎ *305/661–2622*), appealing to families seeking a home-cooked, Cuban-style meal. In North Miami, **Little Havana Restaurant** (⌧ *12727 Biscayne Blvd.* ☎ *305/899–9069*) serves traditional Cuban fare, and in South Beach, **David's Café** (⌧ *1058 Collins Ave.* ☎ *305/534–8736*) is a hole-in-the-wall with excellent eats.

THE CUBAN SANDWICH

A great *cubano* (Cuban sandwich) requires pillowy Cuban bread layered with ham, garlic-citrus-marinated slow-roasted pork, Swiss cheese, and pickles (plus salami, if you're eating in Tampa; lettuce and tomatoes if you're in Key West), butter and/or mustard. The sandwich is grilled in a sandwich press until the cheese melts and all the elements are fused together. Try one, usually about $6, at Enriqueta's Sandwich Shop (⌧ 2830 NE 2nd Ave. ☎ 305/573–4681 ⏱ weekdays 6 AM–4 PM, Sat. 6 AM–2 PM) in the Design District, or Exquisito Restaurant (⌧ 1510 SW 8 St. ☎ 305/643–0227 ⏱ Open daily, 7 AM–midnight) in Little Havana.

KEY CUBAN DISHES

ARROZ CON POLLO

This chicken-and-rice dish is Cuban comfort food. Found throughout Latin America, the Cuban version is typically seasoned with garlic, paprika, and onions, then colored golden or reddish with saffron or achiote (a seed paste), and enlivened with a sizable splash of beer near the end of cooking. Green peas and sliced, roasted red peppers are a standard topping.

BISTEC DE PALOMILLA

This thinly sliced sirloin steak is marinated with lime juice and garlic, and fried with onions. The steak is often served with chimichurri sauce, an olive oil, garlic, and cilantro sauce that is sometimes served with bread as a dip (slather bread with butter and dab on the chimichurri). Also try *Ropa Vieja*, a slow-cooked, shredded flank steak in a garlic-tomato sauce.

LECHON ASADO

Fresh ham or an entire suckling pig marinated in *Mojo Criollo* (parsley, garlic, sour orange, and olive oil) and roasted until fork tender. Served with white rice, black beans, and *tostones* (fried plantains) or yucca (pronounced YU-kah), a starchy tuber with a mild nut taste that's often sliced into fat sticks and deep-fried like fries.

FRITAS

If you're in the mood for an inexpensive, casual Cuban meal, have a *frita*—a hamburger with distinctive Cuban flair. It's made with ground beef that's mixed with ground or finely chopped chorizo, spiced with pepper, paprika, and salt, topped with sautéed onions and shoestring potatoes fries, and then served on a bun slathered with a special tomato-based ketchup-like sauce.

DRINKS

Sip *guarapo* (gwa-RA-poh), a fresh sugarcane juice that isn't really as sweet as you might think, or grab a straw and enjoy a frothy *batido* (bah-TEE-doe), a Cuban-style milk shake made with tropical fruits like mango, *piña* (pineapple), or *mamey* (mah-MAY, a tropical fruit with a melon-cherry taste). For a real twist, try the *batido de trigo*—a wheat shake that will remind you of sugar-glazed breakfast cereal.

DESSERTS

Treat yourself to a slice of *tres leches* cake. The "three milks" come from the sweetened condensed milk, evaporated milk, and heavy cream that are poured over the cake until it's an utterly irresistible gooey mess. Also, don't miss the *pastelitos*, Cuban fruit-filled turnovers. Traditional flavors include plain guava, guava with cream cheese, and cream cheese with coconut. Yum!

(below) Cuban sandwich; (top) *tres leches*

$$$$ ✕ **La Marea.** Come here if you're looking for a sophisticated, intimate
SEAFOOD dining experience in Miami Beach. Choose one of two dining areas—on
the hedge-edged terrace that leads to the entrance of The Tides hotel
or inside the coolly surreal dining room, where dramatic faux tortoise
shells line the walls and hooded wood chairs line the outer tables.
Everything on the menu is tasty, but chef Gonzalo Rivera, a Michael
Mina protégé, shines most in dishes inspired by his Mexican heritage.
Try the Colorado Rack of Lamb with cinnamon and dark mole sauce
complemented by dried bing cherry–quinoa salad and stuffed zucchini
blossom with goat cheese. The tiny little bar in the back, the gorgeous
Coral Room, is a Miami secret. ✉ *1220 Ocean Dr., at The Tides hotel,
South Beach* ☎ *305/604–5070* ▭ *AE, D, DC, MC, V* ✛ *3H.*

$$$ ✕ **Meat Market.** Yes, it's a great name for a steak-inspired restaurant, and
STEAK a name seemingly destined for a place like this on Lincoln Road, where
★ sexy people amble by in skimpy clothes year-round. But here's the great
news: this is a sophisticated place with a large non-steak-house menu.
When this reviewer was there recently with friends, it was a thrilling
night of drinks, plus appetizers that were just sitting at the bar—cedar-
scented hamachi (yellowtail sashimi) topped with mango caviar, white
truffle, fresh lime, and rice-paper tuna tacos with guajillo chili, cab-
bage, grilled watermelon, micro watercress, and roasted garlic. The
seafood selection, like the seared Florida grouper in browned goat but-
ter and bacon-chipotle conch broth, is also excellent. Naturally, there
are the steaks, which range from simple à la carte cuts to thoughtful
creations like the braised prime brisket with coconut, mango, Cuban
sweet potatoes, and wild mushrooms. ✉ *915 Lincoln Rd., South Beach*
☎ *305/532–0088* ⊕ *www.meatmarketmiami.com* ▭ *AE, D, DC, MC,
V* ⊗ *No lunch* ✛ *2G.*

$$ ✕ **Miss Yip Chinese Cafe.** Owner Jennie Yip has helped launch restaurants
CHINESE as fawned over as Blue Door at the Delano and New York's Mercer
Kitchen. At the most popular of only a handful of Chinese restaurants
on South Beach, the hip Miss Yip serves authentic dim sum and steam-
ing fresh Cantonese dishes just off Lincoln Road. Try the Peking duck
and the "Princess Jade" sea bass, made of cubes of tender battered fish
with Chinese mayo sauce. Wash it down with one of Miss Yip's many
specialty cocktails: a few favorites include the lychee mojito and the
ginger martini. A small market sells dozens of sauce and spice mixes.
The crowds here are lively, the design vividly colorful and contemporary, and the food flavorful. ✉ *1661 Meridian Ave., South Beach*
☎ *305/534–5488* ⊕ *www.missyipchinesecafe.com* ▭ *AE, D, DC, MC,
V* ✛ *2G.*

$$$$ ✕ **Nemo.** The SoFi (South of 5th Street) neighborhood may have emerged
SEAFOOD as a South Beach hot spot, but Nemo's location is not why this casually
comfortable restaurant receives rave reviews. It's the menu, which often
changes but always delivers, blending Caribbean, Asian, Mediterranean, and Middle Eastern influences and providing an explosion of cultures in each bite. Popular appetizers include citrus-cured salmon rolls
with tobiko caviar and wasabi mayo, and crispy duck-leg confit served
with lentils in a tangy pineapple sauce. Main courses might include
wok-charred salmon or grilled Indian-spice pork chop. Bright colors

and copper fixtures highlight the tree-shaded courtyard. ✉ *100 Collins Ave., South Beach* ☎ *305/532–4550* ⊕ *www.mylesrestaurantgroup.com* ▤ *AE, DC, MC, V* ⊹ *5G.*

$ ✕ **News Café**. No trip to Miami is complete without a stop at this Ocean
AMERICAN   Drive landmark. The 24-hour café attracts a crowd with snacks, light meals, drinks, periodicals, and the people-parade on the sidewalk out front. Most prefer sitting outside, where they can feel the salt breeze and gawk at the human scenery. Sea-grape trees shade a patio where you can watch from a quiet distance. Offering a little of this and a little of that—bagels, pâtés, chocolate fondue, sandwiches, and a terrific wine list—this joint has something for everyone. Although service can be indifferent to the point of laissez-faire, the café remains a must. ✉ *800 Ocean Dr., South Beach* ☎ *305/538–6397* ⌕ *Reservations not accepted* ⊕ *www.newscafe.com* ▤ *AE, DC, MC, V* ⊹ *4H.*

$$$ ✕ **Osteria del Teatro**. Thanks to word of mouth, this northern Italian
ITALIAN   restaurant is constantly full of the most refined clink and clatter along sometimes-seedy Washington Avenue. Because of inventive and fresh dishes you might stray from the printed menu, and order one of the many daily specials. A representative appetizer is poached asparagus served over polenta triangles with a Gorgonzola sauce. Stuffed pastas, including spinach crepes overflowing with ricotta, can seem heavy but taste light; fish dishes yield a rosemary-marinated tuna or salmon in a rosemary-shiitake-lemon sauce. ✉ *1443 Washington Ave., South Beach* ☎ *305/538–7850* ⌕ *Reservations essential* ⊕ *www. osteriadelteatromiami.com* ▤ *AE, DC, MC, V* ☾ *Closed Sun. No lunch* ⊹ *2H.*

$$$$ ✕ **Prime One Twelve**. This wildly busy steak house is particularly
STEAK   renowned for its highly marbleized prime beef (try the 30-ounce bone-in rib eye for two, $68), creamed corn, truffle macaroni and cheese, and buzzing scene: while you stand at the bar awaiting your table (everyone has to wait—at least a little bit), you'll clamor for a drink with all facets of Miami's high society, from the city's top real-estate developers and philanthropists to striking models and celebrities (Lenny Kravitz, Jay-Z, and Matt Damon are among a big list of celebrity regulars). ✉ *112 Ocean Dr., South Beach* ☎ *305/532–8112* ⊕ *www. mylesrestaurantgroup.com* ▤ *AE, D, DC, MC, V* ⊹ *5H.*

$$$$ ✕ **The Restaurant at The Setai**. With its harmonious courtyard reflecting
ECLECTIC   pool and polished-stone interiors, the setting of the Setai is so dra-
★   matically beautiful that a less-than-heavenly dining experience would be a blow. Even so, The Restaurant, as it's called, exceeds expectations. It has foreign chefs dedicated to producing delicious dishes from their native homelands—Thailand, India, China, Singapore, Malaysia, and Indonesia. Dining here is a culinary tour of Asia. Dishes, such as steamed whole yellowtail with ginger soy and green onions, perfectly cooked dim sum, and curries, come family-style in native crockery. The leather-bound wine list is 45 pages long. ✉ *2001 Collins Ave., South Beach* ☎ *305/520–6400* ⊕ *www.setai.com/dining* ▤ *AE, D, DC, MC, V* ☾ *No lunch* ⊹ *1H.*

$$$ ✕ **SushiSamba Dromo**. This sibling to the New York City SushiSamba
JAPANESE   makes an eclectic pairing of Japanese, Peruvian, and Brazilian cuisines. The results are fabulous if a bit mystifying: miso-marinated sea bass,

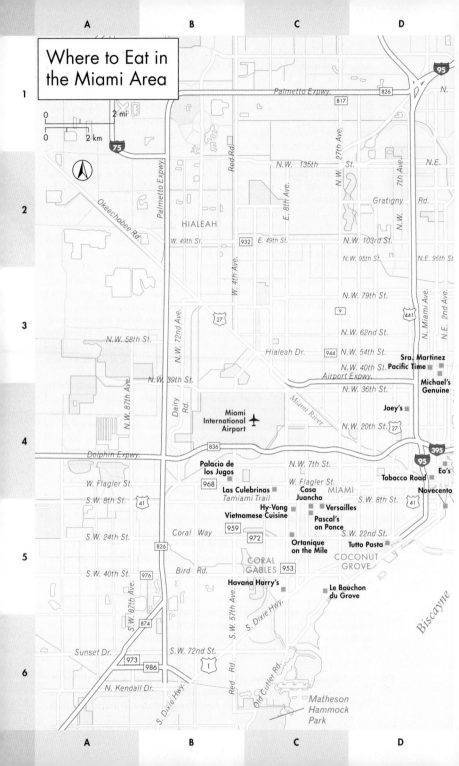

Where to Eat in the Miami Area

0 ___ 2 mi
0 ___ 2 km

HIALEAH

Palmetto Expwy.

Okeechobee Rd.

Palmetto Expwy.

Red Rd.

N.W. 135th St.

E. 8th Ave.

N.W. 27th Ave.

7th Ave.

N.E.

Gratigny   Rd.

N.W.

W. 49th St.

E. 49th St.

N.W. 103rd St.

N.E. 95th St.

N.W. 95th St.

N.W. 4th Ave.

N.W. 79th St.

N.W. 72nd Ave.

N.W. 58th St.

N.W. 62nd St.

N. Miami Ave.

N.E. 2nd Ave.

N.W. 87th Ave.

Hialeah Dr.

N.W. 54th St.

Sra. Martinez

N.W. 40th St.   Pacific Time

Dairy Rd.

Miami International Airport

N.W. 39th St.

Airport Expwy.

N.W. 36th St.

Michael's Genuine

Miami River

Joey's

N.W. 20th St.

Dolphin Expwy.

Eo's

W. Flagler St.

Palacio de los Jugos

N.W. 7th St.

Tobacco Road

Novecento

S.W. 8th St.

Las Culebrinas

Tamiami Trail

W. Flagler St.

Casa Juancho

MIAMI

S.W. 8th St.

Hy-Vong Vietnamese Cuisine

Versailles

S.W. 24th St.

Coral Way

Pascal's on Ponce

S.W. 22nd St.

Ortanique on the Mile

Tutto Pasta

COCONUT GROVE

S.W. 40th St.

Bird   Rd.

CORAL GABLES

S.W. 87th Ave.

S.W. 57th Ave.

Havana Harry's

Le Bouchon du Grove

Biscayne

Sunset Dr.

S.W. 72nd St.

N. Kendall Dr.

S. Dixie Hwy.

Red   Rd.

Old Cutler Rd.

Matheson Hammock Park

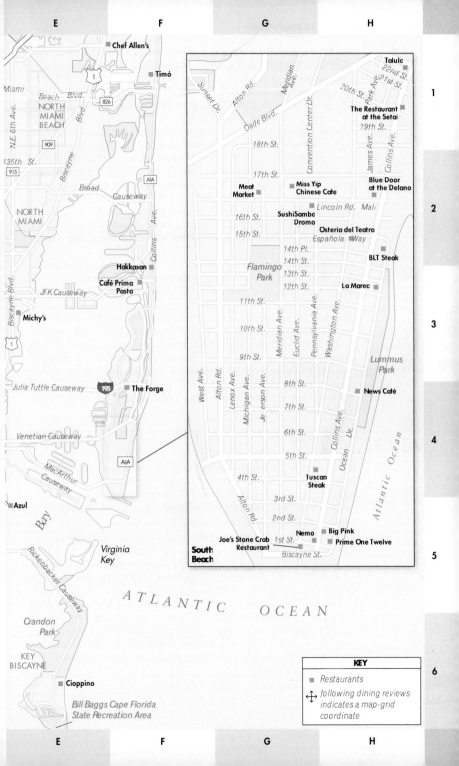

hamachi taquitos (basically a yellowtail tartare), *mocqueca mista* (Brazilian seafood stew), and caramel–passion fruit sponge cake. Loaded with customers in the heart of pedestrian Lincoln Road, SushiSamba has a vibe that hurts the ears but warms the trendy heart. ⊠ *600 Lincoln Rd., South Beach* ☎ *305/673–5337* ⚐ *Reservations essential* ⊕ *www. sushisamba.com* ▭ *AE, MC, V* ✛ *2G.*

$$$$
AMERICAN

✕ **Talula.** Husband-and-wife Frank Randazzo and Andrea Curto share the kitchen while keeping their own cooking styles. The cuisine Curto developed at Wish joins Asian and tropical influences. Randazzo, from the Gaucho Room, grills with a Latin influence. Together they call their style "American creative." Florida wahoo ceviche, barbecued quail, steamed mussels in a saffron broth, grouper with lime and chili, and a tender and moist barbecued pork tenderloin stand out. The key lime pie alone is worth a visit. ⊠ *210 23rd St., South Beach* ☎ *305/672–0778* ⊕ *www.talulaonline.com* ▭ *AE, D, MC, V* ⊗ *No lunch. Sat. Closed Mon.* ✛ *1H.*

$$$$
ITALIAN

✕ **Tuscan Steak.** Dark wood, mirrors, and green upholstery define this chic, masculine place, where big platters of meats and fish are served family-style, assuming yours is a royal family. Tuscan can be as busy as a subway stop, and still the staff is gracious and giving. The chefs take their cues from the Tuscan countryside, where pasta is rich with truffles and main plates are simply but deliciously grilled. Sip red wine with a house specialty: three-mushroom risotto with white-truffle oil, gnocchi with Gorgonzola cream, Florentine T-bone with roasted garlic puree, or filet mignon with a Gorgonzola crust in a red-wine sauce. Portions are enormous. Bring your friends and share, share, share. ⊠ *433 Washington Ave., South Beach* ☎ *305/534–2233* ⊕ *www.chinagrillmgt. com* ▭ *AE, DC, MC, V* ✛ *4G.*

WHERE TO STAY

Updated by
Michael de
Zayas

Room rates in Miami tend to swing wildly. In high season, which is January through May, expect to pay at least $150 per night. In summer, however, prices can be as much as 50% lower than the dizzying winter rates. You can also find great values between Easter and Memorial Day, which is actually a delightful time in Miami.

Business travelers tend to stay in downtown Miami, while most tourists stay on Miami Beach, as close as possible to the water. If money isn't an object, stay in one of the glamorous hotels lining Collins Avenue between 15th and 21st streets. Otherwise, stay on the quiet beaches farther north, or in one of the small boutique hotels on Ocean Drive, Collins, or Washington avenues between 10th and 15th streets. Two important considerations that affect price are balcony and view. If you're willing to have a room without an ocean view, you can sometimes get a price much lower than the standard rate. Many hotels are aggressive with specials and change their rates hour to hour, so it's worth calling around.

WHAT IT COSTS					
	¢	$	$$	$$$	$$$$
FOR TWO PEOPLE	under $150	$150–$200	$200–$300	$300–$400	over $400

Prices for hotels are for two people in a standard double room in high season, excluding 12.5% city and resort taxes.

COCONUT GROVE, CORAL GABLES, AND KEY BISCAYNE

COCONUT GROVE

$$$ **Ritz-Carlton, Coconut Grove.** Although it's the smallest and least exciting of the three Ritz-Carlton properties in the Miami area, it provides the best service experience in Coconut Grove. Overlooking Biscayne Bay, the hotel has rooms that are appointed with marble baths, a choice of down or nonallergenic foam pillows, and private balconies. A 5,000-square-foot spa is on hand to soothe away stress, and the open-air Bizcaya is among Coconut Grove's loveliest dining spots. **Pros:** best service in Coconut Grove; high-quality spa. **Cons:** of the three Miami Ritz-Carltons this one has the least interesting location and the fewest amenities. ✉ *3300 SW 27th Ave.* ☎ *305/644–4680 or 800/241–3333* 🌐 *www.ritzcarlton.com* *88 rooms, 27 suites* *In-room: a/c, safe, refrigerator, Internet, Wi-Fi. In-hotel: 2 restaurants, room service, bar, pool, gym, spa, laundry service, Internet terminal, Wi-Fi hotspot, parking (paid), some pets allowed* *AE, D, DC, MC, V* ⊕ *5D.*

CORAL GABLES

$$$ Fodor's Choice ★ **Biltmore Hotel.** Built in 1926, this landmark hotel has had several incarnations over the years—including a stint as a hospital during World War II—and has changed hands more than a few times. Through it all, this grandest of grandes dames remains an opulent reminder of yesteryear, with its palatial lobby and grounds, enormous pool, and distinctive 315-foot tower, which rises above the canopy of trees shading Coral Gables. Fully updated, the Biltmore has on-site golf and tennis, a spa and fitness center, extensive meeting facilities, and the celebrated Palme d'Or restaurant. The $65 Sunday brunch is a must. **Pros:** historic property; possibly best pool in the Miami area; great tennis and golf. **Cons:** far from Miami Beach. ✉ *1200 Anastasia Ave.* ☎ *305/445–1926 or 800/727–1926* 🌐 *www.biltmorehotel.com* *241 rooms, 39 suites* *In-room: a/c, Wi-Fi. In-hotel: 4 restaurants, room service, bars, golf course, tennis courts, pool, gym, spa, Wi-Fi hotspot, parking (paid)* *AE, D, DC, MC, V* ⊕ *5C.*

KEY BISCAYNE

$$$$ Fodor's Choice ★ **Ritz-Carlton, Key Biscayne.** There is probably no other place in Miami where slowness is lifted to a fine art. On Key Biscayne there are no pressures, there's no nightlife (outside of the hotel's great live Latin music weekends), and the dining choices are essentially limited to the hotel (which has four dining options, including the languorous, Havana-style RUMBAR). In this kind of setting, it's natural to appreciate the Ritz brand of pampering. Need something to do? The "tequilier" at

BEST BETS FOR MIAMI LODGING

Fodor's offers a selective listing of quality lodging experiences in every price range, from the city's best budget beds to its most sophisticated luxury hotels. Here, we've compiled our top recommendations by price and experience. The very best properties are designated in the listings with the Fodor's Choice logo. Find specific details about a hotel in the full reviews, listed alphabetically by neighborhood.

Fodor's Choice ★

Acqualina Resort & Spa on the Beach, p. 209

Biltmore Hotel, p. 199

Circa 39 Hotel, p. 206

Delano Hotel, p. 213

Fisher Island Hotel & Resort, p. 205

Fontainebleau, p. 207

Four Seasons Hotel Miami, p. 204

Mandarin Oriental Miami, p. 204

National Hotel, p. 215

Ritz-Carlton Key Biscayne, p. 199

The Tides, p. 217

Travelodge Monaco Beach Resort, p. 209

By Price

¢

Circa 39 Hotel, p. 206

Travelodge Monaco Beach Resort, p. 209

Villa Paradiso, p. 218

$

Century Hotel, p. 213

Essex House Hotel, p. 214

$$

Cadet Hotel, p. 212

Catalina Hotel & Beach Club, p. 212

The Hotel, p. 214

National Hotel, p. 215

Pelican, p. 216

Townhouse, p. 218

$$$

Biltmore Hotel, p. 199

Fontainebleau, p. 207

$$$$

Acqualina Resort, p. 209

Delano Hotel, p. 213

Fisher Island Hotel, p. 205

Four Seasons Hotel Miami, p. 204

Mandarin Oriental Miami, p. 204

Ritz-Carlton Key Biscayne, p. 199

Setai, p. 217

The Tides, p. 217

By Experience

BEST POOL

Biltmore Hotel, p. 199

National Hotel, p. 215

Ritz-Carlton South Beach, p. 216

The Standard, p. 206

The Viceroy, p. 205

BEST HOTEL BAR

The Hotel, p. 214

Mandarin Oriental Miami, p. 204

National Hotel, p. 215

The Standard, p. 206

The Viceroy (rooftop bar), p. 205

BEST SERVICE

Acqualina Resort, p. 209

Four Seasons Hotel Miami, p. 204

Ritz-Carlton Key Biscayne, p. 199

BEST VIEWS

Mandarin Oriental Miami, p. 204

The Regent Bal Harbour, p. 209

The Tides, p. 217

HIPSTER HOTELS

Catalina Hotel & Beach Club, p. 212

Gansevoort South, p. 214

Shore Club, p. 217

BEST LOCATION

National Hotel, p. 215

Pelican, p. 216

BEST-KEPT SECRET

Acqualina Resort, p. 209

National Hotel, p. 215

Ocean Surf Hotel, p. 207

Travelodge Monaco Beach Resort, p. 209

CHEAP EATS ON SOUTH BEACH

Miami Beach is notorious for over-priced eateries, but locals know better. Half Moon Empanadas (⊠ *1616 Washington Ave., at Lincoln Rd.*) has the colorful and polished look of a national franchise but is a genuine local start-up serving 17 delicious flavors of baked (or fried) empanadas for $1.99 each. Pizza Rustica (⊠ *8th St. and Washington Ave., 14th St. and Washington Ave., and at 667 Lincoln Rd.*) serves up humungous slices overflowing with mozzarella, steak, olives, and barbecue chicken until 4 AM. La Sandwicherie (⊠ *14th St. between Collins Ave. and Washington Ave.*) is a South Beach classic since 1988, serving gourmet French sandwiches, a delicious prosciutto salad, and healthy smoothies from a walk-up bar. Lime Fresh Mexican Grill (⊠ *1439 Alton Rd. at 14th St.*) serves fresh and tangy fish tacos and homemade guacamole.

4

the seaside Cantina Beach can educate you on the finer points of his native region's drink. Hitting the spa? In one of 21 treatment rooms, try signature Coco-Luscious body treatments, a nod to the island's history as the country's largest coconut plantation. An 11-court tennis "garden" with daily clinics, a private beach, and beachside water sports are other options. Recently renovated guestrooms have custom-made touches like mother-of pearl wall coverings. Updated technology includes plasma televisions and jack packs. In-room luxuries like robes, slippers, fine linens and toiletries, are par for the course. The Club Level offers five food presentations throughout the day, and the Ritz Kids club has expanded its full- and half-day and Saturday-night programs to include island history, fishing, beach treasure hunts and a kid-friendly blue and gold macaw. Borrow bikes here to explore Billy Baggs park and its lighthouse. **Pros:** private beach; quiet, luxurious family retreat. **Cons:** it will be too quiet if you're looking for a party—so you have to drive to Miami for nightlife. ⊠ *455 Grand Bay Dr.* ☎ *305/365–4500 or 800/241–3333* ⊕ *www.ritzcarlton.com/resorts/key_biscayne* ⬧ *365 rooms, 37 suites* ⬧ *In-room: a/c, safe, DVD (some), Internet, Wi-Fi. In-hotel: 2 restaurants, room service, bars, tennis courts, pools, gym, spa, beachfront, water sports, bicycles, laundry service, Internet terminal, Wi-Fi hotspot, parking (paid), some pets allowed* ▭ *AE, D, DC, MC, V* ✛ *6E.*

DOWNTOWN MIAMI

$$ 🏨 **Doubletree Grand Hotel Biscayne Bay.** Like the Biscayne Bay Marriott, this elegant waterfront option is at the north end of downtown off a scenic marina, and near many of Miami's headline attractions: the Port of Miami, Bayside, the Arena, and the Carnival Center. Rooms are spacious, and most have a view of Biscayne Bay and the port. Some suites have full kitchens. You can rent Jet Skis or take deep-sea-fishing trips from the marina. **Pros:** great bay views; deli and market on-site. **Cons:** need a cab to get around. ⊠ *1717 N. Bayshore Dr., Downtown Miami*

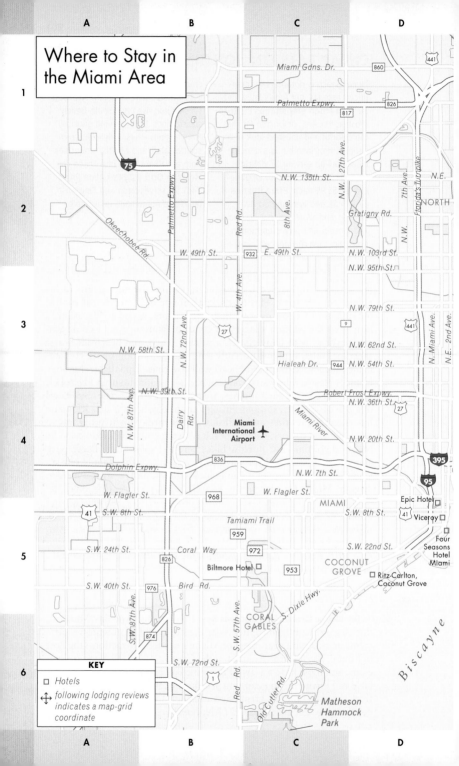

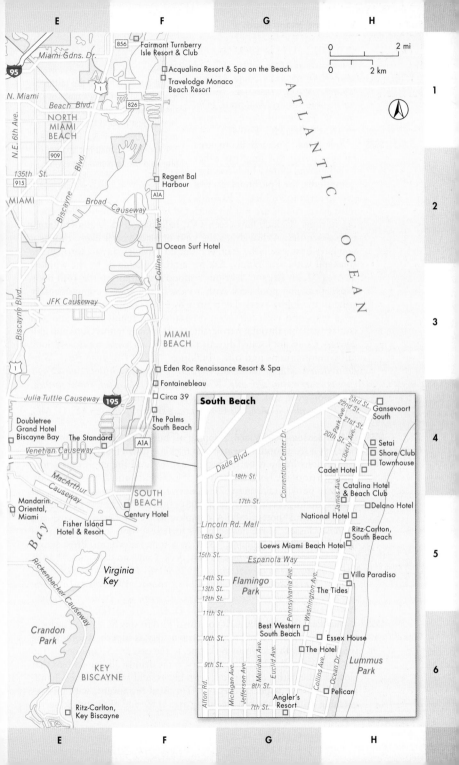

☎ *305/372–0313 or 800/222–8733* ⊕ *www.doubletree.com* ⤵ *152 suites ♿ In-room: a/c, safe, kitchen (some), Wi-Fi. In-hotel: restaurant, room service, bar, pool, gym, spa, Wi-Fi hotspot, parking (paid)* ▭ *AE, D, DC, MC, V ✛ 4E.*

$$$$ ⬚ **Epic Hotel.** Located in an area mostly known for its gritty office buildings and glittery high-rise condominiums, the Epic Hotel is a real gem in downtown Miami. Even the

most basic rooms are plushly outfitted with Frette linens, iPod docking stations, 37-inch flat-screen TVs, balconies, and Acqua Di Parma bath amenities. Although it's the kind of place you'll likely choose if you have business in the area, you should consider staying through the weekend with your family. Ask for a table outside or by the window at Area 31, an elegant, delicious seafood restaurant on the 16th floor. **Pros:** sprawling pool deck with a view of the water; complimentary wine in the lobby every day from 5 to 6 PM; complimentary in-room yoga mats and yoga television programming; tennis courts and golf courts available through partnerships with nearby tennis clubs and golf courses. **Cons:** not located directly near the beach; some rooms overlook tall condominiums and office buildings. ✉ *270 Biscayne Blvd. Way, Downtown Miami* ☎ *305/424–5226* ⊕ *www.epichotel.com* ⤵ *411 rooms ♿ In-room: a/c, safe, Wi-Fi. In-hotel: restaurant, room service, bar, pool, gym, spa, water sports, bicycles, children's programs (ages 2–12), laundry service, Wi-Fi hotspot, parking (paid)* ▭ *AE, D, MC, V ✛ 5D .*

$$$$
Fodor'sChoice
★

⬚ **Four Seasons Hotel Miami.** Stepping off busy Brickell Avenue into this hotel, you see a soothing water wall trickling down from above. Inside, a cavernous lobby is barely big enough to hold the enormous sculptures—part of the hotel's collection of local and Latin American artists. A 2-acre-pool terrace on the 7th floor overlooks downtown Miami, yet makes you forget you're in the middle of the city. The hotel's best feature is the beautiful Sports Club/LA, complete with complimentary yoga and exercise classes. Three heated pools include a foot-deep wading pool with 24 palm tree "islands." Service is tops for Miami. **Pros:** sensational service; amazing gym and pool deck. **Cons:** no balconies. ✉ *1435 Brickell Ave., Downtown Miami* ☎ *305/358–3535 or 800/819–5053* ⊕ *www.fourseasons.com/miami* ⤵ *182 rooms, 39 suites ♿ In-room: a/c, safe. In-hotel: restaurant, bars, pools, gym, spa, Internet terminal, Wi-Fi hotspot, parking (paid)* ▭ *AE, D, DC, MC ✛ 5D.*

$$$$
Fodor'sChoice
★

⬚ **Mandarin Oriental, Miami.** If you can afford to stay here, do. The location, at the tip of Brickell Key in Biscayne Bay, is superb. Rooms facing west overlook the downtown skyline; to the east are Miami Beach and the blue Atlantic. There's also beauty in the details: sliding screens that close off the baths, dark wood, crisp linens, and room numbers hand-painted on rice paper at check-in. The Azul restaurant, with an eye-catching waterfall and private dining area at the end of a catwalk, serves a mix of Asian, Latin, Caribbean, and French cuisine. The hotel has a 20,000-square-foot private beach and an on-site spa. **Pros:** only beach (man-made) in downtown; intimate feeling; top luxury hotel. **Cons:** small pool; few beach cabanas. ⊠ *500 Brickell Key Dr., Downtown Miami* 🕾 *305/913–8288 or 866/888–6780* ⊕ *www.mandarinoriental. com* ⤹ *326 rooms, 31 suites* ⌕ *In-room: a/c, safe, Internet. In-hotel: 2 restaurants, bars, pool, gym, spa, children's programs (ages 5–12), laundry service, Wi-Fi hotspot, parking (paid)* ▭ *AE, D, DC, MC, V* ✛ *5E.*

$ ▦ **Viceroy.** Miami's newest hotel has a brash, super-sophisticated South Beach attitude—something that distinguishes it wholly from every other Miami nonbeach hotel. With game lounges (pool and poker rooms) just off to the side, it's fair to say that the 15th-floor pool deck here is the most stylish, fun-oriented, and impressive of any in America. The main pool is 300 feet long (the longest in Florida) and terminates in mesmerizing view of Biscayne Bay and surrounding islands. The lawn furniture and oversized cabanas the Delano made famous inspire the decor here. It also has a gargantuan hot tub, the size of a regular pool. The rooftop lounge and bar (on the 50th floor) are for guests only, and the views and design of this sophisticated retreat are impressive—the space can function as a lobby aerie. Designed by Kelly Wearstler, the rooms are dramatically contemporary and beautiful. She also designed the restaurant here, Eos, which was opened by two of the biggest names in American gastronomy: chef Michael Psilakis and restaurateur Donatella Arpaia. **Pros:** sensationally designed spa area; fantastic game room and pool deck; sleek rooms. **Cons:** downtown location rather than the beach; tiny lobby. ⊠ *485 Brickell Ave., Downtown Miami* 🕾 *305/503– 4400 or 866/781–9923* ⊕ *www.viceroymiami.com* ⤹ *150 rooms, 18 suites* ⌕ *In-room: a/c, safe, kitchen (some), refrigerator (some), DVD (some), Wi-Fi. In-hotel: restaurant, room service, bars, pools, gym, spa, laundry service, Internet terminal, Wi-Fi hotspot, parking (paid), some pets allowed* ▭ *AE, D, DC, MC, V* ☯ *BP* ✛ *5D.*

FISHER AND BELLE ISLANDS

$$$$ ▦ **Fisher Island Hotel & Resort.** Want to explore Fisher Island? Assuming
Fodor's Choice you don't have a private yacht, there are three ways to gain access to
★   the island just off South Beach: you can either become a club member (initiation fee alone: $25,000), be one of the 750 equity members who have vacation places here (starting price: $8 million), or book a night at the club hotel (basic villa: $900 a night). Once you've made it, you'll be welcomed at reception with champagne. Considering you get a private house, a golf cart, and a fenced-in backyard with a hot tub, villas are a value for a memorable honeymoon or other lifetime event, if not a casual weekend. Families should stay in one of three former guest cottages of the former Italianate mansion of William K. Vanderbilt (in 1925 he swapped Carl Fisher *his* yacht for the island), which forms the centerpiece of this resort. A 9-hole golf course, the surprisingly affordable Spa Internazionale, and 18 lighted tennis courts (hard, grass, and clay), kids' programs, and 1 mi of very private (and very quiet) white-sand beach imported from the Bahamas means there's plenty of sweet nothing to

do here. Oh, and there are eight restaurants and a fun sunset tiki bar to choose from—Porto Cervo is the best Italian restaurant nobody knows about. The Garwood Lounge features nightly piano and seats just 16. Remarkably, this true exclusivity and seclusion is minutes from South Beach. **Pros:** great private beaches; exclusive surroundings; varied dining choices. **Cons:** expensive ferry rides take time. ☒ *1 Fisher Island Dr., Fisher Island* ☎ *305/535–6000 or 800/537–3708* ⊕ *www.fisherisland. com* ⇨ *5 junior suites, 50 condo units, 6 villas, 3 cottages* ⚼ *In-room: a/c, safe, refrigerator, DVD, Wi-Fi. In-hotel: 8 restaurants, golf course, tennis courts, pools, gym, spa, beachfront, water sports, children's programs (ages 4–12), laundry service, Internet terminal, Wi-Fi hotspot, parking (free), some pets allowed* ⊟ *AE, D, DC, MC, V* ✛ *5E.*

$$ ▦ **The Standard.** An extension of André Balazs's trendy, budget hotel chain, the Standard is a Hollywood newcomer that set up shop a few minutes from South Beach on an island just over the Venetian Causeway. The message: we'll do what we please, and the cool kids will follow. The scene is trendy 30- and 40-year-olds interested in the hotel's many "do-it-yourself" spa activities, including mud bathing, scrubbing with sea salts, soaking in hot or arctic-cold waters, and yoga. An 8-foot, 103-degree cascade into a Roman hot tub is typical of the handful of adult pleasures spread around the pool deck. An informal restaurant overlooks the bay's Mediterranean-style mansions and the cigarette boats that float past. If you choose, you can go kayaking around the island. On the hotel facade you'll see the monumental signage of a bygone occupant, the Lido Spa Hotel, and the much smaller sign of its current occupant, hung, with a wink, upside down. The rooms are small and simple, though they have thoughtful touches like a picnic basket and embroidered fabric covers for the small flat-screen TVs. First-floor rooms have outdoor soaking tubs but very limited privacy, so few take that plunge. **Pros:** interesting island location; free bike and kayak rentals; swank pool scene; great spa; inexpensive. **Cons:** removed from South Beach nightlife; small rooms with no views; outdoor tubs are gimmicks; mediocre service. ☒ *40 Island Ave., Belle Isle* ☎ *305/673–1717* ⊕ *www.standardhotel.com* ⇨ *104 rooms, 1 suite* ⚼ *In-room: a/c, safe, refrigerator, DVD, Internet, Wi-Fi. In-hotel: restaurant, room service, bars, pool, gym, spa, water sports, bicycles, laundry service, Wi-Fi hotspot, parking (paid), some pets allowed, no kids under 14* ⊟ *AE, D, DC, MC, V* ✛ *4E.*

MID-BEACH

¢–$ ▦ **Circa 39 Hotel.** This stylish budget boutique hotel pays attention to Fodor'sChoice every detail and gets them all right. In its lobby, inspired in miniature by ★ the Delano hotel, tall candles burn all night. The pool has cabanas and umbrella-shaded chaises that invite all-day lounging. Beyond the pool is a cute bar with board games. Rooms have wood floors and a cool, crisp look with white furnishings dotted with pale-blue pillows. The name Circa 39? It was built in 1939 and is on 39th Street. **Pros:** affordable; chic; intimate; beach chairs provided. **Cons:** not on the beach side of Collins Avenue; no Wi-Fi in rooms (however, there is Wi-Fi in the hotel, for a fee). ☒ *3900 Collins Ave., Mid-Beach* ☎ *305/538–4900* *or 877/824–7223 ⊕ www.circa39.com ↽96 rooms ⟋ In-room: a/c, safe, kitchen, refrigerator, Internet. In-hotel: restaurant, bar, pool, gym, Wi-Fi hotspot, parking (paid), some pets allowed ⊟ AE, D, DC, MC, V ⦶ CP ⊹ 4F.*

$$$$ 🍽 **Eden Roc Renaissance Resort & Spa.** Like its next-door neighbor, the Fontainebleau, this grand 1950s hotel designed by Morris Lapidus just completed a head-to-toe renovation, with the addition of a new 21-story tower and huge pool complex. In the process, the Eden Roc doubled its room count and is now one of the biggest and sleekest hotels in the city. The landmark public areas have retained their grand elegance, including the monumental rosewood columns that surround the social lobby space, centered by an upscale bar. The room renovations have renewed the allure and perhaps returned the swagger of a stay at the Eden Roc to the heights it had reached after opening in the 1950s. For a glimpse of the old glamour, visit Harry's Grille, which has murals of former guests, a veritable roll call of '50s and '60s stars. **Pros:** all-new rooms and facilities; great pools. **Cons:** not on South Beach. ⊠ *4525 Collins Ave., Mid-Beach* ☎ *305/531–0000 or 800/327–8337 ⊕ www. edenrocresort.com ↽631 rooms ⟋ In-room: a/c, safe, kitchen (some), refrigerator, Wi-Fi. In-hotel: 3 restaurants, room service, bars, pools, gym, spa, beachfront, Wi-Fi hotspot, parking (paid) ⊟ AE, D, DC, MC, V ⊹ 3F.*

$$$ 🍽 **Fontainebleau.** Look out, South Beach—Mid-Beach is back. When this
Fodor'sChoice classic property reopened in late 2008 it became Miami's biggest hotel—
★ twice the size of the Loews, with more than 1,500 rooms; it became, indeed, the fruit of the most ambitious and expensive hotel-renovation project in the history of Greater Miami. So what does a $1 billion renovation get you? Eleven restaurants and lounges, a huge nightclub, sumptuous pools with cabana islands, a state-of-the-art fitness center and a 40,000-square-foot spa, and more than 100,000 square feet of meeting and ballroom space—all of it built from scratch. Also, two all-suites lavish towers come with full kitchens including dishwashers. In possibly a first for a big hotel anywhere, all rooms on the property have Apple desktop computers. But not everything is brand-new: two Morris Lapidus–designed, landmarked exteriors and lobbies were restored to their original state. To make way, though, all original rooms were completely gutted, down to the beams, to create new, contemporary rooms. This is a complex of historic proportions. **Pros:** historic design mixed with all-new facilities; fabulous pools. **Cons:** away from the South Beach pedestrian scene; too big to be intimate. ⊠ *4441 Collins Ave., Mid-Beach* ☎ *305/538–2000 or 800/548–8886 ⊕ www.fontainebleau. com ↽1,504 rooms ⟋ In-room: a/c, safe, kitchen (some), refrigerator, DVD (some), Wi-Fi. In-hotel: 11 restaurants, bars, pools, gym, spa, water sports, laundry service, Internet terminal, Wi-Fi hotspot, parking (paid) ⊟ AE, D, DC, MC, V ⊹ 4F.*

¢–$ 🍽 **Ocean Surf Hotel.** Don't expect luxury in this colorful art deco lodge, but if you want a cheap stay away from everybody and ideal beach access, you can't beat the tiny Ocean Surf Hotel. The hotel is on a cute one-block stretch called Ocean Terrace that's directly across the street from the beach. The area will feel like your secret. There's also a small

4

Days Inn here, but the Ocean Surf has more art deco charm. Sure the beds are squishy and look like they're 20 years old, and frankly the hallways are small and humid, but where else will you stay across from the beach for $80 a night? The location off 74th Street puts this quiet hotel well out of the reach of boisterous South Beach. Add in free Continental breakfast, and you've got a great crash pad for a low-key vacation. **Pros:** adorable art deco hotel; cheap; free Continental breakfast. **Cons:** basic rooms; no Internet; spotty service. ⊠ *7436 Ocean Terr., Mid-Beach* ☎ *305/866–1648 or 800/555–0411* ⊕ *www.theoceansurfhotel. com* ⤵ *49 rooms* ⚲ *In-room: a/c, safe, refrigerator. In-hotel: beachfront, parking (paid)* ▭ *AE, MC, V* ⬤ *CP* ⚓ *2F.*

$$ ⬚ **The Palms South Beach.** Stay here if you're seeking an elegant, relaxed property away from the noise but still near South Beach. The Palms has an exceptional beach, an easy pace, and beautiful gardens with soaring palm trees and inviting hammocks. A 2008 renovation has left the rooms looking as fabulous as the grounds, and a 5,000-square-foot Aveda spa was in the works. There are more large palms inside the Great Room lounge just off the lobby and designer Patrick Kennedy used subtle, natural hues of ivory, green, and blue for the homey, well-lighted rooms. **Pros:** tropical garden; relaxed and quiet. **Cons:** no balconies; away from South Beach. ⊠ *3025 Collins Ave., Mid-Beach* ☎ *305/534–0505 or 800/550–0505* ⊕ *www.thepalmshotel.com* ⤵ *220 rooms, 22 suites* ⚲ *In-room: a/c, safe, refrigerator, Wi-Fi. In-hotel: restaurant, room service, bars, pool, beachfront, laundry service, Wi-Fi hotspot, parking (paid)* ▭ *AE, D, DC, MC, V* ⚓ *4F.*

NORTH MIAMI BEACH

AVENTURA

$$$$ ⬚ **Fairmont Turnberry Isle Resort & Club.** Golfers and families will enjoy this upscale resort with one of the best service staffs in the city. The lush resort doesn't just feel like a country club: the LPGA Tour hosts an annual tournament here every April. The sprawling 300-acre resort has a tremendous lagoon pool with a winding waterslide and a lazy river, a wonderful three-story spa, and a delicious new steak house from Michael Mina called Bourbon. The rooms are also jumbo-sized, decorated in calming tan hues and equipped with every amenity you could need. Add two Robert Trent Jones–designed golf courses, four clay tennis courts, and a 117-boat marina, and you've got a corporate vacationer's dream. South Beach may seem a world away—and it's about a 10-minute drive to any beach—but anyone who wants to delve into Ocean Drive madness can access the resort's private Ocean Club at Collins Avenue and 17th Street. **Pros:** great golf, pools, and restaurants; free shuttle to Aventura Mall. **Cons:** far from the beach; no nightlife. ⊠ *19999 W. Country Club Dr., Aventura* ☎ *305/932–6200 or 800/327–7028* ⊕ *www.turnberryisle.com* ⤵ *392 rooms, 41 suites* ⚲ *In-room: a/c, safe, kitchen (some), refrigerator, DVD (some), Wi-Fi. In-hotel: 2 restaurants, bars, golf courses, tennis courts, pools, gym, spa, water sports, bicycles, laundry service, Internet terminal, Wi-Fi hotspot, parking (paid), some pets allowed* ▭ *AE, D, DC, MC, V* ⚓ *1F.*

BAL HARBOUR

$$$$ ▦ **The Regent Bal Harbour.** The tiny, tony town of Bal Harbour finally has a hotel worthy of its ultra-high-end mall. The new Regent is the latest word in contemporary luxury design. Rooms are outfitted with mahogany floors; large terraces offering panoramic views of the water and city (the northwest corner suites have the best views in Miami); bathrooms with 10-foot, floor-to-ceiling windows; and 42-inch flat-screen TVs (plus a small TV incorporated into the bathroom mirror—the latest technological interior-design trick). Suites are furnished with fully equipped kitchens with cooktops, microwaves, convection ovens, dishwashers, and refrigerators. Split your afternoons between the out-doors—enjoying the pool and 750 feet of pristine beachfront—and the hotel's lavish, on-site Guerlain Spa and fitness center, as well as a nice bar and fancy restaurant. **Pros:** great views; beachfront; great contemporary-art collection. **Cons:** pricey; limited lobby socializing. ✉ *10295 Collins Ave., Bal Harbour* ☎ *305/455–5400* ⊕ *www.regenthotels. com* ⬐ *124 rooms, 63 suites* ⚹ *In-room: a/c, safe, kitchen, refrigerator, DVD, Wi-Fi. In-hotel: restaurant, room service, bar, tennis courts, pools, gym, spa, beachfront, water sports, bicycles, laundry service, parking (paid)* ▭ *AE, D, MC, V* ✛ *2F.*

SUNNY ISLES

$$$$

Fodor's Choice
★

▦ **Acqualina Resort & Spa on the Beach.** When it opened in 2006, this hotel raised the bar for luxury in Miami, and it stands as one of the city's best hotels. You'll pay for it, too: Acqualina promises a lavish Mediterranean lifestyle with lawns and pool set below terraces that evoke Vizcaya, and Ferraris and Lamborghinis lining the driveway. There is much to love about the amenities here, including three gorgeous pools, the colossal ESPA spa, and the trendiest of restaurants, including one of only a handful in Miami to offer unobstructed beach views. And, upon arrival, you're escorted to your room for a personal in-room check-in. Rooms are sinfully comfortable, with every conceivable frill. Even standard rooms facing away from the ocean seem grand; they have huge flat-screens that rise out of the foot of the bed, making recumbent TV watching seem like a theater experience. If you're planning to pop the big question on your vacation, a Proposal Concierge will help set the scene. **Pros:** in-room check-in; luxury amenities; huge spa. **Cons:** guests have to pay an extra $40 to use the steam room or sauna. ✉ *17875 Collins Ave., Sunny Isles* ☎ *305/918–8000* ⊕ *www.acqualinaresort.com* ⬐ *54 rooms, 43 suites* ⚹ *In-room: a/c, safe, refrigerator, Wi-Fi. In-hotel: 3 restaurants, room service, bars, pools, gym, spa, beachfront, water sports, children's programs (ages 5–12), laundry service, Internet terminal, Wi-Fi hotspot, parking (paid)* ▭ *AE, D, DC, MC, V* ✛ *1F.*

¢

Fodor's Choice
★

▦ **Travelodge Monaco Beach Resort.** The last of a dying breed, the Travelodge Monaco is a true find. Peek inside the courtyard and you'll see older men and women playing shuffleboard. Some have been coming here for 50 years, and it seems almost out of charity that the Monaco stays open for them today. In high season, rooms peak at only $130, and are nearly half that much of the year. Want a kitchen? Ten dollars more. Naturally the furnishings are simple, but they're clean, and the oceanfront wing literally extends out onto the sand. So there's no

Acqualina Resort & Spa on the Beach

Circa 39 Hotel

Biltmore Hotel

Delano Hotel

Ritz-Carlton, Key Biscayne

Four Seasons Hotel Miami

The Tides South Beach

Mandarin Oriental

wireless Internet in the rooms—who needs it? Read a book under one of the tiki huts on the beach. You don't need to reserve them, and you don't pay extra. This is easily the best value of any hotel in Miami. **Pros:** steps to great beach; wholly unpretentious; bottom-dollar cost. **Cons:** older rooms; not service-oriented; no Wi-Fi in room, and public Wi-Fi in hotel has a fee. ⊠ *17501 Collins Ave., Sunny Isles* ☎ *305/932–2100 or 800/227–9006* ⊕ *www.monacomiamibeachresort.com* ⟿ *110 rooms* ♿ *In-room: a/c, safe, kitchen (some), refrigerator. In-hotel: restaurant, bar, pool, beachfront, Wi-Fi hotspot, parking (paid)* ⊟ *AE, D, DC, MC, V* ⊹ *1F.*

SOUTH BEACH

$ ⬚ Angler's Boutique Resort. Angler's has the feel of a sophisticated private Mediterranean villa community. Duplex apartments here are like wonderful contemporary apartments, complete with private sunning gardens or private rooftop terraces with hot tubs. Single-floor studio options are set around a wonderful pool. This property has a pervasive air of serenity and privacy, largely created by the spotless cleanliness and the wonderful gardens—all of which make you completely forget that the hotel is off busy Washington Avenue, two blocks from the beach. Instead it's a private little oasis. The hotel was originally built in 1930 by architect Henry Maloney. Hemingway was a guest. The property was completely redone and opened again in 2008. There's a good restaurant in the lobby. **Pros:** gardened private retreat. **Cons:** on busy Washington Ave. ⊠ *660 Washington Av., South Beach* ☎ *305/534–9600* ⊕ *www.theanglersresort.com* ⟿ *24 rooms, 20 suites* ♿ *In-room: a/c, safe, kitchen (some), refrigerator (some), DVD (some), Internet (some), Wi-Fi. In-hotel: restaurant, room service, bar, pool, laundry service, Internet terminal, Wi-Fi hotspot, parking (paid), some pets allowed* ⊟ *AE, D, DC, MC, V* ⦿| *BP* ⊹ *G6*

¢ ⬚ Cadet Hotel. You can trace the fact that this is one of the sweetest, quietest hotels in South Beach to the ways of its independent female owner, a local doctor named Vilma Biaggi. (There are very few privately owned hotels here anymore.) The placid patio-garden is the perfect spot to enjoy a full breakfast. Little touches, like candles in the lobby, fresh flowers all around, high-thread-count sheets, and small pouches that contain fresh lavender or seashells, depending on the season, show care and sophistication. The boutique hotel is two blocks from Lincoln Road, two blocks from the beach, across the street from Casa Tua. Clark Gable stayed in Room 225 when he came to Miami for Army Air Corps training in the 1940s; he'd been enrolled at West Point, and thus the hotel's name. A new spa pool and restaurant, Pied-a-Terre, opened in the back in 2010. **Pros:** well run with friendly service; lovely garden; great value. **Cons:** no pool. ⊠ *1701 James Ave., South Beach* ☎ *305/672–6688 or 800/432–2338* ⊕ *www.cadethotel.com* ⟿ *32 rooms, 3 suites* ♿ *In-room: a/c, safe, Wi-Fi. In-hotel: bar, laundry service, Wi-Fi hotspot* ⊟ *AE, D, DC, MC, V* ⦿| *CP* ⊹ *4H.*

$–$$ ⬚ Catalina Hotel & Beach Club. The Catalina is the budget party spot in the heart of South Beach's hottest block. It's across the street from the beach, but makes up for it with free drinks nightly, airport shuttles, bike rentals, two fun pools, and beach chairs, all for south of $300 a night. Each of the Catalina's three buildings has a distinct feel: The original Catalina (with the smallest, most inexpensive rooms) is an exercise in camp, with red-shag carpets, two-story glass windows, and monumental sheer drapes. The midrange rooms are in the old Maxine Hotel, decorated in rock baroque and featuring a karaoke machine in the lobby. Room 400 here is one of the beach's best values, with a private sundeck overlooking the strip. The newest, and most luxurious, addition is the Dorset Hotel, which now houses Catalina's biggest rooms as well as its new sushi restaurant, Kung Fu Chus. Another outdoor restaurant overlooking the passersby on this very sexy strip of Collins Avenue makes the Catalina an entertainment complex in its own right. **Pros:** free drinks; free bikes; free airport shuttle; good people-watching. **Cons:** $15 wireless fee; service not a high priority; loud. ⊠ *1732 Collins Ave., South Beach* ☎ *305/674–1160* ⊕ *www.catalinahotel.com* ⤵ *200 rooms* ⚘ *In-room: a/c, safe, refrigerator, Wi-Fi. In-hotel: restaurant, bars, pool, bicycles, laundry service, Wi-Fi hotspot, parking (paid), some pets allowed* ⊟ *AE, D, DC, MC, V* ✣ *5H.*

4

$ 🛈 **Century Hotel.** If this is your second time staying in South Beach, consider this cheap but tidy hotel at the southern end of the island. It's a dozen blocks south of the big scene but offers the same amazing (though quieter) beach, and it gives you a chance to discover some of the city's best restaurants, which happen to be steps away: Big Pink, Joe's, Prime One Twelve, and Nemo's. Designed in 1939 by art deco master Henry Hohauser, the Century is a cute two-story art deco masterpiece, impeccably maintained down to the terrazzo floors. Rooms are wonderful values for their wood floors, and clean, new furniture. A rarity anywhere in Miami: this is a pet-friendly hotel. Off-season weekend rooms are $199; weekday rooms off-season are $89. The owner, West Tucker, works at the front desk. **Pros:** quiet South Beach location; clean; across from beach; classic art deco building; personal attention. **Cons:** not in the heart of South Beach; no pool; simple rooms. ⊠ *140 Ocean Dr., South Beach* ☎ *305/674–8855 or 888/982–3688* ⊕ *www. centurysouthbeach.com* ⤵ *26 rooms* ⚘ *In-room: a/c, safe, Wi-Fi. In-hotel: Internet terminal, parking (paid), some pets allowed* ⊟ *AE, DC, MC, V* 🍴⦿ *CP* ✣ *F5.*

$$$$ 🛈 **Delano Hotel.** The decor of this grand hotel is inspired by Lewis Carroll's Alice in Wonderland, and as you make your way from the sparse, busy, spacious lobby past cascading white curtains and through rooms dotted with strange, whimsical furniture pieces, you will feel like you are indeed falling down a rabbit hole. Brush by celebrities and expatriates as you make your way to the vast oceanfront gardens and enormous pool outside, where the rich and famous lounge in white cabanas. Like most hotels on South Beach's hottest strip, the Delano boasts glamour and wealth. Unlike some of the other hotels, the Delano's smartly designed rooms and helpful staff make the illusion a reality. Make sure to visit the hotel's brand-new "Florida Room," an über-exclusive lounge designed by Lenny Kravitz with a glass baby grand piano that he plays whenever he's in town. **Pros:** electrifying design; lounging among the beautiful and famous. **Cons:** crowded; scene-y; small rooms; expensive.

Fodor's Choice
★

⊠ 1685 Collins Ave., South Beach ☎ 305/672–2000 or 800/555–5001 ⊕ www.delano-hotel.com ↶ 184 rooms, 24 suites ♿ In-room: a/c, safe, refrigerator, Wi-Fi. In-hotel: 3 restaurants, room service, bars, pool, gym, spa, beachfront, laundry service, Wi-Fi hotspot, parking (paid) ☰ AE, D, DC, MC, V ⊹ 5H.

$ ▦ **Essex House.** You'll get your own South Beach people-watching perch on the outdoor patio at this wonderfully restored art deco gem. A favorite with Europeans, especially the British, Essex House has average-size rooms with midcentury-style red furniture and marble tubs. The suites, reached by crossing a courtyard, are well worth the price: each has a wet bar, king-size bed, pull-out sofa, 100-square-foot bathroom, refrigerator, and hot tub. The lobby mural was created in 1938 by artist Earl Le Pan, and touched up by him 50 years later. Ask for a discount when you're booking; off-season rates are under $100. **Pros:** a social, heated pool; great art deco patio; good service. **Cons:** small pool; not on the beach. *⊠ 1001 Collins Ave., South Beach ☎ 305/534–2700 or 800/815–829 ⊕ www.essexhotel.com ↶ 61 rooms, 15 suites ♿ In-room: a/c, Wi-Fi. In-hotel: bar, pool, laundry service, Wi-Fi hotspot, parking (paid) ☰ AE, D, DC, MC, V ⊹ 6H.*

$$$$ ▦ **Gansevoort South.** For the well-heeled, party-seeking, jet-setting crowd, there's a new South Beach hotel to toy with: this southern cousin of New York's trendsetting Meatpacking District hotel is better than the original, starting with a fantastic beachfront setting. Want to swim or lounge around with a drink? The huge rooftop pool and bar is the best use of a rooftop in Miami; and the 50,000-square-foot plaza level has a big pool and an informal open-air restaurant. The contemporary aesthetic starts in the big, sleek lobby, awash in funky lights and a massive aquarium stocked with small sharks. Not in the thick of South Beach, the hotel has privacy and is relatively quiet. Rooms are quite large, and highly comfortable, though views are disappointing. The hotel has a David Barton Gym and Spa, and fabulous restaurants STK and Phillipe. **Pros:** spacious rooms (averaging 700 square feet); big, fun setting with huge pool deck and rooftop; fancy on-site restaurants. **Cons:** room views aren't amazing; a few blocks too far from most SoBe foot traffic. *⊠ 2377 Collins Ave., South Beach ☎ 305/604–1000 ⊕ www.gansevoortsouth. com ↶ 334 rooms ♿ In-room: a/c, safe, kitchen (some), refrigerator, Internet, Wi-Fi. In-hotel: 2 restaurants, room service, bar, pool, gym, spa, beachfront, water sports, laundry service, Wi-Fi hotspot, parking (paid) ☰ AE, D, MC, V ⊹ 4H.*

$$ ▦ **The Hotel.** Fashion designer Todd Oldham wanted to preserve the art deco roots of the Hotel, which inhabits the historic Tiffany building, while making it modern. So, he made it tie-dye. Everything in this quirky, romantic boutique hotel, from the decor of four-star restaurant, Wish, to the bathrobes hanging in the small but cute bathrooms, is stained blue and green. Somehow the décor, paired with soft browns and whites and accented with the knowing eye of a megadesigner, works. Add soft lighting and two-person bathtubs, and you have all the makings of a romantic retreat. The hotel's most exquisite treat is a rooftop bar, a low-key hangout where locals and hotel guests lounge under the neon light of the Tiffany sign on Thursday, Friday,

and Saturday nights. **Pros:** great service; coolest roof-deck bar in town; good for couples. **Cons:** pool is tiny; rooms have no view. ⊠ *801 Collins Ave., South Beach* ☎ *305/531–2222 or 877/843–4683* ⊕ *www. thehotelofsouthbeach.com* ☞ *48 rooms, 4 suites* ⚬ *In-room: a/c, safe, Wi-Fi. In-hotel: restaurant, room service, bar, pool, laundry service, Internet terminal, Wi-Fi hotspot, parking (paid)* ⊟ *AE, D, DC, MC, V* ✦ *6H.*

$$$$ ☷ **Loews Miami Beach Hotel.** The oldest of South Beach's "new hotels," Loews Miami Beach is marvelous for families, businesspeople, and groups. The 800-room megahotel combines top-tier amenities, a massive new spa, a great pool, and a direct beachfront setting in its pair of enormous 12- and 18-story towers. When it was built in 1998, Loews managed not only to snag 99 feet of beach, but also to take over the vacant St. Moritz next door and restore it to its original 1939 art deco beauty. The entire complex combines boutique charm with updated opulence. How big is it? The Loews has 85,000 square feet of meeting space and an enormous ocean-view grand ballroom. Emeril Lagasse opened a restaurant here, and a three-story spa has 15 treatment rooms and a state-of-the-art fitness center. In the grand lobby you'll find a dozen black-suited staffers behind the counter, and a half dozen other bellboys and valets. Rooms are great: contemporary and very comfortable, with flat-screen TVs and high-end amenities. If you like big hotels with all the services, this is your choice in South Beach. **Pros:** top-notch amenities include a beautiful oceanfront pool and immense spa. **Cons:** intimacy is lost due to its large size. ⊠ *1601 Collins Ave., South Beach* ☎ *305/604–1601 or 800/235–6397* ⊕ *www.loewshotels.com/ miamibeach* ☞ *733 rooms, 57 suites* ⚬ *In-room: a/c, Internet, Wi-Fi. In-hotel: 3 restaurants, room service, bars, pool, gym, spa, beachfront, laundry service, Internet terminal, Wi-Fi hotspot, parking (paid), some pets allowed* ⊟ *AE, D, DC, MC, V* ✦ *5H.*

$$ ☷ **National Hotel.** This luxurious, beautiful hotel serves as a bastion
Fodor's Choice of calm in the sea of white-on-white mod decor and raucous reveling
★ usually reserved for the beachfront masterpieces lining Collins Avenue between 15th and 20th streets. Unlike its neighbors, the National hasn't parted with its art deco past. Most of the chocolate- and ebony-hued pieces in the lobby date back to the 1930s, and the baby grand piano beckons toward a throwback D-Bar Lounge. The most spectacular feature is Miami Beach's longest and most beautiful pool, which stretches from the tower to a duo of tropical tiki bars, a series of comfy black-and-white-striped cabanas and poolside tables, and then the beach. Note, however, that rooms in the main tower are disappointing and far from the pool; stay in the cabana wing if you can. **Pros:** stunning pool; perfect location. **Cons:** tower rooms aren't impressive; neighboring hotels can be noisy on the weekends. ⊠ *1677 Collins Ave., South Beach* ☎ *305/532–2311 or 800/327–8370* ⊕ *www.nationalhotel.com* ☞ *143 rooms, 9 suites* ⚬ *In-room: a/c, safe, DVD, Internet, Wi-Fi. In-hotel: 2 restaurants, room service, bars, pools, gym, beachfront, laundry service, Internet terminal, Wi-Fi hotspot, parking (paid), some pets allowed* ⊟ *AE, DC, MC, V* ✦ *5H.*

$$ ⚏ **Pelican.** The spirit of Diesel clothing company, which owns this Ocean Drive boutique, permeates the hotel. Each room is completely different, fashioned from a mix of antique and garage-sale furnishings selected by the designer of Diesel's clothing-display windows. Each room has its own name, and repeat guests either try to stay in a different one each time, or else fall in love with one room and request it for every stay. For example, the "Me Tarzan, You Vain" room has a jungle theme, with African wood sculptures and a stick lamp; "Up,

WORD OF MOUTH

"If you can get a hotel room at a good price than you should come to Miami during Art Basel week (first weekend in Dec.). It's a very, very cosmopolitan atmosphere. It will be busy but if you like being in a city then you'll enjoy the energy with all sorts of interesting people, art lovers, artists, celebrities, and art everywhere. It's the best week to feel alive in Miami."
—SoBchBud1

Up in the Sky" has a space theme, with a model rocket and off-kilter furniture. The best bet is to head down to the Pelican's porch-front restaurant, which offers one of the most extensive wine lists in town and a bar-none view of Ocean Drive's people parade. **Pros:** unique, over-the-top design; central Ocean Drive location. **Cons:** rooms are so tiny that the quirky charm wears off quickly; no no-smoking rooms. ⊠ *826 Ocean Dr., South Beach* ☎ *305/673–3373 or 800/773–5422* ⊕ *www.pelicanhotel.com* ⤳ *28 rooms, 4 suites* ⚭ *In-room: a/c, safe, refrigerator, Wi-Fi. In-hotel: restaurant, room service, bar, beachfront, laundry service, Wi-Fi hotspot, parking (paid)* ⊟ *AE, D, DC, MC, V* ✛ *6H.*

$$$$ ⚏ **Ritz-Carlton, South Beach.** A sumptuous affair, the Ritz-Carlton is the only truly luxurious property on the beach that *feels* like it's on the beach, because its long pool deck leads you right out to the water. There are all the usual high-level draws the Ritz is known for, that is, attentive service, a kids' club, a club level with five food presentations a day, and high-end restaurants. The spa has exclusive brands of scrubs and creams, and dynamite staff, including a "tanning butler" who will make sure you're not burning, and will apply lotion in the hard-to-reach places. Thursday through Saturday, enjoy Grammy-nominated percussionist Sammy Figueroa, who plays Latin Jazz by the pool. The wonderful diLido Beach club restaurant is, believe it or not, one of the very few places in Miami where you can get a beachside meal. (You may recognize the handsome chef Jeff McInnis from a successful stint on TV's "Top Chef.") The ocean is on one side and the pedestrian Lincoln Road begins on the other: the locale is tops. Overall, this landmarked 1954 art moderne hotel, designed by Melvin Grossman and Morris Lapidus, has never been hotter. **Pros:** luxury rooms; great service; great location. **Cons:** too big to be intimate. ⊠ *1 Lincoln Rd., South Beach* ☎ *786/276–4000 or 800/241–3333* ⊕ *www.ritzcarlton.com* ⤳ *375 rooms* ⚭ *In-room: a/c, safe, refrigerator, Wi-Fi. In-hotel: 4 restaurants, room service, bars, pools, gym, spa, beachfront, children's programs (ages 5–12), laundry service, Wi-Fi hotspot, parking (paid), some pets allowed* ⊟ *AE, D, DC, MC, V* ✛ *5H.*

$$$$ ⬚ **Setai.** Even if you can't afford a stay at Miami's priciest hotel, take time to visit the city's most beautifully designed space. The place feels like an Asian museum, serene and beautiful, with heavy granite furniture lifted by orange accents, warm candlelight, and the soft bubble of seemingly endless pools and ponds. The oceanfront gardens are expansive, lush, and painstakingly manicured. Three infinity pools, heated to 75°F, 85°F, and 95°F lead to an oceanfront terrace and then, white sand. The rooms are as expansive as the premises and furnished in an Asian style that is at once minimalist and cozy. **Pros:** quiet and classy; beautiful grounds. **Cons:** somewhat cold aura; TVs are far from the beds. ⊠ *101 20th St., South Beach* ☎ *305/520–6000 or 888/625–7500* ⊕ *www.setai. com* ➦ *110 rooms* ⑁ *In-room: a/c, safe, refrigerator, DVD, Wi-Fi. In-hotel: restaurant, room service, bars, pools, gym, spa, beachfront, laundry service, Wi-Fi hotspot, parking (paid), some pets allowed* ⊟ *AE, D, DC, MC, V* ✛ *4H.*

$$$$ ⬚ **Shore Club.** Unquestionably the destination for the young, the rich, and the ready to party, Shore Club is the perfect adult playground. Don't spend your time in the rooms—they're nothing special, and the white-on-white decor feels more cold than cool. Instead, venture down to the lobby, where a peek behind the cascading white curtains can yield a celebrity, a scandal, or a make-out session. More debauchery awaits at Sky Bar, the glitziest outdoor bar on the strip. Step into Tuscan restaurant Ago, or Nobu (if you can afford it), and watch Hollywood royalty graze on Japanese-Peruvian delicacies. In terms of lounging, people-watching, and poolside glitz, this is the best of South Beach. **Pros:** good restaurants and bars; nightlife in your backyard. **Cons:** uninviting rooms; snooty service. ⊠ *1901 Collins Ave., South Beach* ☎ *305/695–3100 or 877/640–9500* ⊕ *www.shoreclub.com* ➦ *309 rooms, 79 suites* ⑁ *In-room: a/c, safe, refrigerator, Wi-Fi. In-hotel: 2 restaurants, room service, bars, pools, gym, spa, beachfront, laundry service, Wi-Fi hotspot, parking (paid), some pets allowed* ⊟ *AE, D, DC, MC, V* ✛ *4H.*

$$$$ ⬚ **The Tides.** The Tides is the best boutique hotel in Miami, and the
Fodor's Choice   classiest of the Ocean Drive art deco hotels. The exceptionally tact-
★   ful personalized service makes every guest feel like a celebrity, and the hotel looks like no other in the city. A head-to-toe renovation modeled the interior after a jewelry box: gone is the stark white-on-white minimalism that made it famous, replaced with soft pinks and corals, gilded accents, and marine-inspired decor. The new Coral Bar—a tiny space irresistibly ensconced in the back of the lobby—boasts rums from around the world, and La Marea restaurant offers delectable seafood. The Tides' main competition is its neighbor, Hotel Victor, but the Tides' rooms are large and all have direct ocean views. The pool here is private as can be. Seeking taste and discretion? *Voilà.* **Pros:** superior service; great beach location; ocean views from all suites plus the terrace restaurant. **Cons:** tiny elevators. ⊠ *1220 Ocean Dr., South Beach* ☎ *305/604–5070 or 866/438–4337* ⊕ *www.thetideshotel.com* ➦ *45 suites* ⑁ *In-room: a/c, safe, Internet, Wi-Fi. In-hotel: restaurant, pool, gym, beachfront, laundry service, Wi-Fi hotspot, parking (paid)* ⊟ *AE, D, DC, MC, V* ✛ *5H.*

$　☆ **Townhouse**. Though sandwiched between the Setai and the Shore
★　Club—two of the coolest hotels on the planet—the Townhouse doesn't
try to act all dolled up: it's comfortable being the shabby-chic, light-
hearted, relaxed, no-frills, fun hotel on South Beach. Rooms aren't luxurious, and you won't find many amenities (no gym, no spa, no pool),
but if you want to stay in the middle of the action for under $200, in
simple, clean digs with a good sense of simple style, this may be a good
choice. Enter through a brightly lit, spacious white lobby; after check-
in, head to a small but freshly adorned white-and-red room that comes
with a beach ball you can keep. The hotel has a rooftop terrace with
plush red lounge chairs and a DJ on weekends. A hip sushi restaurant,
Bond St. Lounge, is downstairs, and delivers to rooms during restaurant
hours. With its clean white backdrops and discounts for crew members, there's always a good chance a TV production or magazine shoot
is happening. **Pros:** a great budget buy for the style-hungry. **Cons:** no
pool; small rooms not designed for long stays. ⊠ *150 20th St., east of
Collins Ave., South Beach* ☎ *305/534–3800 or 877/534–3800* ⊕ *www.
townhousehotel.com* ⇆ *69 rooms, 2 suites* ⌂ *In-room: a/c, safe, Internet, Wi-Fi. In-hotel: restaurant, room service, bar, bicycles, laundry
facilities, laundry service, Wi-Fi hotspot, parking (paid)* ⊟ *AE, D, DC,
MC, V* ⏐⊙⏐ *CP* ⊹ *4H.*

¢　☆ **Villa Paradiso**. One of South Beach's best deals, Paradiso has huge
rooms with kitchens and a charming tropical courtyard with benches
for hanging out at all hours. There's even another smaller courtyard
on the other side of the rooms. Peeking out from a sea of tropical foliage, the hotel seems at first to be a rather unassuming piece of art deco
architecture. But for all its simplicity, value shines bright. Rooms have
polished hardwood floors, French doors, and quirky wrought-iron furniture. They are well suited for extended visits—discounts begin at 10%
for a week's stay. **Pros:** great hangout spot in courtyard; good value;
great location. **Cons:** no Wi-Fi; no pool; no restaurant. ⊠ *1415 Collins Ave., South Beach* ☎ *305/532–0616* ⊕ *www.villaparadisohotel.com*
⇆ *17 studios* ⌂ *In-room: a/c, kitchen, refrigerator, Internet. In-hotel:
some pets allowed* ⊟ *AE, D, DC, MC, V* ⊹ *5H.*

The Everglades

WORD OF MOUTH

"Sign up at the Ernest Coe Visitor Center or call ahead to Flamingo Visitor Center for the free ranger-led canoe tour. Fantastic experience. The group met at the Nine-Mile Pond at 8 a.m. and paddled for 4 hours on the pond and through mangroves. Only 4 other couples and 1 family with a 10 year-old on the trip. No experience necessary—maneuvering the long canoe through the twists and turns of the mangroves was a bit of a challenge, but very fun."

—JC98

WELCOME TO THE EVERGLADES

TOP REASONS TO GO

★ **Fun Fishing:** Cast for some of the world's fightingest game fish—600 species of fish in all—in the Everglades' backwaters.

★ **Abundant Birdlife:** Check hundreds of birds off your life list, including— if you're lucky—the rare Everglades snail kite.

★ **Cool Kayaking:** Do a half-day trip in Big Cypress National Preserve or reach for the ultimate—the 99-mi Wilderness Trail.

★ **Swamp Cuisine:** Been hankering for alligator tail and frogs' legs? Or how about swamp cabbage, made from hearts of palm? Better yet, try stone crab claws fresh from the traps.

★ **Great Gator-Spotting:** This is ground zero for alligator viewing in the United States, and you won't leave without spotting your quota.

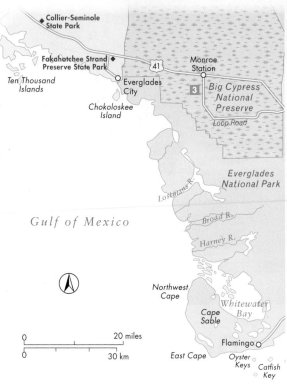

1 **Everglades National Park.** Alligators, Florida panthers, black bears, manatees, dolphins, bald eagles, and roseate spoonbills call this vast habitat home.

2 **Biscayne National Park.** Mostly underwater, here's where the string of coral reefs and islands that form the Florida Keys begin.

Nature tour boat.

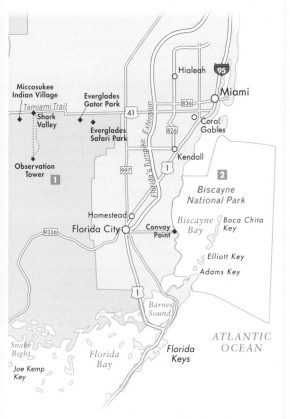

Miccosukee
Indian Village
Tamiami Trail
Shark
Valley
Everglades
Gator Park
41
836
Hialeah
95
Miami
Coral
Gables
826
Everglades
Safari Park
Kendall
997
1
Observation
Tower
1
Florida's Turnpike Extension
2
Biscayne
National Park
Homestead
9336
Florida City
Convoy
Point
Biscayne
Bay
Boca Chita
Key
Elliott Key
Adams Key
1
Barnes
Sound
*Snake
Bight*
*Joe Kemp
Key*
*Florida
Bay*
Florida
Keys
ATLANTIC
OCEAN

GETTING ORIENTED

The southern third of the Florida peninsula is largely taken up by protected government land that includes Everglades National Park, Big Cypress National Preserve, and Biscayne National Park. Miami lies to the northeast, while Naples and Marco Island are northwest. Land access to Everglades National Park is primarily by two roads. The park's main road traverses the southern Everglades from the gateway towns of Homestead and Florida City to the outpost of Flamingo, on Florida Bay. In the northern Everglades, Tamiami Trail (U.S. 41) runs from the Greater Miami area on the east coast or from Naples on the west coast to the western park entrance in Everglades City at Route 29.

5

3 Big Cypress National Preserve. Neighbor to Everglades National Park, it's an outdoor-lover's paradise.

Shark Valley.

THE EVERGLADES PLANNER

When to Go

Winter is the best time to visit the Everglades, and the busiest. Temperatures and mosquito activity are more tolerable, low water levels concentrate the resident wildlife, and migratory birds swell the avian population. In late spring the weather turns hot and rainy, and tours and facilities are less crowded. Migratory birds depart, and you must look harder to see wildlife. Summer brings intense sun and afternoon rainstorms. Water levels rise and mosquitoes descend, making outdoor activity virtually unbearable, unless you swath yourself in netting. Mosquito repellent is a necessity any time of year.

Flying In

Miami International Airport (MIA) is 34 mi from Homestead and 47 mi from the eastern access to Everglades National Park. *For MIA airline carrier information, refer to the Miami chapter.* Shuttles run between MIA and Homestead. Southwest Florida International Airport (RSW) in Fort Myers, a little over an hour's drive from Everglades City, is the closest major airport to the Everglades' western access. On-demand taxi transportation from the airport to Everglades City is available.

About the Restaurants

Dining in the Everglades area centers on mom-and-pop places that serve hearty home-style food, and small eateries that specialize in local fare: alligator, fish, stone crab, frogs' legs, and fresh Florida lobster from the Keys. American Indian restaurants serve local favorites as well as catfish, Indian fry bread (a flour-and-water flatbread), and pumpkin bread. A growing Hispanic population around Homestead means plenty of authentic, inexpensive Mexican cuisine. Restaurants in Everglades City, especially those along the river, have the freshest seafood, particularly stone crab. These places are mostly casual to the point of rustic, and are often closed in late summer or fall. For finer dining, go to Marco Island or Naples.

About the Hotels

Accommodations near the parks range from inexpensive to moderate and offer off-season rates in summer, when rampant mosquito populations essentially preclude going outdoors for any length of time. If you're spending several days exploring the east coast Everglades, stay in one of the park's campgrounds; 11 mi away in Homestead–Florida City, where there are reasonably priced motels and RV parks; or in the Florida Keys or the Greater Miami–Fort Lauderdale area. Lodgings and campgrounds are also available on the Gulf Coast in Everglades City, Naples, and Marco Island. Florida City's selection is mostly of the chain variety and geared toward business travelers.

WHAT IT COSTS

	¢	$	$$	$$$	$$$$
Restaurants	Under $10	$10–$15	$15–$20	$20–$30	over $30
Hotels		Under $80	$80–$100	$100–$140	$140–$220	over $220

Restaurant prices are per person for a main course at dinner. Hotel prices are for a standard double room, excluding 6% sales tax (more in some counties) and 1%–5% tourist tax.

Everglades National Park

More than 1.5 million acres of South Florida's 4.3 million acres of subtropical, watery wilderness were given national-park status and protection in 1947 with the creation of Everglades National Park. It is one of the country's largest national parks and is recognized by the world community as a Wetland of International Importance, an International Biosphere Reserve, and a World Heritage Site. Come here if you want to spend the day biking, hiking, or boating in deep, raw wilderness with lots of wildlife.

Biscayne National Park

To the east of Everglades National Park, Biscayne National Park brings forth a pristine, magical, subtropical Florida. It is the nation's largest marine park and the largest national park within the continental United States boasting living coral reefs. A small portion of the park's 172,000 acres consists of mainland coast and outlying islands, but 95% is under water. Of particular interest are the mangroves and their tangled masses of stiltlike roots that thicken the shorelines. These "walking trees," as locals call them, have curved prop roots, which arch down from the trunk, and aerial roots drop from branches. The trees draw freshwater from saltwater and create a coastal nursery that sustains myriad types of marine life. You can see Miami's high-rise buildings from many of Biscayne's 44 islands, but the park is virtually undeveloped and large enough for escaping everything that Miami and the Upper Keys have become. To truly escape, don scuba diving or snorkeling gear, and lose yourself in the wonders of the coral reefs.

Big Cypress National Preserve

On the northern edge of Everglades National Park is Big Cypress National Preserve, one of South Florida's least-developed watersheds. Established by Congress in 1974 to protect the Everglades, it comprises extensive tracts of prairie, marsh, pinelands, forested swamps, and sloughs. Hunting is allowed, as is off-road-vehicle use. Come here if you like alligators. Stop at the Oasis Visitor Center to walk the boardwalk with alligators lounging underneath and then drive Loop Road for a backwoods experience. If time permits, kayak the Turner River. ■TIP→ **Many activities in the parks and preserve are based on water, so be prepared to get a bit damp on the marshy trails.**

Nearby Towns

Surrounding the parks and preserve are several small communities: Everglades City, Florida City, and Homestead, home to many area outfitters.

⇨ *While outfitters are listed with the parks and preserve, see our What's Nearby section later in this chapter for information about each town.*

Camping in the Everglades

For an intense stay in the "real" Florida, consider one of some four dozen backcountry campsites deep in Everglades National Park, many inland, some on the beach. You'll have to carry in your food, water, and supplies, and carry out all your trash. You'll also need a site-specific permit, available on a first-come, first-served basis from the Flamingo or Gulf Coast visitors centers. Permits cost $10, plus $2 per night for sites, with a 14-night limit, and are only issued up to 24 hours in advance. Front-country camping fees at park campgrounds are $16 per night.

THE FLORIDA
EVERGLADES

by Lynne Helm

Alternately described as elixir of life or swampland muck, the Florida Everglades is one of a kind—a 50-mi-wide "river of grass" that spreads across hundreds of thousands of acres. It moves at varying speeds depending on rainfall and other variables, sloping south from the Kissimmee River and Lake Okeechobee to estuaries of Biscayne Bay, Florida Bay, and the Ten Thousand Islands.

Today, apart from sheltering some 70 species on America's endangered list, the Everglades also embraces more than 7 million residents, 50 million annual tourists, 400,000 acres of sugarcane, and the world's largest concentration of golf courses.

Demands on the land threaten the Everglades' finely balanced ecosystem. Irrigation canals for agriculture and roadways disrupt natural water flow. Drainage for development leaves wildlife scurrying for new territory. Water runoff, laced with fertilizers, promotes unnatural growth of swamp vegetation. What remains is a miracle of sorts, given decades of these destructive forces.

Creation of the Everglades required unique conditions. South Florida's geology, linked with its warm, wet subtropical climate, is the perfect mix for a marshland ecosystem. Layers of porous, permeable limestone create water-bearing rock,

soil, and aquifers, which in turn affects climate, weather, and hydrology.

This rock beneath the Everglades reflects Florida's geologic history—its crust was once part of the African region. Some scientists theorize that continental shifting merged North America with Africa, and then continental rifting later pulled North America away from the African continent but took part of northwest Africa with it—the part that is today's Florida. The Earth's tectonic plates continued to migrate, eventually placing Florida at its current location as a land mass jutting out into the ocean, with the Everglades at its tip.

EXPERIENCING THE ECOSYSTEMS

Eight distinct habitats exist within Everglades National Park, Big Cypress National Preserve, and Biscayne National Park.

ECOSYSTEMS	EASY WAY	MORE ACTIVE WAY
COASTAL PRAIRIE: An arid region of salt-tolerant vegetation lies between the tidal mud flats of Florida Bay and dry land. **Best place to see it: The Coastal Prairie Trail**	Take a guided boat tour of Florida Bay, leaving from Flamingo Marina.	Hike the Coastal Prairie Trail from Eco Pond to Clubhouse Beach.
CYPRESS: Capable of surviving in standing water, cypress trees often form dense clusters called "cypress domes" in natural water-filled depressions. **Best place to see it: Big Cypress National Preserve**	Drive U.S. 41 (also known as Tamiami Trail—pronounced Tammy-Amee), which cuts across Southern Florida, from Naples to Miami.	Hike (or drive) the scenic Loop Road, which begins off Tamiami Trail, running from the Loop Road Education Center to Monroe Station.
FRESH WATER MARL PRAIRIE: Bordering deeper sloughs are large prairies with marl (clay and calcium carbonate) sediments on limestone. Gators like to use their toothy snouts to dig holes in prairie mud. **Best place to see it: Pahayokee Overlook**	Drive there from the Ernest F. Coe Visitor Center.	Take a guided tour, either through the park service or from permitted, licensed guides. You also can set up camp at Long Pine Key.
FRESH WATER SLOUGH AND HARDWOOD HAMMOCK: Shark River Slough and Taylor Slough are the Everglades' two sloughs, or marshy rivers. Due to slight elevation amid sloughs, dense stands of hardwood trees appear as teardrop-shaped islands. **Best place to see it: The Observation Tower**	Take a two-hour guided tram tour from the Shark Valley Visitor Center to the tower and back.	Walk or bike (rentals available) the route to the tower via the tram road and (walkers only) Bobcat Boardwalk trail and Otter Cave Hammock Trail.
MANGROVE: Spread over South Florida's coastal channels and waterways, mangrove thrives where Everglades fresh water mixes with salt water. **Best place to see it: The Wilderness Waterway**	Picnic at the area near Long Pine Key, which is surrounded by mangrove, or take a water tour at Biscayne National Park.	Boat your way along the 99-mi Wilderness Waterway. It's six hours by motorized boat, seven days by canoe.
MARINE AND ESTUARINE: Corals, sponges, mollusks, seagrass, and algae thrive in the Florida Bay, where the fresh waters of the Everglades meet the salty seas. **Best place to see it: Florida Bay**	Take a boat tour from the Flamingo Visitor Center marina.	Canoe or kayak on White Water Bay along the Wilderness Waterway Canoe Trail.
PINELAND: A dominant plant in dry, rugged terrain, the Everglades' diverse pinelands consist of slash pine forest, saw palmettos, and more than 200 tropical plant varieties. **Best place to see it: Long Pine Key trails**	Drive to Long Pine Key, about 6 mi off the main road from Ernest F. Coe Visitor Center.	Hike or bike the 28 mi of Long Pine Key trails.

Habitats within Florida's Everglades ecosystem support a diverse collection of plant and animal species encountered nowhere else. The landscape is dynamic, and the ecosystems are in constant flux, subject to changing elements.

Marine and Estuarine Water Depths
- 0-3 Feet
- 3-6 Feet
- over 6 Feet

Land Cover
- Coastal Prairie
- Cypress
- Fresh Water Marl Prairie
- Fresh Water Slough
- Hardwood Hammock
- Mangrove
- Pinelands
- Urban

Ranger Station
Campground
Picnic Area
Restaurant
······ Walking/Hiking Trails
--- Water/Canoe Trails

FLORA

❶ Cabbage Palm

It's virtually impossible to visit the Everglades and not see a cabbage palm, Florida's official state tree. The cabbage palm (or sabal palm), graces assorted ecosystems and grows well in swamps. **Best place to see them:** At Loxahatchee National Wildlife Refuge (embracing the northern part of the Everglades, along Alligator Alley), throughout Everglades National Park, and at Big Cypress National Preserve.

❷ Sawgrass

With spiny, serrated leaf blades resembling saws, sawgrass inspired the term "river of grass" for the Everglades. **Best place to see them:** Both Shark Valley and Pahayokee Overlook provide terrific vantage points for gazing over sawgrass prairie; you also can get an eyeful of sawgrass when crossing Alligator Alley, even when doing so at top speeds.

❸ Mahogany

Hardwood hammocks of the Everglades live in areas that rarely flood because of the slight elevation of the sloughs, where they're typically found. **Best place to see them:** Everglades National Park's Mahogany Hammock Trail (which has a boardwalk leading to the nation's largest living mahogany tree).

❹ Mangrove

Mangrove forest ecosystems provide both food and protected nursery areas for fish, shellfish, and crustaceans. **Best place to see them:** Along Biscayne National Park shoreline, at Big Cypress National Preserve, and within Everglades National Park, especially around the Caple Sable area.

❺ Gumbo Limbo

Sometimes called "tourist trees" because of peeling reddish bark (not unlike sunburns). **Best place to see them:** Everglades National Park's Gumbo Limbo Trail and assorted spots throughout the expansive Everglades.

FAUNA

❶ American Alligator

In all likelihood, on your visit to the Everglades you'll see at least a gator or two. These carnivorous creatures can be found throughout the Everglades swampy wetlands.

Best place to see them: Loxahatchee National Wildlife Refuge (also sheltering the endangered Everglades snail kite) and within Everglades National Park at Shark Valley or Anhinga Trail. Sometimes (logically enough) gators hang out along Alligator Alley, basking in early morning or late-afternoon sun along four-lane I–75.

❷ American Crocodile

Crocs gravitate to fresh or brackish water, subsisting on birds, fish, snails, frogs, and small mammals.

Best place to see them: Within Everglades National Park, Big Cypress National Preserve, and protected grounds in or around Billie Swamp Safari.

❸ Eastern Coral Snake

This venomous snake burrows in underbrush, preying on lizards, frogs, and smaller snakes.

Best place to see them: Snakes typically shy away from people, but try Snake Bight or Eco Pond near Flamingo, where birds are also prevalent.

❹ Florida Panther

Struggling for survival amid loss of habitat, these shy, tan-colored cats now number around 100, up from lows of near 30.

Best place to see them: Protected grounds of Billie Swamp Safari sometimes provide sightings during tours. Signage on roadway linking Tamiami Trail and Alligator Alley warns of panther crossings, but sightings are rare.

❺ Green Tree Frog

Typically bright green with white or yellow stripes, these nocturnal creatures thrive in swamps and brackish water.

Best place to see them: Within Everglades National Park, especially in or near water.

● =Extremely Common ● =Very Common ● =Somewhat Common ● =Rare

BIRDS

❶ Anhinga

The lack of oil glands for waterproofing feathers helps this bird to dive as well as chase and spear fish with its pointed beak. The Anhinga is also often called a "water turkey" because of its long tail, or a "snake bird" because of its long neck.

Best place to see them: The Anhinga Trail, which also is known for attracting other wildlife to drink during especially dry winters.

❷ Blue-Winged Teal

Although it's predominantly brown and gray, this bird's powder-blue wing patch becomes visible in flight. Next to the mallard, the blue-winged teal is North America's second most abundant duck, and thrives particularly well in the Everglades.

Best place to see them: Near ponds and marshy areas of Everglades National Park or Big Cypress National Preserve.

❸ Great Blue Heron

This bird has a varied palate and enjoys feasting on everything from frogs, snakes, and mice to shrimp, aquatic insects, and sometimes even other birds! The all-white version, which at one time was considered a separate species, is quite common to the Everglades.

Best place to see them: Loxahatchee National Wildlife Refuge or Shark Valley in Everglades National Park.

❹ Great Egret

Once decimated by plume hunters, these monogamous, long-legged white birds with S-shaped necks feed in wetlands, nest in trees, and hang out in colonies that often include heron or other egret species.

Best place to see them: Throughout Everglades National Park, along Alligator Alley, and sometimes even on the fringes of Greater Fort Lauderdale.

❺ Greater Flamingo

Flocking together and using long legs and webbed feet to stir shallow waters and mud flats, color comes a couple of years after hatching from ingesting shrimplike crustaceans along with fish, fly larvae, and plankton.

Best place to see them: Try Snake Bight or Eco Pond, near Flamingo Marina.

❻ Osprey

Making a big comeback from chemical pollutant endangerment, ospreys (sometimes confused with bald eagles) are distinguished by black eyestripes down their faces. Gripping pads on feet with curved claws help them pluck fish from water.

Best place to see them: Look near water, where they're fishing for lunch in the shallow areas. Try the coasts, bays, and ponds of Everglades National Park. They also gravitate to trees. You can usually spot them from the Gulf Coast Visitor Center, or you can observe them via boating in the Ten Thousand Islands.

❼ Roseate Spoonbill

These gregarious pink-and-white birds gravitate toward mangroves, feeding on fish, insects, amphibians, and some plants. They have long, spoon-like bills, and their feathers can have a touch of red and yellow. These birds appear in the Everglades year-round.

Best place to see them: Sandy Key, southwest of Flamingo, is a spoonbill nocturnal roosting spot, but at sunrise these colorful birds head out over Eco Pond to favored day hangouts throughout Everglades National Park.

❽ Wood Stork

Recognizable by featherless heads and prominent bills, these birds submerge in water to scoop up hapless fish. They are most common in the early spring and often easiest to spot in the morning.

Best place to see them: Amid the Ten Thousand Island areas, Nine Mile Pond, Mrazek Pond, and in the mangroves at Paurotis Pond.

THE BEST EVERGLADES ACTIVITIES

HIKING

Top experiences: At Big Cypress National Preserve, you can hike along designated trails or push through unmarked acreage. (Conditions vary seasonally, which means you could be tramping through waist-deep waters.) Trailheads for the Florida National Scenic Trail are at Loop Road off U.S. 41 and Alligator Alley at mile marker 63.

What will I see? Dwarf cypress, hardwood hammocks, prairies, birds, and other wildlife.

For a short visit: A 6.5-mi section from Loop Road to U.S. 41 crosses Robert's Lake Strand, providing a satisfying sense of being out in the middle nowhere.

With more time: A 28-mi stretch from U.S. 41 to I–75 (Alligator Alley) reveals assorted habitats, including hardwood hammocks, pinelands, prairie, and cypress.

Want a tour? Big Cypress ranger-led exploration starts from the Oasis Visitor Center, late November through mid-April.

WALKING

Top experiences: Everglades National Park magnets: wheelchair accessible walkways at Anhinga Trail, Gumbo Limbo Trail, Pahayokee Overlook, Mahogany Hammock, and West Lake Trail.

What will I see? Birds and alligators at Anhinga; tropical hardwood hammock at Gumbo Limbo; an overlook of the River of Grass from Pahayokee's tower; a subtropical tree island with massive mahogany growth along Mahogany Hammock; and a forest of mangrove trees on West Lake Trail.

For a short visit: Flamingo's Eco Pond provides for waterside wildlife viewing.

With more time: Shark Valley lets you combine the quarter-mile Bobcat Boardwalk (looping through sawgrass prairie and a bayhead) with the 1-mi-long round-trip Otter Cave, allowing you to steep in subtropical hardwood hammock.

Want a tour? Pahayokee and Flamingo feature informative ranger-led walks.

The Anhinga Trail near the Royal Palm Visitor Center at Everglades National Park

BOATING

Top experiences: Launch a boat from the Gulf Coast Visitors Center or Flamingo Marina. Bring your own watercraft or rent canoes or skiffs at either location.

What will I see? Birds from bald eagles to roseate spoonbills, plus plenty of mangrove and wildlife—and maybe even some baby alligators with yellow stripes.

For a short visit: Canoe adventurers often head for Hells Bay, a 3-mi stretch about 9 mi north of Flamingo. Or put in at the Turner River alongside the Tamiami Trail in the Big Cypress National Preserve and paddle all the way (about eight hours) to Chocoloskee Bay at Everglades City.

With more time: Head out amid the Ten Thousand Islands and lose yourself in territory once exclusively the domain of only the hardiest pioneers and American Indians. If you've got a week or more for paddling, the 99-mi Wilderness Waterway stretches from Flamingo to Everglades City.

Want a tour? Sign on for narrated boat tours at the Gulf Coast or Flamingo visitor center.

BIRD WATCHING

Top experiences: Anhinga Trail, passing over Taylor Slough.

What will I see? Anhinga and heron sightings are a nearly sure thing, especially in early morning or late afternoon. Also, alligators can be seen from the boardwalk.

For a short visit: Even if you're traveling coast to coast at higher speeds via Alligator Alley, chances are you'll spot winged wonders like egrets, osprey, and heron.

With more time: Since bird-watching at Flamingo can be a special treat early in the morning or late in the afternoon, try camping overnight even if you're not one for roughing it. Reservations are recommended. (Flamingo Lodge remains under reconstruction from 2005 hurricane damage.)

Want a tour? Ranger-led walks at Pahayokee and from Everglades National Park visitor centers provide solid birding background for novices.

(top left) Tourists cruise the Everglades by airboat; (bottom left) Green Heron; (right) Eastern Meadowlark

THE BEST EVERGLADES ACTIVITIES

BIKING

Top experiences: Shark Valley (where bicycling is allowed on the tram road) is great for taking in the quiet beauty of the Everglades. Near Ernest F. Coe Visitor Center, Long Pine Key's 14-mi nature trail also can be a way to bike happily away from folks on foot.

What will I see? At Shark Valley, wading birds, turtles, and, probably alligators. At Long Pine Key, shady pinewood with subtropical plants and exposed limestone bedrock.

For a short visit: Bike on Shark Valley tram road but turn around to fit time schedule.

With more time: Go the entire 15-mi tram road route, which has no shortcuts. Or try the 22-mi route of Old Ingraham Highway near the Royal Palm Visitor Center, featuring mangrove, sawgrass, and birds (including hawks).

Want a tour? In Big Cypress National Preserve, Bear Island Bike Rides (8 mi round-trip over four to five hours) happen on certain Saturdays.

SNORKELING

Top experiences: Biscayne National Park, where clear waters incorporate the northernmost islands of the Florida Keys.

What will I see? Dense mangrove swamp covering the park shoreline, and, in shallow waters, a living coral reef and tropical fish in assorted colors.

For a short visit: Pick a sunny day to optimize your snorkeling fun, and be sure to use sunscreen.

With more time: Advanced snorkel tours head out from the park on weekends to the bay, finger channels, and around shorelines of the barrier islands. Biscayne National Park also has canoe and kayak rentals, picnic facilities, walking trails, fishing, and camping.

Want a tour? You can swim and snorkel or stay dry and picnic aboard tour boats that depart from Biscayne National Park's visitor center.

(top left) Biking near the Shark Valley Visitor Area. (top right) Snorkeling on the surface in the Atlantic Ocean.

DID YOU KNOW?

You can tell you're looking at a crocodile if you can see its lower teeth protruding when its jaws are shut, whereas an alligator shows no teeth when his mouth is closed. Gators are much darker in color—a gray-ish black—compared with the lighter tan color of crocodiles. Alligators' snouts are also much broader than their long, thin crocodilian counterparts.

THE STORY OF THE EVERGLADES

Dreams of draining southern Florida took hold in the early 1800s, expanding in the early 1900s to convert large tracts from wetlands to agricultural acreage. By the 1920s, towns like Fort Lauderdale and Miami boomed, and the sugar industry—which came to be known as "Big Sugar"—established its first sugar mills. In 1947 Everglades National Park opened as a refuge for wildlife.

Meanwhile, the sugar industry grew. In its infancy, about 175,000 tons of raw sugar per year was produced from fields totaling about 50,000 acres. But once the U.S. embargo stopped sugar imports from Cuba in 1960 and laws restricting acreage were lifted, Big Sugar took off. Less than five years later, the industry produced 572,000 tons of sugar and occupied nearly a quarter of a million acres.

Fast-forward to 2008, to what was hailed as the biggest conservation deal in U.S. history since the creation of the national parks. A trailblazing restoration strategy hinged on creating a water flow-way between Lake Okeechobee and the Everglades by buying up and flooding 187,000 acres of land. The country's largest producers of cane sugar agreed to sell the necessary 187,000 acres to the state of Florida for $1.75 billion. Environmentalists cheered.

But within months, news broke of a scaled-back land acquisition plan: $1.34 billion to buy 180,000 acres. By spring 2009, the restoration plan had shrunk to $536,000 to buy 73,000 acres. With the purchase still in limbo, critics claim the state might overpay for acreage appraised at pre-recession values and proponents fear dwindling revenues may derail the plan altogether.

The Big Sugar land deal is part of a larger effort to preserve the Everglades. In 2010, two separate lawsuits charged the state, along with the United States Environmental Protection Agency, with stalling Everglades cleanup that was supposed to begin in 2006. "Glacial delay" is how one judge put it. The state must reduce phosphorus levels in water that flows to the Everglades or face fines and sanctions for violating the federal Clean Water Act. The fate of the Everglades remains in the balance.

EVERGLADES NATIONAL PARK

45 mi southwest of Miami International Airport.

Updated by
Lynne Helm

If you're heading across South Florida on U.S. 41 from Miami to Naples, you'll breeze right through the Everglades. Also known as Tamiami Trail, this mostly two-lane road along much of the route skirts the edge of Everglades National Park and cuts across the Big Cypress National Preserve. You'll also be near the park if you're en route from Miami to the Florida Keys on U.S. 1, which travels through Homestead and Florida City, two communities east of the main park entrance. Basically, if you're in South Florida you can't get away from at least fringes of the Everglades. With tourist strongholds like Miami, Naples, and the Florida Keys so close by, travelers from all over the world typically make day trips to the park.

Everglades National Park has three main entry points: the park headquarters at Ernest F. Coe Visitor Center, southwest of Homestead and Florida City; the Shark Valley area, in the northern reaches and accessed by Tamiami Trail (U.S. 41); and the Gulf Coast Visitor Center, just south of Everglades City to the west and closest to Naples.

You can explore on your own or participate in free ranger-led hikes, bicycle tours, bird-watching tours, and canoe trips; the number and variety of these excursions are greatest from mid-December through Easter, and some (canoe trips, for instance) typically aren't offered in the sweltering summer. Among the more popular are the Anhinga Amble, a 50-minute walk around the Taylor Slough (departs from the Royal Palm Visitor Center), and the Early Bird Special, a 90-minute walk centered on birdlife (departs from Flamingo Visitor Center at 7:30 AM). Ask at the visitor centers for details.

PARK ESSENTIALS

Admission Fees $10 per vehicle, $5 per pedestrian, bicycle, or motorcycle. Admission, payable at gates, is good for seven days. Annual passes are $25.

Admission Hours The park is open daily, year-round, and both the main entrance near Florida City and Homestead, and the Gulf Coast entrance are open 24 hours. The Shark Valley entrance is open 8:30 AM to 6 PM.

COE VISITOR CENTER TO FLAMINGO

About 30 mi from Miami.

The most popular access to Everglades National Park is via the park headquarters entrance just southwest of Homestead and Florida City. If you're coming to the Everglades from Miami, the highway you'll take is Route 836 west to Route 826/874 south to the Homestead Extension of Florida's Turnpike, U.S. 1, and Krome Avenue (Route 997/ old U.S. 27). To reach the Ernest F. Coe Visitor Center from Homestead, go right (west) from U.S. 1 or Krome Avenue onto Route 9336 (Florida's only four-digit route) in Florida City and follow signs to the park entrance.

EXPLORING

To explore this section of the park, follow Route 9336 from the park entrance to Flamingo; there are many opportunities to stop along the way, and an assortment of activities to pursue in the Flamingo area. The following is arranged in geographic order.

Ernest F. Coe Visitor Center. Don't just grab your park map and go; this visitor center has numerous interactive exhibits and films that are well worth your time. The 15-minute film *River of Life,* updated frequently, provides a succinct park overview with emphasis on the river of grass. There is also a movie on hurricanes and a 35-minute wildlife film for children available upon request. A bank of telephones offers differing viewpoints on the Great Water Debate, detailing how last century's gung-ho draining of swampland for residential and agricultural development also cut off water-supply routes for precious wetlands in the Everglades ecosystem. A schedule of daily ranger-led activities parkwide, mainly walks and talks, and information on canoe rentals and boat tours at Flamingo is maintained. The Everglades Discovery Shop stocks books and jewelry including bird-oriented earrings, and you can browse through cool nature, science, and kids' stuff or pick up extra insect repellent. Coe Visitor Center is outside park gates, so you can stop in without paying park admission. ⊠ *11 mi southwest of Homestead on Rte. 9336* ☎ *305/242–7700* ☉ *Daily 8–5; hrs sometimes shortened in off-season.*

Main road to Flamingo. Route 9336 travels 38 mi from the Ernest F. Coe Visitor Center southwest to the Florida Bay at Flamingo. It crosses a section of the park's eight distinct ecosystems: hardwood hammock, freshwater prairie, pinelands, freshwater slough, cypress, coastal prairie, mangrove, and marine-estuarine. Route highlights include a dwarf cypress forest, the transition zone between sawgrass and mangrove forest, and a wealth of wading birds at Mrazek and Coot Bay ponds—where in early morning or late afternoon you can observe the hundreds of birds feeding. Boardwalks, looped trails, several short spurs, and observation platforms help you stay dry. You also may want to stop along the way to walk several short trails (each takes about 30 minutes): the popular, wheelchair-accessible **Anhinga Trail,** which cuts through sawgrass marsh and allows you to see lots of wildlife (be on the lookout for alligators and the trail's namesake, water birds known as anhingas); and junglelike—yet, also wheelchair-accessible—**Gumbo-Limbo Trail;** the **Pinelands Trail,** where you can see the limestone bedrock that underlies the park; the **Pahayokee Overlook Trail,** which ends at an observation tower; and the **Mahogany Hammock Trail** with its dense growth.

■ TIP→ Before you head out on the trails, inquire about insect and weather conditions and plan accordingly, stocking up on bug repellent, sunscreen, and water as necessary. Also, even on seemingly nice days, it's probably smart to bring along a rain jacket.

★ **Royal Palm Visitor Center.** A must for anyone wanting to experience the real Everglades, and ideal for when there's limited time, this small center with a bookstore and vending machines permits access to the **Anhinga Trail boardwalk,** where in winter catching sight of alligators congregating in watering holes is almost guaranteed. Or follow the neighboring **Gumbo Limbo Trail** through a hardwood hammock. Both strolls are short (½ mi) and expose you to two Everglades ecosystems. Rangers conduct daily Anhinga Ambles in season (check for dates by calling ahead) starting at 10:30. At 1:30 the Glades Glimpse program takes place daily in season. Ask also about starlight walks and bike tours in season. ⊠ *4 mi west of Ernest F. Coe Visitor Center on Rte. 9336* ☎ *305/242-7700* ☉ *Daily 8-4:15.*

NEED A BREAK?

Good spots to pull over for a picnic lunch are Paurotis Pond, about 10 mi north of Florida Bay, or Nine Mile Pond, less than 30 mi from the main visitor center. Another option is along Bear Lake, 2 mi north of the Flamingo Visitor Center.

Flamingo. At the far end of the main road to Flamingo lies this community along Florida Bay, where you'll find a marina, visitor center, and campground, with nearby hiking and nature trails. Before hurricanes Katrina and Wilma washed them away in 2005, a lodge, cabins, and restaurants in Flamingo provided Everglades National Park's only accommodations. At press time, rebuilding of Flamingo Lodge was projected to materialize sometime after 2012, but for now, you can still pitch a tent or bring an RV to the campground, where improvements include solar-hot-water showers and electricity for RV sites. A long-popular houseboat rental concession may return in 2011.

Flamingo Visitor Center. Check the schedule here for ranger-led activities, such as naturalist discussions, hikes along area trails, and evening programs in the 100-seat campground amphitheater, opened in winter 2009–10 to replace the old gathering spot destroyed by 2005 hurricanes. Also, find natural history exhibits and pamphlets on canoe, hiking, and biking trails in the small Florida Bay Flamingo Museum on the 2nd floor of the visitor center. ⊠ *1 Flamingo Lodge Hwy., Flamingo* ☎ *239/695-2945, 239/695-3101 marina* ☉ *Exhibits are always open, staffed mid-Nov.–mid-Apr., daily 8-4:30.*

SPORTS AND THE OUTDOORS
BIRDING
Some of the park's best birding is in the Flamingo area.

BOATING

The 99-mi inland **Wilderness Trail** between Flamingo and Everglades City is open to motorboats as well as canoes, although powerboats may have trouble navigating the route above Whitewater Bay. Flatwater canoeing and kayaking are best in winter, when temperatures moderate, rainfall diminishes, and mosquitoes back off—a little, anyway. You don't need a permit for day trips, although there is a $5, 7-day launch fee for all boats brought into the park. The Flamingo area has well-marked canoe trails, but be sure to tell someone where you're going and when you expect to return. Getting lost is easy, and spending the night without proper gear can be unpleasant, if not dangerous.

GOOD READS

■ *The Everglades: River of Grass.* This circa-1947 classic by pioneering conservationist Marjory Stoneman Douglas (1890–1998) is a must-read.

■ *Everglades Wildguide.* Jean Craighead George gives an informative account of the park's natural history in this official National Park Service handbook.

■ *Everglades: The Park Story.* Wildlife biologist William B. Robertson Jr. presents the park's flora, fauna, and history.

OUTFITTER **Flamingo Lodge, Marina, and Everglades National Park Tours** (⊠ *1 Flamingo Lodge Hwy., on Buttonwood Canal, Flamingo* ☎ *239/695–3101*) is the official Everglades National Park concessionaire. The long-popular Flamingo Lodge, a victim of massive hurricane damage in 2005, remains closed pending funding for a new start, but Flamingo's marina and tours are back in action, going strong. The almost two-hour backcountry *Pelican* cruise ($26.50) is the most popular of its tours, winding under a heavy canopy of mangroves, and revealing abundant wildlife—from alligators, crocodiles, and turtles to herons, hawks, and egrets. The marina has charter boats, and rents 17-foot power skiffs from 7 AM for $195 per day (eight hours, if returned by 4 PM) $155 per half day, $80 for two hours. Small (up to two paddlers) and family-size (up to four) canoes rent from $16 per two-hour minimum, $22 for four hours, and $40 for overnight. Two-person charter fishing trips can be arranged for weekends ($350 for a half day or $450 a day; each additional person pays $25). Cost includes tackle, ice, and license. The concessionaire rents rods, reels, and other equipment by the half and full day.

WHERE TO CAMP

■ TIP→ In the dry winter season, be careful with campfires and matches; this is when the wildfire-prone sawgrass prairies and pinelands are most vulnerable.

★ ⚠ **Flamingo.** This campground has 234 drive-in sites; most overlook the bay, and nine of 64 walk-in sites are along water. Ninety sites are available through a reservation system from mid-November through March and on a first-come, first-served basis the rest of the year. In low season, be prepared to pay with cash in case a park employee is not at the campground kiosk when you arrive. If this is the case, just deposit cash into yellow envelopes at what's called the kiosk's "iron ranger." Park personnel cross-check paid envelopes with sites on a regular basis.

♿ *Flush toilets, dump station, drinking water, showers (cold), general store* ⊅ *234 drive-up sites, 64 walk-in sites* ☎ *877/444–6777 campsite reservations, 305/242–7700 park information, 239/695–0124 camping information* ⊕ *www.recreation.gov* ▤ *D, MC, V.*

¢ ⚠ **Long Pine Key.** About 6 mi west of the park's main entrance, Long Pine Key has drive-up sites for tents and RVs, several area hiking trails, and a pond for fishing (permit required). Sites are available on a first-come, first-served basis. Be prepared to pay cash via park-supplied yellow envelope on arrival if a park employee is not at the campground kiosk between December and April. Camping is free the rest of the year. ♿ *Flush toilets, dump station, drinking water, picnic tables* ⊅ *108 drive-up sites* ☎ *305/242–7700* ⊕ *www.nps.gov/ever* ▤ *D, MC, V.*

GULF COAST ENTRANCE

5

To reach the park's western gateway, take U.S. 41 west from Miami for 77 mi, turn left (south) onto Route 29, and travel another 3 mi through Everglades City to the Gulf Coast Ranger Station. From Naples on the Gulf Coast, take U.S. 41 east for 35 mi, then turn right onto Route 29.

Gulf Coast Visitor Center. The best place to bone up on Everglades National Park's watery western side is at this visitor center just south of Everglades City, where rangers are on hand to answer any of your questions. In winter, canoeists check in here for trips to the Ten Thousand Islands and 99-mi Wilderness Waterway Trail, nature lovers view interpretive exhibits on local flora and fauna while waiting for naturalist-led boat trip departures, and backcountry campers purchase permits. In season (Christmas through Easter), rangers lead bike tours and canoe trips. No direct roads run from here to other sections of the park, and admission is free only to this section of the park. ⊠ *Rte. 29, Everglades City* ☎ *239/695–3311* ⊙ *Mid-Nov.–mid-Apr., daily 8–4:30; mid-Apr.–mid-Nov., daily 9–4:30.*

OUTFITTERS On the west side, **Everglades National Park Boat Tours** (⊠ *Gulf Coast Visitor Center, Everglades City* ☎ *239/695–2591 or 866/628–7275* ⊕ *www.nps.gov/ever*), operating in conjunction with boat tours at Flamingo, runs 1½-hour trips ($26.50) through the Ten Thousand Islands National Wildlife Refuge, where passengers often see dolphins, manatees, bald eagles, and roseate spoonbills. In the height of the season, 49-passenger boats run every 30 to 45 minutes daily. Mangrove wilderness tours are also conducted on smaller boats for up to six passengers. These one-hour, 45-minute trips ($35) are the best option to see alligators. The outfitter also rents 16-foot aluminum canoes. Reservations are not accepted.

Fodor'sChoice **Everglades Rentals & Eco Adventures** (⊠ *Ivey House, 107 Camellia St., Everglades City* ✉ *Box 5038, Everglades City 34139* ☎ *877/567–0679 or 239/695–3299* ⊕ *www.evergladesadventures.com*) is an established source for canoes, sea kayaks, and guided Everglades paddling tours year-round, and a Swamp Stomp walking tour ($104, October–April) includes a box lunch. Canoe rentals cost from $35 the first day, $27 for each day thereafter. Day-long kayak rentals are from $45. All half-

Much skill is required to navigate boats through the shallow, muddy waters of the Everglades.

day rentals are from 1 to 5 PM. Shuttles deliver you to major launching areas such as Turner River ($30 for up to two people) and Collier-Seminole State Park ($60). Tour highlights include bird and gator sightings, mangrove forests, no-man's-land beaches, relics of hideouts for infamous and just-plain-reclusive characters, and spectacular sunsets. Longer adventures ($800 for two nights to $1,300 for six nights, with a two-person minimum) include canoe/kayak and equipment rental, all necessary camping equipment, a guide, and meals.

SHARK VALLEY

23½ mi west of Florida's Turnpike, off Tamiami Trail. Approximately 45 minutes west of Miami.

One thing you won't see at Shark Valley is sharks. The name comes from the Shark River, also called the River of Grass, which flows through the area. Several species of shark swim up this river from the coast (about 45 mi south of Shark Valley) to give birth. Young sharks (called pups), vulnerable to being eaten by adult sharks and other predators, gain strength in waters of the slough before heading out to sea to fend for themselves.

EXPLORING

Though Shark Valley is the national park's north entrance, no roads here lead directly to other parts of the park. However, it's still worth stopping here to take a tram tour and climb the observation tower halfway through the ride.

Prefer to do the trail on foot? It takes a bit of nerve to walk the paved 15-mi loop in Shark Valley because in the winter months alligators lie on and alongside the road, basking in the sun—most, however, do move quickly out of the way.

You can also ride a bicycle (the outfitter here rents one-speed, well-used bikes daily 8:30–4 for $7 per hour) or take a two-hour guided tram tour (reservations recommended in winter). Just behind the bike-rental area a short boardwalk trail meanders through the sawgrass, and another one passes through a tropical hardwood hammock. An underwater live camera in the canal behind the center (viewed from the gift shop) lets visitors sporadically see the alligators and otters.

Shark Valley Visitor Center. The small center has rotating exhibits, a bookstore, and park rangers ready for your questions. ⊠ *23½ mi west of Florida's Turnpike, off Tamiami Trail* ☎ *305/221–8776* ☉ *Late Mar.– late Dec., daily 9:15–5:15; late Dec.–late Mar., daily 8:45–5:15; gate daily 8:30–6.*

Observation Tower. At the Shark Valley trail's end (really, the halfway point of the 15-mi loop), you can pause to navigate the now wheelchair-accessible ramp of this tower, first built in 1984, spiraling 50 feet upward. Once on top, the River of Grass gloriously spreads out as far as your eye can see. Observe water birds as well as alligators and, perhaps even river otters crossing the road.

TOUR
★ **Shark Valley Tram Tours.** Starting at the Shark Valley visitor center, two-hour, narrated tours ($16.25) follow a 15-mi loop road—especially good for viewing gators—into the interior, stopping at a 50-foot observation tower. Reservations are recommended December through April. ⊠ *Valley Visitor Center* ☎ *305/221–8455* ⊕ *www.sharkvalleytramtours. com* ⊡ *$16.25 per person* ☉ *Tours Dec.–Apr., hourly 9–4; May–Nov., hourly 9–3.*

SPORTS AND THE OUTDOORS
BOATING

Many Everglades-area tours operate only in season, roughly November through April.

From the Shark Valley area, **Buffalo Tiger's Airboat Tours** (⊠ *5 mi east of Shark Valley* ☎ *305/559–5250* ⊕ *www.buffalotigersairboattours.com*) is operated by a former chief of Florida's Miccosukee tribe, who, at 90 (or so) years old doesn't skipper the boat anymore, but still gets out to meet and greet when he can. Guides narrate the 45-minute trip from the American Indian perspective. Trips run on the north side of Tamiami Trail and include a stop at an old American Indian camp. Tours go from 10–5 Saturday through Thursday and cost $25 per person for two, $20 per person for more than two, up to 12 people. Reservations are not required.

BIG CYPRESS NATIONAL PRESERVE

Through the 1950s and early 1960s the world's largest cypress-logging industry prospered in Big Cypress Swamp. As the industry died out, the government began buying parcels. Today, 729,000 acres, or nearly half of the swamp, form this national preserve. The word "big" refers not to the size of the trees but to the swamp, which juts into the north edge of Everglades National Park like a jigsaw-puzzle piece. Size and strategic location make Big Cypress an important link in the region's hydrological system, where rainwater first flows through the preserve, then south into the park, and eventually into Florida Bay. Its variegated pattern of wet prairies, ponds, marshes, sloughs, and strands provides a wildlife sanctuary, and thanks to a policy of balanced land use—"use without abuse"—the watery wilderness is devoted to recreation as well as research and preservation.

The preserve allows—in limited areas—hiking, hunting, and off-road-vehicle (airboat, swamp buggy, four-wheel-drive vehicles) use by permit. Compared with Everglades National Park, the preserve is less developed and hosts fewer visitors. That makes it ideal for naturalists, birders, and hikers who prefer to see more wildlife than humans.

Several scenic drives link off Tamiami Trail; some require four-wheel-drive vehicles, especially in wet summer months. A few lead to camping areas, and roadside picnic areas.

PARK ESSENTIALS

Admission Fees: There is no admission fee to visit the preserve.

Admission Hours: The park is open daily, year-round. Accessible only by boat, Adams Key is for day use only.

Contact Information: **Big Cypress National Preserve** (✉ *HCR 61, Box 11, Ochopee 34141* ☎ *239/695–1201* ⊕ *www.nps.gov/bicy*).

EXPLORING

Ochopee Post Office. This former irrigation pipe shed is North America's smallest post office. Buy a postcard of the one-room shack and mail it to a friend, to help keep this picturesque outpost in business during times of governmental cutbacks and layoffs. ✉ *4 mi east of Rte. 29, at 38000 E. Tamiami Trail, Ochopee* ☎ *239/695–2099* ⊗ *Weekdays 10–noon and 1–4:30, Sat. 10–11:30.*

Oasis Visitor Center. The biggest attraction here is the observation deck where you can view huge gators as well as fish, birds, and other wildlife. There's also a small butterfly garden where native plants seasonally attract winged wonders. Inside the information center you'll find a small exhibit area, a bookshop, and a theater that shows a dated but informative 15-minute film on the Big Cypress Preserve swamplands.

✉ 24 mi east of Everglades City, 50 mi west of Miami, 20 mi west of Shark Valley ☎ 239/695–1201 ◻ Free ◷ Daily 9–4:30.

RANGER PROGRAMS

From the Oasis Visitor Center you can get in on one of the seasonal ranger-led or self-guided activities, such as campfire and wildlife talks, hikes, slough slogs, and canoe excursions. The 8-mi Turner River Canoe Trail begins nearby and crosses through Everglades National Park before ending in Chokoloskee Bay, near Everglades City. Rangers lead four-hour canoe trips and two-hour swamp walks in season; call for days and times. Bring shoes and long pants for the swamp walks and be prepared to wade at least knee-deep in water. Ranger program reservations are accepted up to 14 days in advance.

SPORTS AND THE OUTDOORS

There are three types of trails—walking (including part of the extensive Florida National Scenic Trail), canoeing, and bicycling. All three trail types are easily accessed from the Tamiami Trail near the preserve visitor center, and one boardwalk trail departs from the center. Canoe and bike equipment can be rented from outfitters in Everglades City, 24 mi west, and Naples, 40 mi west.

Hikers can tackle the Florida National Scenic Trail, which begins in the preserve and is divided into segments 6.5 to 28 mi each. Two 5-mi trails, Concho Billy and Fire Prairie, can be accessed off Turner River Road, a few miles east. Turner River Road and Birdon Road form a 17-mi gravel loop drive that's excellent for birding. Bear Island has about 32 mi of scenic, flat, looped trails that are ideal for bicycling. Most trails are hard-packed lime rock, but a few miles are gravel. Cyclists share the road with off-road vehicles, most plentiful from mid-November through December.

To see the best variety of wildlife from your car, follow 26-mi Loop Road, south of U.S. 41 and west of Shark Valley, where alligators, raccoons, and soft-shell turtles crawl around beside the gravel road, often swooped upon by swallowtail kites and brown-shouldered hawks. Stop at H.P. Williams Roadside Park, west of the Oasis, and walk along the boardwalk to spy gators, turtles, and garfish in the river waters.

WHERE TO CAMP

For lodging options in the area, see the Where to Stay sections under each town in What's Nearby, later in this chapter.

¢ ⚠ **Big Cypress National Preserve.** There are four no-fee primitive campgrounds within the preserve along Tamiami Trail and Loop Road, including Burns Lake, Bear Island, Pinecrest, and Mitchell's Landing. Some open year-round, others seasonally (September to early January); all are subject to closure from flooding or for repairs, so check ahead. A fifth site for both RVs and tents, Monument Lake, has restrooms, a cold shower, an amphitheater, and activities and seasonal

programs (mid-December through March). Campers can use the dump station on Dona Drive in Ochopee. The sixth, Midway, is the only campground with RV electrical hookups and an on-site dump station, free to campers. It is tidily maintained and an improvement upon private campgrounds in the area. All campgrounds are first-come, first-served, and stays are limited to 10 nights. ♿ *Flush toilets, dump station, showers (cold), running water* ☞ *40 sites at Burns Lake; 40 sites at Bear Island; 10 sites at Pinecrest; 15 sites at Mitchell's Landing; 10 tent, 26 RV sites at Monument Lake; 10 tent, 26 RV sites at Midway* ✉ *Tamiami Trail (Hwy. 41), between Miami and Naples* ☎ *HCR 61, Box 110, Ochopee 34141* ☎ *239/695–1201* ▭ *No credit cards.*

¢ ⚠ **Trail Lakes Campground.** Close to Everglades City and Big Cypress National Preserve, Trail Lakes spreads out over 30 acres, is near a canoe launch, and has the added attraction of a nature park and wildlife exhibits. Complex owner David Shealy is the self-proclaimed expert on the Skunk Ape, the Everglades version of Big Foot, and has appeared on national television. RV and tent campsites circle a small lake and front the River of Grass. ♿ *Flush toilets, drinking water, electricity, public telephone, general store* ☞ *80 RV sites, 25 tent sites* ✉ *40904 Tamiami Trail E (Hwy. 41), Ochopee* ☎ *239/695–2275* ⊕ *www.skunkape.info* ▭ *AE, MC, V.*

BISCAYNE NATIONAL PARK

Occupying 172,000 acres along the southern portion of Biscayne Bay, south of Miami and north of the Florida Keys, this national park is 95% submerged, and its altitude ranges from 4 feet above sea level to 60 feet below. Contained within from shore to sea are four distinct zones: mangrove forest along the coast, Biscayne Bay, the undeveloped upper Florida Keys, and coral reefs. Mangroves line the mainland shore much as they do elsewhere along South Florida's protected bay waters. Biscayne Bay functions as a lobster sanctuary and a nursery for fish, sponges, and crabs. Manatees and sea turtles frequent its warm, shallow waters.

GETTING HERE

To reach Biscayne National Park from Homestead, take Krome Avenue to Route 9336 (Palm Drive) and turn east. Follow Palm Drive for about 8 mi until it becomes South West 344th Street and follow signs to park headquarters in Convoy Point. The entry is 9 mi east of Homestead and 9 mi south and east of Exit 6 (Speedway Boulevard/Southwest 137th Avenue) off Florida's Turnpike.

PARK ESSENTIALS

Admission Fees There is no fee to enter Biscayne National Park, and you don't have to pay a fee to access the islands, but there is a $20 overnight camping fee that includes a $5 dock fee to berth vessels at some island docks. The park concessionaire charges for trips to the coral reefs and the islands (⇨ *see Outfitters and Expeditions*).

Admission Hours The park is open daily, year-round.

Contact Information Biscayne National Park (*Dante Fascell Visitor Center* ✉ *9700 SW 328th St., Homestead* ☎ *305/230–7275* ⊕ *www.nps.gov/bisc).*

WHAT TO SEE

Biscayne is a great place if you want to dive, snorkel, canoe, camp, bird-watch, or learn about marine ecology. The best place to hike is Elliott Key *(see Islands, below).*

THE CORAL REEF

Biscayne's corals range from the soft, flagellant fans, plumes, and whips found chiefly in the shallower patch reefs to the hard brain corals, elk-horn, and staghorn forms that can withstand the heavier wave action and depths along the ocean's edge.

THE ISLANDS

To the east, about 8 mi off the coast, lie 44 tiny keys, stretching 18 nautical mi north–south and accessible only by boat. There's no commercial transportation between the mainland and the islands, and only a handful can be visited: Elliott, Boca Chita, Adams, and Sands keys. The rest are wildlife refuges, are too small, or have rocky shores or waters too shallow for boats. It's best to explore the Keys between December and April, when the mosquito population is less aggressive. Repellent is a must.

★ **Boca Chita Key,** 10 mi northeast of Convoy Point, was once owned by the late Mark C. Honeywell, former president of Honeywell Company. A ½-mi hiking trail curves around the south side of the island. Climb the 65-foot-high ornamental lighthouse (by ranger tour only) for a panoramic view of Miami or check out the cannon from the HMS *Fowey.* There's no fresh water, access is by private boat only, and no pets are allowed. Pending restroom upgrades, only portable toilets are on-site. A $20 fee for overnight docking between 6 PM and 6 AM covers a campsite; pay at the automated kiosk near the harbor. Boca Chita Key is listed on the National Register of Historic Places for its 10 historic structures.

The largest of the islands, **Elliott Key,** 9 mi east of Convoy Point, has a mile-long loop trail on the bay side of the island at the north end of the campground. Boaters may dock at any of 36 slips, and a $20 fee for stays between 6 PM and 6 AM covers a campsite. Take an informal, ranger-led nature walk or head out on your own to hike the 6-mi trail along so-called Spite Highway, a 225-foot-wide swath of green that developers mowed down in hopes of linking this key to the mainland. Luckily the federal government stepped in, and now it's a hiking trail through tropical hardwood hammock. Facilities include restrooms, picnic tables, fresh drinking water, showers (cold), grills, and a campground. Leashed pets are allowed in developed areas only, not on trails. A 30-foot-wide sandy beach about a mile north of the harbor on the west (bay) side of the key is the only one in the national park. Boaters like to anchor off it to swim. The beach is for day use only; it has picnic areas and a short trail that follows the shore and cuts through the hammock.

A stone's throw from the western tip of Elliott Key and 9 mi southeast of Convoy Point, **Adams Key, onetime site of the Cocolobo Club, a yacht club famous for once hosting presidents Harding, Hoover, Johnson, Nixon and other luminaries,** is open for day use and has picnic areas, restrooms, dockage, and a short trail that runs along the shore and through a hardwood hammock. Rangers live on-island. Access is by private boat.

VISITOR CENTER

★ **Dante Fascell Visitor Center.** Go out on the wide veranda here to take in views across mangroves and Biscayne Bay. Inside the museum, artistic vignettes and on-request videos including the 11-minute *Spectrum of Life* explore the park's four ecosystems, while the Touch Table gives both kids and adults a feel for bones, feathers, and coral. Facilities include the park's canoe and tour concessionaire, restrooms with showers, a ranger information area, gift shop with books, and vending machines. Various ranger programs take place daily during busy fall and winter seasons. On the second Sunday of each month from January through May, the Family Fun Fest program offers three hours of hands-on activities for kids and families. Rangers also give informal tours of Elliott and Boca Chita keys; arrange in advance. Outside are picnic tables and grills. A short trail and boardwalk lead to a jetty. This is the only area of the park accessible without a boat. ✉ *9700 SW 328th St., Homestead/Convoy Point* ☎ *305/230–7275* ⊕ *www.nps.gov/bisc* ✇ *Free* ⊗ *Daily 9–4:30.*

> ### BISCAYNE IN ONE DAY
>
> Most visitors come to snorkel or dive. Divers should plan to spend the morning on the water and the afternoon exploring the Convoy Point Visitor Center. The opposite is true for snorkelers, as snorkel trips (and one-tank shallow-dive trips) depart in the afternoon. If you want to hike as well, turn to the trails at Elliott Key—just be sure to apply insect repellent (and sunscreen, too, no matter what time of year).

SPORTS AND THE OUTDOORS

BIRD-WATCHING

More than 170 species of birds have been identified around the park. Expect to see flocks of brown pelicans patrolling the bay—suddenly rising, then plunging beak first to capture prey in their baggy pouches. White ibis probe exposed mud flats for small fish and crustaceans. Although all the Keys are excellent for birding, Jones Lagoon (south of Adams Key, between Old Rhodes Key and Totten Key) is outstanding. It's approachable only by nonmotorized craft.

DIVING AND SNORKELING

Diving is great year-around, but best in summer, when calmer winds and smaller seas result in clearer waters. Ocean waters, another 3 mi east of the Keys, showcase the park's main attraction—the northernmost section of Florida's living tropical coral reefs. Some are the size of an office desk, others as large as a football field. You can take a glass-bottom-boat ride to see this underwater wonderland, but you really should snorkel or scuba dive to fully appreciate it.

Native plants along the Turner River Canoe Trail hem paddlers in on both sides, and alligators lurk nearby.

A diverse population of colorful fish—angelfish, gobies, grunts, parrot fish, pork fish, wrasses, and many more—flits through the reefs. Shipwrecks from the 18th century are evidence of the area's international maritime heritage, and a Maritime Heritage Trail is being developed to link six of the major shipwreck and underwater cultural sites. Thus far, three sites, including a 19th-century wooden sailing vessel, have been plotted with GPS coordinates and marked with mooring buoys. Plastic dive cards are being developed that will contain navigational and background information.

WHERE TO CAMP

For lodging options in the area, see the Where to Stay sections under each town in What's Nearby, later in this chapter.

¢ △ **Boca Chita Campground.** This small, flat island has a grassy, waterside campground shaded by palms whispering in the breeze. Views are awesome, and a nature trail circles the island, accessible only by private boat. Campsites are first-come, first-served (if there's an open boat slip, a campsite is available) and cost $20 per night for up to six campers (that includes a boat dockage fee of $5). There's no running fresh water. Campers must carry out all trash. ☺ *Flush toilets, picnic tables* ⟿ *39 sites* ✉ *Visitor center: 9700 SW 328th St., Homestead* ☎ *305/230-7275* 🚍 *No credit cards.*

¢ △ **Elliott Key Campground.** You'll need a private boat to get here, but grassy, beachfront tent sites with awesome views and populated with plenty of native hardwood trees make it worth the inconvenience. Spend the day swimming, snorkeling, hiking trails, and fishing, and spend the night gazing into the brilliant star-strewn, light-pollution-free skies. Parties of up to 25 campers and six tents can reserve one of the three group sites for $30 a night; all other campsites are available on a first-come, first-served basis (if there's an open boat slip, a site is available) and cost $20 per night for up to six (including boat dockage). Bring plenty of insect repellent and drinking water (pumps go out on occasion), and try to pick a breezy spot to pitch your tent. Keep in mind you must carry out all trash. Leashed pets are welcome. *Flush toilets, drinking water, showers (cold), picnic tables, swimming (bay) 40 sites Visitor center: 9700 SW 328th St., Homestead 305/230–7275, 305/230–1100 transportation, 305/230–1144 Ext. 3074 for group campsite www. nps.gov/bisc No credit cards.*

WHAT'S NEARBY

EVERGLADES CITY

35 mi southeast of Naples and 83 mi west of Miami.

Aside from a chain gas station or two, Everglades City is perfect Old Florida. No high-rises (other than an observation tower) mar the landscape at this western gateway to Everglades National Park, just off the Tamiami Trail. It was developed in the late 19th century by Barron Collier, a wealthy advertising entrepreneur, who built it as a company town to house workers for his numerous projects including construction of the Tamiami Trail. It grew and prospered until the Depression and World War II. Today it draws adventure-seekers heading to the park for canoeing, fishing, and bird-watching excursions. Airboat tours, though popular, are banned within the preserve and park because of the environmental damage they cause to the mangroves. The Everglades Seafood Festival, going strong for nearly 40 years and held the first full weekend of February, draws crowds of up to 75,000 for delights from the sea, music, and craft displays. At quieter times, dining choices are limited to a handful of basic eateries. The town is small, fishing-oriented, and unhurried, making it excellent for boating and bicycling. Pedal along the waterfront on a 2-mi ride along the strand out to Chokoloskee Island.

Visitor Information Everglades Area Chamber of Commerce (Rte. 29 and Tamiami Trail 239/695–3172 www.evergladeschamber.com).

EXPLORING

★ **Fakahatchee Strand Preserve State Park.** The ½-mi boardwalk through this linear swamp forest gives you an opportunity to see rare plants, bald cypress, nesting eagles, and North America's largest stand of native royal palms and largest concentration and variety of epiphytic orchids, including more than 30 varieties of threatened and endangered species blooming most extravagantly in hotter months. It's particularly famous for its ghost orchids (as featured in the novel *The Orchid Thief* by Susan Orlean), visible only on guided hikes. In your quest for ghost orchids, also keep a hopeful eye out for white-tailed deer, black bears, bobcats, and the Florida panther. For park nature on parade, take the

12-mi-long (one way) W. J. Janes Memorial Scenic Drive, and, if you have the time, hike the spur trails leading off it. Rangers lead swamp walks and canoe trips November through April. ⊠ *Boardwalk on north side of Tamiami Trail, 7 mi west of Rte. 29; W. J. Janes Scenic Dr., ¾ mi north of Tamiami Trail on Rte. 29; ranger station on W. J. Janes Scenic Dr.* ☎ *239/695–4593* ⊕ *www.floridastateparks.org/fakahatcheestrand* ⊠ *Free* ⊙ *Daily 8 AM–sunset.*

OFF THE
BEATEN
PATH

★ **Collier-Seminole State Park**. Nature trails, biking, hiking, camping, and canoeing into Everglades territory make this park a prime introduction to this often forbidding land. Of historical interest, a Seminole War blockhouse has been re-created to hold the interpretative center, and one of the "walking dredges"—a towering black machine invented to carve the Tamiami Trail out of the muck—stands silent on the grounds amid tropical hardwood forest. Campsites ($22 per night) include electricity, water, and picnic table. Restrooms have hot water, and one has a laundry. ⊠ *20200 E. Tamiami Trail, Naples* ☎ *239/394–3397* ⊕ *www. floridastateparks.org/collier-seminole* ⊠ *$5 per car, $4 with lone driver* ⊙ *Daily 8–sunset.*

Museum of the Everglades. Through artifacts and photographs you can meet the American Indians, pioneers, entrepreneurs, and fishermen who played a role in the development of southwest Florida. Exhibits and a short film chronicle the tremendous feat of building the Tamiami Trail through the mosquito-ridden and gator-infested Everglades wetlands. In addition to the permanent displays, monthly exhibits rotate the work of local artists. ⊠ *105 W. Broadway* ☎ *239/695–0008* ⊠ *Free* ⊙ *Tues.– Sat. 10–4.*

SPORTS AND THE OUTDOORS

BOATING AND CANOEING

On the Gulf Coast explore the nooks, crannies, and mangrove islands of Chokoloskee Bay and Ten Thousand Islands National Wildlife Refuge, as well as the many rivers near Everglades City. The Turner River Canoe Trail, a pleasant day trip with a guarantee of bird and alligator sightings, passes through mangrove, dwarf cypress, coastal prairie, and freshwater slough ecosystems of Everglades National Park and Big Cypress National Preserve.

OUTFITTER   **Glades Haven Marina** (⊠ *801 Copeland Ave. S, Everglades City* ☎ *239/ 695–2628* ⊕ *www.gladeshaven.com*) can put you on the water to explore the Ten Thousand Islands in 16-foot Carolina skiffs and 24-foot pontoon boats. Rates start at $150 a day, with half-day and hourly options. The outfitter also rents kayaks and canoes and has a 24-hour boat ramp and dockage for vessels up to 24 feet long.

WHERE TO EAT

$$–$$$ ✕ **Everglades Seafood Depot**. Count on an affordable, scenic breakfast,
SEAFOOD   lunch, or dinner at this storied 1928 Spanish-style stucco structure fronting Lake Placid. It began its life as the original Everglades train depot, was later deeded to the University of Miami for marine research, and appeared in scenes from the film *Winds across the Everglades,* before becoming a haven for assorted restaurants through the years. Well-prepared seafood including shrimp, frogs' legs, and alligator—much

from local boats—dominates today's menu. For big appetites, there are generously portioned entrées of steak and fish specials and combination platters that include warm, fresh-baked biscuits. All-you-can-eat specials, such as fried chicken, a taco bar, or a seafood buffet are available on selected nights. Ask for a table on the back porch or for a window seat overlooking the lake. Bargain hunters arrive early for the 99¢ breakfast menu, served Friday and Saturday from 5:30 AM–10:30 AM. ✉ *102 Collier Ave.* ☎ *239/695–0075* ⊕ *www.evergladesseafooddepot. com* ☐ *AE, D, MC, V.*

¢ ✕**Havana Cafe**. Cuban specialties are a tasty change from the shanty
CUBAN seafood houses of Everglades City; brightly painted walls and floral tablecloths make this little eatery with 10 indoor tables and four porch tables a cheerful spot. Service is order-at-the-counter for breakfast and lunch (8 AM–3 PM; with dinner on Friday and Saturday nights in season). Jump-start your day with café con leche and a pressed-egg sandwich; For lunch, you'll find the ubiquitous Cuban sandwich, burgers, shrimp, grouper, steak, and pork plates with rice and beans and yucca. ✉ *191 Smallwood Drive, Chocoloskee* ☎ *239/695–2214* ☐ *No credit cards* ◷ *No dinner Apr.–Oct. No dinner Sun.–Thurs. Nov.–Mar.*

$$–$$$ ✕**Oyster House Restaurant**. One of the town's oldest and most old-fash-
SEAFOOD ioned fish houses, Oyster serves all the local staples—shrimp, gator
◔ tail, frogs' legs, oysters, stone crab, and grouper—in a lodgelike setting where mounted wild game decorates walls and rafters. Shrimp and grouper smothered in tomatoes are among the few exceptions to fried preparation. Deep-frying remains an art in these parts, so if you're going to indulge, do it here. Consider the stone crab soup, in season, and try to dine at sunset for golden rays with your watery view. ✉ *Hwy. 29 S* ☎ *239/695–2073* ⊕ *www.oysterhouserestaurant.com* ☐ *AE, D, MC, V.*

$$$ ✕**Rod and Gun Club**. The striking, polished pecky-cypress woodwork
SEAFOOD in this historic building dates from the 1920s when wealthy hunters, anglers, and yachting parties from around the world arrived for the winter season. The main dining room holds the overflow from the popular, enormous screened porch overlooking the river. Like life in general here, servers move slowly and upkeep is minimal. Fresh seafood dominates, from stone crab claws in season to a surf-and-turf combo of steak and grouper, a swamp-and-turf combo of frogs' legs and steak, seafood and pasta pairings, and you can have your catch cooked for $14.95. Pie offerings include key lime and chocolate–peanut butter. The main lobby is worth a look—even if you plan to eat elsewhere. Arrive by boat or land. ✉ *200 Riverside Dr.* ☎ *239/695–2101* ⊕ *www. evergladesrodandgun.com* ☐ *No credit cards.*

$ ✕**Triad Seafood**. Along the Barron River, seafood houses, fishing boats,
SEAFOOD and crab traps populate one shoreline; mangroves the other. Some of the seafood houses, selling fresh off the boat, added picnic tables and eventually grew into restaurants. Family-owned Triad is one, with a screened dining area seating 44, and additional outdoor seating under a breezeway and on a deck overhanging the scenic river where you can savor fresh seafood during stone crab season, October 15 to May 15. Nothing fancy (although smoked salmon and blue crab salad have been

added to the lineup), but you won't find a better grouper sandwich. An all-you-can-eat fresh stone crab jumbo feast will set you back around $80; or $50 for large, $35, medium. Hours vary but it's usually open from 6 AM to 3 PM Monday through Thursday and from 6 AM to 5 PM Friday through Sunday. Lunch starts at 10:30 AM with fried shrimp, oyster, crab cake, and soft-shell blue crab baskets, plus Reubens, hamburgers, Philly cheesesteak sandwiches, and, on Friday, smoked ribs. ✉ *401 School Dr.* ☎ *239/695–0722* ⊕ *www.triadseafood.com* ▤ *AE, D, MC, V* ☺ *Closed May 16–Oct. 15.*

WHERE TO STAY

$–$$ ▦ **Glades Haven Cozy Cabins.** Bob Miller wanted to build a Holiday Inn next to his Oyster House Restaurant on marina-channel shores. When that didn't fly, he sent for cabin kits and set up mobile-home-size units around a pool on his property. Guests renting the cabins get free boat docking. A full cabin, done up in wood, tin roof, and polished floor, has a full kitchen and separate bedroom with screened porch. Duplex cabins—among the best deals in town—have a small fridge and microwave, with or without a screened porch. **Pros:** good food options; convenient to ENP boating; free docking; marina. **Cons:** crowded trailer-park feel; no phones. ✉ *801 Copeland Ave.* ☎ *239/695–2746 or 888/956–6251* ⊕ *www.gladeshaven.com* ⤳ *24 cabins, 4 3-bedroom houses* ♿ *In-room: no phone, kitchen (some). In-hotel: 2 restaurants, pool, laundry facilities* ▤ *AE, D, MC, V.*

$–$$
Fodor's Choice
★

▦ **Ivey House.** A remodeled 1928 boardinghouse originally for workers building the Tamiami Trail, Ivey House today fits many budgets. One part is a friendly B&B bargain with shared baths and a cottage. The newer inn, connected to the B&B, has rooms with private baths—some of Everglades City's plushest accommodations. Most inn rooms surround the screen-enclosed pool and courtyard. Display cases of local flora and fauna decorate the inn, along with Everglades and Ten Thousand Islands photography. The layout is designed to promote camaraderie, but there are secluded patios with chairs and tables for private moments. Rates include breakfast (hot breakfast in season). The owners of 30-year-old NACT-Everglades Rentals & Eco Adventures run Ivey House, so you'll save 20% on their canoe and kayak rentals and tours if you stay here. In 2007, the property became the first Collier County hotel to achieve state "Green Lodging" certification. **Pros:** canoe and kayak rentals and tours; pleasant; affordable. **Cons:** not on water; some small rooms. ✉ *107 Camellia St.* ☎ *877/567–0679 or 239/695–3299* ⊕ *www.iveyhouse.com* ⤳ *31 rooms, 18 with bath; 1 2-bedroom cottage* ♿ *In-room: refrigerator (some), Internet, Wi-Fi (some). In-hotel: restaurant, pool, laundry facilities, Wi-Fi hotspot* ▤ *MC, V* �’⬥ *BP.*

FLORIDA CITY

3 mi southwest of Homestead on U.S. 1.

Florida's Turnpike ends in Florida City, the southernmost town on the peninsula, spilling thousands onto U.S. 1 and eventually west to Everglades National Park, east to Biscayne National Park, or south to the Florida Keys. Florida City and Homestead run into each other, but the

SHUTTLES FROM MIAMI

Airporter (☎ *800/830–3413*) runs shuttle buses three times daily that stop at the Ramada Inn in Florida City on the way between MIA and the Florida Keys. Shuttle service, which takes about an hour, runs 6:10 AM–5:20 PM from Florida City, 7:30 AM–6 PM from the airport. Reserve at least 48 hours in advance. Pickups can be arranged for all baggage-claim areas. The cost is $30 one way.

Super Shuttle (☎ *305/871–2000* ⊕ *www.supershuttle.com*) runs 11-passenger air-conditioned vans 24 hours a day between MIA and the Homestead–Florida City area; pickup is outside baggage claim and costs $53 per person. For the return to MIA, reserve 24 hours in advance and know your pickup zip code for a price quote. Taxi fare from the airport to Everglades City runs about $100.

5

difference couldn't be more noticeable. As the last outpost before 18 mi of mangroves and water, this stretch of U.S. 1 is lined with fast-food eateries, service stations, hotels, bars, dive shops, and restaurants. Hotel rates increase significantly during NASCAR races at the nearby Homestead Miami Speedway. Like Homestead, Florida City is rooted in agriculture, with hundreds of acres of farmland west of Krome Avenue and a huge farmers' market that processes produce shipped nationwide.

VISITOR INFORMATION

Tropical Everglades Visitor Center (✉ *160 U.S. 1* ☎ *305/245–9180 or 800/388–9669* ⊕ *www.tropicaleverglades.com*).

SHOPPING

☾ ★ **Robert Is Here** (✉ *19200 SW 344th St.* ☎ *305/246–1592*), a remarkable fruit stand, sells vegetables, fresh-fruit milk shakes (try the key lime shake), 10 flavors of honey, more than 100 types of jams and jellies, fresh juices, salad dressings, and some 30 kinds of tropical fruits, including (in season) carambola, lychee, egg fruit, monstera, sapodilla, dragonfruit, genipa, sugar apple, and tamarind. The stand started in 1960, when seven-year-old Robert sat at this spot selling his father's bumper crop of cucumbers. Today, Robert (still on the scene daily with his wife and kids), ships all over the United States, donating seconds to needy area families. An odd assortment of animals out back—from goats to emus—adds entertainment value. The stand opens at 8 AM and stays open until at least 7 PM. It shuts down, however, during September and October.

WHERE TO EAT

$$ ITALIAN ✕ **Capri Restaurant.** Locals have been coming to this family-owned enterprise for affordable, traditional Italian-American fare since 1958. Outside it's a rock-walled building with a big parking lot filling up nightly. Interior dining areas have redbrick accent walls with plenty of round tables; a sunny courtyard with umbrellaed tables affords outdoor dining. Tasty options range from pizza with a light, crunchy crust and ample toppings to broiled steaks and seafood-pasta classics, plus spaghetti 16 ways. Bargain hunters have two choices: the daily early-bird entrées, 4:30–6:30 for $12–$14, which include soup or salad and

potato or spaghetti, and the Tuesday family night (after 4 PM), with all-you-can-eat pasta with salad or soup for $6.95. Specialty martinis and fruity cocktails supplement the international wine list. ⊠ *935 N. Krome Ave.* ☎ *305/247–1542* ⊕ *www.dinecapri.com* ⊟ *AE, D, MC, V* ☉ *No lunch Sun.*

$$ ✕ **Captain's Restaurant and Seafood Market.** A comfortable place where
SEAFOOD the chef knows how to do seafood with flair, this is among the town's best bets. Locals and visitors alike gather in the cozy dining room or outdoors on the patio. Blackboards describe a varied menu of sandwiches, pasta, seafood, steak, and nightly specials running up to $23.95. Inventive offerings include lobster Reuben sandwich, crawfish pasta, and pan-seared tuna topped with balsamic onions and shallots. ⊠ *404 SE 1st Ave.* ☎ *305/247–9456* ⊟ *AE, MC, V.*

$ ✕ **Farmers' Market Restaurant.** Although it's in the farmers' market on the
AMERICAN edge of town and serves fresh vegetables, seafood figures prominently
★ on the menu of home-cooked specialties. A family of fishermen runs the place, so fish and shellfish are only hours from the sea, and there's a fish fry on Friday nights. Catering to anglers and farmers, it opens at 5:30 AM, serving pancakes, jumbo eggs, and fluffy omelets with home fries or grits in a pleasant dining room with checkered tablecloths. Lunch and dinner menus have fried shrimp, seafood pasta, country-fried steak, roast turkey, and fried conch, as well as burgers, salads, and sandwiches. ⊠ *300 N. Krome Ave.* ☎ *305/242–0008* ⊟ *MC, V.*

$$$ ✕ **Mutineer Restaurant.** Families and older couples flock to the quirky yet
SEAFOOD well-dressed setting of this roadside steak-and-seafood outpost with a
☾ fish-and-duck pond and a petting zoo for kids. It was built in 1980 to look like a ship, back when Florida City was barely on the map. Etched glass divides the bi-level dining rooms, with velvet-upholstered chairs, an aquarium, and nautical antiques. The menu has 12 seafood entrées, including stuffed grouper (a favorite), Florida lobster tails, and snapper Oscar, plus another half-dozen daily seafood specials, as well as poultry, ribs, and steaks. Burgers and seafood sandwiches are popular for lunch, as is a happy-hour buffet all day until 7 PM in the lounge for $2.25 and the purchase of a drink. You also can dine in the restaurant's Wharf Lounge. Friday and Saturday are dance nights with live entertainment. ⊠ *11 SE 1st Ave. (U.S. 1), at Palm Dr.* ☎ *305/245–3377* ⊕ *www.mutineer.biz* ⊟ *AE, D, DC, MC, V.*

¢ ✕ **Rosita's Restaurante.** With its big Mexican population this area can
MEXICAN boast the authentic flavors that you just don't get in the Tex-Mex chains.
★ Order à la carte specialties or dinners and combos with beans and rice, and salad. Forty-three breakfast, lunch, and dinner entrées are served all day and range from Mexican eggs, enchiladas, and taco salad to stewed beef, shrimp ranchero-style, and fried pork chop. Food is on the spicy side, and if you like more fire, each table is equipped with fresh-tasting salsa, pickled jalapeños, and bottled habanero sauce. Clean (with lingering faint whiffs of bleach to prove it) and pleasant, with an open kitchen, take-out counter, and Formica tables, it's a favorite with locals and budget-minded guests at the Everglades International Hostel across the street. ⊠ *199 W. Palm Dr.* ☎ *305/246–3114* ⊟ *AE, MC, V.*

WHERE TO STAY

$$–$$$ ⚟ **Best Western Gateway to the Keys.** If you want easy access to Everglades and Biscayne national parks as well as the Florida Keys, you'll be well placed at this modern, two-story motel two blocks off Florida's Turnpike. Standard rooms, done in tropical colors, have two queen-size beds or one king-size bed. Rooms around the lushly landscaped pool cost the most. There's high-speed Internet access available in rooms, plus Wi-Fi in the lobby. **Pros:** convenient to national parks and Keys; business services; pretty pool area. **Cons:** traffic noise; generic rooms; fills up fast during high season. ✉ *411 S. Krome Ave.* ☎ *305/246–5100 or 888/981–5100* ⊕ *www.bestwestern.com/gatewaytothekeys* ⟿ *114 rooms ఉ In-room: refrigerator, Internet. In-hotel: pool, laundry facilities, Wi-Fi hotspot* ▭ *AE, D, DC, MC, V* ❙◉❙ *CP.*

$–$$ ⚟ **Econo Lodge.** Close to Florida's Turnpike and with access to the Keys, this is a good overnight pullover spot. Rooms are uncramped, with attractive bedspreads, coffeemakers, and in-room Wi-Fi. The pool sits in the parking lot, but tall ficus hedges separate it from busy U.S. 1. **Pros:** convenient location; business services; microwaves and refrigerators in rooms. **Cons:** urban-ugly location; noisy; lacks character. ✉ *553 NE 1st Ave.* ☎ *305/248–9300 or 800/553–2666* ⊕ *www.econolodge.com* ⟿ *42 rooms ఉ In-room: refrigerator, Internet, Wi-Fi. In-hotel: pool, laundry facilities, Internet terminal* ▭ *AE, D, DC, MC, V* ❙◉❙ *CP.*

¢ ⚟ **Everglades International Hostel.** Stay in clean and spacious private or dorm-style rooms (generally six to a room), relax in indoor or outdoor quiet areas, watch videos or TV on a big screen, and take affordable airboat, hiking, biking, and sightseeing tours (the all-day Everglades Tour is one of the most complete and affordable tours in the area and includes canoeing and a wet-walk). This privately owned facility is in a minimally restored art deco building on a lush, secluded acre between Everglades and Biscayne national parks, 20 mi north of Key Largo. Enjoy a free all-you-can-make pancake breakfast in the communal kitchen, and pitch in for occasional communal dinners ($5 each if one of the on-site volunteers is cooking), or walk to a nearby restaurant. Pets are welcome in private rooms with a $20 refundable deposit. You can make free domestic long-distance calls from the phone in a common room off the lobby. **Pros:** affordable; Everglades tours; free services. **Cons:** communal living; no elevator; old structure. ✉ *20 SW 2nd Ave.* ☎ *305/248–1122 or 800/372–3874* ⊕ *www.evergladeshostel. com* ⟿ *46 beds in dorm-style rooms with shared bath, 2 private rooms with shared bath ఉ In-room: no phone, no TV. In-hotel: water sports, bicycles, laundry facilities, Internet terminal, Wi-Fi hotspot, some pets allowed* ▭ *D, MC, V.*

$–$$ ⚟ **Fairway Inn.** Two stories high with a waterfall pool, this motel has some of the area's lowest chain rates, and it's next to the chamber of commerce visitor center so you'll never be short of reading and planning material. Rooms, with either one king-size bed or two doubles, have tiled bathrooms and closet areas. No-pet policy. **Pros:** affordable; convenient to restaurants, parks, and raceway; free in-room Wi-Fi. **Cons:** no character; plain, small rooms. ✉ *100 SE 1st Ave.* ☎ *305/248–4202 or*

5

888/340–4734 ⤵ 160 rooms ⟐ In-room: refrigerator, Internet, Wi-Fi. In-hotel: pool, laundry facilities ▭ AE, D, MC, V ⏵⦿⏴ CP.

$$ ⊞ **Ramada Inn**. Racing fans can hear the engines roar from this two-
★ story motel next to an outlet mall and within 15 minutes of the race-way and Everglades and Biscayne national parks. If you're looking for an upgrade from the other chains, this one offers more amenities and comfort, such as 32-inch flat-screen TVs, closed closets, and stylish furnishings. Carpeted rooms are bright and clean and have upholstered chairs, a coffeemaker, and an iron and ironing board. Included are a Continental breakfast with some hot items and local calls. **Pros:** extra room amenities; business clientele perks; convenient location. **Cons:** chain anonymity. ⊠ 124 E. Palm Dr. ☏ 305/247–8833 ⊕ www.hotelfloridacity.com ⤵ 123 rooms ⟐ In-room: refrigerator, Internet, Wi-Fi. In-hotel: pool, laundry service ▭ AE, D, DC, MC, V ⏵⦿⏴ CP.

$–$$ ⊞ **Travelodge**. This bargain motor lodge is close to Florida's Turnpike, Everglades and Biscayne national parks, the Florida Keys, and the Homestead Miami Speedway. In fact, many racers stay here, which makes it difficult to get a room when track events are scheduled. Clean, colorful rooms are small, but have more amenities than typical in this price range, including complimentary breakfast and newspaper, coffeemaker, hair dryer, iron with ironing board, and high-speed Internet access (there's free Wi-Fi in rooms, and two computers in the lobby for guest use). Fast-food and chain eateries, gas stations, and a visitor's bureau are within walking distance. **Pros:** in-room refrigerator and microwave; convenience to U.S. 1; complimentary breakfast. **Cons:** lacks character; small rooms; busy location. ⊠ 409 SE 1st Ave. ☏ 305/248–9777 or 800/758–0618 ⊕ www.tlflcity.com ⤵ 88 rooms ⟐ In-room: safe, refrigerator, Internet, Wi-Fi. In-hotel: pool, laundry facilities, Internet terminal ▭ AE, D, MC, V ⏵⦿⏴ CP.

HOMESTEAD

30 mi southwest of Miami.

In recent years Homestead has redefined itself as a destination for tropical agro- and ecotourism. Seated at the juncture between Miami and the Keys as well as Everglades National Park and Biscayne National Park, the area has the added dimension of shopping centers, residential development, hotel chains, and the Homestead Miami Speedway—when car races are scheduled, hotels hike up their rates and require minimum stays. The historic downtown has become a preservation-driven Main Street. Krome Avenue, where it cuts through the city's heart, is lined with restaurants, an arts complex, antiques shops, and low-budget, sometimes undesirable accommodations. West of north–south Krome Avenue, miles of fields grow fresh fruits and vegetables. Some are harvested commercially, and others beckon with U-PICK signs. Stands selling farm-fresh produce and nurseries that grow and sell orchids and tropical plants abound. In addition to its agricultural legacy, the town has an eclectic flavor, attributable to its population mix: descendants of pioneer Crackers, Hispanic growers and farm workers, professionals escaping Miami hubbub, and latter-day Northern retirees.

Are baby alligators more to your liking than their daddies? You can pet one at Everglades Gator Park.

WHAT TO SEE

☉ **Coral Castle**. Driven by unrequited love, 100-pound immigrant Ed Leedskalnin built this castle in the early 1900s out of massive slabs of coral rock, a feat likened to the building of the pyramids. Visitors can learn how he peopled his fantasy world with his imaginary wife and three children, studied astronomy, and created his simple home and elaborate courtyard with no engineering education and tools he mostly fashioned himself. Highlights of this National Register of Historic Places site include the Polaris telescope built to spot the North Star, a working sundial, a 5,000-pound heart-shaped table featured in Ripley's *Believe It or Not*, a banquet table in the shape of Florida, and a playground Ed named "Grotto of the Three Bears." ⊠ *28655 S. Dixie Hwy.* ☎ *305/248–6345* ⊕ *www.coralcastle.com* ⌑ *$9.75* ☉ *Sun.–Thurs. 8–6, Fri. and Sat. 8–8.*

SPORTS AND THE OUTDOORS

AUTO RACING

Homestead-Miami Speedway. This state-of-the-art facility with 65,000 grandstand seats, club seating eight stories above racing action, and two tracks has a 2.21-mi continuous road course and a 1.5-mi oval. There's a schedule of year-round manufacturer and race-team testing, club racing, and other national events. ⊠ *1 Speedway Blvd.* ☎ *866/409–7223* ⊕ *www.homesteadmiamispeedway.com.*

WATER SPORTS

Homestead Bayfront Park. Boaters, anglers, and beach-goers give high ratings to the facilities at this recreational area adjacent to Biscayne National Park. The 174-slip marina has a ramp, dock, bait-and-tackle shop, fuel station, ice, dry storage, and boat hoist, which can handle vessels up to 50 feet long. The park also has a tidal swimming area, a beach with lifeguards, a playground, ramps for people with disabilities (including a ramp that leads into the swimming area), and a picnic pavilion with grills, showers, and restrooms. ✉ *9698 SW 328th St.* ☎ *305/230–3033* 💲 *$6 per passenger vehicle; $12 per vehicle with boat Mon.–Thurs., $15 Fri.–Sun.; $15 per RV; $10 hoist* ⊙ *Daily sunrise–sunset.*

WHERE TO EAT

¢ ╳ **NicaMex.** Among the local Latin population this 68-seat eatery is a

MEXICAN low-budget favorite. It helps if you speak Spanish, but usually some staffers on hand speak English, and the menu is bilingual. Although they term it *comidas rapidas* (fast food), the cuisine is not Americanized. You can get authentic huevos rancheros or *chilaquiles* (corn tortillas cooked in red-pepper sauce) for breakfast, and specialties such as *chicharron en salsa verde* (fried pork skin in hot-green-tomato sauce) and shrimp in garlic all day. Hearty seafood and beef soups are best-sellers. Choose a domestic or imported beer, pop a coin into the Wurlitzer jukebox, select a Latin tune, and escape south of the border. ✉ *32 NW 1st St., across from the Krome Ave. bandstand* ☎ *305/247–0727* 🖃 *AE, D, MC, V.*

¢ ╳ **Sam's Country Kitchen.** For good, old, Southern-style home cooking,

SOUTHERN locals come to Sam's. Burgers, sandwiches, and dinners—including chicken livers, chicken and dumplings, and fried clams—come with fresh-baked corn bread and a daily selection of sides such as okra with tomatoes, turnip greens, pickled beets, or onion rings. Don't miss out on the changing selection of homemade soups and desserts. All this goodness comes cheap, but at the expense of anything-but-glamorous dining environs and often slow service. ✉ *1320 N. Krome Ave.* ☎ *305/246–2990* 🖃 *MC, V* ⊙ *No dinner Sun.*

WHERE TO STAY

$ 🏠 **Grove Inn Country Guesthouse.** Away from downtown but close to

★ Homestead's agricultural attractions, Grove Inn derives much of its personality from co-owners Craig, an artist, and Paul, a former showman. The lush garden is awash in organic, tropical fruit trees and native plants (in addition to a guest book, there's a live signature tree for signing leaves in the courtyard), and rooms named after tropical fruits like Carambola and Mango are decorated with antique furnishings and table settings. The owners go out of their way to pamper you, starting with a country breakfast using local produce, served family-style in a dining room done in Victorian florals. They offer behind-the-scenes tours of orchid nurseries and farms not otherwise open to the public. A vending machine dispenses complimentary cold drinks. **Pros:** fresh fruit; privacy; delicious breakfast; rural location. **Cons:** far from downtown and national parks; no restaurants nearby; not suited to families. ✉ *22540 SW Krome Ave., 6 mi north of downtown* ☎ *305/247–6572 or 877/247–6572* ⊕ *www.groveinn.com* 🛏 *13 rooms, 1 2-bedroom suite, 1 cottage* ⚒ *In-room: kitchen (some), refrigerator, Wi-Fi. In-hotel: pool, laundry facilities, some pets allowed* 🖃 *AE, D, MC, V* ⊙🍴 *BP.*

$-$$ 🏠 **Redland Hotel.** Of downtown Homestead's smattering of mom-and-

★ pop lodging options, this historic inn is the most desirable and has the

most character. When it opened in 1904, the inn was the town's first hotel, later becoming the first mercantile store, first post office, first library, and first boardinghouse. Each room has a different layout and furnishings, and some have access to a shared balcony. The style is Victorian, with lots of pastels and reproduction antique furniture. The pub is popular with locals, and there are good restaurants and antiques shops nearby. A coffee shop–Internet café serving burgers, wings and such, with free Wi-Fi in rooms and public spaces was added in 2006. **Pros:** historic character; convenient to downtown; well maintained. **Cons:** traffic noise; small rooms; ugly street location. ⊠ *5 S. Flagler Ave.* ☎ *305/246–1904 or 800/595–1904* ⊕ *www.redlandhotel.com* ⌔ *13 rooms* ♿ *In-room: Internet, Wi-Fi. In-hotel: restaurant, room service, bar* ⊟ *AE, D, MC, V.*

TAMIAMI TRAIL

5

An 80-mi stretch of U.S. 41 (known as the Tamiami Trail) traverses the Everglades, Big Cypress National Preserve, and Fakahatchee Strand Preserve State Park. The road was conceived in 1915 to link Miami to Fort Myers and Tampa. When it finally became a reality in 1928, it cut through the Everglades and altered natural flow of water and lives of the Miccosukee Indians, who were trying to eke out a living fishing, hunting, farming, and frogging here. The landscape is surprisingly varied, changing from hardwood hammocks to pinelands, then abruptly to tall cypress trees dripping with Spanish moss and back to sawgrass marsh. Slow down to take in the scenery and you'll likely be rewarded with glimpses of alligators sunning themselves along the banks of roadside canals or in the shallow waters, and hundreds of waterbirds, especially in the dry winter season. The man-made landscape has American Indian villages, chickee huts, and airboats parked at roadside enterprises. Between Miami and Naples the road goes by several names, including Tamiami Trail, U.S. 41, 9th Street in Naples, and, at the Miami end, Southwest 8th Street. ■ TIP→ Businesses along the trail give their addresses either based on their distance from Krome Avenue, Florida's Turnpike, and Miami on the east coast or Naples on the west coast.

WHAT TO SEE

☺ **Everglades Gator Park.** Here you can get face-to-face with and even touch an alligator—albeit a baby one—during the park's exciting Wildlife Show. You also can squirm in a "reptilium" of venomous and nonpoisonous native snakes or learn about American Indians of the Everglades through a reproduction of a Miccosukee village. The park also has 35-minute airboat tours and RV campsites ($30 per night) , as well as a gift shop and restaurant serving burgers to gator tail. ⊠ *24050 Tamiami Trail, 12 mi west of Florida's Turnpike, Miami* ☎ *305/559–2255 or 800/559–2205* ⊕ *www.gatorpark.com* ⊠ *Tours, wildlife show, and park $21* ☉ *Daily 9–5.*

Everglades Safari Park. A perennial favorite with tour-bus operators, the park has an arena seating up to 300 for an alligator show and wrestling demonstration. Before and after the show, get a closer look at both alligators and crocodiles on Gator Island; walk through a small wildlife museum, follow the jungle trail, or climb aboard an airboat for a 40-minute ride on the River of Grass (included in admission). There's also a restaurant, gift shop, and an observation platform looking out over the Glades. Small, private airboats are available for an extra charge for tours lasting 40 minutes to 2½ hours. ⊠ *26700 Tamiami Trail, 15 mi west of Florida's Turnpike, Miami* ☎ *305/226– 6923 or 305/223–3804* ⊕ *www.evsafaripark.com* ✉ *$23* ⊙ *Daily 9–5, last tour departs 3:30.*

> **CROCS OR GATORS?**
>
> You can tell you're looking at a crocodile, not an alligator, if you can see its lower teeth protruding when its jaws are shut. Gators are much darker in color—a grayish black—compared with the lighter tan color of crocodiles. Alligator snouts are also much broader than their long, thin crocodilian counterparts.

☸ ★ **Miccosukee Indian Village and Gift Shop.** Showcasing the culture, skills, and lifestyle of the Miccosukee Tribe of Florida, this cultural center offers crafts demonstrations and insight into the interactions between alligators and the American Indians. Narrated 30-minute airboat rides take you into the wilderness where these American Indians hid after the Seminole Wars and Indian Removal Act of the mid-1800s. In modern times many of the Miccosukee have relocated to this village along Tamiami Trail, but most still maintain their hammock farming and hunting camps. The village museum shows a film and displays chickee structures and artifacts. Guided tours run throughout the day, and a gift shop stocks dolls, apparel for adults and children, silver jewelry, beadwork, and other handcrafted items. The Miccosukee Everglades Music and Craft Festival falls on a July weekend, and the 10-day Miccosukee Indian Arts Festival is in late December. ⊠ *Just west of Shark Valley entrance on U.S. 41/Tamiami Trail, 25 mi west of Florida's Turnpike at MM 70, Miami* ☎ *305/552–8365* ⊕ *www.miccosukee.com* ✉ *Village $8, airboat rides $10* ⊙ *Daily 9–5.*

SPORTS AND THE OUTDOORS

BOAT TOURS

Many Everglades-area tours operate only in season, roughly November through April.

Running since 1945, **Coopertown Airboats** (⊠ *11 mi west of Florida's Turnpike, on Tamiami Trail* ☎ *305/226–6048* ⊕ *www.coopertownairboats. com*) operates the oldest airboat rides in the Everglades. The 35- to 40-minute tour ($21) takes you 9 mi to hammocks and alligator holes. Private charters are also available. Southwest of Florida City near the entrance to Everglades National Park, **Everglades Alligator Farm** (⊠ *40351 SW 192nd Ave.* ☎ *305/247–2628* ⊕ *www.everglades.com*) runs a 4-mi, 30-minute airboat tour of the River of Grass with departures 20 minutes after the hour. The tour ($23) includes free hourly alligator, snake, and wildlife shows, or take in shows only ($15.50). **Everglades Safari Park** (⊠ *26700 SW 8th St., 15 mi west of Florida's Turnpike, on Tamiami Trail* ☎ *305/226–6923 or 305/223–3804* ⊕ *www.evsafaripark.com*) runs 40-minute eco-adventure airboat rides for $23 and small, private airboat tours for an extra charge; they last from 40 minutes to 2½ hours. The price includes alligator show, natural-museum admission, and walking-trail access. **Gator Park Airboat Tours** (✉ *12 mi west of Florida's Turnpike, on Tamiami Trail* ☎ *305/559–2255 or 800/559–2205* ⊕ *www.gatorpark.com*) offers 45-minute narrated airboat tours ($21, including park tour and wildlife show).

🐊 A classic Florida roadside attraction, **Wooten's Everglades Airboat Tour** (✉ *Wooten's Alligator Farm, 1½ mi east of Rte. 29 on Tamiami Trail, Ochopee* ☎ *239/695–2781 or 800/282–2781* ⊕ *www.wootensairboats. com* ✉ *$25 for half-hour tour, $8 for animal exhibits* ☉ *Daily 8:30–5; last ride departs at 4:30*) runs airboat tours through the Everglades and swamp-buggy tours through the Big Cypress Swamp lasting approximately 30 minutes each (swamp buggies are giant tractorlike vehicles with oversize rubber wheels). More personalized airboat tours on smaller boats (seating six to eight) are also available for 45 minutes to one hour and start at $37.10. The on-site animal sanctuary offers the typical Everglades array of alligators, snakes, panthers, and other creatures. Discounts are available online.

SHOPPING

Shopping alone might lure you to the **Miccosukee Indian Village** (✉ *Just west of Shark Valley entrance, 25 mi west of Florida's Turnpike at MM 70* ☎ *305/223–8380*). Wares include American Indian crafts such as beadwork, moccasins, dolls, pottery, baskets, and patchwork fabric and clothing.

WHERE TO EAT

$ ✕ **Coopertown Restaurant**. Make this a pit stop for local color and cui-
ECLECTIC sine fished straight from the swamp. Starting a half century ago as a sandwich stand, this small, casual eatery inside an airboat concession storefront has attracted the famous and the humbly hungry. House specialties are frogs' legs and alligator tail breaded in cornmeal and deep-fried, casually served on paper ware with a lemon wedge and Tabasco. More conventional options include catfish, shrimp, burgers, hot dogs, or grilled cheese sandwiches. ✉ *22700 SW 8th St., 11 mi west of Florida's Turnpike, on Tamiami Trail, Miami* ☎ *305/226–6048* ⊕ *www.coopertownairboats.com* ▭ *AE, MC, V.*

$–$$ ✕ **Miccosukee Restaurant**. For a taste of local culture at a reasonable price,
SOUTHWESTERN this roadside cafeteria a quarter mile from the Miccosukee Indian Vil-
★ lage and overlooking the River of Grass, provides the best variety of food along Tamiami Trail in Everglades territory. The River of Grass view, servers wearing traditional Miccosukee patchwork vests, and mural depicting American Indian women cooking and men engaged in a powwow, all provide atmosphere. Favorites are catfish and frogs' legs breaded and deep-fried, Indian fry bread, and pumpkin bread, but you'll also find more common fare, such as huge burgers, sandwiches, salads, and dishes from south of the border. Try the Miccosukee Platter ($24.95) for a sampling of local favorites, including gator bites. Gator Nuggets (slightly larger than gator bites) are $2.25 each. Breakfast and lunch are served daily. ✉ *U.S. 41 (Tamiami Trail), 18 mi west*

of Miccosukee Resort and Gaming; 25 mi west of Florida's Turnpike ☎ *305/894–2374* ▤ *AE, D, MC, V.*

¢–$ ✕**Pit Bar-B-Q.** At the edge of Miami, this old-fashioned roadside eat-
SOUTHERN ery along Tamiami Trail near Krome Avenue was launched in 1965
☺ by the late Tommy Little, who wanted anyone heading into or out of
the Everglades to have access to cold drinks and rib-sticking fare. His
vision remains a holdout from the Everglades' backwoods heritage and
a popular, affordable option for families. Order at the counter, pick up
your food, and eat at one of the picnic tables on the screened porch or
outdoors. Specialties include barbecued chicken and ribs with a tangy
sauce, fries, coleslaw, and a fried biscuit, plus burgers and fish sandwiches. The whopping double-decker beef or pork sandwich with slaw
requires at least five napkins. Latin specialties include corn tamales in
the husk and fried green plantains. Beer is by the bottle or pitcher, wine
by the bottle or glass. Locals flock here with kids on weekends for pony
rides. ⊠ *16400 Tamiami Trail, 5 mi west of Florida's Turnpike, Miami*
☎ *305/226–2272* ⊕ *www.thepitbarbq.com* ▤ *AE, D, MC, V.*

WHERE TO STAY

$$$ ⊞ **Miccosukee Resort & Gaming.** Like an oasis on the horizon of endless
sawgrass, this nine-story resort at the southeastern edge of the Ever-
glades can't help but attract your eye, even if you're not on the lookout
for 24-hour gaming action. The casino occupies the lobby (making for
a cigarette-smoky welcome at check-in), and features over 1,800 video
machines, 58 poker tables, a 1,200-seat Bingo Hall, and nonsmoking
gaming areas. If you ever leave the lobby, you'll find that most rooms
and suites have a view of Everglades sawgrass and wildlife. On-site
there's a well-maintained indoor pool, Jacuzzi, sauna, spa, fitness center,
indoor play area for children, and a game arcade for teens and tweens,
plus Club Egret child care for kids under age 12. There are tours to
the Miccosukee Indian Village, shuttles to area malls, and a 27-hole
golf club and tennis courts just 15 mi away. **Pros:** casino; most modern
resort in these parts; golf. **Cons:** cigarette odor in lobby; parking lot
fills with gamblers; feels incompatible with the Everglades. ⊠ *500 SW
177th Ave., 6 mi west of Florida's Turnpike, Miami* ☎ *305/925–2555
or 877/242–6464* ⊕ *www.miccosukee.com* ↩ *256 rooms, 46 suites*
☖ *In-room: safe, Wi-Fi. In-hotel: 5 restaurants, room service, bars,
golf course, pool, gym, spa, children's programs (up to 12 years old),
laundry service, Internet terminal, Wi-Fi hotspot, parking (free)* ▤ *AE,
D, DC, MC, V.*

The Florida Keys

WORD OF MOUTH

"The keys are definitely a get out on the water type place instead of a driving up and down US 1 kind of place. Bars and restaurants open early and close early. Get out over the water. That is where the most amazing things in the keys are."

—GoTravel

WELCOME TO THE FLORIDA KEYS

TOP REASONS TO GO

★ **John Pennekamp Coral Reef State Park:** A perfect introduction to the Florida Keys, this nature reserve offers snorkeling, diving, camping, and kayaking. An underwater highlight is the massive Christ of the Deep statue.

★ **Under the Sea:** Whether you scuba, snorkel, or ride a glass-bottom boat, don't miss gazing at the coral reef and its colorful denizens.

★ **Sunset at Mallory Square:** Sure it's touristy, but just once while you're here you've got to witness the circus-like atmosphere of this nightly event.

★ **Duval Crawl:** Shop, eat, drink, repeat. Key West's Duval Street and the nearby streets make a good day's worth of window-shopping and people-watching.

★ **Get on the Water:** From angling for trophy-size fish to zipping out to the Dry Tortugas, a boat trip is in your future. It's really the whole point of the Keys.

1 The Upper Keys. As the doorstep to the islands' coral reefs and blithe spirit, the Upper Keys introduce all that is sporting and sea-oriented about the Keys. They stretch from Key Largo to the Long Key Channel (MM 106–65).

2 The Middle Keys. Centered around the town of Marathon, the Middle Keys hold most of the chain's historic and natural attractions outside of Key West. They go from Conch (pronounced *konk*) Key through Marathon to the south side of the Seven Mile Bridge, including Pigeon Key (MM 65–40).

3 The Lower Keys. Pressure drops another notch in this laid-back part of the region, where wildlife and the fishing lifestyle peak. The Lower Keys go from Little Duck Key south through Big Coppitt Key (MM 40–9).

4 Key West. The ultimate in Florida Keys craziness, the party town Key West isn't the place for those seeking a quiet retreat. The Key West area encompasses MM 9-0.

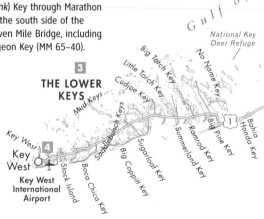

Key West.

THE LOWER KEYS

Gulf of

National Key Deer Refuge

Big Torch Key
Little Torch Key
Cudjoe Key
Mud Keys
No Name Key
Saddlebunch Keys
Big Pine Key
Bahia Honda Key
Key West
Sugarloaf Key
Ramrod Key
Summerland Key
Big Coppitt Key
Boca Chica Key
Stock Island
Key West International Airport

Key West.

Key West.

Homestead
TO MIAMI

905A

Card Sound Bridge

905

U.S. 1

Whitewater Bay

Everglades National Park

9336

Barnes Sound

CAPE SABLE

Flamingo

Key Largo

Key Largo

1

THE UPPER KEYS

Tavernier

John Pennekamp Coral Reef State Park

Windley Key

Plantation Key

Islamorada

Upper Matecumbe Key

Lower Matecumbe Key

2

THE MIDDLE KEYS

Layton

Craig Key

Long Key

Marathon Airport

Marathon

Conch Key

Duck Key

Grassy Key

Vaca Key

Flat Deer Key

Seven Mile Bridges

Mexico

Florida Bay

Straits of Florida

A T L A N T I C   O C E A N

6

0   10 mi

0   10 km

GETTING ORIENTED

The Florida Keys are the dribble of islands off the peninsula's southern tip. From Miami International Airport, Key Largo is a 56-mi drive along the Overseas Highway. The rest of the keys—Islamorada, Marathon, Bahia Honda Key, Big Pine Key—fall in succession for the 106 mi between Key Largo and Key West. At their north end, the Florida Keys front Florida Bay, which separates it from Everglades National Park. The Middle and Lower Keys front the Gulf of Mexico; the Atlantic Ocean borders the length of the chain on its eastern shores.

THE FLORIDA KEYS PLANNER

When to Go

High season in the Keys falls between Christmas and Easter. November to mid-December crowds are thinner, the weather is wonderful, and hotels and shops drastically reduce their prices. Summer, which is hot and humid, is becoming a second high season, especially among Floridians, families, and European travelers. If you plan to attend the wild Fantasy Fest in October, book your room at least six months in advance. Accommodations are also scarce during the first weekend in August, the start of lobster season.

Winter is typically 10°F warmer than on the mainland; summer is usually a few degrees cooler. The Keys also get substantially less rain, around 40 inches annually, compared with an average 55–60 inches in Miami and the Everglades. Most rainfalls are quick downpours on summer afternoons, except in June through October, when tropical storms can dump rain for two to four days. Winter cold fronts occasionally stall over the Keys, dragging overnight temperatures down to the low 50s.

Getting Here and Around

About 450,000 passengers use the **Key West International Airport (EYW)** (☎ 305/296–5439 ⊕ www.keywestinternationalairport.com) each year. In 2009, the airport completed its four-year renovation, which includes a beach where travelers can catch their last blast of rays after clearing security. Because flight schedules can be iffy, many prefer driving via the 110-mi Overseas Highway (aka U.S. 1). Besides Key West International Airport, many visitors to the region fly into Miami International Airport, Fort Lauderdale–Hollywood International Airport, and others on the mainland.

By car, from Miami International Airport (MIA), follow signs to Coral Gables and Key West, which puts you on LeJeune Road, then Route 836 west. Take the Homestead Extension of Florida's Turnpike south (toll road), which ends at Florida City and connects to the Overseas Highway (U.S. 1, currently under construction so expect delays). Tolls from the airport run approximately $3. The alternative from Florida City is Card Sound Road (Route 905A), which has a bridge toll of $1. Continue to the only stop sign and turn right on Route 905, which rejoins Overseas Highway 31 mi south of Florida City. The best Keys road map, published by the Homestead–Florida City Chamber of Commerce, can be obtained for $5.50 from the **Tropical Everglades Visitor Center** (☎ 305/245–9180 or 800/388–9669 ⊕ www.tropicaleverglades.com).

Those unwilling to tackle the route's 43 bridges and peak-time traffic can take Greyhound's (☎ 800/231–2222 ⊕ www.greyhound.com) Keys Shuttle, which has multiple daily departures from Miami International Airport.

Boaters can travel to and along the Keys either along the Intracoastal Waterway through Card, Barnes, and Blackwater sounds and into Florida Bay or along the deeper Atlantic Ocean route through Hawk Channel. The Keys are full of marinas that welcome transient visitors, but there aren't enough slips for all the boats heading to these waters. Make reservations far in advance and ask about channel and dockage depth—many marinas are quite shallow.

About the Restaurants

Seafood rules on the Keys, which is full of chef-owned restaurants with not-too-fancy food. Things get more exotic once you reach Key West. Restaurants serve cuisine that reflects the proximity of the Bahamas and Caribbean. Tropical fruits figure prominently—especially on the beverage side of the menu. Florida spiny lobster should be local and fresh from August to March, and stone crabs from mid-October to mid-May. And don't dare leave the islands without sampling conch, be it in a fritter or in ceviche. Keep an eye out for authentic key lime pie—yellow custard in a graham-cracker crust. If it's green, just say "no." **Note:** Particularly in Key West and particularly during spring break, the more affordable and casual restaurants can get loud and downright rowdy, with young visitors often more interested in drinking than eating. Live music contributes to the decibel levels. If you're more the quiet, intimate dining type, avoid such overly exuberant scenes by eating early or choosing a restaurant where the bar is not the main focus.

About the Hotels

Throughout the Keys, the types of accommodations are remarkably varied, from '50s-style motels to cozy inns to luxurious lodges. Most are on or near the ocean, so water sports reign supreme. Key West's lodging portfolio includes historic cottages, restored Conch houses, and large resorts. Some larger properties throughout the Keys charge a mandatory daily resort fee of $15 or more, which can cover equipment rental, fitness-center use, and other services, plus expect another 12.5% (or more) sales/resort tax. Some guesthouses and inns do not welcome children, and many do not permit smoking.

The Milemarker System

Getting lost in the Keys is almost impossible once you understand the unique address system. **Many addresses are simply given as a mile marker (MM) number.** The markers are small, green, rectangular signs along the side of the Overseas Highway (U.S. 1). They begin with MM 126, 1 mi south of Florida City, and end with MM 0, in Key West. **Keys residents use the abbreviation BS for the bay side of Overseas Highway and OS for the ocean side.** From Marathon to Key West, residents may refer to the bay side as the gulf side.

6

WHAT IT COSTS

	¢	$	$$	$$$	$$$$
Restaurants	under $10	$10–$15	$15–$20	$20–$30	over $30
Hotels	under $80	$80–$100	$100–$140	$140–$220	over $220

Restaurant prices are per person for a main course at dinner. Hotel prices are for a standard double room, excluding 12.5% sales tax (or more) in sales and resort taxes.

Key Biscayne.

THE FLORIDA KEYS BEACHES

Because the Bahama Islands steal the Keys' offshore sand, the region has fewer natural beaches than one might expect. But the ones it does have are award-winning, specifically those at Bahia Honda State Park.

Also, just because a beach is not natural, doesn't mean it should be overlooked. Some of the Keys' public man-made beaches provide solid recreation and sunning options for visitors looking to work on their tan. Many resorts additionally provide their own private beachfronts.

The Keys may not have a surplus of beaches, but one nice perk is the availability of camping on some of them. It's one of many ways to enjoy nature while on the beach. Another is keeping an eye out for sea turtles. April through October female sea turtles lay their eggs into the sand for a nearly two-month period of nesting.

■ TIP→ Don't let pests ruin your day at the beach. To avoid the stings of sea lice, remove your swimsuit and shower thoroughly upon exiting the water. Sand fleas, (aka no-see-ums) are tiny insects with big teeth that are most likely to attack in the morning and around sunset.

BIRD-WATCHING ON THE BEACH

The Florida Keys beaches can be great places to look to the skies and waters for all varieties of birds. Permanent residents include shorebirds—plovers, ruddy turnstones, willets, and short-billed dowitchers; wading birds—great blue herons, great white herons, snowy egrets, tri-colored herons, and white ibis; brown pelicans; osprey; and turkey vultures. In the autumn, hawks migrate through the region, while in winter ducks make their debut. In the summer, white-crowned pigeons are commonly seen.

FLORIDA KEYS' BEST BEACHES

LONG KEY STATE PARK

The beach at Long Key State Park at MM 67.5 is typical of Middle Key's beaches, which are more like sand flats where low tide reveals the coral bedrock of the ecosystem. Here you can snorkel or fish (bonefishing is quite popular) during the day and then be lulled to sleep by the sound of gentle sea waves if you spend the night camping. (The beach is accessible only to campers.)

SOMBRERO BEACH

Something of a local hangout—especially on weekends, when it can get crowded—Sombrero Beach in Marathon is worth getting off the beaten Overseas Highway path for (exit at MM 50 onto Sombrero Beach Road). Families will find much to do on the man-made coved beach and its grassy green, manicured lawn, playground area, and clear, calm waters. Separate sections also accommodate boaters and windsurfers.

BAHIA HONDA STATE PARK

This state park at MM 37 holds three beaches, all of different character. Sandspur Beach is the most removed from crowds with long stretches of powdery sands and a campground. Loggerhead Beach is closer to the park's concession area, where you can rent snorkel equipment and kayaks. Like Sandspur, it faces the Atlantic Ocean, but waves

are typically wimpy. Near Loggerhead, Calusa Beach on the Gulf side near the marina is popular with families, offering a small and safe swimming venue and picnic facilities, as well as camping.

HIGGS BEACH, KEY WEST

Situated on Atlantic Boulevard, this is as urban as beaches in the Keys get, with lots of amenities, activities, and distractions. Visitors can check out a historic site, eat at a popular beachfront Italian restaurant, rent a kayak, play volleyball, tennis, or at the playground—and all within walking distance of the long sweep of man-made beach and sparkling clear, shallow, and calm water.

ZACHARY TAYLOR HISTORIC STATE PARK

This man-made beach is part of a Civil War–era fort complex at the end of Southard Street and is arguably the best beach in Key West with its typically small waves, swaying Australian pines, water-sports rentals, and shaded picnic grounds. It also hosts, from mid-January through mid-April, an alfresco collection of oversized art called Sculpture Key West, which changes annually and showcases artists from across the country.

6

Updated by
Chelle Koster
Walton

Being a Conch is a condition of the heart, and foreclosure on the soul. Many throughout the Florida Keys wear that label proudly, yet there's anything but a shared lifestyle here.

To the south, Key West has a Mardi Gras mood with Fantasy Festivals, Hemingway look-alike contests, and the occasional threat to secede from the Union. It's an island whose melting-pot character allows crusty natives to mingle (more or less peacefully) with eccentrics and escape artists who lovingly call this 4-mi sandbar "Paradise." Although life elsewhere in the island chain isn't quite as offbeat, it's nearly as diverse. Flowering jungles, shimmering seas, and mangrove-lined islands are also, conversely, overburdened. Key Largo, nearest the mainland, is becoming more congested as it evolves into a bedroom community and weekend hideaway for residents of Miami and Fort Lauderdale.

A river of tourist traffic gushes along Overseas Highway, the 110-mi artery linking the inhabited islands. The expansion of U.S. 1 to the mainland to four lanes by 2012 will open the floodgates to increased traffic, population, and tourism. Observers wonder if making Overseas Highway four lanes throughout the Keys can be far away. For now, however, take pleasure as you cruise down Overseas Highway along the islands. Gaze over the silvery blue-and-green Atlantic and its still-living reef, with Florida Bay, the Gulf of Mexico, and the backcountry on your right (the Keys extend southwest from the mainland). At a few points the ocean and gulf are as much as 10 mi apart; in most places, however, they are from 1 to 4 mi apart, and on the narrowest landfill islands they are separated only by the road. Try to get off the highway. Once you do, rent a boat, anchor, and then fish, swim, or marvel at the sun, sea, and sky. In the Atlantic, dive spectacular coral reefs or pursue grouper, blue marlin, dolphinfish, and other deepwater game fish. Along Florida Bay's coastline, kayak and canoe to secluded islands and bays or seek out the bonefish, snapper, snook, and tarpon that lurk in the grass flats and in the shallow, winding channels of the backcountry.

GREAT ITINERARIES

3 DAYS

Spend your first morning diving or snorkeling at John Pennekamp Coral Reef State Park in **Key Largo**. If you aren't certified, sign up for a resort course and you'll be exploring the reefs by the afternoon. Dinner at a bay-side restaurant will give you your first look at a fabulous Keys sunset. On Day 2 get an early start to savor the breathtaking views on the two-hour drive to Key West. Along the way make a stop at the natural-history museum that's part of Crane Point Museum, Nature Center and Historic Site in **Marathon**. Another worthwhile detour is Bahia Honda Key State Park on **Bahia Honda Key**, where you can stretch your legs on a forest trail or snorkel on an offshore reef. Once you arrive in **Key West**, watch the sunset at one of the island's restaurants. The next morning, stroll Duval Street, visit a museum or two, or take a trolley tour of Old Town.

4 DAYS

Spend the first day as you would above, staying overnight in **Key Largo**. Start Day 2 by renting a kayak and exploring the mangroves of Florida Bay, or taking an ecotour of the sandy islands in Everglades National Park. In the afternoon, head down to **Islamorada** and visit Windley Key Fossil Reef Geological State Park. Before day's end, make plans for the next day's fishing. Spend the night in Islamorada. After a morning spent with a rod and reel, stop at one of the many restaurants that happily prepare your catch for you. In the afternoon, set off for **Key West**. Enjoy the sunset celebration at Mallory Square.

6

THE UPPER KEYS

Diving and snorkeling rule in the Upper Keys, thanks to the tropical coral reef that runs a few miles off the seaward coast. Divers of all skill levels benefit from accessible dive sites and an established tourism infrastructure. Fishing is another huge draw, especially around Islamorada, known for its sportfishing in both deep offshore waters and in the backcountry. Offshore islands accessible only by boat are popular destinations for kayakers. In short, if you don't like the water you might get bored here.

Other nature lovers won't feel shortchanged. Within 1½ mi of the bay coast lie the mangrove trees and sandy shores of Everglades National Park, where naturalists lead tours of one of the world's few saltwater forests. Here you'll see endangered manatees, curious dolphins, and other underwater creatures. Although the number of birds has dwindled since John James Audubon captured their beauty on canvas, the rare Everglades snail kite, bald eagles, ospreys, and a colorful array of egrets and herons delight bird-watchers. At sunset flocks take to the skies as they gather to find their night's roost, adding a swirl of activity to an otherwise quiet time of day.

The Upper Keys are full of low-key eateries where the owner is also the chef and the food is tasty and never too fussy. The one exception is Islamorada, where you'll find the more upscale restaurants. Restaurants may close for a two- to four-week vacation during the slow season between mid-September and late October.

In the Upper Keys, the accommodations are as varied as they are plentiful. The majority of lodgings are in small waterfront complexes with efficiencies and one- or two-bedroom units. These places offer dockage and often arrange boating, diving, and fishing excursions. There are also larger resorts with every type of activity imaginable and smaller boutique hotels where the attraction is personalized service.

Depending on which way the wind blows and how close the property is to the highway, there may be some noise from Overseas Highway. If this is an annoyance for you, ask for a room as far from the traffic as possible. Some properties require two- or three-day minimum stays during holiday and high-season weekends. Conversely, discounts apply for midweek, weekly, and monthly stays.

GETTING HERE AND AROUND

Airporter operates scheduled van and bus pick-up service from all Miami International Airport (MIA) baggage areas to wherever you want to go in Key Largo ($50) and Islamorada ($55). Groups of three or more passengers receive discounts. There are three departures daily; reservations are preferred 48 hours in advance. The SuperShuttle charges $102 per passenger for trips from Miami International Airport to the Upper Keys. For trip to the airport, place your request 24 hours in advance.

ESSENTIALS

Transportation Contacts **Airporter** (☎ 305/852–3413 or 800/830–3413). **SuperShuttle** (☎ 305/871–2000 ⊕ www.supershuttle.com).

KEY LARGO

The first of the Upper Keys reachable by car, 30-mi-long Key Largo is also the largest island in the chain. Key Largo—named Cayo Largo ("Long Key") by the Spanish—makes a great introduction to the region.

The history of Largo is similar to that of the rest of the Keys, with its succession of native people, pirates, wreckers, and developers. The first settlement on Key Largo was named Planter, back in the days of pineapple and later key lime plantations. For a time it was a convenient shipping port, but when the railroad arrived Planter died on the vine. Today three communities—North Key Largo, Key Largo, and Tavernier—make up the whole of Key Largo.

If you've never tried diving, Key Largo is the perfect place to learn. Dozens of companies will be more than happy to show you the ropes. Nobody comes to Key Largo without visiting John Pennekamp Coral Reef State Park, one of the jewels of the state-park system. Also popular is the adjacent Key Largo National Marine Sanctuary, which encompasses about 190 square mi of coral reefs, sea-grass beds, and mangrove estuaries. Both are good for underwater exploration.

Fishing is the other big draw, and world records are broken regularly. There are plenty of charter operations to help you find the big ones and teach you how to hook the elusive bonefish, sometimes known as the ghost fish. On land, restaurants will cook your catch or dish up their own offerings with inimitable style.

Key Largo offers all the conveniences of a major resort town, with most businesses lined up along Overseas Highway (U.S. 1), the four-lane highway that runs down the middle of the island. Cars whiz past at all hours—something to remember when you're booking a room. Most lodgings are on the highway, so you'll want to be as far back as possible.

GETTING HERE AND AROUND

Key Largo is 56 mi south of Miami International Airport, with the mile markers going from 106 to 91. The island runs northeast–southwest, with Overseas Highway running down the center. If the highway is your only glimpse of the island, you're likely to feel barraged by its tacky commercial side. Make a point of driving Route 905 in North Key Largo to get a better feel for it.

ESSENTIALS

Visitor Information **Key Largo Chamber of Commerce** (✉ *MM 106 BS, Key Largo* ☎ *305/451–4747 or 800/822–1088* ⊕ *www.keylargochamber.org*) .

EXPLORING

Dagny Johnson Key Largo Hammock Botanical State Park. American crocodiles, mangrove cuckoos, Schaus swallowtail butterflies, mahogany mistletoe, wild cotton, and 100 other rare critters and plants call these 2,400 acres home. The park is also a user-friendly place to explore the largest remaining stand of the vast West Indian tropical hardwood hammock and mangrove wetland that once covered most of the Keys' upland areas. Interpretive signs describe many of the tropical tree species along a 1-mi paved road (2-mi round-trip) that invites walking and biking. There are also more than 6 mi of nature trails accessible to bikes and wheelchairs. Pets are welcome if on a leash no longer than 6 feet. You'll also find restrooms, information kiosks, and picnic tables. ✉ *1 mi north of Overseas Hwy. on Rte. 905 OS, North Key Largo* ☎ *305/451–1202* ⊕ *www.floridastateparks.org/keylargohammock* 💲 *$2.50* ☉ *Daily 8–sundown.*

Jacobs Aquatic Center. Take the plunge at one of three swimming pools: an 8-lane, 25-meter lap pool with a diving well; a 3- to 4-foot-deep pool accessible to people with mobility problems; and an interactive play pool with a waterslide, pirate ship, waterfall, and sloping zero entry instead of steps. ✉ *320 Laguna Ave. (MM 99.6 OS)* ☎ *305/453–7946* ⊕ *www.jacobsaquaticcenter.org* 💲 *$8* ☉ *Daily 10–7.*

John Pennekamp Coral Reef State Park. This state park is on everyone's list for the best diving and snorkeling sites in the Sunshine State. The underwater treasure encompasses 78 square mi of coral reefs, sea-grass beds, and mangrove swamps. Its reefs contain 40 of the 52 species of coral in the Atlantic Reef System and nearly 600 varieties of fish, from the colorful stoplight parrot fish to the demure cocoa damselfish. The park's visitor center has a 30-gallon floor-to-ceiling fish tank surrounded by smaller ones, so you can get a closer look at many of the underwater creatures. When you want to head out to sea, a concessionaire rents kayaks and powerboats, as well as snorkeling and diving equipment. You

Fodor's Choice
★

can also sign up for snorkeling and diving trips ($30 and $60, respectively) and glass-bottom-boat rides to the reef ($24). One of the most popular excursions is the snorkeling trip to see Christ of the Deep, the 2-ton underwater statue of Jesus at Key Largo National Marine Sanctuary. The park also has short nature trails, two man-made beaches, picnic shelters, a snack bar, and a campground. ✉ *102601 Overseas Hwy. (MM 102.5 OS)* ☎ *305/451–1202 for park, 305/451–6300 for excursions* ⊕ *www.pennekamppark.com* 🖅 *$4.50 for 1 person, $9 for 2 people, 50¢ each additional person* ⊘ *Daily 8–sunset.*

SPORTS AND THE OUTDOORS

BOATING

Captain Sterling's **Everglades Eco-Tours** (✉ *Dolphin's Cove, 101900 Overseas Hwy. [MM 102 BS], Key Largo* ☎ *305/853–5161 or 888/224–6044* ⊕ *www.captainsterling.com*) operates Everglades and Florida Bay ecology tours ($49 per person) and sunset cruises ($79 per person). **M.V. Key Largo Princess** (✉ *99701 Overseas Hwy. [MM 100 OS], Key Largo* ☎ *305/451–4655 or 877/648–8129* ⊕ *www.keylargoprincess.com*) offers two-hour glass-bottom-boat trips ($30) and sunset cruises on a luxury 75-foot motor yacht with a 280-square-foot glass viewing area, departing from the Holiday Inn docks three times a day.

CANOEING AND KAYAKING

Sea kayaking continues to gain popularity in the Keys. You can paddle for a few hours or the whole day, on your own or with a guide. Some outfitters even offer overnight trips. The **Florida Keys Overseas Paddling Trail,** part of a statewide system, runs from Key Largo to Key West. You can paddle the entire distance, 110 mi on the Atlantic side, which takes 9–10 days. The trail also runs the chain's length on the bay side, which is a longer route.

At John Pennekamp Coral Reef State Park, **Coral Reef Park Co.** (✉ *102601 Overseas Hwy. [MM 102.5 OS]* ☎ *305/451–6300* ⊕ *www.pennekamppark.com*) has a fleet of canoes and kayaks for gliding around the 2½-mi mangrove trail or along the coast. It also rents powerboats. Rent canoes or sea kayaks from **Florida Bay Outfitters** (✉ *104050 Overseas Hwy. [MM 104 BS]* ☎ *305/451–3018* ⊕ *www.kayakfloridakeys.com*). The company, which helps with trip planning and matches equipment to your skill level, sets up self-guided trips on the Florida Keys Overseas Paddling Trail. It also runs myriad guided tours around Key Largo. Take a full-moon paddle, or a one- to seven-day canoe or kayak tour to the Everglades, Lignumvitae Key, or Indian Key. Trips run $60–$795.

FISHING

Private charters and big head boats (so named because they charge "by the head") are great for anglers who don't have their own vessel.

Sailors Choice (✉ *Holiday Inn Resort & Marina, 99701 Overseas Hwy. [MM 100 OS]* ☎ *305/451–1802 or 305/451–0041* ⊕ *www.sailorschoicefishingboat.com*) has fishing excursions departing twice daily ($40 for half-day trips). The 65-foot boat leaves from the Holiday Inn docks. Rods, bait, and license are included.

SCUBA DIVING AND SNORKELING

Much of what makes the Upper Keys a singular dive destination is variety. Places like Molasses Reef, which begins 3 feet below the surface and descends to 55 feet, have something for everyone from novice snorkelers to experienced divers. The *Spiegel Grove,* a 510-foot vessel, lies in 130 feet of water, but its upper regions are only 60 feet below the surface. On rough days, Key Largo Undersea Park's Emerald Lagoon is a popular spot. Expect to pay about $80 for a two-tank, two-site-dive trip with tanks and weights, or $35–$40 for a two-site-snorkel outing. Get big discounts by booking multiple trips.

Amy Slate's Amoray Dive Resort (⊠ *104250 Overseas Hwy. [MM 104.2 BS]* ☎ *305/451–3595 or 800/426–6729* ⊕ *www.amoray.com*) makes diving easy. Stroll down to the full-service dive shop (NAUI, PADI, TDI, and BSAC certified), then onto a 45-foot catamaran. The rate for a two-dive trip is $80.

★ **Conch Republic Divers** (⊠ *90800 Overseas Hwy. [MM 90.8 BS]* ☎ *305/852–1655 or 800/274–3483* ⊕ *www.conchrepublicdivers.com*) offers instruction as well as scuba and snorkeling tours of all the wrecks and reefs of the Upper Keys. Two-location dives are $80 with tank and weights. **Coral Reef Park Co.** (⊠ *102601 Overseas Hwy. [MM 102.5 OS]* ☎ *305/451–6300* ⊕ *www.pennekamppark.com*), at John Pennekamp Coral Reef State Park, gives 3½-hour scuba ($60) and 2½-hour snorkeling ($30) tours of the park. Besides the great location and the dependability of this operation, it's suited for water adventurers of all levels. **Ocean Divers** (⊠ *522 Caribbean Dr. [MM 105.5 BS]* ⊠ *105800 Overseas Hwy. [MM 100 OS]* ☎ *305/451–0037 or 800/451–1113* ⊕ *www. oceandivers.com*) operates two shops in Key Largo. The PADI five-star Caribbean Drive facility offers day and night dives, a range of courses, and dive-lodging packages. The cost is $80 for a two-tank reef dive with tank and weight rental. Snorkel trips from the other shop cost $5 with snorkel, mask, and fins provided. **Quiescence Diving Services** (⊠ *103680 U.S. 1/Overseas Hwy. [MM 103.5 BS]* ☎ *305/451–2440* ⊕ *www.quiescence.com*) sets itself apart in two ways: it limits groups to six to ensure personal attention and offers day and night dives, as well as twilight dives when sea creatures are most active. Two-dive trips start at $66 without equipment.

SHOPPING

For the most part, shopping is sporadic in Key Largo, with a couple of shopping centers and fewer galleries than you find on the other big islands. If you're looking to buy scuba or snorkel equipment, you'll have plenty of places from which to choose.

You can find lots of shops in the Keys that sell cheesy souvenirs—snow globes, alligator hats, and shell-encrusted anything. **Shellworld** (⊠ *97600 Overseas Hwy. [MM 97.5]* ☎ *305/852–8245*) is the granddaddy of them all. This sprawling building in the median of Overseas Highway has clothing, jewelry, and, delightfully tacky souvenirs, too.

NIGHTLIFE

The semiweekly *Keynoter* (Wednesday and Saturday), weekly *Reporter* (Thursday), and Friday through Sunday editions of the *Miami Herald* are the best sources of information on entertainment and nightlife. Daiquiri bars, tiki huts, and seaside shacks pretty well summarize Key Largo's bar scene.

Mingle with locals over cocktails and sunsets at **Breezers Tiki Bar & Grille** (✉ *103800 Overseas Hwy. [MM 103.8 BS]* ☎ *305/453–0000*), in Marriott's Key Largo Bay Beach Resort. Walls plastered with Bogart memorabilia remind customers that the classic 1948 Bogart-Bacall flick *Key Largo* has a connection with the **Caribbean Club** (✉ *MM 104 BS* ☎ *305/451–4466*). It draws boaters, curious visitors, and local barfly types, happiest while they're shooting the breeze or shooting pool. Post-card-perfect sunsets and live music draw revelers on weekends. **Coconuts** (✉ *528 Caribbean Dr. [MM 100 OS]* ☎ *305/453–9794*) has live music Tuesday to Sunday. The crowd is primarily thirty- and fortysomething, sprinkled with a few more-seasoned townies.

WHERE TO EAT

$ ╳**Alabama Jack's.** Calories be damned—the conch fritters here are
SEAFOOD heaven on a plate. The crab cakes, made from local blue crabs, earn hallelujahs, too. The conch salad is as good as any you'll find in the Bahamas and a third of the price in trendy Keys restaurants. This weath-ered, circa-1950 restaurant floats on two roadside barges in an old fishing community. Regulars include weekend cyclists, Miamians on the lam, and boaters, who come to admire tropical birds in the nearby mangroves, the occasional crocodile in the canal, or the bands that play on weekend afternoons. ■ TIP➔ It's about a half-hour drive from Key Largo, so you may want to plan a visit for your drive in or out. Jack's closes by 7, when the mosquitoes start biting. ✉ *58000 Card Sound Rd., Key Largo* ☎ *305/248–8741* ▤ *MC, V.*

$$$ ╳**The Fish House.** Restaurants not on the water have to produce the
SEAFOOD highest quality food to survive in the Keys. That's how the Fish House
★ has succeeded since the 1980s—so much so that it built The Fish House Encore next door to accommodate fans. The pan-sautéed black grouper will make you moan with pleasure, but it's just one of many headliners in this nautical eatery. On the fin side, the choices include mahimahi, swordfish, tuna, and yellowtail snapper that can be broiled, blackened, baked, or fried. The Matecumbe Catch prepares the day's fresh fish so simply flavorful it should be patented—baked with tomatoes, capers, olive oil, and lemon juice. Prefer shellfish? Choose from shrimp, lobster, and (mid-October to mid-May) stone crab. For a sweet ending, try the homemade key lime pie. ✉ *102341 Overseas Hwy. (MM 102.4 OS)* ☎ *305/451–4665 or 305/451–0650* ⊕ *www.fishhouse.com* ▤ *AE, D, MC, V* ☉ *Closed Sept.*

¢ ╳**Harriette's Restaurant.** If you're looking for comfort food—like melt-
AMERICAN in-your-mouth buttermilk biscuits—try this refreshing throwback. The kitchen makes fresh muffins daily, in flavors like mango, chocolate, and key lime. Little has changed over the years in this yellow-and-turquoise eatery. Owner Harriette Mattson often personally greets guests who come for steak and eggs with hash browns or old-fashioned hotcakes

6

with sausage or bacon. Stick to simple dishes; the eggs Benedict are a disappointment. At lunch and dinner time, Harriette's shines in the burger department, but there are also hot meals such as chicken-fried steak and steak-and-shrimp combo. ⊠ *95710 Overseas Hwy. (MM 95.7 BS)* ☎ *305/852–8689* ▭ *MC, V* ☺ *No dinner Fri.–Sun.*

$
SEAFOOD

✕ **Mrs. Mac's Kitchen.** Townies pack the counters and booths at this tiny eatery, where license plates are stuck on the walls and made into chandeliers. Got a hankering for meatloaf or crab cakes? You'll find them here, along with specials like grilled yellowfin tuna. Bring your appetite for the all-you-can-eat fish specials on Tuesday and Thursday. There's also champagne breakfast, an assortment of tasty burgers and sandwiches, and its famous chili and key lime freeze. Ask about the hogfish special du jour. ⊠ *99336 Overseas Hwy. (MM 99.4 BS)* ☎ *305/451–3722* ⊕ *www.mrsmacskitchen.com* ▭ *AE, D, MC, V* ☺ *Closed Sun.*

$$
SEAFOOD
☾

✕ **Rib Daddy's Chop House.** You'll swoon after tasting the Memphis-style mesquite-smoked prime rib, beef ribs, and pork baby back ribs flavored with specially formulated rubs and sauces. The menu extends beyond barbecue standards to include steak and seafood such as crab cakes and all-you-can-eat lobster and stone crab specials. Try the biscuits and gravy for breakfast or barbecue sandwiches for lunch. Save room for the key lime pie, creamy mango pie, or coconut cake. Kids love staring at the reef aquarium, the highlight of this rather plain, open dining room. ⊠ *102570 Overseas Hwy. (MM 102.2 BS)* ☎ *305/451–0900* ⊕ *www. ribdaddysrestaurant.com* ☖ *Reservations not accepted* ▭ *MC, V.*

$$$
SEAFOOD
★

✕ **Snapper's.** "You hook 'em, we cook 'em" is the motto here. Alas, "cleanin' 'em" is not part of the bargain. If you bring in your ready-for-the-grill fish, dinner here is $13.95 per person. Otherwise, they'll catch and cook you a plank-roasted yellowtail snapper, a grilled tuna steak, fish of the day baked with 36 herbs and spices, or a little something from the raw bar. The ceviche of yellowtail, shrimp, and conch (merrily spiced) wins raves, too. Lunch's seafood burrito is a keeper. All this is served up in a lively, mangrove-ringed waterfront setting with live music, an aquarium bar, Sunday brunch, killer rum drinks, and seating alongside the fishing dock. Three-course early-bird specials are available 5–6 PM for $18.50. ⊠ *139 Seaside Ave. (MM 94.5 OS)* ☎ *305/852–5956* ⊕ *www.snapperskeylargo.com* ▭ *AE, D, MC, V.*

$$$
AMERICAN

✕ **Sundowners.** The name doesn't lie. If it's a clear night and you can snag a reservation, this restaurant will treat you to a sherbet-hued sunset over Florida Bay. If you're here in mild weather—anytime other than the dog days of summer or the rare winter cold snap—the best seats are on the patio. The food is excellent: try the key lime seafood, a happy combo of sautéed shrimp, lobster, and lump crabmeat swimming in a tangy sauce spiked with Tabasco served over penne or rice. Wednesday and Saturday are all about prime rib, and Friday draws the crowds with an all-you-can-eat fish fry ($16). Sunday brunch features beignets and Bloody Marys. ⊠ *103900 Overseas Hwy. (MM 104 BS)* ☎ *305/451–4502* ⊕ *sundownerskeylargo.com* ▭ *AE, D, MC, V.*

WHERE TO STAY

$$$$ ⊞ **Azul del Mar**. The dock points the way to many beautiful sunsets at
★ this adults-only boutique hotel. Advertising executive Karol Marsden
and her husband, Dominic, a commercial travel photographer, transformed a run-down mom-and-pop place into this waterfront gem. As
you'd expect from innkeepers with a background in the image business, the property offers great visuals, from marble floors and granite
countertops to yellow-leather sofas and ice-blue bathroom tiles. Kayaks,
barbecue grills, and a movie library are available for guest use, and
two chickee huts on the beach are equipped with DVD players and
comfortable seating. **Pros:** great garden; good location; sophisticated
design. **Cons:** small beach; close to highway; high-priced. ✉ *104300
Overseas Hwy. (MM 104.3 BS),* ☎ *305/451–0337 or 888/253–2985*
⊕ *www.azulhotels.us* ⤵ *2 studios, 3 1-bedroom suites, 1 2-bedroom
suite* ♿ *In-room: no phone, kitchen, DVD, Wi-Fi. In-hotel: beachfront,
water sports, no kids under 16, Wi-Fi hotspot* ⊟ *AE, D, MC, V.*

$–$$ ⊞ **Coconut Bay Resort & Bay Harbor Lodge**. Some 200 feet of waterfront
is the main attraction at this property, a combination of two lodging options. Coconut palms whisper in the breeze, and gumbo-limbo
trees shade the 2½-acre grounds. Nice features abound, like well-placed
lounge chairs for gazing out over the water, and kayaks and paddleboats (for when you want to get closer). Everybody shows up on the
sundeck or the 16-foot dock to watch the sun slip into Davy Jones's
Locker. Rooms are a bit tight but not without island character. Pale-
yellow cottages are simply furnished. Ask for Unit 25 and 26, a two-
bedroom villa that will give you extra space and a water view. **Pros:**
bay front; neatly kept gardens; walking distance to restaurants; complimentary kayak and paddleboat use. **Cons:** a bit dated; small sea-walled
sand beach. ✉ *97702 Overseas Hwy.2 Overseas Hwy. (MM 97.7 BS)*
☎ *305/852–1625 or 800/385–0986* ⊕ *www.coconutbaykeylargo.com*
⤵ *8 rooms, 5 efficiencies, 1 suite, 1 2-bedroom villa, 6 1-bedroom cottages* ♿ *In-room: kitchen (some), refrigerator, Wi-Fi (some). In-hotel:
pool, beachfront, Wi-Fi hotspot, some pets allowed* ⊟ *AE, D, MC, V.*

$$$–$$$$ ⊞ **Dove Creek Lodge**. Old-school anglers will likely be scandalized by
this 2004 fishing camp's sherbet-hued paint and plantation-style fur-
nishings. But when they get a load of the massive flat-screen TV, the
comfy leather couch, and the stack of fishing magazines in the lobby,
they might never want to leave. You can head out on a boat from the
marina, chase billfish offshore or bonefish on the flats, and come to brag
to your buddies about the one that got away. The surprisingly plush
rooms range in size from simple lodge rooms to luxury suites, all with
private screened porch or balcony. Avoid rooms 201 and 202, and you'll
avoid the "lively" noise from the seafood restaurant next door. **Pros:**
great for fishing enthusiasts; luxurious rooms; close to Snapper's restau-
rant with charging privileges. **Cons:** Formica countertops in suites; loud
music next door. ✉ *147 Seaside Ave. (MM94.5 OS)* ☎ *305/852–6200
or 800/401–0057* ⊕ *www.dovecreeklodge.com* ⤵ *14 rooms* ♿ *In-room:
safe, kitchen (some), refrigerator, Internet, Wi-Fi. In-hotel: pool, Wi-Fi
hotspot* ⊟ *AE, D, MC, V* ⏅ *CP.*

6

$$$$
Fodor's Choice
★

⊞ Kona Kai Resort & Gallery. Brilliantly colored bougainvilleas, coconut palms, guava trees, and a new botanical garden make this 2-acre hideaway one of the prettiest places to stay in the Keys. Each of the intimate cottages has furnishings that add to the tropical feel. Spacious studios and one- and two-bedroom suites—with full kitchens and original art—are filled with natural light. Outside, kick back in a lounge chair or hammock, soak in the hot tub, or contemplate sunset from the deck. The resort also has an art gallery and an orchid house with more than 225 plants. Maid service is every third day to prolong your privacy; however, fresh linens and towels are available at any time. At the pool, help yourself to complimentary bottled water and fruit. **Pros:** lush landscaping; free use of sports equipment; knowledgeable staff. **Cons:** expensive rates; some rooms are very close together. ⊠ 97802 Overseas Hwy. (MM 97.8 BS) ☎ 305/852–7200 or 800/365–7829 ⊕ www. konakairesort.com ➷ 8 suites, 3 rooms ⚒ In-room: no phone, kitchen (some), refrigerator, DVD. In-hotel: tennis court, pool, beachfront, Wi-Fi hotspot, no kids under 16 ⊟ AE, D, MC, V ⊙ Closed Sept.

$$$
★

⊞ Largo Lodge. When you drive under the dense canopy of foliage at the entrance of Largo Lodge you'll feel like you've gone back in time. Vintage 1950s cottages are tucked amid 3 acres of palm trees, sea grapes, and orchids. Baby-boomer couples seem right at home here in rooms that might call to mind places they stayed as kids (though their own kids are not allowed here now!). Cottage accommodations—surprisingly spacious—feature small kitchen and dining areas and large screened porches. A lavish swath of bay frontage is perfect for communing with the friendly squirrels, iguanas, and ibises. For swimming, you'll need to drive about 1 mi to John Pennekamp Coral Reef State Park, but kayak use is complimentary here. **Pros:** lush grounds; great sunset views; affordable rates; boat docking. **Cons:** no pool; some traffic noise outdoors. ⊠ 101740 Overseas Hwy. (MM 101.7 BS) ☎ 305/451–0424 or 800/468–4378 ⊕ www.largolodge.com ➷ 2 rooms, 6 cottages ⚒ In-room: no phone, kitchen (some), refrigerator, Wi-Fi. In-hotel: beachfront, Wi-Fi hotspot, no kids under 16 ⊟ MC, V.

$$$$
☺
★

⊞ Marriott's Key Largo Bay Beach Resort. Park the car and toss the keys in the bottom of your bag; there's no need to go anywhere else (except maybe John Pennekamp Coral Reef State Park, just a half mile north). This 17-acre bay-side resort has plenty of diversions, from diving to parasailing to a day spa. Given all that, the pool still rules, so a stroll to the tiki bar could well be your most vigorous activity of the day. The resort's lemon-yellow facade exudes an air of warm, indolent days. This isn't the poshest chain hotel you've ever encountered, but it's fresh looking and suitably tropical in style. Some of the best rooms and suites offer sunset views. **Pros:** lots of activities; free covered parking; lovely pool. **Cons:** rooms facing highway can be noisy. ⊠ 103800 Overseas Hwy. (MM 103.8 BS) ☎ 305/453–0000 or 866/849–3753 ⊕ www. marriottkeylargo.com ➷ 132 rooms, 20 2-bedroom suites, 1 penthouse suite ⚒ In-room: safe, kitchen (some), Wi-Fi. In-hotel: 3 restaurants, room service, bars, pool, gym, spa, beachfront, diving, water sports, bicycles, children's programs (ages 5–13), laundry facilities, laundry service, Wi-Fi hotspot, some pets allowed ⊟ AE, D, DC, MC, V.

¢–$ ⬚ **The Pelican.** This 1950s throwback is reminiscent of the days when parents packed the kids into the station wagon and headed to no-frills seaside motels, complete with an old-timer fishing off the dock. The owners have spiffed things up with cute, artsy touches and added a small sunning beach, but basically it's just a motel, not fancy but comfortable. Guests here don't mind skimping on space and a few frills in favor of homey digs, socializing under the chickee, and a low price tag. **Pros:** free use of kayaks and paddleboats; well-maintained dock; reasonable rates. **Cons:** some small rooms; basic accommodations and amenities. ✉ *99340 Overseas Hwy. (MM 99.3)* ☎ *305/451–3576 or 877/451–3576* ⊕ *www.thepelicankeylargo.com* ⤏ *13 rooms, 4 efficiencies, 4 suites* ⬦ *In-room: no phone, kitchen (some), refrigerator, DVD (some), Wi-Fi. In-hotel: beachfront, water sports, Wi-Fi hotspot* 🖴 *AE, D, DC, MC, V.*

> **WORD OF MOUTH**
>
> "Went on the snorkeling trip out of John Pennekamp State Park. The total was $44 for snorkel trip, full rental including wet suit. Really enjoyed the trip, but wished I had driven down for the 9 AM trip—there were fewer snorkelers and the Web site offered a discount coupon for the morning tour." —starrsville

$–$$ ⬚ **Seafarer Resort.** It's budget lodging, but the Seafarer Resort is not without its charms. There's a pond and hammocks, and most rooms have water views, and some have private patios. Rooms 3 and 4 are spacious and best for families. Unit 6, a one-bedroom cottage called the "beach house," has a large picture window with an awesome view of the bay. Guests gather at the beachfront picnic table for alfresco dining and on the dock and lounge chairs for sunset-watching. **Pros:** sandy beach; complimentary kayak use. **Cons:** some rooms close to road noise; basic accommodations. ✉ *97684 Overseas Hwy. (MM 97.6 BS)* ☎ *305/852–5349* ⊕ *www.seafarerresort.com* ⤏ *8 rooms, 3 studios, 3 1-bedroom cottages, 1 2-bedroom cottage, 2 apartments* ⬦ *In-room: no phone, kitchen (some), refrigerator, Wi-Fi. In-hotel: beachfront, water sports, laundry facilities, Wi-Fi hotspot* 🖴 *MC, V.*

CAMPING

☺ ⛺ **John Pennekamp Coral Reef State Park.** Divers and snorkelers won't find
★ a better location in the Upper Keys. Pennekamp's campsites are carved out of hardwood hammock, providing shade and privacy away from the heavy day-use areas. Activities include boating, fishing, scuba diving, snorkeling, and hiking. There's no restaurant, but there are vending machines for late-night snack attacks. ⬦ *Flush toilets, partial hookups (electric and water), dump station, drinking water, showers, fire pits, picnic tables, electricity, public telephone, general store, ranger station, swimming (ocean)* ⤏ *47 partial hookups for RVs and tents* ✉ *102601 Overseas Hwy. (MM 102.5 OS)* ☎ *305/451–1202 park, 800/326–3521 reservations* ⊕ *www.reserveamerica.com* 🖴 *AE, D, MC, V.*

⛺ **Kings Kamp.** Florida Bay breezes keep things cool at this campground, and the neighboring waterway gives boaters direct access to John Pennekamp Coral Reef State Park. The campground has a marina for storing boats ($10 per day). The park can accommodate RVs up to 40 feet long, and if you don't want to bring your own, you can rent one ($110–$125). This property also has a cottage ($195–$220), motel-style units ($55–$75), and tent sites ($50). ☼ *Partial hookups (electric and water), dump station, drinking water, picnic tables, electricity, public telephone, swimming (ocean), Wi-Fi hotspot* ⤴ *60 hookups for RVs and tents* ✉ *103620 Overseas Hwy. (MM 103.5 BS)* ☎ *305/451–0010* ⊕ *www.kingskamp.com* ▭ *MC, V.*

ISLAMORADA

Islamorada is between mile markers 90.5 and 70.

Early settlers named this key after their schooner, *Island Home*, but to make it sound more romantic they translated it into Spanish: *Isla Morada*. The chamber of commerce prefers to use its literal translation "Purple Island," which refers either to a purple-shelled snail that once inhabited these shores or to the brilliantly colored orchids and bougainvilleas.

Early maps show Islamorada as encompassing only Upper Matecumbe Key. But the incorporated "Village of Islands" is made up of a string of islands that the Overseas Highway crosses, including Plantation Key, Windley Key, Upper Matecumbe Key, Lower Matecumbe Key, Craig Key, and Fiesta Key. In addition, two state-park islands accessible only by boat—Indian Key and Lignumvitae Key—belong to the group.

Islamorada (locals pronounce it "*eye*-la-mor-*ah*-da") is one of the world's top fishing destinations. For nearly 100 years, seasoned anglers have fished these clear, warm waters teeming with trophy-worthy fish. There are numerous options for those in search of the big ones, including chartering a boat with its own crew or heading out on a vessel rented from one of the plethora of marinas along this 20-mi stretch of the Overseas Highway. More than 150 backcountry guides and 400 offshore captains are at your service.

Islamorada is one of the more affluent resort areas of the Keys. Sophisticated resorts and restaurants meet the needs of those in search of luxury, but there's also plenty for those looking for something more casual and affordable. Art galleries and boutiques make Islamorada's shopping scene the best in the Upper Keys, but if you're shopping for groceries, head to Marathon or Key Largo.

ESSENTIALS

Visitor Information **Islamorada Chamber of Commerce** (✉ *MM 83.2 BS, Upper Matecumbe Key, Islamorada* ☎ *305/664–4503 or 800/322–5397* ⊕ *www. islamoradachamber.com*).

EXPLORING

History of Diving Museum. Adding to the region's reputation for world-class diving, this museum plunges into the history of man's thirst for undersea exploration. Among its 13 galleries of interactive and other interesting displays are a submarine and helmet from the film *20,000 Leagues Under the Sea*. Historic equipment, sunken treasures, and photographs are part of the extensive collection donated by a local

Islamorada's warm waters attract large fish and the anglers, including charters, who want to catch them.

couple. ⊠ *82990 Overseas Hwy. (MM 83 BS), Upper Matecumbe Key* ☎ *305/664-9737* ⊕ *www.divingmuseum.org* 🎟 *$12* ⊙ *Daily 10–5.*

The fossilized-coral reef at **Windley Key Fossil Reef Geological State Park,** dating back about 125,000 years, shows that the Florida Keys were once beneath the ocean. Excavation of Windley Key's limestone bed by the Florida East Coast Railway exposed the petrified reef, full of beautifully fossilized brain coral and sea ferns. The park contains the **Alison Fahrer Environmental Education Center,** with historic, biological, and geological displays about the area. There also are guided and self-guided tours along trails that lead to the railway's old quarrying equipment and cutting pits, where you can make rubbings of the interesting quarry walls. The first Saturday in March is Windley Key Day, when the park sells native plants and hosts environmental exhibits. ⊠ *MM 85.5 BS, Windley Key* ☎ *305/664-2540* ⊕ *www.floridastateparks.org/windleykey* 🎟 *Education center free, $2.50 for park, $1 for ranger-guided tours* ⊙ *Education center Thurs.–Mon. 8–5; tours at 10 and 2.*

ⓒ The second-oldest marine-mammal center in the world, **Theater of the Sea** doesn't attempt to compete with more modern, more expensive parks. Even so, it's among the better attractions north of Key West, especially if you have kids in tow. Like the pricier parks, there are dolphin, sea lion, and stingray encounters ($55–$175, including general admission) where you can get up close and personal with underwater creatures. These are popular, so reserve in advance. Ride a "bottomless" boat to see what's below the waves and take a guided tour of the marine-life exhibits. Entertaining educational shows highlight conservation issues. You can stop for lunch at the grill, shop in the boutique, or sunbathe at a lagoon-side beach. This easily could be an all-day attraction. ⊠ *84721 Overseas Hwy. (MM 84.5 OS), Windley Key* ☎ *305/664–2431* ⊕ *www. theaterofthesea.com* 🖃 *$26* ⊙ *Daily 9:30–5 (last ticket sold at 3:30).*

Upper Matecumbe Key was one of the first of the Upper Keys to be permanently settled. Early homesteaders were so successful at growing pineapples in the rocky soil that at one time the island yielded the country's largest annual crop. However, foreign competition and the hurricane of 1935 killed the industry. Today, life centers on fishing and tourism, and the island is filled with bait shops, marinas, and charter-fishing boats. ⊠ *MM 84–79.*

OFF THE BEATEN PATH

Indian Key Historic State Park. Mystery surrounds 10-acre Indian Key, on the ocean side of the Matecumbe islands. Before it became one of the first European settlements outside of Key West, it was inhabited by American Indians for several thousand years. The islet served as a base for 19th-century shipwreck salvagers until an Indian attack wiped out the settlement in 1840. Dr. Henry Perrine, a noted botanist, was killed in the raid. Today his plants grow in the town's ruins. Most people kayak or canoe here from Indian Key Fill to explore the nature trails and the town ruins or snorkel. Florida Keys Kayak has an office at Robbie's Marina. There are no restrooms or picnic facilities on the island. ⌂ *Box 1052* ☎ *305/664–2540* ⊕ *www.floridastateparks.org/indiankey* 🖃 *Free* ⊙ *Daily sunrise–sunset.*

OFF THE BEATEN PATH

Lignumvitae Key Botanical State Park. On the National Register of Historic Places, this 280-acre bay-side island is the site of a virgin hardwood forest and the 1919 home of chemical magnate William Matheson. His caretaker's cottage serves as the park's visitor center. Access is by boat—your own, a rented vessel, or a ferry operated by Robbie's Marina at 10 AM and 2 PM Thursday to Monday. (Paddling here from Indian Key Fill, at MM 78.5, is a popular pastime.) The only way to do the trails is by a guided ranger walk, offered Thursday through Monday for ferry passengers on the 10 and 2 excursions. Wear long sleeves and pants, and bring mosquito repellent. On the first weekend in December is the Lignumvitae Christmas Celebration. ⌂ *Box 1052* ☎ *305/664–2540* park, *305/664–9814* ferry ⊕ *www.floridastateparks.org/lignumvitaekey* 🖃 *Free; ferry and tour $20* ⊙ *Park open Thurs.–Mon. 9–5; house tours Fri.–Sun 10 and 2.*

☺
★

Huge, prehistoric-looking denizens of the not-so-deep, silver-sided tarpon congregate around the docks at **Robbie's Marina** on Lower Matecumbe Key. Children—and lots of adults—pay $4 to feed them sardines or $1 just to watch. Spend some time hanging out at this authentic Keys community, where you can grab a bite to eat, do a little shopping, or charter a boat. ⊠ *77522 Overseas Hwy. (MM 77.5 BS), Lower Matecumbe Key* ☎ *305/664–9814 or 877/664–8498* ⊕ *www.robbies.com* 🖃 *Dock access $1* ⊙ *Daily 8–5.*

On Lower Matecumbe Key, **Anne's Beach Park** is a popular village park whose "beach" (really a typical Keys-style sand flat) is best enjoyed at low tide. The nicest feature here is a ½-mi, elevated, wooden boardwalk that meanders through a natural wetland hammock. Covered picnic areas along the way give you places to linger and enjoy the view.

Restrooms are at the north end. Weekends are packed with Miami day-trippers as it's the only public beach until you reach Marathon. ⊠ *MM 73.5 OS, Lower Matecumbe Key* ☎ *305/853–1685.*

BOATING

Marinas pop up every mile or so in the Islamorada area, so finding a rental or tour is no problem. Robbie's Marina is a prime example of a salty spot where you can find it all—from fishing charters and kayaking rentals to lunch and tarpon feeding.

Bump & Jump (⊠ *81197 Overseas Hwy. [MM 81.2 OS], Upper Mate-cumbe Key* ☎ *305/664–9404 or 877/453–9463* ⊕ *www.keysboatrental. com*) is a one-stop shop for windsurfing, sailboat and powerboat rent-als, sales, and lessons. This company delivers to your hotel or house, or drops it off right at the beach.

See the islands from the comfort of your own boat (captain's cap optional) when you rent from **Houseboat Vacations of the Florida Keys** (⊠ *85944 Overseas Hwy. [MM 85.9 BS], Plantation Key* ☎ *305/664–4009* ⊕ *www.floridakeys.com/houseboats*). The company maintains a fleet of 42- to 55-foot boats that accommodate up to 10 people and come outfitted with everything you need besides food. (You may provision yourself at a nearby grocery store.) The three-day minimum starts at $1,112; one week costs $1,950 and up. Kayaks, canoes, and skiffs suitable for the ocean are also available.

Robbie's Boat Rentals & Charters (⊠ *77522 Overseas Hwy. [MM 77.5 BS], Lower Matecumbe Key* ☎ *305/664–9814 or 877/664–8498* ⊕ *www. robbies.com*) does it all. The company will give you a crash course on how not to crash your boat. The rental fleet includes an 18-foot skiff with a 60-horsepower outboard for $150 for four hours and $200 for the day to a 23-foot deck boat with a 130-horsepower engine for $185 for a half day and $235 for eight hours. Robbie's also rents fishing and snorkeling gear (there's good snorkeling nearby) and sells bait, drinks and snacks, and gas. Want to hire a guide who knows the local waters and where the fish lurk? Robbie's offers offshore-fishing trips, patch-reef trips, and party-boat fishing. Backcountry flats trips are a specialty. Captains Pam and Pete Anderson of **Treasure Harbor Marine** (⊠ *200 Trea-sure Harbor Dr. [MM 86.5 OS], Plantation Key* ☎ *305/852–2458 or 800/352–2628* ⊕ *www.treasureharbor.com*) provide everything you'll need for a vacation at sea. Best of all, they give excellent advice on where to find the best anchorages, snorkeling spots, or lobstering sites. Vessels range from a 23.5-foot Hunter to a 41-foot Morgan Out Island. Rates start at $160 a day; $700 a week. Hire a captain for $175–$200 a day. Marina facilities are basic—water, electric, ice machine, laundry, picnic tables, and restrooms with showers. A store sells snacks, bever-ages, and sundries.

FISHING

Here in the self-proclaimed "Sportfishing Capital of the World," sailfish is the prime catch in the winter and dolphinfish in the summer. Buch-anan Bank just south of Islamorada is a good spot to try for tarpon in the spring. Blackfin tuna and amberjack are generally plentiful in the

Renting wave runners is a fun way to catch some surf and sun in Florida Keys. Each fits one to three people.

area, too. ■TIP→ The Hump at Islamorada ranks highest among anglers' favorite fishing spots in Florida (declared *Florida Monthly* magazine's best for seven years in a row) due to the incredible offshore marine life.

Captain Ted Wilson (✉ *79851 Overseas Hwy. [MM 79.9 OS], Upper Matecumbe Key* ☎ *305/942–5224 or 305/664–9463* ⊕ *www. captaintedwilson.com*) takes you into the backcountry for bonefish, tarpon, redfish, snook, and shark aboard a 17-foot boat that accommodates up to three anglers. For two people, half-day trips run $350, full-day trips $525, and evening excursions $375. There's a $100 charge for an extra person.

Long before fly-fishing became popular, Sandy Moret was fishing the Keys for bonefish, tarpon, and redfish. Now he attracts anglers from around the world with the **Florida Keys Outfitters** (✉ *Green Turtle, 81219 Overseas Hwy. [MM 81.2], Upper Matecumbe Key* ☎ *305/664–5423* ⊕ *www.floridakeysoutfitters.com*). Weekend fly-fishing classes, which include classroom instruction, equipment, and daily lunch, cost $985. Add $1,070 for two additional days of fishing. Guided fishing trips cost $395 for a half day, $535 for a full day. Packages combining fishing and accommodations at Islander Resort are available. The 65-foot party boat ***Miss Islamorada*** (✉ *Bud n' Mary's Marina, 79851 Overseas Hwy. [MM 79.8 OS], Upper Matecumbe Key* ☎ *305/664–2461 or 800/742–7945*) has full-day trips for $60. Bring your lunch or buy one from the dockside deli.

★ Captain Ken Knudsen of the **Hubba Hubba Charters** (✉ *MM 79.8 OS, Upper Matecumbe Key* ☎ *305/664–9281* ⊕ *www.capthubbahubba. com*) quietly poles his flatboat through the shallow water, barely making a ripple. Then he points and his clients cast. Five seconds later there's a zing, and the excitement of bringing in a snook, redfish, trout, or tarpon begins. Knudsen has fished Keys waters for more than 40 years. Now a licensed backcountry guide, he's ranked among Florida's top 10 by national fishing magazines. He offers four-hour sunset trips for tarpon ($400–$425) and two-hour sunset trips for bonefish ($200), as well as half- ($375) and full-day ($550) outings. Prices are for one or two anglers, and tackle and bait are included.

Like other top fly-fishing and light-tackle guides, Captain Geoff Colmes of **Florida Keys Fly Fish** (✉ *105 Palm La., Upper Matecumbe Key* ☎ *305/853–0741* ⊕ *www.floridakeysflyfish.com*) helps his clients land trophy fish in the waters around the Keys ($500–$550).

SCUBA DIVING AND SNORKELING
About 1¼ nautical mi south of Indian Key is the **San Pedro Underwater Archaeological Preserve State Park,** which includes the wreck of a Spanish treasure-fleet ship that sank in 1733. The state of Florida protects the site for divers; no spearfishing or souvenir collecting is allowed. Resting in only 18 feet of water, its ruins are visible to snorkelers as well as divers and attract a colorful array of fish.

Florida Keys Dive Center (✉ *90451 Overseas Hwy. [MM 90.5 OS], Plantation Key* ☎ *305/852–4599 or 800/433–8946* ⊕ *www.floridakeysdivectr.com*) organizes dives from John Pennekamp Coral Reef State Park to Alligator Light. The center has two 46-foot Coast Guard–approved dive boats, offers scuba training, and is one of the few Keys dive centers to offer nitrox and trimix (mixed gas) diving. With a resort, pool, restaurant, lessons, and twice-daily dive and snorkel trips, **Holiday Isle Dive Shop** (✉ *84001 Overseas Hwy. [MM 84 OS], Windley Key* ☎ *305/664–3483 or 800/327–7070* ⊕ *www.diveholidayisle.com*) is a one-stop dive shop. Rates start at $75 for a two-tank dive without equipment.

WATER SPORTS
Florida Keys Kayak (✉ *Robbie's Marina, 77522 Overseas Hwy. [MM 77.5 BS], Lower Matecumbe Key* ☎ *305/664–4878*) rents kayaks for trips to Indian and Lignumvitae keys, two favorite destinations for paddlers. Kayak rental rates are $20 per hour for a single, and $27.50 for a double. Half-day rates (and you'll need plenty of time to explore those mangrove canopies) are $40 for a single kayak and $55 for a double. The company also offers guided two- and three-hour tours ($39 and $49 per person).

SHOPPING
Art galleries, upscale gift shops, and the mammoth World Wide Sportsman (if you want to look the part of a local fisherman, you must wear a shirt from here) make up the variety and superior style of Islamorada shopping.

At the **Banyan Tree** (✉ *81197 Overseas Hwy. [MM 81.2 OS], Upper Matecumbe Key* ☎ *305/664–3433 or 877/453–9463* ⊕ *www.banyantreegarden.com*), a sharp-eyed husband-and-wife team successfully combines antiques and contemporary gifts for the home and garden with plants, pots, and trellises in a stylishly sophisticated indoor–outdoor setting. The go-to destination for one-of-a-kind gifts is **Gallery**

Continued on page 299

DID YOU KNOW?

The coral making up the Barrier Reef is living and provides an ecosystem for small marine creatures. Bumping against or touching the coral can kill these creatures as well as damage the reef itself.

UNDER THE SEA
SNORKELING AND DIVING
IN THE FLORIDA KEYS by Lynne Helm

Up on the shore they work all day ...

While we devotin',

Full time to floatin',

Under the sea ...

—"Under the Sea,"
from Disney's *Little Mermaid*

All Floridians—even those long-accustomed to balmy breezes and swaying palms—turn ecstatic at the mere thought of tripping off to the Florida Keys. Add the prospect of underwater adventure, and hot diggity, it's unparalleled bliss.

Perennially laid back, the Keys annually attract nearly 800,000 snorkeling and scuba diving aficionados, and why not? There's arguably no better destination to learn these sports that put you up close to the wonders of life under the sea.

THE BARRIER REEF
The continental United States' only living coral barrier reef stretches 5 mi offshore of the Keys and is a teeming backbone of marine life, ranging from brilliant corals to neon-colored fish from blue-striped grunts to green moray eels. This is the prime reason why the Keys are where you descend upon intricate natural coral formations and encrusted shipwrecks, some historic, others sunk by design to create artificial reefs that attract divers

and provide protection for marine life. Most diving sites have mooring buoys (nautical floats away from shore, sometimes marking specific sites); these let you tie up your boat so you don't need to drop anchor, which could damage the reef. Most of these sites also are near individual keys, where dozens of dive operators can cater to your needs.

Reef areas thrive in waters as shallow as 5 feet and as deep as 50 feet. Shallow reefs attract snorkelers, while deeper reefs suit divers of varying experience levels. The Keys' shallow diving offers two benefits: longer time safely spent on the bottom exploring, and more vibrant colors because of sunlight penetration. Most divers log maximum depths of 20 to 30 feet.

(left) Shallow-water coral reef, (top) Nine Foot Stake is a popular site for underwater photography.

WHERE TO SNORKEL AND DIVE

KEY WEST
Mile Marker 0–4

You can soak up a mesmerizing overview of submerged watery wonders at the Florida Keys Eco-Discovery Center, opened in 2007 on Key West's Truman

Nine Foot Stake

Annex waterfront. Both admission and parking are free at the 6,000 square–foot center (🕘 *9–4 Tues.-Sat.* ☎ *305/809–4750);* interactive exhibits here focus on Keys marine life and habitats. Key West's offshore reefs are best accessed via professional charters, but it's easy to snorkel from shore at Key West Marine Park. Marked by a lighthouse, Sand Key Reef attracts snorkelers and scuba divers. Joe's Tug, at 65-foot depths, sets up encounters with Goliath grouper. Ten-Fathom Ledge, with coral caves and

dramatic overhangs, shelters lobster. The Cayman Salvor, a buoy tender sunk as an artificial reef in 1985, shelters baitfish. Patch reef Nine Foot Stake, submerged 10 to 25 feet, has soft corals and juvenile marine life. Kedge Ledge features a pair of coral-encrusted anchors from 18th-century sailing vessels. 🚩 *Florida Keys main visitor line at ☎ 800/FLA-KEYS (352-5397).*

BIG PINE KEY/LOWER KEYS
Mile Marker 4–47

Many devotees feel a Florida dive adventure would not be complete without heading 5 mi from Big Pine Key to Looe Key National Marine Sanctuary, an underwater preserve named for the HMS Looe running aground in 1744. If you time your visit for July, you might hit the one-day free underwater music festival for snorkelers

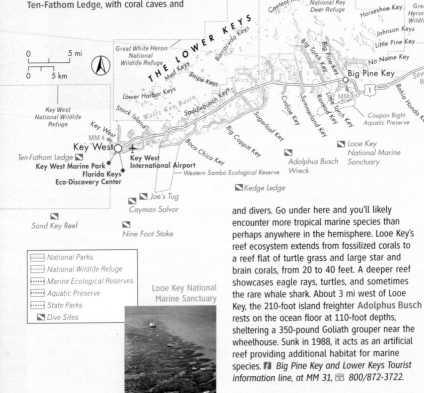

Looe Key National Marine Sanctuary

Legend:
- National Parks
- National Wildlife Refuge
- Marine Ecological Reserves
- Aquatic Preserve
- State Parks
- Dive Sites

and divers. Go under here and you'll likely encounter more tropical marine species than perhaps anywhere in the hemisphere. Looe Key's reef ecosystem extends from fossilized corals to a reef flat of turtle grass and large star and brain corals, from 20 to 40 feet. A deeper reef showcases eagle rays, turtles, and sometimes the rare whale shark. About 3 mi west of Looe Key, the 210-foot island freighter Adolphus Busch rests on the ocean floor at 110-foot depths, sheltering a 350-pound Goliath grouper near the wheelhouse. Sunk in 1988, it acts as an artificial reef providing additional habitat for marine species. 🚩 *Big Pine Key and Lower Keys Tourist information line, at MM 31, ☎ 800/872-3722.*

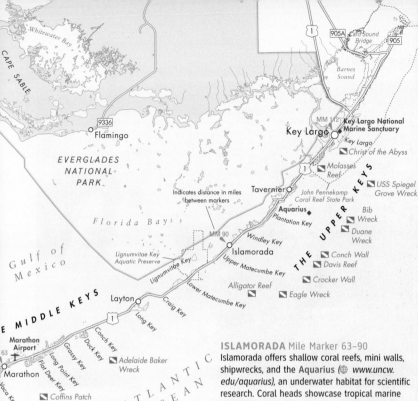

ISLAMORADA Mile Marker 63–90

Islamorada offers shallow coral reefs, mini walls, shipwrecks, and the **Aquarius** (⊕ www.uncw. edu/aquarius), an underwater habitat for scientific research. Coral heads showcase tropical marine life, from grunt to regal queen angelfish. Green moray eels populate spur-and-groove channels, and nurse sharks linger around overhangs. Submerged attractions include the **Eagle**, a 287-foot ship in 110 feet of water; **Davis Reef**, with gorgonian coral; **Alligator Reef**, where the *USS Alligator* sank while fighting pirates; the sloping **Conch Wall**, with barrel sponges and gorgonian; and **Crocker Wall**, featuring spur-and-groove and block corals. 🚹 *Islamorada Chamber and visitor center at MM 83.2,* ☎ *800/322-5397.*

KEY LARGO Mile Marker 90–112

Key Largo marine conservation got a big leg up with creation of **John Pennekamp Coral Reef State Park** in 1960, the nation's first undersea preserve, followed by 1975's designation of the **Key Largo National Marine Sanctuary**. A popular underwater attraction is the bronze statue of **Christ of the Abyss** between coral formations. Explorers with a "lust for rust" can dive down to 60 to 90 feet and farther to see the murky cemetery for two twin 327-foot U.S. Coast Guard cutters, *Duane* and *Bibb*, used during World War II; *USS Spiegel Grove*, a 510-foot Navy transport ship sunk in 2002 to create an artificial reef; and **Molasses Reef**, showcasing coral heads. 🚹 *Key Largo Chamber at MM 106,* ☎ *800/822-1088.*

MARATHON/MIDDLE KEYS
Mile Marker 47–63

The Middle Keys yield a marine wilderness of a spur-and-groove coral and patch reefs. The **Adelaide Baker** historic shipwreck has a pair of stacks in 25 feet of water.

Sombrero Reef

Popular **Sombrero Reef**, with coral canyons and archways, is marked by a 140-foot lighted tower. Six distinct patch reefs known as **Coffin's Patch** have shallow elkhorn forests. **Delta Shoals**, a network of coral canyons fanning seaward from a sandy shoal, attracts divers to its elkhorn, brain, and star coral heads. Marathon's **Thunderbolt**, a 188-foot ship sunk in 1986, sits upright at 115-foot depths, coated with sponge, coral, and hydroid, and attracting angelfish, jacks, and deep-water pelagic creatures. 🚹 *Greater Marathon Chamber and visitors center at MM 53.5,* ☎ *800/262-7284.*

6

IN FOCUS UNDER THE SEA

SCUBA DIVING

A diver explores the coral reef in the Florida Keys National Marine Sanctuary off Key Largo.

Florida offers wonderful opportunities to spend your vacation in the sun and become a certified diver at the same time. In the Keys, count on setting aside three to five days for entry-level or so-called "Open Water" certification offered by many dive shops. Basic certification (covering depths to about 60 feet) involves classroom work and pool training, followed by one or more open-water dives at the reef. After passing a knowledge test and completing the required water training (often starting in a pool), you become a certified recreational scuba diver, eligible to rent dive gear and book dive trips with most operations worldwide. Learning through video or online computer programs can enable you to complete classroom work at home, so you can more efficiently schedule time in the Keys for completing water skills and getting out to the reef for exploration.

Many would-be divers opt to take the classroom instruction and pool training at home at a local dive shop and then spend only two days in the Keys completing four dives. It's not necessarily cheaper, but it can be far more relaxing to commit to only two days of diving.

Questions you should ask: Not all dive shops are created equal, and it may be worthwhile to spend extra money for a better diving experience. Some of the larger dive shops take out large catamarans that can carry as many as 24 to 40 people. Many people prefer the intimacy of a smaller boat.

Good to know: Divers can become certified through PADI *(www.padi.com)*, NAUI *(www.naui.org)*, or SSI *(www. divessi.com)*. The requirements for all three are similar, and if you do the classroom instruction and pool training with a dive shop associated with one organization, the referral for the open water dives will be honored by most dive shops. Note that you are not allowed to fly for at least 24 hours after a dive, because residual nitrogen in the body can pose health risks upon decompression. While there are no rigid rules on diving after flying, make sure you're well-hydrated before hitting the water.

Cost: The four-day cost can range from $300 to $475, but be sure to ask if equipment, instruction manuals, and log books are extra. Some dive shops have relationships with hotels, so check for dive/stay packages. Referral dives (a collaborative effort among training agencies) run from $285 to $300 and discover scuba runs around $175 to $200.

SNUBA

Beyond snorkeling or the requirements of scuba, you also have the option of "Snuba." The word is a trademarked portmanteau or combo of snorkel and scuba. Marketed as easy-to-learn family fun, Snuba lets you breathe underwater via tubes from an air-supplied vessel above, with no prior diving or snorkel experience required.

NOT CERTIFIED?

Not sure if you want to commit the time and money to become certified? Not a problem. Most dive shops and many resorts will offer a discover scuba day-long course. In the morning, the instructor will teach you the basics of scuba diving: how to clear your mask, how to come to the surface in the unlikely event you lose your air supply, etc. In the afternoon, instructors will take you out for a dive in relatively shallow water—less than 30 feet. Be sure to ask where the dive will take place. Jumping into the water off a shallow beach may not be as fun as actually going out to the coral. If you decide that diving is something you want to pursue, the open dive may count toward your certification.

■ **TIP→** You can often book the discover dives at the last minute. It may not be worth it to go out on a windy day when the currents are stronger. Also the underwater world looks a whole lot brighter on sunny days.

6

IN FOCUS UNDER THE SEA

(top) Scuba divers; (bottom) Diver ascending line.

SNORKELING

Snorkling lets you see the wonders of the sea from a new perspective.

The basics: Sure, you can take a deep breath, hold your nose, squint your eyes, and stick your face in the water in an attempt to view submerged habitats . . . but why not protect your eyes, retain your ability to breathe, and keep your hands free to paddle about when exploring underwater? That's what snorkeling is all about.

Equipment needed: A mask, snorkel (the tube attached to the mask), and fins. In deeper waters (any depth over your head), life jackets are advised.

Steps to success: If you've never snorkeled before, it's natural to feel a bit awkward at first, so don't sweat it. Breathing through a mask and tube, and wearing a pair of fins take getting used to. Like any activity, you build confidence and comfort through practice.

If you're new to snorkeling, begin by submerging your face in shallow water or a swimming pool and breathing calmly through the snorkel while gazing through the mask.

Next you need to learn how to clear water out of your mask and snorkel, an essential skill since splashes can send water into tube openings and masks can leak. Some snorkels have built-in drainage valves, but if a tube clogs, you can force water up and out by exhaling through your mouth. Clearing a mask is similar: lift your head from water while pulling forward on mask to drain. Some masks have built-in purge valves, but those without can be cleared underwater by pressing the top to the forehead and blowing out your nose (charming, isn't it?), allowing air to bubble into the mask, pushing water out the bottom. If it sounds hard, it really isn't. Just try it a few times and you'll soon feel like a pro.

Now your goal is to get friendly with fins—you want them to be snug but not too tight—and learn how to propel yourself with them. Fins won't help you float, but they will give you a leg up, so to speak, on smoothly moving through the water or treading water (even when upright) with less effort.

Flutter stroking is the most efficient underwater kick, and the farther your foot bends forward the more leg power you'll be able to transfer to the water and the farther you'll travel with each stroke. Flutter kicking movements involve alternately separating the legs and then drawing them back together. When your legs separate, the leg surface encounters drag from the water, slowing you down. When your legs are drawn back together, they produce a force pushing you forward. If your kick creates more forward force than it causes drag, you'll move ahead.

Submerge your fins to avoid fatigue rather than having them flailing above the water when you kick, and keep your arms at your side to reduce drag. You are in the water—stretched out, face down, and snorkeling happily away—but that doesn't mean you can't hold your breath and go deeper in the water for a closer look at some fish or whatever catches your attention. Just remember that when you do this, your snorkel will be submerged, too, so you won't be breathing (you'll be holding your breath). You can dive head-first, but going feet-first is easier and less scary for most folks, taking less momentum. Before full immersion, take several long, deep breaths to clear carbon dioxide from your lungs.

If your legs tire, flip onto your back and tread water with inverted fin motions while resting. If your mask fogs, wash condensation from lens and clear water from mask.

TIPS FOR SAFE SNORKELING

■ Snorkel with a buddy and stay together.

■ Plan your entry and exit points prior to getting in the water.

■ Swim into the current on entering and then ride the current back to your exit point.

■ Carry your flippers into the water and then put them on, as it's difficult to walk in them.

■ Make sure your mask fits properly and is not too loose.

■ Pop your head above the water periodically to ensure you aren't drifting too far out, or too close to rocks.

■ Think of the water as someone else's home—don't take anything that doesn't belong to you, or leave any trash behind.

■ Don't touch any sea creatures; they may sting.

■ Wear a T-shirt over your swimsuit to help protect you from being fried by the sun.

■ When in doubt, don't go without a snorkeling professional; try a guided tour.

Cayman Salvor

TOP OUTFITTERS

COMPANY	ADDRESS & PHONE	COST	DESCRIPTION
AMY SLATE'S AMO-RAY DIVE CENTER ⊕ www.amoray.com	✉ 104250 Overseas Hwy. (MM 104.2), Key Largo ☎ 305/451–3595	⊙ Daily ✒ Scuba classes for kids ages 8 and up and adults $100-$200.	Sign up for dive/snorkel trips, scuba instruction and kid programs.
DIVE KEY WEST ⊕ www.divekeywest.com	✉ 3128 N. Roosevelt Blvd., Key West ☎ 305/296–3823	✒ Snorkel from $49, dive from $69	Operating nearly 40 years. Has charters, instruction, and gear.
ECO SCUBA KEY WEST ⊕ www.ecoscuba.com	✉ 5930 Peninsular Ave. (MM 5), Key West ☎ 305/851–1899	⊙ Daily ✒ Snorkel from $35, scuba from $99.	Debuted in 2009. Offers eco-tours, lobstering, snorkeling, and scuba.
FLORIDA KEYS DIVE CENTER ⊕ www.floridakeysdivectr.com	✉ 90451 Old Hwy. (MM 90.5), Tavernier ☎ 305/852–4599	⊙ Daily ✒ Classes from $175.	Charters for snorkerlers and divers go to Pennekamp, Key Largo, and Islamorada.
HORIZON DIVERS ⊕ www.horizondivers.com	✉ 100 Ocean Dr. #1, Key Largo ☎ 305/453–3535	⊙ Daily ✒ Snorkel from $50, scuba from $80.	Take customized dive/snorkel trips on a 45-foot catamaran.
ISLAND VENTURES ⊕ www.islandventure.com	✉ 103900 Overseas Hwy. (MM 103.9), Key Largo ☎ 305/451–4957	⊙ Two trips daily ✒ Snorkel $45, scuba from $80.	Go on snorkeling and scuba explorations to the Key Largo reef and shipwrecks.
KEYS DIVER SNORKEL TOURS ⊕ www.keysdiver.com	✉ 99696 Overseas Hwy. (MM 99.6), Key Largo ☎ 305/451–1177	✒ Three daily snorkel tours from $28. Includes gear.	Family-oriented snorkel-only tours head to coral reefs such as Pennekamp.
LOOE KEY REEF RE-SORT & DIVE CENTER ⊕ www.diveflakeys.com	✉ 27340 Overseas Hwy. (MM 27.5), Ramrod Key ☎ 305/872–2215	⊙ Daily ✒ Snorkel from $44, scuba from $85.	Beginner and advanced scuba instruction, a photographer course, and snorkel gear rental.
RON JON SURF SHOP ⊕ www.ronjons.com	✉ 503 Front St., Key West ☎ 305/293–8880	⊙ Daily ✒ Sells snorkel gear.	Several locations in Florida; its HQ is in Cocoa Beach.
SNUBA OF KEY WEST ⊕ www.snubakeywest.com	✉ 600 Palm Ave., Key West ☎ 305/292–4616	⊙ Daily ✒ $99 per person, $44 for ride-alongs.	Swimmers ages 8 and up can try Snuba.
TILDENS SCUBA CENTER ⊕ www.tildensscuba-center.com	✉ 4650 Overseas Hwy. (MM 49.5), Marathon ☎ 305/743–7255	⊙ Daily ✒ Snorkel from $35.99, scuba from $60.99.	Operating for 25 years. Has lessons, tours, snorkeling, scuba, snuba, gear, and a kids club.

Morada (✉ *81611 Old Hwy. [MM 81.6 OS], Upper Matecumbe Key* ☎ *305/664–3650* ⊕ *www.gallerymorada.com*) , where blown-glass objects are beautifully displayed, as are the original sculptures, paintings, lithographs, and jewelry, of top South Florida artists. Among the best buys in town are the used best-sellers at **Hooked on Books** (✉ *82681 Overseas Hwy. [MM 82.6 OS], Upper Matecumbe Key* ☎ *305/517–2602* ⊕ *www.hookedonbooksfloridakeys.com*), which also sells new titles, audiobooks, and CDs. **Island Silver & Spice** (✉ *81981 Overseas Hwy. [MM 82 OS], Upper Matecumbe Key* ☎ *305/664–2714*) has tropical-style furnishings, rugs, and home accessories. The shop also stocks women's and men's resort wear and a large jewelry selection with high-end watches and marine-theme pieces. The **Rain Barrel** (✉ *86700 Overseas Hwy. [MM 86.7 BS], Plantation Key* ☎ *305/852–3084*) is a natural and unhurried shopping showplace. Set in a tropical garden of shady trees, native shrubs, and orchids, the crafts village has shops with works by local and national artists and resident artists in studios, including John Hawver, noted for Florida landscapes and seascapes. The **Redbone Gallery** (✉ *200 Industrial Dr. [MM 81.5 OS), Upper Matecumbe Key* ☎ *305/664–2002* ⊕ *www.redbone.org*), one of the largest sportfishing–art galleries in Florida, stocks hand-stitched clothing and giftware, in addition to work by wood and bronze sculptors such as Kendall van Sant; watercolorists Chet Reneson, Jeanne Dobie, and Kathleen Denis; and painters C.D. Clarke and Tim Borski. Proceeds benefit cystic fibrosis research.

Former U.S. presidents, celebrities, and record holders beam alongside their catches in black-and-white photos on the walls at **World Wide Sportsman** (✉ *81576 Overseas Hwy. [MM 81.5 BS], Upper Matecumbe Key* ☎ *305/664–4615 or 800/327–2880*), a two-level retail center that sells upscale fishing equipment, resort clothing, sportfishing art, and other gifts. When you're tired of shopping, relax at the Zane Grey Long Key Lounge just above World Wide Sportsman.

NIGHTLIFE
Islamorada is not known for its raging nightlife, but for local fun Lorelei's is legendary. Others cater to the town's sophisticated clientele and fishing fervor.

★ Behind a larger-than-life mermaid, the **Lorelei Restaurant & Cabana Bar** (✉ *81924 Overseas Hwy. [MM 82 BS], Upper Matecumbe Key* ☎ *305/664–2692* ⊕ *www.loreleifloridakeys.com*) is the kind of place you fantasize about during those long, cold winters up north. It's all about good drinks, tasty pub grub, and beautiful sunsets set to live bands playing island tunes and light rock.

WHERE TO EAT
$$$ ✕ **Green Turtle Inn.** This circa-1928 landmark inn and its vintage neon
SEAFOOD sign is a slice of Florida Keys history. Period photographs decorate the wood-paneled walls. Breakfast and lunch options include surprises like coconut French toast and yellowfin tuna tartare. Award-winning chef Andy Niedenthal relies heavily on Continental classics tossed with a few Latin touches for his dinner menu; think turtle chowder (don't gasp; it's made from farm-raised freshwater turtles), churrasco steak with

yucca hash, and rum-glazed duck with sweet plantain mash. Naturally, there's a Turtle Sundae on the dessert menu. The chef uses organic produce wherever possible. ⊠ *81219 Overseas Hwy. (MM 81.2 OS), Upper Matecumbe Key* ☎ *305/664–2006* ⊕ *www.greenturtlekeys.com* ⚓ *Reservations essential* ⊟ *AE, MC, V* ⊙ *Closed Mon.*

$$ ✕ **Island Grill.** Don't be fooled by appearances; this shack on the water-
SEAFOOD   front takes island breakfast, lunch, and dinner cuisine up a notch. The
★   eclectic menu tempts you with such dishes as guava-barbecue shrimp wrapped in bacon, and lobster rolls. Southern-style shrimp and andouille sausage with grits join island-style specialties such as grilled mahi-mahi with black bean and corn salsa on the list of entrées. There's an air-conditioned dining room and bar as well as outdoor seating under the trees. The outdoor bar hosts live entertainment Wednesday to Sunday. ⊠ *85501 Overseas Hwy. (MM 85.5 OS), Windley Key* ☎ *305/664–8400* ⊕ *www.keysislandgrill.com* ⊟ *AE, D, MC, V.*

$$ ✕ **Kaiyó.** Kaiyó's decor—an inviting setting that includes colorful
JAPANESE   abstract mosaics, polished wood floors, and upholstered banquettes—
★   almost steals the show here, but the food is equally interesting. The menu, a fusion of East and West, offers sushi and sashimi and rolls that combine local ingredients with traditional Japanese tastes. The key lime lobster roll is a blend of Florida lobster with hearts of palm and essence of key lime ($18). The baby conch roll surrounds tempura conch, ponzu mayo, and kimchi with sushi rice for an inside-out effect. Entrees in the $19-and-up range include a noodle seafood bowl, teriyaki chicken, and a grilled-fillet-and-lobster-tail combo. ⊠ *81701 Overseas Hwy. (MM 81.5 OS), Upper Matecumbe Key* ☎ *305/664–5556* ⊕ *www.kaiyokeys. com* ⊟ *AE, MC, V* ⊙ *Closed Sun.*

$$ ✕ **Marker 88.** A few yards from Florida Bay, this seafood restaurant
SEAFOOD   has been popular for more than 40 years. Large picture windows offer
★   great sunset views, but the bay is lovely no matter what time of day you visit. Chef Sal Barrios serves such irresistible entrées as grilled yellowfin tuna and yellowtail snapper in a tomato-basil sauce. Landlubbers find dishes like Parmesan-crusted filet mignon. If you're not that hungry, there's also a long list of sandwiches. The extensive wine list is an oenophile's delight. ⊠ *88000 Overseas Hwy. (MM 88 BS), Plantation Key* ☎ *305/852–9315* ⊕ *www.marker88.info* ⚓ *Reservations essential* ⊟ *AE, D, MC, V.*

$$$ ✕ **Morada Bay Beach Café.** This bay-front restaurant wins high marks for
ECLECTIC   its surprisingly stellar cuisine, tables planted in the sand, and tiki torches
☾   that bathe the evening in romance. Entrées feature alluring combina-
★   tions like broiled lobster with tropical fruit salsa and caramelized jumbo sea scallops with wild mushroom risotto. Seafood takes center stage, but you can always get roasted organic chicken (flavored with lemon) or a steak. Nightly specials like triple tail fish and lobster with green curry sauce strut the kitchen's stuff. Sit in a dining room outfitted with surfboards or outdoors on a beach, where the sunset puts on a mighty show and kids (and your feet) play in the sand. There's nightly live music and a monthly full-moon party. ⊠ *81600 Overseas Hwy. (MM 81 BS), Upper Matecumbe Key* ☎ *305/664–0604* ⊕ *www.moradabay-restaurant.com* ⊟ *AE, MC, V.*

$$$$ ✕**Pierre's.** One of the Keys' most elegant restaurants, Pierre's marries

FRENCH   colonial style with modern food trends. Full of interesting architec-

Fodor's Choice   tural artifacts, the place oozes style, especially the wicker chair–strewn

★   veranda overlooking the bay. Save your best "tropical chic" duds for dinner here, so you don't stand out from your surroundings. The food, drawn from French and Floridian influences, is multilayered and beautifully presented. Among the appetizer choices, few can resist the lamb ravioli or shrimp bisque. A changing list of entrées might include hogfish meunière and pan-seared duck breast with caramelized sweet potatoes. The downstairs bar is a perfect spot for catching sunsets, sipping martinis, and enjoying light eats. ⊠ *81600 Overseas Hwy. (MM 81.5 BS), Upper Matecumbe Key* ☎ *305/664–3225* ⊕ *www.pierres-restaurant. com* ⚂ *Reservations essential* ▭ *AE, MC, V.*

$$$ ✕**Uncle's Restaurant.** Former fishing guide Joe LePree adds flair to

ITALIAN   standard seafood dishes by expanding the usual grilled, broiled, or blackened options. Here you can also have your seafood almandine, Milanese (breaded and fried), or LePree (with artichokes, mushrooms, and lemon-butter wine sauce). You also can feast on mussels or little-neck clams in a marinara or garlic sauce. Specials sometimes combine game (bison, caribou, or elk) with seafood. Portions are huge, so share dishes or take home a doggie bag, or order off the $13.95 light menu. Weather permitting, sit outdoors in the garden; poor acoustics make dining indoors unusually noisy. ⊠ *80900 Overseas Hwy. (MM 81 OS), Upper Matecumbe Key* ☎ *305/664–4402* ▭ *AE, D, DC, MC, V* ⊘ *Closed Mon.*

6

WHERE TO STAY

$$$$ ⌂ **Casa Morada.** This relic from the 1950s was rescued and restyled

Fodor's Choice   into a suave, design-forward, all-suites property in 2000. Subsequent

★   renovations have added outdoor showers and Jacuzzis to some of the suites, each of which claims its own design personality, many with an Asian feel. Lush landscaping, a pool surrounded by a sandy "beach" on its own island accessible by a bridge, and lounge chairs at the water's edge lend a spalike vibe; complimentary yoga classes, a Zen garden, and a rock waterfall complete the scene. Cool tile-and-terrazzo floors invite you to kick off your shoes and step out onto your private patio overlooking the gardens and the bay. Breakfast and lunch are served on the waterside terrace. **Pros:** cool design; complimentary snacks and bottled water; complimentary use of bikes, kayaks, and snorkel gear. **Cons:** trailer park across the street; beach is small and inconsequential. ⊠ *136 Madeira Rd. (MM 82 BS), Upper Matecumbe Key* ☎ *305/664–0044 or 888/881–3030* ⊕ *www.casamorada.com* ⇆ *16 suites* ⚃ *In-room: safe, DVD, Wi-Fi. In-hotel: restaurant, room service, bar, pool, water sports, bicycles, laundry service, no kids under 16* ▭ *AE, MC, V* ⎮⊙⎮ *CP.*

$$$$ ⌂ **Cheeca Lodge & Spa.** Newly renovated after a fire closed it down for

★   a year, Cheeca came back better than ever in December 2009. The fire demolished its historic main lodge, but in its place are West Indian–style rooms boasting luxurious touches like elegant balcony tubs that fill from the ceiling. If soaking in the tub is not your thing, soak in the great views from the updated showers. The renovation includes a newly formatted main dining room plus a sushi bar and an upgraded swimming pool with underwater speakers and new tiki bar. The resort's other buildings have remained much as they were, but the spa got a face-lift with the addition of mud baths, an adults-only lap pool, and a fitness center. For families, there's the 1,200-foot private beach, a nature trail, and Camp Cheeca—a fun and educational program that makes use of a playground. Golf (nine holes), tennis, and all manner of water sports cater to sports enthusiasts. **Pros:** beautifully landscaped grounds; new designer rooms; plenty of activities. **Cons:** expensive rates; $39 resort fee for activities; busy. ⊠ *MM 82 OS, Box 527, Upper Matecumbe Key* ☎ *305/664–4651 or 800/327–2888* ⊕ *www.cheeca.com* ⤴ *214 rooms, 44 1-bedroom suites, 4 2-bedroom suites* ⚿ *In-room: safe, kitchen (some) refrigerator, DVD, Wi-Fi. In-hotel: 2 restaurants, room service, bar, golf course, tennis courts, pools, gym, spa, beachfront, diving, water sports, bicycles, children's programs (ages 5–12), laundry service, Wi-Fi hotspot* ⊟ *AE, D, DC, MC, V.*

$$–$$$ ★ 🏠 **Drop Anchor Resort and Marina.** It's easy to find your cottage here, as they are painted in an array of Crayola colors. Immaculately maintained, this place has the feel of an old friend's beach house. Inside you'll find soothing West Indies–type furnishings and kitschy-cool, 1950s-era tile in the bathrooms. Welcoming as the rooms may be, you didn't come to the Keys to sit indoors: there's a luscious expanse of white sand awaiting, and you can catch ocean breezes from either your balcony, a comfy Adirondack chair, or a picnic table perched in the sand. There's a boat ramp to accommodate anglers. **Pros:** bright and colorful; attention to detail; laid-back charm. **Cons:** noise from the highway; beach is better for fishing than swimming. ⊠ *84959 Overseas Hwy. (MM 85 OS), Windley Key* ☎ *305/664–4863 or 888/664–4863* ⊕ *www.dropanchorresort.com* ⤴ *18 rooms and suites* ⚿ *In-room: kitchen (some), refrigerator. In-hotel: pool, beachfront, laundry facilities* ⊟ *AE, D, DC, MC, V.*

$$$$ 🏠 **The Islander Resort.** Although the vintage sign is straight out of a *Happy Days* rerun, this property has undergone a top-to-bottom transformation while the general layout retained a 1950s feel. The decor is modern yet comfortable, with white cottage-style furnishings, elegant fabrics, and sunny yellow bedrooms. Private screened porches lead to a coral-shell oceanfront beach with palm trees bending in the sea breeze. Families snap up suites in the oceanfront Beach House; couples looking for more privacy head to rooms set back from the beach. The pools—one saltwater, one freshwater—win raves, as do the full kitchens. A 200-foot dock, lighted at night, plus shuffleboard, basketball, and volleyball add to the resort feel. **Pros:** spacious rooms; nice kitchens; eye-popping views. **Cons:** pricey for what you get; beach has rough sand; no a/c in the screened gym. ⊠ *82200 Overseas Hwy. (MM 82.1 OS), Upper Matecumbe Key* ☎ *305/664–2031 or 800/753–6002* ⊕ *www.islanderfloridakeys.com* ⤴ *114 rooms* ⚿ *In-room: safe, kitchen, Wi-Fi. In-hotel: restaurant, bar, pools, gym, beachfront, water sports, bicycles, laundry facilities, Wi-Fi hotspot, some pets allowed* ⊟ *AE, D, DC, MC, V* ⦿ *CP.*

$$$$ Fodor's Choice ★ 🏠 **The Moorings Village.** This tropical retreat is everything you imagine when you think of the Keys—from hammocks swaying between towering trees to sugar-white sand (arguably the Keys' best resort beach) lapped by aqua-green waves. West Indies–style cottages with cypress and Dade County pine accents, colorful shutters, private verandas, and wicker furniture sit in a canopy of coconut palms and old forest landscaping on a residential street off the highway. This is a high-end slice of Old Florida, so don't expect tacky tiki bars. The one-, two-, and three-bedroom cottages all have modern kitchens with modern appliances. A palm-lined walkway leads to the beach, where a swimming dock awaits. The spa offers massages (in the beach chickee, if you desire) and beauty treatments. During busy season, there may be a two-night minimum-stay requirement for one-bedroom cottages, and a one-week minimum on other lodgings. Neighboring Cheeca Lodge, the Moorings has the same high standards but is less cramped, more private and exclusive, and possibly the most beautiful property in the Keys. **Pros:** romantic setting; good dining options with room-charging privileges; beautiful beach. **Cons:** no room service; extra fee for housekeeping; daily resort fee for activities. ⊠ *123 Beach Rd. (MM 81.6 OS), Upper Matecumbe Key* ☎ *305/664–4708* ⊕ *www.themooringsvillage.com* ➷ *4 cottages, 14 houses* ⚑ *In-room: kitchen, Wi-Fi. In-hotel: tennis court, pool, gym, spa, beachfront, water sports, laundry facilities, Wi-Fi hotspot* ⊟ *AE, D, MC, V.*

6

$ **Ragged Edge Resort.** Tucked away in a residential area at the ocean's edge, this hotel is big on value but short on style. Ragged Edge draws returning guests who would rather fish off the dock and hoist a brew than loll around in Egyptian cotton sheets. Even those who turn their noses up at the cheap plastic deck furniture and pine paneling admit that the place has a million-dollar setting, with fabulous ocean views all around. There's no beach to speak of, but you can ride a bike across the street to Islamorada Founder's Park, where you'll find a nice little beach and water toys for rent. If a bit of partying puts you off, look elsewhere. Although the rooms are plain-Jane, they are clean and fairly spacious. Ground-floor units have screened porches; upper units have large decks, more windows, and beam ceilings. **Pros:** oceanfront location; boat docks and ramp; cheap rates. **Cons:** dated decor; guests can be noisy. ⊠ *243 Treasure Harbor Rd. (MM 86.5 OS), Plantation Key* ☎ *305/852–5389 or 800/436–2023* ⊕ *www.ragged-edge.com* ➷ *10 units* ⚑ *In-room: kitchen (some), refrigerator, Wi-Fi. In-hotel: pool, bicycles, Wi-Fi hotspot* ⊟ *AE, MC, V.*

LONG KEY

Long Key isn't a tourist hot spot, making it a favorite destination for those looking to avoid the masses and enjoy some cultural and ecological history in the process.

GETTING HERE AND AROUND

Long Key runs from mile markers 70 to 65.5, with the tiny town of Layton at its heart. Many people get around by bike.

EXPLORING

Long Key State Park. Come here for solitude, hiking, fishing, and camping. On the ocean side, the Golden Orb Trail leads to a boardwalk that cuts through the mangroves (may require some wading) and alongside a lagoon where waterfowl congregate (as do mosquitoes, so be prepared). A 1¼-mi canoe trail leads through a tidal lagoon, and a broad expanse of shallow grass flats is perfect for bonefishing. Bring a mask and snorkel to observe the marine life in the shallow water. The park is particularly popular with campers who long to stake their tent at the campground on a beach. In summer, no-see-ums (local reference for biting sand flies) also love the beach, so again—be prepared. The picnic area is on the water, too, but lacking beach. Canoes rent for $5 per hour, and single kayak rentals start at $17 for two hours, $21.50 for a double. ⊠ *67400 Overseas Hwy. (MM 67.5 OS)* ☎ *305/664–4815* ⊕ *www.floridastateparks. org/longkey* ▣ *$4.50 for 1 person, $5.50 for 2 people, and 50¢ for each additional person in the group* ⊙ *Daily 8–sunset.*

SPORTS AND THE OUTDOORS

BEACH

Long Key State Park. Camping, snorkeling, and bonefishing are the favored activities along this narrow strip of natural, rocky beach. It lines the park's campground, which is open only to registered campers. ⊠ *67400 Overseas Hwy. (MM 67.5 OS)* ☎ *305/664–4815* ⊕ *www. floridastateparks.org/longkey* ▣ *$4.50 for 1 person, $5.50 for 2 people, and 50¢ for each additional person in the group* ⊙ *Daily 8–sunset.*

WHERE TO EAT AND STAY

$ ✕ **Little Italy.** It's your basic Italian joint that looks like it's been around
ITALIAN forever. In 2009, the chef who once made the place locally famous returned with a standard-issue Italian menu but with a few surprises like conch parmigiana and mahimahi with sherry and mushroom sauce. The lunch and dinner menus offer plenty of variety—dishes include lobster po'boy, steaks, and a fisherman's platter—but few can resist the pull of the pasta. (Maybe it's the garlicky aroma that permeates the place.) ⊠ *68500 Overseas Hwy. (MM 68.5 BS)* ☎ *305/664–4472* ▭ *AE, MC, V* ⊙ *Closed Wed.*

$$ 🏠 **Lime Tree Bay Resort.** Easy on the eye and the wallet, this 2½-acre resort on Florida Bay is far from the hustle and bustle of the larger islands. Walls are painted in faux finishes and display tropical art. The five apartments offer stunning gulf views, while four deluxe rooms have cathedral ceilings and skylights. The best bet for two couples traveling together is the upstairs Tree House. Most units have a shared balcony or porch. Hammocks and chickee huts dot the gravelly beach. Water sports and bicycle rentals are close by. **Pros:** great views; friendly staff; close to Long Key State Park. **Cons:** only one restaurant nearby, shared balconies. ⊠ *68500 Overseas Hwy. (MM 68.5 BS), Layton* ☎ *305/664–4740 or 800/723–4519* ⊕ *www.limetreebayresort.com* ↳ *10 rooms, 10 studios, 8 suites, 5 apartments* ♿ *In-room: kitchen (some), refrigerator. In-hotel: tennis court, pool, beachfront, Wi-Fi hotspot* ▭ *AE, D, DC, MC, V.*

EN
ROUTE

As you cross Long Key Channel, look beside you at the old **Long Key Viaduct.** The second-longest bridge on the former rail line, this 2-mi-long structure has 222 reinforced-concrete arches. The old bridge is popular with anglers who fish off the sides day and night.

THE MIDDLE KEYS

Most of the activity in this part of the Florida Keys centers around the town of Marathon—the region's third-largest metropolitan area. On either end of it, smaller keys hold resorts, wildlife research and rehab facilities, a historic village, and a state park. The Middle Keys make a fitting transition from the Upper Keys to the Lower Keys not only geographically but mentally. Crossing Seven Mile Bridge prepares you for the slow pace and don't-give-a-damn attitude you'll find a little farther down the highway. Fishing is one of the main attractions—in fact, the region's commercial-fishing industry was founded here in the early 1800s. Diving is another popular pastime. There are many beaches and natural areas to enjoy in the Middle Keys, where mainland stress becomes an ever more distant memory.

If you get bridge fever—the heebie-jeebies when driving over long stretches of water—you may need a pair of blinders (or a couple of tranquilizers) before tackling the Middle Keys. Stretching from Conch Key to the far side of the Seven Mile Bridge, this zone is home to the region's two longest bridges: Long Key Viaduct and Seven Mile Bridge, both historic landmarks.

Overseas Highway takes you from one end of the region to the other in a direct line that takes in most of the sights, but you'll find some interesting resorts and restaurants off the main drag.

6

GRASSY KEY

Grassy Key is between mile markers 60 and 57.

Local lore has it that this sleepy little key was named not for its vegetation—mostly native trees and shrubs—but for an early settler by the name of Grassy. There's no marked definition between it and Marathon, so it feels sort of like a suburb of its much larger neighbor to the south. Grassy Key's sights-to-see tend toward the natural, including a worthwhile dolphin attraction and a small state park.

EXPLORING

🕲
★ **Dolphin Research Center.** The 1963 movie *Flipper* popularized the notion of humans interacting with dolphins, and Milton Santini, the film's creator, also opened this center, which is home to a colony of dolphins and sea lions. The nonprofit center has tours, narrated programs, and programs that allow you to greet the dolphins from dry land or play with them in their watery habitat. You can even paint a T-shirt with a dolphin—you pick the paint, the dolphin "designs" your shirt ($55). The center also offers five-day programs for children and adults with disabilities. ⊠ *58901 Overseas Hwy. (MM 59 BS)* ☎ *305/289–1121 or 305/289–0002* ⊕ *www.dolphins.org* 🖃 *$19.50* ⊙ *Daily 9–4:30.*

OFF THE
BEATEN
PATH

Looking for a slice of the Keys that's far removed from tiki bars? On the ocean and bay sides of Overseas Highway, **Curry Hammock State Park** (⊠ *56200 Overseas Hwy. [MM 57 OS], Crawl Key* ☎ *305/289–2690* ⊕ *www.floridastateparks.org/curryhammock* 🖃 *$4.50 for 1 person, $6 for 2, 50¢ per additional person* ⊙ *Daily 8–sunset*) covers 260 acres of

CLOSE UP

Swimming with Dolphins

Here in the Florida Keys, where the 1963 movie *Flipper* was filmed, close encounters of the mammalian kind are an everyday occurrence. There are a handful of facilities that allow you to commune with trained dolphins. In-water programs, where you actually swim with these intelligent creatures, are extremely popular and require advance reservations. All programs begin with a course on dolphin physiology and behavior. Afterward you learn a few important dos and don'ts. Finally, you take the plunge, quite literally.

The best time to swim with dolphins is when it's warm, from March through December. You spend a lot of time in and out of the water, and you can feel your teeth chattering on a chilly day. Waterside programs let you feed, shake hands, and do tricks with dolphins from a submerged platform. These are great for people who aren't strong swimmers or for youngsters who don't meet a facility's minimum age requirements for in-water programs.

Dolphin Connection. Hawk's Cay Resort's Dolphin Connection offers three programs, including Dockside Dolphins, a 30-minute encounter from the dry training docks ($60); Dolphin Discovery, an in-water program that lasts about 45 minutes and lets you kiss, touch, and feed the dolphins ($155); and Trainer for a Day, a three-hour session with the animal training team ($295). ⊠ *61 Hawks Cay Blvd. (MM 61 OS), Duck Key* ☎ *305/743–7000* ⊕ *www.dolphinconnection.com.*

Dolphin Cove. This educational program begins during a 30-minute boat ride on adjoining Florida Bay. Afterward, you slip into the water for some frolicking with your new dolphin pals. The cost is $125–$185 for the interactive Wade Program, Natural Swim (no interaction), and hands-on Structured Swim. ⊠ *101900 Overseas Hwy. (MM 101.9 BS), Key Largo* ☎ *305/451–4060 or 877/365–2683* ⊕ *www.dolphinscove.com.*

Dolphin Research Center. This nonprofit organization has a colony of bottlenose dolphins and California sea lions. Programs range from a stay-dry Meet the Dolphin program for $50 to get-wet Dolphin Dip ($104), Dolphin Encounter ($189), and Trainer for a Day ($650) programs. You can even paint with a dolphin. ⊠ *58901 Overseas Hwy. (MM 59 BS), Marathon Shores* ☎ *305/289–1121 or 305/289–0002* ⊕ *www.dolphins.org.*

Dolphins Plus. A sister property to Dolphin Cove, Dolphins Plus offers some of the same programs. Costing $135, the Natural Swim program begins with a one-hour briefing; then you enter the water to become totally immersed in the dolphins' world. In this visual orientation, participants snorkel and are not allowed to touch or interact with the dolphins. For tactile interaction (kissing, fin tows, etc.), sign up for the Structured Swim program ($165–$185 depending on time of year). Other interactions include the sea lion swim ($120) and Cuddle with Castaway shallow-water experience ($150). ⊠ *31 Corrine Pl. (MM 99), Key Largo* ☎ *305/451–1993 or 866/860–7946* ⊕ *www.dolphinsplus.com.*

DID YOU KNOW?

Dolphins come in various forms, from the Atlantic bottlenose dolphin to the killer whale. These playful and smart creatures love to leap out of the water and synchronize their movements with others. By swimming next to ships, dolphins can conserve energy.

upland hammock, wetlands, and mangroves. On the bay side, there's a trail through thick hardwoods to a rocky shoreline. The oceanside is more developed, with a sandy beach, a clean bathhouse, picnic tables, a playground, grills, and a 28-site campground open November to May. Locals consider the paddling trails under canopies of arching mangroves one of the best kayaking spots in the Keys. Manatees frequent the area, and it's a great spot for bird-watching. Herons, egrets, ibis, plovers, and sanderlings are commonly spotted. Raptors are often seen in the park, especially during migration periods.

WHERE TO EAT AND STAY

$$$ ✕ **Hideaway Café.** The name says it all. Tucked between Grassy Key and
AMERICAN Marathon, it's easy to miss if you're barnstorming through the middle islands. When you find it (upstairs at Rainbow Bend Resort), you'll discover a favorite of locals who appreciate a well-planned menu, lovely ocean view, and quiet evening away from the crowds. For starters, dig into escargots à la Edison (sautéed with vegetables, pepper, cognac, and cream). Then feast on several specialties, such as a rarely found chateaubriand for one, a whole roasted duck, or the seafood medley combining the catch of the day with scallops and shrimp in a savory sauce. ⊠ *Rainbow Bend Resort, 57570 Overseas Hwy. (MM 58 OS), Grassy Key* ☎ *305/289–1554* ⊕ *www.hideawaycafe.com* ▭ *AE, MC, V* ⊗ *No lunch.*

$–$$ 🛏 **Bonefish Resort.** Set on a skinny lot bedecked with palm trees, banana trees, and hibiscus plantings, this motel-style hideaway is the best choice among the island's back-to-basics properties. It's not fancy, but it's cheap, clean, and a good base for paddling a kayak, wading for bonefish, and watching the waves roll in from a lounge chair. Rooms are decorated with tropical motifs like the colorful metal lizards on the doors. A narrow gravel courtyard lined with umbrella-shaded tables leads to a small beach and a waterfront pool. The kayaks and paddleboats encourage exploration of the waterfront. The communal deck is scattered with hammocks and chaises. Check-in is at next-door sister property Yellowtail Inn, which has cottages and efficiencies. **Pros:** decent price for the location; oceanside setting. **Cons:** decks are small; simple decor. ⊠ *58070 Overseas Hwy. (MM 58 OS)* ☎ *305/743–7107 or 800/274–9949* ⊕ *www.bonefishresort.com* ↰ *3 rooms, 11 efficiencies* ⟡ *In-room: kitchen (some), refrigerator, Wi-Fi. In-hotel: beachfront, pool, bicycles, laundry facilities, Wi-Fi hotspot, some pets allowed* ▭ *D, MC, V.*

MARATHON

Marathon runs from mile markers 53 to 47.5. Most of what there is to see lies right off the Overseas Highway, with the exception of a couple of hidden restaurants.

Marathon is a bustling town, at least compared to other communities in the Keys. As it leaves something to be desired in the charm department, Marathon will probably not be your first choice of places to stay. But there are a number of good dining options, so you'll definitely want to stop for a bite even if you're just passing through on the way to Key West.

Outside of Key West, Marathon has the most historic attractions, which merit a visit. Fishing, diving, and boating are the main events here. It throws tarpon tournaments in April and May, more fishing tournaments in June and September, a birding festival in September, and lighted boat parades around the holidays.

GETTING HERE AND AROUND

The SuperShuttle charges $102 per passenger for trips from Miami International Airport to the Upper Keys. To go farther into the Keys, you must book an entire 11-person van, which costs about $250 to Marathon. For a trip to the airport, place your request 24 hours in advance.

Miami Dade Transit provides daily bus service from MM 50 in Marathon to the Florida City Walmart Supercenter on the mainland. The bus stops at major shopping centers as well as on-demand anywhere along the route during daily round trips on the hour from 6 AM to 10 PM. The cost is $1.85 one way, exact change required. The Lower Keys Shuttle bus runs from Marathon to Key West ($2 one way), with scheduled stops along the way.

ESSENTIALS

Transportation Contacts **Lower Keys Shuttle** (☎ *305/809–3910* ⊕ *www. kwtransit.com*). **Miami Dade Transit** (*formerly the Dade–Monroe Express* ☎ *305/770–3131*). **SuperShuttle** (☎ *305/871–2000* ⊕ *www.supershuttle.com*).

Visitor Information **Greater Marathon Chamber of Commerce and Visitor Center** (✉ *12222 Overseas Hwy. [MM 53.5 BS], Marathon* ☎ *305/743–5417 or 800/262–7284* ⊕ *www.floridakeysmarathon.com*).

EXPLORING

✪ ★ **Crane Point Museum, Nature Center, and Historic Site.** Tucked away from the highway behind a stand of trees, Crane Point—part of a 63-acre tract that contains the last-known undisturbed thatch-palm hammock—is delightfully undeveloped. This multiuse facility includes the **Museum of Natural History of the Florida Keys,** which has displays about local wildlife, a seashell exhibit, and a marine-life display that makes you feel you're at the bottom of the sea. Also here is the **Children's Activity Center,** with a replica of a 17th-century galleon and pirate dress-up room where youngsters can play swashbuckler. On the 1-mi indigenous loop trail, visit the **Wild Bird Center** and the remnants of a Bahamian village, site of the restored **George Adderly House.** It is the oldest surviving example of Bahamian tabby (a concrete-like material created from sand and seashells) construction outside of Key West. A re-created Cracker house demonstrates the vernacular housing of the early 1900s. A boardwalk crosses wetlands, rivers, and mangroves before ending at Adderly Village. From November to Easter docent-led tours, are available; bring good walking shoes and bug repellent during warm weather. Events include a Bahamian Heritage Festival in January. ✉ *5550 Overseas Hwy. (MM 50.5 BS)* ☎ *305/743–9100* ⊕ *www.cranepoint.net* 💰 *$11* ☉ *Mon.–Sat. 9–5, Sun. noon–5; call to arrange trail tours.*

QUICK BITES

If you don't get a buzz from breathing in the robust aroma at **Leigh Ann's (More Than Just A) Coffee House** (✉ *7537 Overseas Hwy. [MM 50 OS]* ☎ *305/743–2001* ⊕ *www.leighannscoffeehouse.com*), order an espresso shot, Cuban or Italian, for a satisfying jolt. Pastries are baked fresh daily, but the biscuits with sausage gravy and the Italian frittata cooked without added fat are among the big movers. Leigh Ann's also serves lunch—quiche, chicken potpie, and hot and cold sandwiches. It's open weekdays 7–5, Saturday 7–3, and Sunday 8–noon.

Seven Mile Bridge. This is one of the most photographed images in the Keys. Actually measuring slightly less than 7 mi, it connects the Middle and Lower Keys and is believed to be the world's longest segmental bridge. It has 39 expansion joints separating its various concrete sections. Each April runners gather in Marathon for the annual Seven Mile Bridge Run. The expanse running parallel to Seven Mile Bridge is what remains of the **Old Seven Mile Bridge,** an engineering and architectural marvel in its day that's now on the National Register of Historic Places. Once proclaimed the Eighth Wonder of the World, it rested on a record 546 concrete piers. No cars are allowed on the old bridge today, but a 2-mi segment is open for biking, walking, and fishing.

OFF THE BEATEN PATH

Pigeon Key. There's much to like about this 5-acre island under the Old Seven Mile Bridge. You can reach it by walking across a 2-mi section of the bridge or by ferry. Once there, tour the island on your own or join a guided tour to explore the buildings that formed the early-20th-century work camp for the Overseas Railroad that linked the mainland to Key West. Later the island became a fish camp, a state park, and then government-administration headquarters. Exhibits in a small museum recall the history of the Keys, the railroad, and railroad baron Henry M. Flagler. Pick up the ferry outside the gift shop, which occupies an old railroad car on Knight's Key (MM 47 OS), for a two-hour excursion. ⊠ *1 Knights Key Blvd. (MM 45 OS), Pigeon Key* ☎ *305/289–0025 general information, 305/743–5999 tickets* ⊕ *www.pigeonkey.net* ✉ *$11* ☉ *Daily 9:30–4; ferryboat departures at 10, 11:30, 1, 2:30.*

☼ **The Turtle Hospital.** More than 70 injured sea turtles check in here every year. The guided tours take you into recovery and surgical areas at the world's only state-certified veterinary hospital for sea turtles. If you're lucky, you can visit hatchlings. Call ahead—tours are sometime cancelled due to medical emergencies. ⊠ *2396 Overseas Hwy. (MM 48.5 BS)* ☎ *305/743–2552* ⊕ *www.turtlehospital.org* ✉ *$15* ☉ *Daily 9–5; tours at 10, 1, and 4.*

SPORTS AND THE OUTDOORS

BEACH

Sombrero Beach. Here, pleasant, shaded picnic areas overlook a coconut palm–lined grassy stretch and the Atlantic Ocean. Separate areas allow swimmers, boaters, and windsurfers to share the narrow cove. Facilities include barbecue grills, showers, and restrooms, as well as a large playground, a pier, and a volleyball court. Sunday afternoons draw lots of local families toting coolers. The park is accessible for those with disabilities and allows leashed pets. Turn east at the traffic light in Marathon and follow signs to the end. ⊠ *Sombrero Beach Rd. (MM 50 OS)* ☎ *305/743–0033* ✉ *Free* ☉ *Daily 8–sunset.*

BIKING

Tooling around on two wheels is a good way to see Marathon. There's easy cycling on a 1-mi off-road path that connects to the 2 mi of the Old Seven Mile Bridge leading to Pigeon Key.

"Have bikes, will deliver" could be the motto of **Bike Marathon Bike Rentals** (☎ *305/743–3204*), which gets beach cruisers to your hotel door for $45 per week, including a helmet. It's open Monday through Saturday 9–4 and Sunday 9–2. **Overseas Outfitters** (✉ *1700 Overseas Hwy. [MM 48 BS]* ☎ *305/289–1670*) rents aluminum cruisers and hybrid bikes for $10 to $12 per day. The company also rents tandem bikes and children's bikes. It's open weekdays 9–6, and Saturday 9–5.

BOATING

Sail, motor, or paddle—whatever your choice of modes, boating is what the Keys is all about. Brave the Atlantic waves and reefs or explore the backcountry islands on the gulf side. If you don't have a lot of boating and chart-reading experience, it's a good idea to tap into local knowledge on a charter.

Captain Pip's (✉ *1410 Overseas Hwy. [MM 47.5 OS]* ☎ *305/743–4403 or 800/707–1692* ⊕ *www.captainpips.com*) rents 19- to 24-foot outboards, $175–$330 per day, as well as tackle and snorkeling gear. You also can charter a small boat with a guide, $500–$685 for a half day and $750–$925 for a full day. **Fish 'n Fun** (✉ *4590 Overseas Hwy. [MM 49.5 OS] at Banana Bay Resort & Marina* ☎ *305/743–2275 or 800/471–3440* ⊕ *www.fishnfunrentals.com*) lets you get out on the water on 19- to 26-foot powerboats starting at $140 for a half day, $190 for a full day. The company offers free delivery in the Middle Keys. You also can rent Jet Skis and kayaks.

FISHING

For recreational anglers, the deepwater fishing is superb in both bay and ocean. Marathon West Hump, one good spot, has depths ranging from 500 to more than 1,000 feet. Locals fish from a half-dozen bridges, including Long Key Bridge, the Old Seven Mile Bridge, and both ends of Tom's Harbor. Barracuda, bonefish, and tarpon all frequent local waters. Party boats and private charters are available.

★ Morning, afternoon, and night, fish for mahimahi, grouper, and other tasty catch aboard the 73-foot **Marathon Lady** (✉ *MM 53 OS, at 117th St.* ☎ *305/743–5580* ⊕ *fishfloridakeys.com/marathonlady*), which departs on half-day ($45) excursions from the Vaca Cut Bridge, north of Marathon. Join the crew for night fishing ($50) from 6:30 to midnight from Memorial Day to Labor Day; it's especially beautiful on a full-moon night. Captain Jim Purcell, a deep-sea specialist for ESPN's *The American Outdoorsman,* provides one of the best values in Keys fishing. **Sea Dog Charters** (✉ *1248 Overseas Hwy. [MM 47.5 BS]* ☎ *305/743–8255* ⊕ *www.seadogcharters.net*), next to the Seven Mile Grill, has half- and full-day offshore, reef and wreck, and backcountry fishing trips, as well as fishing and snorkeling trips aboard 30- to 37-foot boats. The cost is $60 per person for a half day, regardless of whether your group fills the boat, and includes bait, light tackle, ice, coolers, and fishing licenses. If you prefer an all-day private charter on a 37-foot boat, he offers those, too, for $600 for up to six people. A fuel surcharge may apply.

SCUBA DIVING AND SNORKELING

Local dive operations take you to Sombrero Reef and Lighthouse, the most popular down-under destination in these parts. For a shallow dive and some lobster-nabbing, Coffins Patch, off Key Colony Beach, is a good choice. A number of wrecks such as *Thunderbolt* serve as artificial reefs. Many operations out of this area will also take you to Looe Key Reef.

Hall's Diving Center & Career Institute (⌧ *1994 Overseas Hwy. [MM 48.5 BS]* ☎ *305/743–5929 or 800/331–4255* ⊕ *www.hallsdiving.com*) has been training divers for more than 40 years. Along with conventional twice-a-day snorkel and two-tank dive trips ($40–$55) to the reefs at Sombrero Lighthouse and wrecks like the *Thunderbolt*, the company has more unusual offerings like digital and video photography.

Twice daily, **Spirit Snorkeling** (⌧ *1410 Overseas Hwy., Slip No. 1 [MM 47.5 BS]* ☎ *305/289–0614* ⊕ *www.spiritsnorkeling.net*) departs on snorkeling excursions to Sombrero Reef and Lighthouse Reef for $30 a head.

WHERE TO EAT

$$$ ⤫**Barracuda Grill**. Sparsely decorated with fish and bird art and filled
ECLECTIC with tables covered with butcher paper, this restaurant is not much to look at. But when it comes to the food, Barracuda Grill delivers. The sophisticated, eclectic menu capitalizes on local seafood (take a test drive with the mangrove snapper), but gives equal treatment to aged Angus beef, rack of lamb, and braised pork shank. Smaller entrées such as mini-mahi and baby steak appeal to light appetites. Favorite main courses include Francesca's spicy voodoo stew with scallops, shrimp, and vegetables in a tomato-saffron stock; a 22-ounce cowboy rib eye; and sashimi of yellowfin tuna accompanied by wasabi and tamari. For dessert, slices of oh-so-rich key lime cheesecake fly out of the kitchen. The well thought out wine list is heavily Californian. Call ahead, as the owners often close during the off-season. ⌧ *4290 Overseas Hwy. (MM 49.5 BS)* ☎ *305/743–3314* ⤫ *Reservations not accepted* ▭ *AE, MC, V* ☉ *No lunch. Closed Sun.–Tues.*

¢ ⤫**Fish Tales Market and Eatery**. This roadside eatery with its own seafood
SEAFOOD market serves signature dishes such as oysters on a roll and snapper on grilled rye with coleslaw and melted Muenster cheese. You also can slurp lobster bisque or red-conch chowder. There are burgers, chicken, and dogs for those who don't do seafood. Plan to dine early; it's only open until 6:30 PM. This is a no-frills kind of place with a loyal local following, a couple of picnic tables, and friendly service. ⌧ *11711 Overseas Hwy. (MM 52.5 OS)* ☎ *305/743–9196 or 888/662–4822* ⊕ *www.floridalobster.com* ▭ *AE, MC, V* ☉ *Closed Sun.*

$$ ⤫**Key Colony Inn**. The inviting aroma of an Italian kitchen pervades
ITALIAN this family-owned favorite with a supper club atmosphere. As you'd expect, the service is friendly and attentive. For lunch there are fish and steak entrées served with fries, salad, and bread in addition to Italian specialties. At dinner you can't miss with traditional dishes like veal

Oscar and New York strip, or such specialties as seafood Italiano, a dish of scallops and shrimp sautéed in garlic butter and served with marinara sauce over a bed of linguine. The place is renowned for its Sunday brunch, served from November to April. ⊠ *700 W. Ocean Dr. (MM 54 OS), Key Colony Beach* ☎ *305/743–0100* ⊕ *www.kcinn.com* ⊟ *AE, MC, V.*

$$ ✕ **Keys Fisheries Market & Marina.** From the parking lot, this commer-
SEAFOOD cial warehouse flanked by fishing boats and lobster traps barely hints
★ at the restaurant inside. Order at the window outside, pick up your food, then dine at one of the waterfront picnic tables outfitted with rolls of paper towels. Fresh seafood (and a token hamburger) are the only things on the menu. A huge lobster Reuben ($14.95) served on thick slices of toasted bread is the signature dish. Other delights include the shrimpburger, very rich whiskey-peppercorn snapper, and the Keys Kombo (broiled or grilled lobster, shrimp, scallops, and mahimahi for $29). There's also an eight-flavor ice-cream station and a bar serving beer and wine. ⊠ *3390 Gulfview Ave. (turn west on 35th St.), end of 35th St. (MM 49 BS)* ☎ *305/743–4353 or 866/743–4353* ⊕ *www. keysfisheries.com* ⊟ *MC, V.*

¢ ✕ **The Stuffed Pig.** With only eight tables and a counter inside, this break-
AMERICAN fast-and-lunch place is always hopping. When the weather's right, grab a table out back. The kitchen whips up daily lunch specials like burgers, seafood platters, or pulled pork with hand-cut fries, but a quick glance around the room reveals that the all-day breakfast is the main draw. You can get the usual breakfast plates, but most newcomers opt for oddities like the lobster omelet, alligator tail and eggs, or "grits and grunts" (that's fish, to the rest of us). ⊠ *3520 Overseas Hwy. (MM 49 BS)* ☎ *305/743–4059* ⊕ *www.thestuffedpig.com* ⊟ *No credit cards* ☾ *No dinner.*

WHERE TO STAY

$$$$ ⊞ **Tranquility Bay.** Ralph Lauren might have designed the rooms at this
★ luxurious beach resort. The 87 two- and three-bedroom town houses have gingerbread trim, white-picket fences, and open-floor-plan interiors decorated in trendy cottage style. The picture-perfect theme continues with the palm-fringed pool and the sandy beach edged with a ribbon of blue bay (and echoed in the blue-and-white stripes of the poolside umbrellas). Guests look like models on a photo shoot: attractive young families enjoying themselves at the sunny decks, casual outdoor bar, or elegant restaurant. **Pros:** secluded setting; gorgeous design; lovely crescent beach. **Cons:** a bit sterile; no real Keys atmosphere; cramped building layout. ⊠ *2600 Overseas Hwy. (MM 48.5 BS)* ☎ *305/289–0888 or 866/643–5397* ⊕ *www.tranquilitybay.com* ⇲ *45 2-bedroom suites, 41 3-bedroom suites* ⌂ *In-room: kitchen, refrigerator, DVD, Wi-Fi. In-hotel: 2 restaurants, bars, pools, gym, beachfront, diving, water sports, Wi-Fi hotspot* ⊟ *AE, D, MC, V.*

6

THE LOWER KEYS

Beginning at Bahia Honda Key, the islands of the Florida Keys become smaller, more clustered, and more numerous—a result of ancient tidal water flowing between the Florida Straits and the gulf. Here you're likely to see more birds and mangroves than other tourists, and more refuges, beaches, and campgrounds than museums, restaurants, and hotels. The islands are made up of two types of limestone, both denser than the highly permeable Key Largo limestone of the Upper Keys. As a result, freshwater forms in pools rather than percolating through the rock, creating watering holes that support alligators, snakes, deer, rabbits, raccoons, and migratory ducks. (Many of these animals can be seen in the National Key Deer Refuge on Big Pine Key.) Nature was generous with her beauty in the Lower Keys, which have both Looe Key Reef, arguably the Keys' most beautiful tract of coral, and Bahia Honda State Park, considered one of the best beaches in the world for its fine-sand dunes, clear warm waters, and panoramic vista of bridge, hammocks, and azure sky and sea. Big Pine Key is fishing headquarters for a laid-back community that swells with retirees in the winter. South of it, the dribble of islands can flash by in a blink of an eye if you don't take the time to stop at a roadside eatery or check out tours and charters at the little marinas.

EXPLORING THE LOWER KEYS

In truth, the Lower Keys include Key West, but since it is as different from the rest of the Lower Keys as peanut butter is from jelly, it is covered in its own section.

GETTING HERE AND AROUND

The Lower Keys in this section include the keys between MM 37 and MM 9. The Seven Mile Bridge drops you into the lap of this homey, quiet part of the Keys.

Heed speed limits in these parts. They may seem incredibly strict given the traffic is lightest of anywhere in the Keys, but the purpose is to protect the resident Key deer population, and officers of the law pay strict attention and will readily issue speeding tickets.

BAHIA HONDA KEY

Bahia Honda Key is between mile markers 38 and 36.

All of Bahia Honda Key is devoted to its eponymous state park, which keeps it in a pristine state. Besides the park's outdoor activities, it offers an up-close look at the original railroad bridge.

EXPLORING

Fodor's Choice ★ **Bahia Honda State Park.** Most first-time visitors to the region are dismayed by the lack of beaches—but then they discover sun-soaked Bahia Honda Key. The 524-acre park here sprawls across both sides of the highway, giving it 2½ mi of fabulous sandy coastline. The snorkeling isn't bad, either; there's underwater life (soft coral, queen conchs, random little fish) just a few hundred feet offshore. Although swimming,

DID YOU KNOW?

An old railroad bridge used to connect Bahia Honda Key with Key West until a hurricane destroyed it in 1935. While it is no longer in operation, the bridge is used by visitors as a place for viewing the island.

kayaking, fishing, and boating are the main reasons to visit, you shouldn't miss biking along the 2½ mi of flat roads or hiking the Silver Palm Trail, with rare West Indian plants and several species found nowhere else in the nation. Along the way you'll be treated to a variety of butterflies. Seasonal ranger-led nature programs take place or depart from the Sand and Sea Nature Center. There are rental cabins, a campground, snack bar, gift shop, 19-slip marina, nature center, and facilities for renting kayaks and arranging snorkeling tours. Get a panoramic view of the island from what's left of the railroad—the Bahia Honda Bridge. ⊠ *36850 Overseas Hwy. (MM 37 OS)* ☎ *305/872–2353* ⊕ *www.floridastateparks.org/bahiahonda* ⊡ *$4.50 for 1 person, $9 for 2 people, 50¢ per additional person* ☉ *Daily 8–sunset.*

SPORTS AND THE OUTDOORS

BEACH

Bahia Honda State Park contains three beaches in all—on both the Atlantic Ocean and the Gulf of Mexico. Sandspur Beach, the largest, is regularly declared the best beach in Florida, and you'll be hard pressed to argue. The sand is baby-powder soft, and the aqua water is warm, clear, and shallow. With their mild currents, the beaches are great for swimming, even with small fry. ⊠ *36850 Overseas Hwy. (MM 37 OS)* ☎ *305/872–2353* ⊕ *www.floridastateparks.org/bahiahonda* ⊡ *$4.50 for 1 person, $9 for 2 people, 50¢ per additional person* ☉ *Daily 8–sunset.*

SCUBA DIVING AND SNORKELING

Bahia Honda Dive Shop (⊠ *36850 Overseas Hwy. [MM 37 OS]* ☎ *305/ 872–3210* ⊕ *www.bahiahondapark.com*), the concessionaire at Bahia Honda State Park, manages a 19-slip marina; rents wet suits, snorkel equipment, and corrective masks; and operates twice-a-day offshore-reef snorkel trips ($30 plus $9 for equipment). Park visitors looking for other fun can rent kayaks ($10 per hour for a single, $18 for a double) and beach chairs.

WHERE TO STAY

$$$ 🏨 **Bahia Honda State Park.** Elsewhere you'd pay big bucks for the won-
★   derful water views available at these cabins on Florida Bay. Each of three cabins have two, two-bedroom units with a full kitchen and bath and air-conditioning (but no television, radio, or phone). The park also has popular campsites ($43 per night) suitable for either tents or motor homes. Some are directly on the beach—talk about a room with a view! Cabins and campsites book up early, so reserve up to 11 months before your planned visit. **Pros:** great bay-front views; beach-front camping; affordable rates. **Cons:** books up fast; area can be buggy. ⊠ *36850 Overseas Hwy. (MM 37 OS)* ☎ *305/872–2353 or 800/326– 3521* ⊕ *www.reserveamerica.com* ⤝ *80 partial hookup campsites, 6 cabin units* ☖ *In-room: no phone, kitchen, no TV. In-hotel: beachfront, water sports, bicycles, dump station* ▭ *AE, D, MC, V.*

BIG PINE KEY

Big Pine Key runs from mile marker 32 to 30.

Welcome to the Keys' most natural holdout, where wildlife refuges protect rare and endangered animals. Here you have left behind the commercialism of the Upper Keys for an authentic backcountry atmosphere.

ESSENTIALS

Visitor Information Big Pine and the Lower Keys Chamber of Commerce (✉ *31020 Overseas Hwy. [MM 31 OS], Big Pine Key* ☎ *305/872–2411 or 800/872–3722* ⊕ *www.lowerkeyschamber.com*).

EXPLORING

★ **National Key Deer Refuge.** This 84,351-acre refuge was established in 1957 to protect the dwindling population of the Key deer, one of more than 20 animals and plants classified as endangered or threatened in the Florida Keys. The Key deer, which stands about 30 inches at the shoulders and is a subspecies of the Virginia white-tailed deer, once roamed throughout the Lower and Middle Keys, but hunting, destruction of their habitat, and a growing human population caused their numbers to decline to 27 by 1957. The deer have made a comeback, increasing their numbers to approximately 750. The best place to see Key deer in the refuge is at the end of Key Deer Boulevard and on No Name Key, a sparsely populated island just east of Big Pine Key. Mornings and evenings are the best time to spot them. Deer may turn up along the road at any time of day, so drive slowly. They wander into nearby yards to nibble tender grass and bougainvillea blossom, but locals do not appreciate tourists driving into their neighborhoods after them. Feeding them is against the law and puts them in danger. The refuge also has 21 other listed endangered and threatened species of plants and animals, including five that are found nowhere else.

Blue Hole. A quarry left over from railroad days, the Blue Hole is the largest body of freshwater in the Keys. From the observation platform and nearby walking trail, you might see the resident alligator (its mate died recently from ingesting a plastic toy), turtles, and other wildlife. There are two well-marked trails: the Jack Watson Nature Trail (.6 mi), named after an environmentalist and the refuge's first warden; and the Fred Mannillo Nature Trail, one of the most wheelchair-accessible places to see an unspoiled pine-rockland forest and wetlands. The visitor center has exhibits on Keys biology and ecology. The refuge also provides information on the Key West National Wildlife Refuge and the Great White Heron National Wildlife Refuge. Accessible only by water, both are popular with kayak outfitters. ✉ *Visitor Center–Headquarters, Big Pine Shopping Center, MM 30.5 BS, 28950 Watson Blvd.* ☎ *305/872–2239* ⊕ *www.fws.gov/nationalkeydeer* 🎟 *Free* ☉ *Daily sunrise–sunset; headquarters weekdays 8–5.*

SPORTS AND THE OUTDOORS

BIKING

A good 10 mi of paved roads run from MM 30.3 BS, along Wilder Road, across the bridge to No Name Key, and along Key Deer Boulevard into the National Key Deer Refuge. Along the way you might see some Key deer. Stay off the trails that lead into wetlands, where fat tires can do damage to the environment.

Marty Baird, owner of **Big Pine Bicycle Center** (⊠ *31 County Rd. [MM 30.9 BS]* ☎ *305/872–0130*), is an avid cyclist and enjoys sharing his knowledge of great places to ride. He's also skilled at selecting the right bike for the journey, and he knows his repairs, too. His old-fashioned single-speed, fat-tire cruisers rent for $8 per half day and $10 for a full day. Helmets, baskets, and locks are included. Although the shop is officially closed on Sunday, join Marty there most Sunday mornings at 8 from December to Easter for a free off-road fun ride.

BOATING

Strike Zone Charters (⊠ *29675 Overseas Hwy. [MM 29.6 BS], Big Pine Key* ☎ *305/872–9863 or 800/654–9560* ⊕ *www.strikezonecharter.com*) has glass-bottom-boat excursions into the backcountry and Atlantic Ocean. The five-hour Island Excursion ($55 plus fuel surcharge) emphasizes nature and Keys history; besides close encounters with birds, sea life, and vegetation, there's a fish cookout on an island. Snorkel and fishing equipment, food, and drinks are included. This is one of the few nature outings in the Keys with wheelchair access.

KAYAKING

★ **Big Pine Kayak Adventures** (⊠ *Old Wooden Bridge Fishing Camp, MM 30 BS, turn right at traffic light, continue on Wilder Rd. toward No Name Key* ☎ *305/872–7474* ⊕ *www.keyskayaktours.com*) makes it very convenient to rent kayaks by delivering them to your lodging or anywhere between Seven Mile Bridge and Stock Island. The company, headed by *The Florida Keys Paddling Guide* author Bill Keogh, will rent you a kayak and then ferry you—called taxi-yakking—to remote islands with clear instructions on how to paddle back on your own. Rentals are by the half day or full day. Group kayak tours ($50 for three hours) explore the mangrove forests of Great White Heron and Key Deer National Wildlife Refuges. Custom tours ($125 and up, four hours) transport you to exquisite backcountry areas teeming with wildlife. Kayak fishing charters are also popular.

SCUBA DIVING AND SNORKELING

Strike Zone Charters (⊠ *29675 Overseas Hwy. [MM 29.5 BS]* ☎ *305/872–9863 or 800/654–9560*) leads dive excursions to the wreck of the 110-foot *Adolphus Busch* ($55), and scuba ($45) and snorkel ($35) trips to Looe Key Reef aboard glass-bottom boats. Strike Zone also offers a five-hour island excursion that combines snorkeling, fishing, and an island cookout for $55 per person. A large dive shop is on-site.

WHERE TO EAT

¢ ✕ **Good Food Conspiracy.** Like good wine, this small natural-foods eatery and market surrenders its pleasures a little at a time. Step inside to the aroma of brewing coffee, and then pick up the scent of fresh

VEGETARIAN

strawberries or carrots blending into a smoothie, the green aroma of wheatgrass juice, followed by the earthy odor of hummus. Order raw or cooked vegetarian and vegan dishes, organic soups and salads, and organic coffees and teas. Bountiful sandwiches (available halved) include the popular tuna melt or hummus and avocado. If you can't sit down for a bite, stock up on healthful snacks like dried fruits, raw nuts, and carob-covered almonds. Dine early: the shop closes at 7 PM Monday to Saturday, and at 5 PM on Sunday. ⊠ *30150 Overseas Hwy. (MM 30.2 OS)* ☎ *305/872–3945* ⊟ *AE, D, MC, V.*

$ ✕**No Name Pub.** This no-frills honky-tonk has been around since 1936,
AMERICAN delighting inveterate locals and intrepid vacationers who come for the excellent pizza, cold beer, and *interesting* companionship. The decor, such as it is, amounts to the autographed dollar bills that cover every inch of the place. The full menu printed on place mats includes a tasty conch chowder, a half-pound fried-grouper sandwich, spaghetti and meatballs, and seafood baskets. The lighting is poor, the furnishings are rough, and the music is oldies. This former brothel and bait shop is just before the No Name Key Bridge. It's a bit hard to find, but worth the trouble if you want a singular Keys experience. ⊠ *MM 30 BS, turn west on Wilder Rd., left on South St., right on Avenue B, right on Watson Blvd.* ☎ *305/872–9115* ⊕ *www.nonamepub.com* ⊟ *D, MC, V.*

WHERE TO STAY

$ ▦**Big Pine Key Fishing Lodge.** There's a congenial atmosphere at this
★ lively family-owned lodge-campground-marina. It's a happy mix of tent campers (who have the fabulous waterfront real estate), RVers (who look pretty permanent), and motel-dwellers who like to mingle at the rooftop pool and challenge each other to a game of poker. Rooms have tile floors, wicker furniture, and doors that allow sea breezes to waft through. A skywalk joins the upper story rooms with the pool and deck. Campsites range from rustic to full hookups. Everything is spotless— even the campground's bathhouse—and the service is good-natured and efficient. The staff will book you a room, sell you bait, or hook you up with a fishing charter. There are plenty of family-oriented activities, so the youngsters will never complain about being bored. Discounts are available for weeklong or longer stays. **Pros:** local fishing crowd; nice pool; great price. **Cons:** RV park is too close to motel; deer will eat your food if you're camping. ⊠ *33000 Overseas Hwy. (MM 33 OS)* ☎ *305/872–2351* ↘ *16 rooms; 158 campsites, 97 with full hookups, 61 without hookups* ♿ *In-room: no phone, kitchen (some), refrigerator. In-hotel: pool, laundry facilities, Internet terminal, Wi-Fi hotspot* ⊟ *D, MC, V.*

$$$$ ▦**Deer Run Bed & Breakfast.** Key deer wander the grounds of this beachfront B&B, set on a quiet street lined with buttonwoods and mangroves. Innkeepers Jen DeMaria and Harry Appel were way ahead of the green-lodging game when they opened in 2004. They continue to make strides in environmental- and guest-friendliness, and were recognized as one of the most sustainable inns in the United States by *Islands* magazine in 2009. Two large oceanfront rooms are decorated in soothing earth tones and furnished with mahogany and pecan-wood furnishings. The beach-level unit is decorated in key lime and flamingo-pink, with wicker

6

furnishings, and the garden-view room is an eclectic mix that includes Victorian farmhouse doors serving as the headboard of the queen-size bed. Guests share a living room and a veranda. The mostly organic breakfast menu is suitable for vegans. Guest rooms are stocked with organic cotton towels and cruelty-free toiletries. **Pros:** quiet location; healthy breakfasts; complimentary bike and kayak use. **Cons:** price is a bit high; hard to find. ⊠ *1997 Long Beach Dr. (MM 33 OS)* ☎ *305/872–2015* ⊕ *www.deerrunfloridabb.com* ↪ *4 rooms* ⚓ *In-room: no phone, refrigerator, Wi-Fi. In-hotel: pool, beachfront, water sports, bicycles, no kids under 18* ▭ *D, MC, V* ⦶ *BP.*

LITTLE TORCH KEY

Little Torch Key is between mile markers 29 and 10.

Little Torch Key and its neighbor islands, Ramrod Key and Summerland Key, are good jumping-off points for divers headed for Looe Key Reef. The islands also serve as a refuge for those who want to make forays into Key West but not stay in the thick of things.

The undeveloped backcountry at your door makes Little Torch Key an ideal location for fishing and kayaking. Nearby **Ramrod Key,** which also caters to divers bound for Looe Key, derives its name from a ship that wrecked on nearby reefs in the early 1800s.

NEED A BREAK?

The aroma of rich roasting coffee beans at Baby's Coffee (⊠ *3178 Overseas Hwy. [MM 15 OS], Saddlebunch Keys* ☎ *305/744–9866 or 800/523–2326* ⊕ *www.babyscoffee.com*) arrests you at the door of "the Southernmost Coffee Roaster." Buy it by the pound or by the cup along with fresh baked goods.

SPORTS AND THE OUTDOORS

For something with more of an adrenaline boost, book with **White Knuckle Thrill Boat Ride** (⊠ *Sunset Marina, Overseas Hwy., 5555 College Rd., Key West* ☎ *305/797–0459* ⊕ *www.whiteknucklethrillboatride.com*). The speedboat holds up to 12 people and does 360s, fishtails, and other water stunts in the gulf. Cost is $59 each, and includes pickup shuttle.

SCUBA DIVING AND SNORKELING

★ In 1744 the HMS *Looe,* a British warship, ran aground and sank on one of the most beautiful coral reefs in the Keys. Today **Looe Key Reef** (⊠ *216 Ann St. [MM 27.5 OS], Key West* ☎ *305/292–0311*) owes its name to the ill-fated ship. The 5.3-square-nautical-mi reef, part of the **Florida Keys National Marine Sanctuary,** has strands of elkhorn coral on its eastern margin, purple sea fans, and abundant sponges and sea urchins. On its seaward side, it drops almost vertically 50 to 90 feet. In its midst, **Shipwreck Trail** plots the location of nine historic wreck sites in 14 to 120 feet of water. Buoys mark the sites, and underwater signs tell the history of each site and what marine life to expect. Snorkelers and divers will find the sanctuary a quiet place to observe reef life—except in July, when the annual Underwater Music Festival pays homage to Looe Key's beauty and promotes reef awareness with six hours of music broadcast via underwater speakers. Dive shops, charters, and private boats transport about 500 divers and snorkelers to hear the spectacle, which includes classical, jazz, and new age, Caribbean music, as well as a little Jimmy Buffett. There are even underwater Elvis impersonators. Rather than the customary morning and afternoon two-tank, two-location trips offered by most dive shops, **Looe Key Reef Resort & Dive Center** (✉ *Looe Key Reef Resort, 27340 Overseas Hwy. [MM 27.5 OS], Ramrod Key* ☎ *305/872–221 or 800/942–5397* ⊕ *www.diveflakeys.com*), the closest dive shop to Looe Key Reef, runs a single three-tank, three-location dive ($80 for divers, $40 for snorkelers). The maximum depth is 30 feet, so snorkelers and divers go on the same boat. On Wednesday it runs a dive-only trip that visits the wreck and reefs in the area ($80). The dive boat, a 45-foot catamaran, is docked at the full-service Looe Key Reef Resort.

WATER SPORTS
Rent a paddle-propelled vehicle for exploring local gulf waters at **Sugarloaf Marina** (✉ *17015 Overseas Hwy. [MM 17 BS], Sugarloaf Key* ☎ *305/745–3135*); rates for one- or two-person kayak, and canoes start at $15 for one hour to $35 for a full day. Extra days are $25. Delivery is free for multiple-day rentals.

WHERE TO EAT

$ ✕ **Geiger Key Marina Smokehouse.** There's a strong hint of the Old Keys at this oceanside marina restaurant, on the backside of paradise, as the sign says. Locals usually outnumber tourists; they come for the daily dinner specials: meat loaf on Monday, pasta on Tuesday, and so on. For lunch, try the fresh catch or lobster BLT. Weekends are the most popular; the place is packed on Saturday for steak-on-the-grill night and on Sunday for the chicken and ribs barbecue. In season, local fishermen stop here for breakfast before heading out in search of the big ones. ✉ *Geiger Key at 5 Geiger Key Rd., off Boca Chica Rd. (MM 10)* ☎ *305/296–3553 or 305/294–1230* ⊕ *www.geigerkeymarina.com* ▭ *MC, V* ⊘ *Closed for breakfast Apr.–Dec.*

AMERICAN

$$$$ ✕ **Little Palm Island Restaurant.** The oceanfront setting calls to mind St. Barts and the other high-end destinations of the Caribbean. Keep that in mind as you reach for the bill, which can also make you swoon. The restaurant at the exclusive Little Palm Island Resort—its dining room and adjacent outdoor terrace lit by candles and warmed by live music—is one of the most romantic spots in the Keys. The seasonal menu is a melding of French and Caribbean flavors, with exotic little touches. Think shrimp and yellowtail ceviche or coconut lobster bisque as a starter, followed by mahimahi with cilantro and creamy polenta. The Saturday and Sunday brunch buffet, the full-moon dinners with live entertainment, and Chef's Table Dinner are very popular. The dining room is open to nonguests on a reservations-only basis. ✉ *28500 Overseas Hwy. (MM 28.5 OS)* ☎ *305/872–2551* ⊕ *www.littlepalmisland. com* ⚞ *Reservations essential* ▭ *AE, D, DC, MC, V.*

ECLECTIC
★

WHERE TO STAY

$$$$ ▦ **Little Palm Island Resort & Spa.** *Haute tropicale* best describes this luxury retreat, and "second mortgage" might explain how some can afford the extravagant prices. But for those who can, it's worth the price. This property sits on a 5-acre palm-fringed island 3 mi offshore from

Fodor'sChoice
★

6

Little Torch Key. The 28 oceanfront thatch-roof bungalow suites have slate-tile baths, mosquito-netting-draped king-size beds, and British colonial–style furnishings. Other comforts include an indoor and outdoor shower, private veranda, separate living room, and comfy robes and slippers. Two Island Grand Suites are twice the size of the others and offer his-and-hers bathrooms, an outdoor hot tub, and uncompromising ocean views. To preserve the quiet atmosphere, cell phones are highly discouraged in public areas. **Pros:** secluded setting; heavenly spa; easy wildlife viewing. **Cons:** expensive; might be too quiet for some. ⊠ *28500 Overseas Hwy. (MM 28.5 OS)* ☎ *305/872–2524 or 800/343–8567* ⊕ *www.littlepalmisland.com* ⊃ *30 suites* ⌂ *In-room: no phone, safe, refrigerator, no TV, Internet. In-hotel: restaurant, room service, bars, pool, gym, spa, beachfront, diving, water sports, Wi-Fi hotspot, parking (free), no kids under 16* ⊟ *AE, D, DC, MC, V* ⦿ *MAP.*

$–$$ ⊡ **Looe Key Reef Resort & Center.** If your Keys vacation is all about diving, you'll be well served at this scuba-obsessed operation. The closest place to stay to the stellar reef and affordable to boot, it's popular with the bottom-time crowd. Rooms are basic but perfect for sleeping between dives and hanging out at the tiki bar. The one suite is equipped with a fridge and microwave. Single rooms are available. **Pros:** guests get discounts on dive and snorkel trips; fun bar. **Cons:** small rooms; unheated pool; close to road. ⊠ *27340 Overseas Hwy. (MM 27.5 OS), Ramrod Key* ☎ *305/872–2215 Ext. 2 or 800/942–5397* ⊕ *www.diveflakeys. com* ⊃ *23 rooms, 1 suite* ⌂ *In-room: Wi-Fi. In-hotel: bar, pool, Wi-Fi hotspot* ⊟ *D, MC, V.*

$$–$$$ ⊡ **Parmer's Resort.** Almost every room at this budget-friendly option has a view of South Pine Channel, with the lovely curl of Big Pine Key in the foreground. Waterfront cottages, with decks or balconies, are spread out on 6 landscaped acres, with a heated swimming pool and a five-hole putting green. There are water sports galore, and the staff will book you a kayak tour, a fishing trip, or a bike excursion, or tell you which local restaurants will deliver dinner to your room. So what if the decor feels a little like Grandma's house and you have to pay extra ($10) if you want your room cleaned daily? **Pros:** bright rooms; pretty setting; good value. **Cons:** a bit out of the way; housekeeping costs extra; little shade around the pool. ⊠ *565 Barry Ave. (MM 28.7 BS)* ☎ *305/872–2157* ⊕ *www.parmersresort.com* ⊃ *18 rooms, 12 efficiencies, 15 apartments, 1 penthouse* ⌂ *In-room: no phone, kitchen (some). In-hotel: pool, laundry facilities, Wi-Fi hotspot* ⊟ *AE, D, MC, V* ⦿ *CP.*

EN ROUTE The huge object that looks like a white whale floating over Cudjoe Key (MM 23–21) is not a figment of your imagination. It's Fat Albert, a radar balloon that monitors local air and water traffic.

KEY WEST

Situated 150 mi from Miami, 90 mi from Havana, and an immeasurable distance from sanity, this end-of-the-line community has never been like anywhere else. Even after it was connected to the rest of the country— by the railroad in 1912 and by the highway in 1938—it maintained a strong sense of detachment.

Key West reflects a diverse population: Conchs (natives, many of whom trace their ancestry to the Bahamas), freshwater Conchs (longtime residents who migrated from somewhere else years ago), Hispanics (primarily Cuban immigrants), recent refugees from the urban sprawl of mainland Florida, military personnel, and an assortment of vagabonds, drifters, and dropouts in search of refuge. The island was once a gay vacation hot spot, and it remains a decidedly gay-friendly destination. Some of the most renowned gay guesthouses, however, no longer cater to an exclusively gay clientele. Key Westers pride themselves on their tolerance of all peoples, all sexual orientations, and even all animals. Most restaurants allow pets, and it's not surprising to see stray cats, dogs, and even chickens roaming freely through the dining rooms. The chicken issue is one that government officials periodically try to bring to an end, but the colorful fowl continue to strut and crow, particularly in the vicinity of Old Town's Bahamian Village.

Although the rest of the Keys are known for outdoor activities, Key West has something of a city feel. Few open spaces remain, as promoters continue to churn out restaurants, galleries, shops, and museums to interpret the city's intriguing past. As a tourist destination, Key West has a lot to sell—an average temperature of 79°F, 19th-century architecture, and a laid-back lifestyle. Yet much has been lost to those eager for a buck. Duval Street looks like a miniature Las Vegas lined with garish signs for T-shirt shops and tour company offices. Cruise ships dwarf the town's skyline and fill the streets with day-trippers gawking at the hippies with dogs in their bike baskets, gay couples walking down the street holding hands, and the oddball lot of locals, some of whom bark louder than the dogs.

GETTING HERE AND AROUND

Between mile markers 4 and 0, Key West is the one place in the Keys where you could conceivably do without a car, especially if you plan on staying around Old Town. If you've driven the 106 mi down the chain, you're probably ready to abandon your car in the hotel parking lot anyway. Trolleys, buses, bikes, scooters, and feet are more suitable alternatives. To explore the beaches, New Town, and Stock Island, you'll probably need a car.

Greyhound Lines runs a special Keys shuttle two times a day (depending on the day of the week) from Miami International Airport (departing from Concourse E, lower level) and stops throughout the Keys. Fares run about $39 for Key West (3535 S. Roosevelt, Key West International Airport). Keys Shuttle runs scheduled service six times a day in 15-passenger vans between Miami Airport and Key West with stops throughout the Keys for $70 to $90 per person. Key West Express operates air-conditioned ferries between the Key West Terminal (Caroline and Grinnell streets) and Miami, Marco Island, and Fort Myers Beach. The trip from Fort Myers Beach takes at least four hours each way and costs $85.50 one way, $145 round-trip. Ferries depart from Fort Myers Beach at 8:30 AM and from Key West at 6 PM. The Miami and Marco Island ferry costs $85.50 one way and $119 round-trip, and departs at 8:30 am. A photo ID is required for each passenger. Advance reservations are recommended. The SuperShuttle charges $102 per passenger for trips

KEY WEST'S COLORFUL HISTORY

The United States acquired Key West from Spain in 1821, along with the rest of Florida. The Spanish had named the island Cayo Hueso, or Bone Key, after the American Indians' skeletons they found on its shores. In 1823, President James Monroe sent Commodore David S. Porter to chase pirates away. For three decades the primary industry in Key West was wrecking—rescuing people and salvaging cargo from ships that foundered on the nearby reefs. According to some reports, when pickings were lean the wreckers hung out lights to lure ships aground. Their business declined after 1849 when the federal government began building lighthouses.

In 1845 the army began construction on Fort Taylor, which kept Key West on the Union side during the Civil War even though most of Florida seceded. After the fighting ended, an influx of Cubans unhappy with Spain's rule brought the cigar industry here. Fishing, shrimping, and sponge-gathering became important industries, as did pineapple canning. Through much of the 19th century and into the 20th, Key West was

Florida's wealthiest city in per-capita terms. But in 1929 the local economy began to unravel. Cigar-making moved to Tampa, Hawaii dominated the pineapple industry, and the sponges succumbed to blight. Then the Depression hit, and within a few years half the population was on relief.

Tourism began to revive Key West, but that came to a halt when a hurricane knocked out the railroad bridge in 1935. To help the tourism industry recover from that crushing blow, the government offered incentives for islanders to turn their charming homes—many of them built by shipwrights—into guesthouses and inns. The wise foresight has left the town with more than 100 such lodgings, a hallmark of Key West vacationing today. In the 1950s the discovery of "pink gold" in the Dry Tortugas boosted the economy of the entire region. Harvesting Key West shrimp required a fleet of up to 500 boats and flooded local restaurants with sweet, luscious shrimp. The town's artistic community found inspiration in the colorful fishing boats.

from Miami International Airport to the Upper Keys. To go farther into the Keys, you must book an entire 11-person van, which costs about $350 to Key West. You need to place your request for transportation back to the airport 24 hours in advance.

The City of Key West Department of Transportation has six color-coded bus routes traversing the island from 6:30 AM to 11:30 PM. Stops have signs with the international bus symbol. Schedules are available on buses and at hotels, visitor centers, and shops. The fare is $2 one way. The Lower Keys Shuttle bus runs from Marathon to Key West ($3 one way), with scheduled stops along the way.

Old Town Key West is the only place in the Keys where parking is a problem. There are public parking lots that charge by the hour or day (some hotels and B&Bs provide parking or discounts at municipal lots). If you arrive early, you can sometimes find a spot on side streets off Duval and Whitehead, where you can park for free—just be sure it's not marked for residential parking only. Your best bet is to bike or take the trolley around town if you don't want to walk. You can disembark and reboard at will.

ESSENTIALS

Transportation Contacts **City of Key West Department of Transportation** (☎ 305/809–3910). **Greyhound Lines** (☎ 800/410–5397 or 800/231–2222). **Keys Shuttle** (☎ 305/289–9997 or 888/765–9997 ⊕ www.floridakeysshuttle.com). **Key West Express** (✉ 100 Grinnell St. ☎ 888/539–2628 ⊕ www.seakeywestexpress. com). **Lower Keys Shuttle** (☎ 305/809–3910 ⊕ www.monroecounty-fl.gov). **SuperShuttle** (☎ 305/871–2000 ⊕ www.supershuttle.com).

Visitor Information **Greater Key West Chamber of Commerce** (✉ 402 Wall St. ☎ 305/294–2587 or 800/527–8539 ⊕ www.keywestchamber.org).

EXPLORING

Numbers in the margin correspond to the Key West map.

OLD TOWN

TOP ATTRACTIONS

The heart of Key West, this historic Old Town area runs from White Street to the waterfront. Beginning in 1822, wharves, warehouses, chandleries, ship-repair facilities, and eventually in 1891 the U.S. Custom House sprang up around the deep harbor to accommodate the navy's large ships and other sailing vessels. Wreckers, merchants, and sea captains built lavish houses near the bustling waterfront. A remarkable number of these fine Victorian and pre-Victorian structures have been restored to their original grandeur and now serve as homes, guesthouses, shops, restaurants, and museums. These, along with the dwellings of famous writers, artists, and politicians who've come to Key West over the past 175 years, are among the area's approximately 3,000 historic structures. Old Town also has the city's finest restaurants and hotels, lively street life, and popular nightspots.

❺ Audubon House and Tropical Gardens. If you've ever seen an engraving by ornithologist John James Audubon, you'll understand why his name is synonymous with birds. See his works in this three-story house, which was built in the 1840s for Captain John Geiger and filled with period furniture. It now commemorates Audubon's 1832 stop in Key West while he was traveling through Florida to study birds. A children's room makes his work accessible to youngsters. Docents lead a guided tour that points out the rare indigenous plants and trees in the garden. An art gallery sells lithographs of the artist's famed portraits. ✉ 205 Whitehead St. ☎ 305/294–2116 or 877/294–2470 ⊕ www.audubonhouse. com ▱ $11 ☉ Daily 9:30–5, last tour starts at 4:30.

❶ ★ Ernest Hemingway Home and Museum. Amusing anecdotes spice up the guided tours of Ernest Hemingway's home, built in 1801 by the town's most successful wrecker. While living here between 1931 and 1942, Hemingway wrote about 70% of his life's work, including classics like *For Whom the Bell Tolls*. Few of his belongings remain aside from some books, and there's little about his actual work, but photographs help you visualize his day-to-day life. The supposed six-toed descendants

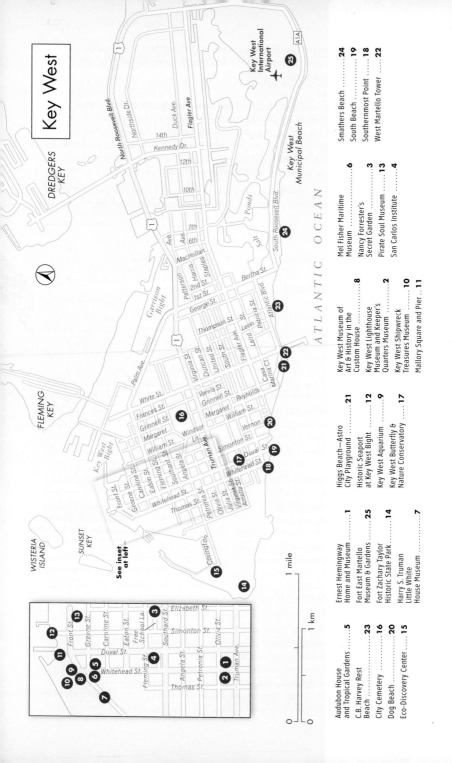

Key West

WISTERIA ISLAND

SUNSET KEY

DREDGERS KEY

FLEMING KEY

Key West Bight

Garrison Bight

See inset at left

ATLANTIC OCEAN

Key West Municipal Beach

Key West International Airport

A1A

DREDGERS KEY

North Roosevelt Blvd.
Northside Dr.
Duck Ave.
Flagler Ave.
14th
Kennedy Dr.
12th
10th
7th
6th
Ave.
Ave.
Macmillan
Patterson
2nd St.
Harris
1st St.
Staples
George St.
Thompson St.
Bertha St.
Leon St.
Laird St.
Patricia St.
Atlantic Blvd.
South Roosevelt Blvd.
Salt Ponds
Casa Marina Ct.
Palm Ave.
White St.
Frances St.
Grinnell St.
Margaret
William St.
Windsor Ln.
Simonton St.
Duval St.
Whitehead St.
Thomas St.
Petronia St.
Olivia St.
Julia St.
Virginia St.
Amelia St.
Covington
Front St.
Greene St.
Eaton St.
Fleming St.
Southard St.
Angela St.
Caroline St.
Truman Ave.
Virginia St.
Duncan St.
United St.
South St.
Flagler Ave.
Reynolds
Vernon
Margaret
Varela St.
Grinnell St.
Palm Ave.

Inset map:

Elizabeth St.
Simonton St.
Caroline St.
Eaton St.
Free School La.
Southard St.
Greene St.
Front St.
Duval St.
Whitehead St.
Fleming St.
Angela St.
Thomas St.
Petronia St.
Olivia St.
Truman Ave.

1 mile
1 km

KEY WEST: A GOOD TOUR

To cover many sights, take the **Old Town Trolley**, which lets you get off and reboard a later trolley. Old Town is also manageable on foot, bicycle, moped, or electric cars. The area is expansive, so you'll want either to pick and choose from the stops on this tour or break it into two or more days. Start on Whitehead Street at the ❶ **Ernest Hemingway Home and Museum**, and then cross the street and climb to the top of the ❷ **Key West Lighthouse Museum & Keeper's Quarters Museum** for a spectacular view. Return to Whitehead Street and follow it north to Angela Street, where you'll turn right. At Margaret Street, the ⑯ **City Cemetery** is worth a look for its aboveground vaults and unusual headstone inscriptions. Head north on Margaret Street, turn left onto Southard Street, then right onto Simonton Street. Halfway up the block, ❸ **Nancy Forrester's Secret Garden** occupies Free School Lane. Follow Southard Street south through Truman Annex to ⑭ **Fort Zachary Taylor Historic State Park**.

Walk west into Truman Annex to see the ❼ **Harry S. Truman Little White House Museum**, President Truman's vacation residence. Return east on Caroline and turn left on Whitehead to visit the ❺ **Audubon House and Tropical Gardens**, honoring the famed artist and naturalist. Follow Whitehead north to Greene Street and turn left to see the salvaged sea treasures of the ❻ **Mel Fisher Maritime Museum.** At Whitehead's northern end are the ❾ **Key West Aquarium** and the ❽ **Key West Museum of Art & History**, the historic former U.S. Custom House. By late afternoon you should be ready to cool off with a dip or catch a few rays at the beach. From the aquarium, head east about a mile, where you'll find ⑲ **South Beach**, located at Southernmost Hotel at the Beach and named for its location at the southern end of Duval Street. If you've brought your pet, stroll a few blocks east to ⑳ **Dog Beach**, at the corner of Vernon and Waddell streets. A little farther east is ㉑ **Higgs Beach–Astro City Playground**, on Atlantic Boulevard between White and Reynolds streets. As the sun starts to sink, return to the west side of Old Town and follow the crowds to Mallory Square, behind the aquarium, to watch Key West's nightly sunset spectacle. (Those lucky enough may see a green flash—the brilliant splash of green or blue that sometimes appears as the sun sinks into the ocean on a clear night.) For dinner, head east on Caroline Street to ⑫ **Historic Seaport at Key West Bight**, a renovated area where there are numerous restaurants and bars.

TIMING

Allow two full days to see all the Old Town museums and homes, especially with a little shopping thrown in. For a narrated trip on the tour train or trolley, budget 1½ hours to ride the loop without getting off, or an entire day if you plan to get off and on the trolley at sights and restaurants.

6

Sailboats big and small make their way into Key West Harbor; photo by John Franzis, Fodors.com member.

of Hemingway's cats—many named for actors, artists, authors, and even a hurricane—have free rein of the property. Tours begin every 10 minutes and take 25–30 minutes; then you're free to explore on your own. ⊠ *907 Whitehead St.* ☎ *305/294–1136* ⊕ *www.hemingwayhome. com* ⊡ *$12* ☉ *Daily 9–5.*

⓮ **Fort Zachary Taylor Historic State Park.** Construction of the fort began in
★ 1845 but was halted during the Civil War. Even though Florida seceded from the Union, Yankee forces used the fort as a base to block Confederate shipping. More than 1,500 Confederate vessels were detained in Key West's harbor. The fort, finally completed in 1866, was also used in the Spanish-American War. Take a 30-minute guided walking tour of the fort, a National Historic Landmark, at noon and 2. In February a celebration called Civil War Heritage Days includes costumed reenactments and demonstrations. From mid-January to mid-April the park serves as an open-air gallery for pieces created for Sculpture Key West. One of its most popular features is its man-made beach. ⊠ *Box 6565; end of Southard St., through Truman Annex* ☎ *305/292–6713* ⊕ *www. floridastateparks.org/forttaylor* ⊡ *$4.50 for 1 person, $7 for 2 people, 50¢ per additional person* ☉ *Daily 8–sunset, tours noon and 2.*

NEED A BREAK? Check out the pretty palm garden next to the Key West Library at 700 Fleming Street, just off Duval. This leafy, outdoor reading area, with shaded benches, is the perfect place to escape the frenzy and crowds of downtown Key West. There's free Internet access in the library, too.

❼ **Harry S. Truman Little White House Museum.** Recent renovations to this circa-1890 landmark have restored the home and gardens to the Truman era, down to the wallpaper pattern. A free photographic review of visiting dignitaries and presidents—John F. Kennedy, Jimmy Carter, and Bill Clinton are among the chief executives who passed through here—is on display in the back of the gift shop. Engaging 45-minute tours begin every 15 minutes until 4:30. They start with an excellent 10-minute video on the history of the property and Truman's visits. On the grounds of **Truman Annex,** a 103-acre former military parade grounds and barracks, the home served as a winter White House for presidents Truman, Eisenhower, and Kennedy. Note: the tour does require climbing steps. ⊠ *111 Front St.* ☎ *305/294–9911* ⊕ *www.trumanlittlewhitehouse.com* 💲 *$12* ☉ *Daily 9–5, grounds sunrise–6; last tour at 4:30.*

㉑ **Higgs Beach–Astro City Playground.** This Monroe County park with its groomed pebbly sand is a popular sunbathing spot. A nearby grove of Australian pines provides shade, and the West Martello Tower provides shelter should a storm suddenly sweep in. Kayak and beach-chair rentals are available, as is a volleyball net. The beach also has a marker and cultural exhibit commemorating the gravesite of 295 enslaved Africans who died after being rescued from three South America–bound slave ships in 1860. Across the street, **Astro City Playground** is popular with young children. ⊠ *Atlantic Blvd. between White and Reynolds Sts.* ☎ *No phone* 💲 *Free* ☉ *Daily 6* AM*–11* PM.

⑫ **Historic Seaport at Key West Bight.** What used to be a funky—in some places even seedy—part of town is now an 8½-acre historic restoration project of 100 businesses, including waterfront restaurants, open-air bars, museums, clothing stores, bait shops, dive shops, docks, a marina, water-sports concessions, and the Waterfront Market. It's all linked by the 2-mi waterfront **Harborwalk,** which runs between Front and Grinnell streets, passing big ships, schooners, sunset cruises, fishing charters, and glass-bottom boats. ⊠ *100 Grinnell St.* ☎ *305/293–8309.*

NEED A BREAK?

Get your morning (or afternoon) buzz at Coffee Plantation (⊠ *713 Caroline St.* ☎ *305/295-9808* ⊕ *www.coffeeplantationkeywest.com*), where you can also hook up to the Internet in the comfort of a homelike setting in a circa-1890 Conch house. Poets, writers, and minstrels sometimes show up to perform while you munch pastries or luncheon sandwiches and wraps and sip your hot or cold espresso beverage.

⑰ **Key West Butterfly & Nature Conservatory.** This air-conditioned refuge for butterflies, birds, and the human spirit gladdens the soul with hundreds of colorful wings—more than 45 species of butterflies alone—in a lovely glass-encased bubble. Waterfalls, artistic benches, paved pathways, birds, and lush, flowering vegetation elevate this above most butterfly attractions. The gift shop and gallery are worth a visit on their own. ⊠ *1316 Duval St.* ☎ *305/296–2988 or 800/939–4647* ⊕ *www. keywestbutterfly.com* 💲 *$12* ☉ *Daily 9–5 (last admission 4:30); gallery and shop open until 5:30.*

⑧ **Key West Museum of Art & History in the Custom House.** When Key West was designated a U.S. port of entry in the early 1820s, a custom house was established. Salvaged cargoes from ships wrecked on the reefs were brought here, setting the stage for Key West to become for a time the

Fodor's Choice

See the typewriter Hemingway used at his home-office in Key West. He lived here from 1931 to 1942.

richest city in Florida. The imposing redbrick-and-terra-cotta Richardsonian Romanesque–style building reopened as a museum and art gallery in 1999. Smaller galleries have long-term and changing exhibits about the history of Key West, including a Hemingway room and a fine collection of folk artist Mario Sanchez's wood paintings. ✉ *281 Front St.* ☎ *305/295–6616* ⊕ *www.kwahs.com* 🎫 *$10* ⊙ *Daily 9:30–4:30.*

❷ Key West Lighthouse Museum & Keeper's Quarters Museum. For the best view in town, climb the 88 steps to the top of this 1847 lighthouse. The 92-foot structure has a Fresnel lens, which was installed in the 1860s at a cost of $1 million. The keeper lived in the adjacent 1887 clapboard house, which now exhibits vintage photographs, ship models, nautical charts, and lighthouse artifacts from all along the Key reefs. ✉ *938 Whitehead St.* ☎ *305/295–6616* ⊕ *www.kwahs.com* 🎫 *$10* ⊙ *Daily 9:30–5; last admission at 4:30.*

⓫ Mallory Square and Pier. For cruise-ship passengers, this is the disembarkation point for an attack on Key West. For practically every visitor, it's the requisite venue for a nightly sunset celebration that includes street performers—human statues, sword swallowers, tightrope walkers, musicians, and more—plus craft vendors, conch fritter fryers, and other regulars who defy classification. (Wanna picture with my pet iguana?) With all the activity, don't forget to watch the main show: a dazzling tropical sunset. ✉ *Mallory Sq.* ☎ *No phone.*

⓳ The Southernmost Point. Possibly the most photographed site in Key West, this is a must-see for many visitors. Who wouldn't want his picture taken next to the big striped buoy that marks the southernmost point in the continental United States? A plaque next to it honors Cubans

CLOSE UP

Hemingway Was Here

In a town where Pulitzer Prize–winning writers are almost as common as coconuts, Ernest Hemingway stands out. Bars and restaurants around the island claim that he ate or drank there (except Bagatelle, where the sign reads "Hemingway never liked this place").

Hemingway came to Key West in 1928 at the urging of writer John dos Passos and rented a house with wife number two, Pauline Pfeiffer. They spent winters in the Keys and summers in Europe and Wyoming, occasionally taking African safaris. Along the way they had two sons, Patrick and Gregory. In 1931, Pauline's wealthy uncle Gus gave the couple the house at 907 Whitehead Street. Now known as the Ernest Hemingway Home & Museum, it's Key West's number-one tourist attraction. Renovations included the addition of a pool and a tropical garden.

In 1935, when the visitor bureau included the house in a tourist brochure, Hemingway promptly built the brick wall that surrounds it today. He wrote of the visitor bureau's offense in a 1935 essay for *Esquire,* saying, "The house at present occupied by your correspondent is listed as number eighteen in a compilation of the forty-eight things for a tourist to see in Key West. So there will be no difficulty in a tourist finding it or any other of the sights of the city, a map has been prepared by the local F.E.R.A. authorities to be presented to each arriving visitor. This is all very flattering to the easily bloated ego of your correspondent but very hard on production."

During his time in Key West, Hemingway penned some of his most important works, including *A Farewell to Arms, To Have and Have Not, Green Hills of Africa,* and *Death in the Afternoon.* His rigorous schedule consisted of writing almost every morning in his 2nd-story studio above the pool, then promptly descending the stairs at midday. By afternoon and evening he was ready for drinking, fishing, swimming, boxing, and hanging around with the boys.

One close friend was Joe Russell, a craggy fisherman and owner of the rugged bar Sloppy Joe's, originally at 428 Greene Street but now at 201 Duval Street. Russell was the only one in town who would cash Hemingway's $1,000 royalty check. Russell and Charles Thompson introduced Hemingway to deep-sea fishing, which became fodder for his writing. Another of Hemingway's loves was boxing. He set up a ring in his yard and paid local fighters to box with him, and he refereed matches at Blue Heaven, then a saloon at 729 Thomas Street.

Hemingway honed his macho image dressed in cutoffs and old shirts and took on the name Papa. In turn, he gave his friends new names and used them as characters in his stories. Joe Russell became Freddy, captain of the *Queen Conch* charter boat in *To Have and Have Not.*

Hemingway stayed in Key West for 11 years before leaving Pauline for wife number three. Pauline and the boys stayed on in the house, which sold in 1951 for $80,000, 10 times its original cost.

—Jim and Cynthia Tunstall

6

who lost their lives trying to escape to America and other signs tell Key West history. ⊠ *Whitehead and South Sts.* ☎ *No phone.*

WORTH NOTING

🔟 **City Cemetery.** You can learn almost as much about a town's history through its cemetery as through its historic houses. Key West's celebrated 20-acre burial place may leave you wanting more, with headstone epitaphs such as "I told you I was sick," and, for a wayward husband, "Now I know where he's sleeping at night." Among the interesting plots are a memorial to the sailors killed in the sinking of the battleship USS *Maine,* carved angels and lambs marking graves of children, and grand aboveground crypts that put to shame many of the town's dwellings for the living. There are separate plots for Catholics, Jews, and refugees from Cuba. You're free to walk around the cemetery on your own, but the best way to see it is on a 60-minute tour given by the staff and volunteers of the Historic Florida Keys Foundation. Tours leave from the main gate, and reservations are required. ⊠ *Margaret and Angela Sts.* ☎ *305/292–6718* ⟡ *Tours $15* ☉ *Daily sunrise–6 PM, tours Tues. and Thurs. at 9:30 year-round; call for additional times.*

🔟 **Dog Beach.** Next to Louie's Backyard, this tiny beach—the only one in Key West where dogs are allowed unleashed—has a shore that's a mix of sand and rocks. ⊠ *Vernon and Waddell Sts.* ☎ *No phone* ⟡ *Free* ☉ *Daily sunrise–sunset.*

🔟 **Eco-Discovery Center.** While visiting Fort Zachary Taylor Historic State Park, stop in at this 6,400-square-foot interactive attraction, which encourages visitors to venture through a variety of Florida Keys habitats from pinelands, beach dunes, and mangroves to the deep sea. Walk through a model of NOAA's (National Oceanic and Atmospheric Administration) Aquarius, a unique underwater ocean laboratory 9 mi off Key Largo, to virtually discover what lurks beneath the sea. Touch-screen computer displays, a dramatic movie, a 2,450-gallon aquarium, and live underwater cameras show off North America's only contiguous barrier coral reef. ⊠ *35 E. Quay Rd., at end of Southard St. in Truman Annex* ☎ *305/809–4750* ⊕ *floridakeys.noaa.gov* ⟡ *Free, donations accepted* ☉ *Tues.–Sat. 9–4.*

🔟 **Key West Aquarium.** Pet a nurse shark and explore the fascinating underwater realm of the Keys without getting wet at this historic aquarium. Hundreds of tropical fish and enormous sea creatures live here. A touch tank enables you to handle starfish, sea cucumbers, horseshoe and hermit crabs, even horse and queen conchs—living totems of the Conch Republic. Built in 1934 by the Works Progress Administration as the world's first open-air aquarium, most of the building has been enclosed for all-weather viewing. Guided tours, included in the admission price, feature shark feedings. ⊠ *1 Whitehead St.* ☎ *305/296–2051* ⊕ *www. keywestaquarium.com* ⟡ *$12* ☉ *Daily 10–6; tours at 11, 1, 3, and 4:30.*

🔟 **Key West Shipwreck Treasures Museum** (⊠ *1 Whitehead St.,* ☎ *305/292–8990* ⊕ *www.shipwreckhistoreum.com* ⟡ *$12* ☉ *Daily 9:40–5).* Much of Key West's history, early prosperity, and interesting architecture come from ships that ran aground on its coral reef. Artifacts from the circa-

1856 *Isaac Allerton,* which yielded $150,000 worth of wreckage, comprises the museum portion of this multifaceted attraction. Actors and films add a bit of Disneyesque drama. The final highlight is climbing to the top the 65-foot lookout tower, a reproduction of the 20 or so towers used by Key West wreckers during the town's salvaging heydays.

6 **Mel Fisher Maritime Museum.** In 1622 two Spanish galleons laden with riches from South America foundered in a hurricane 40 mi west of the Keys. In 1985 diver Mel Fisher recovered the treasures from the lost ships, the *Nuestra Señora de Atocha* and the *Santa Margarita.* Fisher's incredible adventure tracking these fabled hoards and battling the state of Florida for rights is as amazing as the loot you'll see, touch, and learn about in this museum. Artifacts include a gold bar (that you can lift to get an idea what $15,000 feels like) and a 77.76-carat natural emerald crystal worth almost $250,000. Exhibits on the 2nd floor rotate and might cover slave ships, including the excavated 17th-century *Henrietta Marie,* or the evolution of Florida maritime history. ⊠ *200 Greene St.* ☎ *305/294–2633* ⊕ *www.melfisher. org* 🎫 *$12* ⊗ *Weekdays 8:30–5, weekends 9:30–5.*

3 **Nancy Forrester's Secret Garden.** It's hard to believe that this green escape still exists in the middle of Old Town Key West. Despite damage by hurricanes and pressures from developers, Nancy Forrester has maintained her naturalized garden for more than 40 years. Growing in harmony are rare palms and cycads, ferns, bromeliads, bright gingers and heliconias, gumbo-limbo trees strewn with orchids and vines, and a colorful crew of birds, reptiles, cats, and a few surprises. An art gallery has botanical prints and environmental art. One-hour private tours cost $15 per person, four-person minimum. ⊠ *1 Free School La.* ☎ *305/294–0015* ⊕ *www.nancyforrester.com* 🎫 *$10* ⊗ *Daily 10–5.*

13 **Pirate Soul Museum.** Enter if you dare! This swashbuckling attraction combines an animatronic Blackbeard's head, hands-on exhibits about buccaneers, and a collection of nearly 500 artifacts, including the only authentic surviving pirate chest in America, dating back to the 1600s. Don't miss the Disney-produced, three-dimensional sound program that takes you below decks into a completely dark mock prison cell. ⊠ *524 Front St.* ☎ *305/292–1113* ⊕ *www.piratesoul.com* 🎫 *$14* ⊗ *Weekdays 9–5, weekends 10–5.*

4 **San Carlos Institute.** South Florida's Cuban connection began long before Fidel Castro was born. The institute was founded in 1871 by Cuban immigrants. Now it contains a research library and museum rich with the history of Key West and 19th- and 20th-century Cuban exiles. Cuban patriot Jose Martí delivered speeches from the balcony of the auditorium, and opera star Enrico Caruso sang in the opera house, which has exceptional acoustics. It's frequently used for concerts, lectures, films, and exhibits. ⊠ *516 Duval St.* ☎ *305/294–3887* ⊕ *www.institutosancarlos.org* ☜ *Free* ⊙ *Fri.–Sun. noon–6.*

⑲ South Beach. On the Atlantic, this stretch of sand, also known as City Beach, is popular with travelers staying at nearby motels. It is now part of the new Southernmost Hotel on the Beach resort, but is open to the public with a fun beach bar and grill. There's no parking however, so visitors must walk or bike to the beach. ⊠ *Foot of Duval St.* ☎ *No phone* ☜ *Free* ⊙ *Daily 7 AM–11 PM.*

NEW TOWN

The Overseas Highway splits as it enters Key West, the two forks rejoining to encircle New Town, the area east of White Street to Cow Key Channel. The southern fork runs along the shore as South Roosevelt Boulevard (Route A1A) skirting Key West International Airport. Along the north shore, North Roosevelt Boulevard (U.S. 1) passes the Key West Welcome Center. Part of New Town was created with dredged fill. The island would have continued growing this way had the Army Corps of Engineers not determined in the early 1970s that it was detrimental to the nearby reef.

㉓ C. B. Harvey Rest Beach. This beach and park were named after Cornelius Bradford Harvey, former Key West mayor and commissioner. It has half a dozen picnic areas, dunes, and a wheelchair and bike path. ⊠ *Atlantic Blvd., east side of White St. Pier* ☎ *No phone* ☜ *Free* ⊙ *Daily 7 AM–11 PM.*

㉕ ★ **Fort East Martello Museum & Gardens.** This Civil War citadel was *semper paratus,* or "always ready" as the U.S. Coast Guard motto says, but, like most of Florida during the war, it never saw a lick of action. Today it serves as a museum, with historical exhibits about the 19th and 20th centuries. Among the latter are relics of the USS *Maine,* a Cuban refugee raft, and books by famous writers—including seven Pulitzer Prize winners—who have lived in Key West. The tower, operated by the Key West Art and Historical Society, also has a collection of Stanley Papio's "junk art" sculptures and Cuban folk artist Mario Sanchez's chiseled and painted wooden carvings of historic Key West street scenes. ⊠ *3501 S. Roosevelt Blvd.* ☎ *305/296–3913* ⊕ *www.kwahs.com* ☜ *$6* ⊙ *Weekdays 10–4, weekends 9:30–4:30.*

㉔ Smathers Beach. This wide beach has nearly 2 mi of sand, plus restrooms, picnic areas, and volleyball courts, all of which make it popular with the spring-break crowd. Trucks along the road rent rafts, windsurfers, and other beach "toys." Metered parking is on the street. ⊠ *S. Roosevelt Blvd.* ☎ *No phone* ☜ *Free* ⊙ *Daily 7 AM–11 PM.*

㉒ West Martello Tower. Among the arches and ruins of this redbrick Civil War–era fort the Key West Garden Club maintains lovely gardens of native and tropical plants, fountains, and sculptures. It also holds art, orchid, and flower shows February through April and leads private garden tours one weekend in March. ⊠ *Atlantic Blvd. and White St.* ☎ *305/294–3210* ⊕ *www.keywestgardenclub.com* ☜ *Donation welcome* ⊙ *Tues.–Sat. 9:30–3:15.*

THE CONCH REPUBLIC

Beginning in the 1970s, pot smuggling became a source of income for islanders who knew how to dodge detection in the maze of waterways in the Keys. In 1982, the U.S. Border Patrol threw a roadblock across the Overseas Highway just south of Florida City to catch drug runners and undocumented aliens. Traffic backed up for miles as Border Patrol agents searched vehicles and demanded that the occupants prove U.S. citizenship. Officials in Key West, outraged at being treated like foreigners by the federal government, staged a protest and formed their own "nation," the so-called Conch Republic. They hoisted a flag and distributed mock border passes, visas, and Conch currency. The embarrassed Border Patrol dismantled its roadblock, and now an annual festival recalls the city's victory.

OFF THE BEATEN PATH

History buffs might remember long-deactivated Fort Jefferson as the prison that held Dr. Samuel Mudd for his role in the Lincoln assassination. But today's "guests" are much more captivated by this sanctuary's thousands of birds and marine life. **Dry Tortugas National Park** (⌂ *Box 6208, Key West 33040* ☎ *305/242–7700* ⊕ *www.nps.gov/drto* ☞ *$5*) is 70 mi off the shores of Key West and consists of seven small islands. Tour the fort; then lay out your blanket on the sunny beach for a picnic before you head out to snorkel on the protected reef. Many people like to camp here ($3 per person per night, eight sites plus group site and overflow area; first come, first served), but note that there's no freshwater supply and you must carry off whatever you bring onto the island.

The fast, sleek, 100-foot catamaran *Yankee Freedom II,* of the **Dry Tortugas National Park Ferry** (⊠ *Lands End Marina, 240 Margaret St., Key West* ☎ *305/294–7009 or 800/634–0939* ⊕ *www.yankeefreedom.com* ☞ *$160, plus $5 park fee* ☉ *Trips daily at 8* AM), cuts the travel time to the Dry Tortugas to 2¼ hours. The time passes quickly on the roomy vessel equipped with three restrooms, two freshwater showers, and two bars. Stretch out on two decks: one an air-conditioned salon with cushioned seating, the other an open sundeck with sunny and shaded seating. Continental breakfast and lunch are included. On arrival, a naturalist leads a 40-minute guided tour, which is followed by lunch and a free afternoon for swimming, snorkeling (gear included), and exploring. The vessel is ADA–certified for visitors using wheelchairs.

■ TIP➔ The Dry Tortugas lies in the central time zone.

SPORTS AND THE OUTDOORS

Unlike the rest of the region, Key West isn't known for outdoor pursuits. But everyone should devote at least half a day to relaxing on a boat tour, heading out on a fishing expedition, or pursuing some other adventure at sea. The ultimate excursion is a boat trip to Dry Tortugas National Park for snorkeling and exploring Fort Jefferson. Other excursions cater to nature lovers, scuba divers and snorkelers, and those who would just like to get out in the water and enjoy the scenery and sunset. For those who prefer their recreation land based, biking is the way to go. Hiking is limited, but walking the streets of Old Town provides plenty of exercise.

BEACH

⑬ **Fort Zachary Taylor Historic State Park.** The park's beach is the best and saf-
★ est to swim in Key West. There's an adjoining picnic area with barbecue grills and shade trees, a snack bar, and rental equipment, including snorkeling gear. A café serves sandwiches and other munchies. ⊠ *Box 6565; end of Southard St., through Truman Annex* ☎ *305/292–6713* ⊕ *www. floridastateparks.org/forttaylor* ☜ *$4.50 for 1 person, $7 for 2 people, 50¢ per additional person* ⊘ *Daily 8–sunset, tours noon and 2.*

BIKING

Key West was practically made for bicycles, but don't let that lull you into a false sense of security. Narrow and one-way streets along with car traffic result in several bike accidents a year. Some hotels rent or lend bikes to guests; others will refer you to a nearby shop and reserve a bike for you. Rentals usually start at about $12 a day, but some places also rent by the half-day. ■TIP→ Lock up; bikes—and porch chairs!—are favorite targets for local thieves.

Eaton Bikes (⊠ *830 Eaton St.* ☎ *305/295-0057* ⊕ *www.eatonbikes. com*) has tandem, three-wheel, and children's bikes in addition to the standard beach cruisers ($18 for first day) and seven-speed cruisers ($18). It delivers free to all Key West rentals. **Keys Moped & Scooter** (⊠ *523 Truman Ave.* ☎ *305/294–0399*) rents beach cruisers with large baskets for $10 a day. Rates for scooters start at $35. Look for the huge American flag on the roof. **Moped Hospital** (⊠ *601 Truman Ave.* ☎ *305/296–3344 or 866/296–1625* ⊕ *www.mopedhospital.com*) supplies balloon-tire bikes with yellow safety baskets for adults and kids ($12 per day), as well as mopeds ($40) and double-seater scooters ($65). **Paradise Scooter Rentals** (⊠ *112 Fitzpatrick St.* ☎ *305/923–6063* ⊕ *www. paradisescooterrentals.com*) rents bikes starting at $8 for two hours and scooters for $60–$70 a day.

FISHING

Key West Bait & Tackle (⊠ *241 Margaret St.* ☎ *305/292–1961* ⊕ *www. keywestbaitandtackle.com*) carries live bait, frozen bait, and fishing equipment. It also has the Live Bait Lounge, where you can sip ice-cold beer while telling fish tales.

Key West Pro Guides (⊠ *G-31 Miriam St.* ☎ *866/259–4205* ⊕ *www. keywestproguides.com*) has several different trips, including flats and backcountry fishing ($400 for a half day) and reef and offshore fishing ($600 for half day).

GOLF

Key West Resort Golf Course (⊠ *6450 E. College Rd.* ☎ *305/294–5232* ⊕ *www.keywestgolf.com*) is an 18-hole, par 70 course on the bay side of Stock Island; greens fees are $70–$95.

KEY WEST TOURS

BICYCLE TOURS

Lloyd's Original Tropical Bike Tour (✉ Truman Ave. and Simonton St., Key West ☎ 305/304–4700 ⊕ www.lloydstropicalbiketour.com), led by a 30-year Key West veteran, explores the natural, noncommercial side of Key West at a leisurely pace, stopping on backstreets and in backyards of private homes to sample native fruits and view indigenous plants and trees; at City Cemetery; and at the Medicine Garden, a private meditation garden. The behind-the-scenes tours run two hours and cost $35, including bike rental.

Victoria Impallomeni, a 34-year wilderness guide and marine scientist, invites up to six nature lovers—especially children—aboard the *Imp II*, a 25-foot Aquasport, for four-hour ($500) and seven-hour ($700) **Dancing Dolphin Spirit Charters** (✉ MM 5 OS at Murray's Marina, 5710 Overseas Hwy., Key West ☎ 305/304–7562 or 888/822–7366 ⊕ www.captainvictoria.com) ecotours that frequently include encounters with wild dolphins. While island-hopping, you visit underwater gardens, natural shoreline, and mangrove habitats. For her Dolphin Day for Humans tour, Impallomeni pulls you through the water, equipped with mask and snorkel, on a specially designed "dolphin water massage board" that simulates dolphin swimming motions. Sometimes dolphins follow the boat and swim among participants. All equipment is supplied. Tours leave from Murray's Marina (☎ 305/296–0364 ⊕ www.murraymarine.com).

KAYAK TOURS

Lazy Dog Kayak Guides (✉ 5114 Overseas Hwy., Key West ☎ 305/295–9898 ⊕ www.lazydog.com) runs four-hour guided sea kayak–snorkel tours around the mangrove islands just east of Key West. The $60 charge covers transportation, bottled water, a snack, and supplies, including snorkeling gear. A $35 two-hour guided kayak tour is also available.

WALKING TOURS

In addition to publishing several good guides on Key West, the **Historic Florida Keys Foundation** (✉ 510 Greene St., Old City Hall, Key West ☎ 305/292–6718) conducts tours of the City Cemetery Tuesday and Thursday at 9:30.

KAYAKING

Key West is surrounded by marinas, so it's easy to find what you're looking for, whether it's sailing with dolphins or paddling in the mangroves. At **Key West Eco-Tours** (✉ *Historic Seaport, 100 Grinnell St.* ☎ *305/294–7245* ⊕ *keywestecotours.co*), the sail-kayak-snorkel excursions take you into backcountry flats and mangrove forests. The 4½-hour trip costs $95 per person and includes lunch. Sunset sails and private charters are also available.

SCUBA DIVING AND SNORKELING

Captain's Corner (✉ *125 Ann St.* ☎ *305/296–8865* ⊕ *www.captainscorner.com*), a PADI–certified dive shop, has classes in several languages and twice-daily snorkel and dive trips ($40–$45) to reefs and wrecks aboard the 60-foot dive boat *Sea Eagle*. Equipment rental is extra. Safely dive the coral reefs without getting a scuba certification with **Snuba of Key**

West (✉ *Garrison Bight Marina, Palm Ave. between Eaton St. and N. Roosevelt Blvd.* ☎ *305/292–4616* ⊕ *www.snubakeywest.com*). Ride out to the reef on a catamaran, then follow your guide underwater for a one-hour tour of the coral reefs. You wear a regulator with a breathing hose that is attached to a floating air tank on the surface. No prior diving or snorkeling experi-

---

THE FISH GUIDE

Chambers of commerce, marinas, and dive shops offer free **Teall's Guides** (✉ *Box 522409, Marathon Shores 33052* ☎ *305/872–3123*) with land and nautical charts pinpointing popular fishing and diving areas throughout the Keys.

---

ence is necessary, but you must know how to swim. The $99 price includes beverages.

SHOPPING

On these streets you'll find colorful local art of widely varying quality, key limes made into everything imaginable, and the raunchiest T-shirts in the civilized world. Browsing the boutiques—with frequent pub stops along the way—makes for an entertaining stroll down Duval Street.

Where to start? **Bahama Village** is an enclave of spruced-up shops, restaurants, and vendors responsible for the restoration of the colorful historic district where Bahamians settled in the 19th century. The village lies roughly between Whitehead and Fort streets and Angela and Catherine streets. Hemingway frequented the bars, restaurants, and boxing rings in this part of town.

ARTS AND CRAFTS

Key West is filled with art galleries, and the variety is truly amazing. Much is locally produced by the town's large artist community, but many galleries carry international artists from as close as Haiti and as far away as France. Local artists do a great job of preserving the island's architecture and spirit.

Cuba, Cuba! (✉ *814 Duval St.* ☎ *305/295–9442* ⊕ *cubacubastore.com*) stocks paintings, sculptures, and photos by Cuban artists. The **Gallery on Greene** (✉ *606 Greene St.* ☎ *305/294–1669* ⊕ *www.galleryongreene. com*) showcases politically incorrect art by Jeff MacNelly and three-dimensional paintings by Mario Sanchez. This is the largest gallery-exhibition space in Key West. The oldest private art gallery in Key West, **Gingerbread Square Gallery** (✉ *1207 Duval St.* ☎ *305/296–8900* ⊕ *www.gingerbreadsquaregallery.com*), represents local and internationally acclaimed artists, including Sal Salinero and Michael Palmer, in media ranging from graphics to art glass. **Glass Reunions** (✉ *825 Duval St.* ☎ *305/294–1720* ⊕ *www.glassreunions.com*) showcases a collection of wild and impressive fine-art glass. It's worth a stop in just to see the imaginative and over-the-top glass chandeliers, jewelry, dishes, and platters.

Historian, photographer, and painter Sharon Wells opened **KW Light Gallery** (✉ *1203 Duval St.* ☎ *305/294–0566* ⊕ *www.kwlightgallery.com*) to showcase her own fine-art photography and painted tiles and canvases,

Nightlife, shops, and some interesting street art can all be found on Key West's Duval Street.

as well as the works of other national artists. You can find historic photos here as well. **Lucky Street Gallery** (✉ *1130 Duval St.* ☎ *305/294–3973* sells high-end contemporary paintings. There are also a few pieces of jewelry by internationally recognized Key West–based artists. Changing exhibits, artist receptions, and special events make this a lively venue. **Pelican Poop Shoppe** (✉ *314 Simonton St.* ☎ *305/296–3887* ⊕ *www.pelicanpoopshoppe.com*) sells Caribbean art in a tropical courtyard garden. The owners buy directly from the artisans every year, so the prices are very attractive. Potters Charles Pearson and Timothy Roeder can be found at **Whitehead St. Pottery** (✉ *322 Julia St.* ☎ *305/294–5067* ⊕ *www. whiteheadstreetpottery.com*, where they display their porcelain stoneware and raku-fired vessels. The setting, around two koi ponds with a burbling fountain, is as sublime as the art.

BOOKS

The **Key West Island Bookstore** (✉ *513 Fleming St.* ☎ *305/294–2904*) is a home away from home for the large Key West writers' community. It carries new, used, and rare titles. It specializes in Hemingway, Tennessee Williams, and South Florida mystery writers.

CLOTHING AND FABRICS

Don't leave town without a browse through the legendary **Fairvilla Megastore** (✉ *520 Front St.* ☎ *305/292–0448* ⊕ *www.fairvilla.com*), where you'll find an astonishing array of fantasy wear, outlandish costumes (check out the pirate section), and other interesting souvenirs. Take home a shopping bag full of scarlet hibiscus, fuchsia heliconias, blue parrot fish, and even pink flamingo fabric from the **Seam Shoppe**

($\boxtimes$ *1114 Truman Ave.* ☎ *305/296–9830* ⊕ *www.tropicalfabricsonline. com*), which has the city's widest selection of tropical-print fabrics.

FOOD AND DRINK

★ The **Blond Giraffe** ($\boxtimes$ *802 Duval St.* ☎ *305/293–7874* $\boxtimes$ *614 Front St.* ☎ *305/296–2020* $\boxtimes$ *1209 Truman Ave.* ☎ *305/295–6776* ⊕ *www. blondgiraffe.com*) turned an old family recipe for key lime pie into one of the island's success stories. You'll often encounter a line out the door waiting for a pie with delicate pastry, sweet-tart custard filling, and thick meringue topping. The key lime rum cake is the best-selling product for shipping home. For a snack on the run, try the pie on a stick. **Fausto's Food Palace** ($\boxtimes$ *522 Fleming St.* ☎ *305/296–5663* $\boxtimes$ *1105 White St.* ☎ *305/294–5221*) is a market in the traditional town-square sense. Since 1926 Fausto's has been the spot to catch up on the week's gossip and to chill out in summer—it has groceries, organic foods, marvelous wines, a sushi chef on duty from 8 AM–6 PM, and box lunches to go. You'll be pleasantly surprised with the fruit wines sold at the **Key West Winery** ($\boxtimes$ *103 Simonton St.* ☎ *305/292–1717 or 866/880–1717* ⊕ *www.thekeywestwinery.com*). Display crates hold bottles of wines made from blueberries, blackberries, pineapples, cherries, mangoes, watermelons, tomatoes, and, of course, key limes. Stop in for a free tasting. If you like it hot, you'll love **Peppers of Key West** ($\boxtimes$ *602 Greene St.* ☎ *305/295–9333 or 800/597–2823* ⊕ *www.peppersofkeywest.com*). The shop has hundreds of sauces, salsas, and sweets guaranteed to light

★ your fire. A sea-life mural cleverly hides the fact that **Waterfront Market** ($\boxtimes$ *201 William St.* ☎ *305/296–0778*) occupies a big and ugly concrete building. The family-owned, upscale market sells items from around the world, including health food, organic produce, fresh salads, gourmet coffees, imported cheeses, baked goods, and more. Don't miss the fish market, arguably the best in town; there's also a juice bar, sushi, and vegan dishes.

GIFTS AND SOUVENIRS

Part museum, part shopping center, **Cayo Hueso y Habana** ($\boxtimes$ *410 Wall St., Mallory Sq.* ☎ *305/293–7260*) occupies a circa-1879 warehouse with a hand-rolled cigar shop, one-of-a-kind souvenirs, a Cuban restaurant, and exhibits that tell of the island's Cuban heritage. Outside, a memorial garden pays homage to the island's Cuban ancestors. **Fast Buck Freddie's** ($\boxtimes$ *500 Duval St.* ☎ *305/294–2007* ⊕ *www.fastbuckfreddies. com*) sells a classy, hip selection of gifts, including every flamingo item imaginable. It has a whole department called "Tropical Trash," and carries such imaginative items as an electric fan in the shape of a rooster. **Half Buck Freddie's** ($\boxtimes$ *920 Caroline St.* ☎ *305/294–2007* is the discount-outlet store for Fast Buck Freddie's.

★ For that unique (but slightly overpriced) souvenir of your trip to Key West head to **Montage** ($\boxtimes$ *512 Duval St.* ☎ *305/395–9101 or 877/396–4278* ⊕ *montagekeywest.com*), where you'll discover hundreds of hand-crafted signs of popular Key West guesthouses, inns, hotels, restaurants, bars, and streets. If you can't find what you're looking for, they'll make it for you.

NIGHTLIFE

Rest up: much of what happens in Key West does so after dark. Open your mind and have a stroll. Scruffy street performers strum next to dogs in sunglasses. Brawls tumble out the doors of Sloppy Joe's. Drag queens strut across stages in Joan Rivers garb. Tattooed men lick whipped cream off of women's body parts. And margaritas flow like a Jimmy Buffett tune.

BARS AND LOUNGES

Capt. Tony's Saloon (⊠ *428 Greene St.* ☎ *305/294–1838* ⊕ *www. capttonyssaloon.com*) was the original Sloppy Joe's in the mid-1930s, when Hemingway was a regular. Later, a young Jimmy Buffett sang here and made this watering hole famous in his song "Last Mango in Paris." Bands play nightly. No matter your mood, **Durty Harry's** (⊠ *208 Duval St.* ☎ *305/296–5513* ⊕ *www.ricksanddurtyharrys.com*) can fill the bill. The megasize entertainment complex has live music in a variety of indoor-outdoor bars including Rick's Dance Club Wine & Martini Bar and the tiny Red Garter strip club. Pause for a libation at the open-air **Green Parrot Bar** (⊠ *601 Whitehead St., at Southard St.* ☎ *305/294–6133* ⊕ *www.greenparrot.com*). Built in 1890, the bar is said to be Key West's oldest. The sometimes-rowdy saloon has locals outnumbering out-of-towners, especially on weekends when bands play. Belly up to the bar for a cold mug of the signature Hog's Breath Lager at the infamous **Hog's Breath Saloon** (⊠ *400 Front St.* ☎ *305/296–4222* ⊕ *www.hogsbreath.com*), a must-stop on the Key West bar crawl. Live bands play daily 1 PM–2 AM. A youngish, touristy crowd, sprinkled with aging Parrot Heads, frequents **Margaritaville Café** (⊠ *500 Duval St.* ☎ *305/292–1435* ⊕ *www.margaritaville.com*), owned by former Key West resident and recording star Jimmy Buffett, who has been known to perform here. The drink of choice is, of course, a margarita. There's live music nightly, as well as lunch and dinner. Nightlife at the **Pier House** (⊠ *1 Duval St.* ☎ *305/296–4600 or 800/327–8340* ⊕ *www. pierhouse.com*) begins with a steel-drum band to celebrate the sunset on the beach (on select Thursdays and Fridays), then moves indoors to the Wine Galley piano bar for live jazz. The **Schooner Wharf Bar** (⊠ *202 William St.* ☎ *305/292–3302* ⊕ *www.schoonerwharf.com*), an open-air waterfront bar and grill in the historic seaport district, retains its funky Key West charm and hosts live entertainment daily. Its margarita ranks among Key West's best. There's history and good times at **Sloppy Joe's** (⊠ *201 Duval St.* ☎ *305/294–5717* ⊕ *www.sloppyjoes.com*), the successor to a famous 1937 speakeasy named for its founder, Captain Joe Russell. Decorated with Hemingway memorabilia and marine flags, the bar is popular with travelers and is full and noisy all the time. A Sloppy Joe's T-shirt is a de rigueur Key West souvenir, and the gift shop sells them like crazy. **The Top** (⊠ *430 Duval St.* ☎ *305/296–2991* ⊕ *www. laconchakeywest.com/thetop.htm*) is on the 7th floor of the La Concha Crowne Plaza and is one of the best places in town to view the sunset and enjoy live entertainment.

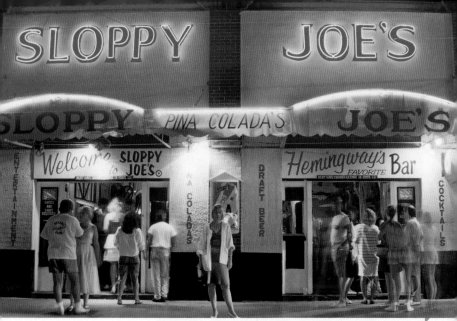

Sloppy Joe's is one stop on most Key West visitors' bar-hop stroll, also known as the Duval Crawl.

In the best traditions of a 1950s cocktail lounge, **Virgilio's** (✉ *524 Duval St.* ☎ *305/296–8118* ⊕ *www.virgilioskeywest.com*) serves chilled martinis to the soothing tempo of live jazz and blues nightly.

WHERE TO EAT

$$-$$$
JAPANESE

✕ **Ambrosia.** Ask any savvy local where to get the best sushi on the island and you'll undoubtedly be pointed to this tiny wood-and-tatami-paneled dining room with indoor waterfall tucked away into a resort near the beach. Grab a seat at the sushi bar and watch owner and head sushi chef Masa prepare an impressive array of superfresh sashimi delicacies. Sushi lovers can't go wrong with the Ambrosia special ($35), a sampler of five kinds of sashimi, seven pieces of sushi and sushi rolls. There's an assortment of lightly fried tempura and teriyaki dishes and a killer bento box at lunch. Enjoy it all with a glass of premium sake or a cold glass of Sapporo beer. ✉ *Santa Maria Resort, 1401 Simonton St.* ☎ *305/293–0304* 🟰 *AE, MC, V* ⊘ *No lunch weekends. Closed 2 weeks after Labor Day.*

$$$
CARIBBEAN
★

✕ **Blue Heaven.** The outdoor dining area here is often referred to as "the quintessential Keys experience," and it's hard to argue. There's much to like about this historic restaurant where Hemingway refereed boxing matches and customers cheered for cockfights. Although these events are no more, the free-roaming chickens and cats add that "what-a-hoot" factor. Nightly specials include black bean soup, Provençal sea scallops, jerk chicken, and sautéed yellowtail snapper in citrus beurre blanc sauce. Desserts and breads are baked on the premises; the banana bread and lobster Benedict with key lime hollandaise are hits

Continued on page 346

EVERYTHING'S FISHY IN THE KEYS

Fish. It's what's for dinner in the Florida Keys. The Keys' runway between the Gulf of Mexico or Florida Bay and Atlantic warm waters means fish of many fin. Restaurants take full advantage by serving it fresh, whether you caught it or a local fisherman did.

Menus at a number of colorful waterfront shacks such as **Snapper's** (✉ *139 Seaside Ave., Key Largo* ☎ *305/852–5956*) in Key Largo and **Half Shell Raw Bar** (✉ *231 Margaret St., Key West* ☎ *305/294–7496*) range from basic raw, steamed, broiled, grilled, or blackened fish to some Bahamian and New Orleans–style interpretations. Other seafood houses dress up their tables in linens and their fish in creative haute-cuisine styles, such as **Pierre's** (✉ *MM 81.5 BS, Islamorada* ☎ *305/664–3225*) hogfish *meunière* or sashimi of yellowfin tuna at **Barracuda Grill** (✉ *4290 Overseas Hwy., Marathon* ☎ *305/743–3314*). And if you're looking for that seafood breakfast Keys-style, try the "grits and grunts"—fried fish and grits—at **The Stuffed Pig** (✉ *3520 Overseas Hwy., Marathon* ☎ *305/743–4059*).

BUILT-IN FISH

You know it's fresh when you see a fish market as soon as you open the door to the restaurant where you're dining. It happens all the time in the Keys. You can even peruse the seafood showcases and pick the fish fillet or lobster tail you want.

Many of the Keys' best restaurants are found in marina complexes, where the commercial fishermen bring their catches straight from the sea. Some, however, such as the seafood restaurants in **Stock Island** (one island north of Key West) and at **Keys Fisheries Market & Marina** (✉ *End of 35th St., Marathon, MM 49 BS* ☎ *305/743-4353 or 866/743-4353*), take some finding.

FLORIDA LOBSTER

What happened to the claws? Stop looking for them: Florida spiny lobsters don't have 'em, never did. The sweet tail meat, however, makes up for the loss. Commercial and sports divers harvest these glorious crustaceans from late July through March. Check with local dive shops on restrictions, then get ready for a fresh feast. Restaurants serve them broiled with drawn butter or in creative dishes such as lobster Benedict, lobster sushi rolls, lobster Reuben, and lobster tacos.

CONCH

One of the tastiest legacies of the Keys' Bahamian heritage, conch shows up on nearly every restaurant menu. It's so prevalent in local diets, that natives refer to themselves as Conchs. Conch fritter is the most popular culinary manifestation, followed by cracked (pounded, breaded, and fried) conch, and conch salad, a ceviche-style refresher. Since the harvesting of queen conch is now illegal, most of the islands' conch come from the Bahamas.

STONE CRAB

In season October 15 through May 15, it gets its name from its rock-hard shell. Most fishermen take only one of its claws, which it can regenerate in a sustainable manner. Connoisseurs prefer it chilled with tangy mustard sauce. Some restaurants give you a choice of hot claws and drawn butter, but this means the meat will be cooked twice, because it's usually boiled or steamed quickly after taken from its crab trap.

YELLOWTAIL SNAPPER

The preferred species of snappers, it is more plentiful in the Keys than any other Florida waters. As pretty as it is tasty, it's a favorite of divers and snorkelers. Mild, sweet, and delicate, its meat lends itself to any number of preparations. It is available pretty much year-round, and many restaurants will give you a choice of broiled, baked, fried, or blackened. Chefs top it with everything from key lime beurre blanc to mango chutney. **Ballyhoo's** in Key Largo (⊠ *MM 97.8, In the median* ☎ *305/852–0822*) serves it seven different ways.

GROUPER

Once central to Florida's trademark seafood dish—fried grouper sandwich—its populations have been overfished in recent years, meaning that the state has exerted more control over bag regulations and occasionally closes grouper fishing on a temporary basis. Some restaurants have gone anti-grouper to try to bring back the abundance, but most grab it when they can. Black grouper is the most highly prized of the several varieties.

6

(left) conch fritters; (above) stone crabs

during "breakfast with the roosters." Breakfast is the signature meal here. ⊠ *729 Thomas St.* ☎ *305/296–8666* ⊕ *www.blueheavenkw.com* ⚲ *Reservations not accepted* ⊟ *AE, D, MC, V* ⊗ *Closed after Labor Day for 6 weeks.*

¢–$
SEAFOOD

✕ **B.O.'s Fish Wagon.** What started out as a fish house on wheels appears to have broken down on the corner of Caroline and William Streets and is today the cornerstone for one of Key West's junkyard-chic dining institutions. Step up to the wood-plank counter window and order the specialty: a grouper sandwich fried or grilled and topped with key lime sauce. Other choices include fish nuts (don't be scared, they're just fried nuggets), hot dogs, and shrimp or soft-shell-crab sandwich. Talk sass with your host and find a picnic table or take a seat at the plank. Grab some paper towels off one of the rolls hanging around and busy yourself reading graffiti, license plates, and irreverent signs. It's a must-do Key West experience. ⊠ *801 Caroline St.* ☎ *305/294–9272* ⊟ *No credit cards.*

$
VEGETARIAN

✕ **The Café, A Mostly Vegetarian Place.** You don't have to be a vegetarian to love this new-age café decorated with bright artwork and a corrugated tin–fronted counter. Local favorites include homemade soup, veggie burgers (order them with a side of sweet potato fries), grilled portobello mushroom salad, seafood, vegan specialties, and grilled Gorgonzola pizza. For bigger appetites there are offerings like the Szechuan-style vegetable stir-fry. ⊠ *509 Southard St.* ☎ *305/296–5515* ⊟ *MC, V.*

$$$
CONTINENTAL
Fodor'sChoice
★

✕ **Café Marquesa.** Chef Susan Ferry presents seven or more inspired entrées on her changing menu each night; delicious dishes can include yellowtail snapper with pear, ricotta pasta purses with caponata, and red pepper coulis; and Australian rack of lamb crusted with goat cheese and a port-cranberry sauce. End your meal on a sweet note with key lime napoleon with tropical fruits and berries. There's also a fine selection of wines and custom martinis such as the key limetini and the Irish martini. Adjoining the intimate Marquesa Hotel, the dining room is equally relaxed and elegant. ⊠ *600 Fleming St.* ☎ *305/292–1244* ⊕ *www.marquesa.com* ⊟ *AE, DC, MC, V* ⊗ *No lunch.*

$$$
FRENCH
★

✕ **Café Solé.** Welcome to the "home of the hog snapper," a deliciously roasted local fish seasoned with a red-pepper-custard sauce. This little piece of France is concealed behind a high wall and a gate in a residential neighborhood. Inside, chef John Correa marries his French training with local ingredients, creating delicious takes on classics, including portobello mushroom soup, snapper with mango salsa, and some of the best bouillabaisse that you'll find outside of Marseilles. From the land, there is filet mignon with a wild-mushroom demi-glace. If you can't decide, a three-course tasting dinner costs $27. Creative salads, carpaccios, and sandwiches star on the lunch menu. ⊠ *1029 Southard St.* ☎ *305/294–0230* ⊕ *www.cafesole.com* ⊟ *AE, D, DC, MC, V.*

$$
CARIBBEAN

✕ **El Meson de Pepe.** If you want to get a taste of the island's Cuban heritage, this is the place. Perfect for after Mallory Square sunset, you can dine alfresco or in the dining room on refined versions of Cuban classics. Begin with a megasized mojito while you enjoy the basket of bread and savory sauces. The expansive menu offers *tostones rellenos* (green plantains with different traditional fillings), ceviche (raw fish "cooked" in lemon juice), and more. Choose from Cuban specialties such as roasted pork in a cumin mojo sauce and *ropa vieja* (shredded beef stew). At lunch, the local Cuban population and cruise-ship passengers enjoy Cuban sandwiches and smaller versions of dinner's most popular entrées. A salsa band performs outside at the bar during sunset celebration. ⊠ *Mallory Sq., 410 Wall St.* ☎ *305/295–2620* ⊕ *www. elmesondepepe.com* ⊟ *AE, D, MC, V.*

$ ✕ **El Siboney**. Dining at this family-style restaurant is like going to Mom's
CARIBBEAN for Sunday dinner—if your mother is Cuban. The dining room is noisy, and the food is traditional *cubano*. There are well-seasoned black beans, a memorable paella, traditional ropa vieja (shredded beef and roast pork), and local seafood served grilled, stuffed, and breaded. Dishes come with Cuban bread, salad or plantains, and rice or fries. To make a good thing even better, the prices are very reasonable. ⊠ *900 Catherine St.* ☎ *305/296–4184* ⊕ *www.elsiboneyrestaurant.com* ⊟ *AE, DC, MC, V.*

$ ✕ **Finnegan's Wake Irish Pub and Eatery**. "Come for the beer. Stay for the
IRISH food. Leave with the staff," is the slogan of this popular pub. The pictures of Beckett, Shaw, Yeats, and Wilde on the walls and the creaky wood floors underfoot exude Irish country warmth. The certified Angus beef is a bit pricey ($30 for an 18-ounce rib eye), but most of the other dishes are bargains. Traditional fare includes bangers and mash, chicken potpie, and colcannon—rich mashed potatoes with scallions, sauerkraut, and melted white cheddar cheese. Bread pudding soaked with a honey-whiskey sauce is a true treat. Live music on weekends and daily happy hours from 4 to 7 and midnight to 2 featuring nearly 30 beers on tap make it popular with the spring break and sometimes noisy drinking crowd. ⊠ *320 Grinnell St.* ☎ *305/293–0222* ⊕ *www.keywestirish. com* ⊟ *AE, D, MC, V.*

$–$$ ✕ **Half Shell Raw Bar**. Smack-dab on the docks, this legendary institution
SEAFOOD gets its name from the oysters, clams, and peel-and-eat shrimp that are a
☺ departure point for its seafood-based diet. It's not clever recipes or fine dining (or even air-conditioning) that packs 'em in; it's fried fish, po'boy sandwiches, and seafood combos. For a break from the deep fryer, try the fresh and light conch ceviche "cooked" with lime juice. The potato salad is flavored with dill, and the "Pama Rita" is a new twist in Margaritaville. ⊠ *Lands End Village at Historic Seaport, 231 Margaret St.* ☎ *305/294–7496* ⊕ *www.halfshellrawbar.com* ⊟ *AE, MC, V.*

¢ ✕ **Lobo's Mixed Grill**. White Castle attained national cult status with its
AMERICAN burgers; the equivalent among Key West denizens is Lobo's belly buster. The 8-ounce, charcoal-grilled chunk of ground chuck is thick and juicy and served with lettuce, tomato, and pickle on a toasted bun. The 30 wraps (rib eye, oyster, grouper, and others) are equally popular. The menu includes salads and quesadillas, as well as a fried shrimp and oyster combo. Beer and wine are served. This courtyard food stand closes at 6, so eat early. Most of Lobo's business is takeout (it has a half-dozen outdoor picnic tables), and it offers free delivery within Old Town. ⊠ *5 Key Lime Sq., east of intersection of Southard and Duval Sts.* ☎ *305/296–5303* ⊕ *www.loboskeywest.com* ⊟ *No credit cards* ⊙ *Closed Sun. Apr.–early Dec.*

$$$$
ECLECTIC
★
╳ **Louie's Backyard.** Feast your eyes on a steal-your-breath-away view and beautifully presented dishes prepared by executive chef Doug Shook. Once you get over sticker shock on the seasonally changing menu (appetizers cost around $9–$18; entrées hover around the $35 mark), settle in on the outside deck and enjoy dishes like shrimp with bacon and stone-ground grits, pistachio-crusted king salmon and potato cake with horseradish cream, and chicken breast with sour-orange mustard and farro. Louie's key lime pie has a gingersnap crust and is served with a berry sauce. If you come for lunch, the menu is less expensive but the view is just as fantastic. For night owls, the tin-roofed Afterdeck Bar serves cocktails on the water until the wee hours. ⌧ *700 Waddell Ave.* ☎ *305/294–1061* ⊕ *www.louiesbackyard.com* ⌂ *Reservations essential* ▤ *MC, V* ⊗ *Closed Labor Day to mid-Sept.*

$–$$
ITALIAN
★
╳ **Mangia Mangia.** This longtime favorite serves large portions of homemade pastas that can be matched with any of the homemade sauces. Tables are arranged in a brick garden hung with twinkling lights and in a nicely dressed-up dining room in an old house. Everything out of the open kitchen is outstanding, including the *bollito misto di mare* (fresh seafood sautéed with garlic, shallots, white wine, and pasta) or the memorable spaghettini "schmappellini," homemade pasta with asparagus, tomatoes, pine nuts, and Parmesan. The wine list—with more than 350 offerings—includes old and rare vintages, and also has a good by-the-glass selection. ⌧ *900 Southard St.* ☎ *305/294–2469* ⊕ *www.mangia-mangia.com* ▤ *AE, D, MC, V* ⊗ *No lunch.*

$$$
AMERICAN
╳ **Michaels Restaurant.** White tablecloths, subdued lighting, and romantic music give Michaels the feel of an urban eatery. Garden seating reminds you that you are in the Keys. Chef-owner Michael Wilson flies in prime rib, cowboy steaks, and rib eyes from Allen Brothers in Chicago, which has supplied top-ranked steak houses for more than a century. Also on the menu is a melt-in-your-mouth grouper stuffed with jumbo lump crab, veal saltimbocca, and a variety of made-to-order fondue dishes (try the pesto pot, spiked with hot pepper and basil). The Hemingway (mojito-style) and the Third Degree (raspberry vodka and white crème de cacao) top the cocktail menu. ⌧ *532 Margaret St.* ☎ *305/295–1300* ⊕ *www.michaelskeywest.com* ▤ *AE, MC, V* ⊗ *No lunch.*

$$$
ECLECTIC
╳ **Nine One Five.** Twinkling lights draped along the lower- and upper-level outdoor porches of a 100-year-old Victorian mansion set an elegant—though unstuffy—stage at this very cool tapas-style eatery. If you like to sample and sip, you'll appreciate the variety of smaller plate selections and wines by the glass. Taster-portioned tapas include olives, cheese, shrimp, and pâté, or try a combination with the tapas platter or the signature "tuna dome" with fresh crab, lemon-miso dressing, and an ahi tuna–sashimi wrapping. There are also larger plates if you're craving something like seafood soup or steak au poivre frites.

Dine outdoors and people-watch along upper Duval, or sit at a table inside while listening to light jazz. ⊠ *915 Duval St.* ☎ *305/296–0669* ⊕ *www.915duval.com* ☰ *AE, MC, V* ☾ *No lunch.*

$$$$
CONTINENTAL
★

✕ **Pisces.** In a circa-1892 former store and home, chef William Arnel and staff create a contemporary setting with a stylish granite bar, Andy Warhol originals, and glass oil lamps. On the menu of this reinvented restaurant, once known as Café des Artistes, favorites include "lobster tango mango," flambéed in cognac and served with saffron butter sauce and sliced mangoes. Other dishes include Pisces Aphrodite (seafood in puff pastry), veal chops with wild mushrooms, and champagne-braised black grouper. ⊠ *1007 Simonton St.* ☎ *305/294–7100* ⊕ *www.pisceskeywest. com* ☰ *AE, MC, V* ☾ *No lunch.*

$$
ITALIAN
★

✕ **Salute Ristorante at the Beach.** This colorful restaurant sits on Higgs Beach, giving it one of the island's best lunch views—and a bit of sand and salt spray on a windy day. Owners of the popular Blue Heaven restaurant recently took it over and have designed an intriguing dinner menu that includes linguine with mussels, vegetable or three-meat lasagna, and white bean soup with grilled bread. At lunch there are calamari marinara, antipasti sandwich, and pasta primavera, as well as a fresh-fish sandwich. New this year, breakfast is also served. ⊠ *1000 Atlantic Blvd., Higgs Beach* ☎ *305/292–1117* ☰ *AE, D, MC, V.*

$$
SEAFOOD
★

✕ **Seven Fish.** A local hot spot, this off-the-beaten-track eatery is good for an eclectic mix of dishes like tropical shrimp salsa, wild-mushroom quesadilla, seafood marinara, and sometimes even an old-fashioned meat loaf with real mashed potatoes. Those in the know arrive for dinner early to snag one of the 12 or so tables clustered in the bare-bones dining room. ⊠ *632 Olivia St.* ☎ *305/296–2777* ⊕ *www.7fish. com* ☰ *AE, D, MC, V* ☾ *Closed Tues. No lunch.*

$$
SEAFOOD
♨

✕ **Turtle Kraals.** Named for the kraals, or corrals, where sea turtles were once kept until they went to the cannery, this place calls to mind the island's history. The menu offers an assortment of marine cuisine that includes seafood enchiladas, mesquite grilled lobster and oyster combo, and mango crab cakes. The newest addition, a slow-cook wood smoker, results in wonderfully tender ribs, brisket, and North Carolina–style pork with peppered vinegar sauce topped with coleslaw. Breakfast offers some interesting and quite tasty options like barbecued hash and eggs or huevos rancheros. The open restaurant overlooks the marina at the Historic Seaport. ⊠ *231 Margaret St.* ☎ *305/294–2640* ⊕ *www. turtlekraals.com* ☰ *AE, MC, V.*

WHERE TO STAY

Historic cottages, restored century-old Conch houses, and large resorts are among the offerings in Key West, the majority charging from $100 to $300 a night. In high season, December through March, you'll be hard pressed to find a decent room for less than $200, and most places raise prices considerably during holidays. Many guesthouses and inns do not welcome children under 16, and most do not permit smoking indoors; rates often include an expanded Continental breakfast and afternoon wine or snack.

$$$$ ⊞ **Ambrosia Key West.** If you desire personal attention, a casual atmo-
★ sphere, and a dollop of style, stay at these twin inns spread out on
nearly 2 acres. Ambrosia is more intimate, with themed rooms such
as the Treetop, Sailfish Suites, and Havana Cabana. Ambrosia Too is
a delightful art-filled hideaway. Rooms and suites have original work
by local artists, wicker or wood furniture, and spacious bathrooms.
Each has a private entrance and deck, patio, or porch. Poolside Continental breakfast is included, and children are welcome. **Pros:** spacious
rooms; poolside breakfast; friendly staff. **Cons:** on-street parking can
be tough to come by; a little too spread out. ⊠ *615, 618, 622 Fleming
St.* ☎ *305/296–9838 or 800/535–9838* ⊕ *www.ambrosiakeywest.com*
⤸ *22 rooms, 3 town houses, 1 cottage, 6 suites* ⚏ *In-room: kitchen
(some), refrigerator, Wi-Fi. In-hotel: pools, bicycles, Wi-Fi hotspot,
parking (free), some pets allowed* ⊟ *AE, D, MC, V* ❘◎❘ *BP.*

$$–$$$ ⊞ **Angelina Guest House.** The high rollers and ladies of the night were
chased away long ago, but this charming guesthouse revels in its past as
a gambling hall and bordello. In the heart of Old Town Key West, it's
a home away from home that offers simple, clean, attractively priced
accommodations. Accommodations range from small rooms sharing a
bath to spacious rooms with king beds and sleeper sofas. Built in the
1920s, this yellow-and-white clapboard building has 2nd-floor porches,
gabled roofs, and a white picket fence. The current owners prettied the
rooms with flower-print curtains and linens and added homemade cinnamon rolls, which receive rave reviews in the guest book, to the breakfast bar. A lagoon-style pool, fountain, and old-brick walkways accent
a lovely garden. **Pros:** good value; nice garden; friendly staff. **Cons:** thin
walls; basic rooms; shared balcony. ⊠ *302 Angela St.* ☎ *305/294–4480
or 888/303–4480* ⊕ *www.angelinaguesthouse.com* ⤸ *13 rooms* ⚏ *In-
room: no phone, refrigerator (some), no TV, Wi-Fi. In-hotel: pool, no
kids under 18, Wi-Fi hotspot* ⊟ *D, MC, V* ❘◎❘ *CP.*

$$$ ⊞ **Azul Key West.** The ultramodern—nearly minimalistic—redo of this
classic circa-1903 Queen Anne mansion is a break from the sensory
overload of Key West's other abundant Victorian guesthouses. The
adults-only boutique hotel, 3½ blocks from Duval Street, combines
original trim, high ceilings, and shiny wood floors with sleek furnish-
ings, including a curved frosted-glass-and-chrome check-in desk, leather
loungers, and a state-of-the-art sound system. Spacious, serene rooms,
some with private verandas, have leather headboards, flat-screen TVs,
and remote-controlled fans and lights. **Pros:** lovely building; marble-
floored baths; luxurious linens. **Cons:** on a busy street. ⊠ *907 Truman
Ave.* ☎ *305/296–5152 or 888/253–2985* ⊕ *www.azulhotels.us* ⤸ *10
rooms, 1 suite* ⚏ *In-room: Wi-Fi. In-hotel: pool, Wi-Fi hotspot, no kids
under 21* ⊟ *AE, D, MC, V* ❘◎❘ *CP.*

$$$$ ⊞ **Casa Marina Resort & Beach Club.** At any moment, you expect the
☾ landed gentry to walk across the oceanfront lawn, just as they did
★ when this 13-acre resort was built back in the 1920s. Set on a private,
1,100-foot rocky beach, it has the same richly appointed lobby with
beamed ceilings, polished pine floor, and original art. Guest rooms
are stylishly decorated with Italian tiled floors, sleeper sofas, and teak
captain's chairs that add a lot of warmth. Fluffy bathrobes, espresso

machines, iHome clock radios, and luxurious designer toiletries make it feel like a boutique hotel. Two-bedroom loft suites with balconies face the ocean. The main building's rooms open onto large outdoor living rooms, and the pools have a nice view of the Atlantic. Guests also have privileges at its nearby sister property, the Reach Resort. **Pros:** nice beach; historic setting; away from the crowds. **Cons:** long walk to Old Town. ⊠ *1500 Reynolds St.* ☎ *305/296–3535 or 866/203–6392* ⊕ *www.casamarinaresort.com* ⤳ *239 rooms, 72 suites* ♿ *In-room: safe, refrigerator, Internet, Wi-Fi. In-hotel: restaurant, room service, bars, tennis courts, pools, gym, spa, beachfront, diving, water sports, bicycles, children's programs (ages 4–12), laundry service, some pets allowed* ☐ *AE, D, DC, MC, V.*

$$$ ⚐ **Courtney's Place.** If you like kids, cats, and dogs, you'll feel right at home in this collection of accommodations ranging from cigar-maker cottages to shotgun houses. The interiors are equally varied in coloring and furnishings, but all rooms have at least a refrigerator, microwave, and coffeepot, if not a full kitchen. The family-owned property is tucked into a residential neighborhood, though within easy walking distance of Duval Street. All rooms are not created equal here; tiny loft rooms are tucked into attic space. **Pros:** near Duval Street; fairly priced. **Cons:** small parking lot; small pool. ⊠ *720 Whitemarsh La., off Petronia St.* ☎ *305/294–3480 or 800/869–4639* ⊕ *www.courtneysplacekeywest. com* ⤳ *6 rooms, 2 suites, 2 efficiencies, 8 cottages* ♿ *In-room: kitchen (some), refrigerator. In-hotel: pool, bicycles, parking (free), some pets allowed.* ☐ *AE, D, MC, V* ⦵ *CP.*

$$$–$$$$ ⚐ **Eden House.** From the vintage metal rockers on the street-side porch
★ to the old neon hotel sign in the lobby, this 1920s rambling Key West mainstay hotel is high on character, low on gloss. You'll get a taste of authentic Old Key West, without sacrificing convenience or comfort. Rooms come in all shapes and sizes, from shared-bath basic to large apartments with full kitchens and private decks or porches. The spacious outdoor area is shaded by towering palms. Grab a book and plop in a hammock in the outdoor library, tucked into a sun-dappled corner with a gurgling waterfall and potted bonsai. **Pros:** sunny garden; hot tub is actually hot; daily happy hour around the pool. **Cons:** cutesy signage is overdone; pricey. ⊠ *1015 Fleming St.* ☎ *305/296–6868 or 800/533–5397* ⊕ *www.edenhouse.com* ⤳ *36 rooms, 8 suites.* ♿ *In-room: kitchen (some), refrigerator (some), Wi-Fi. In-hotel: restaurant, pool, bicycles, Internet terminal, parking (free), Wi-Fi hotspot* ☐ *MC, V.*

$$$ ⚐ **The Gardens Hotel.** Built in 1875, this gloriously shaded property cov-
Fodor'sChoice ers a third of a city block in Old Town. Peggy Mills, who bought it as a
★ private estate in 1931, coiffed it with orchids, ponytail palms, and black bamboo. She added walks, fountains, and earthen pots imported from Cuba. After her death in 1971, the property was turned into a romantic inn that offers several types of accommodations, from standard rooms with garden and courtyard views to a two-bedroom carriage house suite. Decorated with Bahamian plantation-style furnishings, the quiet and elegant rooms are a luxurious tropical retreat. Most have private verandas. **Pros:** luxurious bathrooms; secluded garden seating; free phone calls. **Cons:** hard to get reservations; expensive. ⊠ *526 Angela*

St. ☎ *305/294–2661 or 800/526–2664* ⊕ *www.gardenshotel.com* ⤳ *17 rooms* ☖ *In-room: safe, refrigerator, Wi-Fi. In-hotel: bar, pool, parking (free), no kids under 16, Wi-Fi hotspot* ⊟ *AE, D, MC, V* ⬚ *CP.*

$$$$ ☷ **Hyatt Key West Resort and Spa.** With its own man-made beach, the Hyatt Key West is one of few resorts where you can dig your toes in the sand, then walk a short distance away to the streets of Old Town. A top-to-bottom renovation in 2007 transformed this hotel into a tropical escape with plenty of panache. It offers a wide range of water sports, two good restaurants, and fitness amenities—all with an eye toward keeping green. Rooms are bright and airy, with walk-in showers with rain showerheads, and balconies that overlook the gulf. It pampers you with little extras such as down comforters and fluffy robes. **Pros:** a little bit away from the bustle of Old Town; plenty of activities. **Cons:** beach is small; cramped-feeling property; chain-hotel feel. ⊠ *601 Front St.* ☎ *305/809–1234* ⊕ *www.keywest.hyatt.com* ⤳ *118 rooms* ☖ *In-room: safe, Internet, Wi-Fi. In-hotel: 2 restaurants, room service, bars, pool, gym, spa, beachfront, diving, water sports, laundry service, parking (paid), no-smoking rooms* ⊟ *AE, D, DC, MC, V.*

$$$–$$$$ ☷ **Key Lime Inn.** This 1854 Grand Bahama–style house on the National Register of Historic Places succeeds by offering amiable service, a great location, and simple rooms with natural-wood furnishings. The cluster of pastel-painted cottages, surrounded by white picket fences, has a residential feel, a bit like a beach colony without the beach, or the backlot of a movie set. The Garden Cottages have one room; a few include a porch or balcony. Some rooms in the historic Maloney House have a porch or patio. **Pros:** free parking; some rooms have private outdoor spaces. **Cons:** standard rooms are pricey; pool faces a busy street; mulch-covered paths. ⊠ *725 Truman Ave.* ☎ *305/294–5229 or 800/549–4430* ⊕ *www.keylimeinn.com* ⤳ *37 rooms* ☖ *In-room: safe, refrigerator (some), Internet, Wi-Fi. In-hotel: pool, Wi-Fi hotspot, parking (free)* ⊟ *AE, D, MC, V* ⬚ *CP.*

$$–$$$ ☷ **Key West Bed and Breakfast/The Popular House.** Local art—large, splashy
★ canvases and a Gauguinesque mural—decorates the walls, while handmade textiles (owner Jody Carlson is a talented weaver) drape chairs, couches, and beds at this historic home. There are accommodations for every budget, but the owners reason that budget travelers deserve as pleasant an experience (and lavish a tropical Continental breakfast) as their well-heeled counterparts. Less expensive rooms burst with bright colors (hand-painted dressers add a whimsical flourish) and balconies on the 2nd-floor rooms overlook the gardens. Spacious, and more expensive, 3rd-floor rooms are decorated with a paler palette and original furniture. **Pros:** lots of art; tiled outdoor shower; hot tub and sauna area is a welcome hangout. **Cons:** some rooms are small. ⊠ *415 William St.* ☎ *305/296–7274 or 800/438–6155* ⊕ *www.keywestbandb.com* ⤳ *8 rooms, 6 with bath* ☖ *In-room: no phone, no TV, Wi-Fi (some). In-hotel: pool, bicycles, Wi-Fi hotspot, no kids under 18, no-smoking rooms* ⊟ *AE, D, DC, MC, V* ⬚ *CP.*

$$$$ ☷ **Marquesa Hotel.** In a town that prides itself on its laid-back luxury,
Fodor'sChoice this complex of four restored 1884 houses stands out. Guests—typi-
★ cally shoeless in Marquesa robes—relax among two richly landscaped

pools, rock waterfalls, and peaceful gardens. Elegant rooms surround a courtyard and have antique and reproduction furnishings, earthy tones with black-and-white accents, marble baths, and outdoor sitting areas. Six off-site cottages are also for rent. The lobby resembles a Victorian parlor, with Audubon prints, vases overflowing with flowers, and photos of early Key West. The clientele is mature, well traveled, and affluent, mostly straight, but the hotel is gay-friendly. **Pros:** elegant setting; romantic atmosphere; turndown service. **Cons:** street-facing rooms can be noisy; expensive rates. ⊠ *600 Fleming St.* ☎ *305/292–1919 or 800/869–4631* ⊕ *www.marquesa.com* ⮌ *27 rooms* ⬧ *In-room: safe, refrigerator, DVD, Wi-Fi. In-hotel: restaurant, room service, pools, laundry service, Internet terminal, Wi-Fi hotspot, parking (free), no kids under 14* ⊟ *AE, DC, MC, V.*

$$$–$$$$ 🏨 **Marriott Key West Beachside Hotel.** This new hotel, branded a Marriott in 2008, vies for convention business with the biggest ballroom in Key West. It also appeals to families with its spacious condo units decorated with impeccable good taste. Designer furnishings reflect the resort's waterfront location. Frette linens on the beds, real china in the kitchens, and marble hot tubs add touches of luxury. Rooms have spiral staircases down to the gardens and up to the rooftop sundecks. Families enjoy the beach and pool area. Complimentary shuttles take guests to Old Town and the airport. **Pros:** private beach; poolside cabanas. **Cons:** small beach; can't walk to Old Town; cookie-cutter facade. ⊠ *3841 N. Roosevelt Blvd., New Town* ☎ *305/296–8100 or 800/546–0885* ⊕ *www.beachsidekeywest.com* ⮌ *93 rooms, 80 1-bedroom suites, 15 2-bedroom suites, 21 3-bedroom suites* ⬧ *In-room: kitchen (some), Internet. In-hotel: 2 restaurants, room service, bars, pool, gym, Wi-Fi hotspot, parking (paid)* ⊟ *AE, D, DC, MC, V.*

$$$ 🏨 **Merlin Guesthouse.** Key West guesthouses don't usually welcome fami-
★ lies, but this laid-back jumble of rooms and suites is an exception. If you can live with a few flaws, you'll grab a bargain. Accommodations in the 1930s Simonton House, with four-poster beds, are most suitable for couples. The one- and two-bedroom suites are popular with families. Bright, roomy cottages are perfect if you want a bit more privacy. Get a room in the back if you are bothered by noise. The leafy courtyard and pool area are where guests hang out day and night. **Pros:** good location near Duval Street; good rates. **Cons:** neighbor noise; common areas are dated; street parking. ⊠ *811 Simonton St.* ☎ *305/296–3336 or 800/642–4753* ⊕ *www.merlinguesthouse.com* ⮌ *10 rooms, 6 suites, 4 cottages* ⬧ *In-room: no phone, safe, kitchen (some), refrigerator (some). In-hotel: pool, Internet terminal, Wi-Fi hotspot* ⊟ *AE, D, MC, V* ⦿ *CP.*

$$$–$$$$ 🏨 **Mermaid & the Alligator.** An enchanting combination of flora and fauna
★ makes this 1904 Victorian house a welcoming retreat. The property is bathed in palms, banyans, birds of paradise, and poincianas, with cages of colorful, live parrots and swarms of butterflies adding tropical punch. Rooms are Caribbean colonial–inspired, with wood-slat floors, elegant trim, and French doors. The color scheme—key lime, cantaloupe, and other rich colors—couldn't be more evocative of the Keys. Some downstairs rooms open onto the deck, pool, and gardens

designed by one of the resident owners, a landscape designer. Upstairs rooms overlook the gardens. A full breakfast is served poolside, and guests can take advantage of complimentary bottled waters, soda, and evening wine. **Pros:** hot plunge pool; massage pavilion; island-getaway feel. **Cons:** minimum stay required (length depends on season); dark public areas; plastic lawn chairs. ⊠ *729 Truman Ave.* ☎ *305/294–1894 or 800/773–1894* ⊕ *www.kwmermaid.com* ⬭ *9 rooms* ⌂ *In-room: no phone, no TV, Wi-Fi. In-hotel: pool, Internet terminal, no kids under 16* ▭ *AE, D, MC, V* ⥾⃝⃓ *BP.*

$$$$ ★ 🛏 **Ocean Key Resort & Spa.** A pool and lively open-air bar and restaurant sit on Sunset Pier, a popular place to watch the sun sink into the horizon. Toast the day's end from private balconies that extend from spacious rooms that are both stylish and homey. High ceilings, hand-painted furnishings, sleigh beds, wooden chests, and lavish whirlpool tubs create a personally designed look. This is a full-service resort, with excellent amenities such as a Thai-inspired spa—small and without locker rooms, but each treatment room comes with a Japanese-style tub on the balcony—and a (new in 2009) pool bar. Its 2nd-floor elegant restaurant is cleverly named Hot Tin Roof, a reference to its construction as well as to Tennessee Williams' Key West connection. **Pros:** well-trained staff; lively pool scene; best spa on the island. **Cons:** confusing layout; too bustling for some. ⊠ *Zero Duval St.* ☎ *305/296–7701 or 800/328–9815* ⊕ *www.oceankey.com* ⬭ *64 rooms, 36 suites* ⌂ *In-room: kitchen (some), refrigerator, Wi-Fi In-hotel: 2 restaurants, room service, bars, pool, spa, diving, water sports, bicycles, laundry service, parking (paid), Wi-Fi hotspot* ▭ *AE, D, DC, MC, V.*

$$$$ ★ 🛏 **Pier House Resort and Caribbean Spa.** The location—on a quiet stretch of beach at the foot of Duval—is ideal as a buffer from and gateway to the action. Its sprawling complex of weathered gray buildings includes an original Conch house. The courtyard is riotous with tall coconut palms and hibiscus blossoms, and rooms are cozy and colorful, with a water, pool, or garden view. Six top-of-the-line suites extend over the water with sunset views. Rooms nearest the public areas can be noisy. **Pros:** beautiful beach; good location; nice spa. **Cons:** lots of conventions; cookie-cutter feel; poolside rooms are small. ⊠ *1 Duval St.* ☎ *305/296–4600 or 800/327–8340* ⊕ *www.pierhouse.com* ⬭ *113 rooms, 29 suites* ⌂ *In-room: refrigerator, Wi-Fi. In-hotel: 2 restaurants, room service, bars, pool, gym, spa, beachfront, bicycles, laundry service, Wi-Fi hotspot* ▭ *AE, D, DC, MC, V.*

$$$$ ★ 🛏 **The Reach Resort.** Embracing Key West's only natural beach, this recently reinvented and reopened full-service resort has its roots in the 1980s when locals rallied against the loss of the topless beach it displaced. As a tip of the hat to the city's bohemian spirit, the resort devotes a portion to topless sunbathing. And then there's the Strip House, its naughty little steak house with nude images and a bordello feel. Top luxury prevails these days from turndown service and plushly lined seersucker robes in the room to life-sized chess and boccie in the courtyard and a pool concierge delivering popsicles and drinks du jour. In addition to its own facilities, guests are privy to the spa, tennis, and other amenities at sister resort Casa Marina nearby. Sleek

Sunset Key cottages are right on the water's edge, far away from the action of Old Town.

rooms with various layouts contain all the conveniences, including iPod docks, espresso machines, and wet bars. The private pier-gazebo makes a perfect spot for weddings and watching the sun rise. **Pros:** removed from Duval hubbub; great sunrise views; pullout sofas in most rooms. **Cons:** $20 per day per room resort fee; expensive. ⊠ *1435 Simonton St.* ☎ *305/296–5000 or 888/318–4316* ⊕ *www.reachresort.com* ⮑ *150 rooms, 76 suites* ⚲ *In-room: safe, refrigerator, Wi-Fi. In-hotel: restaurant, room service, bars, pools, gym, beachfront, water sports, laundry service, Internet terminal, Wi-Fi hotspot, parking (paid), some pets allowed* ⊟ *AE, D, DC, MC, V.*

$$$$ ★ **Simonton Court.** A small world all of its own, this lodging makes you feel deliciously sequestered from Key West's crasser side, but close enough to get there on foot. The "basic" rooms are in an old cigar factory, each with its own unique decor. There's also a restored shotgun house and cottages. But top-of-the-line units occupy a Victorian home and the town house facing the property's pool and brick-paved breakfast courtyard. **Pros:** lots of privacy; well-appointed accommodations; friendly staff. **Cons:** minimum stays required in high season. ⊠ *320 Simonton St.* ☎ *305/294–6386 or 800/944–2687* ⊕ *www. simontoncourt.com* ⮑ *17 rooms, 6 suites, 6 cottages* ⚲ *In-room: safe, kitchen (some), refrigerator, Wi-Fi. In-hotel: pools, no kids under 18, Wi-Fi hotspot* ⊟ *D, DC, MC, V* ⋈ *CP.*

$$$–$$$$ **Southernmost Hotel.** This hotel's location on the quiet end of Duval means you don't have to deal with the hustle and bustle of downtown unless you want to—it's within a 20-minute walk (but around sunset, this end of town gets its share of car and foot traffic). Cookie-cutter rooms are spacious, bright, and airy, and have cottage-style furnishings

and the required tropical color schemes. Grab a cold drink from the Tiki Hut bar and join the crowd around the pool, or venture across the street to the beach, where there's a restaurant and a beach resort. **Pros:** pool attracts a lively crowd; access to nearby properties; free parking. **Cons:** public beach is small; can get crowded around the pool and public areas. ⊠ *1319 Duval St.* ☎ *305/296–6577 or 800/354–4455* ⊕ *www. southernmostresorts.com* ⤺ *127 rooms* ⚹ *In-room: safe, refrigerator, Internet, Wi-Fi. In-hotel:, pool, laundry facilities, Wi-Fi hotspot* ⊟ *AE, D, DC, MC, V.*

$$$ ⊞ **Speakeasy Inn.** During Prohibition, Raul Vasquez made this place popular by smuggling in liquor from Cuba. Today the booze is legal, and there's a daily happy hour so you can fully appreciate it. The Speakeasy Inn is still well known, only now its reputation is for having reasonably priced rooms within walking distance of the beach. Accommodations have bright-white walls offset by bursts of color in rugs, pillows, and seat cushions. Queen-size beds and tables are fashioned from salvaged pine. The rooms are basic, but some have nice touches like claw-foot tubs. Room 1A has a deck that's good for people-watching. **Pros:** good location; reasonable rates; high-quality cigar store attached. **Cons:** no pool; basic decor. ⊠ *1117 Duval St.* ☎ *305/296–2680 or 800/217–4884* ⊕ *www.speakeasyinn.com* ⤺ *2 suites, 4 studios* ⚹ *In-room: refrigerator, Wi-Fi. In-hotel: Internet terminal Wi-Fi hotspot* ⊟ *AE, D, MC, V* ❑│ *CP.*

$$$$ ⊞ **Sunset Key.** This private island retreat feels completely cut off from the
Fodor's Choice   world, yet you're just minutes away from the action. Board a 10-minute
★   launch to 27-acre Sunset Key, where you'll find sandy beaches, swaying palms, flowering gardens, and a delicious sense of privacy. A favorite of yacht owners, the hotel has a 40-slip marina. The comforts are first-class at the cluster of one-, two-, and three-bedroom cottages at the water's edge. Baked goods, freshly squeezed juice, and a newspaper are delivered each morning. Each of the accommodations has a kitchen, but you can use the grocery shopping service or hire a private chef (both for a fee, of course). You can use all the facilities at the Westin Key West Resort in Old Town, but be warned: you may never want to leave Sunset Key and its great restaurants, pretty pool, and very civilized beach complete with attendants and cabanas. **Pros:** peace and quiet; roomy verandas; free 24-hour shuttle. **Cons:** luxury doesn't come cheap. ⊠ *245 Front St.* ☎ *305/292–5300 or 888/477–7786* ⊕ *www.sunsetkeyisland. com* ⤺ *37 cottages* ⚹ *In-room: safe, kitchen, DVD, Internet, Wi-Fi. In-hotel: restaurant, room service, bars, tennis courts, pool, gym, beach-front, laundry facilities, laundry service, Internet terminal, parking (paid), no-smoking rooms* ⊟ *AE, D, DC, MC, V* ❑│ *CP.*

Travel Smart
South Florida

WORD OF MOUTH

"[T]he trip to the car rental areas [from Miami International Airport] is somewhat hellish. That will change in the next year as the Miami Intermodal Rental Car Center (http://www.micdot.com/) opens. All the car rental agencies will be housed in one building on the main road with a people mover to and from the airport terminal. By 2012 the Intermodal Center will be a Grand Central for all ground transportation with connections to Metrorail, buses, and trains. That is good news for travelers who find it a pain to get in and out of Miami International."

—SoBchBud1

GETTING HERE AND AROUND

■ AIR TRAVEL

Flying times to Florida vary based on the city you're flying to, but typical times are 3 hours from New York, 4 hours from Chicago, 2¾ hours from Dallas, 4½–5½ hours from Los Angeles, and 8–8½ hours from London.

AIRPORTS

Four airports serve southeast Florida. If you're destined for the north side of Miami-Dade County (metro Miami) or are renting a car at the airport, consider flying into Fort Lauderdale–Hollywood International; it's much easier to use than Miami International, and often—if not always—cheaper. The airports are only 40 minutes apart by car.

Airport Information Fort Lauderdale–Hollywood International (FLL) (☎ 954/359–6100 or 866/435–9355 ⊕ www.broward.org/airport). **Key West International Airport (EYW)** (☎ 305/296–5439 ⊕ www.monroecounty-fl. gov/Pages/MonroeCoFL_Airport/keywest). **Miami International Airport (MIA)** (☎ 305/876–7000 ⊕ www.miami-airport.com). **Palm Beach International (PBI)** (☎ 561/471–7420 ⊕ www.pbia.org).

GROUND TRANSPORTATION

SuperShuttle has service to and from Miami International airport. Downtown Miami to Miami International Airport is typically $15 and takes 30 minutes. Downtown Miami to Palm Beach International Airport is typically $92 and takes 1½ hours. SuperShuttle will pick you up from a hotel, office, or residence; it's best to make reservations at least two days in advance. Inside the airports there are hubs where you can obtain SuperShuttle tickets to go from the airport to your desired local destination.

Taxis are available at Miami International's arrival zone; flat rates vary by the zone you will be traveling to but run between $22 and $52 in the immediate Miami area—the flat rate to Miami Beach is $32.

FLIGHTS

Major Airlines American Airlines (☎ 800/433–7300 ⊕ www.aa.com). **Delta Airlines** (☎ 800/221–1212 for U.S. reservations, 800/241–4141 for international reservations ⊕ www.delta.com). **jetBlue** (☎ 800/538–2583 ⊕ www.jetblue.com). **Southwest Airlines** (☎ 800/435–9792 ⊕ www.southwest.com). **United Airlines** (☎ 800/864–8331 for U.S. reservations, 800/538–2929 for international reservations ⊕ www.united.com). **US Airways** (☎ 800/428–4322 for U.S. and Canada reservations, 800/622–1015 for international reservations ⊕ www.usairways.com).

Smaller Airlines AirTran (☎ 800/247–8726 ⊕ www.airtran.com) to Miami, Fort Lauderdale, and West Palm Beach. **jetBlue** (☎ 800/538–2583 ⊕ www.jetblue.com) to Fort Lauderdale and West Palm Beach. **Midwest Airlines** (☎ 800/452–2022 ⊕ www.midwestairlines. com) to Fort Lauderdale. **Southwest Airlines** (☎ 800/435–9792 ⊕ www.southwest.com) to Fort Lauderdale and West Palm Beach.

■ BUS TRAVEL

Greyhound passes through practically every major city in Florida. For schedules and fares, contact your local Greyhound Information Center.

Using a major credit card, you can purchase Greyhound tickets online or by using the carrier's toll-free phone numbers. You can also purchase tickets—using cash, traveler's checks, or major credit cards—at any Greyhound terminal where tickets are sold or through one of the many independent agents representing Greyhound. A complete state-by-state list of agents is available at the Greyhound Web site.

Bus Information Greyhound Lines (☎ 800/231–2222 ⊕ www.greyhound.com).

▌ CAR TRAVEL

Three major interstates lead to Florida. Interstate 95 begins in Maine, runs south through the mid-Atlantic states, and enters Florida just north of Jacksonville. It continues south past Daytona Beach, the Space Coast, Vero Beach, Palm Beach, and Fort Lauderdale, ending in Miami.

Interstate 75 begins in Michigan at the Canadian border and runs south through Ohio, Kentucky, Tennessee, and Georgia, then moves south through the center of the state before veering west into Tampa. It follows the west coast south to Naples, then crosses the state through the northern section of the Everglades, and ends in Fort Lauderdale.

California and most Southern and Southwestern states are connected to Florida by Interstate 10, which moves east from Los Angeles through Arizona, New Mexico, Texas, Louisiana, Mississippi, and Alabama; it enters Florida at Pensacola and runs straight across the northern part of the state ending in Jacksonville.

TYPICAL TRAVEL TIMES

	Miles	Hours
Ft. Lauderdale–Orlando	210	3:10
Ft. Lauderdale–Palm Beach	45	1
Ft. Lauderdale–Miami	28	0:35
Miami–Key Largo	64	1:15
Key Largo–Key West	98	2
Miami–Key West	162	3:30–4

RENTAL CARS

Car rental is highly recommended for travelers in Florida, since public transportation is limited and restrictive. In-season rates in Miami begin at $36 a day and $170 a week for an economy car with air-conditioning, automatic transmission, and unlimited mileage. Rates in Fort Lauderdale begin at $36 a day and $159 a week. This does not include tax on car rentals, which varies from county to county. Bear in mind that rates fluctuate tremendously—both above and below these quoted figures—depending on demand and the season.

In the past, major rental agencies were at the airport, whereas cheaper firms weren't. Now, however, all over Florida, even the majors might be off airport property. Speedy check-in and frequent shuttle buses make off-airport rentals almost as convenient as on-site service. However, it's wise to allow a little extra time for bus travel between the rental agency and the airport.

In Florida you must be 21 to rent a car, and rates are higher if you're under 25.

CAR RENTAL RESOURCES

Local Agencies

Continental Florida Auto Rental	800/327–3791 or 954/764–1125 in Fort Lauderdale
Sunshine Rent-A-Car	888/786–7446 or 954/467–8100 in Fort Lauderdale

Major Agencies

Alamo	800/462–5266	www.alamo.com
Avis	800/230–4898	www.avis.com
Budget	800/527–0700	www.budget.com
Hertz	800/654–3131	www.hertz.com
National Car Rental	800/227–7368	www.nationalcar.com

GASOLINE

There are many gas stations, many open late, in the major cities and surrounding areas of Florida. The cost of a gallon of 87-octane gasoline averages approximately $3.15 to $3.75 in the state. Keep in mind that fuel prices have been fluctuating wildly over the past couple of years; therefore this price range may change. At most gas stations you are able to pay at the pump with your credit or debit card, and a receipt is typically provided if you request one. Most stations require you to pay before you pump.

PARKING

Florida's cities have meters in the major downtown areas, typically with two-hour time limits. Miami is converting their meters to Pay and Display machines that accept credit cards, debit cards, and dollar bills in addition to coins—the rate per hour in Miami is 75¢ to $1.50.

ROAD CONDITIONS

Florida has its share of traffic problems. Downtown areas of such major cities as Miami can be extremely congested during rush hours, usually 7–9 AM and 3:30–6 PM on weekdays. When you drive the interstate system in Florida, try to plan your trip so that you are not entering, leaving, or passing through a large city during rush hour when traffic can slow to 10 mph for 10 mi or more. In addition, snowbirds usually rent in Florida for a month at a time, which means they all arrive on the first of the month and leave on the 31st. Believe it or not, from November to March, when the end and beginning of a month occur on a weekend, north–south routes like Interstate 75 and Interstate 95 almost come to a standstill during daylight hours. It's best to avoid traveling on these days if possible.

ROADSIDE EMERGENCIES

If you need emergency assistance while traveling on roads in Florida, dial 911 or *FHP (*347) from your cell phone. The Florida Highway Patrol's Web site provides real-time traffic information—including areas congested with construction or accidents.

Emergency Services **Florida Highway Patrol** (☎ *911 or *FHP [*347]* ⊕ *www.dot.state.fl.us*).

RULES OF THE ROAD

Speed limits are 60 mph on state highways, 30 mph within city limits and residential areas, and 70 mph on interstates and Florida's Turnpike. Be alert for signs announcing exceptions.

In Florida you must strap a child six or younger into a child-restraint device: children up to three years old must be in a separate carrier or child seat; children four through six can be secured in a separate carrier, integrated child seat, or by a seat belt. The driver will be held responsible for passengers 15 and younger who are not wearing seat belts. All front-seat passengers are required to wear seat belts.

Florida's Alcohol/Controlled Substance DUI Law is one of the toughest in the United States. A blood-alcohol level of .08 or higher can have serious repercussions even for the first-time offender.

ESSENTIALS

▌ACCOMMODATIONS

Florida has every conceivable type of lodging—from tree houses to penthouses, from mansions for hire to hostels. Even with occupancy rates inching above 70%, there are almost always rooms available, except maybe at Christmas and other holidays.

Children are welcome generally everywhere in Florida. Pets are another matter, so inquire ahead of time if you're bringing an animal with you.

In the busy seasons—over Christmas and from late January through Easter in the southern half of the state and all over Florida during holiday weekends in summer—always reserve ahead for the top properties. Fall is the slowest season: rates are low and availability is high, but this is also the prime time for hurricanes. Key West is jam-packed for Fantasy Fest at Halloween. If you're not booking through a travel agent, call the visitors bureau in the area you'll be visiting to check whether a special event is scheduled for the period of your trip.

▌TIP→ Assume that hotels operate on the European Plan (**EP**, no meals) unless we specify that they use the Breakfast Plan (**BP**, with full breakfast), Continental Plan (**CP**, continental breakfast), Full American Plan (**FAP**, all meals), or Modified American Plan (**MAP**, breakfast and dinner), or are all-inclusive (**AI**, all meals and most activities).

APARTMENT AND HOUSE RENTALS

Contacts **American Realty** (✉ *Box 1133, Captiva 33924* ☎ *800/547–0127* ⊕ *www. captiva-island.com*). **Florida Keys Rental Store/Marr Properties** (✉ *99980 Overseas Hwy., Key Largo 33037* ☎ *800/585–0584 or 305/451–3879* ⊕ *www.floridakeysrentalstore. com*). **Freewheeler Vacations** (✉ *85992 Overseas Hwy., MM 86, Islamorada 33036* ☎ *866/664–2075 or 305/664–2075* ⊕ *www. freewheeler-realty.com*). **Interhome**

(☎ *954/791–8282 or 800/882–6864* ⊕ *www. interhome.us*). **ResortQuest International** (✉ *546 Mary Esther Cut-off, Suite 3, Fort Walton Beach 32548* ☎ *800/336–4853* ⊕ *www.resortquest.com*). **Sand Key Realty** (✉ *2701 Gulf Blvd., Indian Rocks Beach 33785* ☎ *800/377–4971 or 727/595–5441* ⊕ *www. sandkey.com*). **Suncoast Vacations Rentals** (✉ *224 Franklin Blvd., St. George Island 32328* ☎ *800/341–2021* ⊕ *www.uncommonflorida. com*). **Villas International** (☎ *415/499–9490 or 800/221–2260* ⊕ *www.villasintl.com*). **Wyndham Vacation Resorts** (✉ *5259 Coconut Creek Pkwy., Margate 33063* ☎ *800/251–8736* ⊕ *www.wyndhamvacationresorts.com*).

BED-AND-BREAKFASTS

Small inns and guesthouses are increasingly numerous in Florida, but they vary tremendously, ranging from economical places that are plain but serve a good home-style breakfast to elegantly furnished Victorian houses with four-course breakfasts and rates to match. Many offer a homelike setting. In fact, many are in private homes with owners who treat you almost like family; others are more businesslike. The associations listed below offer descriptions and suggestions for B&Bs throughout Florida.

Reservation Services **Bed & Breakfast.com** (☎ *512/322–2710 or 800/462–2632* ⊕ *www. bedandbreakfast.com*). **Bed & Breakfast Inns Online** (☎ *800/215–7365* ⊕ *www.bbonline. com*). **BnB Finder.com** (☎ *888/547–8226* ⊕ *www.bnbfinder.com*). **Florida Bed & Breakfast Inns** (☎ *877/303–3224* ⊕ *www.florida-inns.com*).

HOTELS

Wherever you look in Florida you'll find lots of plain, inexpensive motels and luxurious resorts, independents alongside national chains, and an ever-growing number of modern properties as well as quite a few timeless classics. In fact, since Florida has been a favored travel destination for some time, vintage hotels are everywhere: there are grand edifices like the Breakers in Palm Beach, Boca Raton Resort & Club in Boca Raton, the Biltmore in Coral Gables, and Casa Marina in Key West.

All hotels listed have private bath unless otherwise noted.

■TIP→ You know you can save a bundle on trips to warm-weather destinations by traveling in rainy season. But there's also a chance that a severe storm will disrupt your plans. The solution? Look for hotels and resorts that offer storm/hurricane guarantees. Although they rarely allow refunds, most guarantees do let you rebook later if a storm strikes.

■ EATING OUT

An antismoking amendment endorsed in 2002 by Florida voters bans smoking statewide in most enclosed indoor workplaces, including restaurants. Exemptions are permitted for stand-alone bars where food takes a backseat to the libations.

A cautionary word: raw oysters have been identified as a potential problem for people with chronic illness of the liver, stomach, or blood, or who have immune disorders. All Florida restaurants that serve raw oysters are required to post a notice in plain view of all patrons, warning of the risks associated with consuming them.

FLORIBBEAN FOOD

A trip to South Florida is not complete without a taste of Cuban food. The cuisine is heavy, with pork dishes like *lechon asado*, served in garlic-based sauces. The two most typical dishes are *arroz con frijoles* (the staple side dish of rice and black beans) and *arroz con pollo* (chicken in sticky yellow rice). Key West is a mecca for lovers of key lime pie (the best is found here) and conch fritters. Stone-crab claws, a South Florida delicacy, can be savored from November through May.

WORD OF MOUTH

Was the service stellar or not up to snuff? Did the food give you shivers of delight or leave you cold? Did the prices and portions make you happy or sad? Rate restaurants and write your own reviews or start a discussion about your favorite places in the Forums on ⊕ *www.fodors.com*. Your comments might even appear in our books. Yes, you, too, can be a correspondent!

MEALS AND MEALTIMES

Unless otherwise noted, the restaurants listed in this guide are open daily for lunch and dinner.

RESERVATIONS AND DRESS

Regardless of where you are, it's a good idea to make a reservation if you can. We mention them specifically only when reservations are essential (there's no other way you'll ever get a table) or when they are not accepted. For popular restaurants, book as far ahead as you can (often 30 days), and reconfirm as soon as you arrive. (Large parties should always call ahead to check the reservations policy.) We mention dress only when men are required to wear a jacket or a jacket and tie.

Contacts OpenTable (⊕ *www.opentable.com*). **DinnerBroker** (⊕ *www.dinnerbroker.com*).

WINE, BEER, AND SPIRITS

Beer and wine are usually available in Florida's restaurants, whether you're dining first class or at a beachside bistro. A few chain restaurants in the major cities are also microbreweries and have a variety of premise-made beers that change with the season. Liquor is generally available at fine-dining establishments only.

■ HEALTH

If you are unaccustomed to strong subtropical sun, you run a risk of sunburn and heat prostration, even in winter. So hit the beach or play tennis, golf, or another outdoor sport before 10 AM or after 3 PM. If you must be out at midday, limit strenuous exercise, drink plenty of liquids, and wear a hat. If you begin to feel faint, get out of the sun immediately and sip water slowly. Even on overcast days, ultraviolet rays shine through the haze, so use a sunscreen with an SPF of at least 15, and have children wear a waterproof SPF 30 or higher.

While you're frolicking on the beach, steer clear of what look like blue bubbles on the sand. These are Portuguese man-of-wars, and their tentacles can cause an allergic reaction. Also be careful of other large jellyfish, some of which can sting.

If you walk across a grassy area on the way to the beach, you'll probably encounter sand spurs. They are quite tiny, light brown, and remarkably prickly. You'll feel them before you see them; if you get stuck with one, just pull it out.

■ HOURS OF OPERATION

Many museums in Florida are closed Monday, but offer extended hours on another weekday and are usually open on weekends. Some museums reserve a day of the week for free admission. Popular visitor attractions are usually open daily, with the exception of Thanksgiving and Christmas Day.

■ MONEY

Prices throughout this guide are given for adults. Substantially reduced fees are almost always available for children, students, and senior citizens.

CREDIT CARDS

Throughout this guide, the following abbreviations are used: **AE**, American Express; **D**, Discover; **DC**, Diners Club; **MC**, MasterCard; and **V**, Visa.

It's a good idea to inform your credit-card company before you travel. Otherwise, the credit-card company might put a hold on your card owing to unusual activity—not a good thing halfway through your trip. Record all your credit-card numbers—as well as the phone numbers to call if your cards are lost or stolen—in a safe place, so you're prepared should something go wrong. Both MasterCard and Visa have general numbers you can call if your card is lost, but you're better off calling the number of your issuing bank, since MasterCard and Visa usually just transfer you to your bank; your bank's number is usually printed on your card.

Reporting Lost Cards American Express (🖀 800/992–3404 ⊕ www.americanexpress. com). **Diners Club** (🖀 800/234–6377 ⊕ www. dinersclub.com). **Discover** (🖀 800/347–2683 ⊕ www.discovercard.com). **MasterCard** (🖀 800/622–7747 ⊕ www.mastercard.com). **Visa** (🖀 800/847–2911 in U.S., 410/581–9994 collect from abroad ⊕ www.visa.com).

■ PACKING

Even in summer, ocean breezes can be cool, so always take a sweater or jacket just in case.

Miami is warm year-round and often extremely humid in summer months. Be prepared for sudden storms all over Florida in summer, but keep in mind that plastic raincoats are uncomfortable in the high humidity. Often storms are quick and the sun comes back in no time.

Dress is casual throughout the state—sundresses, jeans, or walking shorts are appropriate during the day. A few restaurants request that men wear jackets and ties, but most do not. Be prepared for air-conditioning working in overdrive; another reason to pack a sweater.

You can generally swim year-round in peninsular Florida from about New Smyrna Beach south on the Atlantic coast and from Tarpon Springs south on the Gulf coast. Be sure to take a sun hat and sunscreen—the sun can be fierce even in winter and even if it's chilly or overcast. Don't leave valuables on your beach blanket while you walk the beach or go for a dip.

FOR INTERNATIONAL TRAVELERS

CURRENCY

The dollar is the basic unit of U.S. currency. A dollar has 100 cents. Coins are the penny (1¢); the nickel (5¢), dime (10¢), quarter (25¢), half-dollar (50¢), and the very rare golden $1 coin and even rarer silver $1. Bills are denominated $1, $5, $10, $20, $50, and $100, all mostly green and identical in size; designs and background tints vary. You may come across a $2 bill, but the chances are slim.

CUSTOMS

Information U.S. Customs and Border Protection (⊕ www.cbp.gov).

DRIVING

Driving in the United States is on the right. Speed limits are posted in miles per hour (usually between 55 mph and 70 mph). Watch for lower limits in small towns and on back roads (usually 30 mph to 40 mph). Most states require front-seat passengers to wear seat belts; many states require children to sit in the back seat and to wear seat belts. In major cities rush hour is 7–10 AM; afternoon rush hour is 4–7 PM. To encourage carpooling, some freeways have special lanes, ordinarily marked with a diamond, for high-occupancy vehicles (HOV)—cars carrying two people or more.

Highways are well paved. Interstates—limited-access, multilane highways designated with an "I–" before the number—are fastest. Interstates with three-digit numbers circle urban areas, which may also have other limited-access expressways, freeways, and parkways. Tolls may be levied on limited-access highways. U.S. and state highways aren't necessarily limited access, but may have several lanes.

ELECTRICITY

The U.S. standard is AC, 110 volts/60 cycles. Plugs have two flat pins set parallel to each other.

EMBASSIES

Contacts Australia (☎ 202/797–3000 ⊕ www.austemb.org).

Canada (☎ 202/682–1740 ⊕ www.canadianembassy.org).

United Kingdom (☎ 202/588–7800 ⊕ uki-nusa.fco.gov.uklen).

EMERGENCIES

For police, fire, or ambulance, dial 911 (0 in rural areas).

HOLIDAYS

New Year's Day (Jan. 1); Martin Luther King Jr. Day (3rd Mon. in Jan.); Presidents' Day (3rd Mon. in Feb.); Memorial Day (last Mon. in May); Independence Day (July 4); Labor Day (1st Mon. in Sept.); Columbus Day (2nd Mon. in Oct.); Thanksgiving Day (4th Thurs. in Nov.); Christmas Eve and Christmas Day (Dec. 24 and 25); and New Year's Eve (Dec. 31).

MAIL

You can buy stamps and aerograms and send letters and parcels in post offices. Stamp-dispensing machines can occasionally be found in airports, bus and train stations, and convenience stores. U.S. mailboxes are dark blue steel bins; pickup schedules are posted on the bin. Parcels weighing more than 13 ounces must be mailed from a post office or from a private mailing center.

Within the United States a first-class letter weighing 1 ounce or less costs 44¢; each additional ounce costs 17¢. Postcards cost 28¢. A 1-ounce airmail letter or a postcard to most countries costs 98¢; a 1-ounce letter or a postcard to Canada or Mexico costs 75¢ or 79¢, respectively.

To receive mail on the road, have it sent C/O GENERAL DELIVERY at your destination's main post office (use the correct five-digit ZIP code). You must pick up mail in person within 30 days, with a driver's license or passport for identification.

Contacts **DHL** (☎ *800/225-5345* ⊕ *www.dhl.com*).

Federal Express (☎ *800/463-3339* ⊕ *www.fedex.com*).

Mail Boxes, Etc./The UPS Store (☎ *800/789-4623* ⊕ *www.mbe.com*).

United States Postal Service (⊕ *www.usps.com*).

PASSPORTS AND VISAS

Visitor visas aren't necessary for citizens of Australia, Canada, the United Kingdom, and most citizens of European Union countries coming for tourism and staying for fewer than 90 days. If you require a visa, the cost is $100—waiting time can be substantial depending on where you live. Apply for a visa at the U.S. consulate in your place of residence; check the U.S. State Department's special visa Web site for further information.

VISA INFORMATION

Destination USA (⊕ *www.travel.state.gov/visa/visa_1750.html*).

PHONES

Phone numbers consist of a three-digit area code and a seven-digit local number. Within many local calling areas you dial only the seven digits; in others you dial "1" first and all 10 digits—just as you would for calls between area-code regions. The same is true for calls to numbers prefixed by "800," "888," "866," and "877"—all toll-free. For calls to numbers prefixed by "900" you must pay—usually dearly.

For international calls, dial "011" followed by the country code and the local number. For help, dial "0" and ask for an overseas operator. Most phone books list country codes and U.S. area codes. The country code for Australia is 61, New Zealand 64, and the United Kingdom 44. Calling Canada is the same as calling within the United States, whose country code, by the way, is 1.

For operator assistance, dial "0." For directory assistance, call 555-1212 or occasionally 411 (free at many public phones). You can reverse long-distance charges by calling "collect"; dial "0" instead of "1" before the 10-digit number.

Instructions are generally posted on pay phones. Usually you insert coins in a slot (usually 25¢–50¢ for local calls) and wait for a steady tone before dialing. On long-distance calls the operator tells you how much to insert; prepaid phone cards, widely available in various denominations, can be used from any phone. Follow the directions to activate the card (there's usually an access number, then an activation code), then dial your number.

CELL PHONES

The United States has several GSM (Global System for Mobile Communications) networks, so multiband mobiles from most countries (except for Japan) work here. Unfortunately, it's almost impossible to buy a pay-as-you-go mobile SIM card in the United States—which allows you to avoid roaming charges—without also buying a phone. However, cell phones with pay-as-you-go plans are available for well under $100. The cheapest ones with decent national coverage are the GoPhone from AT&T and Virgin Mobile, which only offers pay-as-you-go service.

Contacts **AT&T** (☎ *888/333-6651* ⊕ *www.att.com*).

Virgin Mobile (☎ *888/322-1122* ⊕ *www.virginmobileusa.com*).

SAFETY

Stepped-up policing of thieves who prey on tourists in rental cars has helped address what was a serious issue in the early 1990s. Still, visitors should be especially wary when driving in strange neighborhoods and leaving the airport, especially in the Miami area. Don't assume that valuables are safe in your hotel room; use in-room safes or the hotel's safety-deposit boxes. Try to use ATMs only during the day or in brightly lighted, well-traveled locales.

GOVERNMENT ADVISORIES

If you are visiting Florida during the June through November hurricane season and a hurricane is imminent, be sure to follow directions from local authorities.

Safety Transportation Security Administration (*TSA*; ⊕ *www.tsa.gov*).

TAXES

Florida's sales tax is 6% or higher depending on the county, and local sales and tourist taxes can raise what you pay considerably, especially for certain items, such as lodging. Miami Beach hoteliers, for example, collect 14% for city and resort taxes. It's best to ask about additional costs up front, to avoid a rude awakening.

TIME

Mainland Florida is in the Eastern time zone.

TIPPING

Whether they carry bags, open doors, deliver food, or clean rooms, hospitality employees work to receive a portion of your travel budget. In deciding how much to give, base your tip on what the service is and how well it's performed.

In transit, tip airport valets $1–$3 per bag and taxi drivers 15%–20% of the fare.

For hotel staff, recommended amounts are $1–$3 per bag for bellhops, $1–$2 per night per guest for chambermaids, $5–$10 for special concierge service, $1–$3 for a doorman who hails a cab or parks a car, 15% of the greens fee for caddies, 15%–20% of the bill for a massage, and 15% of a room-service bill (bear in mind that sometimes 15%–18% is automatically added to room-service bills, so don't add it twice).

In a restaurant, give 15%–20% of your bill before tax to the server, 15% to bartenders, and 15% of the wine bill for a wine steward who makes a special effort in selecting and serving wine.

VISITOR INFORMATION

Welcome centers are on Interstate 10, Interstate 75, and Interstate 95. ⇨ *For regional tourist bureaus and chambers of commerce, see individual chapters.*

Contacts Visit Florida (✉ *2540 W. Executive Center Circle, Suite 200, Tallahassee* ☎ *850/488–5607* ⊕ *www.visitflorida.com*).

INDEX

PHOTO CREDITS

NOTES

ABOUT OUR WRITERS

Miami native Michael de Zayas spent nights in 50 hotels and had dozens more meals to bring you the lodging and dining coverage for Miami and Miami Beach. When not on assignment for Fodor's (he's contributed to titles on Bermuda, Mexico, Argentina, Chile, Spain, New York City, New England, the Caribbean, among many others), he now lives in Brooklyn and Vermont and runs the clothing website Neighborhoodies.com. He's also at work on a novel about a travel writer in Cuba.

Native Floridian and freelance writer Teri Evans updated the beaches, shopping, nightlife and exploring sections of the Miami and Miami Beach chapter. While Teri currently lives in New York City, she still visits Florida as often as possible for a breath of fresh air and an always welcome dose of sunshine.

After being hired sight unseen by a South Florida newspaper, Fort Lauderdale-based freelance travel writer and editor Lynne Helm arrived from the Midwest anticipating a few years of palm-fringed fun. More than a quarter century later (after covering the state for several newspapers, consumer magazines, and trade publications), she's still enamored of Florida's sun-drenched charms. Lynne updated the Greater Fort Lauderdale and the Everglades chapters.

Snowbird Susan MacCallum-Whitcomb spends as much time as possible in the Sunshine State. Little wonder: winters in her Nova Scotian hometown can be *looong*. Having already contributed to Fodors.com and over two dozen Fodor's guide books, she jumped at the chance to write the Experience chapter for this edition.

Palm Beach and the Treasure Coast writer Mary Thurwachter, a Florida resident since 1979, writes travel stories for *The Palm Beach Post, Miami Herald* and www.innsideflorida.com, a travel site she launched in 2008. She and her husband INNspector Alex have cased all sorts of Sunshine State joints, from the Panhandle to the Keys.

From her home of more than 25 years on Sanibel Island, Chelle Koster Walton—author of the Keys chapter—has written and contributed to a dozen guidebooks, two of which have won Lowell Thomas Awards. She has penned thousands of articles about Florida and the Caribbean for *Miami Herald, USA Today,* Concierge.com, FoxNews.com, and other print and electronic media, including an iTunes guidebook application for Sanibel and Captiva islands.